TRUE
CHRISTIANITY

The New Century Edition
of the Works of Emanuel Swedenborg

TRUE CHRISTIANITY

Containing

a Comprehensive Theology

*of the New Church That Was Predicted by the Lord
in Daniel 7:13–14 and Revelation 21:1, 2*

EMANUEL SWEDENBORG

Volume 1

Translated from the Latin by Jonathan S. Rose

With an Introduction by R. Guy Erwin

And Notes by Glen M. Cooper, George F. Dole,
R. Guy Erwin, Jonathan S. Rose, and Stuart Shotwell

SWEDENBORG FOUNDATION

West Chester, Pennsylvania

Originally published in Latin as *Vera Christiana Religio,* Amsterdam, 1771

Printed in the United States of America

ISBN (library)   Volume 1: 0-87785-484-X
                    Volume 2: 0-87785-501-3
ISBN (paperback)   Volume 1: 0-87785-485-8
                    Volume 2: 0-87785-502-1
ISBN (slipcase set) Volumes 1 and 2: 0-87785-506-4

Library of Congress Cataloging-in-Publication Data

Swedenborg, Emanuel, 1688–1772.
    [Vera Christiana religio. English]
    True Christianity, containing a comprehensive theology of the new church that was predicted by the Lord in Daniel 7:13–14 and Revelation 21:1, 2 / by Emanuel Swedenborg ; translated from the Latin by Jonathan S. Rose ; with an introduction by R. Guy Erwin ; and notes by Stuart Shotwell . . . [et al.].
        p. cm. — (The new century edition of the works of Emanuel Swedenborg)
    Includes bibliographical references and indexes.
    ISBN 0-87785-506-4 (two-volume set, slipcase : alk. paper) — ISBN 0-87785-484-X (hardcover, v. 1 : alk. paper) — ISBN 0-87785-501-3 (hardcover, v. 2 : alk. paper) — ISBN 0-87785-485-8 (pbk., v. 1 : alk. paper) — ISBN 0-87785-502-1 (pbk., v. 2 : alk. paper)
    1. New Jerusalem Church—Doctrines.   2. Theology, Doctrinal.   I. Rose, Jonathan S.   II. Erwin, R. Guy.   III. Shotwell, Stuart, 1953– .   IV. Title.

BX8712.T8 2006
230'.94—dc22
                                                                2004018105

This book is printed on acid-free paper that meets the American National Standards Institute Z39.48-1992 standard.

Senior Copyeditor, Alicia L. Dole
Cover design by Caroline Kline
Text designed by Joanna V. Hill
Ornaments from the first Latin edition, 1771
Typesetting by Alicia L. Dole
Design consultant, Mary Greene

For information contact:
        Swedenborg Foundation
        320 North Church Street
        West Chester, PA 19380 USA

Contents

For the author's own, more detailed table of contents, see the end of volume 2.

Translator's Preface

Outline

EMANUEL Swedenborg was apparently not intending *Vera Christiana Religio* (True Christianity) to be his final published work, although when it appeared in 1771 he was eighty-three years of age and therefore must have known it was likely to be among the last. He left indications in the work itself that he planned an appendix;[1] and after *True Christianity* was published he also mentioned in a letter of August 24, 1771, to Duke Ludwig IX, the Landgrave of Hesse-Darmstadt (1719–1790), that he planned four more small volumes (Acton 1948–1955, 756). Two of these projected works were apparently never written, and the other two have come down to us as only sketches or outlines. Thus it seems to have been by default rather than design that *True Christianity* was the last of Emanuel Swedenborg's major theological publications.

Both by its birth order, so to speak, and by its own intrinsic nature, *True Christianity* occupies a place of particular importance in the family of theological texts Swedenborg produced. In some ways, it is an encapsulation of his theology, and indeed borrows quite heavily from a variety of theological works he had published earlier. Yet in other ways it is intriguingly unique: it contains by far the most imagery and the greatest number of similes of any of his published theological works; it displays arguably the widest range of styles and even, one might say, "emotions," from outrage to playful humor; it addresses all of Swedenborg's multiple audiences in an unprecedented way; and it is the only major work (if "major" means longer than a few pages) published in at least partial response to an attack.

I. The Western European Backdrop

To understand the original audience for Swedenborg's theology, one first needs to know a little about the situation then existing in western Europe. Ten generations before *True Christianity*, the Christian church had suffered and survived fundamental divisions during what came to be called the Reformation.[2] By the time the dust settled, Western Christianity had split into three main groups: Roman Catholics; Lutherans (also known as Evangelicals); and Calvinists (also known as the Reformed). In Swedenborg's Europe, the northern lands on the Baltic were generally Lutheran, Holland was Calvinist, and France, Spain, and Italy were Catholic. Germany was divided into many political units with different

---

1. For mentions in *True Christianity* of a projected appendix see §§177:2, 4; 343; 627; 758; for a mention of a seemingly related possible future work, see §123:2. As is common in Swedenborgian studies, text citations here refer not to page numbers but to Swedenborg's own section numbers, which are uniform in most editions.

2. For accessible works on the Reformation, see MacCulloch 2003, Chadwick 1964, McGrath 1999.

religious orientations, depending on who was in power. Britain had its own form of Protestantism known as Anglicanism. (The Orthodox forms of Christianity in Russia and Asia Minor were known to Swedenborg but seem to have been quite far off on the periphery of his consciousness.)[3]

In Swedenborg's lifetime, Christianity was experiencing another significant upheaval as a result of the Enlightenment. After centuries in which great authority was attributed to the texts of the past, recent developments in science and philosophy had called those texts into question to an unprecedented degree. Although it was first the authority of Aristotle (384–322 B.C.E.) and ancient views of cosmology that came under critical review, the doubt of received authority soon spread to include the authority of Christianity and its written revelation, the Bible. The intellectual leaders of society in Swedenborg's day therefore could be roughly divided into two camps: the leaders of the Christian church (of whatever branch), who were greatly enriched and empowered by the intimate relationship of church and state at the time; and free-thinking philosophers and scientists, many of whom were questioning the validity of belief in Christ, Christianity, or the Bible, although nearly all of them retained a belief in God.[4] Of course, the Western world was largely populated by people who fell into neither camp, and simply went about their daily lives: getting their bread and eating it, interacting with society at large for better or worse, and going to church on Sundays—the overwhelming majority of Europeans being at that time Christian. For the sake of convenience in the present discussion (and admitting that in reality there were not always sharp dividing lines between the people in these categories), I will refer to these three groups as "Christian leaders," "philosophers," and "ordinary people" respectively.

II. Swedenborg's Three Audiences and His Earlier Work

Over the course of his theological publications, Swedenborg addressed all three of these audiences in different ways, showing understanding yet also giving corrective advice, and telling stories to illustrate the way our worldly lives affect our circumstances after death.

---

3. The only mentions of Eastern Orthodox Christianity in Swedenborg's published theological works occur in *True Christianity* 153, 647:3, and *Survey* 18.

4. The label of atheist has been more readily applied to many Enlightenment philosophers and scientists than a reading of their writings would support (Kors 2003, 1:96). For a survey of the relationship between religion and philosophy at the time, see Byrne 1997; see also Waring 1967, Young 1998.

Throughout these works Swedenborg's primary audience—the audience he clearly was holding in mind as he wrote—was ordinary people. (The apparent contradiction that he wrote in Latin, the language of the learned classes, will be addressed below.) Changes in topic and approach in his later works suggest, however, that some of those works address philosophers more specifically, and other works, Christian leaders. Three works seem particularly designed to appeal to philosophers: *Divine Love and Wisdom* (1763), *Divine Providence* (1764), and *Soul-Body Interaction* (1769); these are the twelfth, thirteenth, and seventeenth of Swedenborg's eighteen theological titles. Three other works question and challenge Christian leaders and their doctrinal outlook: *Revelation Unveiled* (1766), *Survey* (1769), and *True Christianity;* these are the fourteenth, sixteenth, and eighteenth titles.[5]

In the eighteenth century there was often polarization between philosophers on the one hand and Christian leaders on the other. Swedenborg's family, however, did not fit this pattern. His father, Jesper Swedberg (1653–1735), was a prominent bishop in the Swedish Lutheran church, and Swedenborg himself had a distinguished career as a scientist, philosopher, and engineer who held a government position supervising Sweden's most important economic asset: its mining industry.[6]

In his mid-fifties, during the years 1743 to 1745, Swedenborg underwent profound spiritual experiences, including at least one reported visionary interaction with Jesus Christ, and had a gradual supersensory awakening that culminated in a daily awareness of the spiritual world. He found himself in theological territory, his father's bailiwick. Yet unlike his father, he approached that realm as a lay person—a scientist and a philosopher—rather than as a trained theologian.

a. Works for Ordinary People and for Philosophers

As a researcher and a lifelong servant of the public and the state who was used to publishing his scientific findings, Swedenborg was strongly moved to publish his spiritual findings as well. He started with biblical

---

5. For a list of Swedenborg's published theological works, see pages 105–107 below. For more detailed bibliographies, see Hyde 1906; Rose 2005b.

6. For a brief overview of Swedenborg's life, see Smoley 2005. The best complete biographies are Sigstedt 1981 and Benz 2002. For a list of selected biographies of Swedenborg, see Eller 2005, 377–379. Swedenborg's father was not his only clerical relative: his family constituted something of a dynasty in the Swedish church, holding many of the top positions (Benz 2002, 498–499).

exegesis based on his new spiritual perspective. His first major published work of theology, *Secrets of Heaven* (1749–1756; 8 volumes), a verse-by-verse presentation of deeper meaning in Genesis and Exodus, was by far his largest; if quantity of words is the measure, it constitutes 64 percent of the published theological corpus he left behind. As he often did when publishing in a field that was new for him (see Sigstedt 1981, 156), Swedenborg published *Secrets of Heaven* anonymously. Although the work is clearly religious in nature, it avoids directly addressing doctrinal flaws in the existing Christian church and labeling them as such. It does, however, imply throughout that heaven and hell exist and that the Bible is indeed holy and worthy of study (presumably because philosophers of his day were questioning these very assumptions); and it does assert that love and life are more important than faith, and that they determine the eternal outcome that awaits the individual after death. The work has much to say about the process an individual needs to go through in order to reach heaven, and draws parallels between that and the process Jesus Christ went through in order to become one with the Father. Therefore it was not lost on its clergy readers that in both its Christology and its nonliteral approach to Scripture *Secrets of Heaven* departed from the standard Christian theology of the day;[7] yet the work was not overtly polemical toward Christian leaders and barely mentions Lutheranism, Calvinism, or other recent doctrinal developments.[8]

---

7. See, for example, the negative review of *Secrets of Heaven* by Johann August Ernesti (1701–1781), professor of rhetoric and theology at Leipzig (Ernesti 1760).

8. In only one passage in the whole of *Secrets of Heaven* do the words "Lutheran" or "Calvinist" occur, and that passage describes in very conditional terms the disappearance of such denominational distinctions:

> In the Christian world, it is doctrine that differentiates churches. Doctrine is the basis on which people call themselves Roman Catholic, Lutheran, Calvinist (Protestant), Evangelical, and other names as well. These names grow out of doctrine alone, which would never happen if we considered love for the Lord and charity for our neighbor the chief concern of faith. If we did, those distinctions would simply be differences of opinion on the mysteries of faith. True Christians would leave such issues up to the individual and the individual's conscience. In their hearts they would say, "A person who lives as a Christian—who lives as the Lord teaches—is a real Christian." One church would come out of all the different churches, and all disagreement due to doctrine alone would vanish. Even personal hatred would melt away in a moment, and the Lord's kingdom would come on earth. (*Secrets of Heaven* 1799:4; translation by Lisa Hyatt Cooper)

The language Swedenborg chose for his published theological works tells us something about his intended audience. To have written in Swedish would have given him the potential to reach readers in his native Sweden, but would have denied his works to virtually all other Europeans. Instead he chose Latin, which was still spoken and read by almost all educated people at the time, both clergy and lay, and which thus made his works available to an international readership. Two facts show that he still had ordinary people in mind as well, however. The first is that he wrote in a very accessible and simple Latin style; anyone with a year or two of Latin schooling could read his originals with some understanding.[9] The other fact is that he paid for three of his titles to be translated into English almost immediately upon their publication in Latin (*Secrets of Heaven* volume 2, *Survey,* and *Soul-Body Interaction*), and was pleased to learn of translations of his works into Swedish and German.[10]

Secrets of Heaven is the least self-conscious of Swedenborg's works, in the sense that it describes features of the spiritual world without apology. The reader sees Swedenborg's awe and wonder at his new insights into the nature of the spiritual world, and his delight in sharing what he has discovered. The work shows a baroque passion for minute detail in specifying the substructures of the human spirit, the nuances of the various steps of regeneration, and the many different heavens and hells.[11] Its

---

9. Swedenborg's friend Johann Christian Cuno (1708–1796), a merchant and banker in Amsterdam, gives an appraisal of the simplicity of Swedenborg's Latin style: "One dare not accuse Swedenborg of lack of clearness, else one would do him great injustice. He writes very simply, clearly, and understandably; indeed his relations [that is, accounts of memorable occurrences in the spiritual world] are so circumstantial and frequently so picturesque that one could paint his narratives" (Cuno 1947, 5). (Translations in this preface are those of the source cited, unless specified otherwise.) In his survey of Neo-Latin literature, the Neo-Latin scholar Jozef IJsewijn calls Swedenborg's Latin "straightforward": "Somewhere between . . . strictly scientific Latin and literary prose we find some remarkable works of a very peculiar character, namely Swedenborg's natural, theosophical, and moral writings written in a straightforward modern Latin" (IJsewijn 1990, 279).

10. For Swedenborg's pleasure at hearing that his most loyal friend and follower, Gabriel Beyer (1720–1779), professor of theology at the Göteborg Academy, was working on a translation of *Soul-Body Interaction* into Swedish, see Acton 1948–1955, 703. Cuno gives an eyewitness account of Swedenborg's response to learning that his *Other Planets* had been translated into German and published: "The news which I brought him, that his work *De Telluribus,* etc., had appeared in translation, gave him singular pleasure, and his eyes, always smiling, became twice as bright" (Cuno 1947, 160).

11. For more on the baroque passion for detail, see Lang 2004, 15.

chapters, which present deeper meanings behind Scripture's literal sayings and stories, are complemented by doctrinal and experiential material at the beginnings and ends of chapters. As the work unfolds, the reader's attention is repeatedly launched from points in the literal meaning of Genesis and Exodus on journeys that traverse a great variety of spiritual topics and then head home again to the words of Scripture.

Secrets of Heaven was followed in 1758 by five works that are considerably smaller and more accessible.[12] The preface of the largest of these, *Heaven and Hell,* explicitly states that its purpose is to protect the faith of ordinary people from being undermined by the philosophers who were questioning Scripture and Christianity.[13]

Those five works were followed by a five-year hiatus in publishing. When it ended, Swedenborg put out no fewer than seven small works in just over a year (1763 to early 1764). The first four of these, collectively referred to as the Four Doctrines, aim at more central and contentious issues in Christianity—the Lord, Sacred Scripture, life (and repentance), and faith—but are again not overtly polemical toward Christian leaders.

The next two volumes are the first to speak to philosophers more directly. *Divine Love and Wisdom* and *Divine Providence* minimize the use of Scripture quotation and use terminology to describe God that comes clearly from the philosopher's glossary rather than the cleric's. In fact, when

---

12. The five works Swedenborg published in 1758 are *Heaven and Hell, New Jerusalem, Last Judgment, White Horse,* and *Other Planets. Secrets of Heaven* by itself contains 4,559 pages in the Latin first edition; taken together, the five works just listed total only 584 pages. For more bibliographic information on these works, see pages 105–106 below.

13. *Heaven and Hell* 1. A key statement there is the following (George F. Dole's translation, emphasis mine):

> Church people these days know practically nothing about heaven and hell or their life after death, even though there are descriptions of everything available to them in the Word. In fact, many who have been born in the church deny all this. In their hearts they are asking who has ever come back to tell us about it.
>
> *To prevent this negative attitude—especially prevalent among people who have acquired a great deal of worldly wisdom—from infecting and corrupting people of simple heart and simple faith,* it has been granted me to be with angels and to talk with them person to person. I have also been enabled to see what is in heaven and in hell, a process that has been going on for thirteen years. *Now I am being allowed therefore to describe what I have heard and seen, in the hopes of shedding light where there is ignorance, and of dispelling skepticism.*

Swedenborg cites Scripture in these works, he seems to do so in order to
defend Scripture and interest those readers in it, rather than calling on it as
something that would have authority for them (Swedenborg [1763] 2003,
273 note 70).

b. A Change in Targeted Audience and Approach

After 1765, Swedenborg's approach changed in two significant ways: he
began to include material that was explicitly critical of Christian leaders
(although he rarely mentions names); and he began to distribute his works
more actively. He sent his works with cover letters directly to those very
Christian leaders, as well as to prominent politicians and university professors and libraries, not only in Sweden but also elsewhere in Europe. In
this last period of his theological publishing, Swedenborg saw five works
through the press, all of which were widely distributed, and three of which
not only sharply criticized existing Christian doctrines, attitudes, and
practices, but also clearly assigned to Christian leaders the primary
responsibility for problems in these areas. Swedenborg's purpose in so
doing was not to join the philosophers in tearing Christianity down—as
has already been noted, he wished to protect ordinary Christians from the
undermining effect of the philosophical assault against Christ and the
Bible. His purpose was instead to urge change and reform, and to provoke
a reexamination of Christianity's teachings and a return to its original
focuses on love, usefulness, and actual repentance. But it seems clear that
Swedenborg knew that any such changes would not happen smoothly—
they would not pass unresisted by those in power. Swedenborg apparently
decided that it was time to stop treading carefully around the church leadership. A letter Swedenborg wrote on December 29, 1769, to his friend,
Gabriel Beyer (1720–1779), clarifies his attitude and purpose during this
period. In it he refers to an earlier letter of October 1769, which was published at his request in Göteborg, accusing two unnamed local priests of
being in league with spirits who were "followers of the Dragon"—an epi-
thet all his Christian readers would understand to be synonymous with
evil (see Revelation 12:7–9).

> I have . . . received the printed letter, about which, in the beginning, a
> large number in the House of Clergy [one of four parts of the Swedish
> government] made a great noise; yet such noise does no harm, for it
> acts in the same way as ferment in wine when it is being made, of
> which it later clears itself; for if that which is unright does not come to

be ventilated and so driven off, that which is right cannot be seen and received. (Acton 1948–1955, 701–702)

The first work to show this new, more aggressive approach was *Revelation Unveiled*. In preparation for writing it, Swedenborg expanded his understanding of Catholic and Lutheran doctrine through intense study of their credos. At the beginning of the work he presents two lengthy sections detailing first Catholic and then Protestant teachings on various topics, something he had never done before. This opening by itself will have signaled to contemporary readers that those doctrinal positions, which dominated the Christian world, would be subject to close scrutiny and refutation in this volume. *Revelation Unveiled* also includes a new feature not found in previous works in exactly the same explicitly defined and delimited form: memorable occurrences—that is, lengthy narrative accounts of Swedenborg's experiences in the spiritual world. In the memorable occurrences in *Revelation Unveiled,* clergy in the spiritual world, both Protestant and Catholic, generally appear corrupt, arrogant, obstructionist, deaf to criticism, and more interested in power and wealth than in saving the souls entrusted to their care. Leaving aside the memorable occurrences, the expository portion of the work, which presents the inner meaning of the Book of Revelation, is unflattering to the Christian clergy of all branches at the time, although Protestants bear the brunt. From start to finish, *Revelation Unveiled* shows no care to protect the egos of contemporary church authorities.

The impact of these criticisms was heightened by Swedenborg's distribution of the work. His largest previous effort of this kind had been limited geographically to a single country: he had sent complimentary copies of his 1758 works to British bishops and nobility.[14] In the case of *Revelation Unveiled,* however, he distributed the volume to political and

---

14. The 1758 works were *Heaven and Hell, New Jerusalem, Last Judgment, White Horse,* and *Other Planets;* for more information on them, see pages 105–106. For evidence that Swedenborg sent copies of these works to all the British bishops and many nobles in the House of Lords, see *Revelation Unveiled* 716; Cuno 1947, 103. His distribution of *Revelation Unveiled* took place on an even wider scale, as he indicates in the following letter to the secretary of state in Sweden: "I have at last finished the Explication of St. John's Revelations, circulated them round to all the Universities in Holland, Germany, France, and England; and am going to send seventy copies to Stockholm, of which your honor will please to take 10, and give 5 to the following Senators: Senator Höpken, Senator Scheffer, and Nordencrantz, Councillor of Commerce; Bishop Mennander, and Bishop Serenius; the other five you will be pleased to dispose of amongst your friends. I desire the remaining 60 to be kept safe until I return home, meaning to distribute them amongst the Academies and Libraries in Sweden, and to Clergymen qualified for a more than ordinary station. I design to present 4 to the Court, and the remainder to the Universities and Seminaries in foreign parts" (Acton 1948–1955, 610–611).

ecclesiastical leaders across Europe. He sent copies via Beyer to Eric Lamberg (1719–1780), bishop of Göteborg, and Olof Andreas Ekebom (1716–1784), dean of the Consistory[15] in Göteborg (Acton 1948–1955, 610 and note 8), both of whom would later become leading enemies of his. Furthermore, in two extant cover letters that he sent out with the volumes he urged the recipients to read the accounts of memorable occurrences first, noting that these passages were marked off in the text by special asterisks (Acton 1948–1955, 610, 611–612). An advertisement for *Revelation Unveiled* in Britain written in a mixture of Latin and English also encourages the study of these accounts:

> *The Book of Revelation Unveiled,* uncovering the secrets that were foretold there and have lain hidden until now, together with memorable occurrences at the end of the chapters, *some of which concern the English and their bishops in the spiritual world.* The memorable occurrences are found there at §§67, 153, 224, 255, 294, 341, 386, 417, 463, 484, 531, 566, 611, 655, 675, 716, 752, 802, 839, 875, 926, 961, 962.[16]

III. *Survey* and the First Stage of *True Christianity*

After publishing and distributing *Revelation Unveiled,* Swedenborg seems to have turned back to his primary audience of ordinary people as he wrote and published a work on marriage: *Marriage Love* (1768). It, too, features memorable occurrences and was widely distributed, but it contains little in the way of criticism of the Christian leadership, although it does question Christian attitudes to women and marriage, as well as the common Christian understanding of the statement that there is no marriage in heaven. This work is significant in that it was the first of the theological works to present Swedenborg's name on the title page.[17]

Since his identity had now been revealed, Swedenborg apparently had no qualms about including on the last page of the volume a list of

---

15. On the nature of the Consistory, see note 21 below.

16. Hyde 1906, page 455; translation and emphasis mine.

17. In addition to giving Swedenborg's name, the title page of *Marriage Love* identified him as "a Swede." Swedenborg's identity as the author of the earlier theological works had become known to an indeterminable but relatively small number of people prior to his application to the Swedish censor in March 1760 for permission to import his writings; it thereafter became widely known (Acton 1948–1955, 529; Tafel 1877, 397).

theological works he had published up to that point, with information about two bookstores in England where his works were for sale. At the end of the list he added the following paragraph:

> Within two years you will see the complete Doctrine of the New Church foretold by the Lord in Revelation 21 and 22.[18]

This is the first notice of the work that was to become *True Christianity.* As we will see, as the work evolved it had at least three different titles. The first working title seems to have been *The Doctrine of the New Church* (in Latin, *Doctrina Novae Ecclesiae*), or perhaps *The Complete Doctrine of the New Church.* Since *Marriage Love* bore the date 1768 on its title page, and appeared before October of that year, it can be assumed that *The Doctrine of the New Church* was predicted to appear some time in 1770. It may be that Swedenborg had already begun work on it when he drafted the last page of *Marriage Love.*

Swedenborg was well able to estimate accurately the time it would take to write and print the projected work; after all, he had published more than a hundred works since the age of twelve. But circumstances of which he was not then aware were soon to change both that schedule and the nature of the work itself.

a. *Survey* as a Precursor to *True Christianity*

Late in 1768 Swedenborg began work on *The Doctrine of the New Church* and laid out an outline for it. As he worked on it and reflected on it, however, he apparently came to feel that a volume that appeared in 1770 would arrive too late to maintain the momentum for change (see the statement quoted just below). Therefore he decided to put out an interim work with the title *Summaria Expositio Doctrinae Novae Ecclesiae* (Survey of the Doctrine of the New Church), which is here referred to with the short title *Survey.* The words "the doctrine of the new church" in the title could simply refer to the theological perspective of the new church. However, the overlap with the title of the work then in progress *(The Doctrine of the New Church),* and the fact that *Survey* is the precursor of

---

18. My translation. In that same list on the last page of *Marriage Love,* the words *Doctrina Novae Hierosolymae* ("the Doctrine of the New Jerusalem") are used as a collective title for the so-called Four Doctrines, as if Swedenborg intended to imply that those four works on the Lord, Sacred Scripture, life, and faith addressed only four key aspects of the theology, while the projected work, *The Complete Doctrine of the New Church,* would present that theology fully or comprehensively.

that work, suggest instead that the title identifies the book as a "survey of *The Doctrine of the New Church.*" Swedenborg explains the purpose of *Survey* in its preface:

> After producing over a period of some years several large and small works on the New Jerusalem (that is, the new church being established by the Lord) and unveiling the Book of Revelation, I planned to bring to light the complete or comprehensive Doctrine of that Church. But because this will take several years, I have decided to issue this precursor to it, in order to give people at least a general idea of that church and its doctrine.[19]

After the preface, *Survey* follows the example of *Revelation Unveiled:* it begins with carefully documented doctrinal presentations, first of the teachings of Roman Catholics and then of Lutheran Protestants. Swedenborg adds a note at the end of that introduction to the effect that the Calvinist Protestant teachings found in England and Holland were essentially the same as the Lutheran teachings just cited (§15). Again the teachings of the Christian leaders are specifically and explicitly targeted.

Survey goes on to present a table of contents (§16) of the forthcoming work itself (which will later evolve into *True Christianity*). This table of contents allows us a rare glimpse into Swedenborg's thinking about a future volume. *Survey* states that the coming work will be divided into three parts, and gives titles and numbers to individual chapters of the first two parts. The third part is described in a prose paragraph that then leads directly into the main body of *Survey* itself.[20] The main portion of *Survey* that follows consists of twenty-five points of disagreement between the existing Christian churches and what Swedenborg calls the "new church," with brief discussions. To these are added two memorable occurrences from *Revelation Unveiled,* followed by a quote from Jeremiah, a statement in large print of the faith of the new heaven and the new church, and finally three more memorable occurrences from *Revelation Unveiled.* In *Survey*'s sixty-seven pages, then, Swedenborg outlines a new form of Christianity and details its differences from the prevailing version.

This little work was in print by January or early February 1769, as we gather from a letter to Swedenborg from his friend Cuno. That letter

---

19. *Survey* 1; my translation.

20. For this table of contents and its contrast with the finished work, see figure 1 on page 18.

indicates that the printing of the work and its initial distribution were completed "scarcely a month" before March 8, 1769, the date of the letter (Acton 1948–1955, 651). In addition Cuno comments on Swedenborg's active distribution of the work, makes a tongue-in-cheek conjecture about the strategy behind that distribution (see the portion set in italics in the quotation below), and expresses an opinion on whether it will work:

> You have again sent out your last work, and distributed it among the clergy of all sects in this city—not the Reformed only but also the Papists. You have distributed it throughout other cities and universities of Holland. From that time, scarcely a month has now passed and I do not hear of any one murmuring. *It seems, therefore, that you are seeking adversaries,* but, if I may be allowed to speak openly, I fear you will not find them. . . . (Acton 1948–1955, 651, emphasis mine)

b. The Göteborg Consistory's Attack on Swedenborg's Teachings

A week later, on March 15, 1769, Swedenborg wrote home from Amsterdam to his friend Beyer, who was a member of the Göteborg Consistory.[21] In his letter, Swedenborg proposed a plan for distributing *Survey* in Sweden:

> I am thinking of sending 12 copies to the Herr Doctor *[Beyer]* by the first ship that goes from here. These the Herr Doctor will please give: 1 to the Herr Bishop [Lamberg], 1 to the Herr Dean [Ekebom], and the rest, except his own copy, to the Lectors of Theology and to the Priests in the city; for no one can judge the work so well as one who has fundamentally entered into the secrets of justification. After the little work has been read by the Herr Dean *[Ekebom],* may it please the Herr Doctor *[Beyer]* kindly to request him to express his opinion of it in the Consistory. All those here who are able and willing to see the truth, will assent.[22]

During a single week in Göteborg back in July 1765, Swedenborg had met Lamberg, Ekebom, Beyer, and Johan Rosén (1726–1773), professor of poetry and elocution at the Göteborg Academy; they had all seemed open to Swedenborg's point of view at the time. At this moment in mid-March 1769, Swedenborg evidently still thought of Ekebom as supportive

---

21. The Göteborg Consistory was the governing council of those members of the clergy who served in and around the mercantile city of Göteborg on the west coast of Sweden.

22. Acton 1948–1955, 659. The names in brackets have been added for clarity; those not in italics were added by Acton, those in italics by me.

of his message, and therefore as someone particularly well suited to read *Survey* and report on it to the Göteborg Consistory.

There was great irony in this request, of which Swedenborg was apparently not at all aware when he wrote. Just a week later—though actually not in response to Swedenborg's letter—Ekebom presented an official statement before the Göteborg Consistory[23] in which he declared Swedenborg's writings to be "corrupting, heretical, injurious, and in the highest degree to be rejected" (Acton 1948–1955, 662). This strong statement was the culmination of an investigation of several months' duration into the status and acceptability of Swedenborg's teachings. The investigation had been prompted during the previous fall (September and October 1768) when the Göteborg Consistory had received two or three questions or complaints about Swedenborgianism.[24] In the course of the investigation, Ekebom and later Bishop Lamberg had proven hostile to Swedenborgianism and had launched a joint attack against it, including an eventually successful effort to have Beyer, their colleague, fired from his teaching position and replaced.

Swedenborg, busy writing and publishing far away in Amsterdam, was still unaware of the entire business. He first learned of the crisis in a letter sent to him in the beginning of April 1769 (Acton 1948–1955, 661) by a lay friend from Göteborg, the merchant and banker Peter Hammarberg (1720–1807), who was Beyer's brother-in-law (Tafel 1877, 1144).

As soon as Swedenborg knew that Ekebom had proven to be an enemy to what he was writing, he immediately changed his plans for distribution of *Survey* in Sweden. As we saw above, he had previously been thinking of sending a dozen copies of the work to Göteborg alone (Acton 1948–1955, 659), and presumably planned to send more to Stockholm and Uppsala. He had already sent copies of it to each of the priests,

---

23. Ekebom was then acting head of the Consistory while Bishop Lamberg was away (Acton 1948–1955, 672).

24. These questions apparently arose in response to four events, three of which involved a presentation of Swedenborg's thought to Swedish people in their own tongue rather than in Latin—something that had not occurred before: (1) On October 20, 1766, Rosén published in *Göteborgske Spionen* (The Göteborg Spy) a brief extract of *Revelation Unveiled* translated into Swedish (Swedenborg 1766). (2) In 1767, Beyer wrote and published anonymously a volume of sermons in Swedish whose content drew upon Swedenborg's teachings ([Beyer] 1767). (3) In April 1768 Rosén published a Swedish translation of a review by Ernesti of *Revelation Unveiled* in *Preste-Tidningar* (Pastoral News; Ernesti 1768). And (4) at Göteborg's annual clergy meetings in September 1768, Magnus Roempke (1717–1784), professor of theology at the Göteborg Academy, presented a paper on redemption that took a Swedenborgian view (Acton 1948–1955, 660).

clergy, and professors in Holland and to the "foremost" priests and universities in Germany; he had also distributed it in Paris and commissioned a translation of it into English (Acton 1948–1955, 659, 672). Upon learning of the crisis, however, he decided to send just a single copy to Sweden, to his trusted friend Beyer, with instructions not to circulate it (Acton 1948–1955, 659); he now planned instead to await a reaction to *Survey* from those other countries before actively distributing the work in Sweden:

> It must wait for judgment concerning it from abroad before being made generally known in Sweden. Until then, therefore, keep it for yourself alone. (Acton 1948–1955, 672)

Swedenborg did send one other copy into Sweden, to his nephew, Lars Benzelstierna (1719–1800), bishop of Västerås, but again he did so with "the strict proviso, that it shall in no way be communicated to any other person."[25]

Cuno's prophecy that there would be little response turned out to be true for the rest of Europe—no storm of controversy arose there; but Swedenborg's homeland favored him with a full-blown crisis. As he was continuing to write the first draft of *True Christianity* in April 1769 he became aware of and at least peripherally involved in the storm. Swedenborg apparently adjusted the work in progress, at least in part, to address and defend against the attack in Sweden.

c. *The Doctrine of the New Church* as a Digest

In developing a book, Swedenborg's usual practice was to create preliminary studies and drafts in outline form. These outlines were complete down to the numbered points he wished to make under each section.[26] He would copy these points into a rough draft and write material to

---

25. Acton 1948–1955, 697. From the fact that *Survey* appeared two or three months before Swedenborg learned of the trouble with the Göteborg Consistory and that upon being apprised of it he changed the distribution he had planned in Sweden, it becomes clear that although *Survey* and the storm of controversy may seem to be linked, they had no cause-and-effect relationship, but merely coincided in time (late 1768 and early 1769). Sweden had not seen the volume when the crisis and trial began, and Swedenborg had not heard of the crisis when he wrote and published the volume.

26. Compare the outline in *Summary of New Church Teachings* (= Swedenborg 1996, 2:561–567) with the topics in the finished work *Survey;* compare also the outline in *Sketch for "True Christianity"* (= Swedenborg 1996, 1:177–239) with the points made in the first three chapters of *True Christianity.* Also see Regamey 1935.

explain each point. Then he would rewrite this rough copy in a more careful, legible hand as a fair copy for the printer, with instructions on typefaces and type sizes in the margins and indications for the placement of ornaments. The fair copy would therefore closely match the rough copy. In the case of *True Christianity,* however, Swedenborg may have produced as many as three rough drafts. He started the first draft in the fall of 1768 before turning to *Survey* or learning that his works were under attack in Sweden.

Since his topic was the complete doctrine of the new church, and since he had written many works already on specific teachings for or related to the new church, Swedenborg seems to have based at least some of the chapters on other volumes he had already published. This borrowing is still visible in the finished product—especially in the first half of the work, but also in the supplement at the end concerning the spiritual world. The basic content of the first chapter is very similar to material in *Divine Love and Wisdom,* but the approach is quite different.[27] The second chapter borrows concepts and lists of passages from *The Lord* (1763). The fourth chapter is probably the heaviest borrowing of all; it is a minimally edited version of *Sacred Scripture* (1763). The fifth chapter parallels some material in *Life* (1763). The sixth chapter shows some dependence on *Faith* (1763). The seventh chapter reworks an earlier unpublished manuscript titled *Sketch on Goodwill* (= Swedenborg 1995). Chapters 8 through 14 are more original, but the closing section is very closely modeled on *Supplements* (1763; see part IVb of this preface below). There are also many smaller passages in the work that are imported from earlier works (see the table of parallel passages at the end of volume 2). The text is generally silent about these many borrowings and instances of close dependence, but there are occasionally passages, such as §§397–402, that are lifted wholesale from earlier works and flagged as quotations. In addition, fully two-thirds of the memorable occurrences in the volume were first published in *Revelation Unveiled* or *Marriage Love.*[28]

---

27. See Dole 2005, 115.

28. If the original plan had been carried out (see *Survey* 16), there would likely have been even more borrowings. Presumably the projected chapter 5 in part 1, "Teachings about Life Drawn from the Ten Commandments," would have owed something to Swedenborg's 1763 work *Teachings about Life: Drawn from the Ten Commandments* (currently known by the short title *Life*); chapters 10 through 12 in part 1, on heaven and hell and eternal life, would have borrowed from *Heaven and Hell;* and chapter 3 in part 2, "The Last Judgment," would have been based on Swedenborg's 1758 work *Last Judgment* and on *Supplements,* which included a supplement to *Last Judgment.*

In every case, the material is reworked to suit its new home. Nevertheless, some minor inconsistencies remain. The work's fourteen chapters, for example, contain four different types of subheadings: one type appears in chapters 1 through 3; a second type, in chapters 4 and 6; a third type, in chapter 5; and a fourth type, in chapters 7 through 14. Another example of inconsistency is less superficial: most chapters have many similes and analogies, but chapter 4 has virtually none, presumably because it was largely copied from an earlier work that lacked such features.

At the time in early April 1769 when Swedenborg first learned of trouble in Sweden, he had progressed far enough in the composition of *The Doctrine of the New Church* that he was planning to travel to Paris the following week in order to have a censor read the work, a necessary step in having the book printed there.[29] The work must have been sufficiently complete to be ready for the censor's review. It was presumably a complete first draft of the work, with the title *The Doctrine of the New Church*.

IV. Changes in Response to Attack

Since we have a published outline of *The Doctrine of the New Church* as Swedenborg conceived of it shortly before February 1769, we can clearly see that the work underwent significant changes between then and its appearance as *True Christianity* in June 1771 (see figure 1, page 18). It seems highly likely that Swedenborg made these changes in response to learning in April 1769 that his works and his followers were under attack.

a. Changes in the Outline

By the time *True Christianity* appeared in June 1771, the work looked quite different than it had in January or February 1769. The opening chapter on the Lord and on the divine Trinity within him had expanded into three large chapters, one on the Father, one on the Son, and one on

---

29. This trip did in fact happen, but the work was not published in Paris. The censor in Paris said that though the work could be printed there, Swedenborg would not be allowed to use the word "Paris" on the title page. The censor suggested that "London" or "Amsterdam" be placed there instead. Presumably those cities were chosen as the most plausible substitutes because they were the most religiously liberal and tolerant cities in western Europe. Swedenborg was unwilling to go along with this deception, and instead arranged to have the work published in Amsterdam (Tafel 1877, 700–701; Sigstedt 1981, 376).

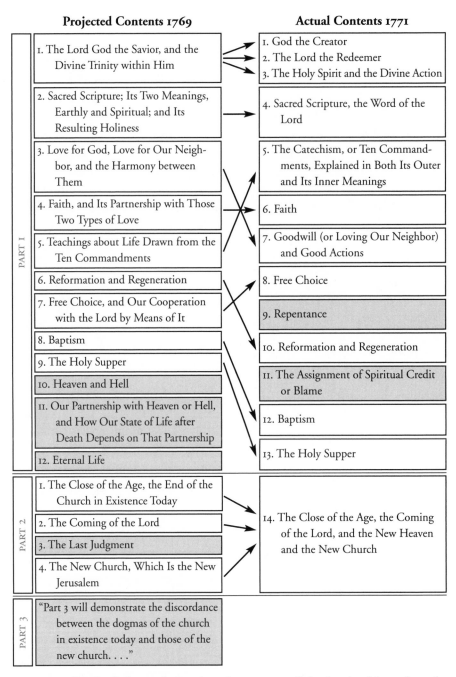

Figure 1. On the left are the projected contents of the book ultimately published under the title *True Christianity,* quoted from *Survey* 16. On the right are the actual contents of the book as it was published. Arrows show the rearrangement of topics that took place between 1769 and 1771. Shaded topics have no parallel in the opposing list.

the Holy Spirit. This three-part treatment of God is without precedent in Swedenborg's earlier works; but it does reflect common practice in the Protestant theology of that time.[30] A chapter on living in accordance with the Ten Commandments was retitled, and presumably also reworked, as an explanation of the Catechism, a term and topic very familiar to contemporary Lutheran readers, who had to memorize the Catechism from an early age.[31] A chapter on repentance was added, as was a chapter on "imputation," or the assignment of spiritual credit or blame, a significant theological topic in recent Protestant thought. The original plan for *The Doctrine of the New Church* indicates that the book was to contain three chapters on heaven and hell and eternal life. Given the centrality of these topics in Swedenborg's theology, it is surprising that these chapters were omitted from the later plan. As Swedenborgian scholar George F. Dole has suggested, perhaps the reason behind this particular change was that life after death was not a standard topic of Lutheran theology.[32] A chapter on the Last Judgment was also dropped.

b. Changes in the Supplement

A shift toward a Lutheran audience also appears when we compare the supplement on the spiritual world in *Supplements* with the supplement on the spiritual world in *True Christianity.* The latter material is clearly based on the former, and generally follows it closely; therefore the differences become informative (see figure 2, page 20).

The most notable change is that a new section, not found in *Supplements* but inserted toward the beginning of the otherwise parallel material in *True Christianity,* concerns the Protestant religious leaders Martin Luther (1483–1546), Philipp Melanchthon (1497–1560), and John Calvin

---

30. See pages 76–77, 83 below; and Dole 1988, 352.

31. See pages 60, 82–84 below; and see also Smoley 2005, 5.

32. Dole 2005, 114. It should be noted as well that *True Christianity* quotes Acts and Epistles much more often than Swedenborg's previous works do, a discrepancy that suggests that the work is aimed at a new audience, or at least addresses an existing audience in a new way. Although Swedenborg had earlier compiled five Bible indexes (see the works designated U118–U119, U123–U124, U126 in Rose 2005b, 481–485), around this time he compiled yet another concordance, this time to Acts and Epistles, and also included further concordance material on the prophets for specific topics dealt with in *True Christianity* (see *Bible Concordance for "True Christianity"* = Swedenborg 1996, 2:241–347). Hyde 1906, entry 2711, dates this manuscript to September 1769, a few months after Swedenborg learned of the trial in Göteborg. For Swedenborg's position before this time on Acts and Epistles, see Acton 1948–1955, 612–613.

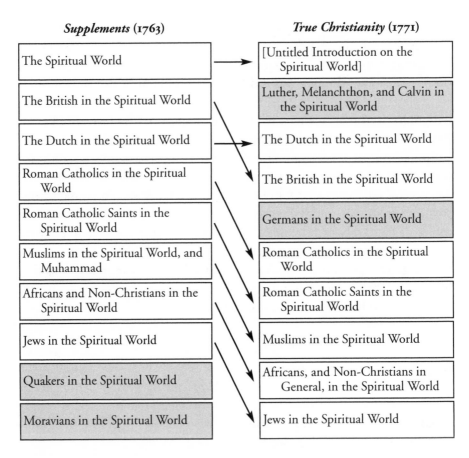

Figure 2. On the left are items in the contents of the material on the spiritual world in *Supplements* 32–90 (published late summer 1763). On the right are the contents of the supplement on the spiritual world in *True Christianity* 792–845 (published June 1771). Arrows show related topics. Shaded topics have no parallel in the opposing list.

(1509–1564) in the spiritual world. There could hardly be a clearer indication that they and their followers had become a primary focus of the volume as it evolved. Swedenborg also added a section on Germans and omitted sections on Quakers and Moravians. In neither volume is there a section on the Swedes or the Danes in the spiritual world—a striking and no doubt deliberate omission. Indeed, the geographical sequence itself at the end of *True Christianity* suggests a Lutheran worldview, omitting

Swedenborg's country and its neighbor Denmark; then turning from predominantly Protestant countries nearby to Protestant countries farther away; then to Germany, which straddled both Protestantism and Catholicism in its various duchies; to Catholic lands; and finally to non-Christian religions and regions of the world.

Such extensive changes to the manuscript must have required some time and rewriting. In fact, there are clues that this is the case. *True Christianity* 791, a passage that comes at the very end of the main text and before the supplement on the spiritual world, explicitly states that "this work" was completed before June 19, 1770. What work was completed on this date? It seems highly unlikely that it was the first draft, since the material presented to the French censor in April 1769 must have been sufficiently complete to allow him to judge it. It was probably not the final draft either, since after this, five months elapsed before printing began around December 1770 (see part V of this preface below). Therefore the work whose completion by June 19, 1770, warranted this celebratory statement at the end of the main text may well have been a second draft, representing a completely rewritten version of the first.

Biographer Alfred Acton (1867–1956) conjectures that in the five or so months that intervened between this statement and the time Swedenborg began to see pages through the press, he "busied himself with copying and enlarging" the work he was about to publish (Acton 1948–1955, 734). To state the case more explicitly, we may see Swedenborg's work during this period as consisting of actually preparing yet another draft of the whole work.

c. One Last Change: A New Title

During the time in which it seems likely that Swedenborg was rewriting the work, its title apparently changed slightly: whereas it had been referred to as *The Doctrine of the New Church,* it became *A Comprehensive Theology of the New Church.* We first learn of this new version of the title in Swedenborg's letter to Beyer of April 30, 1770 (Acton 1948–1955, 715). Letters Swedenborg wrote on July 20 and July 23 of that same year show that this continued to be the working title while the final revision was underway (Acton 1948–1955, 730, 732).

By December 1770, when printing began, the title had apparently gained a new phrase to become *A Comprehensive Theology of the New*

Heaven and the New Church, to judge by the running heads in the first edition of the work. (The running heads are the words repeated at the top of every page.) In the finished work, from the first signature to the end of the main text on page 502, the running heads read *UNIVERSA THEOLOGIA* (A Comprehensive Theology) on the verso (left-hand) pages and *NOVI CAELI ET NOVAE ECCLESIAE* (of the New Heaven and the New Church) on the recto (right-hand) pages. In Swedenborg's theological publications, the running heads usually contain the title of the work; the presence of these words in the running heads suggests therefore that when printing began, this was what Swedenborg intended as the title.

The printing of the volume lasted from around December 1770 to shortly before June 18, 1771. Late in that process, Swedenborg was still using *A Comprehensive Theology of the New Heaven and the New Church* as the title of the work, as we gather from a letter he wrote to Beyer on April 30, 1771, just six weeks before the work was completed and bound (Acton 1948–1955, 735). In that same letter, Swedenborg makes it clear that he is still thinking about the Göteborg trial; when the work is in print he plans to send two copies of it to each of the four estates, or houses, of the Swedish Diet, the governing assembly.

During the seven weeks between May 1 and June 18, 1771, however, as the last pages were coming off the press, it appears that Swedenborg modified the title yet again: he introduced the words *Vera Christiana Religio* ("True Christianity," or, if translated word-for-word, "True Christian Religion")[33] and the word *Continens* ("Containing") before the rest of the title. In effect this became the new main title, and the old title became a subtitle. Because the old title page must have already been printed as part of the first signature (that is, the first eight pages, which had been printed as a unit), Swedenborg must have ordered the first signature redone and the obsolete signatures destroyed.

The main evidence for this conjectured change in title is the contrast between the main title given in the running heads *(Comprehensive Theology . . .)* and the main title that appears on the title page and at the top of page 3 *(True Christianity)*. In addition, as we will see below, there is

---

33. On the choice of the phrase "True Christianity" rather than "True Christian Religion" to translate the title, see note 44 below.

no evidence that Swedenborg used the title *Vera Christiana Religio* before June 7, 1771; after that date, it was the only title he used for the work. Another piece of possible evidence for this late change in title is its placement at the top of page 3 of the first edition. This was a departure from Swedenborg's usual pattern. In his published works, on the first recto page after the title page, that is, on the first full page of text (usually numbered page 3), a full-width headpiece ornament virtually always appears above the opening title, which is then followed by the text itself; at the very least there is a double line.[34] *True Christianity* is the lone exception; it has no ornament or double line at that location. Instead the words *VERA CHRISTIANA RELIGIO* (True Christianity, or True Christian Religion) appear at the very top of the page; and *CONTINENS* (Containing) appears on a second line down. It is highly likely, then, that the first version of page 3 had a headpiece ornament there, as well as the words *UNIVERSA THEOLOGIA NOVI CAELI ET NOVAE ECCLESIAE* (A Comprehensive Theology of the New Heaven and the New Church), matching the title given in the letters mentioned just above.

If this conjecture is correct, the change must have been made in the last weeks of production. The first definite instance of the use of the new title can be dated to June 7, 1771, when Swedenborg wrote out the title page in its entirety on a slip of paper for Duke Ludwig IX, the Landgrave of Hesse-Darmstadt (Benz 1947, 309–310), beginning with the words *Vera Christiana Religio.*

The reason for the change is not clear—to the best of my knowledge Swedenborg never comments on it. But the change was decisive: from

---

34. For an example of a headpiece ornament, see Swedenborg 1763, 3; the same example is reproduced in Swedenborg [1763] 2003, 51. The placing of an ornament on the first right-hand page after the title page is the single most consistent rule in Swedenborg's use of such decorative elements: an ornament can be found after all of the twenty-eight title pages of his theological works before *True Christianity* (see Rose 1998, 306–317). Only the twenty-three-page *Soul-Body Interaction* does not fully conform, and not just in this respect: this work, which has no title page at all and presents the place and date of publication on the last page instead, has a simple ornament of a full-width double line instead of the usual more elaborate headpiece. Ever since he had first begun publishing major works in 1734, Swedenborg had been consistently placing headpiece ornaments in these locations. (It should be noted that *Secrets of Heaven* was published in multiple volumes and even in parts of volumes; thus there are more title pages than there are actual individual works in Swedenborg's theological corpus. All these "extra" title pages also fit the pattern described here.)

June 7, 1771, onward in both his manuscripts and letters Swedenborg always refers to this volume as *Vera Christiana Religio* (True Christianity, or True Christian Religion).[35]

The new title has many interesting parallels and precedents. The simpler concept of the "true religion" goes back to the early days of the clash between Christianity and ancient religions; the Christian philosopher Augustine (354–430), for example, wrote a work titled *On the True Religion.* The expression can later be seen in European statements intended to assert the primacy of Christianity over Islam.[36] When Christianity itself fractured, the terms "true religion,"[37] "true Christianity," and especially "true Christian religion" became code phrases for the form of Christianity espoused by a particular individual or branch of Christianity. It appears conspicuously at the beginning of a portion of the Formula of Concord known as the Solid Declaration (1577):

> Fundamental, enduring unity in the church requires above all else a clear and binding summary and form in which a general summary of teaching is drawn together from God's Word, to which the churches that hold the *true Christian religion* confess their adherence.[38]

The phrase "true Christian religion" in Latin and other European languages appears in a number of book titles between the sixteenth and

---

35. Outside of one mention on the title page of the first edition and one at the top of page 3 (above the beginning of the main text), the phrase that serves as the title, *vera christiana religio,* is not mentioned in the text itself. When in the body of the work Swedenborg refers to the work itself, he uses vague language such as "this book" or "this work" (see §§75:7, 485, 791). Manuscripts and letters written on or after June 7, 1771, however, consistently refer to the work as *Vera Christiana Religio:* see *Draft for "Coda to True Christianity"* (= Swedenborg 1996, 1:23–106) §§18, 21, 22, 28, 39; *Draft Invitation to the New Church* (= Swedenborg 1996, 1:125–150) §§syllabus:2, 32, 39, 43; Acton 1948–1955, 738, 744, 747, 749, 751.

36. See, for example, the four-volume Catholic work by Lodovico Marracci (1612–1700) titled *Precursor to a Refutation of the Alcoran* [the Qur'an], *in Which the Falsity of the Muhammadan Sect Is Shown through Four Indications of True Religion; [and] the Truth of the Christian Religion Is Proven* (Latin, 1691). In the following discussion I have translated titles into English; further publication information including the original titles is given in the list of works cited at the end of this preface.

37. See, for example, John Milton's (1608–1674) treatise "Of True Religion, Haeresie, Schism, Toleration, and . . . the Growth of Popery" (English, 1673).

38. Kolb and Wengert 2000, 526; emphasis mine. Composed of a number of texts ranging from 1524 to 1580, the *Book of Concord* is an anthology of definitive and authoritative Lutheran teachings; for a recent edition see Kolb and Wengert 2000. Swedenborg used an edition of 1756, published in Leipzig (*Concordia* 1756).

eighteenth centuries. For example, Georg Calixt (1586–1656), a professor of theology at the University of Helmstedt who wished to reunite the various branches of Christianity, wrote a work titled *The True Christian Religion and Church* (Latin, 1633); and Edward Burrough wrote a Quaker tract titled "The True Christian Religion Again Discovered, after a Long and Dark Night of Apostasy . . ." (English, 1658). The phrase was sometimes used on works that heralded a new movement within Christianity: see, for example, the Reformed creed known as the Second Helvetic Confession, penned by theologian Heinrich Bullinger (1504–1575), *A Brief and Plain Confession and Declaration of . . . the True Christian Religion* (Latin, 1566); the Baptist declaration by one of its founders, John Smyth (1570?–1612), *Propositions and Conclusions Concerning True Christian Religion* (English, 1612–1614; see Smyth 1915); and the controversial Anglican sermon published by John Thomas, rector of Saint Nicholas in Cardiff, *A Vindication of the True Christian Religion, in Opposition to the Abominations of Popery* (English, 1679).[39]

A number of works had titles with closely related phrases, such as "the true ancient Christian religion" or "the truth of the Christian religion."[40] Though it is not likely that all of these were known to Swedenborg, two were definitely prominent in his life. The German theologian Johann Arndt (1555–1621) wrote a highly popular work, *True Christianity* (German, 1605); it was very familiar to Swedish readers in Swedenborg's day.[41] The prolific Dutch scholar and jurist Hugo Grotius (1583–1645) published

---

39. Other examples of the phrase are found in the titles of Swithune Butterfield's *The Principles of the True Christian Religion* (English, 1590); Daniel Tossanus's *Theological Theses on These Three Questions Much Ventilated Today; How the True Christian Religion Is to Be Defined and Acknowledged . . .* (Latin, 1593); Johann David Wunderer's *Unprejudiced Consideration of and Answer to the Question of Whether the Holy Gospels, That Is, the True Christian Religion, Should Be Defended with the Worldly Sword* (German, 1619); Thomas Emes's *The Atheist Turn'd Deist, and the Deist Turn'd Christian: Or, The Reasonableness and Union of Natural and the True Christian Religion* (English, 1698); and Adam Struensee's *Theological Dissertation on Joy in the Holy Spirit as a Genuine Criterion of the True Christian Religion* (Latin, 1751).

40. As examples of a few of the many such titles, see Antoine Lescaille's *Antithesis of the True, Ancient Christian Religion and the New Anti-Christian Religion* (Latin, 1597); Augustin Fuhrman's *Preservation of the Ancient True Christian Catholico-Evangelical Religion* (German, 1658); Gilbert Burnet's *Rational Method for Proving the Truth of the Christian Religion, As It Is Professed in the Church of England* (English, 1675); François Lamy's *The Obvious Truth of the Christian Religion* (French, 1694); Andreas Hasselquist's *Light That Was Shed by the Light . . . or the True and Legitimate Christian Religion* (Latin, 1697); and in the same year as Swedenborg's *True Christianity,* Jean Pey's two-volume work, *The Truth of the Christian Religion, Proven to a Deist* (French, 1771).

41. See page 60 below.

a defense of Christianity titled *On the Truth of the Christian Religion* (Latin, 1627). Swedenborg quotes this work dozens of times in his commonplace book (a collection of quotations from various authors); in fact he owned a copy of the 1662 edition published in Amsterdam.[42]

Aside from these literary and doctrinal forerunners, there is another striking precedent for the title in a letter Swedenborg himself wrote to Gabriel Beyer on April 12, 1770. This letter was intended for publication; it was composed in response to the published minutes of the Göteborg Consistory and to a plea from Beyer for help as he was being threatened with exile. In it Swedenborg wrote of his own works as described by the Consistory: "There they call this Swedenborgianism, but I for my part, True Christianity."[43]

Since the early days of Christianity, then, authors and theologians had marked certain teachings and positions as "true Christian religion," "true Christianity," or the like, much the way explorers plant a flag on a high point of land in a newly discovered territory. Perhaps Swedenborg chose this title because he wished to place a familiar and readily recognizable flag atop the summit of the theological territory he had discovered.[44]

---

42. For Swedenborg's citations of Grotius, see the index entry under "Grotius" in Swedenborg 1976, 528. For the edition Swedenborg owned, see Grotius [1627] 1662; and also Alfelt 1969, 120; Swedenborg 1976, 528 note.

43. Acton 1948–1955, 709. The words that Acton translates as "True Christianity" are "rätta *Christianismus*," a Swedish word followed by a Latin word; for the original see Swedenborg 1787, page G5. One might be tempted to think that this letter shows the birth of the new title, but that position would be hard to reconcile with Swedenborg's use of *A Comprehensive Theology* . . . as the main title for at least a year after this letter was written, and the lack of any reference to the title *True Christianity,* or *True Christian Religion,* until June 1771. Since no pages had been printed when this letter was written, Swedenborg would have had every opportunity to specify that the words *Vera Christiana Religio* (True Christianity or True Christian Religion) be placed in the running heads, but he did not do so.

44. The term "Christianity" rather than "the Christian religion" is used in the title of this translation because it captures the broad and inclusive sense Swedenborg clearly intended his Neo-Latin title to have. As the similar titles just quoted suggest, the Neo-Latin term *Christiana religio* (literally, "the Christian religion") was commonly used to mean "Christianity." In contemporary English the phrase "Christian religion," on the other hand, is generally limited to academic usage. Although Neo-Latin writers, including Swedenborg, also used another term, *Christianismus* (literally "Christianism"), this term was somewhat problematic. First, it was ambiguous, since it sometimes denoted no more than the geographical extent of Christianity. Second, it carried negative overtones, as many terms ending in *ism* do in modern English. Although technically there could have been a noun form *Christianitas,* like the English term "Christianity," in actual practice this form was extremely rare in Neo-Latin literature, and nonexistent in Swedenborg's writing. Thus his use of *Christiana religio* rather than some other term for "Christianity" reflects the best option available to him.

Whatever significance the conjectured last-minute addition of a new main title and the demotion of the old main title into a subtitle may have in and of themselves, these decisions take on greater importance when they are seen as the last and most visible of a whole series of changes to the work since Swedenborg learned of the trial in Sweden.

This analysis does not seek to deny that *True Christianity* truly did begin as a digest of the doctrine or theology of the new church. It does maintain, however, that as the work evolved it took on an additional role: that of a defense of the authenticity and Scriptural soundness of that theology, a defense directed against a faction in the Swedish Lutheran clergy bitterly hostile to it.

The main impact of all these changes on the final product is that the tone of the book varies enormously. It ranges from the warm, personal, and spiritual tone of most of Swedenborg's former works to a harsher and more confrontational tone. The latter was no doubt a response to the adversarial climate in Sweden at the time the work was revised, and which in fact caused that thorough-going revision.[45]

---

45. Although the heresy trial continued after *True Christianity* appeared in print and therefore falls partly outside the scope of this preface, its course and outcome can be briefly stated as follows. After much back and forth in the Göteborg Consistory, in December 1769 the issue of whether Swedenborg's works were indeed heretical and should be banned was brought to the House of the Clergy, which was meeting as part of the Diet in Stockholm, by Bishop Lamberg of Göteborg, who had been appointed the speaker in the House of the Clergy. Swedenborg was so well connected with the Swedish ecclesiastical hierarchy that he himself was never placed on trial, and many favorable things about his works were said in the discussion in the House of the Clergy. The opposition was strong, however, and the issue was referred at several points to King Adolph Frederick himself (1710–1771). The king seems to have been quite favorable to Swedenborg. He had earlier invited Swedenborg to dine with him, in company with the queen, the royal family, and five members of the court, at which time the conversation had largely concerned Swedenborg's awareness of the spiritual world and his revelatory writings (Acton 1948–1955, 724); and the king spoke reassuring words about the probable outcome of the trial to Swedenborg on one occasion in July 1770 (Tafel 1875, 72). Beyer was called on to testify in writing before the king on the issue of the truth and usefulness of what Swedenborg had written, which he did eloquently (Tafel 1877, 323–345). The final royal judgment was unfavorable, but could have been worse; Swedenborg's works were not declared *heretical*, but were said to contain *errors* (Tafel 1877, 365–368; Benz 2002, 512). All translations and reviews of Swedenborg's works were banned, and importation of his works was allowed only if the local consistory approved. Beyer and Rosén were forced out of their teaching positions. This may seem a harsh judgment, but it was far milder than Lamberg or Ekebom had apparently hoped for. Rosén and Beyer stood firm and were unwilling to renounce Swedenborgianism. The case was therefore referred to the Court of Appeals in June 1772. The Court decided not to act until the Uppsala Consistory had reviewed Swedenborg's writings and had ruled on the issue of heresy. In September 1778, years after Swedenborg himself had died, the Court of Appeals reported to King Gustaf III (1746–1792) that it had still not heard from the Uppsala Consistory, and asked that the case be dropped. To this request the king gave his consent (Acton 1948–1955, 734 note 9a).

V. The Speed of Production

All told, these changes caused the publication schedule to slip by a year. Once production of the printed volume finally began, however, it progressed at an impressive rate. In a letter written on January 26, 1771, Cuno gives us a window into Swedenborg's progress on the printing:

> He is now working on his book indefatigably; indeed, I must say in an astonishing and superhuman way. Sixteen sheets in type twice as small as his previous book are already printed. Just think! for every printed sheet he must fill four sheets in writing. He is now having two sheets printed every week. He reads the proof himself. Consequently he must write eight sheets every week. And, what is completely incomprehensible, he never has even a single line in reserve. His work, as he says, will consist in print of eighty sheets; consequently, he has calculated that the printing cannot be finished before Michaelmas [September 29]. (Cuno 1947, 160–161)

Several statements in this letter warrant a comment. The type in *True Christianity* is indeed smaller than that of all Swedenborg's previous theological publications. It is not literally half the size, however; in Anglo-American units his previous works appear in eleven-point type with twelve points of leading from baseline to baseline. *True Christianity* was set in nine-point type with ten points of leading. Therefore many more words fit on each page. By a "sheet" Cuno means a large piece of paper printed on front and back with 4 pages on each side. When folded in half and in half again, this sheet would form a signature, or bundle (called an "ark" in the jargon of Swedenborg's printers), of 8 printed pages. Therefore the first 128 pages of the work were printed by January 26, 1771. When Cuno says that Swedenborg is writing eight sheets (or 64 pages) a week, we are not to imagine that he was composing those pages from scratch—he had begun writing the work over two years earlier. Presumably this refers instead to Swedenborg's writing out a final copy, the fair copy for the printer. It is surprising, however, to learn that Swedenborg kept only one step ahead of the printer, copying just enough for the following day's work. This suggests that he had been so busy with revising or that the revision was so extensive that he had not prepared the fair copy before printing began.[46]

---

46. This last-minute preparation of a fair copy had not been Swedenborg's practice a dozen years earlier; back then, when he was working on *Revelation Explained* (= Swedenborg 1994–1997), immediately after writing a few paragraphs of rough copy he would draft a fair copy of the same material.

Cuno's letter allows us to calculate back and determine that if the printing proceeded from its commencement at the same pace of two sheets or sixteen pages per week, the first pages must have been printed around December 3, 1770.

In January 1771, Swedenborg projected that the finished work would fill eighty sheets, or 640 pages. As it turned out, the finished work filled just sixty-eight sheets, or 544 pages (it formally ends on page 541, but this is followed by a brief page listing typographical errors and two blank pages). Although it is possible that Swedenborg simply miscalculated, it is much more likely that in January 1771 Swedenborg was still thinking of including the appendix he mentions in several places in the volume.[47] At some point between then and the end of April he must have changed his mind and decided to publish the volume without the appendix; although he had earlier projected that the volume would appear at the end of September 1771, in a letter of April 30, 1771, he tells Beyer the work will "at last" leave the press in June 1771 (Acton 1948–1955, 735), a prediction that proved accurate.

Either Cuno actually understates the rate of progress on the volume, or Swedenborg and the press accelerated. Between page 128 on January 26 and page 544 around June 18, the volume was completed at an average rate of twenty-one pages per week (or eighty-four pages of handwritten fair copy). The speed, the small type, and the age of the eyes of the proofreader (Swedenborg himself) took a toll on the volume. The percentage of words with typographical errors is much higher than in previous volumes. The list of errors on the last printed page, which is itself full of mistakes, ends abruptly at the notations for page 296, with the added comment: "Not to mention many trivial errors."[48] Swedenborg later wrote corrections in his own copy, and Samuel H. Worcester (1824–1891) incorporated them in his Latin edition of 1906 (see the selected list of editions at the end of this preface, pages 50 to 51). The present translation takes Swedenborg's corrections into account.

---

47. See note 1 above.

48. The minor mistakes to which Swedenborg was evidently referring are easily detected and compensated for by the reader, however unprofessional those errors may appear. For example, if the reader of an English text were to encounter an *n* instead of an *h* in the word "del016" the mistake would be irritating, but the intended word obvious. This is the superficial nature of the vast majority of typographical errors in *True Christianity*.

VI. The Three Audiences of the Work in Its Finished Form

True Christianity in its final form seems to have been written with all three of the audiences mentioned above in mind: Christian leaders, philosophers, and ordinary people. Although the revisions mentioned placed a greater emphasis on the teachings and attitudes of Christian leaders, the shortcomings of philosophers and especially materialist philosophy and atheism are not ignored. In addition to criticisms in the main text, a number of memorable occurrences highlight the folly of the people who espouse these philosophies, and the dire outcome that awaits them after death (see, for example, §§77:5, 79, 80, 121:2, 133, 333:2).

And Swedenborg has not forgotten the ordinary people, who, as has already been noted, have been the primary audience for many of his earlier works. He expressly states that he adorns the doctrinal argument with many analogies "for the sake of ordinary people" (§131); indeed, these analogies occur copiously throughout the work (there are some four hundred instances of just one particularly elaborate type; see Rose 1994, 871). In the memorable occurrences, people who are neither clergy nor philosophers often provide the voice of wisdom and sanity (see §389, for example, in which lay people are theologically enlightened, but their episcopal governors are obtuse). And the theological teachings themselves are highly practical, often appealing to common sense and common experience. For example, the discussion of different ways to show love for one's neighbor in the chapter on goodwill is down-to-earth and practical, including mentions of the attitude we should have toward paying taxes and fulfilling our obligations to family members (§§430–431). Similarly, the instructions on repentance in chapter 9 apply to everyone, not just to the educational and ecclesiastical elite.

VII. Extant Manuscripts Written in Preparation for *Survey* and *True Christianity*

Survey was the only work written in preparation for *True Christianity* that was actually published, though a few other preparatory manuscripts that were not published in Swedenborg's lifetime also survive. The titles given here are drawn from the annotated bibliography of Swedenborg's writings (Rose 2005b) that appears in the companion volume to this edition (Rose and others, 2005). Because identifying these manuscripts without ambiguity requires a degree of care, I shall also give reference numbers (for example, "U166") keyed to the same annotated bibliography. (For evidence and argumentation that most of the theological manuscripts left unpublished by Swedenborg were written in preparation for the published works, see Rose 2005a.)

Surprisingly little survives of what must have been quite a stack of paper written in preparation for *True Christianity*. All rough and fair copies of the work itself were apparently destroyed when the work was published. The few fragments that have come down to us do, however, tell us some interesting things about both the focus of the work and Swedenborg's method of assembling it.

For instance, the *Brief Index of Catholic Teachings* (U166, around 1769; = Swedenborg 1996, 2:539–549), the *Bible Concordance for "True Christianity"* (U172, September 1769; = Swedenborg 1996, 2:241–347), and even the very brief *Index to "The Book of Concord" for "True Christianity"* (U173, late 1769; = Swedenborg 1975, 58–73) show that Swedenborg felt the need for further research into contemporary Christian theology before writing *True Christianity*. (These index and concordance titles are posthumous creations by scholars; Swedenborg did not title these works.) The *Index to "The Book of Concord" for "True Christianity"* presents something of a puzzle. It consists of over 180 pages, but contains only brief entries scattered about under rubric letters; most of it is blank. The few entries Swedenborg did make in it relate to only the first 44 pages of the *Book of Concord*.[49] The topic of justification by faith alone—a central concern—has only two entries, from pages 10 and 11 of the *Book of Concord*.[50] However, in actual practice Swedenborg cites a much wider range of pages than those referenced in his index, not only in several passages in *True Christianity* (§§101; 137:7, 10; 356), but in the summary in *Survey* (§§9–15) and in letters he wrote to the Göteborg Consistory in April 1769 (Acton 1948–1955, 667, 670, 671). The presence of an index in the 1756 version of the *Book of Concord* he used (*Concordia* 1756) may have made his own indexing unnecessary.

Other preparatory manuscripts give us some insights into how *True Christianity* was written. I have discussed above (part IIIc) how Swedenborg outlined his intended work: he first chose general topics that were to

---

49. See Swedenborg 1975, 71.

50. See Swedenborg 1975, 67.

become chapters, and then arranged under each topic a list of items that were to appear as numbered points:

> general topics (to become chapters)
>> item (to become a numbered point)
>> item (to become a numbered point), and so on

The preparatory manuscripts *Outline about God the Savior* (U168; = Swedenborg 1996, 2:557–560), *Sketch on Goodwill* (U160), *Sketch for "True Christianity"* (U170), and *Draft Memorable Occurrences for "True Christianity"* (U174; = Swedenborg 1996, 1:157–172) reflect this organizational method and give glimpses of how the work evolved.[51] For example, when Swedenborg wrote *Sketch for "True Christianity"* around mid-1769 he had apparently already departed from the outline he had published in *Survey* earlier that year: the numbered points and even the division of topics differ from those previously outlined.

VIII. Editions and Translations of *True Christianity*

The present translation is based on the first edition of the work, which was published in Amsterdam in 1771 and sold and distributed by John Christian Sepp of that city.[52]

A second Latin edition of *True Christianity*, in two volumes, was published by Johann Friedrich Immanuel Tafel in both London and Tübingen in 1857 and 1858. A third edition, edited by Samuel H. Worcester, was published in New York in 1906. In 1964, the Swedenborg Institut of Basel, Switzerland, published a facsimile of the first edition.

The first English translation, that of John Clowes, was published in London in 1781. Clowes's translation appeared in numerous later editions and revisions as well, published on both sides of the Atlantic. The first English translation completed in the United States, that of T. G. Worcester, appeared in Boston in 1833.

J. B. Lippincott published R. Norman Foster's translation in Philadelphia in 1869. In 1906 and 1907, the American Swedenborg Printing and

---

51. See also note 26 above.

52. See Acton 1948–1955, 649 (where the last name is misspelled "Seep"), 741, 745, 753–754. Notice of Sepp was omitted from the title page at the time, and further information about him has not to the best of my knowledge been unearthed since.

Publishing Society (later renamed the Swedenborg Foundation) issued a new translation in two volumes by John C. Ager; the Ager translation later became part of the Swedenborg Foundation's standard edition. In 1933, the Everyman's Library series, distributed in Great Britain and Canada by J. M. Dent and in the United States by E. P. Dutton, published a new translation by Francis Bayley, with an introduction by Helen Keller.

The Swedenborg Society in London issued a translation by William C. Dick in 1950. In 1988, on the occasion of the three-hundredth anniversary of Swedenborg's birth, the same publisher issued a new English translation by John Chadwick.

Arguably the most unusual English version of the work is the unpublished translation by Clarence Hotson, who in 1973 rendered *True Christianity* in English blank verse, varied with heroic couplets; the typescript is kept in the Swedenborg Library in Bryn Athyn, Pennsylvania.

The work has also been translated into Chinese, Danish, Dutch, French, German, Italian, Japanese, Latvian, Portuguese, Spanish, and Swedish. Extracts of the work have been published in Dutch, English, French, German, Italian, Japanese, Latin, Latin combined with English, Latvian, Norwegian, Polish, Russian, Sesotho, Spanish, Swedish, and Zulu.[53]

IX. Reviews of and Reactions to *True Christianity*

Francis Okely (1718–1794), an ordained Moravian deacon, wrote a letter to John Wesley (1703–1791), the founder of Methodism, on December 10, 1772, in which Okely mentioned both something Swedenborg had said to him about reading *True Christianity,* and his own reaction to the work:

> Baron Swedenborg is to me a riddle. Certainly, as you say, he speaks many great and important truths; and as certainly seems to me to contradict Scripture in other places. But, as he told me, I could not understand his *Vera Christiana Religio* without a Divine illumination; and I am obliged to confess that I have not yet a sufficiency of it for that

---

53. Hyde 1906, entries 2836–2874; Wainscot 1967, entries 2837/a–2874/7. As indicated in the selected list of editions at the end of this preface, most if not all previous English translations have used the title *True Christian Religion,* either with or without a definite article.

purpose. I am thankful, my present course does not seem absolutely to require it. (Tafel 1877, 696)

Two things are of interest about this letter: that Swedenborg would tell someone *True Christianity* was unintelligible without divine illumination; and that Okely had a mixed response to the work.

On the first point, Swedenborg had written and even published similar statements before. In the last section of the published work *Heaven and Hell* he writes:

> What I have been saying in this book about heaven, the world of spirits, and hell will be obscure to people who find no delight in knowing about spiritual truths; but it will be clear to people who do have this delight, especially to people involved in an affection for truth for its own sake—that is, people who love truth because it is true.[54]

In a rough note to himself written less than two years before his death Swedenborg suggests that he actually crafted his prose to have this polarizing effect—to seem clear to some readers and obscure to others:

> The books that have been written by the Lord through me . . . have been written in such a way that they shine before the very eyes of those who believe in the Lord and the new revelation; but they are darkness and of no importance for those who deny those things, and who, for various external reasons, are not inclined to accept them. (Swedenborg 1975, 193)

As for Okely's mixed response, some others apparently felt similarly. Samuel Taylor Coleridge (1772–1834), whose careful, reflective notes on *True Christianity* and several other works by Swedenborg are preserved in the British Museum, also seems to have found some things to like and some to dislike in the work. In the margins of *True Christianity* Coleridge writes, for example, "no man of good heart will doubt Swedenborg's Veracity who has also truly read his works" (Edmisten 1954, 271). Yet he also criticizes *True Christianity* for exaggerating the differences between its theology and that of contemporary Protestantism:

> The point, I like least in Swedenborg, . . . is his evident disposition and constant efforts, to interpret the phrases of the Churches, to whose tenets he opposes his own, into meanings of the greatest possible difference that might be conveyed in these words, and then burthening them

---

54. *Heaven and Hell* 603; George F. Dole's translation.

with consequences which they themselves disclaim, and which (as in the doctrine of Faith & Works common to the Lutheran and Calvinist) do not appear in their lives. Hence he often, nay most often, mistakes their opinions, which, in substance at least, he might have found reconcilable with his own, & with little other difference than arises almost inevitably when the same Object is contemplated by several persons from several different points of view.[55]

The work also received some cold responses. There were only two published contemporary reviews of *True Christianity*, one in Swedish, the other in English ("Berättelse" 1771; Review of *Vera Christiana Religio* 1771); the review in English was reprinted in a second journal (Review of *Vera Christiana Religio* 1772). Both reviews are brief, negative, and intriguingly devoid of engagement with Swedenborg's theology; they focus instead almost exclusively on the reviewers' skepticism about Swedenborg's claim to have had spiritual experiences. Both conclude that he was out of his mind.

Friedrich Christoph Oetinger (1702–1782), a German author and clergyman with theosophical interests, was disappointed by *True Christianity*. He had started reading Swedenborg's works in 1762, and became sufficiently intrigued with them to publish *Swedenborgs und anderer irdische und himmlische Philosophie* (The Earthly and Heavenly Philosophy of Swedenborg and Others; 1765), a two-volume German work that included translated passages from Swedenborg's works. He also initiated a friendly correspondence with Swedenborg. Oetinger was very interested in Swedenborg's spiritual experiences, but was not keen on his nonliteral interpretation of Scripture. When Swedenborg sent him the much-awaited *True Christianity* shortly after it was published, Oetinger made it clear to Swedenborg and to several other correspondents that he was dissatisfied with the work. He was particularly dismayed by Swedenborg's statement that the Second Coming was not to be a literal reappearance of Jesus, but had already taken place in the form of what Swedenborg himself had written.[56]

---

55. Edmisten 1954, 276. For wider context, see also Preus 1970, 1:33, in which Lutheran theologian Robert Preus (1924–1995) describes polemics as having been "the order of the day" in the Lutheran theology of the sixteenth and seventeenth centuries. Preus writes that it was a "general practice among theologians" then to press the arguments of their adversaries "to their logical but absurd conclusions," a practice he characterizes as "particularly annoying to us today."

56. Tafel 1877, 1059; Acton 1948–1955, 754; see *True Christianity* 779.

John Wesley, too, received the Latin first edition of *True Christianity* from Swedenborg himself. He later purchased Clowes's English translation of it (Wesley 1783, 439 = Tafel 1877, 585–586), and read other works by Swedenborg as well. In 1783 he presented in his own publication, *Arminian Magazine,* a series of criticisms titled "Thoughts on the Writings of Baron Swedenborg."[57] A majority of these criticisms are aimed at *True Christianity.* Wesley criticizes every major aspect of the work: Swedenborg's expounding of Scripture, his doctrinal teachings, and both the style and the content of the memorable occurrences. Wesley makes his points by interspersing lengthy quotations from Swedenborg with comments of his own, though his criticisms have more the flavor of entertaining mockery than serious engagement. For instance, after quoting one passage from *True Christianity* (a single brief sentence without its context), Wesley responds by declaring it "as errant nonsense as was ever pronounced by any man in Bedlam" (Wesley 1783, 496). Wesley expresses disagreement with Swedenborg's position that there are not three persons in God, and that angels are not a separately created race; in both cases he argues that these teachings depart from the clear, literal statements of Scripture (Wesley 1783, 496, 678). He objects particularly strongly to Swedenborg's description of the conditions in hell. In *True Christianity* 281, a passage that Wesley quotes at some length, male evil spirits are described as being confined to workhouses where they have to work in order to get food. When they have done something evil to someone else, they are put on a bed of "accursed dust," a highly noxious substance, until they show some sign of repentance; only then are they allowed to return to their labors. At the end of each workday, they are allowed to go for a walk or socialize and then go to sleep; each of them is also allowed to take a harlot as a partner. It is of these teachings that Wesley is writing when he says, "The most dangerous part of all [Swedenborg's] Writings I take to be the account which he gives of hell. It directly tends to familiarize it to unholy men, to remove all their terror, and to make them consider it, not as a *place of torment,* but a very tolerable habitation" (Wesley 1783, 674).

---

57. Wesley 1783; for further analysis of Wesley's criticisms of Swedenborg's works, along with a lengthy collection of negative words he uses of them, see Rogal 1988, 299. It may be noted in passing that though Wesley refers to Swedenborg as "Baron," the title is not one Swedenborg himself used. Some British writers, whether favorable to Swedenborg or not, gave him this title as a recognition of his membership in the third tier of the Swedish nobility. (The third tier of the British nobility, that of barons, parallels the third tier of the Swedish nobility, which is without title.)

"O how much more comfortable is the condition of these spirits in hell, than that of the galley slaves at *Marseilles,* or the Indians in the mines of *Potosi!*" (Wesley 1783, 678). Of their association with harlots in specific, Wesley says, "Amazing! So the Christian Koran exceeds even the Mahometan! Mahomet allowed such to be in paradise: but he never thought of placing them in hell! The Baron should have concluded here; for nothing can exceed this" (Wesley 1783, 678). Chief of all Wesley's responses, however, is the charge that Swedenborg's teachings and accounts of spiritual experiences are at odds with Scripture. He concludes, "True, his tales are often exceedingly lively; and as entertaining as the tales of the faries [*sic*]. But I dare not give up my Bible for them: and I must give up one or the other" (Wesley 1783, 680).

Several others, however, reported powerful positive reactions to the same work. John Clowes (1743–1831), an Anglican pastor in Manchester, never met Swedenborg and was not aware of *True Christianity* when it was first published. He first heard of the book from an acquaintance in the spring of 1773 (Clowes 1834, 30). Clowes purchased a copy, but was initially put off by the size of the volume, and concluded from a glance at the structure and nature of its argument that a reading would require more sustained attention than he was willing to give it. Looking back, he later reports that he felt content with his religious beliefs at that time, and decided not to expend the effort (Clowes 1834, 20).

However, one evening in October 1773, before leaving to visit a friend for an extended period, Clowes chanced to open *True Christianity* once more. He happened to notice the term *Divinum Humanum,* which he read as meaning "Divine Humanity."[58] He thought little of it at the time, but several days later, at his friend's house, he awoke to have an hour-long spiritual experience of peace, joy, and divine glory that he associated with the divine humanity of Jesus Christ. All that day he could not stop thinking about this experience. The following morning it was repeated, but even more profoundly. Then a sudden, persistent, and overwhelming desire came over him to return home and read *True Christianity.* He made apologies to his friend and rushed back to Manchester, as he puts it, "rather with the impetuosity of a lover, than with the sedateness of a man, who had no other object of pursuit but to consult the pages of an

---

58. Clowes 1834, 31. The phrase appears some thirty times in *True Christianity,* so the passage in which Clowes noticed it cannot be determined.

unknown and heretofore slighted *book*" (Clowes 1834, 31–32). Clowes eagerly read the volume, and reports in his memoirs that as he did so

> it seemed as if a continually increasing blaze of new and recreating light was poured forth on the delighted understanding, opening it to the contemplation of the most sublime mysteries of wisdom, and convincing it of the being of a God, of the existence of an eternal world, of the interior sanctities of the Holy Scriptures, of the true nature of creation, redemption, and regeneration, in a manner and degree, and with a force of satisfactory evidence, in which those interesting subjects had never been viewed before. The mind, therefore, was no longer perplexed about the proper object of its worship, because it was enlightened to see clearly, as by the light of a meridian sun, that Jesus Christ, in His Divine Humanity, is that object, He being the Creator from eternity, the Redeemer in time, and the Regenerator to eternity. . . . (Clowes 1834, 35–36)

Although the passionate language with which Clowes describes his initial encounter with Swedenborg's theology might suggest that he had fallen prey to a passing enthusiasm, the permanent effect the experience had on his life proves otherwise. He devoted the next twenty years to translating Swedenborg's works, an effort that ultimately included the first English translation of almost three-quarters of Swedenborg's published theological volumes (Clowes 1834, 42). In 1780 he founded an organization dedicated to publishing Swedenborg's works in English; by 1828 that organization had distributed over 260,000 books and tracts by or about Swedenborg (Clowes 1834, 50).

Another remarkable, yet quite different, response to reading *True Christianity* was that of Robert Carter III (1728–1804) of Virginia. Although he is now all but forgotten, Carter had more land and more slaves—and a larger library—than anyone else in colonial Virginia, including many of the Framers of the United States.[59] In 1790 he first

---

59. Levy 2002, 188–189. It is worth mentioning in passing that *True Christianity* also found its way into the hands of some of the Framers themselves. John Hargrove (1750–1839), a Swedenborgian minister in Baltimore, sent copies of *True Christianity* to President George Washington (1732–1799) in 1793 and to President Thomas Jefferson (1743–1826) in 1801. Both responded in gracious if vague terms, and Hargrove was invited to preach in the Capitol Rotunda on two occasions, in 1802 and 1804. For the correspondence with Washington, see Hindmarsh 1861, 154–155; for that with Jefferson, see Hindmarsh 1861, 180–181.

encountered Swedenborg's theology in the form of the little work *Soul-Body Interaction*. He immediately ordered *True Christianity* and read it. After that, he remained a lifelong Swedenborgian (Kirven and Eller 2005, 266–268). The effect of his reading, however, extended beyond his personal devotions. Struck by the material toward the end of *True Christianity* about the spiritual excellence of Africans (§§837–840), Carter began in the very next year (1791, over seventy years before the Emancipation Proclamation) a detailed legal process that eventually emancipated all his slaves as well as generations of their unborn descendants.[60]

In 1909 a black minister of the African Holy Catholic Church named David Mooki (1876–1927) happened on *True Christianity* in a pile of second-hand books in an old furniture shop in Krugersdorp, South Africa. Upon purchasing and reading the volume, he felt certain that the Second Coming of Jesus Christ had in fact already taken place, as Swedenborg claimed. Like Robert Carter, Mooki was affected by the statements toward the end of the volume about the spirituality of black Africans. He convinced many in his church to become Swedenborgians; *True Christianity* became their chief doctrinal authority. Later they left the African Holy Catholic Church and formed the New Church of Africa (Williams-Hogan 2005, 321–323).

Helen Keller (1880–1968) can serve as a final example. This author and social advocate for the handicapped, who was herself blind and deaf, was greatly influenced by Swedenborg's works, including *True Christianity* (see Keller 2000). In an introduction to a new translation of *True Christianity* in 1933, she writes:

> The theological teachings of Swedenborg are in many long volumes. The summation, the universal theology, is found in this *magnum opus, The True Christian Religion,* which is now being brought to new thousands of reverent readers. Yet his central doctrine is simple. It consists of three main ideas: God as Divine Love, God as Divine Wisdom, and God as Power for use. These ideas come as waves from an ocean which floods every bay and harbour of life with new potency of will, of faith, and of effort. To our conception of God, the Word, and the Hereafter, which we have received on trust from ages of unproved

60. Levy 2002, 189, 199, 203. The exact number of slaves freed is uncertain, but it exceeds five hundred (Levy 2002, 189, 200). The emancipation Carter brought about continued for a long time; as a direct result of the Deed of Gift he drafted, descendants of his slaves were still being freed in 1852 (Levy 2002, 203).

faith, Swedenborg gives a new actuality, which is as startling, as thrilling as the angel-sung tidings of the Lord's birth. He brings fresh testimony to support our hope that the veil shall be drawn from unseeing eyes, that the dull ear shall be quickened, and dumb lips gladdened with speech. There is among us a distressing indifference to all things of faith, and an impatience at any effort to explain the laws of life in spiritual terms. The only really blind are those who will not see the truth—those who shut their eyes to the spiritual vision. For them alone darkness is irrevocable. Those who explore the dark with love as a torch and trust as a guide find it good. Blind people who have eyes[61] know that they live in a spiritual world inconceivably more wonderful than the material world that is veiled from them. The landscapes they behold never fade. The flowers they look upon are the immortal flowers which grow in God's garden. Swedenborg's message is like the rock smitten by Moses, yielding sweet streams of healing water, even an abundance of truths for those who hunger and thirst in their pilgrimage through an age of materialism and selfishness. (Keller 1933, vii–viii)

True Christianity has provoked a wide range of reactions; it has also played a significant role in establishing Swedenborgianism around the world, and has remained over the centuries one of Swedenborg's most read and best-loved works.

X. Issues in Translating *True Christianity*

The purpose of this and the other translations in this series is to bring both the thought content and the tone and style of Swedenborg's originals across the great distance between the eighteenth century and the twenty-first.

Swedenborg could presume that his readership was thoroughly familiar with the Bible; he could also assume that many of his readers would be educated Christians and would therefore be aware of the major issues and associated terminology of Christian theology in general and Lutheran theology in specific, as well as the common philosophical heritage of western Europe at the time. A translation today should not presume

---

61. The phrase "blind people who have eyes" is from Isaiah 43:8.

familiarity with any of those things. Therefore where I have been aware of a choice, I have sought to use a broadly familiar vocabulary rather than the religious vocabulary of various branches of the Christian church today—including Swedenborgianism—even though those alternatives might have communicated more clearly or more familiarly to those specific groups. For example, I translate *imputatio* as "the assignment of spiritual credit or blame" rather than as "imputation." In this case, the loss of a link to the doctrine of imputation for the theologically initiated reader seemed less critical to me than the loss of meaning those readers might experience who were not familiar with the word "imputation" or the concept it represents. A note on the first occurrence of the term allows readers to mentally substitute "imputation" for the phrase if it is clearer and more helpful for them. The same applies to many other terms.

The most important consideration that encouraged me to choose this mode of translation is that Swedenborg is not a terminologist. As context indicates, when he uses familiar terms from the Christian vocabulary of his times, he often gives them new meanings; his own favorite words and phrases, too, tend to shift meanings from one passage to another. Careful attention to his diction in context shows that in most cases, no single English equivalent will adequately cover all occurrences.

I should amplify this statement. The Neo-Latin language Swedenborg employed had a much smaller vocabulary than modern English; as a result, its individual words generally needed to carry a broader range of meanings than English words. Thus Swedenborg often uses a single word in varied senses, each of which might well be represented by its own word in English. Furthermore, he was pointedly opposed to scholastic theology's tendency to focus on definitions of and argumentation about terms, and he deliberately made more elastic use of standard theological terms than the scholastic philosophers of medieval times. Because of this elasticity, context alone shows the changing force of a given word in his texts; therefore I have sought to translate his *meaning*, which is shown only by his words *in context*, including the context of his entire theological corpus. I have allowed different translations of the same *word* or *phrase* in different passages, where context demanded it.

Another challenge in turning Swedenborg's Neo-Latin into English is presented by Neo-Latin's tendency to favor substantive adjectives (an adjective used as a noun). In fact, Neo-Latin seems to prefer to give an adjective and no noun, where we English-speakers would prefer to learn the noun, even if we have to give up the adjective along the way. In English we could and would not say "The witness spoke trues"; Neo-Latin could and would. Because many of the nouns in this work are implied rather than stated, and yet English generally demands that those nouns be stated, I have had to conjecture what those implied nouns might be. Here again, context offers some help, but not always enough.

This situation is complicated by differences in the basic nature of Neo-Latin and English. Neo-Latin uses different word endings to indicate the grammatical function of a word in a sentence, whereas English often uses additional words for this purpose, particularly prepositions. The various Neo-Latin word endings, when they are attached to nouns, signal various forms of those nouns, which have been organized by grammarians into classes called *cases*. One of these classes, the genitive case, is particularly problematic for the translator. Among its uses is the denotation of possession, where it functions much like the English apostrophe-plus-*s* (which is itself, by the way, a case ending). However, the rest of the range of possible functions of the genitive is far larger than the simple English possessive that is often chosen to represent it. In fact, it can be said that in Neo-Latin the genitive case ending does little more than link one noun to another, without necessarily clarifying the nature of their relationship. A further complication is that often the words in question are not nouns, strictly speaking, but substantive adjectives—the problematic not-quite-nouns discussed in the previous paragraph. English and Neo-Latin are so different in this respect that it is challenging to find English examples that effectively convey the problem. However, if we use the word *of* to indicate that the second noun is in the genitive case, and artificially pluralize English adjectives to reflect a very normal Latin substantive plural usage, we could say that Swedenborg's pages are crowded with expressions that would be rendered "good of love," "trues of faith," "falses of evil," and so on. These expressions are just two words long in the original; they occur like language molecules that attach in many places to Swedenborg's sentences. Sometimes they attract another linguistic atom and become three words long. They are almost always paired or contrasted with other language molecules of similar size: "pleasants of love of good" are paired with "delightfuls of faith of true," and both are contrasted with "pleasants of love of evil" that are paired with "delightfuls of faith of false." It would be an understatement to say that translating these phrases meaningfully is not easy. After much study, reflection, and consultation with others, I have come to render all the examples just given with phrases such as the following, depending again on context: "goodness that comes from love," "true insights related to faith," "false perspectives that arise from evil," "the pleasure of loving what is good," "the delight that accompanies true faith," "the pleasure of loving what is evil," and "the delight that accompanies false faith."

As scholars of Latin and Swedenborg's own contemporaries have testified,[62] his Latin original possessed great simplicity, accessibility, and an engaging, vivid, and (sometimes) even amusing style. It has been my hope to achieve something equivalent in English. The effort to move closer to the tone of the original has often necessitated a move away from word-for-word literalism, especially in narrative passages.

My overwhelming feeling as I present this translation to the public is one of humility. I can only hope that despite its imperfections it may stimulate fresh thinking about Swedenborg's work and afford new perspectives for readers.

XI. Acknowledgments

A very large team contributed its expertise to improve this translation—a team not only of scholars and readers I know and shall always remember well, but also of researchers in various institutions who remain personally unknown to me. At the risk of inadvertently omitting important members of this host of supporters, I must nevertheless list some of those who stand at the forefront of my memory. I am deeply grateful to N. Bruce Rogers, whose mentorship prepared me and whose professional courtesy allowed me to undertake this translation; to Chara Cooper Daum for reading the entire work with great care against the Latin, and making countless helpful suggestions; to Shirley G. Gladish for polishing my English style; to Wendy E. Closterman, Lisa Hyatt Cooper, George F. Dole, Alice Blackmer Skinner, and Stuart Shotwell for their careful reading of the English; to Alicia Dole for editing and checking the finished product; to Allegra Asplundh-Smith, Carolyn Andrews Cole, Chara M. Odhner, and Chelsea Rose for their help in researching various issues; to Benjamin J. Bibler for scanning the ornaments; to Carroll Odhner, director of the Swedenborg Library; to Erik E. Sandström, Curator of Swedenborgiana,

---

62. See note 9 above.

and to Rachel Longstaff and David Perry, reference librarians, at the same; to Stephen D. Cole for lending me Samuel H. Worcester's own annotated copy of Swedenborg's first edition; to Reuben P. Bell for his penetrating insights into difficult scientific issues; to Glen M. Cooper and R. Guy Erwin for the research they contributed for notes besides those which they themselves directly wrote; to Fredrik Bryntesson and Sean Lawing for help with Swedish; to Michael A. Ivie and Chris Carlton for coleopterological information; to David B. Eller for taking the first steps toward making the New Century Edition a reality; to the members of the New Century Edition Editorial Committee itself for their cama-raderie, support, and good humor; to the Swedenborg Foundation for its visionary and unwavering commitment to this project; to the Asplundh, Brickman, Elder, Glencairn, Iungerich, and Rotch Foundations for their tremendous generosity; and finally, to the many individuals whose finan-cial and moral support have made the New Century Edition possible.

JONATHAN S. ROSE
Bryn Athyn, Pennsylvania
December 2005

Works Cited
in the Translator's Preface

Acton, Alfred. 1948–1955. *The Letters and Memorials of Emanuel Swedenborg.* 2 vols. Bryn Athyn, Pa.: Swedenborg Scientific Association.

Alfelt, Lennart O. 1969. "Swedenborg's Library: An Alphabetical List." *The New Philosophy* 72:115–126.

Arndt, Johann. 1605. *Von wahrem Christenthumb.* Frankfurt am Main: Rosen.

Benz, Ernst. 1947. *Swedenborg in Deutschland: F. C. Oetingers und Immanuel Kants Auseinandersetzung mit der Person und Lehre Emanuel Swedenborgs.* Frankfurt am Main: Vittorio Klostermann.

———. 2002. *Emanuel Swedenborg: Visionary Savant in the Age of Reason.* Translated by Nicholas Goodrick-Clarke. West Chester, Pa.: Swedenborg Foundation.

"Berättelse om Herr Assessor Swedenborgs nya theologie och dess syner." 1771. *Postillionen, med bihang ti dagligt allehanda eller berättelser om märkwärdiga och til sörre delen nyligen timade händelser; jämte angra handlingar* 92:361–362.

[Beyer, Gabriel]. 1767. *Nya försök til upbyggelig förklaring öfwer evangeliska sön- och högtidsdags texterne.* Göteborg: Langiska Boktryckeriet.

Bullinger, Heinrich. 1566. *Confessio et Expositio Simplex Orthodoxae Fidei et Dogmatum Catholicorum Sincerae Religionis Christianae.* Zürich: Christopher Froschover. In later editions this work came to be known as the *Confessio Helvetica Posterior.*

Burnet, Gilbert. 1675. *A Rational Method for Proving the Truth of the Christian Religion, As It Is Professed in the Church of England.* London: Richard Royston.

Burrough, Edward. 1658. *The True Christian Religion Again Discovered, after a Long Dark Night of Apostacy.* London: Roger Norton for Giles Calvert.

Butterfield, Swithune. 1590. *The Principles of the True Christian Religion.* London: John Hill.

Byrne, James M. 1997. *Religion and the Enlightenment: From Descartes to Kant.* Louisville, Ky.: Westminster John Knox Press.

Calixt, Georg. 1633. *De Vera Christiana Religione et Ecclesia.* Helmstedt: Hamm.

Chadwick, Owen. 1964. *The Reformation.* Baltimore: Penguin.

Clowes, John. 1834. *A Memoir of the Late Rev. John Clowes.* Manchester: J. Gleave.

Concordia Pia et Unanimi Consensu Repetita Confessio Fidei. 1756. Leipzig: Grossiana.

Cuno, J. C. 1947. *J. C. Cuno's Memoirs on Swedenborg.* Translated by Claire E. Berninger. Bryn Athyn, Pa.: Academy Book Room.

Dole, George F. 1988. "*True Christian Religion* as Apologetic Theology." In *Swedenborg and His Influence,* edited by Erland J. Brock and others. Bryn Athyn, Pa.: Academy of the New Church.

———. 2005. "Swedenborg's Modes of Presentation, 1745–1771." In *Emanuel Swedenborg: Essays for the New Century Edition on His Life, Work, and Impact,* edited by Jonathan S. Rose and others. West Chester, Pa.: Swedenborg Foundation.

Edmisten, Leonard Martin. 1954. *Coleridge's Commentary on Swedenborg.* Dissertation, University of Missouri, Columbia.

Eller, David B. 2005. "Recommended Works." In *Emanuel Swedenborg: Essays for the New Century Edition on His Life, Work, and Impact,* edited by Jonathan S. Rose and others. West Chester, Pa.: Swedenborg Foundation.

Emes, Thomas. 1698. *The Atheist Turn'd Deist, and the Deist Turn'd Christian: or The Reasonableness and Union of Natural and the True Christian Religion.* London.

Ernesti, Johann August. 1760. Review of *Secrets of Heaven,* by Emanuel Swedenborg. *Neue Theologische Bibliothek* 1:515–527.

———. 1768. Review of *Revelation Unveiled,* by Emanuel Swedenborg. Translated into Swedish and annotated by Johan Rosén. *Preste-Tidningar* (April):97–109.

Fuhrman, Augustin. 1658. *Rettung der alten wahren christlichen catholisch-evangelischen Religion.* Amsterdam: Betkius.

Grotius, Hugo. 1627. *Sensus Librorum Sex, Quos pro Veritate Religionis Christianae Batavice Scripsit H. Grotius.* Paris: Ruart. In later editions this work came to be known as *De Veritate Religionis Christianae.*

———. [1627] 1662. *De Veritate Religionis Christianae.* Amsterdam: Elzevir.

Hasselquist, Andreas Benedicti. 1697. *Lumen de Lumine Sparsum . . . seu Vera et Gnesios Christiana Religio . . .* Åbo: J. L. Wall.

Hindmarsh, Robert. 1861. *Rise and Progress of the New Jerusalem Church.* London: Hodson & Son.

Hyde, James. 1906. *A Bibliography of the Works of Emanuel Swedenborg, Original and Translated.* London: Swedenborg Society.

IJsewijn, Jozef. 1990. *Companion to Neo-Latin Studies. Part I: History and Diffusion of Neo-Latin Literature.* 2nd ed. Leuven: Leuven University Press.

Keller, Helen. 1933. Introduction to *The True Christian Religion Containing the Universal Theology of the New Church,* by Emanuel Swedenborg, [translated by F. Bayley]. London and Toronto: J. M. Dent and Sons, and New York: E. P. Dutton.

———. 2000. *Light in My Darkness.* 2nd ed. Edited by Ray Silverman. West Chester, Pa.: Swedenborg Foundation. Revision of 1927 edition of *My Religion,* with added material, Garden City: Doubleday, Page.

Kirven, Robert H., and David B. Eller. 2005. "Selected Examples of Swedenborg's Influence in Great Britain and the United States." In *Emanuel Swedenborg: Essays for the New Century Edition on His Life, Work, and Impact,* edited by Jonathan S. Rose and others. West Chester, Pa.: Swedenborg Foundation.

Kolb, Robert, and Timothy J. Wengert, eds. 2000. *The Book of Concord.* Minneapolis: Fortress Press.

Kors, Alan Charles, ed. 2003. *Encyclopedia of the Enlightenment.* 4 vols. Oxford: Oxford University Press.

Lamy, François. 1694. *Vérité évidente de la religion chrétienne, ou Élite de ses preuves et de celles de sa liaison avec la divinité de Jésus-Christ.* Paris: E. Couterot.

Lang, Bernhard. 2004. "'Auch noch andere Menschen und andere Geschlechter der Tiere': Menschliches Leben im außerirdischen Weltall aus der Sicht von Fontenelle (1686), Huygens (1698) und Swedenborg (1758)." In *Science & Fiction II: Leben auf anderen Sternen,* edited by Thomas P. Weber. Frankfurt am Main: Fischer Taschenbuch Verlag.

Lescaille, Antoine. 1597. *Antithesis Verae, Antiquae Christianae Religionis et Novae Antichristianae.* Freiburg im Breisgau: Böckler.

Levy, Andrew. 2002. "The Anti-Jefferson." In *Best American Essays,* edited by Stephen Jay Gould. New York and Boston: Houghton Mifflin.

MacCulloch, Diarmaid. 2003. *The Reformation.* New York: Penguin Group.

Marracci, Lodovico. 1691. *Prodromus ad Refutationem Alcorani. In Quo per Quatuor Praecipuas Verae Religionis Notas Mahumetanae Sectae Falsitas Ostenditur; Christianae Religionis Veritas Comprobatur.* 4 vols. Rome: Sacra Congregatio de Propaganda Fide.

McGrath, Alister E. 1999. *Reformation Thought: An Introduction.* Oxford: Blackwell.

Milton, John. 1673. *Of True Religion, Haeresie, Schism, Toleration, and What Best Means May Be Us'd against the Growth of Popery.* London.

Oetinger, Friedrich Christoph. 1765. *Swedenborgs und anderer irdische und himmlische Philosophie.* Edited by Karl C. E. Ehmann. Reutlingen: Rupp & Baur.

Pey, Jean. 1771. *La Verité de la religion chrétienne prouvée à un déiste.* 2 vols. Paris: Humblot.

Preus, Robert D. 1970. *The Theology of Post-Reformation Lutheranism.* 2 vols. St. Louis: Concordia.

Regamey, Alfred G. 1935. *Swedenborg au travail.* Lausanne: Agence des Publications de la Nouvelle Église.

Review of *Vera Christiana Religio,* by Emanuel Swedenborg. 1771. *Monthly Review* 45:580–583.

Review of *Vera Christiana Religio,* by Emanuel Swedenborg. 1772. *Scots Magazine* 34:27–28.

Rogal, Samuel J. 1988. "Swedenborg and the Wesleyans: Opposition or Outgrowth?" In *Swedenborg and His Influence,* edited by Erland J. Brock and others. Bryn Athyn, Pa.: Academy of the New Church.

Rose, Frank S. 2005a. "Swedenborg's Manuscripts." In *Emanuel Swedenborg: Essays for the New Century Edition on His Life, Work, and Impact,* edited by Jonathan S. Rose and others. West Chester, Pa.: Swedenborg Foundation.

Rose, Jonathan S. 1994. "Similes in Emanuel Swedenborg's *Vera Christiana Religio* (1771)." In *Acta Conventus Neo-Latini Hafniensis.* Binghamton: Medieval & Renaissance Texts & Studies.

———. 1998. "The Ornaments in Swedenborg's Theological First Editions." *Covenant: A Journal Devoted to the Study of the Five Churches* 1:293–362.

———. 2005b. "Annotated Bibliography of Swedenborg's Writings." In *Emanuel Swedenborg: Essays for the New Century Edition on His Life, Work, and Impact,* edited by Jonathan S. Rose and others. West Chester, Pa.: Swedenborg Foundation.

Rose, Jonathan S., and others, eds. 2005. *Emanuel Swedenborg: Essays for the New Century Edition on His Life, Work, and Impact*. West Chester, Pa.: Swedenborg Foundation. Also issued in paperback format under the title *Scribe of Heaven*.

Sigstedt, Cyriel Odhner. 1981. *The Swedenborg Epic: The Life and Works of Emanuel Swedenborg*. London: Swedenborg Society. First edition: 1952, New York: Bookman Associates.

Smoley, Richard. 2005. "The Inner Journey of Emanuel Swedenborg." In *Emanuel Swedenborg: Essays for the New Century Edition on His Life, Work, and Impact*, edited by Jonathan S. Rose and others. West Chester, Pa.: Swedenborg Foundation.

Smyth, John. 1915. *The Works of John Smyth, Fellow of Christ's College, 1594–8*. Edited by William Thomas Whitley. 2 vols. Cambridge: Cambridge University Press.

Struensee, Adam. 1751. *Dissertatio Theologica de Gaudio in Spiritu Sancto Tanquam Genuino Verae Religionis Christianae Criterio*. Halle: Gebauer.

Swedenborg, Emanuel. 1763. *Sapientia Angelica de Divino Amore et de Divina Sapientia*. Amsterdam.

———. 1766. Extract from *Revelation Unveiled*, translated into Swedish by Johan Rosén. *Göteborgske Spionen* 42 (October 20): 329–334.

———. 1787. *Tankar om falska propheter*. Vol. 1 of *Samlingar för philantroper*. Stockholm: A. J. Nordström.

———. 1975. *Small Theological Works and Letters of Emanuel Swedenborg*. Translated and edited by John E. Elliott. London: Swedenborg Society.

———. 1976. *A Philosopher's Note Book*. Translated by Alfred Acton. Bryn Athyn, Pa.: Swedenborg Scientific Association. First edition: 1931, Philadelphia: Swedenborg Scientific Association.

———. 1994–1997. *Apocalypse Explained*. 6 vols. Translated by John C. Ager, revised by John Whitehead, and edited by William Ross Woofenden. West Chester, Pa.: Swedenborg Foundation.

———. 1995. *Charity: The Practice of Neighborliness*. 2nd ed. Translated by William F. Wunsch and edited by William Ross Woofenden. West Chester, Pa.: Swedenborg Foundation. First edition: 1931, Philadelphia: J. B. Lippincott.

———. 1996. *Posthumous Theological Works*. 2 vols. Translated by John Whitehead and edited by William Ross Woofenden. West Chester, Pa.: Swedenborg Foundation.

———. 2002. *Emanuel Swedenborg's Diary Recounting Spiritual Experiences During the Years 1745 to 1765*. Vol. 3. Translated by J. Durban Odhner. Bryn Athyn, Pa.: General Church of the New Jerusalem.

———. [1763] 2003. *Angelic Wisdom about Divine Love and about Divine Wisdom*. Translated by George F. Dole. West Chester, Pa.: Swedenborg Foundation.

Tafel, R. L. 1875. *Documents Concerning the Life and Character of Emanuel Swedenborg*. Vol. 1. London: Swedenborg Society.

———. 1877. *Documents Concerning the Life and Character of Emanuel Swedenborg*. Vol. 2, parts 1 and 2. London: Swedenborg Society.

Thomas, John. 1679. *A Vindication of the True Christian Religion, in Opposition to the Abominations of Popery*. London: Isaac Cleave.

Tossanus, Daniel. 1593. *Theses Theologicae de His Tribus Quaestionibus Hodie Tantopere Agitatis: Quomodo Definienda et Agnoscenda Sit Vera Religio Christiana* . . . Heidelberg: Smesmannus.

Wainscot, A. Stanley, comp. 1967. *List of Additions to the Bibliography [of the Works of Emanuel Swedenborg, Original and Translated, by the Rev. James Hyde] Since Its Publication in 1906.* London: [Swedenborg Society]. Mimeographed.

Waring, E. Graham, ed. 1967. *Deism and Natural Religion: A Source Book.* New York: F. Ungar.

Wesley, John. 1783. "Thoughts on the Writings of Baron Swedenborg." *Arminian Magazine* 6:437–441, 495–498, 550–552, 607–614, 669–680.

Williams-Hogan, Jane. 2005. "Examples of Internationalization: The New Church in Africa." In *Emanuel Swedenborg: Essays for the New Century Edition on His Life, Work, and Impact,* edited by Jonathan S. Rose and others. West Chester, Pa.: Swedenborg Foundation.

Wunderer, Johann David. 1619. *Unvorgreiffliches Bedencken und Antwort auff die Frage ob das H. Evangelium, das ist die wahre christliche Religion vnd Freyheit dess Gewissens mit dem weltlichen Schwerd zuverfechten seye?* Frankfurt am Main: J. C. Vuckel.

Young, B. W. 1998. *Religion and Enlightenment in Eighteenth-Century England: Theological Debate from Locke to Burke.* Oxford: Clarendon Press.

Selected List of Editions
of *True Christianity*

———

1. Latin Editions

Swedenborg, Emanuel. 1771. *Vera Christiana Religio, Continens Universam Theologiam Novae Ecclesiae a Domino apud Danielem Cap. VII: 13–14, et in Apocalypsi Cap. XXI: 1, 2. Praedictae.* Amsterdam.

————. [1771] 1857–1858. *Vera Christiana Religio, Continens Universam Theologiam Novae Ecclesiae a Domino apud Danielem Cap. VII: 13–14, et in Apocalypsi Cap. XXI: 1, 2. Praedictae.* 2 vols. Edited by J. F. Immanuel Tafel. Tübingen: Verlagsexpedition, and London: Swedenborg Society.

————. [1771] 1906. *Vera Christiana Religio Continens Universam Theologiam Novae Ecclesiae a Domino apud Danielem VII: 13, 14, et in Apocalypsi XXI: 1, 2, Praedictae.* 2 vols. Edited by Samuel H. Worcester. New York: American Swedenborg Printing and Publishing Society.

————. [1771] 1964. *Vera Christiana Religio.* Basel: Swedenborg Institut. Facsimile of the first edition.

2. English Translations

Swedenborg, Emanuel. [1771] 1781. *True Christian Religion Containing the Universal Theology of the New Church: Which Was Foretold by the Lord, in Daniel, Chap. vii. 5, 13, 14, and in the Apocalypse, Chap. xxi. 1, 2.* 2 vols. [Translated by John Clowes.] London.

————. [1771] 1833. *The True Christian Religion Containing the Universal Theology of the New Church Foretold by the Lord in Daniel VII. 13, 14; and in Revelation XXI. 1, 2.* Translated by T. G. W[orcester]. Boston: John Allen.

————. [1771] 1869. *The True Christian Religion Containing the Entire Theology of the New Church, Foretold by the Lord in Dan. vii, 13, 14; and Rev. xxi. 1, 2.* 2 vols. Translated by R. Norman Foster. Philadelphia: J. B. Lippincott.

————. [1771] 1906–1907. *The True Christian Religion Containing the Universal Theology of the New Church Foretold by the Lord in Daniel VII. 13, 14; and in Revelation XXI. 1, 2.* 2 vols. Translated by John C. Ager. New York: American Swedenborg Printing and Publishing Society. Several reprintings, the most recent of which was a two-volume set issued as part of the Redesigned Standard Edition by the Swedenborg Foundation, West Chester, Pa., 1996.

————. [1771] 1933. *The True Christian Religion Containing the Universal Theology of the New Church.* [Translated by F. Bayley], with an introduction by Helen Keller. London and Toronto: J. M. Dent and Sons, and New York: E. P. Dutton.

———. [1771] 1950. *The True Christian Religion Containing the Universal Theology of the New Church Foretold by the Lord in Daniel vii 13, 14, and in the Revelation xxi 1, 2.* Translated by William C. Dick. London: Swedenborg Society.

———. [1771] 1988. *The True Christian Religion Containing the Complete Theology of the New Church as Foretold by the Lord in Daniel 7:13,14 and in Revelation 21:2,3.* 2 vols. Translated by John Chadwick. London: Swedenborg Society.

On *True Christianity*

*An Introduction to Swedenborg's Most Comprehensive
and Systematic Theological Writing
from the Standpoint of the Religion of His Contemporaries*

R. GUY ERWIN

Outline

AT the time of Emanuel Swedenborg's birth in 1688, Europe was still feeling strong aftershocks from the century of religious warfare that had formally ended four decades earlier: in the year of his birth a "revolution" in England shifted its crown from one dynasty to another largely to avoid the possibility of a Catholic monarchy; the death of the ex-queen of Sweden the following year in self-imposed Roman exile was a reminder of the costs of conversion to Catholicism; and the infamous revocation of the Edict of Nantes three years before had forced the emigration of much of France's talented and industrious Protestant minority to other, more tolerant lands. By the time of Swedenborg's death in 1772, some aspects of this world had greatly changed: "enlightened" governments and edicts of official toleration of religious minorities were much more the norm in Europe, although they were still not yet universal; and an "age of reason," which was proud of its self-liberation from religious dogma, had made open questioning of traditional religious truths not only common but actually fashionable among the educated elite (Hazard 1963, 44–58). The new religious spectrum ranged from nearly medieval superstition to open skepticism about the existence of a powerful God. The northern Europe of the mid-eighteenth century was also in the midst of a number of intellectual and cultural struggles. Failing philosophical and scientific paradigms as well were being challenged and replaced with new ones.

Into this mix came Swedenborg, in many ways a perfect man of his times: an inquisitive and intrepid scientist, a gifted observer of nature, an ardent student of all forms of knowledge—and then, from the beginnings of his spiritual experiences in 1743, also a communicator and interpreter of religious truths and insights. Swedenborg became, without setting out to do so, a defender of a new view of Christianity that built upon but also deeply challenged the received wisdom and religious teaching of his times (Hazard 1963, 431–433).

When the last of the pages of Swedenborg's *Vera Christiana Religio* (True Christianity) came off the press in Amsterdam in June 1771, its author had reason both for deep satisfaction in his work and for at least mild concern: satisfaction, because the book that lay before him ready for public attention contained the most comprehensive account of his new religious doctrine that he had ever published in a single volume; concern perhaps, for he was presenting his views to a world that had not generally welcomed them. *True Christianity* was, in fact, a work with more than one purpose: in a positive vein, it was a systematic presentation—a *summa theologica*[1]—of Swedenborg's teaching; and at the same time it was an apologetic—a defense of his spiritual insights against the putative criticism of a skeptical audience of theologians, church leaders, and educated laypeople.

As will be demonstrated, the defensive purpose of this work shaped its content and structure just as much as its positive purpose did; for there were some in Sweden who opposed Swedenborg so strongly that they were willing to take action to have his writings suppressed. In an age in which established churches and control of the press were still commonplaces, this threat to silence a dissenting voice was a very real one. Thus in order to understand Swedenborg's text it is necessary to have a clear picture of the Lutheran religious and church-political background both of Swedenborg's personal life and of the Sweden of his time.

Furthermore, the Lutheranism of Sweden did not exist in a vacuum, but was part of a vital and largely shared Lutheran religious culture common to all of the lands of the Reformation and especially strong around the great Lutheran lake of the Baltic Sea. Lutherans themselves called their understanding of the Christian faith simply "Evangelical"; but it was distinct from other forms of Protestantism, and the distinctiveness and difference were deeply cherished.

To some extent, other aspects of the Protestant landscape are important in Swedenborg's religious environment, too: Reformed (Calvinist) Christians were part of his world, some few in Sweden itself, but far more beyond it—particularly in the Netherlands and in England, where he encountered Anabaptists, Quakers, and other nonmainstream Protestants. All of these left their impression on Swedenborg. He was also aware to a degree of the Roman Catholicism of his time, albeit rather unsympathetically; certainly his negative views on Catholicism, and Jesuits in particular, are similar to those held by many of his northern European Protestant contemporaries. The theological warfare of the sixteenth century had set the terms of religious discourse that persisted well into Swedenborg's time; theological positions were in the eighteenth century still almost always defined and argued over and against the errors of others.

---

1. A *summa theologica* (theological summary) is a compendium, summary, or manual of theology, containing all one needs to know; perhaps the most well-known model is that of the Catholic theologian Thomas Aquinas (1224 or 1225–1274).

Concerned most of all to communicate the truth of his personal revelations, Swedenborg nonetheless attempts in *True Christianity* to be intelligible even about doctrines he personally rejects and opposes, and shows this by trying to refute them not only by the higher authority of what was revealed to him but also by more generally accepted means: the use of reason and the witness of Scripture.[2]

Swedenborg realizes fully what sort of world he lives in; he knows that the knowledge of the spiritual world he has experienced since 1743 will not be welcomed by the religious establishment of his day. Nor does he expect his views to be persuasive to all seekers; but the urgency with which he argues them in *True Christianity* expresses a strong optimism that he will succeed in at least weakening the theological edifice tradition had built in the 250 years that had elapsed since the Reformation began in the theological challenge issued by Martin Luther (1483–1546).

True Christianity is a work of high originality, but it is also a work that strives to be comprehensible in conventional Christian terms. As such, it is both surprising and predictable, familiar and startlingly new.

I. Emanuel Swedenborg's Place in Church History

As a religious figure and a theologian, Swedenborg has been largely neglected by historians of Christianity; in standard church histories written for use by undergraduates, seminarians, and the educated public, Swedenborg and the Church of the New Jerusalem movement that his writings inspired are often simply overlooked.[3] One notable exception is Justo González's popular two-volume work *The Story of Christianity* (1964), which grants Swedenborg just under a page and a half of text in a short chapter titled "The Spiritualist Option." In this chapter of González's textbook, Swedenborg is lined up after the Lutheran mystic Jacob Boehme (1575–1624) and the English Quaker George Fox (1624–1691) as representative of a strain of Christian piety that reacted

---

2. I am grateful for the valuable insights of George F. Dole in his essay "*True Christian Religion* as Apologetic Theology" (Dole 1988); they have stimulated an important new way of thinking about *True Christianity.*

3. Three examples, of different eras and degrees of technical detail, but united in ignoring Swedenborg: Walker 1970, Dowley 2002, and Johnson 1976. Another work used today in seminary schools that does mention Swedenborg's influence is Ahlstrom 1972.

against the over-technical and hairsplitting orthodoxy of their day by an inward turn—to spiritual knowledge through personal experience or insight or revelation. Such knowledge, unchallengeable by learned experts or powerful prelates, was then the personal treasure of the one who enjoyed it. But Swedenborg—as González admits—does not fit very well into the spiritualist mold he has constructed. Boehme and Fox do fit his schema; both men came from very humble origins and were only very modestly educated, and therefore the internalization of spirituality was their only means to develop and express a personal faith in a religious world where they had little authority. But Swedenborg is anomalous in his fairly grand social status and his high education; all González can do is point to an unspecified "similarity" in their teachings and restate the point that the inward turn of such visionaries is in part a result of their outsider status, relative powerlessness, and social-critical stance toward conditions prevailing in their times. Swedenborg not only did not suffer these disadvantages, but (as his critics sometimes enviously pointed out) represented quite the opposite position. Not many intellectual iconoclasts have had independent means enough to travel freely, live abroad (albeit modestly) for long periods of time, and publish lavish editions of their writings at their own expense.

By any paradigm, Swedenborg's place in the history of Christianity is not a clear one—but that he lived and taught as he did, that he was deeply, if not widely, influential to a group of "receivers," and that numbered among his critics were some of Europe's most distinguished thinkers, all make it strange that he should not have received more attention from those attempting to survey the history of Christianity. As much as anything, though, this habitual omission is probably due to the assumption (happily not shared by González) that importance in Christian history is determined less by the profundity and originality of a theologian's ideas than by his or her ability to make converts or create controversy.

In works that concentrate on eighteenth-century religion or theology in particular, or on the history of religious ideas, Swedenborg of course makes a regular appearance, though usually as a marginal figure, and often as a counterfoil to others not much like him, such as Nikolaus von Zinzendorf (1700–1760), charismatic Lutheran Pietist and patron of the Unity of Brethren, or "Moravians"; Johann Georg Hamann (1730–1788), German irrationalist philosopher; or at the other end of the spectrum, Immanuel Kant (1724–1804), German rationalist philosopher. Only in studies of eighteenth-century science or in the realm of the history of ideas, though, does Swedenborg seem to get much attention. From the standpoint of a historian of religion, it seems that his impact on the Christianity of his day as it was believed and practiced was simply too slight, his historical footprint too faint, to warrant much notice.[4] Perhaps some of what follows will provide explanatory background for this unjust omission.

a. The Swedish Church of Swedenborg's Day

The Church of Sweden in Swedenborg's time was only part of a larger Lutheran religious world, and that in turn was only part of a much wider Protestant community of northern Europe. Great similarities in structure and leadership, worship and piety, and clergy training and theology extended through this Lutheran community. The Scandinavian churches usually absorbed new ideas and made gradual change after German models and at a certain distance of time, frequently in a transmission from northwestern Germany through Denmark, or from the Baltic coast directly to Sweden. The internationalism of this Lutheran religious consensus was great, aided by a common language among the learned, some similarities in national and political culture, and frequent commercial and political interaction among the lands of northern Europe in the era since the Reformation. The Latin language used in writing by all educated persons in this period (particularly among those writing on theological topics, who also maintained the custom longer) made it possible to exchange books easily and correspond and converse over language boundaries, but the close relationship of the German and Scandinavian languages also made translation of works intended for ordinary readers easy and straightforward. The strong commercial relationship between the major Lutheran cities of northern Germany and the trading ports of Denmark and Sweden (and their tributary lands of Norway, Finland, Estonia, and Livonia) made the transfer of ideas even more direct. Though the great day of the medieval Hanseatic League of merchant cities was over, the trading nexus of the Baltic and North Seas remained a powerful cultural connector, and goods and people moved along time-worn paths. The greater cultural richness

---

4. Even in the best modern history of the actual church life of the time and place, Swedenborg is only mentioned once, and then only as the prominent son of Jesper Swedberg (for whom see further mention in the text). The nature of the prominence, interestingly, is assumed to require no further specification (Hope 1995, 7).

of the European mainland made connections to German culture particularly desirable for Scandinavians; the Germany-to-Scandinavia transmission was much greater than the reverse. A rich example pertinent to our topic: one leading historian of German and Scandinavian Protestantism points out that German books were widely sold in the Stockholm book trade throughout the seventeenth and eighteenth centuries, and that it is not until well into the eighteenth century that Swedish-language books outnumber German titles in Stockholm booksellers' catalogs (Hope 1995, 22). Latin books of course dominated the field of theology; religious books in the vernacular languages were mostly devotional in character, though many of these had a wide readership and deep religious influence.

Another major area of connection between Sweden and the wider Lutheran world was in higher education. The Reformation had to some degree begun as a university movement, as Luther and many of the principal reformers had been professors, and one of its results was the foundation of a number of new Protestant universities. During the span of Swedenborg's life, there were five universities on Swedish territory, two on the Swedish mainland: Uppsala (founded 1477) and Lund (founded 1666); and three in the Swedish-ruled tributary lands: Åbo (founded 1640) in Finland (lost to Russia 1809), Dorpat (founded 1632, closed 1710) in Estonia (lost to Russia 1721), and Greifswald (founded 1456) in Pomerania (lost to Prussia 1815). All but Greifswald were Reformation-inspired Lutheran foundations, including Uppsala.[5] The university in nearby Copenhagen was also firmly Lutheran. From their foundation, the Swedish universities maintained close ties with the Lutheran universities of Germany; even in the eighteenth century most Swedish professors had received at least part of their education outside Sweden, most often in Germany. Students were also highly mobile, often attending more than one university and thus gaining a broader perspective on scholarship and the world, but most of them seem to have restricted themselves to universities of their own religious persuasion. Scandinavian students most

---

5. To be precise, the University of Uppsala, though medieval in origin, had disbanded in the sixteenth century and had been revived and reorganized along Lutheran lines as a result of a religious conference in Uppsala in 1593—the same epoch-making conference at which the Lutheran faith was made Sweden's legal religion (see page 61 below).

frequently studied at the nearby German Lutheran universities of Rostock and Greifswald, to a lesser degree at Wittenberg and Leipzig, and
(beginning in Swedenborg's time as a student) at the relatively new
(1694) university in Halle (Hope 1995, 101–102).

Culturally and religiously, Sweden had been since the 1530s part of a
greater, and predominantly German-influenced, Lutheran religious community characterized by theological orthodoxy, a conservative approach
to forms of worship, and a strong devotional and scholarly focus on the
Bible. Three books were at the heart of the religious knowledge (and
perhaps the library) of a seventeenth- or eighteenth-century Lutheran:
the Bible, the hymnal approved for that country, and the catechism. In
Swedenborg's Sweden, a specific, authoritative Swedish-language text of
all three had been set by law two years before his birth: a definitive
translation of the Scriptures, based on Luther's German version; a hymnal containing chorales (mostly German in origin); and an annotated
version of the Small Catechism written by Martin Luther and published
in 1529 for the instruction of young people and the ongoing religious
education of the unlettered classes (= Kolb and Wengert 2000, 345–375).
Beyond these three basic texts of the church, eighteenth-century Swedish
Lutherans were shaped in their faith and habits of piety by prayer books
and devotional texts of various kinds, the most popular of which (in
Sweden as in Germany) was the *True Christianity* of Johann Arndt (1555–
1621), a German devotional writer of the period of consolidation after
Luther's death and before the Thirty Years' War. Arndt's book, and others
like it, served as a bridge between the often mysterious and inaccessible
scriptural texts and the need of individual Christians for a meaningful,
profound, and simple expression of Christian faith and life. Arndt's *True
Christianity* was first published in Sweden during 1647 and 1648; and second and third Swedish editions were printed in 1695 and 1732 respectively. In addition to *True Christianity*, German devotional books
common during Swedenborg's youth would have included Arndt's *The
Little Garden of Paradise* (1612; Swedish translation 1648) and the sermons and meditations known as *The Soul's Treasure* by the much-read
north German preacher Christian Scriver (1629–1693).[6] The works of
devotional writers of the Church of England were also fairly readily

6. During Swedenborg's lifetime, Scriver's sermons and meditations were available both in German editions (for the original German edition see Scriver 1675–1696) and in a Swedish translation
(Scriver 1723–1727).

available, and Swedish church leaders who had visited Britain, like Jesper Swedberg, Swedenborg's father,[7] were especially fond of translating and publishing English devotional works. Upon his elevation to the episcopacy in 1702, one of Swedberg's first acts was to set up a printing shop at the episcopal residence in Brunsbo, where devotional works, Bibles, hymnals, and catechisms could be cheaply produced for an increasingly literate and spiritually hungry public (Hope 1995, 33). Of the English devotional works of wide interest in Sweden (as elsewhere in Protestant Europe), the works of the Puritan bishop of Bangor, Lewis Bayly (died 1631), were especially widely distributed, particularly his *Practice of Piety,* published in a Swedish edition in 1643. A guide to Christian life called *Christian Directory* (1582) was also translated into Swedish and reprinted a number of times (in spite of the fact that its author, Robert Parsons [1546–1610], was actually a Jesuit); likewise the *Art of Divine Meditation* (1606) by Joseph Hall (1574–1656), bishop of Exeter, another prominent Puritan divine.

One of the central points of all these devotional manuals was that the Christian life was not simply a matter of assent to belief in particular doctrines (however forcefully those might also have been communicated) but of interior conversion, a growth in cheerful, unforced obedience to God's laws and the development of a more sincere love for one's neighbor. They were moralistic tomes, to be sure, but were also promoted by a clergy wrestling with the challenge of "Christianizing" a largely illiterate, poor population and enforcing minimal moral standards. The element of social control is never far from the surface; church laws were as much a part of the life of the ordinary Swede as the laws of the king. This became still clearer as the seventeenth century progressed and Sweden's church became even more a part of its political system.

The 1686 *Kyrkolag* (Church Law) forcefully reemphasized the well-established point that to be Swedish was also to be Lutheran. Since a dramatic assembly of the clergy in Uppsala in 1593 had forced a permanent decision for Luther's doctrines, the Swedish realm had been committed to them—Lutheranism was expected of Sweden's monarch as much as of

---

7. Swedberg was the family surname of Swedenborg's family until 1719, when the family was ennobled. In such cases, the family name was usually slightly changed as a mark of elevation in status, and thus the Swedbergs became the Swedenborgs. However, because as a bishop Jesper Swedberg himself already was a member of the Swedish Diet, or parliament, he was not ennobled, and his name did not change.

that monarch's subjects. The governing texts decreed in 1593 to be authoritative interpretations of the Christian faith for Sweden were relatively few: the three historic creeds (Apostles', Nicene, and Athanasian) and the Augsburg Confession of 1530 (which summarized Lutheran doctrine; = Kolb and Wengert 2000, 27–105) were the only binding theological statements; the addition of the earlier Church Order of 1571 as equally binding secured to the Swedish church of 1593 and beyond a full-blown system of episcopal government of a kind not common to all Lutheran lands. The strength and independence of the sixteenth- and seventeenth-century Swedish bishops enabled them to defend Lutheranism as central to the national religious heritage even at times in which the monarchs were less than fully committed to it personally or politically.

The decision in the reign of Charles XI (1655–1697) to restructure the Church Law was made against a background in which the church's independence from the monarchy had lessened considerably; though conservative in its theological assumptions, the 1686 law which ruled the Swedish church in Swedenborg's time, and which in some aspects has continued in force into modern times, was as much a victory for royal authority as for ecclesial cohesiveness. The new church law was supported by two groups in particular: those who wanted to see the monarch's role in the church strengthened, particularly when that role was played by subordinate Crown counselors; and those who wanted to commit the Swedish church more formally to the doctrines of Lutheranism as a way of resisting religious change. The one party gained a shift toward royal power over customary law in church affairs; the other secured the formal approval of the entire *Book of Concord* of 1580 (the collected doctrinal statements of German Lutheranism; = Kolb and Wengert 2000) as an "authorized" interpretation of the Augsburg Confession that had already been definitive since 1593. This pleased the ultra-Lutherans among the clergy and laity, and effectively closed Sweden off from the twin threats of Calvinism and Catholicism. A guiding spirit behind the drafting of the 1686 law was Haquin Spegel (1645–1714), bishop of Skara, close associate and patron (in this as in the later attempt to produce a new hymnal and Bible translation) of the ambitious young Jesper Swedberg, who himself succeeded Spegel as bishop of Skara upon the latter's elevation to the archiepiscopal see of Uppsala.

In a modern secular worldview, the symbolic importance and usefulness of a state church and national confession of faith is hard to imagine, but at the end of a century and a half of religious warfare, to lay down an absolute national standard for faith seemed indispensable for national unity and cohesiveness. This is precisely what the *Kyrkolag* of 1686 did in its opening sentence: "In this kingdom . . . all shall confess . . . to the Christian teaching and faith, grounded in God's holy Word, . . . the three main creeds, . . . and the unaltered Augsburg Confession of the year 1530 . . . as explained in the *Book of Concord*. . . ."[8]

The era ushered in by the new church law corresponded precisely with Swedenborg's youth and the rise of his father to churchly prominence. A spirit of modernization and reform followed the new law—the church became, more than it had ever been before, an instrument of royal power and social control. All community records of births, marriages, and deaths were now in the control and the responsibility of the parish priest; most schools at the local level were parish-run; and from 1695 all children were to be taught to read and catechized—in fact, two aspects of the same educational function. In 1693 a new prayer book was approved for use in churches as well. As has been mentioned, Swedenborg's father then participated (with Haquin Spegel) in editing a new hymnal, which was printed in 1698 in many copies, but which ultimately failed to secure formal approval for use, as a result of professional jealousy on the part of rival clergymen (or so Jesper Swedberg insisted). Certainly the Swedberg hymnal was a great step forward, including a number of new and original hymns along with the German Lutheran classics. Swedberg himself composed many (some apparently believed too many) of the new hymns.

Swedenborg's family was immersed in the formal life of the church, conventional Lutheran piety, and ecclesiastical politics. Its members were intimately connected to the ecclesial aristocracy of the time: Emanuel's elder sister Anna (1686–1766) married Erik Benzelius the younger (1675–1743), son of Erik Benzelius, archbishop of Uppsala (1632–1709). The younger Benzelius himself later became successively bishop of Göteborg (1726–1731), bishop of Linköping (1731–1742), and for a few months archbishop of Uppsala (1742–1743). Benzelius's brothers Jacob (1683–1747) and Henrik (1689–1758) became bishops of Göteborg and Lund respectively,

---

8. Rydholm 1902, 5. Aside from passages quoted from *True Christianity*, all translations in this essay are my own, unless further ascription is given in the notes or bibliography.

and then the former succeeded the latter as archbishop of Uppsala.[9] One of Erik and Anna's sons later became a bishop as well (Karl Jesper Benzelius [1714–1793], bishop of Strängnäs), and their daughter Ulrika (died 1766) married Peter Filenius (1704–1780), a future bishop of Linköping, who ultimately became one of Emanuel Swedenborg's ecclesiastical opponents in the controversy among the clergy of Göteborg in 1769–1771.

Jesper Swedberg himself became rector of the University of Uppsala in 1693 and bishop of Skara in 1702, necessitating his family's move to the episcopal residence at Brunsbo. Young Emanuel, who had just begun his university studies at Uppsala, remained behind in the household of his brother-in-law Erik Benzelius. In the Swedberg household, young Emanuel had been exposed to a Lutheran piety of a warm, but a strict, moralistic, and somewhat unimaginative kind; in the Benzelius household a more "modern" and "enlightened" spirit prevailed, though the piety was no less strong—Benzelius himself was a forward-looking man and an intellectual leader. All his life, Emanuel Swedenborg was closely related by blood or marriage to the religious and intellectual leaders of Swedish church and academic life; his remarkable network of clerical relatives in the next generation testifies to the inbred nature of church leadership in eighteenth-century Sweden, but also goes far in explaining why ecclesiastical censure of Swedenborg for his later theological views came so late and so mildly.

Swedish church life in the era of Charles XI is characterized by one historian as "military," because of the prominence of former regimental chaplains among its bishops and leaders, the rather intolerant and regimented system of church government, and the absolutist claims of monarch and bishop alike (Wordsworth 1911, 311). Certainly the theology of the time was unimaginative and reductive as well: confessional orthodoxy and its theological corollary, emphasis on the Lutheran core doctrine of "justification by faith,"[10] in addition to a rigid moralism left

---

9. Another brother, Lars Benzelius (1680–1755), married Swedenborg's sister Hedwig (1690–1728). Lars was, like Swedenborg, a mine administrator. Among his children were Erik (1715–1745), who became a notary on the Board of Mines, and Lars the younger (1719–1800), who became bishop of Västerås in 1759. Like the Swedberg children, the Benzelius family was ennobled in 1719, and later members used the name Benzelstjerna (see note 7 above).

10. The phrase "justification by faith" refers to the doctrinal concept that God forgives people's sins and counts people righteous on the basis of their faith, through God's grace rather than because of any merit on their part. For a discussion of modern Lutheran perspectives on this doctrine, see Mannermaa 2005.

some, even the conservative Jesper Swedberg, worried that the church was more concerned with doctrinal conformity than with faithfulness to Christ's example of goodness and love. In the Swedberg household, the doctrine of justification by grace through faith would have been accompanied by a clear teaching that a justifying faith must manifest itself in works of self-sacrifice and love for one's neighbor (Tottie 1885–1886, 1:48–49). Bishop Swedberg himself was highly critical of those who turned the central Lutheran doctrine of salvation as a free gift of God into an excuse for moral laxity and indifference. As we will see, this implied criticism of a too one-sided doctrinal Lutheranism soaked deeply into the young Emanuel Swedenborg.

b. The Wider Protestant World

Though Swedenborg's lifetime would see a steep decline in the fortunes of Sweden as a great power, certainly in his youth his natal land was a kingdom to be reckoned with in all of Europe: the military legacy of Gustav II Adolf, or Gustavus Adolphus (1594–1632), the Protestant hero of the Thirty Years' War, still lived on strongly in Sweden, as in Europe generally, at the time of Swedenborg's birth in 1688. At that point the Thirty Years' War was only four decades in the past, and the three formally recognized forms of Western Christianity that came out of the Westphalian peace treaty of 1648 (Roman Catholicism, Lutheranism, and Calvinism) were still settling into a state of permanent (and increasingly secure) opposition to one another. Sweden had emerged from the seventeenth century still a great power—it was not until 1721, well into Swedenborg's adulthood, that Sweden's ultimate defeat in the Great Northern Wars against Russia reduced her position in the world and threatened her dominance even in Scandinavia and the Baltic. In Swedenborg's early adulthood, in fact, Sweden's young king Charles XII (1682–1718) was idolized by many continental Lutherans as a kind of second Gustav Adolf, ready to take leadership as the head of international Protestantism.

The hardening of an "orthodox" line on the church's doctrinal statements was not unique to Lutheranism at the time of Swedenborg's birth; well into the eighteenth century, both Calvinist churches and even the Roman Catholic world continued to fight, or at least practice fighting, confessional battles against each other and between conservatives and progressives within each tradition.

Even the conservative religious circles that had idealized Sweden's own Charles XII as the perfect Protestant hero took alarm when he sought refuge in Turkey after the failed 1709 military campaign against Russia. During his stay as a guest of Sultan Ahmed III (1673–1736), which was admittedly mysteriously long (from 1709 to 1714), apocalyptic-minded Christians in northern Germany and Scandinavia pondered whether Charles's conversion to Islam was pending, an event that they thought might well be the opening act in the end of the world (Schneider 1992, 118). Such was the significance of the faith of princes. Though by Swedenborg's time the Reformation and the Thirty Years' War were receding into the distant historical past, the confessional position of nations and their rulers remained critical not only for religious but also for political life.

1. The Lutheran Sphere

Within Lutheranism, the hardening of confessional lines was most severe in Germany and Sweden and their dependencies. Although Copenhagen and Hamburg were both centers of an irenic, open-minded moderate Lutheranism, the principalities that made up Luther's native land of Saxony were threatened by the proximity of Catholic Poland and Austria, and the rise in the north of a new power, Prussia, a Lutheran land ruled by a Calvinist royal house. This helped foster a sense of religious insecurity among Saxon Lutherans, who (particularly the professors in the Lutheran intellectual fortresses of Leipzig, Wittenberg, Jena, and Halle) were sensitive to every shift in the political winds and watchful for even hints of change in church policy on the part of the now-Catholic Saxon royal house. In this setting, "confessionalism," the extreme emphasis on doctrinal definition and conformity over and against other faiths, was a significant shaping factor in German Lutheranism, particularly in the universities of the major German Lutheran lands. Sweden fits to some degree into this same mold, as a nation struggling to hold on to a Baltic-wide empire against a number of rivals.

Theological Lutheranism in Sweden and Germany at the end of the seventeenth century was fairly narrowly focused on the confessions of faith contained in the *Book of Concord* and the ongoing struggle for doctrinal purity and clarity against (real or imagined) Calvinist or Catholic foes. But not all Lutherans found this exercise either personally edifying or socially useful; in fact, by the last quarter of the seventeenth century a large and influential movement of moral and religious renewal—not doctrinal, but life centered—had developed throughout the Lutheran world. Called "Pietism" by its detractors, this movement took many forms, but emphasized personal renewal in faith, a life of self-sacrifice and helpfulness to others, and generally an avoidance of divisive argument on the finer points of doctrinal theology. Pietism attempted to be a religion of the heart as well as of the mind—a faith active in love, to use Luther's own expression. As such, the Pietist movement was a useful and, for many people, highly welcome corrective to the arid academic teaching and preaching of orthodox Lutheran clergy and professors. Many of the figures with whom Swedenborg is often compared shared with him an early exposure to Pietist ideas and practices. The incipient movement corresponded well to Jesper Swedberg's own criticism of his contemporaries for being unable to translate faith into action, and he was warmly welcoming of its ideas in his area of influence.

The most famous of the early Pietists was Philipp Jakob Spener (1635–1705), an Alsatian Lutheran clergyman active as a pastor in Frankfurt am Main. In the cosmopolitan and open setting that Frankfurt's status as an imperial free city could provide, Spener preached an attractive, warm, and inclusive message of faith and redemption, and revitalized religious life in his community by closer attention to the actual life-experiences of his parishioners. This too was an important aspect of Pietism that made it appealing to sincere lay believers and committed clergy alike—that parish life and pastoral ministry to individuals and families were at least as important to the church as teaching and monitoring right doctrine. Spener's writings, particularly his *Pia Desideria oder herzliches Verlangen nach gottgefälliger Besserung der wahren evangelischen Kirche* (*Pia Desideria,* or Heartfelt Longing for a God-Pleasing Improvement in the True Evangelical Church; 1675), were widely circulated throughout the Lutheran world, including Sweden, but it was his example that was most influential. A generation of Lutheran clergy took his preaching and his parish work as their model and injected new religious energy and sincerity into the pastoral office, a position that had become formal and authoritarian. Bishops like Jesper Swedberg openly encouraged and supported such a renewal of parish life through the clerical office, though the approbation was not universal, and in some places where it was identified as a challenge to the status quo, Pietism was opposed by the local church authorities.

In addition to the return to questions of personal faith and spiritual growth that Pietism brought about, it also introduced two new emphases:

reliance on the Bible for answers to all questions, and a spirit of evangel-
ism and missionary feeling. The Bible emphasis was intended to correct
what was perceived as an overscholastic and hyperconfessional form of
preaching, which used the Scriptures as a sort of great quiver full of arrows
against false doctrine, and preached not to warm the heart or convert the
wavering, but instead to slay the theological foe. The missionary emphasis
was in part a renewal of the sense of the church as a believing community,
in which the spiritual growth of one's neighbor is a matter of one's own
religious concern. In that understanding, it is not enough to be part of the
right-believing group, but it is also necessary to promote the faith to those
outside it, and support and intensify it for those already within the fold.
This resulted in a late outpouring of Lutheran interest in missionary work
both at home and abroad.

Yet another new emphasis the Pietist movement brought into view
was the idea of social improvement as part of the Christian mission in a
time in which it was clear that the institutions of most countries were
inadequate to the purpose of ensuring a decent life to their citizens. In
an age before the existence of programs of national health care and
other social services, those who were poor, sick, aged, orphaned, or otherwise marginalized were the responsibility of the community in which
they lived, and were often largely neglected. Since the Reformation, in
Lutheran lands social services were usually offered through the town government, or more rarely, on a national level through caritative institutions established or endowed by the monarch. The Pietist clergy and laity
took up with enthusiasm and dedication the task of helping the less for-
tunate in society, and reformed old and created new institutions for
social service, most famously the great orphanage school founded by the
renowned German Pietist clergyman and educator August Hermann
Francke (1663–1727) in Halle in 1695, which helped disadvantaged youth
receive an education that prepared them for a trade or for university
study. The Franckean institutions in Halle were also a seedbed of missionary work; the Tranquebar mission in India and many far-flung
Lutheran outposts, including that in Pennsylvania pastored by Henry
Melchior Mühlenberg (1711–1787), were led by clergy brought up or educated at Halle. Francke also established a printing office at Halle, which
produced a vast literature of Pietist devotional and theological works. On
the parish level, Lutheran pastors like Johann Friedrich Oberlin (1740–
1826) in Alsace were sometimes able to organize their villages into truly
integrated Christian communities. Other Pietist groups took the reorganization of society along Christian lines even further; the believers who

gathered on the estates of the Pietist Saxon nobleman Nikolaus von Zinzendorf in Upper Lusatia organized themselves into a model of the godly community, foregoing old customs of social and even family organization for a structure they saw as mirroring more closely the original Christian community and as more practical for the spiritual development of individuals. Zinzendorf's followers called their first new community *Herrnhut* (Under the Lord's Care). By Swedenborg's maturity, Herrnhuter, or as they came to be called in the English-speaking world, "Moravian," fellowships existed all over Protestant Germany and parts of Sweden, and had even spread to England and the British colonies in America. In many places, their separatist tendencies brought them under suspicion by the churchly authorities, but Zinzendorf's own basic belief was that those inspired by the Moravian example ought not separate themselves from their churches, but intensify through their own lives and examples the religious life within them. Their methods of promoting spiritual growth and their popularity in England influenced John Wesley (1703–1791), Charles Wesley (1707–1788), and early Methodism; Swedenborg certainly had contact, though it was not entirely happy, with Moravians in England during his time of spiritual crisis in 1744 and counted Pietists of a Moravian type among his friends in Sweden. Both their concern for sincerity and neighbor-love and their relative lack of interest in confessional or denominational affiliation are to some degree reflected in Swedenborg's own description of Christian life in *True Christianity*.

In the Swedish Lutheranism of the eighteenth century, then, the ardent confessionalism of Jesper Swedberg's generation was gradually being softened by Pietism, which was well represented among people of Swedenborg's class as well as among the more pious segments of society. It was not acceptable, though, to take these new ideas to extremes; a conventicle act was passed in Sweden in 1725 that forbade illicit gatherings of a religious nature and provided penalties for those who organized or attended them. "Illicit" in this context meant any not approved by the local church authorities; the new law was provoked by a growing popularity, even among the well-to-do, of lay-led independent religious meetings in private homes and outside of regular worship. The fear behind this prohibition was that, without appropriate church supervision, false doctrine might be taught and divisiveness in society fostered, and thus ultimately both the Gospel and the realm would be endangered.

The Swedish antiseparatist edict of 1725 was strengthened and renewed ten years later. The penalties were real, and the implications would not be lost on anyone active in Stockholm church circles. They had a powerful and famous example of imprisonment on religious principles right at hand, in the person of Lars Ulstadius (died 1732). Ulstadius, a Swede from Swedish-controlled Finland, had been tried and convicted in 1693 for disrupting church services and for unauthorized preaching, and had been in Stockholm's infamous Smedjegården prison ever since that time.

2. The Ecumenical Scene

Though the confessional battles that would have influenced Sweden and Swedenborg most directly were largely an intra-Lutheran struggle, the issue was not confined to the Lutheran world. In the countries where a Calvinist or Calvinist-inspired Protestantism was dominant, like England, Scotland, and the Netherlands, similar conflicts between rigorists and moderates had broken out—in England in particular, questions of church order in fact dominated political life in the seventeenth century and led to a revolution of government and a destructive civil war. In Swedenborg's year of birth, 1688, a coup in England had deposed James II (1633–1701) and replaced him with his Protestant cousin, Mary (1631–1694), and her husband, William of Orange (1626–1692), ruler of the Netherlands; and the argument for this "Glorious Revolution" had been principally religious. The dominance of Calvinism in Scotland kept the situation there relatively calm, while the traditional commercial openness of the Netherlands meant that though theological debates raged there between radical and moderate Calvinists and members of other Protestant splinter groups, no coercive policies were enforced by the Calvinist establishment. The same situation tended to apply to the small Calvinist communities in north Germany and the Calvinist territories of the Rhine, the latter falling in the course of Swedenborg's lifetime increasingly into the orbit of France.

Roman Catholicism also participated to some degree in this struggle for orthodoxy and clarity; of all the players in the European political scene at the end of the Thirty Years' War in 1648, only the pope had been excluded from the Westphalian settlement, and he and his successors did not feel obligated by a treaty that had recognized the political, if not the religious, legitimacy of the heresies of Lutheranism and Calvinism as established faiths within the old (Catholic) Holy Roman Empire. The canons of the Council of Trent (1545–1563), Rome's answer to Protestant claims to reform in doctrine and practice, had a centralizing tendency as they were gradually implemented in Catholic lands through the seventeenth century. This centralization gave the pope greater authority within the diocesan structure of the church, but its resulting authority could not simply be claimed; it also had to be won. The rise of new movements and organizations within the Roman Church, the success of the new Jesuit order (officially recognized in 1540) as a source of missionaries and teachers, and a general sense that the catholicity of Europe should be its continuing goal kept Roman Catholicism a vital and energetic force in Europe, one that its Protestant opponents could not afford to ignore. In the 1700s the papacy was relatively weak in relation to the Catholic monarchies (the Jesuit organization was suppressed in 1773 by Pope Clement XIV [1705–1774] on the demand of the French, Spanish, and Portuguese governments), but to a great degree, eighteenth-century Protestants still saw Catholicism as a threat and were sensitive to the challenge presented by eloquent and learned Catholic apologists, such as Jacques Bénigne Bossuet (1627–1704).[11] Swedenborg's references to Roman Catholicism and the Jesuits in *True Christianity* are uniformly unflattering, but they reflect their time accurately—as has been noted, the religious polarization of Europe that had caused a century of war was still a powerful reality of Swedenborg's day. The Jesuits were somehow suspect from both Protestant and Catholic perspectives. Even among those within the three traditions whose advanced ideas of "enlightenment" made them critics of their own traditions, fear of and prejudice against those of other faiths was still pervasive.

This is not to say that Protestants at least were incapable of cooperation across confessional lines when it was needed; indeed the missionary work that began to be popular among Lutherans in the mid-eighteenth century was a significantly ecumenical endeavor. In fact, the general Pietist emphasis on personal faith and neighbor-love was an engine of ecumenism: some of the Pietist leaders (most notably Zinzendorf) were markedly ecumenical in outlook, believing that adherents of all confessions (even Roman Catholics) would be represented in the kingdom of God. This emphasis can also be seen in Swedenborg's *True Christianity*, which depicts Christians of all confessional groups present in every level of the spiritual world.

---

11. See Hazard 1963, 198–202.

II. *True Christianity* as a System of Theology

Into this mixed world of confessional stances and degrees of piety came Swedenborg's distinctive set of doctrines, derived from his own experience of religious life and faith in his father's house and beyond, his love of science and philosophical argument and nuance, and (above all) his direct personal experience of the spiritual world, which began in 1743 and intensified to a life-changing degree by 1745. In his new, second career as a communicator of religious ideas, the now fifty-seven-year-old Swedenborg, recently retired from his work as an official on the Board of Mines, set forth to experience and to communicate his new revelation of a parallel spiritual world, of unity in God, and of the loving fellowship to which God had called humankind. Swedenborg's own experience of the supernatural was gradual and progressive, developed over years of unique experience of the spiritual world he described as existing in tandem with the sense-world of physical life. Not until late in his life does Swedenborg seem to feel a need to systematize his doctrines into anything like a conventional comprehensive theology; when he does, it is clearly with an eye both to challenges looming in the present and to the possibility that there might be greater openness to his message in the future.

a. A New Faith

In *True Christianity,* Swedenborg takes pains to be both clear and thorough—he shapes teachings that are powerful and unique to him into chapters that correspond to what the world and the church expected from theology, and that could be set side by side with other, similar systems. It does not minimize either the uniqueness or the particular depth of Swedenborg's work to see *True Christianity* as his attempt to fit his unique revelations into a tradition of academic theological reflection, and though Swedenborg does present us with a work of startling originality, the categories, the style, and the purpose of the work are in many ways apologetic—that is, a comprehensive defense of his views to a potentially skeptical audience. In this, *True Christianity* is highly accessible to those to whom Swedenborg's revelations are not well known, as indeed they were not to most of his contemporaries.

The very title of Swedenborg's work, *Vera Christiana Religio,* or (translated very literally) *The True Christian Religion,*[12] itself describes

---

12. For the reason that the Latin title has here been translated as *True Christianity,* see page 26 note 44.

Swedenborg's intentions and the scope of his work; clearly this is to be a full, complete, and self-contained summary of the Christian faith as Swedenborg perceives it, with an assertion of this faith as true and sufficient. The title alone serves as a signal to the reader that Swedenborg here is offering something that is whole and entire, the validity and truth of which is clear and demonstrable. In this stance, *True Christianity* is reminiscent of many other important works of theology, most notably the great *Institutes of the Christian Religion* (many editions from 1536) of John Calvin (1509–1564). In the Lutheran tradition, the pattern had been set by an earlier work, the *Commonplaces* (many editions from 1521)[13] of Philipp Melanchthon (1497–1560), Luther's friend and colleague, and author of the Augsburg Confession. Its successors included the *Commonplaces or Compendium of Theology* (1600) of Matthias Hafenreffer (1561–1619) of Tübingen, which was especially widely used in Sweden, and of which Jesper Swedberg prepared an abridgement in both Latin and Swedish (Hafenreffer 1714a, 1714b; Tottie 1885–1886, 2:63–64); the *Commonplaces* (1610) of Leonhard Hutter (1563–1616) of Wittenberg; the *Theologia Positiva Acromatica* (1664) of Johann Friedrich König (1619–1664) of Rostock; and finally—in Sweden itself—the *Syntagma Theologicum* (1641) of Olaus Laurelius (1585–1670), professor of theology at Uppsala and later bishop of Västerås. Each of these works held a more or less prominent place in Protestant theological education at the end of the seventeenth century; each was an attempt to summarize and recapitulate all the essential doctrines necessary to a full understanding of the Christian faith as revealed in Scripture, interpreted by the Protestant Reformers, and (as was to be hoped) taught by the clergy and believed by the people; and furthermore, they are only a small fraction of the important works of the kind that were still in use in Swedenborg's time. By writing a comprehensive work of Christian theology and attempting to have the "last word" on the Christian faith, Swedenborg is being very bold. His boldness is all the more striking because, unlike the other theological writers mentioned, as a layman he possessed only a very slight formal authority, at least by the academic standards of church and society.

Swedenborg addresses the issue of his authority to write such a work on the title page of *True Christianity,* where he describes himself as

---

13. The pattern of "commonplaces" established by Melanchthon, which involved listing theological topics in a logical order and addressing each with biblical and logical arguments, became a standard for Lutheran dogmatic theology. It was also an approach used in other fields of learning, and continued into the eighteenth century (Burke 2000, 95).

"Emanuel Swedenborg, Servant of the Lord Jesus Christ." This is the place where one would expect the author of such a work to list his credentials as a professor, or a bishop, or a doctor of theology, or a member of the clergy at least. Instead, Swedenborg trumps the other titles of authority and status with the ultimately humble title of "servant." Now, Swedenborg was not at all without fame or status in Europe. The stories of his telepathic gifts were very well known, and seem to have made him a subject of general interest. Three of them in particular are reported: his long-range experience of the Stockholm fire of 1759; his relating to Queen Lovisa Ulrika (1720–1782) a family story only she could have known; and his relaying a message to the widow de Marteville[14] from her late husband (the latter two events in 1761). In the late 1760s, the final flurry of controversy about the Consistory case against his supporters in Göteborg, with its potential for censure or even punishment, again focused public attention on Swedenborg, though in a not altogether flattering light. That he was gifted as a scientist and extremely talented in every form of human knowledge would have been acknowledged by most; he was certainly far ahead of most of his peers in the Swedish House of Nobles, where his reports on finance policy (among other things) drew the appreciative attention of many of his colleagues.

But as a writer of theology, Swedenborg did not enjoy high status. Most obviously, he was not a member of the clergy—in a time in which there was an almost complete monopoly on theology by university-trained specialists. In a sense, his self-identification on the title page of *True Christianity* as "Emanuel Swedenborg, Servant of the Lord Jesus Christ" could be seen as an attempt to forestall criticism that he was writing beyond his competence. Whatever one might think of Swedenborg's spiritual experiences, one could not deny a Christian's right to style himself a "servant of Christ," which humble status would shame all those who use their position as leaders in the Christian church for worldly glory. From the title page of *True Christianity,* then, it is already clear that this compendium of the faith is not of the ordinary kind.

Swedenborg opens the work with a pair of quotations from Scripture: one from Daniel 7 and the other from Revelation 21, each of which proclaims the coming of a great and new thing. The Daniel passage

---

14. Biographical details concerning the principal figure of this celebrated incident, Marie Louisa Ammon de Marteville, are difficult to obtain. For a summary of this event and the others mentioned here, with further references, see Smoley 2005, 33–36.

promises that the "Son of Humankind" shall come in clouds and glory to rule the nations in an everlasting kingdom; the Revelation passage predicts the new abode of the blessed, the New Jerusalem, to which the writer has been carried in the spirit and is now instructed to communicate these things to all humans: "The One sitting on the throne said, 'Behold, *I am making all things new*'; and said to me, 'Write, because these words are true and trustworthy'" (Revelation 21:5). If one had not already known from the title page that this was no ordinary theological text, these epigraphs would make it clear; this work is a new message to the world, whose author believes that he is opening a door to a new age.

This belief is then made explicit in *True Christianity*'s introductory section, "The Faith of the New Heaven and the New Church," in which Swedenborg describes briefly the presuppositions that guide him in communicating the teachings that follow. He sets the work up architecturally, describing the faith that is the heart of this message as being like the "doorway that allows entry into the temple" (§1).[15] He introduces, in rapid and almost bewildering juxtaposition, the concepts that he will carry through the work like the bass in a fugue: faith, goodness, love, truth. These traditional theological and spiritual virtues are here (as we will see) made to carry new meanings. This entryway, Swedenborg insists, is what the reader needs to know about the intention of God in establishing a new heaven and a new church. This is the new faith in a nutshell.

This new faith, according to Swedenborg, has both a universal and a specific form: universal, in God the Lord from eternity; particular, in the person and work of Jesus Christ, in whom God has come into the world in human form. The universal points of faith are summarized by Swedenborg as two sets of three points each: first, God's unity; God's Trinity; and that Jesus Christ is God; second, the impossibility of salvation without God's coming into the world; the desire of God to save humanity from hell; and that God overcame hell through struggle and conquest. Those who believe in this and lead good lives, the text declares, will be saved (§2).

A second series then follows with implications for the believer's faith and life, this time in five points: (1) the unity and Trinity of God, and God's identity with Jesus Christ; (2) that "believing in him is a faith that saves"; (3) that evil is to be avoided; (4) and good is to be done; and

---

15. References to Swedenborg's works are by section number. These were inserted by Swedenborg himself and are standard in most editions of his works.

finally (5) that humans are to live as though the good they do comes from themselves, while knowing that it comes from God. Points 1 and 2, Swedenborg describes, are matters of faith; points 3 and 4 matters of goodwill or love; and point 5 is the partnership between goodwill and faith, which is "the partnership between the Lord and us" (§3).

Each of these ideas—the unity of God; the identity of God and Christ; the purpose of God's coming in human form; the nature of faith and its relationship to good works; eternal life; heaven and hell; and the meaning of faith, goodwill, and truth—has its part to play in the text to come. From the opening section it is clear again that Swedenborg is presenting here a complete and self-contained system of doctrine, one that will explain the whole workings of God and the implications of faith in God and that will recast Christianity according to new understandings.

b. A Reasonable Faith

Like most systematic statements of theology in the Christian tradition, *True Christianity* basically moves from the most abstract to the most concrete principles, in this case through fourteen chapters in four rough and unequal groupings: first, God and the things of God (God the Creator, the relationship of God to Christ and to the Holy Spirit, then God's communication with humankind, through Scripture in general and the Ten Commandments in particular—chapters 1 through 5); second, the life of the believer (faith in this understanding of God and faith's role in the life of the believer with respect to love, freedom of choice, repentance, reformation, regeneration, and the assignment of spiritual credit or blame—chapters 6 through 11); third, the practical ways in which the believer lives in this faith (through baptism and the Lord's Supper—chapters 12 and 13); and fourth and finally, the "last things" (the return of the Lord, eternal life, and the new church to come—chapter 14). The first two groups, of God and the things of God, and of faith and life, are the largest by far; the practices of the faith, the sacraments, and the final chapter on the coming of the Lord seem to be—at least from the space they occupy in the work—of secondary importance. This variation in itself is a significant marker both of Swedenborg's intentions in the book and of its relationship to other, earlier dogmatic theologies, for Swedenborg's stress on prior truths (the nature of God, Christ, and the Scriptures) and the spiritual development of the believer (from faith to the assignment of faith), though conventional in theme, are highly unconventional both in the way they are treated and in the length at which they are treated. The latter part of *True Christianity* (the sections dealing with the sacraments and the life to come) are likewise fairly conventional both in theme and, at least in comparison with what went before them, in treatment. By the time the reader reaches them, of course, the distance between Swedenborg's new faith and the traditional faith as understood in his day is very clearly apparent, and Swedenborg can concentrate more exclusively on the areas of difference without having to describe them in as much detail as earlier.

Above all, Swedenborg stresses in his opening chapters the reasonableness of this new faith. More than once he emphasizes not only that his reworking of traditional Christian formulas is affirmed by his own spiritual experience, but that the need for that reworking is patent from the illogical nature of the traditional doctrines themselves. The doctrine of the Trinity, in particular, is to Swedenborg the evidence of an extremely disordered way of thinking in Christianity. Only a "brain fever," he insists, could have induced Christian leaders to have formulated the relationship of Father, Son, and Holy Spirit in such a way as to make it a Trinity not just of "persons" but actually of gods (§4). That modern people are turning their backs on such ancient doctrines is, in Swedenborg's judgment, a natural result and in fact their only recourse when faced with such illogical formulations. Here Swedenborg hits a note he is to carry through the work: the internal contradictions in Christian teaching have weakened it to the point (in Swedenborg's own day) that it simply has no credibility as taught, and is begging to be replaced with a true and authoritative teaching. This is a characteristic aspect of Swedenborg's thought: a traditional emphasis on the necessity of religious belief, and on faith as the apprehension and internalization of that belief, combined with a very modern understanding of the corrosive nature of rational doubt on revealed religion.

Beyond the doctrine of the Trinity, the other conventional teaching that most distresses Swedenborg is the Lutheran core doctrine of justification by faith.[16] Lutherans asserted this belief in their confessional writings not only as the central explanation of God's love for humankind but also as a key to understanding all God's promises manifest in Christ and communicated in Scripture. Swedenborg believes this doctrine has

---

16. For the definition of justification by faith, see note 10 above; for further discussion, see pages 90–92 below.

completely undermined faith in God and discouraged the good that
believers must do. As has been mentioned, this antagonism toward what
Lutheran churches held to be essential doctrine was not entirely unique to
Swedenborg; in fact, it had already been a theme in his father's teaching
and was the constant refrain of Pietist-influenced Lutherans. However,
Swedenborg's position on this was sufficiently far from the contemporary
mainstream and so uncompromisingly expressed that it would necessarily
preclude *True Christianity* from being considered by its contemporaries as
a work of orthodox Protestant teaching. Again, it was in large part what
he saw as the illogical and irrational nature of these doctrines and the
erroneous picture of God he felt they created that caused Swedenborg to
reject them so emphatically.

It is striking, in the historical view, to observe that during Swedenborg's
lifetime a new movement in northern Europe was applying similarly rationalist methods to the examination of Scripture. These "neologians" (as theologians of that time called them) were in their new way of thinking on a
vastly different wavelength from Swedenborg, but they and he attacked the
same targets in conventional theology, and on the same grounds—that
those theological commonplaces were irrational. Unfortunately for the
legacy of Swedenborg's work, their skepticism toward revealed truths
would in the end make them as disdainful of Swedenborg's revelations as of
the orthodox theology they (and he) rejected.[17]

c. The Centrality of Scripture

One area in which Swedenborg seems quite conventional, at least on the
surface, is in his use of Scripture. Never, in the text of *True Christianity,*
are we far from a citation from Scripture; in some places he inserts line
after line of them as proofs for a particular point. Particularly, of course,
in the chapters on God, Swedenborg can back up each of his contentions
with at least one reference to the Bible, and he is very generous in sharing
with the reader all the biblical knowledge at his disposal. His use of

---

17. The term "neologians" refers to "adherents of the new teaching," that is, about how to inter-
pret the Bible, specifically in the rationalist terms so popular during the Enlightenment. Their
movement, called in German the *Neologie,* flourished particularly in Germany between 1740 and
1790. One of the most significant neologians was Johann Jakob Griesbach (1745–1812). While at
the University of Halle he studied under Johann David Michaelis (1717–1791) and Johann Salamo
Semler (1725–1791), who were among the founders of the modern scientific study of the New Testament and are by some scholars included in the *Neologie.* See Bray 1996, 257–264.

Scripture, furthermore, is not only conventional but consistent with his own evaluation of its many parts: he uses particular books of the Bible far more often than others. As Swedenborg had already made his own assessment of the canonical status of the various books of the Bible, one is not surprised to find that in *True Christianity* he has very strongly emphasized some old favorites: the Pentateuch, the Psalms, Isaiah and Jeremiah, the Gospels, and the Revelation of John.[18]

To a modern critical reader, Swedenborg's "proof-texting," or heaping up of biblical citations in support of a particular point in his argument, might seem strange, and certainly even in *True Christianity*'s own time (1771) it was somewhat outmoded, but it was a conventional thing to do in theological treatises like this. In fact, the citation of whole lists of biblical references without attention to context or setting might have a deeper justification for Swedenborg personally than for most theologians of his time, for he believed quite firmly that Scripture contained within it divine messages at every level—that even the very letters themselves can be revelatory of a divine intent to those gifted with understanding (§191). This interpretive method is, by the standards of the 1770s, a very distinctive and unusual view of the appropriate way to read Scripture, and is one of the reasons Swedenborg's learned critics reject his views so completely. Critical acceptance and analysis of the uncertainties and inconsistencies in the biblical text had been commonplaces in the scholarly conversation of academic theologians since the time of Erasmus (1466?–1536) and Luther in the sixteenth century, and by Swedenborg's time were the stuff of basic university-level study of Scripture. Swedenborg had made himself a proficient reader of Hebrew since 1748, but other than demonstrating on occasion that he understands the Hebrew terms and feels empowered to retranslate them, he shows in *True Christianity* little connection to and less interest in the new forms of biblical criticism that were coming to fruition in the middle of the eighteenth century and were engaging theological scholarship intensely in his time. In light of his lack of interest in contemporary biblical interpretation, and of the importance of the Scriptures to theology in the Protestant traditions, it is unsurprising that one of Swedenborg's most vocal critics, Johann August Ernesti of Leipzig (1701–1781), was himself a renowned Bible scholar and notable exegete.

---

18. For a description of Swedenborg's full canon of the Bible, see page 679 note 17.

d. Swedenborg's "Memorable Occurrences"

The well-educated eighteenth-century Lutheran reader who picked up a copy of *True Christianity* out of general interest, or perhaps because of Swedenborg's reputation as a seer, would likely have had particular interest in the "memorable occurrences" that Swedenborg put at the end of every chapter. These events are brief accounts of Swedenborg's visits to the spiritual world or conversations with individual spirits. In each case, the one or more "occurrences" at the end of the section illustrate or illuminate in one way or another the point made in the chapter in which they appear. Sometimes they add a supernatural layer of evidence to Swedenborg's logical and scriptural argument; in others, they show the folly of belief in the view Swedenborg has just attacked by illustrating the consequences in the spiritual world for those who have held such erroneous views.

Occasionally the "occurrences" are like biblical parables, in that the moral is not clear until the end, if at all; in others, the point is made from the outset, and the figures in the recounting simply carry Swedenborg's argument further. In this latter instance they are somewhat like the lists of biblical citations that precede them: a source of additional authority for Swedenborg's position. Putting them side by side with Scripture, of course, claims for these experiences a divine revelatory authority that would have been at least mildly shocking to an orthodox Protestant reader, but this is consistent with Swedenborg's whole position on authority throughout *True Christianity*. He consistently maintains that the truth of the positions he takes is rationally apparent, scripturally defensible, and verified by his own experience. This pattern: reason, Holy Writ, and personal revelation, is the standard way in which each of *True Christianity*'s chapters presents Swedenborg's arguments.

III. *True Christianity* as an Attack on Lutheran Theology

One of the things a modern reader of *True Christianity* quickly notices is the tendentious and assertive tone the book takes almost from its beginning. After a gentle introductory passage (§§1–3), at the very start of chapter 1 Swedenborg blasts a trumpet against the error and complacency of the church in his own time. He insists that the church as it exists is "so close to its end today that scarcely any of it remains in existence," and as a consequence the Lord has recently ("several months ago") called out the twelve disciples (now angels) and sent them throughout the spiritual world to preach the Gospel anew. The reason that this has become necessary, Swedenborg declares, is that the church has waned to the point of near extinction. He blames this decline on the fact that the Christian church, though established by God, has done something unthinkable; it has misunderstood the Trinity of God by splitting God "into three persons, each of whom is God and Lord" (§4:1).

This error, ultimately, has meant for Swedenborg the destruction of the church's theology and the forfeiture of the very name "Christian"; for he insists that no church built on such a basis can survive. It is "deranged," is at "cross-purposes" with itself, has indeed "torn to pieces" the idea of God (§4:2, 3). Swedenborg takes no conciliatory position here; he has fired more than a rhetorical shot across traditional theology's bows: he has unleashed a full salvo to its waterline. How can a work that so determinedly challenges one of the oldest and most fundamental doctrines of Christianity see itself as a "True" exposition of the same? It is clear that Swedenborg wants the reader to ask that question, and that he knows that by making this bold statement, he either drives readers away or draws them forward into a new way of thinking about God and God's relationship to humankind. "Brain fever," Swedenborg calls the conventional language of the Trinity, as we have seen. His opponents, for their part, have earlier declared him "fanatical."[19] How can constructive theology be hammered out this way?

For Swedenborg, the path is clear and straight. A "mending" can occur for that which has been ripped apart, and the solution is obvious. Human reason now must be convinced anew "from the Word and its light" that the Trinity exists and is fundamental to faith, not in the way that the "orthodox" claim, but in a natural, relational way—as the soul to the body. Swedenborg is writing here of nothing less than the fundamental nature of God's self-revelation to humanity. The field of contest has here been claimed, and the weapons for the duel are chosen: human reason, the "Word," and the Word's "light" (§4:3). So the theological battle begins.

Nevertheless, *True Christianity* in its very form, structure, and content owes more to Lutheran theology than its use of that theology as a foil would suggest. To produce a blow-by-blow comparison would go beyond the scope of this introduction; instead it will highlight just the signal differences between Swedenborg's system and Lutheran theology.

---

19. Johann August Ernesti, mentioned above in the text, had branded Swedenborg a fanatic in his review of *Secrets of Heaven* (Ernesti 1760, 527).

a. The Influence of the Catechism

In Swedenborg's experience of the Christian church as a young man, the most common (in fact, universal) way of learning about, understanding, and expressing the basic truths of the Christian faith was through the Small Catechism (1529) of Martin Luther. In that brief and simple work, intended by Luther for the instruction of children and unlettered adults, the claims for Christian truth are reduced to their most basic and ancient level, using texts so sacred to the Christian church's heritage that many Christians even today have committed them to memory: the Apostles' Creed, the Ten Commandments, and the Lord's Prayer. It is safe to say not only that Swedenborg knew these classic Christian texts by heart (and many more besides) but indeed that every part of the text of the whole Small Catechism would have been accessible to him in stored memory. In his day, the gateway to adulthood and to full membership of the church in Sweden or any Lutheran land was through a single rite of passage: memorization of Luther's Small Catechism. This feat provided the practical minimum of the religious knowledge of even the humblest member of the community. Inability to master this rudimentary text would put one, in a sense, outside the community. For it was in the rite of confirmation that a person was admitted to the fellowship of the church's principal sacrament, the Lord's Supper or Holy Communion. This ceremony had become mandatory in Sweden in the time of Swedenborg's grandfather, as it already had been elsewhere in the Lutheran world. The cornerstone of the confirmation rite was the public examination, when the confirmand would be asked in the face of the congregation to recite from it. One of the commandments, an article of the creed, or a phrase of the Lord's Prayer would be read forth, Luther's traditional catechetical question, "What is this?" would be asked, and the confirmand would be expected to answer in Luther's own words.[20]

Memorizing the catechism for confirmation, which took place in about one's fourteenth year (often later, for those otherwise uneducated or in remote locales), was a long project, often spanning more than one year. In many places a head start was gained by the use of the catechism and other traditional religious texts as material from the very beginning

---

20. An example: after the reading of the Third Commandment ("You are to hallow the day of rest"), the correct answer to "What is this?" is "We are to fear and love God, so that we do not despise preaching or God's Word, but instead keep that Word holy and gladly hear and learn it" (Kolb and Wengert 2000, 352).

of the process of learning to read. Reading and religion then grew up together. In the household of Jesper Swedberg, perfect knowledge of the catechism would have been expected of every child, and the good bishop doubtless perfected his own method of teaching and explaining the catechism by practice on his own children. About the time of Swedenborg's completion of his university studies at Uppsala, Jesper Swedberg published his own version of the catechism, including the traditional text but extending it many times over with explanations and interpretation. Although doing so was not a new technique, Swedberg thus made the catechism his own personal textbook of the faith.[21] Through this more advanced kind of commentary, the basic textbook of a child's faith could become a lifelong learning tool, useful in nurturing the faith of believers of every age.

The influence of the catechism on Swedenborg's *True Christianity* is obvious both in its content and, almost more significantly, in its structure. In content, because the catechism is referred to more frequently than any other work besides the Bible, the *Book of Concord* (which actually contains the Small Catechism as one of its component parts), and the other works of Swedenborg. In structure, because like the catechism, *True Christianity* contains a section on each of the three articles of the Apostles' Creed (chapters 1 through 3); a section on the Ten Commandments with a subsection for each (chapter 5); a fairly lengthy passage that repeatedly touches on the Lord's Prayer (chapter 2, §§112–113); and sections on each of the two sacraments, Baptism and the Lord's Supper (chapters 12 and 13). *True Christianity*, to be sure, also includes long chapters on deeper theological subjects not dealt with in the catechism, like the nature of Scripture (chapter 4); two of the theological virtues, faith (chapter 6) and goodwill (chapter 7); the question of free will (chapter 8); repentance (chapter 9); reformation and regeneration (chapter 10); and the assignment of spiritual credit or blame (chapter 11). After the two chapters on the sacraments, *True Christianity* ends with a chapter on the end of the ages, the coming of the Lord, and the new church (chapter 14). These additional subjects do not receive detailed attention in the catechism, but they would have been found in most other standard theology texts of the time.

---

21. Swedberg dedicated his *Catechism: or Godly Exercise Together with Comforting Conversation* (1709) to his surviving children and grandchildren. Emanuel is listed second, after Anna, an older brother having already died.

What is unusual about *True Christianity* compared to contemporary works of systematic theology is the inclusion of a detailed, separate section on the Ten Commandments in addition to one on Scripture in general. Except for the importance these sacred laws held for ordinary Christians, there is no special theological or exegetical reason for the Ten Commandments to be separated out from the rest of the biblical text. Swedenborg does so in order to use these familiar texts to support his argument that the most profound aspects of faith are also deeply reasonable. The Decalogue (then as now) has often been seen as a kind of religious "basic law" for which parallels in other religious cultures can be found. Swedenborg does this, claiming that these great divine laws are "universally recognized on earth" (§282). The fundamental role Swedenborg believes the Ten Commandments play in Christian belief is also underscored by his choice of the resonant word "catechism" to describe them in that chapter's title: "The Catechism, or Ten Commandments, Explained in Both Its Outer and Its Inner Meanings" (chapter 5).

b. The Role of the Confessions

Another important source of specifically Lutheran doctrinal authority that Swedenborg uses as a foil in *True Christianity* is the *Book of Concord,* the compilation of "confessional" (doctrinally binding) statements of faith of the Lutheran Church. Composed of a number of texts ranging in date from 1524 to 1580, the *Book of Concord* is an anthology of definitive and authoritative Lutheran teachings. Some of the texts it contains, like the Small Catechism, the Large Catechism (1529; = Kolb and Wengert 2000, 377–480), and the Smalcald Articles (1537; = Kolb and Wengert 2000, 295–328), were written by Martin Luther himself; several others, including the Augsburg Confession and its explanation, the Apology of the Augsburg Confession (1531; = Kolb and Wengert 2000, 107–294), were composed by Luther's friend and colleague Philipp Melanchthon. The last of the confessional writings was the Formula of Concord of 1577 (Kolb and Wengert 2000, 562–573), which in 1580 gave its name to the entire collection, called from that point the *Book of Concord.* These texts were all attempts to clarify and define the theology of the "Evangelical" or Lutheran party in the Empire. Most of the confessions were written to distinguish the evangelical faith from what Luther's followers saw as Catholic errors and abuses. The later texts add the dual purposes of mediating disputes among Lutherans on questions Luther had left unclear, and distinguishing Lutheran from Calvinist views. In Swedenborg's time, the Church of Sweden—as it was directed to do in the 1686 *Kyrkolag*—required of its theologians a commitment of doctrinal fidelity to the Augsburg Confession specifically, but also recognized the whole *Book of Concord* as a correct and definitive expression of the essence of the Gospel message and the faith of the church. In the German Lutheran lands, the *Book of Concord* was generally recognized as definitive in its entirety, and those ordained to the church's ministry were expected to subscribe to it. The Augsburg Confession had binding validity in every Lutheran land; the two catechisms written by Luther followed it in authority and surpassed it in popularity.

Swedenborg makes it very clear in *True Christianity* that he rejects specific doctrines central to the Lutheran confessional writings. He sets up the *Book of Concord* as a sort of formal opponent and in doing so challenges the entire Lutheran tradition it represents. In many ways, Swedenborg's challenge was a timely one; as we have seen, he was not alone in his era as a critic of the excessively narrow confessionalism of much Lutheran theology. In fact, though, a new and growing historical consciousness among Lutheran theologians in the eighteenth century had renewed the old Lutheran principle of the priority of Scripture, with the consequence that the confessions' claim to be valid interpretations of Scripture was being reexamined. In the same way, a new historical perspective on the person of Luther had put the Reformation in a clearer (and clearly more distant) context. This trend is illustrated also by the eighteenth-century rise in interest in Luther; a major new edition of Luther's writings (with the many Latin texts translated into German for a lay audience) was edited and published by Johann Georg Walch (1693–1775) of Jena between 1740 and 1753 (Luther 1740–1753). Swedenborg, though he reports in the supplement to *True Christianity* concerning his conversations with Luther in the spiritual world, seems largely untouched by the expansion of historical knowledge of Luther in his own era. His concentration on the *Book of Concord* as the source of the theology he opposes is at the same time reasonable and slightly odd: it remained the traditional source of authoritative Lutheran teaching, but by Swedenborg's time the major debates among Lutheran theologians had moved far beyond the material of the confessions themselves. From the perspective of his contemporaries, Swedenborg would be much more current in his criticism of "naturalist" (materialist) theologians than in what could only be seen as a somewhat quixotic attack on the confessions themselves, codified as they were in dogma and in law, and far from the theological "cutting edge" in the 1770s.

c. The Creeds and the Doctrine of the Trinity

Of the major doctrinal traditions Swedenborg challenges in *True Christianity,* the doctrine of the Trinity was the most venerable. Taken from the statement at the end of the Gospel of Matthew (28:19) in which Jesus commissions the apostles to "go therefore and make disciples of all nations, baptizing them in the name of the Father, Son, and Holy Spirit," the idea that God can best be described as coexisting in the forms of "Father, Son, and Holy Spirit" took hold of the church's imagination early in its history, and is one of early Christianity's first attempts to express a distinctively Christian understanding of God. The doctrine of the Trinity is associated particularly with the early church's creeds, which were attempts to express fundamental truths of Christianity in short, clear formulations that could be easily memorized and recited by the community or used as personal statements of faith. The creeds took the trinitarian form (Father, Son, Holy Spirit), and expressed faith in God as each of these three forms, building on to each statement a short explanation of the way God is manifested in each case.

The first creed known to have been used in liturgy and doctrine was the "Old Roman" Creed of the early third century, which in modified form is known to the Christian world today as the "Apostles' Creed." Most Christian communities today continue to use some version of this formula in worship and particularly at baptisms, though the doctrinal status of the creeds varies among churches. To combat a variety of heresies about the relationship of the two natures in Christ, and to clarify further the symmetrical nature of the Trinity, the Councils of Nicaea (325) and Constantinople (381) took a basic baptismal creed like the Roman one and added more text, producing what is known today as the Nicene Creed. Reaffirmed by later councils in 431 and 451, the Nicene Creed remains for most of the world's Christians the definitive statement of faith on the humanity and divinity of Christ and the relationship of the Father to the Son and Holy Spirit. Some tinkering in the Western Church in the fifth century led to the insertion of a clause ("and from the Son") to the third article, which made it clear that the Holy Spirit came equally from the Father and Son, an addition that was rejected by the Eastern (Greek) Church. An additional form of creed, the so-called Athanasian Creed, probably arose in fifth-century Gaul. It is a long recapitulation of the doctrines of the Trinity and the incarnation, and includes condemnations of those holding other views. Its authorship by Athanasius (about 293–373), first disputed in the seventeenth century by the Dutch theologian Gerhard Jan Voss (1577–1649), is now no longer believed, but was still accepted as fact at the time of the Reformation. All three creeds came to have binding authority in Western Christianity, which has called them (somewhat misleadingly, as the Athanasian Creed has never been definitive in the Eastern Church) the "ecumenical creeds."

The Reformation brought a general reaffirmation of the three historic creeds by all of the various Protestant confessional groupings: both Lutherans and Calvinists took pains in their debates with Rome to assert their continued loyalty to these ancient formulations. They were not all three uniformly emphasized in Protestant statements of faith, however: Calvinists, though they accepted all three, put their stress on the Apostles' Creed; Anglicans (though again, accepting all three) have tended to de-emphasize the Athanasian Creed, which is no longer definitive in some Anglican churches today; only Lutherans have consistently held up all three creeds as definitive and inseparable.[22]

In challenging this trinitarian formulation, therefore, Swedenborg strikes at the root of a venerable and basic theological assertion, one that, though perhaps poorly understood and badly articulated, nonetheless had stood the test of time and had acquired, on that basis, an almost totemic status in the Christian church. Swedenborg rejects the traditional understanding of the Trinity, the definition of the three aspects of God as "persons," as a form of polytheism. This is not a new objection, even in Swedenborg's own time, but it is not one that was very likely to find widespread support among Lutherans or Calvinists of a traditional frame of mind.

Swedenborg's rejection of this traditional formula results in his being labeled as an antitrinitarian heretic—to be precise, as a "Socinian." This label, which Swedenborg sharply rejects in *True Christianity*, was a natural and easy, if superficial, one to place on him, as it tended in that time to be loosely applied to any questioning of or deviation from the accepted formulas and description of the Trinity (Dilthey 1923, 139–140). The term derives from a pair of Italian antitrinitarians named Lelio (1525–1562) and Fausto (1539–1604) Sozzini (or in Latinized form, Socinus), uncle and nephew, who became famous throughout sixteenth-century Europe for their boldness in questioning this basic doctrine. They also denied the

---

22. The fact that Swedenborg addresses all three creeds in *True Christianity* suggests again that the work is aimed primarily at a Lutheran audience.

usefulness of the sacraments and most religious practices. The Sozzinis were not the first to hold such views, but they were unusual in the degree to which they were able to move around Europe promoting their ideas and seeking kindred spirits. Communities of antitrinitarian Protestants flourished in Transylvania, Poland, and a few places in Switzerland until the mid-seventeenth century. Socinian views were, however, generally proscribed, and their adherents persecuted in most Roman Catholic, Lutheran, and Calvinist lands, and by the eighteenth century few real Socinians remained. Their ideas, though, found a receptive audience among the English deists and the later English Unitarians, and their name remained a standard theological byword long after their movement waned. In Swedenborg's lifetime the leading English antitrinitarian was Joseph Priestley (1733–1804), like Swedenborg a doubter of many standard Christian doctrines and a gifted scientist, who is remembered today chiefly for his writings on the nature of air and his identification of oxygen. Shortly after *True Christianity* appeared, Priestley began to publish his own major theological work, *Institutes of Natural and Revealed Religion,* which appeared in three volumes between 1772 and 1774. It is in Priestley's time that the antitrinitarian movement becomes significant enough again to acquire a positive name of its own choice: Unitarian. It is not clear that Swedenborg ever knew of Priestley's scientific or religious views, but the similarity between the two men is striking, and they both were tagged by their opponents with the "Socinian" label.[23]

Why is the issue of the Trinity so important to Swedenborg, and who does he see as his opponents in this controversy? First and foremost, he targets the dogmatic theologians, people whose love of terms and formulations have, in his view, led them far from a lively understanding of God's love for humankind and God's intimate activity in sustaining and guiding the world. On the other side, Swedenborg also takes aim at those he calls "naturalists," whose rationalist and mechanical explanations for God's work in creating and maintaining the world have stripped all divine meaning from the physical world. The distance between these two positions is great, and not only Swedenborg but the mainstream of Christian belief probably fall somewhere in between.

---

23. There is of course the distinction between Swedenborg and antitrinitarians such as Priestley that the latter rejected the divinity of Christ, a stance that was to become one of the distinguishing features of Unitarianism.

It is in the second half of chapter 3 that Swedenborg deals with the Trinity (§§163–184), after his discussion of the ways God works through the Holy Spirit (§§138–158). As we saw above, the list of the conclusions he proposes can be subdivided into groups of three—in this case, three groups of three (§163). The three initial points are that there is a Trinity; that the Father, Son, and Holy Spirit are "essential components" of one God; and that this Trinity was not eternal, but came into being after the world was created, and specifically, through the incarnation of the Son. Swedenborg follows these positive conclusions with three negative ones: (1) to say there is an eternal Trinity is to say there are three Gods; (2) the apostolic church knew nothing of a "trinity of persons"; and (3) the later (Nicene and Athanasian) definitions of the Trinity have "perverted the whole Christian church." The consequences of this are also threefold: (1) "abomination of desolation" and affliction has come into the church like none that has existed before; (2) this affliction is so bad that without God's recent intervention to create a new church all would be doomed to perish; and (3) the Athanasian definition of the persons of God has completely distorted and skewed Christian thinking and theology. Each of these nine points is given a fairly full exposition in a section of chapter 3.

How do the three manifestations of God relate to God's ultimate unity? For Swedenborg, who calls them "essential components" *(essentialia),* the interrelationship can be seen as analogous with the relationship between a person's soul, body, and deeds. In a more technical sense, Swedenborg explains them as reflecting two levels of essence: what he calls "general essential components" *(essentialia communia)* and "specific essential components" *(essentialia particularia),* which "combine to make one essence" (§166). In the analogy to soul, body, and deeds, the more fundamental produces the more ephemeral: the soul, which is basic, produces the body, which in turn produces the body's deeds. This is how God works, too: the Father is the Creator, who shapes and brings about the Son (§167), whose work in creation, in the hells, and in the heavens is through the Holy Spirit.

Much of the way Swedenborg writes of these relationships could fit within the various doctrinal explanations traditional in his time. The point at which he draws a distinction between his views and those of the tradition, and distances himself from it, lies in his description of how these three "components" of God are defined; he firmly opposes the use of the word *person* to describe the three parts of the Trinity. Where does this word *person* come from, and what did it mean to the churchly tradition and to Swedenborg? The tradition, at least as manifested by the

Lutheran dogmaticians of the post-Reformation period, defined a theological "person" *(hypostasis)* in these terms: "an individual, intelligent, incommunicable substance, which is not sustained, either upon another or from another" (Chemnitz [1591] 1608–1609, 1:39; Schmid 1889, 144), or, in another, similar vein, "a person is an independent and communicable subsistence of singular, complete, and intelligent substance" (Hollatz [1707] 1718, 284; Schmid 1889, 144). Compare this to the formulation Swedenborg so strongly criticizes in chapter 1: "The term *person* means that which is not a role of, or a quality in, someone else, but an entity subsisting on its own" (§17). Swedenborg has simplified the language, but has accurately recapitulated the tradition. At issue is the relationship between the central, unified divine essence *(ousia)* and the "personal" substance that makes each of the aspects of the Trinity distinctive.

The formulations that prevailed in the Christian tradition attempted to keep the "persons" clearly distinct and to prevent any blurring of them; what loses out in this formulation, as Swedenborg astutely observes, is the preservation of God's ultimate unity. By making a distinction between God in essential terms and God in "personal" manifestation, the intention was to keep both aspects in balance: God's unity and the divinity of the Son and the Spirit. Whether that theological intention was ever matched by the reality of the dogmatic language is questionable; the sixteenth- and seventeenth-century Lutheran dogmaticians, in gamely attempting to revivify the old distinctions and give them a more solidly logical basis, had to admit that they were forced ultimately by the limitations of language to refer the inquirer to the realm of mystery. That Swedenborg should have found this logically unsatisfying is not at all surprising; when his spiritual experience provided him with a new understanding, it is natural that he would greatly prefer it. Swedenborg does not share the early church's preoccupation with the relationship of the two natures in Christ; his spiritual experience has equipped him with a new certainty and a better language to describe them. Armed as Swedenborg is with what he knows to be a deeper and more intimate knowledge of the real relationships, the fact that any deviance from the accepted formulas would be a point of criticism by theologians would not hinder or deflect him in the least.

d. Justification by Faith

It is difficult to say whether Swedenborg's challenge to the Lutheran doctrine of justification by faith would have been more scandalous to his

Lutheran contemporaries than his attack on the conventional understanding of the Trinity, but it might well have been. Certainly in this challenge they would have known that it was Lutheran teaching in particular, and not just Christian dogmatics in general, that was under attack. The doctrine of "justification by faith," better described as "justification by grace through faith," was so much the central doctrine of the Lutheran rethinking of the Catholic tradition that it had acquired—for Lutherans—the same sort of totemic importance as the doctrine of the Trinity had long held for Catholic Christians.[24] It was, Lutheran theologians were fond of saying, the "article on which the church stands or falls";[25] in other words, the boundary line separating the truly Christian from the unchristian in theology.

The justification doctrine was not only an objective and fundamental assertion about the interaction of God with humanity; it was also—for Lutherans in particular but in a general way for all Protestants—a hermeneutical and exegetical key through which the scriptural witness could be understood and theology derived from Scripture could be judged. No less a figure than Luther had made it clear that this single doctrine was the lens through which even Scripture could (and should) be read and understood (Luther 1883–, 6:2–11 = Luther 1955, 35:357–362). In fact, Luther's intense promotion of this special doctrine had been intended by him as a corrective to a medieval Catholic misunderstanding of the nature of God's grace, which Luther thought had distorted the whole theology of the church of his day. Much in the same fashion, Swedenborg attacks the justification doctrine itself because of the manner in which he believes it has distorted the whole Protestant view of God's intentions for humankind. In this, ironically, Swedenborg could be said to have been employing a "Lutheran" critical principle to the very doctrine Luther himself used to critique the theology and church practice of his own time. Both men, Luther and Swedenborg, also felt strongly enough about their respective understandings of the issue—the role of God's grace in human salvation—to feel empowered to read the whole Bible through them: but where Luther's justification-based interpretive principle led him to emphasize the letters of Paul and the Gospel of John and downplay the synoptic

---

24. For a definition of justification by faith alone, see note 10 above.

25. The Latin form of this often-used phrase is *articulus stantis et cadentis ecclesiae.* Its origin is obscure. For a similar comment by Luther himself, see the end of the preface to the Smalcald Articles: "on this article stands all we teach and practice. . . ." (Kolb and Wengert 2000, 301).

Gospels and the pastoral Epistles (particularly the letter of James, which he felt to be nearly useless), Swedenborg's view of the inner meaning of Scripture and the dangers of the doctrine of "faith alone" led him to reject Paul's Epistles and favor instead the Gospels and the Revelation of John, particularly because of their clearer call to holy living in preparation for the new advent of Christ.

Swedenborg's idea of what the justification doctrine meant in Lutheran theology, though accurate in some ways, is strangely one-sided. Swedenborg's view of Luther seems to have been skewed by an assumption (derived most likely from the *Book of Concord* and the tradition he grew up with) that Luther was almost exclusively interested in the idea of imputed righteousness he found in the letters of Paul, which, of course, Swedenborg thought had caused so much harm in the church. In fact, Luther's emphasis on justification by faith as a first principle of theology was closely balanced with a belief that the life of faith was inevitably a life of neighbor-love. As to the doctrine itself, and its theological description and explanation, however, Swedenborg is highly accurate. He had before him in the Formula of Concord the most precise formulation of this doctrine Lutheran theologians had ever written.

Swedenborg's attack on the misuse of the justification doctrine is not in itself surprising; it is a commonplace of the preaching of the time that an understanding of doctrine is not itself a justifying faith. But why, in light of this, does he take it on so passionately? To some degree, the answer may lie less in Swedenborg's concept of a merciful God than in his view of a capable humanity. The sections of *True Christianity* in which Swedenborg most clearly reveals his anthropology are the chapter on Jesus the Redeemer (chapter 2) and the set of chapters in which he discusses repentance and regeneration (chapters 8 through 11). In these, as in the sections where he discusses the future life in the spirit, Swedenborg describes a free, aware, and perfectible humankind, who through an understanding of the Lord's example and inspiration can rise to a higher level of purity and holiness. Described in chapter 10 as "reformation" and "regeneration," this potential for human improvement is essential to Swedenborg's whole theology.

e. The Person and Work of Christ

For a Lutheran of traditional views, perhaps the most deeply shocking of Swedenborg's challenges to Lutheran doctrine would have been his rejection of the received understanding that the atoning death of Christ was necessary to the divine plan for salvation. This underlying doctrine supports the key teaching of justification by faith itself; without the atoning death of Christ to restore the broken relationship between God and humanity and bridge the gap created by human sin, salvation was not thought to be possible. The incarnation of Christ comes in here: in appearing on earth in human form, God broke down the barrier between the heavenly and eternal realm and the physical and mortal world; by suffering and dying, the Divine Human reestablished the relationship that had been broken at Adam and Eve's fall and opened anew the possibility of salvation.

For Swedenborg, the unity of God and Jesus is again as much an assertion of the perfectibility and future potential of humanity as it is a mark of divine mercy. Salvation, then, rests not in some abstract decision on God's part to forgive for Jesus' sake, but in the entire process through which God demonstrates love for humanity by becoming human, showing how the "human" can be perfected and made holy in love, and demonstrating that the ultimate destination of the true believer is heaven. Swedenborg's system eliminates the old distinction between Christ's "person," which demonstrates God's mercy, and Christ's "work" of satisfaction for human guilt. Instead, Swedenborg presents Jesus as manifesting God to humankind and then showing humanity how to live in faith and grow in perfection. The "atonement" of the tradition is thus replaced with a "preparation" by God in human form of a new home, a new church, for all the faithful. This Swedenborg calls "gaining control of the hells" and "restructuring the heavens" (§§114–115). From Swedenborg's perspective, the work of God is not a way for God to satisfy self-created and abstract divine ideas of justice and appropriateness but rather a way to provide for human benefit and growth.

f. Faith and the Assignment of Spiritual Credit or Blame

This same emphasis on human cooperation is visible as well in Swedenborg's views of faith and of the assignment of spiritual credit or blame (traditionally called imputation). He diverges most dramatically from Lutheran and Calvinist orthodoxy—and does so intentionally—in §§355–359, in which he describes how, though faith and goodwill both come from God, human abilities play a role in securing them. As Swedenborg describes it, the Scriptures offer objective truths about God that can be gained by sincere seekers, which, when they lead those seekers to love God, are the beginning of faith. Swedenborg knows he is here denying the Protestant principle of the human inability to bring about or secure salvation. Swedenborg's main point seems to be polemical; he wants to overturn Protestant orthodoxy's insistence on the primacy of God's action not because he has a lower view of God, but because he wants to intensify human responsibility and draw the rationally believing away from the abstraction of faith to the reality of loving action. Where the Protestant tradition's principal concern was human over-confidence, Swedenborg's target is human complacency. Each view diagnoses and treats the main spiritual malady of its own time; Swedenborg has the historical advantage of understanding the earlier view and supplementing it with his own.

On the question of how spiritual credit or blame is assigned (chapter 11), Swedenborg once again parts company from the mainstream. A fairly long introduction describes the concept as understood in the tradition (§§626–635): it had come to mean the righteousness of Christ imputed to the believer by God for the sake of Christ, which then counted as righteousness for the believer toward salvation. In the conventional Protestant understanding of the time, the assignment of spiritual credit or blame is not an experienced stage in a process of gaining saving faith, but a technical step in an abstract and theological understanding of God's work through grace. But Swedenborg makes something quite original out of this. He first demolishes the tradition by rejecting the separation of Christ's righteousness from Christ himself and linking this to the old christological and trinitarian debates of the early church. Just as those debates erroneously and falsely divided God, now Protestant theologians, says Swedenborg, divide Christ from Christ's righteousness (§96).

For Swedenborg, the assignment of spiritual credit or blame is part of the process by which the soul, upon arrival in the world of spirits, learns of its true disposition and destiny. God in all of this has a purely positive role, willing heaven to all and calling all souls to come there for judgment—and thus the judgment, when it occurs, is not made by God, but comes about from the subject's own faith and life. A pure faith and life receives reward; an impure and evil one, punishment. In this, Swedenborg is so different in his view from the traditional or the contemporary church that he cannot do more than simply list the two views side by side to be contrasted. One section contains a series of paragraphs in which he simply declares the old to be superseded by the new: "the faith of the former church is . . ." and "the faith of the new church is . . ." (§647). Backing his exposition up with four memorable occurrences, Swedenborg here constructs a new system of judgment and eternal life that must have been completely foreign, but was highly interesting, to his contemporaries.

g. The Future of the Faith

Swedenborg's final chapter is unique and untraditional; it has less obvious connection to the Lutheran theological background than many other aspects of *True Christianity*. Its theme is the end of days, the return of Christ, and the establishment of the new church. Swedenborg here optimistically replaces the customary description of the "four last things" (death, judgment, heaven, and hell) common to Lutheran books of systematic theology with a vision of the restoration of the kingdom of God as he experienced it in his interactions with the spiritual world. In this last formal chapter, Swedenborg also describes the history of the "church" in the sense of the history of God's relationship with humankind.

It was not unusual in Swedenborg's time to write human history in divine terms or to see the actual lapse of time and course of human events as conforming to a scheme of "salvation history" in God's terms. The Reformation had brought about a spate of history-writing that tended to see the beginnings of Protestantism as the dawn of a new golden age; Swedenborg is in good company in thinking of his own age as the ultimate one. In his division of history, the "old church" is described as having existed in four epochs, each individually described as a "church" in itself: one that lasted from creation to the Flood; one from the Flood to the giving of the law to Moses; one from Mount Sinai to Calvary; and the final one from the time of Jesus to the lifetime of Swedenborg. This is not a very unusual pattern; indeed it is almost the same schema that the biblical "church history" written in 1699 by Swedenborg's brother-in-law Erik Benzelius the younger took as its point of departure.[26] But in Swedenborg's version the period since Jesus has a subdivision: first the faithful church of the apostolic age; and then the church since the Council of Nicaea's fateful trinitarian formulations, which Swedenborg believes drove the church into a theological ditch. Most Protestant church histories of Swedenborg's time would have seen

---

26. Benzelius 1699; the pattern had been set earlier in the century by Johannes Elai Terserus (1605–1678), professor of theology at Uppsala and later bishop in Åbo and Linköping, who wrote a history of "the church" in the form of an extended commentary on Genesis and Exodus; see Terserus 1655, Terserus 1657, Terserus 1660, and Lindroth 1976, 67.

the church's period of decline as coinciding with the millennium of papal authority and power, framed by purer periods before the sixth century and since the sixteenth. Swedenborg's historical schema would be attractive to those who felt that the end of the eighteenth century was likely to be the end of the world; millenarian feeling (as we have seen), though still rare, was a strong current among dissenters from the Protestant mainstream in that era.[27]

IV. Conclusion

As an apologetic, *True Christianity* is a very assertive and confident statement of a radically challenging set of theological positions. There is no question from this text that if Swedenborg's conservative opponents in Sweden were looking for heresy, Swedenborg gives them here all the heresy they could want. And Swedenborg is not only clearly aware of this, he seems to revel in it. As a text that is making a case in a skeptical context, *True Christianity* is bold, and right from the opening section insists on the correctness and validity of its position. Swedenborg is not concerned to word his positions delicately or to make things easy for those who are well disposed toward him personally but are theologically skeptical; he comes right out and says things he knows are deeply at odds with the teaching of the church into which he was born. He is, he asserts, empowered to do this by a divine calling and by the attendant experience he has been granted of the spiritual world. A view as divergent from the mainstream as Swedenborg's could not be camouflaged into respectability, even if Swedenborg were interested in thus disguising it—which he is not; it could only be proclaimed with conviction and with as much corroboration as possible from Scripture and reason as supporting witnesses.

Nevertheless, the general reaction at first to *True Christianity* was muted and mixed, with a few very warm and a few very harsh responses.[28] That Swedenborg did not receive more attention from contemporary theologians was due in part to the number of issues in the air during that

---

27. Many Pietist millenarianists occupied themselves with Revelation; see Beyreuther 1978, 262–263.

28. For an account of early responses both warm and harsh, see pages 33–40 above in the translator's preface.

period, but also in part to the timing of Swedenborg's message, which
did not fit neatly into the ongoing debates. His unique combination of
rationalism (which, at least in its Wolffian[29] form, was passing out of
fashion) and spiritualism (the golden days of which still lay ahead in the
nineteenth century) kept him from being neatly classified. His new spiritual experiences tended to alarm traditionalists; his stress on the priority
of such experience alienated rationalists. In an increasingly active and
international scholarly debate, Swedenborg's distance from the conventional alignments of academic theology kept him out of the journals
except on a few occasions.

In all this, Swedenborg was simply too unusual to be easily classified
by his contemporaries; more than an individualist, in the term used in
his time he was an *individuum,* a self-contained and unique whole entity,
combining scientific authority with more than a touch of the mystical. In
an era that relished novelty and controversy it is natural that he would
attract some attention, but without a strong following or some institu-
tional authority he would not have an automatic audience. Yet in time an
audience found him.

Swedenborg lived in what saw itself as a new age of freedom, but the
intellectual ferment that had begun in the seventeenth century and found
expression in his lifetime would come to yet fuller expression in the century
to follow. Swedenborg's religious views, not widely accepted in his lifetime,
still had their greatest influence ahead of them. His ideas had sunk tender
but tenacious roots: in England among those who had known him and
continued to read his works; in Sweden among his friends and supporters;
in Germany, particularly among the pupils of Oetinger[30] in Swabia; and
after all of them, in the new religious societies founded in Swedenborg's

---

29. In the early and mid-eighteenth century, the philosophical system of Christian Wolff
(1679–1754), which Wolff perfected while teaching in Marburg, was influential in every Lutheran
university, including those in Sweden. In Uppsala, where Wolffian philosophy had become synonymous with opposition to atheism, deism, and naturalism, it had dominated the field in the
1730s. By the end of Swedenborg's lifetime, however, the influence of Wolffian rationalism was on
the wane.

30. The Pietist and polymath Friedrich Christoph Oetinger (1702–1782) was a high-ranking
clergyman of the Lutheran church of Württemberg in southern Germany. Oetinger was a rest-
less and imaginative thinker who explored questions of natural theology, the nature of the
spiritual world, and the interpretation of Scripture, with openness to new ideas but a firm
grounding in his Lutheran tradition and the Pietist ethos of Christianity. He lent qualified
support to Swedenborg's concepts, especially in a controversial work he published during
Swedenborg's lifetime (Oetinger 1765).

spirit in the United States. Time would bring about a wider acceptance of Swedenborg's insights; the great changes that lay just ahead and beneath the surface, in political life as in the world of thought, would create an atmosphere in the new century more open to Swedenborg's inspiration. The fundamental questions about human knowledge and human dignity that had effected a rethinking of basic assumptions concerning human society in the decade of Swedenborg's birth, and arose again a century later in an age of violent revolution and societal renewal, forever changed the religious and social framework in which theological texts like *True Christianity* would be read and understood.

Works Cited in the Introduction

1. Sources

Arndt, Johann. 1647–1648. *Fyra böcker om een sann christendom.* Translated by Carl Carlsson Gyllenhielm. 4 vols. Stockholm: Ignatius Meurer.

———. [1612] 1648. *Paradijs lustgård.* Translated by Ericus Schroderus. Nyköping: Amund N. Grefwe.

———. 1695. *Fyra böcker om een sann christendom.* Translated by Carl Carlsson Gyllenhielm. 4 vols. Stockholm: Johann Billingsley.

———. 1732. *Fyra anderika böcker om en sann christendom.* Norrköping: Broocman.

Bayly, Lewis. 1643. *Praxis Pietatis: Thet är, Gudachtigheetz öfnings andre deel.* Translated by Justus Gesenius. Stockholm: Henrich Keyser.

Benzelius, Erik. 1699. *Breviarium Historiae Ecclesiasticae, Veteris et Novi Testamenti.* Strängnäs: Johannes Rönberg.

Calvin, John. 1536. *Christianae Religionis Institutio, Totam Fere Pietatis Summam, et Quicquid Est in Doctrina Salutis Cognitu Necessarium, Complectens.* Basel: Thomas Platter and Balthasar Lasius.

Chemnitz, Martin. [1591] 1608–1609. *Loci Theologici.* Frankfurt: Hofmann.

Ernesti, Johann August. 1760. Review of *Secrets of Heaven,* by Emanuel Swedenborg. *Neue Theologische Bibliothek* 1:515–527.

Hafenreffer, Matthias. 1600. *Loci Theologici.* Tübingen: G. Gruppenbach.

———. 1714a. *Doctrinae Coelestis Compendium Minus, ex Locis Theologicis Matth. Hafenrefferi Collectum et in Usum Scholarum Editum.* Edited by Jesper Swedberg. Skara: Anders Kiellberg.

———. 1714b. *En liten bok, innehållande ens christens tro och lefwerne. Utdragen af d. Matth. Hafenrefferi här wedertagen scholebok.* Edited and translated by Jesper Swedberg. Skara: Anders Kiellberg.

Hall, Joseph. 1606. *The Arte of Diuine Meditation.* London: Macham and Cooke.

Hollatz, David. [1707] 1718. *Examen Theologicum Acromaticum.* Leipzig: Russworm.

Hutter, Leonhard. 1610. *Compendium Locorum Theologicorum ex Scripturis Sacris et Libro Concordiae . . . Collectum.* Wittenberg: Helwig.

Kolb, Robert, and Timothy J. Wengert, eds. 2000. *The Book of Concord: The Confessions of the Evangelical Lutheran Church.* Minneapolis: Fortress Press.

König, Johann Friedrich. 1664. *Theologia Positiva Acromatica.* Rostock: Kilius.

Laurelius, Olaus. 1641. *Syntagma Theologicum in Thesi et Antithesi Adornatum.* Uppsala: Laurelius.

Luther, Martin. 1740–1753. *D. Martin Luthers sowol in deutscher als lateinischer Sprache verfertigte und aus der lezteren in die erstere übersetzte sämtliche Schriften.* Edited by Johann Georg Walch. 24 vols. Halle: Johann Justinus Gebauer.

———. 1883–. *D. Martin Luthers Werke: Kritische Gesamtausgabe. Abteilung 3: Die Deutsche Bibel.* Weimar: Hermann Böhlau.

———. 1955. *Luther's Works: American Edition.* Edited by Jaroslav Pelikan and Helmut T. Lehmann. 55 vols. St. Louis: Concordia, and Philadelphia: Fortress.

Melanchthon, Philipp. 1521. *Loci Communes Rerum Theologicarum.* Basel: A. Perri.

Oetinger, Friedrich Christoph. 1765. *Swedenborgs und anderer irdische und himmlische Philosophie.* 2 vols. Edited by Karl C. E. Ehmann. Reutlingen: Rupp & Baur.

Parsons, Robert. 1582. *Christian Directory.* Rouen: Parsons.

Priestley, Joseph. 1772–1774. *Institutes of Natural and Revealed Religion.* 3 vols. London: J. Johnson.

Rydholm, P. 1902. *Sveriges kyrkolag af år 1686.* Stockholm: Bonnier.

Scriver, Christian. 1675–1696. *Seelen-Schatz.* 5 vols. Leipzig: Johann and Friedrich Lüderwalt.

———. 1723–1727. *Siäle-skatt.* 6 vols. Norrköping: Broocman.

Spener, Philipp Jakob. 1675. *Pia Desideria oder herzliches Verlangen nach gottgefälliger Besserung der wahren evangelischen Kirche.* Frankfurt am Main.

Swedberg, Jesper. 1709. *Catechismi gudliga öfning: Jemte tröstrikt samtal med en högt bedröfwad siäl.* Skara: Anders Kiellberg.

Terserus, Johannes Elai. 1655. *Annotationes in Genesin.* Uppsala: Johannes Pauli.

———. 1657. *Sacra Chronologia Inde ab Ortu Mundi Usque ad Natum Christum.* Uppsala: Johannes Pauli.

———. 1660. *Exodus et in Eam Annotationes.* Stockholm: Ignatius Meurer.

2. Secondary Literature

Acton, Alfred. 1948–1955. *The Letters and Memorials of Emanuel Swedenborg.* 2 vols. Bryn Athyn, Pa.: Swedenborg Scientific Association.

Ahlstrom, Sidney E. 1972. *Religious History of the American People.* New Haven: Yale University Press.

Beyreuther, Erich. 1978. *Geschichte des Pietismus.* Stuttgart: J. F. Steinkopf.

Bray, Gerald. 1996. *Biblical Interpretation, Past and Present.* Downers Grove, Ill.: Inter-Varsity.

Burke, Peter. 2000. *A Social History of Knowledge: From Gutenberg to Diderot.* Oxford: Blackwell.

Dilthey, Wilhelm. 1923. *Weltanschauung und Analyse des Menschen seit Renaissance und Reformation.* 3rd ed. Wilhelm Diltheys gesammelte Schriften 2. Leipzig: B. G. Teubner.

Dole, George F. 1988. "*True Christian Religion* as Apologetic Theology." In *Swedenborg and His Influence,* edited by Erland J. Brock and others. Bryn Athyn, Pa.: Academy of the New Church.

Dowley, Tim, ed. 2002. *Introduction to the History of Christianity.* Minneapolis: Fortress.

González, Justo L. 1964. *The Story of Christianity.* 2 vols. San Francisco: Harper & Row.

Hazard, Paul. 1963. *The European Mind: 1680–1715.* Cleveland and New York: Meridian.

Hope, Nicholas. 1995. *German and Scandinavian Protestantism from 1700 to 1918.* Oxford: Oxford University Press.

Johnson, Paul. 1976. *A History of Christianity.* New York: Atheneum.

Lindroth, Sten. 1976. *A History of Uppsala University 1477–1977.* Uppsala: Almqvist & Wiksell.

Mannermaa, Tuomo. 2005. *Christ Present in Faith: Luther's Views of Justification.* Translated by Kirsi Stjerna. Minneapolis: Fortress Press.

Schmid, Heinrich. 1889. *The Doctrinal Theology of the Evangelical Lutheran Church, Exhibited and Verified from the Original Sources.* Translated by Charles A. Hay and Henry E. Jacobs. Philadelphia: Lutheran Bookstore.

Schneider, Hans. 1992. "Beziehungen deutscher radikaler Pietisten zu Skandinavien." In *Der Pietismus in seiner europäischen und außereuropäischen Ausstrahlung,* edited by Esko M. Laine. Suomen Kirkkohistoriallisen Seuran Toimituksia 157. Helsinki: Suomen Kirkkohistoriallinen Seura.

Smoley, Richard. 2005. "The Inner Journey of Emanuel Swedenborg." In *Emanuel Swedenborg: Essays for the New Century Edition on His Life, Work, and Impact,* edited by Jonathan S. Rose and others. West Chester, Pa.: Swedenborg Foundation.

Tottie, Henry W. 1885–1886. *Jesper Svedbergs lif och verksamhet: Bidrag till svenska kyrkans historia.* 2 vols. Uppsala: Edvard Berling.

Walker, Williston. 1970. *A History of the Christian Church.* 3rd ed. New York: Charles Scribner's Sons.

Wordsworth, John. 1911. *The National Church of Sweden.* The Hale Lectures, 1910. London: A. R. Mowbray.

Short Titles and Other Conventions
Used in This Work

———

ALTHOUGH *True Christianity* was originally published as a single
volume, in this edition it has been broken into two volumes.

Following a practice common in his time, Swedenborg divided his
published theological works into sections numbered in sequence from
beginning to end. His original section numbers have been preserved in
this edition; they appear in red boxes in the outside margins. Because
many sections throughout Swedenborg's works are too long for precise
cross-referencing, Swedenborgian scholar John F. Potts (1838–1923) further divided them into subsections; these have since become standard.
They are indicated by bracketed arabic numbers that appear in the text
itself: [2], [3], and so on. Since the beginning of the first subsection
coincides with the beginning of the section, it is not labeled in the text.

As is common in Swedenborgian studies, text citations of Swedenborg's
works refer not to page numbers but to section numbers, which are uniform in most editions. Thus "*Secrets of Heaven* 29" refers to section 29 (§29)
of Swedenborg's *Secrets of Heaven*. Subsection numbers are given after a
colon; a reference such as "29:2" indicates subsection 2 of section 29.

Biblical citations in this edition follow the accepted standard: a semi-
colon is used between book references and between chapter references, and
a comma between verse references. Therefore "Matthew 5:11, 12; 6:1; 10:41,
42; Luke 6:23, 35" refers to Matthew chapter 5, verses 11 and 12; Matthew
chapter 6, verse 1; Matthew chapter 10, verses 41 and 42; and Luke chapter
6, verses 23 and 35.

Some features of the original Latin text of *True Christianity* have been
modernized in this edition. For example, Swedenborg's first edition relies
on context or italics rather than quotation marks to indicate passages
taken from the Bible or from his other works. The manner in which
these conventions are used in the original suggests that Swedenborg did
not belabor the distinction between direct quotation and paraphrase;
neither did he mark his omissions from or changes to material, whether
biblical or his own. This edition follows Swedenborg's practice of not
marking omissions or changes in quotations; but it reserves the use of

either block quotes or quotation marks for directly quoted material, and presents paraphrased material instead as regular text. Words in italics in the biblical quotations of this edition reflect a similar emphasis in the first edition. In passages of dialog as well, quotation marks have been introduced that were not present as such in the original.

This translation is based on the first Latin edition, published by Swedenborg himself. It incorporates the silent emendation of minor errors, not only in the text proper but in Bible verse references and in section references to Swedenborg's other published theological works. The text has also been changed without notice where the verse numbering of the Latin Bible cited by Swedenborg differs from that of modern English Bibles. Biblical references that occur in parentheses in passages of dialog are present in the first edition. In these passages and elsewhere throughout the translation, references or cross-references that were implied but not stated have been inserted in brackets. Unless an endnote indicates otherwise, all square brackets [] represent an insertion of material that was not present in the first edition.

Comments on the text are printed as endnotes, which are referenced by superscript numbers appearing in the main text. A reverse reference is given in the endnote itself. To find the location of the text treated in endnote 34, for example, the reader would turn back to the indicated section, §8, and the indicated subsection, [2]. The initials of the writer or writers are given in square brackets at the end of each note. Translations of material quoted in the endnotes are those of the indicated writer, except where otherwise specified or in cases in which the cited source is a translated text. Indexes to the entire work appear at the end of the second volume.

References to Swedenborg's writings in this work accord with the short titles listed below, except where he gives his own version of a title in the text of the translation, or where other translations are cited by the annotators. In this list, the short title is followed by the traditional translation of the title; by the original Latin title, with its full translation; and finally by the place and date of original publication if Swedenborg published it himself, or the approximate date of writing if he did not. The list is chronological within each of the two groups shown—the published theological works, and the nontheological and posthumously published works. The titles given below as theological works published by Swedenborg are generally not further referenced in lists of works cited in the preface, introduction, and endnotes.

Theological Works Published by Swedenborg

Secrets of Heaven
Traditional title: *Arcana Coelestia*
Original title: *Arcana Coelestia, Quae in Scriptura Sacra, seu Verbo Domini Sunt, Detecta: . . . Una cum Mirabilibus Quae Visa Sunt in Mundo Spirituum, et in Coelo Angelorum* [A Disclosure of Secrets of Heaven Contained in Sacred Scripture, or the Word of the Lord, . . . Together with Amazing Things Seen in the World of Spirits and in the Heaven of Angels]. London: 1749–1756.

Heaven and Hell
Traditional title: *Heaven and Hell*
Original title: *De Coelo et Ejus Mirabilibus, et de Inferno, ex Auditis et Visis* [Heaven and Its Wonders and Hell: Drawn from Things Heard and Seen]. London: 1758.

New Jerusalem
Traditional title: *New Jerusalem and Its Heavenly Doctrine*
Original title: *De Nova Hierosolyma et Ejus Doctrina Coelesti: Ex Auditis e Coelo: Quibus Praemittitur Aliquid de Novo Coelo et Nova Terra* [The New Jerusalem and Its Heavenly Teaching: Drawn from Things Heard from Heaven: Preceded by a Discussion of the New Heaven and the New Earth]. London: 1758.

Last Judgment
Traditional title: *The Last Judgment*
Original title: *De Ultimo Judicio, et de Babylonia Destructa: Ita Quod Omnia, Quae in Apocalypsi Praedicta Sunt, Hodie Impleta Sunt: Ex Auditis et Visis* [The Last Judgment and Babylon Destroyed, Showing That at This Day All the Predictions of the Book of Revelation Have Been Fulfilled: Drawn from Things Heard and Seen]. London: 1758.

White Horse
Traditional title: *The White Horse*
Original title: *De Equo Albo, de Quo in Apocalypsi, Cap. XIX: Et Dein de Verbo et Ejus Sensu Spirituali seu Interno, ex Arcanis Coelestibus* [The White Horse in Revelation Chapter 19, and the Word and Its Spiritual or Inner Sense (from *Secrets of Heaven*)]. London: 1758.

Other Planets
Traditional title: *Earths in the Universe*
Original title: *De Telluribus in Mundo Nostro Solari, Quae Vocantur Planetae, et de Telluribus in Coelo Astrifero, deque Illarum Incolis, Tum de Spiritibus et Angelis Ibi: Ex Auditis et Visis* [Planets or Worlds in Our Solar System, and Worlds in the Starry Heavens, and Their Inhabitants, As Well as the Spirits and Angels There: Drawn from Things Heard and Seen]. London: 1758.

The Lord
Traditional title: *Doctrine of the Lord*
Original title: *Doctrina Novae Hierosolymae de Domino* [Teachings for the New Jerusalem on the Lord]. Amsterdam: 1763.

Sacred Scripture
Traditional title: *Doctrine of the Sacred Scripture*
Original title: *Doctrina Novae Hierosolymae de Scriptura Sacra* [Teachings for the New Jerusalem on Sacred Scripture]. Amsterdam: 1763.

Life
Traditional title: *Doctrine of Life*
Original title: *Doctrina Vitae pro Nova Hierosolyma ex Praeceptis Decalogi* [Teachings about Life for the New Jerusalem: Drawn from the Ten Commandments]. Amsterdam: 1763.

Faith
Traditional title: *Doctrine of Faith*
Original title: *Doctrina Novae Hierosolymae de Fide* [Teachings for the New Jerusalem on Faith]. Amsterdam: 1763.

Supplements
Traditional title: *Continuation Concerning the Last Judgment*
Original title: *Continuatio de Ultimo Judicio: Et de Mundo Spirituali* [Supplements on the Last Judgment and the Spiritual World]. Amsterdam: 1763.

Divine Love and Wisdom
Traditional title: *Divine Love and Wisdom*
Original title: *Sapientia Angelica de Divino Amore et de Divina Sapientia* [Angelic Wisdom about Divine Love and Wisdom]. Amsterdam: 1763.

Divine Providence
Traditional title: *Divine Providence*
Original title: *Sapientia Angelica de Divina Providentia* [Angelic Wisdom about Divine Providence]. Amsterdam: 1764.

Revelation Unveiled
Traditional title: *Apocalypse Revealed*
Original title: *Apocalypsis Revelata, in Qua Deteguntur Arcana Quae Ibi Praedicta Sunt, et Hactenus Recondita Latuerunt* [The Book of Revelation Unveiled, Uncovering the Secrets That Were Foretold There and Have Lain Hidden until Now]. Amsterdam: 1766.

Marriage Love
Traditional title: *Conjugial Love*
Original title: *Delitiae Sapientiae de Amore Conjugiali: Post Quas Sequuntur Voluptates Insaniae de Amore Scortatorio* [Wisdom's Delight in Marriage Love: Followed by Insanity's Pleasure in Promiscuous Love]. Amsterdam: 1768.

Survey
Traditional title: *Brief Exposition*
Original title: *Summaria Expositio Doctrinae Novae Ecclesiae, Quae per Novam Hierosolymam in Apocalypsi Intelligitur* [Survey of Teachings for the New Church Meant by the New Jerusalem in the Book of Revelation]. Amsterdam: 1769.

Soul-Body Interaction
Traditional title: *Intercourse between the Soul and Body*
Original title: *De Commercio Animae et Corporis, Quod Creditur Fieri vel per Influxum Physicum, vel per Influxum Spiritualem, vel per Harmoniam Praestabilitam* [Soul-Body Interaction, Believed to Occur either by a Physical Inflow, or by a Spiritual Inflow, or by a Preestablished Harmony]. London: 1769.

True Christianity
Traditional title: *True Christian Religion*
Original title: *Vera Christiana Religio, Continens Universam Theologiam Novae Ecclesiae a Domino apud Danielem Cap. VII:13–14, et in Apocalypsi Cap. XXI:1, 2 Praedictae* [True Christianity: Containing a Comprehensive Theology of the New Church That Was Predicted by the Lord in Daniel 7:13–14 and Revelation 21:1, 2]. Amsterdam: 1771.

Nontheological and Posthumously Published Works by Swedenborg Cited in This Volume

Small Vibrations
Traditional title: *On Tremulation.*
Original title: "Bewis at wårt lefwander wesende består merendels i små darringar thet är tremulationer [A Proof That Our Vital Essence Consists for the Most Part of Small Vibrations, That Is, of Tremulations]." *Daedalus Hyperboreus* 6 (April–June 1717):10–14.

Another Draft on Small Vibrations
Traditional title: *On Tremulation*
Original title: [Untitled]. Written between summer 1719 and February 1720.

Basic Principles of Nature
Traditional title: *Principia*
Original title: *Principia Rerum Naturalium sive Novorum Tentaminum Phaenomena Mundi Elementaris Philosophice Explicandi* [Basic Principles of Nature or of New Attempts to Explain Philosophically the Phenomena of the Natural World]. Dresden and Leipzig: 1734.

The Infinite
Traditional title: *The Infinite*
Original title: *Prodromus Philosophiae Ratiocinantis de Infinito, et Causa Finali Creationis: Deque Mechanismo Operationis Animae et Corporis* [Precursor to a Philosophy Reasoning about the Infinite and about the Final Cause of Creation; Also about the Operative Mechanism between the Soul and the Body]. Dresden and Leipzig: 1734.

Notes about a Pathway to Knowledge of the Soul
Traditional title: *Knowledge of the Soul*
Original title: *De Via ad Cognitionem Animae* [On the Pathway to a Knowledge of the Soul]. Written during or after March 1739.

Dynamics of the Soul's Domain
Traditional title: *Economy of the Animal Kingdom*
Original title: *Oeconomia Regni Animalis in Transactiones Divisa* [Dynamics of the Soul's Domain, Divided into Treatises]. Amsterdam: 1740–1741.

Quotations on Various Philosophical and Theological Topics
Traditional title: *A Philosopher's Note Book*
Original title: [Untitled]. Written around 1741.

Draft on the Soul and the Body
Traditional title: *Soul and Body*
Original title: *Transactio Prima de Anima et Ejus et Corporis Harmonia in Genere* [First Treatise on the Soul and the Harmony between It and the Body in General]. Written before or during 1742.

Draft of a Rational Psychology
Traditional title: *Rational Psychology*
Original title: [Untitled]. Written before or during 1742.

Draft on Ontology
Traditional title: *Ontology*
Original title: *Ontologia* [Ontology]. Written before or during 1742.

Draft on the Fiber
Traditional title: *The Fiber*
Original title: [Untitled]. Written around 1742.

Draft on the Five Senses
Traditional title: *The Five Senses*
Original title: [Untitled]. Written before or during July 1744.

The Soul's Domain
Traditional title: *The Animal Kingdom*
Original title: *Regnum Animale, Anatomice, Physice, et Philosophice Perlustratum* [The Soul's Domain Thoroughly Examined by Means of Anatomy, Physics, and Philosophy]. The Hague: 1744–1745.

Worship and Love of God
Traditional title: *Worship and Love of God*
Original title: *Pars Prima de Cultu et Amore Dei; Ubi Agitur de Telluris Ortu, Paradiso, et Vivario, Tum de Primogeniti seu Adami Nativitate, Infantia, et Amore. Pars Secunda de Cultu et Amore Dei; Ubi Agitur de Conjugio Primogeniti seu Adami, et Inibi de Anima, Mente Intellectuali, Statu Integritatis, et Imagine Dei. Pars Tertia, de Vita Conjugii Paris Primogeniti.* [Part 1: Concerning the Worship and Love of God; In Which Is Discussed the Earth's Origin, Paradise, and the Garden, and Then the Birth of the Firstborn, or Adam, His Infancy, and Love. Part 2: Concerning the Worship and Love of God; In Which Is Discussed the Marriage of the Firstborn, or Adam, and Therein the Soul, the Understanding Mind, the State of Wholeness, and the Image of God. Part 3: Concerning the Life of the Firstborn Married Couple]. London: 1745.

Notes on the Creation Story
Traditional title: *History of Creation*
Original title: *In Nomine Domini. Historia Creationis a Mose Tradita. Ex Smidio et ex Castellione* [In the Name of the Lord. The Creation Story Passed Down by Moses. Based on Schmidt and Castellio]. Written during summer 1745.

The Old Testament Explained
Traditional title: *The Word Explained*
Original title: *Explicatio in Verbum Historicum Veteris Testamenti* [The Historical Word of the Old Testament Explained]. Written during November 1745 to February 1747.

Spiritual Experiences
Traditional title: *The Spiritual Diary*
Original title: *Experientiae Spirituales* [Spiritual Experiences]. 1745–1765.

Revelation Explained
Traditional title: *Apocalypse Explained*
Original title: *Apocalypsis Explicata secundum Sensum Spiritualem, Ubi Revelantur Arcana, Quae Ibi Praedicta, et Hactenus Recondita Fuerunt* [The Book of Revelation Explained as to Its Spiritual Meaning, Which Reveals Secret Wonders That Were Predicted There and Have Been Hidden until Now]. 1757–1759.

Draft of "Sacred Scripture"
Traditional title: *De Verbo*
Original title: *De Scriptura Sacra seu Verbo Domini ab Experientia* [On Sacred Scripture, or the Word of the Lord, from Experience]. Written around 1762.

Draft of "Supplements"
Traditional title: *Last Judgment (Posthumous)*
Original title: *De Ultimo Judicio* [On the Last Judgment]. Written around 1762 to early 1763.

Draft on Divine Wisdom
Traditional title: *On Divine Wisdom*
Original title: *De Divina Sapientia* [On Divine Wisdom]. Written in early 1763.

Sketch on Goodwill
Traditional title: *Charity*
Original title: *De Charitate* [On Charity]. Written between April and September 1766.

Brief Index of Catholic Teachings
Traditional title: *De Justificatione*
Original title: [Untitled]. Written around 1769.

Outline about God the Savior
Traditional title: *God the Savior Jesus Christ*
Original title: [Untitled]. Written around 1769.

Summary of New Church Teachings
Traditional title: *Specimen and Sketch of the New Church*
Original title: [Untitled]. Written around 1769.

Sketch for "True Christianity"
Traditional title: *Canons of the New Church*
Reported original title: *Canones Novae Ecclesiae, seu Integra Theologia Novae Ecclesiae . . .* [Canons of the New Church, or the Entire Theology of the New Church . . .]. Written around 1769.

Bible Concordance for "True Christianity"
Traditional title: *Dicta Probantia*
Original title: [Untitled]. Written after September 1769.

Index to "The Book of Concord" for "True Christianity"
Traditional title: *Index to the Formula Concordiae*
Original title: [Untitled]. Written around late 1769.

Draft Memorable Occurrences for "True Christianity"
Traditional title: *Additions to True Christian Religion*
Original title: [Untitled]. Written during or after July 1770.

Reply to Ernesti
Traditional title: *Reply to Ernesti*
Original title: [Untitled]. [Amsterdam: 1771.]

Sketch for "Coda to True Christianity"
Traditional title: *Sketch of the Coronis*
Original title: *Coronis seu Appendix ad Veram Christianam Religionem . . .* [Coda or Appendix to "True Christianity" . . .]. Written around 1771.

Draft for "Coda to True Christianity"
Traditional title: *Coronis*
Original title: *Coronis seu Appendix ad Veram Christianam Religionem . . .*
[Coda or Appendix to "True Christianity" . . .]. Written around 1771.

Sketch for "End of the Age"
Traditional title: *Consummation of the Age*
Original title: *De Consummatione Saeculi, de Adventu Secundo Domini, et de Nova Ecclesia* [On the End of the Age, the Second Coming of the Lord, and the New Church]. Written around 1771.

Outlines for "End of the Age"
Traditional title: *Abomination of Desolation*
Original title: [Untitled]. Written around 1771.

Draft Invitation to the New Church
Traditional title: *Invitation to the New Church*
Original title: [Untitled]. Written around 1771.

Biblical Titles

Swedenborg refers to the Hebrew Scriptures as the Old Testament and to the Greek Scriptures as the New Testament; his terminology has been adopted in this edition. As was the custom in his day, he refers to the Pentateuch (Genesis, Exodus, Leviticus, Numbers, and Deuteronomy) as the books of Moses, or simply as "Moses"; for example, in §218 he writes "in Moses we read the following" and then quotes a passage from Exodus. Similarly, in sentences or phrases introducing quotations he sometimes refers to the Psalms as "David," and to both the Gospel and the Epistles of John as simply "John"; references given in parentheses after the quotations specify their sources.

True Christianity

By Emanuel Swedenborg
Servant of the Lord Jesus Christ

Daniel 7:13, 14

I saw visions in the night, and behold, there was someone coming with the clouds of the heavens—someone like *the Son of Humankind*.[1] He was given dominion, glory, and a kingdom. All peoples, nations, and tongues will worship him. His dominion is a dominion of an age that will not pass, and his kingdom is one that will not perish.

Revelation 21:1, 2, 5, 9, 10

I, John, saw a new heaven and a new earth. And I saw the holy city, the new Jerusalem, coming down from God out of heaven, prepared as a bride adorned for her husband. And the angel spoke with me saying, "Come, I will show you *the bride, the wife of the Lamb.*" And [the angel] carried me away in the spirit to the top of a mountain great and high, and showed me the great city, holy Jerusalem, coming down out of heaven from God.

The One sitting on the throne said, "Behold, *I am making all things new*"; and said to me, "Write, because these words are true and trustworthy."[2]

True Christianity

Containing

a Comprehensive Theology
of the New Heaven and the New Church

The Faith of the New Heaven and the New Church

THE faith of the new heaven and the new church[3] is stated here in both universal and specific forms to serve as the face of the work that follows, the doorway that allows entry into the temple, and the summary that in one way or another contains all the details to follow.[4] I say "the faith of the new heaven and the new church" because heaven, where there are angels,[5] and the church, in which there are people, act together like the inner and the outer levels[6] in a human being. People in the church who love what is good because they believe what is true and who believe what is true because they love what is good[7] are angels of heaven with regard to the inner levels of their minds. After death they come into heaven, and enjoy happiness there according to the relationship between their love and their faith. It is important to know that the new heaven that the Lord[8] is establishing today has this faith as its face, doorway, and summary.

The faith of the new heaven and the new church in universal form is this: The Lord from eternity, who is Jehovah,[9] came into the world to gain control over the hells[10] and to glorify[11] his own human nature. If he had not done this, not one mortal could have been saved; those who believe in him are saved.

[2] I say "in universal form" because this concept is universal to the faith and something universal to the faith is going to be present in each and every aspect of it. It is universal to the faith to believe that God is one in essence and in person,[12] to believe that in God there is a divine Trinity, and to believe that the Lord God the Savior Jesus Christ is God. It is universal to the faith to believe that if the Lord had not come into

1

2

115

the world not one mortal could have been saved. It is universal to the faith to believe that the Lord came into the world to separate hell from the human race, and that he accomplished this by repeatedly doing battle with hell and conquering it. In this way he gained control over it, forced it back into the divine design,[13] and made it obey him. It is universal to the faith to believe that he came into the world to glorify the human nature he took on in the world, that is, to unite it to its divine source. This is how he keeps hell eternally in its place and in obedience to himself. Since this could not have been accomplished except by allowing his human nature to be tested, including even the ultimate test, the suffering on the cross, therefore he underwent that experience. These are universal points of faith regarding the Lord.

[3] For our part, it is universal to the faith that we believe in the Lord, for our believing in him gives us a partnership[14] with him, and through this partnership comes salvation. To believe in him is to have confidence that he saves; and because only those who live good lives can have such confidence, this too is meant by believing in him. In fact, the Lord says in John: "This is the will of the Father, that everyone who believes in the Son has eternal life" (John 6:39–40). And in another passage, "Those who believe in the Son have eternal life. But those who do not believe the Son will not see life; instead the anger of God remains on them" (John 3:36).[15]

3 *The faith of the new heaven and the new church in a specific form* is this: Jehovah God[16] is love itself and wisdom itself, or goodness itself and truth itself. As divine truth, or the Word,[17] which was "God with God," he came down and took on a human manifestation for the purpose of forcing everything in heaven, everything in hell, and everything in the church back into the divine design. The power of hell had become stronger than the power of heaven, and on earth the power of evil had become stronger than the power of goodness; therefore total damnation stood threatening at the door. By means of his human manifestation, which was divine truth, Jehovah God lifted this pending damnation and redeemed both people and angels. Afterward, in his human manifestation, he united divine truth to divine goodness, or divine wisdom to divine love. In this way he returned to the divine nature that he had had from eternity, together with and in the human manifestation, which had been glorified. These things are meant by this statement in John: "The Word was with God, and the Word was God. And the Word became flesh" (John 1:1, 14).

And in the same Gospel, "I went out from the Father and came into the world; again I am leaving the world and am going to the Father" (John 16:28). And also by this: "We know that the Son of God came and gave us understanding so that we would know the truth. And we are in the truth in the Son of God, Jesus Christ. He is the true God and eternal life" (1 John 5:20). From all this it is clear that if the Lord had not come into the world no one could have been saved.

The situation today is similar. Therefore if the Lord does not come into the world again in the form of divine truth, which is the Word, no one can be saved.

[2] For our part, the specifics of faith are these: (1) There is one God, the divine Trinity exists within him, and he is the Lord God the Savior Jesus Christ. (2) Believing in him is a faith that saves. (3) We must not do things that are evil—they belong to the Devil[18] and come from the Devil. (4) We must do things that are good—they belong to God and come from God. (5) We must do these things as if we ourselves were doing them, but we must believe that they come from the Lord working with us and through us.

The first two points have to do with faith, the second two have to do with goodwill;[19] and the fifth has to do with the partnership between goodwill and faith, the partnership between the Lord and us.[20]

Chapter 1

God the Creator

SINCE the time of the Lord, the Christian church has passed through various ages; it has gone from infancy to extreme old age. Its infancy occurred when the apostles were alive and were preaching two things throughout the whole world: *repentance* and *faith in the Lord God the Savior,* as one can see from these words in the Acts of the Apostles: "To both Jews and Greeks Paul proclaimed repentance before God and faith in our Lord Jesus Christ" (Acts 20:21).

4

It is worth noting that several months ago the Lord called together his twelve disciples, who are now angels, and sent them out to the entire spiritual world[21] with the command to preach the gospel there anew, since the church established by the Lord through those disciples is so close to its end today that scarcely any of it remains in existence. Also worth noting is that the church's deterioration was the result of its splitting the divine Trinity into three persons, each of whom is God and Lord.[22] [2] As a result, a kind of brain fever spread throughout the whole theology and infected the church that calls itself Christian from the name of the Lord. I call it a brain fever because this development has so deranged human minds that they do not know whether there is one God or three. The mouth says there is one, but the mind thinks there are three. The mind, then, is at cross-purposes with its own mouth, and thought with its own speech; this results in no knowledge of God at all. The materialist philosophy[23] that rules today has no other source. As long as "one" is what the mouth is saying and "three" is what the mind is thinking, do they not inwardly meet halfway and obliterate each other? Then if thinking about God occurs at all, it scarcely goes beyond thinking the word "God." The word is denuded of any meaning that would entail actually having a concept of him.

[3] Because the idea of God and every notion of him has been torn to pieces, I intend to discuss in sequence God the Creator, the Lord the Redeemer, and the Holy Spirit the Effecter, and then to discuss the divine Trinity, with the purpose of mending what has been torn. This mending will occur when human reason is convinced from the Word and its light that there is a divine Trinity; that it exists within the Lord God the Savior Jesus Christ like the soul,[24] the body, and the effect of one person; and that the following statement in the Athanasian Creed[25] is valid:

> In Christ, God and a human being, or the divine nature and the human nature, are not two; they are in one person. Just as the rational soul[26] and the flesh is one human being, so God and a human being is one Christ.

The Oneness of God

5 The very essence and soul of everything in a comprehensive theology is the acknowledgment of God [arising] from a concept of him. Therefore

it is necessary to begin with the oneness of God, and to prove it point by point:[27]

1. The whole of Sacred Scripture teaches that there is one God, and therefore so do the theologies of the churches in the Christian world.

2. The recognition that God exists and that there is one God flows universally into human souls.

3. As a result, every nation in the whole world that possesses religion and sound reason acknowledges that God exists and that there is one God.

4. For various reasons, different nations and peoples have had and still have a diversity of opinions on the nature of that one God.[28]

5. On the basis of many phenomena in the world, human reason is capable of perceiving and concluding, if it wants to, that God exists and that there is one God.

6. If there were not one God the universe could not have been created or maintained.

7. Those who do not acknowledge God are cut off from the church and damned.

8. Nothing about the church is integrated in people who acknowledge many gods rather than one.

These points will be explored one by one.

1. *The whole of Sacred Scripture teaches that God exists and that there is one God, and therefore so do all the theologies of the churches in the Christian world.* The whole of Sacred Scripture teaches that God exists, because at the core of Sacred Scripture there is nothing but God, or the divine quality that comes from God. Scripture was dictated by God and nothing else can come from God except what is God and is called divine. This is what lies at the heart of Scripture. In the derivative layers of Scripture that come from that heart and lie below it, however, Sacred Scripture has been adapted to the comprehension of both angels and people in the world. In these layers too there is divineness, but in different forms that are called heavenly, spiritual, and earthly[29] divine qualities. They are in fact the layered clothes of God. What God himself is like at the heart of the Word is something that cannot be seen by any created person or thing. When Moses prayed to see the glory of Jehovah, Jehovah replied that no one can see God and live [Exodus 33:20]. The situation at the heart of the Word is similar, where God exists in his own underlying reality[30] and his own essence.

[2] Although that inmost divine quality is covered over with elements adapted to the comprehension of both angels and people in the

world, it nevertheless shines through like light through crystalline forms. Its radiance varies depending on the condition of mind that we have formed for ourselves either from God or on our own. For all those who have formed the state of their mind from God, Sacred Scripture is like a mirror in which they see God, although each in a different way. The mirror is made of truths that they learn from the Word and become steeped in through living a life according to them. A first conclusion from this is that Sacred Scripture is the fullness of God.[31]

[3] Sacred Scripture teaches not only that God exists, but also that there is one God. This can be established from the truths that form a mirror, as I just indicated. These truths are connected to each other and have the effect that we cannot think of God except as one entity. As a result, everyone whose reason has been at all steeped in holiness from the Word knows almost intuitively that there is one God, and senses that it would be insane to say there are many gods. Angels cannot even open their mouths to say "gods," because the heavenly atmosphere in which they live resists it. Sacred Scripture teaches the oneness of God not only in the universal way just described but also specifically in many passages such as the following:

> Israel, hear this: Jehovah our God is one Jehovah. (Deuteronomy 6:4; Mark 12:29)

> The only God is among you, and there is no God except me. (Isaiah 45:14–15)

> Am not I Jehovah? There is no other God except me. (Isaiah 45:20–21)

> I am Jehovah your God, and you are not to acknowledge a God except me. (Hosea 13:4)

> Thus said Jehovah, the King of Israel: "I am the First and the Last, and there is no God except me." (Isaiah 44:6)

> In that day, Jehovah will be king over the whole earth; in that day there will be one Jehovah, and his name will be one. (Zechariah 14:9)

7 The churches in the Christian world teach one God; this is common knowledge. They teach this because all their teachings come from the Word, and those teachings are all integrated as long as one God is acknowledged not only orally but also with the heart. It is common in Christianity today, however, for people to confess one God with their lips but three with their hearts. To such people God is no more than a verbal expression. To them theology as a whole is a kind of golden idol locked up in a case, and the key to unlock it is held by church leaders alone. When such people read the Word they do not detect any light in it or from it—not even the impression that there is one God. To them the Word is marred with blotches, and the oneness of God in it is obscured. The Lord described people like this in Matthew: "You will hear with your hearing but you will not understand; and you will see by seeing, but you will not perceive. They have closed their eyes to avoid ever seeing with their eyes, hearing with their ears, understanding with their hearts, turning themselves around, and being healed by me" (Matthew 13:14–15). All such Christians are like people who go into windowless rooms to avoid the light and who grope for food and coins by feeling their way along the walls. Eventually they develop eyesight like that of owls and see in the dark. They are like a woman who has many husbands—she is a promiscuous woman rather than a wife. They are like a young woman who accepts rings from multiple suitors, and after the wedding, rents out her nights not only to one of them but also to the rest.

2. *The recognition that God exists and that there is one God flows universally from God into human souls.* There is an inflow[32] from God into us. This is obvious from everyone's ready admission that everything good that is truly good and that exists in us and is done by us is from God. The same admission applies to everything related to goodwill and faith. For we read, "We cannot receive anything unless it is given to us from heaven" (John 3:27). And Jesus said, "Without me you cannot do anything" (John 15:5), meaning anything having to do with goodwill and faith.

This inflow comes into our souls because the soul is the inmost and highest[33] part of us. The inflow from God reaches that part first and then comes down into the things below and enlivens them, depending on our openness to what flows in. Of course, truths that will become part of our faith do indeed flow in through our hearing and are implanted in our mind, which is below the soul; but all these truths do is prepare us to accept what flows in from God through our soul. The quality of that preparation determines the quality of our acceptance and of the transformation of our earthly faith into spiritual faith.

[2] The notion that there is one God flows into our souls from God because everything that is divine, as a whole and in every detail, is

God. And because everything that is divine is integrated into a unity, it cannot help but inspire in us the idea of one God. This idea grows ever stronger as God lifts us into the light of heaven. In angelic light, the angels cannot force themselves to say "gods." In fact, every phrase of their speech ends rhythmically on a single beat,[34] a phenomenon that arises from no other cause than the notion inflowing into their souls that there is one God.

[3] Now, even though the idea of one God flows into all our souls, many of us think nonetheless that God's divinity has been divided among many gods who share the same essence. This is because as that inflow comes down it takes forms that do not correspond to one another,[35] and the forms themselves cause variation. This variation also occurs in every entity in the three kingdoms of nature.[36] The same God who gives life to us gives life to every animal, so it is the form on the receiving end that makes the animal an animal and the human a human.[37] A comparable variation happens when humans render their minds beastly. The sun flows the same way into every tree; the difference in trees is a result of each one's form. The sun flows the same way into a grapevine as into a thorn bush, but if a thorn branch is grafted onto a grapevine, the inflow is changed and adapts to the form of the thorn branch.

[4] A similar thing happens to the things in the mineral kingdom. The light that flows into a diamond and into a piece of limestone is the same; but in one it shines through while in the other it is darkened.

Our minds are varied according to their forms, which are inwardly spiritual depending on our faith in God and also on our life from God. These forms become translucent and angelic when we believe in one God, but become opaque and beastly when we believe in many gods, which is virtually the same as not believing in God.

9 3. *As a result, every nation in the whole world that possesses religion and sound reason acknowledges that God exists and that there is one God.* From the divine inflow into human souls, discussed just above, it follows that in everyone there is an inner voice saying that God exists and that there is one God. Nevertheless there are people who deny God, people who worship nature as God, people who worship many gods, and people who worship idols as gods. The reason for this is that they have let worldly and bodily[38] perspectives block off the inner reaches of their reason or intellect[39] and obliterate their first childhood idea of God; they have rejected religion from their heart and have put it behind them.

The Christian confessional creed[40] shows that Christians acknowledge one God and shows how they view the unity of God:

> The catholic faith is this, that we venerate one God in a trinity, and the Trinity in unity. There are three divine persons, the Father, the Son, and the Holy Spirit, and yet there are not three gods; there is one God. The Father is a person, the Son another, and the Holy Spirit another, and yet they have one divinity, equal glory, and coeternal majesty. The Father, then, is God, the Son is God, and the Holy Spirit is God; but just as Christian truth compels us to confess each person individually as God and Lord, so the catholic religion forbids us to say that there are three gods or three lords.

This is the Christian faith regarding the unity of God. (In the chapter that discusses the divine Trinity [§§163–184] you will see that the trinity of God and the unity of God presented in this confession are incompatible.)

[2] The other nations in the world that possess religion and sound reason agree that there is one God: all Muslims in their countries; the Africans in the many countries on their continent; and the Asians as well, in the many countries on theirs. So too do modern-day Jews. In the Golden Age,[41] the most ancient people who were religious worshiped one God, whom they named Jehovah.[42] So did the ancient people in the following age, up to the time when monarchies were created. In the time of the monarchies, upper levels of the intellect that had previously been open, and had been like sanctuaries and temples of worship to the one God, were increasingly closed off by worldly loves, and then by bodily loves.[43] The Lord God, in order to unblock those upper levels of the intellect and restore worship of one God, instituted a church among the descendants of Jacob and set the following precept above all the other precepts in their religion: "There is to be no other God before my face" (Exodus 20:3).

[3] "Jehovah," which he named himself anew for the Jews, means the highest and only Being, and the origin of everything that exists and occurs in the universe. People in the preclassical period acknowledged Jove as the highest God (perhaps so named from Jehovah),[44] and deified many others who made up his court. In the age that followed, however, sages like Plato and Aristotle admitted that the other [Olympians] were not gods but different properties, qualities, and attributes of the one God, called gods because there was divinity in each of them.[45]

10   Every multifaceted entity falls apart unless it depends on one thing, a fact recognized by all sound reasoning whether religious or not. For example, a human being, made up of many limbs, internal organs, sensory organs, and motor organs all interconnected, would fall apart if it did not depend on one soul; and the body itself would fall apart if it did not depend on one heart. A country would fall apart but for its one monarch; a household would fall apart but for its one head; every one of the many workplaces in every country would fall apart but for its one person in charge. What army would prevail against its enemies without a leader who has supreme power, and officers with authority over their soldiers? Likewise a church would fall apart unless it acknowledged one God; and even the angelic heaven would fall apart. Heaven acts as the head of the church on earth; the soul of both is the Lord; this is why heaven and the church are called his body. So if heaven and the church did not acknowledge one God, each would be like a lifeless corpse that would be thrown away and buried because it was good for nothing.

11   *4. For various reasons, different nations and peoples have had and still have a diversity of opinions on the nature of that one God.* The first reason for this is that knowledge about God and therefore acknowledgment of God is not possible without *revelation;*[46] and knowledge of the Lord and therefore acknowledgment that all the fullness of divinity dwells physically in him is not possible without *the Word,* which is a garland of revelations.[47] From the revelation they have been given, people are able to meet God, receive an inflow, and thus be made spiritual instead of earthly.

Early revelation spread throughout the whole world, and the earthly self distorted it in many different ways, giving rise to divergences, disagreements, heresies, and schisms among religions.

The second reason [for the diversity of opinions on God] is that the earthly self cannot comprehend anything about God; it can comprehend only the world, and conform it to itself. This is why it is among the axioms of the Christian church that the earthly self is against the spiritual self, and that they battle each other.[48] People then have come to acknowledge from the Word [or] from some other revelation that there is a God, and yet in both the past and the present they have had a diversity of opinions on the nature and the oneness of God.

[2] Therefore people whose mental sight was dependent on their physical senses and who nevertheless wished to see God made idols for themselves out of gold, silver, stone, and wood. They intended to adore God in those forms as objects of sight. Others with the same desires but

with religious principles that forbade idols pictured the sun and moon, the stars, and various things on earth as images of God. Those who believed themselves to be wiser than most but who remained earthly were led by the immensity and omnipresence God displayed in creating the world to acknowledge nature as God, in some cases in its innermost, in others in its outermost aspects.⁴⁹ And some who wished to see God as separate from nature thought up some thing that was as all-encompassing as possible and that they called the Entity of All; but because they know nothing more of God than this, this "Entity of All" turns out to be an entity of their minds alone, utterly without any real meaning.⁵⁰

[3] As anyone can see, concepts of God are mirrors of God, and people who know nothing about God do not see God in a mirror facing their eyes, but in a mirror that is facing the wrong way, the back of which is covered with quicksilver or some black, sticky substance that absorbs rather than reflects the light.

Faith in God enters us on a pathway that comes down from above, from the soul into the higher reaches of the intellect. Concepts of God enter us on a pathway that comes up from below, because the intellect takes them in from the revealed Word through our bodily senses. In mid-intellect the different inflows come together. There an earthly faith, which is mere belief, becomes a spiritual faith, which is actual acknowledgment. The human intellect, then, is a kind of trading floor on which exchanges occur.

5. *On the basis of many phenomena in the world the human reason is capable of perceiving and concluding, if it wants to, that God exists and that there is one God.*⁵¹ This truth can be corroborated by countless phenomena in the visible world [around us], for the universe is like a stage on which proofs are constantly being demonstrated that God exists and that there is one God.

By way of illustration I will cite a *memorable occurrence*⁵² that I experienced in the spiritual world: Once when I was having a conversation with angels, there were several people present who had recently arrived from the physical world.⁵³ When I saw them I wished them a happy arrival and told them a number of things they would not otherwise have known about the spiritual world. After that I asked them what considered opinions about God and nature they were bringing with them from the world.

Their answer was this: "Nature produces everything that occurs in the created universe. After creation, God endowed nature with this productive power and ability; he imprinted this power on it. God's only role [now] is to maintain nature's productive power and ability and keep them from failing. Therefore these days everything in the world that comes about and is produced or reproduced is attributed to nature."[54]

I replied that nature of itself does nothing; it is God who produces things through nature. They asked me to prove it. So I said,[55] "People who believe that the Divine is at work in every detail of nature find support for a belief in God in many of the phenomena they observe in the world. They find much more evidence to support a belief in God than to support a belief in nature.

[2] "Those who see evidence of God at work in the details of nature ponder the obvious yet astounding phenomena in the reproduction of plants and animals.

"In *the reproduction of plants,* a tiny seed is put in the ground, and a root comes out. Up through the root comes a stem, and then in succession come branches, twigs, leaves, flowers, and fruit, leading to new seeds, completely as if the seed knew the sequence of events or procedure to follow in order to create itself anew! What rational person could think that the sun, which is nothing but fire, knows how to achieve this? Or that the sun can empower its heat and light to bring about these developments? Is the sun capable of intending to be useful? Those with an elevated rational mind, when they see and consider these phenomena in the proper light, cannot help but think that these phenomena come from One whose wisdom is infinite—namely, God. Others as well who do recognize the divine handiwork in the details of nature find additional support for their belief in these phenomena.

"On the other hand, those who do not acknowledge that God is at work in nature move the eyes of their reason to the back of their heads rather than the front when looking at these phenomena. They are the type who derive every idea of their thought process from their bodily senses, and let themselves be convinced by false sensory evidence, saying, 'You *see* the sun producing all these changes through its heat and light, don't you? What is a thing you *can't even see?* Is it in fact anything at all?'

[3] "People who are strengthening their belief in the Divine take note of the astounding things they see in *the reproduction of animals:* Here I should first mention eggs as an example. In the seed of an egg there is a potential chick, together with everything required for its formation and for every stage it will go through after hatching until it becomes a bird just like its mother.

"Furthermore, if it considers flying creatures of every kind, a mind capable of deep thought will encounter stupefying things. For example, in the smallest thing that flies, just as in the largest, in the microscopic, just as in the plainly visible, in tiny insects, just as in songbirds and giant birds of prey, there are sensory organs of sight, smell, taste, and touch, and motor organs or muscles allowing them to fly and walk; and there are internal organs attached to their hearts and lungs[56] that are activated by their brains.

"Those who attribute everything to nature do indeed see these phenomena, but their only thought is that they exist. They simply say that nature has that effect. They say this because they turn their minds away from thoughts about the Divine; and when people who turn away from the Divine see astounding things in nature they cannot think about them rationally, much less spiritually. They think with their senses and in a material way. They think in nature, from nature, and not beyond it. The only difference between them and animals is that they have rational capability, meaning that they could understand if they wanted to.

[4] "Those who are averse to thinking about the Divine and have therefore become mindlessly sense-oriented, fail to realize that their eyesight is so dull and limited to physical matter that it sees a mass of tiny insects as a single vague object, although in fact every single one of those insects has organs for sensing and moving. They are equipped with fibers and vessels, with tiny little hearts, windpipes that function like lungs, internal organs, and brains that have all been woven out of the finest substances in nature. Those structures respond to life at the lowest level; that life individually activates their most minuscule parts. Eyesight, then, is so dull that it sees many things, each of which has countless elements, as nothing more than a little blur; and yet sense-oriented people think and pass judgment on the basis of their eyesight. Obviously, then, their minds are dulled, and they are in darkness regarding what is spiritual.

[5] "All of us, if we want to, can use phenomena in nature to support a belief in the Divine; and we do so when we think about God, about the omnipotence he displayed in creating the universe, and about his omnipresence in preserving the universe.

"For example, when we see the birds that fly in the sky we can reflect on the fact that each species of them knows its own food and where to find it, and recognizes its companions by sight and sound. In fact it knows which birds among all others are friendly and which are hostile. Birds know the mating of their kind; they pair off with a mate, they artfully arrange nests, and in them they lay their eggs and brood over them; they know how long to incubate them; and when the time comes they hatch their young, give them tender love, nurture them under their wings, and gather food and feed them, until the young come of age and can take on those tasks for themselves. All who are willing to think about a divine inflow through the spiritual world into the physical world can see that inflow from these examples. If they are willing, they can say in their hearts that such knowledge cannot be acquired from the sun through its heat and light. The sun, nature's origin and essence,[57] is nothing but a fire. The flow of heat and light from it is utterly dead. From this they can conclude that these phenomena are the result of divine inflow through the spiritual world into the outermost aspects of nature.

[6] "When they look at caterpillars, too, all people can put the visible features of nature to use to strengthen their belief in the Divine. The delight of some love impels caterpillars to long and strive for a change from their earthly condition to something like a heavenly state. So they crawl into a suitable place, wrap themselves in a covering, and create for themselves a kind of womb in which to be reborn. In that womb they become chrysalises, pupas, nymphs, and finally butterflies. After they have undergone their metamorphosis and have been adorned with beautiful wings that reflect their species, they fly into the air as if it were their own heaven and cheerfully play there. They find a partner, lay eggs, and provide for the next generation. During their butterfly phase they nourish themselves with sweet and pleasant food from flowers. Surely all who use the phenomena visible in nature to strengthen their belief in the Divine see an image of our earthly state in the caterpillars, and an image of our heavenly state in the butterflies. Those who convince themselves in favor of nature do indeed see these phenomena, but because they reject the existence of a heavenly human state, they call these phenomena the mere workings of nature.

[7] "By focusing on what is known about bees[58] as well, anyone can use things visible in nature to strengthen a belief in the Divine. Bees know how to collect wax from roses and other flowers, and how to extract honey. They know how to build cells like little apartments and lay them out in the form of a city with passages for coming and going. From far away they smell the flowers and plants from which they get wax for their hive and honey for food. Once stuffed with these, they fly in a straight line back to their own beehive. By doing so they store up food for themselves for the coming winter as if they saw it coming. They set

over themselves a female to lead them as their queen. She gives birth to the next generation. They also set over themselves a kind of court for her, complete with bodyguards. When the time comes for her to give birth, she takes an entourage of these bodyguards, called drones, and goes from cell to cell laying eggs, which her crowd of followers covers with daub to protect the eggs from the air. This results in new offspring. Later on, when they have grown to the age at which they can take on these tasks, the young bees are expelled from the hive. They first gather into a swarm in order to stay together and then fly to look for a new home. In the fall the drones are taken away because they have contributed no wax or honey. Their wings are removed to prevent them from coming back and consuming the hive's food, for which they did no work.

"All this and more besides serves to show that because bees are useful to the human race, a divine inflow through the spiritual world gives bees a form of government like the one among people on earth, and even like the one among angels in the heavens.

[8] "Surely everyone of sound reason sees that it is not because of the *physical* world that bees behave this way. What does the sun, the origin of nature, have in common with a government that emulates and is analogous to a government in heaven?

"Those who believe in nature and worship it use these and similar animal phenomena to support their belief in nature. Those who believe in and worship God use the same phenomena to support their belief in God. The spiritual person sees something spiritual in these phenomena, while the earthly person sees something earthly; everyone sees it in her or his own way. To me, these phenomena have been evidence of an inflow of the spiritual world into the physical world—an inflow from God.

"While you are at it, ponder whether it would be possible for you to think analytically about a form of government, or about a civil law, or about a moral virtue, or about a spiritual truth, if the Divine were not flowing in from its wisdom through the spiritual world. It has not been possible for me, nor is it now. I have been aware of and have sensed this inflow continually for twenty-six years now.[59] Therefore I speak from personal experience.

[9] "Can nature have usefulness as a goal? Can it sort useful functions into well-ordered sequences and forms? This is impossible except for one who is wise. And to arrange and form the whole universe like this is impossible except for God, whose wisdom is infinite. Who else could foresee and provide substances for people to eat and to wear—food from

the field's harvest, from the earth's fruit, and from animals; and clothing from the same sources? Among the marvels of the universe is that those lowly insects called silkworms clothe with silk and magnificently adorn both women and men from queens and kings down to maids and butlers. And those lowly insects called bees supply wax for the lamps that give churches and royal courts their splendor. These and many other things are obvious proof that everything occurring in nature is produced by God himself through the spiritual world."

[10] To that statement I should add that in the spiritual world I have had a chance to observe people who used phenomena visible in the physical world to support a belief in nature even to the point that they became atheists. In spiritual light it became apparent that their intellect was open at the bottom but closed at the top, because they had looked downward toward the earth in their thought rather than upward to heaven. Just above the lowest level of their intellect, the sensory level, I saw a kind of covering that was flickering with hellish fire. In some it was as black as soot; in others, gray like a corpse.

Everyone needs to beware of affirming a belief in nature. Affirm a belief in God instead. There is no shortage of support for it.

13 6. *If there were not one God the universe could not have been created or maintained.* We can infer the oneness of God from the creation of the universe, because the universe is a work connected together as one thing from beginning to end, all dependent on one God as the body depends on its soul. The universe was designed to allow God to be omnipresent, keep every detail of it under his supervision, and maintain it perpetually as one entity, that is, preserve it. This is why Jehovah God says he is "the First and the Last, the Beginning and the End, the Alpha and the Omega"[60] (see Isaiah 44:6; Revelation 1:8, 17); and why he says elsewhere that he makes all things, stretches out the heavens, and extends the earth by himself (see Isaiah 44:24).

This vast system called the universe is a work connected as one thing from beginning to end because God had a single purpose in creating it: an angelic heaven populated by the human race. All the things that make up the world are means of fulfilling that purpose, because someone who intends an end result also intends the means to achieve it.

[2] If we view this world as a work containing the means of fulfilling the aforementioned purpose, we can see the created universe as a work connected together into one thing; and see that this world is a complex structure of useful functions arranged and prioritized for the sake of the human race, the source of the angelic heaven.

Divine love cannot intend anything other than that people should forever have the blessings of its divineness. Divine wisdom cannot produce anything other than useful things that are means of fulfilling that purpose.

Upon examining the world with this universal idea in mind, every wise person is capable of grasping that there is one Creator of the universe and that his essence is love and wisdom. For this reason every single thing in this world is of benefit to us; if it seems of no direct benefit, at least it is of indirect benefit. The fruits of the earth and the animals benefit us with food and also with clothing.

[3] Among the marvels of this world is that the lowly insects called silkworms clothe with silk and magnificently adorn both women and men from queens and kings down to maids and butlers. And the lowly insects called bees supply wax for the lamps that give churches and royal courts their splendor.[61]

Some people examine certain aspects of the world in isolation rather than looking at everything as a chain from purposes through intermediate means to results.[62] Therefore those people cannot see that the universe is the handiwork of one God. The same is true for people who do not see creation as the product of divine love acting through divine wisdom. Neither group is able to see that God dwells in individual useful things because he dwells in the purpose behind them. Yet everyone who has some purpose is also involved in the means of achieving it, because deep within every one of the means lies the purpose as the force that drives and guides it.

[4] Some do not view the universe as the handiwork of God and the home of his love and wisdom, but view it instead as a product of nature and as the home of the sun's heat and light. They close the higher levels of their mind toward God and open the lower levels of their mind toward the Devil. In the process, they take off their humanity and put on the nature of a wild animal. It is not just a belief of theirs that humans are like animals; they themselves actually become like animals. They become as crafty as foxes, as fierce as wolves, as deceptive as leopards, as savage as tigers; or they take on the nature of crocodiles, snakes, horned owls, or night birds. In the spiritual world they even look like these wild animals from a distance. Their love for evil takes these shapes.

7. *Those who do not acknowledge God are cut off from the church and damned.* People who do not acknowledge God are cut off from the church because the whole point of the church is God, and because the things related to God that are called theological teachings give the church its

structure. Therefore to deny the existence of God is to deny everything having to do with the church. The denial itself is what cuts them off; that is, they cut themselves off. God does not cut them off.

They are damned as well because those who are cut off from the church are also cut off from heaven. The church on earth and the angelic heaven act as a unit, just like the inner and outer self, and like the spiritual part and the physical part in each of us. God created us in such a way that our inner self is in the spiritual world and our outer self is in the physical world. Therefore to make us permanent and everlasting beings, God made us citizens of both worlds[63] so that the spiritual part of us, which belongs in heaven, could be planted in the physical part belonging to this world the way a seed is planted in the ground.

[2] People who cut themselves off from the church and from heaven by denying the existence of God close their inner selves on the side of the will[64] and shut themselves off from its positive love. (The will in us is a vessel for love and becomes its dwelling place.) Their inner selves on the side of the intellect, however, they are unable to close, because if they could and did they would no longer be human; but [evil] love in their will does befuddle their higher intellect with false ideas. As a result, their intellect becomes virtually closed to truths related to faith and good qualities related to goodwill and becomes more and more closed to the Lord and the spiritual teachings of the church. As a result, those denying the existence of God lose their partnership with angels in heaven. Once that is gone, they establish a partnership with satans[65] in hell and think what the satans are thinking. All satans deny the existence of God and have absurd thoughts about God and about the church's spiritual teachings; and so do people on earth who are in partnership with them.

[3] Such people come into their spirit,[66] so to speak, when they are at home alone and let their thoughts be guided by their pleasure in the evil and the falsity they have conceived and given birth to in themselves. In that state, their thought about God is that he does not exist—God is only a word intoned in the pulpit to constrain the lower classes to obey the laws of justice that are society's rules. The Word, the source of ministers' pronouncements about God, they see as a haphazard and fanciful text to which authorities have attributed holiness. The Ten Commandments or the Catechism they see as a little book that is to be tossed aside once it has been worn out by the hands of the young. After all, that book prescribes that we honor our parents, that we not murder, whore, steal, or testify falsely, and who does not know all that from civil law? The church they think of as nothing more than a herd of uneducated,

gullible, and timid people, who [think they] see what they do not see. Humans, including themselves, they think of as being much like animals; they think the same fate awaits humans and animals after death.[67]

[4] This is what their inner selves think, no matter how differently their outer selves may talk. For, as I said, all people have an inner and an outer self. Their inner self is their real self, called their spirit. It is the part that lives after death. Their outer self, in which they practice hypocrisy through [apparent] morality, will be buried in the grave. Then because they denied the existence of God they will be condemned.

All of us on earth are associated in spirit with those in the spiritual world who are like ourselves; we are in a sense united to them. Quite often, in fact, I have been allowed to see the spirits of people who were still alive on earth. In some cases the spirits of these people were in angelic communities; in some cases, in hellish communities. I have even been allowed to spend days talking with the spirits of people. It has amazed me that the people themselves still alive in their bodies were completely unaware that this was happening. From these experiences it became clear to me that those who deny the existence of God are already among the damned. After death they are gathered to their people.[68]

8. *Nothing about the church is integrated in people who acknowledge many gods rather than one.* People who acknowledge one God in their belief and worship one God in their heart are in the communion of saints[69] on earth and the communion of angels in the heavens. Each of these groups or communions is called a partnership, and is a partnership, because there is one God among its people, and they are in the one God. These same people also have a partnership with the entire angelic heaven. I would even go so far as to say they have a partnership with each and every one in heaven. For they are all like children and descendants of one parent, with such similar minds, mannerisms, and looks that they recognize each other as relatives. The angelic heaven is laid out in communities on the basis of all the varieties of love for what is good. All these kinds of love aim at one most universal love: love for God. All people who direct the acknowledgment of their faith and the worship of their heart to one God who is the Creator of the universe and also the Redeemer and the Regenerator[70] are descended from that love.

[2] Exactly the opposite is true of people who adore, and seek help from, many gods instead of one. The opposite is also true of those who say one God but think three. This is the practice of people in the church today who divide God into three persons and hail each person as a God in his own right, and who attribute different qualities or properties to

each one that the others do not have. This leads to actual divisions not only in the unity of God but also in [Christian] theology itself, and even in the human mind in which that theology has to live. What other result could there be except confusion and discontinuity in the teachings of the church? In the appendix at the end of this work[71] I will show that this is the state of the church today.

The truth is that dividing God or the divine essence into three persons, each of whom is individually a god in his own right, causes denial of God. It is like someone entering a church for worship and seeing a triptych above the altar with one god portrayed as the ancient of days, another god as a high priest, and a third god as Aeolus flying in the air,[72] with an inscription reading, *These Three Are One God.* Or perhaps it is like the same person seeing a painting above the altar that portrays God's unity and trinity as a deformed person with three heads protruding from one body or three bodies sharing a single head.[73] If people enter heaven with this as their picture of God, they will definitely be thrown out head-first, even if they plead that the head or heads stand for God's essence and the body or bodies stand for God's distinctly different properties.

To these points I will add a *memorable occurrence.* I saw some people who had recently left the physical world and arrived in the spiritual world talking among themselves about three divine persons from eternity. They were ministers; one of them was a bishop.

They came over to me. After I talked to them about the spiritual world—something they had known nothing about before—I said to them, "I heard your conversation about three divine persons from eternity. Could I ask you to explain this great mystery by telling me your view of it? I'm interested in the mental images you had of it when you were in the physical world that you recently left behind."

The leader looked me up and down. He said, "I see that you are a layperson, so I shall disclose the view I have had of this great mystery and instruct you.

"My view has been and still is that God the Father, God the Son, and God the Holy Spirit sit in the middle of heaven on exalted and majestic chairs or thrones. God the Father sits on a throne made of pure gold and has a scepter in his hand. God the Son sits to his right on a throne of pure silver and has a crown on his head. And God the Holy Spirit sits next to both of them on a throne of dazzling crystal and holds a dove in his hand. Surrounding them are three tiers of hanging lamps glittering with precious stones. At quite a distance from this inner circle stand countless angels, all adoring and glorifying them.

"Furthermore, God the Father is continually discussing with his Son which people should be granted justification.74 Between the two they arrive at a decision and they decree which people on earth are worthy to be accepted by them among the angels and crowned with eternal life. God the Holy Spirit hears the names and immediately rushes across the world to those people, bringing gifts of justice as proof of salvation for those granted justification. As soon as he arrives and breathes on them, he blows away their sins like someone with a fan blowing the smoke out of a furnace and then whitewashing it. He also takes from their hearts the hardness of stone and gives them instead the softness of flesh. At the same time he renews their spirits or minds and makes them born again, giving them the face of a child. Finally, he marks their foreheads with the sign of the cross and calls them the chosen ones and children of God."

When his lecture came to an end, the leader said to me, "When I was in the world that is how I untangled this great mystery. And because many of our priests there applauded the views I have expressed to you, I am convinced that you as a layman will likewise put your faith in them."75

[2] After the leader said this I observed him and the ministers with him, and I perceived that they were all in complete agreement. So, launching into a reply, I said, "I have considered the beliefs you just uttered, and from them I gather that you are attached to, and you cherish, an utterly physical and sensory picture of the triune God; in fact I would even call your view materialistic. The idea of three gods inevitably flows from your picture. Isn't it a sensory idea of God the Father to think of him sitting on a throne with a scepter in his hand? And to think of the Son as sitting on his own throne with a crown on his head? And to think of the Holy Spirit sitting on his own throne with a dove in his hand and then rushing all over the world following the orders he has heard? Since your depiction leads to a physical picture of God, I cannot put my faith in what you said. Ever since I was a little child I have not been able to allow any other idea of God into my mind except the idea of one God. And because I have allowed this idea and it is the only one I hold, nothing you have said has any effect on me.

"Later I came to see that the throne on which Jehovah sits, according to Scripture, means his kingdom. His scepter and his crown mean his governing and his power. Sitting at the right hand means the omnipotence God has through his human manifestation. And the things said about the Holy Spirit refer to the actions of the divine omnipresence.

"Please, my lord, give consideration to the idea of one God, and use your reason to ponder the idea appropriately. In time you will come to see clearly that it is true.

[3] "Now, all of you do indeed say there is one God, because you give the three persons one essence, as well as giving each person an individual essence; but you do not allow anyone to say that that one God is one person. You maintain that there are three persons, because you do not want to lose your idea of three gods. You give each person different characteristics from the others. Yet doesn't that divide this divine essence of yours?

"Given all that, how could you think and say that there is one God? I would understand if you had said there is one divineness; but when someone hears that 'The Father is God, the Son is God, the Holy Spirit is God, and each person is individually God,'[76] how can that person think there is one God? It is a contradiction to which faith could never adhere.

"Therefore you cannot say 'one God,' though you could have said 'the same divineness.' For example, many people go together to make one senate, one committee, or one council. You cannot call them one person; but when each and every one of them has the same opinion, you can say that they share one point of view. Three diamonds are made of the same substance; you cannot call them one diamond, but you can say they are of one substance. Yet you can also say that the diamonds differ in value according to each one's weight, which you couldn't say if there was one diamond rather than three.

[4] "I gather, however, that you call three divine persons, each of whom is God by himself or individually, one God. You order each person in the church to speak in this way, because sound and enlightened reason across the globe recognizes that there is one God; so you would blush with shame if you did not do the same. And yet, while you are pronouncing 'one God,' even though you are thinking 'three,' somehow that sense of shame does not keep the two sets of words stuck in your throat, but instead you utter them both."

After this exchange the bishop and his ministers left. While he was walking away, he turned back and wanted to shout, "There is one God," but he could not do it, since his thought stopped his tongue. Instead he opened his mouth wide and thundered, "There are three gods!"[77] When the people who had been standing nearby saw this bizarre occurrence they burst out laughing and went elsewhere.

Afterward I asked where I might run into the scholars with the sharpest wits who stand in favor of a divine Trinity divided into three persons. There happened to be three such people present. I asked them, "How can you divide the divine Trinity into three persons and claim that each person is individually or by himself God and Lord? Surely your verbal confession that there is one God is as distant from your thought as the south is from the north."

"There is no distance at all," they replied. "Those three persons have one essence, and the divine essence is God. In the world, we were tutors teaching the trinity of persons; the pupil we were responsible for was our faith. In our faith each divine person plays his own role: God the Father's role is to give spiritual credit or blame[78] and to bestow [grace], God the Son's role is to intercede and mediate, and God the Holy Spirit's role is to put into effect the actual credit or blame and the mediation."

[2] So I asked, "What do you mean by 'divine essence'?"

They said, "We mean omnipotence, omniscience, omnipresence, immensity, eternity, and equality of majesty."[79]

To this I said, "If that essence makes many gods one God, couldn't you add even more? How about a fourth god mentioned by Moses, Ezekiel, and Job: God Shaddai?[80] The ancient people in Greece and Italy did something similar. They assigned equal attributes and a similar essence to their gods, such as Saturn, Jupiter, Neptune, Pluto, Apollo, Juno, Diana, Minerva; and Mercury and Venus as well.[81] But nonetheless they couldn't call all of them one God. In fact, you are three people, and to my mind you seem academically similar, so you have a similar essence as far as scholarship goes; but you couldn't combine yourselves into one scholar."

They laughed at this, and said, "You're joking! It is different with the divine essence. The divine essence is one thing; it doesn't come in three parts. It is single and undivided. Partition and division don't apply to it."

[3] When I heard this I retorted, "Then let's go down into the ring and fight.—What do you understand a 'person' to be?" I asked. "What does that mean?"

They answered, "The term *person* means that which is not a role of, or a quality in, someone else, but an entity subsisting on its own.[82] This is the definition of *person* used by all—by the leaders of the church and by us as well."

"Is this truly your definition of *person?*" I asked.

"It is," they said.

So I replied, "Then the Father and the Son have nothing in common, and neither of them has anything in common with the Holy Spirit. Therefore each one has his own free choice, responsibility, and power. They share nothing, then, other than the fact that each one has a will, which he can communicate if he wishes. Aren't these three persons three distinct gods? And listen to this: You have in fact defined a *person* as someone who subsists on his or her own. Therefore there are three 'subsistings' or substances into which you have divided the divine essence, and yet you said that the divine essence is indivisible; you said there was one undivided essence. Furthermore you attribute to each substance or person characteristics that are not in the others and could not be shared with them: giving spiritual credit or blame, mediating, and putting into effect. What other conclusion is possible except that the three persons are three gods?"

At my saying this, they drew back and said, "We will discuss these points among ourselves, and after our discussion we will give you our response."

[4] A wise person was standing nearby. On hearing all this, the wise person said to them, "I do not wish to sift such a sublime topic with such a fine mesh. Setting subtleties aside, I see in a clear light that there are three gods in the ideas of your thought. If you publicized your views before the whole world it would cause you shame, because you would be labeled either insane or stupid. Therefore saying that there is one God helps you avoid losing respect."

The three scholars, however, held on to their opinion and paid no attention. As they went away they were muttering terms borrowed from metaphysics.[83] This alerted me that metaphysics was the oracle they planned to consult in giving their response.

The Underlying Divine Reality or Jehovah

18 First I will discuss the underlying divine reality, and afterward the divine essence.[84] These two might seem to be one and the same thing, but underlying reality is even more universal than essence. Essence presupposes an underlying reality and arises from it. The underlying reality of God, the underlying divine reality, cannot be described. It is beyond the reach of any idea in human thought. Everything human thought can conceive of is created and finite; it cannot conceive of what was not created and is infinite. Therefore it cannot conceive of the underlying divine reality. The underlying divine reality is the reality itself from which all things exist, and which must be in every thing in order for that thing to exist. Some further notion of the underlying divine reality may, however, be gained from the following points:

1. The one God is called Jehovah from "being," that is, from the fact that he alone is and was and will be, and that he is the First and the Last, the Beginning and the End, the Alpha and the Omega.
2. The one God is substance itself and form itself.[85] Angels and people are substances and forms from him. To the extent that they are in him and he is in them, to that extent they are images and likenesses of him.
3. The underlying divine reality is intrinsic reality and is also an intrinsic capacity to become manifest.[86]
4. The intrinsic, underlying divine reality and intrinsic capacity to become manifest cannot produce anything else divine that is intrinsically real and has an intrinsic capacity to become manifest. Therefore another God of the same essence is impossible.
5. The plurality of gods in ancient times, and nowadays as well, has no other source than a misunderstanding of the underlying divine reality.

These points need to be clarified one by one.

1. *The one God is called Jehovah from "being," that is, from the fact that he alone is [and was] and will be, and that he is the First and the Last, the Beginning and the End, the Alpha and the Omega.* "Jehovah" means "I am" and "to be," as is generally known. We know from the Book of Creation, or Genesis, that God was called "Jehovah" from most ancient times. In the first chapter he is called "God," but in the second and subsequent chapters he is called "Jehovah God."[87] Later on the descendants of Abraham through Jacob forgot the name of God owing to their long sojourn in Egypt. Then in the event recorded in the following passage it was recalled to memory:

> Moses said to God, "What is your name?" God said, "*I Am I Who Am.*[88] So you will say to the Children of Israel, '*I Am* sent me to you.' And you will say, '*Jehovah, the God* of your fathers, sent me to you.' This is my name to eternity, and this is how I will be remembered from generation to regeneration."[89] (Exodus 3:13–15)

Since God alone is "*I Am*" and being, or "Jehovah," therefore nothing exists in the created universe that does not derive its underlying reality from him. (How this happens will be discussed below [§§21, 75, 76, 78].)

The same thing is meant by these words: "I am the First and the Last, the Beginning and the End, the Alpha and the Omega" (Isaiah 44:6 and Revelation 1:8, 11; 22:13). This means that on every level of existence he is the one and only entity, the source of all things. [2] God is called the Alpha and the Omega, the Beginning and the End, because alpha is the first letter in the Greek alphabet and omega is the last; so together they mean all things as a whole.

In the spiritual world, every alphabetical letter has a meaning. A vowel, because it carries tone, means a feeling or some kind of love. Spiritual and angelic speech, and also writing, depends on these meanings—but this is a mystery that has not been known until now. There is in fact a universal language shared by all angels and spirits. It has nothing in common with any human language in our world. After death everyone inherits that language, because it is latent in everyone from creation. In the spiritual world, then, everyone can understand everyone else. I have often been allowed to hear that language. I have compared it with languages in the physical world[90] and have ascertained that it has not even the least thing in common with any earthly language. It differs by its very origin, which is that every letter of every word has a meaning. This is why God is here called the Alpha and the Omega, meaning that on every level of existence he is the one and only entity, the source of all things. (For more on how this language and its written form flow from angels' spiritual thought, see the work *Marriage Love* 326–329;[91] see also what follows in this work [§280].)

20   2. *The one God is substance itself and form itself. Angels and people are substances and forms from him. To the extent that they are in him and he is in them, to that extent they are images and likenesses of him.* Because God is the underlying reality, he is also substance. Unless the underlying reality becomes substance it is a figment of the imagination; but as a substance it becomes an entity. And one who is substance is also form, for substance without form is another figment of the imagination. We can attribute both of these to God, provided he is seen as the sole, the only, and the archetypal substance and form.

The work *Divine Love and Wisdom,* published in Amsterdam in 1763, demonstrates that God's form is the human form itself, that is, that God is the Human Being, and all God's attributes are infinite. That work also shows that angels and people are substances and forms that have been created and arranged to receive divine qualities flowing into them through heaven. In the Book of Creation they are called images and likenesses of

God (Genesis 1:26–27). Elsewhere they are called God's children and people born of God.[92]

As the sequence of topics in this book will show in many ways, the more we live under divine guidance, meaning the more we submit to God's leading, the more and more deeply we become an image of God.

If human minds do not form an idea of God as the archetypal substance and form, and of God's form as the Human Form itself, they render themselves highly susceptible to delusions and speculations about God, about the development of the human race, and about the creation of the world. Their thought of God is restricted to a thought of the expanse of nature underlying the universe, or else a thought about emptiness or nothing at all.[93] The development of the human race they think of as a lucky coincidence—elements just happened to come together in this form.[94] As for the creation of the world, they see its substances and forms as originating in geometry's points and then lines; and because these are nondimensional and one-dimensional they are actually nothing.[95] In such minds, everything that has to do with the church is like the river Styx or the thick darkness in Tartarus.[96]

3. *The underlying divine reality is intrinsic reality, and is also an intrinsic capacity to become manifest.* Jehovah God is intrinsic reality because from eternity to eternity he is the I Am, the Absolute, and the first and only thing from which comes everything that exists and to which everything owes its existence. Because of this and nothing else he is the Beginning and the End, the First and the Last, and the Alpha and the Omega.

One cannot say that his underlying reality comes *from* himself, because *coming from himself* implies before and after, and therefore time, and time cannot apply to the infinite underlying reality that is described as existing from eternity. *Coming from* also either implies another god who is the real god, and then you have a god from a god; or it implies that God formed himself. In either case God would not be uncreated or infinite, because he would have boundaries and limitations that were imposed either by himself or by some other god.

From the fact that God is the intrinsic underlying reality, it follows that God is love in itself, wisdom in itself, and life in itself.[97] It also follows that God is the Absolute from which all things come and to which all things are connected so that they may exist. God is God because he is life in itself, as the Lord's words in John 5:26 make clear.[98] Likewise in Isaiah: "I, Jehovah, am the maker of all things. I alone stretch out the

21

heavens. I extend the earth by myself" (Isaiah 44:24); and he alone is God, and there is no God except him (Isaiah 45:14, 21; see also Hosea 13:4).

God is not only the intrinsic underlying reality but is also an intrinsic capacity to become manifest. For unless the underlying reality is capable of manifesting, it is nothing. It is equally true that the capacity to become manifest is nothing without the underlying reality. Neither one can exist without the other. The same is true for substance unless it takes a form. A substance without a form has no properties or attributes, and something that has no quality is in fact nothing.

I speak specifically here of underlying reality and capacity to become manifest, not of essence and actual manifestation,[99] because the relationship between underlying reality and essence is the relationship between something that comes before and something that comes afterward; the same goes for the capacity to become manifest and actual manifestation. What comes before is more universal than what comes afterward. The underlying divine reality has the attributes of infinity and eternity, but the divine essence and manifestation have the attributes of divine love and divine wisdom, and through them, omnipotence and omnipresence, which I will get to when it is their turn.

22 Using its own reasoning, the earthly self has no way of knowing that God is the Absolute and the first and only thing that is called the intrinsic underlying reality and the intrinsic capacity to become manifest from which come all things that exist and take form. Under its own power of reasoning the earthly self cannot draw on anything other than what belongs to nature. Earthly things fit with the earthly self's essence because from our infancy and childhood onward nothing but what is earthly comes into the self. Nevertheless, we were created to be spiritual as well as earthly, since we are going to live after death and will then be among spiritual people in their world. Therefore God has provided the Word.

In the Word God has revealed not only himself but also the existence of heaven and hell, and the fact that every single one of us is going to live in one or the other realm to eternity, each of us according to our life as well as our faith. God has also revealed in the Word that he is "I Am" or the underlying reality, and is the Absolute and the only one to exist in and of himself; he revealed therefore that he is the First or the Beginning from which all things come.

[2] This revelation makes it possible for the earthly self to rise above nature, even above itself, and see what belongs in the realm of God. It appears to be far away. Yet God is actually close to each of us, for God is in

us with his essence. Because he is, he is near to those who love him—people who live by his instructions and believe in him. In a sense they see him.

What else is faith except spiritually seeing what is real? And what else is living by God's instructions except an actual acknowledgment that he is the source of salvation and eternal life?

But people whose faith is earthly and not spiritual and consists of mere factual knowledge, and who have an earthly but not a spiritual way of life, do indeed see God, but from far away, and then only when they talk about him.

Spiritual people compared to earthly ones are like people who are standing in broad daylight, seeing others near themselves and touching them, compared to people standing in a heavy fog that makes it difficult to tell whether the objects nearby are people or perhaps trees or rocks.

[3] Spiritual people compared to earthly ones are like people in a town on a high mountain, walking around and talking to their friends in the town, compared to people who look down from that mountain and cannot make out whether they are seeing people or animals or statues below.

Spiritual people compared to earthly ones are also like people standing on a planet and seeing their friends and loved ones right there, compared to people looking at another planet through hand-held telescopes. People in the second group look at the planet and say they see people there, when in fact all they have is a vague impression of landmasses, like the moon's lighter areas, and bodies of water, like the moon's darker patches.[100]

The same difference exists between people who are in faith and also live a life of goodwill, who see God and divine attributes that emanate from him in their mind, compared to those who have nothing more than knowledge about these things. This is the difference between spiritual and earthly people.

Those, however, who deny the divine holiness of the Word but still carry their religion around in a pack on their back do not see God at all.[101] They only sound out the word God, not much differently from parrots.

4. *The intrinsic, underlying divine reality and intrinsic capacity to become manifest cannot produce anything else divine that is intrinsically real and has an intrinsic capacity to become manifest. Therefore another God of the same essence is impossible.* Up to this point I have shown that the one God, the Creator of the universe, is the intrinsic underlying reality and capacity to become manifest. Therefore he is intrinsically God. From this

23

it follows that a god from a god is not possible, because such a god would necessarily lack absolute and essential divinity in the form of intrinsic underlying reality and capacity to become manifest. It does not matter whether that god is said to be "born" of God or to emanate from him, he would still be produced by God, which is scarcely different from being created by him.

To introduce into the church the belief that there are three divine persons, each of whom is individually God, although they share a single essence, and to say that one of them was eternally begotten and the third has been having an effect from eternity, is to destroy completely the concept of one God. Along with that it is also to eradicate the whole notion of divinity and to drive all reasoned spirituality into exile. No longer truly human, human beings are becoming earthly in every respect. The only difference between them and wild animals is that they can talk. They are against anything and everything spiritual about the church—the earthly self calls all that delusional.

These hideous heresies about God have poured out of one source alone: the earthly self. Dividing the divine Trinity into persons has brought about not only nighttime in the church, but also death.

[2] The concept of three divine essences that are the same is an offense to reason, as I learned from angels. They said that even pronouncing "three equal divinities" is impossible for them. They said that if someone came to them and tried to say it, that person would automatically turn away. After saying it the person would become like a human log and would be thrown away downward, headed for those in hell who do not acknowledge the existence of any God.

Truly, to implant in toddlers, children, and teenagers the idea of three divine persons—which inevitably entails the idea of three gods—is to take away all their spiritual breast milk, and then all their spiritual solid food, and later on all the spiritual food for their reason, and, in the case of those who convince themselves of that point of view, to cause their spiritual death.

On the one hand, those who direct heartfelt, faithful worship to one God alone as Creator of the universe, and as Redeemer and Regenerator as well, are comparable to the city of Zion in the time of David, and the city of Jerusalem in the time of Solomon after the Temple was built. On the other hand, the church that believes in three persons and views each person as an individual god is like Zion and Jerusalem after they had been destroyed by Vespasian and the Temple there had been burned down.[102]

Those who worship one God in whom there is a divine trinity and who is therefore one person become more and more alive, and become angels on earth. Those, however, who convince themselves to believe in a plurality of gods because there is a plurality of divine persons become more and more like a statue with movable joints, inside which stands Satan, talking through its hinged mouth.[103]

5. *The plurality of gods in ancient times, and nowadays as well, has no other source than a misunderstanding of the underlying divine reality.* In §8 above I showed that the oneness of God is written into each human mind at the deepest level, since it is central to all things that flow from God into our souls. It has not yet come down from there into our intellect, however, because we have been lacking concepts we need in order to go up toward God. Each of us needs to make a pathway for God [Isaiah 40:3], meaning we need to prepare ourselves to receive God, and this preparation requires certain concepts.

The concepts we have been lacking are listed below. Their lack has deprived our intellect of the penetration to see that there is one God, that there can be only one underlying divine reality, and that all things in the material world come from that underlying reality.

(a) Until now, no one has known anything about the spiritual world, where there are spirits and angels and where we go after we die. (b) The spiritual world has a sun[104] that is pure love from Jehovah God, who is within that sun. (c) The heat from that sun is essentially love, and its light is essentially wisdom. (d) As a result, everything in that world is spiritual and affects us in our inner selves, forming our will and our intellect at that level. (e) By means of that sun, Jehovah God produced not only the spiritual world and all the countless spiritual things in it, which are substantial,[105] but also the material world and all the countless material things in it, which are physical. (f) Until now, no one has known the difference between "spiritual" and "earthly," or even what "spiritual" essentially means. (g) No one has known that there are three levels of love and wisdom that have been used to structure the angelic heavens. (h) No one has known that the human mind is differentiated into the same number of levels so that we can be lifted to one of the three heavens after death, depending on our life and faith. (i) Lastly, none of the above would be the case for one instant were it not for the underlying divine reality—the Absolute in itself; the First and the Beginning from which all things exist.

Even though these are the concepts we need in order to go higher and recognize the divine reality, they have been lacking until now.

24

[2] I say that we go higher, but I really mean that we are taken up by God. We have free will; we can use it to gain religious knowledge. When we exercise our intellect and gain religious knowledge from the Word, we smooth a pathway that God can use to come down and lift us up.

The concepts that can lift our intellect higher, and let God take us by the hand and lead us, can be compared to the steps on the ladder that Jacob saw. It was set up on the ground but the top of it stretched into heaven. Angels were climbing up on it and Jehovah was standing above it (Genesis 28:12–13).

When we lack these concepts or reject them with contempt, the situation is quite the opposite. Under these conditions, the reach of our intellect can be compared to a ladder on the grounds of a magnificent mansion, but the ladder extends only to a window on the first floor, where people are staying, and does not reach the windows of the second floor where there are spirits, let alone the windows of the third floor, where there are angels.

If we lack or reject these concepts, we are limited to the atmospheres and matter in nature that we experience with our eyes, ears, and noses. From these sources we get only atmospheric and material ideas about heaven and about God's underlying reality and essence. Thinking on the basis of them, we will never decide anything about whether God exists or not, or whether there is one God or many, much less what the underlying reality and essence of God are like. As a result, in ancient times, and nowadays as well, people have come to believe in a plurality of gods.

25   To these points I will add the following memorable occurrence.

One time just after I woke up from sleeping I fell into a deep meditation on God. Looking up I saw above me in heaven an oval of intensely shining light.[106] As I fixed my gaze on the light, it gradually receded toward the sides and merged into the periphery [of my vision].

Then, behold, heaven opened up to me! I saw magnificent things, and angels standing in a circle on the south side of the opening, talking to each other. Because a burning desire came over me to hear what they were saying, I was allowed to hear it—first the sound of it, which was full of heavenly love; then the conversation itself, which was full of the wisdom that goes with that love.

They were having a conversation about the only God, about being in partnership with God, and about the salvation that results. What they were saying was ineffable—most of it could not be expressed in the words of any earthly language. Several times before, however, I had been in gatherings of angels in heaven itself, and had been able to join in their conversation because I was then in a state similar to theirs. This enabled me to understand them now, and to select from their discussion a few points that could be expressed in a rational way using the words of earthly language.

[2] They were saying that the underlying divine reality is united, uniform, absolute, and undivided. They used spiritual images as illustration.

They said, "The underlying divine reality cannot be divided into many entities, each of which possesses an underlying divine reality, and still remain united, uniform, absolute, and undivided. Otherwise each separate entity would think on its own from its own separate underlying divine reality. If it also happened to be of the same mind as the others, there would be a number of deities in agreement; there would not be one God. Agreement, or the consensus of many, each one acting on its own or by itself, is not an attribute of one God but of many."

They did not say "gods" because they were unable to. It was suppressed by the light of heaven that shaped their thought and by the atmosphere in which their conversation took place. They also said that when they tried to utter the word "gods" and to describe each one as a person by himself, the effort to say that immediately veered off toward "one," and in fact toward "the one only God."

They added, "The underlying divine reality is a reality in itself, not from itself, because if it were from itself, that would imply an underlying reality that existed in itself from some prior underlying reality. It would mean there was a god from a god, which is not possible. What comes from God is called 'divine,' but it is not called 'God.' What is 'a god from God,' what is 'an eternally begotten god from God,' and what is 'a god emanating from an eternally begotten god from God'[107] except words devoid of heavenly light?"

[3] Later on they said, "The underlying divine reality, which in itself is God, is uniform—and uniform not just in a simple way but in an infinite number of ways. It is uniform from eternity to eternity. It is uniform everywhere, and it is uniform with everyone and in everyone. (It is the condition of the recipient that causes all the variety and change in reception.)"

The angels demonstrated the absoluteness of the underlying divine reality, which in itself is God, as follows: "God is the Absolute, because he is absolute love and absolute wisdom, or to put it another way, because he is absolute good and absolute truth. As a result, he is life itself.

If these qualities were not absolute in God they would never exist in heaven or in the world, because they would be relatively nonexistent compared to the Absolute. Every quality is what it is because it comes from the Absolute, both as its source and as its point of reference.

"The Absolute (meaning the underlying divine reality) has no specific location. It is with those and in those who are in specific locations, depending on their locations. Love and wisdom, goodness and truth, and the life these qualities give are absolute in God; in fact, they are God himself. A specific location cannot be attributed to them, and neither can a progression from place to place as the source of their omnipresence. For this reason the Lord says he is in the midst of people [Matthew 18:20]; and he is in them and they are in him [John 6:56; 14:20; 15:4, 5].

[4] "Nevertheless, no one can comprehend God as he is in himself. Therefore he is visible above the angelic heavens as a sun, which is the form his essence takes. He himself as wisdom emanates from that sun in the form of light, and he himself as love emanates from that sun in the form of heat. That sun is not God himself. The divine love and wisdom surrounding him as they first go forth from him come to angels' view as a sun.

"The Absolute in that sun is *the Human Being*. It is *our Lord Jesus Christ, including both the Divine Source and the Divine Human Manifestation.* Since the Absolute, which is absolute love and absolute wisdom, was in him as his soul from the Father, therefore divine life or life in itself was in him. None of us is like this. The soul in us is not life; it is merely a vessel for receiving life.

"In fact, the Lord teaches this when he says, 'I am the way, the truth, and *the life*' [John 14:6]; and in another passage, 'As the Father has *life in himself*, so he has granted the Son *to have life in himself*' (John 5:26). 'Life in himself' is God."

They added that people who have any spiritual light at all can see from all this that the underlying divine reality cannot be shared among many, because it is united, uniform, absolute, and undivided. If anyone were to claim that the divine reality could be shared, further points that person made on the subject would contain obvious contradictions.

26 Then the angels became aware that my thoughts included common Christian ideas of God: ideas of a trinity of persons in unity, and a unity of persons in the Trinity, and also of the Son of God's birth from eternity. At that point they said, "What are you thinking? Surely you are thinking those thoughts from an earthly light that is incompatible with our spiritual

light. We are closing heaven to you and leaving unless you get rid of the
ideas that go with that point of view."

So I said, "Please go deeper into my thinking. Perhaps you will see a
compatibility."

They went deeper and saw that three persons to me meant three
emanating divine activities: creating, redeeming, and regenerating, which
are activities of the one only God. The birth of a Son of God from eternity to me meant his birth foreseen from eternity and carried out in time.
To think of some son actually born of God from eternity seemed to me
not to transcend but to oppose what is natural and rational. It is another
thing altogether to view the Son of God born to the Virgin Mary in time
as the sole and only begotten Son of God—in fact, believing anything
else is a monstrous error.

Then I explained that my earthly thoughts about the trinity and the
unity of persons and about the eternally begotten Son of God were based
on the church's statement of faith that was named after Athanasius.[108]

The angels then said, "Good."

They asked me to pass on a statement from them: "Anyone who does
not seek help from the absolute God of heaven and earth cannot come
into heaven, because heaven is heaven from the one only God. *The
absolute God is Jesus Christ, who is the Lord Jehovah, Creator from eternity,
Redeemer in time, and Regenerator to eternity.* He is the Father, the Son,
and the Holy Spirit combined. This is the gospel that needs to be
preached."

Afterward the heavenly light I had seen above the opening came back.
It came down bit by bit and filled the inner reaches of my mind, enlightening my ideas of the trinity and the unity of God. Then I saw my former
merely earthly ideas being separated out, just as husks are shaken off
wheat tossed in a winnowing basket.[109] I saw my old notions carried off as
if by a wind to the north of heaven and scattered.

The Infinity of God: His Immensity and Eternity

Two properties of the physical world limit all things in it: one is space
and the other is time. Because God created this world and concurrently
created space and time as limitations on it, I need to discuss the origins

27

of space and time; namely, immensity and eternity. God's immensity relates to space and his eternity relates to time. Infinity includes both immensity and eternity.

Infinity transcends what is finite. A concept of infinity is therefore beyond the finite mind. To give at least some sense of it, I will discuss it in the following sequence:

1. God is infinite because he is intrinsic reality and manifestation, and all things in the universe have reality and manifestation from him.
2. God is infinite because he existed before the world—before space and time came into being.
3. Ever since he made the world, God has existed in space independently of space, and in time independently of time.
4. Infinity in relation to space is called immensity; in relation to time it is called eternity. Yet although these are related, there is nonetheless no space in God's immensity, and no time in his eternity.
5. From many things in the world, enlightened reason can see the infinity of God the Creator.
6. Every created thing is finite. The Infinite is in finite objects the way something is present in a vessel that receives it; the Infinite is in people the way something is present in an image of itself.

I need to explain these statements separately.

28   1. *God is infinite because he is intrinsic reality and manifestation, and all things in the universe have reality and manifestation from him.* So far I have shown that God is one, that he is the Absolute, that he is the primary reality that underlies all things, and that all that exists, takes shape, and endures in the universe is from him. It follows then that he is infinite.

Just below [§32] I will show that many phenomena in the created universe enable human reason to see the infinity of God. Yet although the human mind can use those phenomena to support an acknowledgment that the first entity or primary being is infinite, still it cannot come to know what the Infinite is like. The only way it can define the Infinite is to say that it is utterly without limits and self-sufficient, and is therefore the absolute and only substance. Because substance has no attributes without form, it is also the absolute and only form. What substance and form are in their full infinity, however, is not apparent. The human mind itself, even the most highly analytical and elevated mind, is finite; it cannot be rid of its own limitations.[110] It will never have the capacity to see the infinity of God as it truly is, or God as he truly is. It can see God in a shadow from behind, as Moses was told to do when he begged to see God. He was put in a crevice in the rock and saw God's back (Exodus 33:20–23). "God's back" has as a general meaning the phenomena visible in the world and has as a specific meaning the things that are comprehensible in the Word.

It is obviously pointless then to aim to find out what God is like in his own underlying reality or in his own substance. It is enough to acknowledge him from finite, created things, in which he is infinitely present.

The person who goes farther than that could be compared to a fish hauled out into the air; or to a bird put in a vacuum pump, gasping as the air is pumped out, and soon expiring;[111] or to a ship overcome by a storm, no longer responsive to the helm, drifting onto reefs and sandbanks. Something comparable happens to people who want to know the infinity of God from the inside and are not content to acknowledge it from the outside on good evidence.

We read that a philosopher among the ancients threw himself into the sea because in the mental light he had he could not envision or comprehend the eternity of the world.[112] What if he had tried to see the infinity of God?

2. *God is infinite because he existed before the world, before space and time came into being.* The physical world has time and space. The spiritual world, on the other hand, lacks actual time and space, although it does have apparent time and space.[113]

Time and space were introduced into both worlds for the sake of distinguishing one thing from another, large from small, many from few—one quantity from another, and one quality from another. Time and space allow our bodily senses to discern the objects they are sensing; and they allow our mental senses to discern the objects they are sensing—to be affected, to think, and to choose.

Units of time were introduced into our physical world by the spinning of the earth on its axis and its orbit from point to point along the zodiac.[114] (The sun, the source of heat and light for this whole globe of lands and seas, only seems to be the cause of these cycles.) The result is the times of day: morning, afternoon, evening, and night; and the seasons of the year: spring, summer, fall, and winter. The times of day vary from light to dark; the seasons of the year vary from hot to cold.

Units of space are part of our physical world because the earth was formed into a globe composed of substances whose elements are differentiated from each other and also extended.[115]

In the spiritual world, there are no physical units of space or corresponding units of time. Yet there appear to be. Apparent space and time follow the different states of mind that spirits and angels go through there. The units of spiritual time and space match the desires of their will and the resulting thoughts in their intellect. Apparent space and time, then, are real—they are predictably determined by one's state of mind.

[2] The general opinion on the state of souls after death, as well as of angels and spirits, is that they have no extension—they are not in space or time. This has led to the saying about souls after death that they are in limbo, and that spirits and angels are ghosts, which are thought of as ether,[116] air, breath, or wind.

In fact, souls after death are substantial[117] people who live together like people in the physical world, only with units of space and time that are determined by their states of mind. If the spiritual universe—destination of souls and home of angels and spirits—lacked its own space and time then it could be passed through the eye of a needle or compressed onto the tip of a single hair. This would be possible if there were no substantial extension there. Since there is substantial extension there, however, angels live among each other with clear and distinct boundaries, in fact with even clearer boundaries than people on earth do, where there is material extension.

Time in the spiritual world is not marked by days, weeks, months, and years, because the sun there does not seem to rise and set or to swing across the sky. It stands still in the east, halfway between the horizon and the point directly overhead. Because everything that is physical in our world is substantial in the spiritual world, there are units of space there. I will say more on this topic in the part of this chapter that deals with creation [§§75–80].

[3] From what I have just said, you can see that there are space and time limitations on each and every thing in both worlds; and that people have limitations not only to their bodies but even to their souls. The same goes for spirits and angels.

From all the above we can draw the conclusion that God is infinite or without limits.[118] As Creator, Shaper, and Maker of the universe, he gave everything a limit or a boundary. He did so by means of the sun that surrounds him. That sun consists of the divine essence that goes out as a sphere around him. In that sun and from it, the first limitedness occurs. Things are increasingly limited the closer they are to the lowest level of nature in the world. Since God was not created, in himself he is without limits, or infinite.

What is infinite may seem to us to be nothing, because we are finite and limited, and we base our thinking on things that are limited. If the limitations in our thought were taken away, we would see whatever was left as nothing. Yet the truth is that God is infinitely everything; of ourselves, we are relatively nothing.

3. *Since the world was made, God has existed in space independently of space, and in time independently of time.* God, and the divine emanation that comes directly from him, is not in space, yet he is omnipresent and is with every human being in the world, every angel in heaven, and every spirit below heaven. This fact is inaccessible to thinking that is merely earthly, but spiritual thinking can comprehend it to some extent. Thinking that is merely earthly cannot comprehend it because space is part of the thinking. Earthly thinking is based on things in the world; and everything visible in the world has spatial dimensions. Size here, whether large or small, has to do with space; length, width, and height here have to do with space. In fact, every measurement, shape, and form in our world has to do with space.

Still, we can to some extent understand God's relationship to space through material thinking, provided we let in some spiritual light; but first I will say something about spiritual thinking. Ideas in spiritual thought have no relationship to space; they relate in every way to state. State applies to love, life, wisdom, emotions and inclinations, and enjoyment—generally to goodness and truth. A truly spiritual conceptualization of these things has nothing in common with space. It is higher. It sees spatial concepts below itself the way heaven sees earth.

[2] God is present in space independently of space and in time independently of time because God is always the same, from eternity to eternity. What God was like before creation, God was like after creation. Before creation, there was no space or time in and with God. After creation, there was. Because God remained the same, then, he is in space independently of space, and in time independently of time. As a result, nature is separate from him and yet he is omnipresent in it. It is similar with the life that is present in every substantial and every physical part of us, but does not integrate itself into those parts. A similar thing is true of light in relation to our eyes, sound in relation to our ears, and taste in relation to our tongues.[119] A similar thing is also true of the ether in landmasses and

oceans that allows this terraqueous planet to be held together and spun around;[120] and so on. If those active forces—light, sound, taste, and ether—were taken away, the receptors made of substance and matter would soon collapse and fall apart. In fact, if God were not present in the human mind everywhere and always, the mind would dissolve like a bubble popping in the air, and both brains,[121] on whose primary structures the mind depends, would turn to froth. Everything that is human would become the dust of the earth or a smell floating in the atmosphere.

[3] Because God is present in all time independently of time, his Word speaks of past and future in the present tense. For example, in Isaiah: "A Child is born to us, a Son is given to us, whose name is Hero, Prince of Peace" (Isaiah 9:6). In David as well, "I will announce this decision: Jehovah said to me, 'You are my Son. Today I fathered you'" (Psalms 2:7). These statements refer to the Lord who was to come. In the same source it also says, "In your eyes, a thousand years are like yesterday" (Psalms 90:4).

From many other passages in the Word about seeing and being vigilant we can see that God is present everywhere in the entire world, and yet there is nothing belonging to the world in him, that is, nothing limited in space and time. For example, this passage in Jeremiah:

> Am I not a God near you, rather than a God far away? Can a man be covered over in hiding places so that I would not see him? I fill the whole heaven and the whole earth. (Jeremiah 23:23–24)

31   *4. God's infinity in relation to space is called immensity; in relation to time it is called eternity. Yet although these are related, there is nonetheless no space in God's immensity, and no time in his eternity.*[122] God's infinity in relation to space is called immensity because "immense" is associated with "large" and "huge," and also with extension and spaciousness within extension. God's infinity in relation to time, however, is called eternity because the phrase "to eternity" means "in an endless succession of stages measurable in units of time." To clarify: we describe the earth itself and its surface in spatial terms and the earth's rotation and orbit in temporal terms. The earth's motions anchor our measurements of time, and the earth itself anchors our measurements of space. In consequence of our senses, space and time are also present in a similar way in the perception of our minds as we reflect. In God, however, there is no space and time, as I have shown just above, yet space and time originate from God. Therefore "immensity" means his infinity in relation to space, and "eternity" means his infinity in relation to time.

[2] Angels in heaven see God's immensity as the divineness of his underlying reality and God's eternity as the divineness of his capacity to become manifest. They also see God's immensity as the divineness of his love and God's eternity as the divineness of his wisdom. The reason is that angels remove space and time from divinity; this gives rise to the concepts just mentioned. Since we on earth cannot help basing our thinking on ideas that are spatial and temporal, we cannot conceive of the immensity of God before there was space or the eternity of God before there was time. In fact, if we try to conceive of them, our mind more or less loses consciousness, like a shipwrecked person who has fallen in the ocean or like someone being swallowed in an earthquake. Indeed, if we rashly persevere in that pursuit, we can easily go insane and end up denying the existence of God.

[3] Once I myself was in a state like that. I thought and thought about what God did from eternity, what he did before the world was constructed.[123] I wondered whether he debated the act of creation and worked out a sequence he would follow. I pondered whether mental debate was possible in a pure vacuum, and other useless questions. To prevent these considerations from driving me insane, the Lord lifted me into the atmosphere and light of inner angels.[124] As factors related to space and time in my former thinking were somewhat removed there, I became able to understand that God's eternity is not an eternity of time. Since there was no time before the world came about, I realized that it was completely pointless to ponder such questions about God. Furthermore, since the Divine "from eternity," that is, the Divine independent of time, did not involve days, years, and centuries—they were all an instant for God—I concluded that God did not create the world in a preexisting context of time; time was first introduced by God as part of creation.

[4] In addition, I would like to relate something worth mentioning. At one extreme end of the spiritual world, two statues of monstrous human forms appear with wide open mouths and gaping jaws. People whose thinking about God from eternity is pointless and insane seem to themselves to be swallowed up by these statues. The statues are really the delusions people hurl themselves into when they think discordant and unseemly thoughts about God before he created the world.

5. *From many things in the world, enlightened reason can see the infinity of God.* I will list a number of things that human reason can view as evidence of God's infinity.

32

(a) In the entire created universe, no two things can possibly be the same. It is impossible for any two things to be identical at any given point in time, as human scholarship and reasoning have seen and verified.[125] Yet the substantial[126] and physical things in the universe viewed one by one add up to an infinite number. Neither can the world have two identical situations over time. As you can see from the wobbling of the earth caused by the misalignment of the axis to the poles, the earth never comes back to the same spot.[127]

This is also provable from human faces. In the whole world, not one face exists that is the same as another or similar in every way. Nor will there ever be two identical faces to eternity. Infinite variety like this could occur only as the result of God the Creator's infinity.

[2] (b) No one's character is completely like another's. As the saying goes, there are as many opinions as there are people.[128] Therefore no mind, that is, no will and intellect, is the same as another or similar in every way. As a result, no one's speech is identical to anyone else's, either in tone or in the thought behind it. Nor does anyone's action copy another's to a *T*, either in manner or in the emotion and inclination behind it. This infinite variety as well is like a mirror in which we can see the infinity of God the Creator.

[3] (c) In all animal sperm and in all plant seeds there is an intrinsic kind of immensity and eternity—immensity because it can be replicated to infinity, and eternity because its replication has continued without interruption from the creation of the world until now and will continue perpetually.[129] As an example from the animal kingdom, take fish in the ocean. If there were as many fish as there are fish sperm, within twenty to fifty years fish would fill the ocean to the point where it contained nothing else, causing the water to flood the whole planet and destroy it. To prevent this, God has provided that fish become food for other fish.

The same would happen with plant seeds. If all the seeds that one plant produces each year were planted, within twenty or thirty years they would cover the surface of not just one planet but many. In the case of some bushes, each seed will produce hundreds or even thousands of other seeds [in a year]. Calculate it for yourself, multiplying the production of one such seed twenty or thirty times over, and you will see.[130]

The divine immensity and eternity cannot help but be reflected in some way. The two commonly experienced phenomena just discussed make these divine qualities visible.

[4] (d) To an enlightened reason the infinity of God can become apparent from the fact that every academic discipline can grow to an infinite extent. So, therefore, can our intelligence and wisdom. Both intelligence and wisdom are capable of growing from a seed into a tree, and from a tree into forests and gardens of trees—intelligence and wisdom have no end. Our memory is their soil. They germinate in our intellect; they bear fruit in our will. In fact, these two faculties, our intellect and our will, are capable of being cultivated and improved to the end of our lives in this world, and afterward to eternity.

[5] (e) You can also see the infinity of God the Creator in the infinite number of stars, which are all suns, and all have solar systems.[131] Elsewhere, in a short work that I wrote as an eyewitness, I have shown that out in space there are planets that have people, animals, birds, and plants.[132]

[6] (f) The angelic heaven and also hell have made the infinity of God even more obvious to me. God has arranged and ordered both places into countless communities and groups according to every type of love for good or love for evil, allotting every individual a location according to what she or he loves. All members of the human race have gathered there since the creation of the world; they will continue to gather there throughout the ages of ages. Although each person has his or her own place and situation, still all who are there have such a partnership with each other that the entire angelic heaven is like one divine human being, and the entirety of hell is like one monstrous devil. From the entirety of heaven and the entirety of hell and from the infinite number of astounding things in them, both the immensity and the omnipotence of God stand in plain view.

[7] (g) If we raise the level of our mental reasoning a little, surely we can all understand that the life to eternity we will all have after death is impossible unless God is eternal.

[8] (h) There are further aspects of infinity that become visible to us, some in physical light and others in spiritual light. As examples that become visible in physical light, there are various geometrical series that go on to infinity. On each of the three vertical levels as well, there is a progression to infinity. The first level, called the earthly level, cannot be refined and raised to the perfection of the second level, called the spiritual level. Neither can this level be refined and raised to the perfection of the third level, called the heavenly level. It is like the purpose, the means, and

the result. No matter how developed the result becomes, it cannot take the place of the means to itself; nor can these means take the place of the purpose behind them.

Take the three levels of atmospheres as another illustration. The aura is supreme, the ether is below it, and the air is under the ether.[133] No type of air can ever have such high quality that it becomes a type of ether, nor can any type of ether ever have such high quality that it becomes a type of aura. Yet the qualities of each of these atmospheres can be developed and improved to infinity.

As for examples that become visible in spiritual light, the earthly type of love an animal has cannot have such a high quality that it becomes the spiritual love that creation has endowed us with. Likewise an animal's earthly intelligence cannot have such a high quality that it becomes human, spiritual intelligence. Because these last points are not yet known, they will be explained elsewhere [§§48:8–15; 335].

From all the above examples you can see that features that are universal to our world are everlasting tokens of God the Creator's infinity. As for the way specific things imitate those universal features, however, and reflect the infinity of God, this is an abyss; it is an ocean the human mind can navigate, as long as it remains watchful for storms arising from the earthly self that would sink the ship—masts, sails, and all—starting with the helm where the earthly self stands confident.

33   *6. Every created thing is finite. The Infinite is in finite objects the way something is present in a vessel that receives it; the Infinite is in people the way something is present in an image of itself.* Every created thing is finite because Jehovah God [created] all things through the sun of the spiritual world, which most closely surrounds him. That sun is made of a substance that went out from him, the essence of which is love. The universe from beginning to end was created from that sun through its heat and light. This is not the place, however, to lay out the steps of creation in sequence. A rough outline of them will be presented in sections to come [§§76, 78]. The only point relevant to the current discussion is that things were formed from what went before. As a result, levels were created—three levels in the spiritual world; three corresponding levels in the physical world; and the same number for the inert substances that make up the lands and waters of the world. Information on the origin and nature of those levels was published in *Angelic Wisdom about Divine Love and Wisdom* (Amsterdam 1763). It was fully laid out in the little work *Soul-Body Interaction* (published in London, 1769). Because of these levels, all things that came later were vessels for earlier things.

These in turn were vessels for things earlier still, which were vessels for the primary substances that constitute the sun of the angelic heaven. This is how finite vessels that could receive the Infinite came about. (This process squares with ancient wisdom: every single thing can be divided without end.)[134]

There is an idea in circulation that finite things are not large enough to hold the Infinite and therefore they could not be vessels for the Infinite.[135] On the contrary, points that I made in my works on creation[136] show that God first made his infinity finite in the form of substances put out from himself. The first sphere that surrounds him consists of those substances, and forms the sun of the spiritual world. By means of that sun, he then completed the remaining spheres even to the farthest one, which consists of inert elements. He increasingly limited the world, then, stage by stage. I lay this out here to appease human reason, which never rests until it knows how something was done.

In people, the Infinite Divine is present the way something is present in an image of itself. The Word shows this, when we read the following:

> Finally God said, "Let us make human beings in our image, according to our likeness." Therefore God created human beings in his own image; in the image of God he created them. (Genesis 1:26–27)

From this statement it follows that human beings are organisms that are open to God, and organisms whose quality depends on their response.

[2] The human mind—the source and determiner of our humanness—has been formed into three areas to match three levels. On the first level the human mind is heavenly; angels of the highest heaven are on that level. On the second level it is spiritual; angels of the middle heaven are on that level. On the third level it is earthly; angels of the lowest heaven are on that level.

Organized as it is to accommodate these three levels, the human mind is a vessel for receiving divine inflow. Yet what is divine does not flow in beyond our smoothing of the way [Isaiah 40:4] or our opening of the door [Revelation 3:20]. If we smooth the way and open the door all the way to the highest level, the heavenly one, then we truly become an image of God. After death we will become an angel of the highest heaven. If we smooth the way or open the door only to the middle or spiritual level, then we still become an image of God, but one that is not as complete. After death we will become angels of the middle heaven. But if we smooth the way or open the door only to the lowest or earthly level, then we become an image of God at the lowest level, provided we acknowledge God and worship him with acts of devotion. After death we will become angels of the lowest heaven.

If we do not acknowledge God and do not worship him with acts of devotion, we divest ourselves of the image of God and become like one type of animal or another, except for the fact that we still enjoy the ability to understand and therefore to speak. If under those circumstances we close our highest earthly level, which corresponds to the highest heavenly level, we become like farm animals in what we love. If we close our middle earthly level, which corresponds to the middle spiritual level, we become like foxes in what we love, and like birds that come out in the evening, as far as our intellectual discernment goes. If we close even our lowest earthly level to its spiritual counterpart, we become like wild animals in what we love and like fish in our understanding of truth.[137]

[3] Divine life flows in from the sun of the angelic heaven and energizes us much the way light from our sun flows into a transparent object. Our highest level receives life the way light flows into a diamond; our second level receives life the way light flows into a crystal; our lowest level receives life the way light flows into translucent glass[138] or parchment.

If the lowest degree is totally closed spiritually, as happens when we deny the existence of God and worship Satan,[139] life flows into us from God much the way light flows into opaque things on earth: rotten wood, swamp sod, dung, and so on. At that stage we become spiritual cadavers.

35 To these points I will add the following memorable occurrence.

At one point I was struck with amazement at the vast number of people who attribute creation—everything under the sun and everything beyond it as well—to nature. No matter what they see, they say with heartfelt conviction, "Surely this is nature's doing."

I have asked them why they say nature is responsible for everything, and why not God, especially since they repeatedly use the common expression, "God created nature," and therefore could as easily say that God, rather than nature, is responsible for what they see. Beneath their breath, in an almost inaudible voice, they reply, "What God is there except nature?"

Their conviction that the universe was created by nature—an insanity that seems like wisdom to them—makes them all feel so glorious that they look down on all who acknowledge that the universe was created by

God. They picture these faithful people as ants that crawl on the ground and tread a well-worn path. Some they picture as butterflies that flit around in the air. "Dreams"—that is what they call the dogmas of the faithful, who see what they themselves do not see. "Who has seen God?" they say; "Who has *not* seen nature?"

[2] While I stood amazed at the vast number of such people, an angel appeared at my side and said, "What are you thinking about?"

I replied, "I'm thinking about the vast number of people who believe that nature exists from itself—that nature itself created the universe."

"All hell is made up of such people," the angel told me. "There they are called satans and devils. The satans are those who have come to deny the existence of God because they have convinced themselves to believe in nature. The devils are those whose acknowledgment of God has been driven from their hearts because they have spent their lives committing crimes. I will take you to lecture halls in the southwest where there are people like this who are not yet in hell."

The angel took me by the hand and led me there. I saw humble buildings that contained the lecture halls. In the middle I saw a building that looked like the main hall for the rest. It was built out of stones as black as tar that had been covered with little glasslike disks made to look as though they were sparkling with gold and silver, much like what we call selenite or mica; shiny seashells had also been worked in here and there.

[3] We went up to the building and knocked. Soon a man[140] opened the door, saying, "Welcome!" Then he hurried over to a table and picked up four books [he had written]. He said, "These books contain wisdom that has now been hailed by a host of nations. This book here, this wisdom, has been hailed by many people in France; this one, by many people in Germany; this one, by some people in the Netherlands; and this one, by some people in Britain." He added, "If you'd like to see it, I'll make these four books shine before your eyes!" Then he poured forth on all sides the glory of his own reputation, and soon the books seemed to gleam with light; but the light immediately disappeared before our eyes.

Then the angel and I asked what he was writing now. He replied that he was currently extracting matters of inmost wisdom from their hidden treasuries, in summary namely: (1) *whether nature comes from life or life comes from nature;* (2) *whether the center comes from the expanse or the expanse from the center;* and (3) *a discussion of the center of the expanse and of life.*

[4] After he said this, he sat back down on a chair at the table. We meanwhile wandered around his lecture hall, which was very spacious. Because no sunlight penetrated the building, only a light like that of a moonlit night, he had a candle on his table. To my amazement I saw the candle move around the building, illuminating it, although because the wick had not been trimmed it did not shed much light. As he was writing, we saw images of various kinds flying from the table toward the walls. In that light like a moonlit night, they looked like gorgeous indigo birds. In the light of day when we opened the door, though, they looked like the webbed-winged creatures that come out in the evening. They were in fact things basically true becoming false through his argumentation as he ingeniously chained them together.

[5] After seeing those visions we went over to the table and asked him what he was writing now. He said, "I'm on point one: *whether nature comes from life or life comes from nature.*" He said that he could argue this point either way and make it true; but because of some deeply hidden fear, he dared argue only that nature comes from and originates in life. He did not dare say that life comes from and originates in nature. We asked him in a kindly way what his deeply hidden fear was. He said he feared the possibility that clergy would call him a nature-worshiper, meaning an atheist, and that lay people would call him a man whose reason was not sound, since both lay people and clergy either believe on the basis of blind faith or adopt the perspective of those who argue for faith.

[6] At that point, feeling rather indignant because of our passion for the truth, we spoke to him and said, "Friend, you are seriously wrong. Your wisdom (which is really a genius for writing) has led you astray, and your glorious reputation has seduced you into arguing what you don't believe. Surely you are aware that the human mind can be raised above things on the sensory level—things taken into our thoughts from our bodily senses—and that when the mind is raised up, it sees above it things that relate to life, but below it things that relate to nature. What else is life but love and wisdom? What else is nature but a vessel to receive love and wisdom, through which they achieve results and accomplish useful things? Life and nature can become one only if life is the primary force and nature is its agent. Can light be one with the eye, or sound with the ear? Where do our sensations of light and sound come from if not from life? Where do the forms of our organs of sensation come from if not from nature? What else is the human body but an organ of life?

Surely, all the things in the body have been formed into organs to carry out what love wants and what the intellect thinks. Aren't the organs of the body derived from nature? Aren't love and thought derived from life? Aren't they completely different from each other?

"Lift the focus of your genius just a little higher and you'll see that being moved and thinking come from life. Being moved has to do with love, and thinking has to do with wisdom. Both have to do with life, because love and wisdom are life, as we stated before.

"If you raise your intellectual faculty even a little higher, you will see that love and wisdom do not exist unless they have a source somewhere. Their source is love itself and wisdom itself, and therefore life itself. These are the God from whom nature comes."

[7] Next we spoke with him about point two: *whether the center comes from the expanse or the expanse from the center.* The angel and I asked him why he was discussing this. He replied that his purpose was to arrive at a conclusion about the center and the expanse of nature and of life—about the origin, then, of one and the other.

When we asked what his position was, his answer was similar to the one he had given before: he could argue it either way, but because he feared losing his reputation he argued that the expanse comes from or originates in the center. "I know, though," he added, "that before the sun existed there was something. That something was throughout the expanse. Of its own accord it flowed together into some order, namely, the center."[141]

[8] Again indignant because of our passion for the truth, we spoke to him and said, "Friend, you are insane!"

When he heard this he pushed his chair away from the table and looked at us nervously. Then he gave us his attention again, but with a smile on his face.

"What is more insane," we continued, "than saying that the center comes from the expanse? When you say 'center,' we take you to mean the sun. When you say 'expanse,' we take you to mean the universe. You seem to be saying that the universe came into existence without the sun. Doesn't the sun make nature? Doesn't it make all the features of nature that depend solely on heat and light emanating from the sun through the atmospheres? Where were those things before [there was a sun]? (But we'll say where they came from in a moment.) Surely the atmospheres, and everything else on the earth, are like outer surfaces that have the sun as their center. What were all those things before the sun took shape? Could they have continued to exist for one moment? What would all those things do without the sun? Could they have come into being? Continuing to exist is the same as perpetually coming into being.[142] Since the continued existence of all things in nature depends on the sun, it follows that their original coming into being also depended on the sun. Everyone sees this and acknowledges it from personal observation. [9] As something subsequent comes into existence from something prior, so it also continues to exist from that something prior. If the outer surface came first and the center came later, something prior would be dependent on something subsequent for its continued existence. But that is against the laws of the divine design. How can things that come later produce things that come first? How can outer things produce inner things? How can denser things produce purer things? How then can the superficial things that make up the expanse produce the center? This is against the laws of nature, as anyone can see. We have presented these arguments from rational analysis in order to convince you that the expanse comes into existence from the center, and not the reverse, although anyone who thinks well sees this without these arguments.

"You said that the expanse of its own accord flowed together into the center. Was it just by accident, then, that it fell into such a miraculous and astounding design that one thing exists for the next, and they all exist for the sake of humankind and our eternal life? Is nature capable of drawing on some love and using some wisdom to find a purpose, make means available, and accomplish results so that things may come into existence in their own design? Can nature turn people into angels, make a heaven out of them, and provide that this heaven's inhabitants will live to eternity? Give enough thought to these questions and you will let go of your idea that nature created nature."

[10] After that we asked him what his past and current thinking was about point three: *on the center and the expanse of nature and of life.* We asked whether he believed that the center and the expanse of life was the same as the center and the expanse of nature. He said that he was now stuck. He had thought before that the inner energy in nature was life, that the love and the wisdom that essentially constituted human life came from nature, and that the sun's fire produced our life through the heat and light conveyed to us by the atmospheres. But now, from these points about human life after death, he was becoming uncertain. The uncertainty was

causing his mind to go up one moment and down the next. When his mind was up, he was acknowledging a Center about which he had previously known nothing. When his mind was down, he was looking at the center that he had previously thought to be the only center. He was seeing that life comes from the Center about which he had previously known nothing, that only nature comes from the center that he had previously thought to be everything, and that both centers have expanses around them.[143] [11] We said that these realizations were good, provided he tried in addition to see the center and expanse of nature as coming from the center and expanse of life, and not the other way around. We explained to him that above the angelic heaven there is a sun that is pure love. It looks as fiery as the earth's sun. From the heat that radiates from that sun, angels and people have volition and love; from its light they have understanding and wisdom. Things derived from that sun are called spiritual. Things derived from earth's sun are containers or vessels of life; they are called physical.

We told him that the expanse around the center of life is called *the spiritual world*. That expanse has continued existence because of its sun. The expanse around the center of nature is called *the physical world*. It has continued existence because of its sun. Now, because units of space and time do not apply to love and wisdom, but states apply instead, it follows that the expanse around the sun of the angelic heaven is not physically extended. It is nonetheless present in the physical extension around the physical sun and is present with living entities in nature according to how receptive they are; they are receptive according to their forms and their states.

[12] Then he asked, "Where does the fire in the earth's or nature's sun come from?"

"It comes from the sun of the angelic heaven," we replied, "which is not fire; it is divine love most closely emanating from God, who is within it."

He was stunned by this, so we proved it as follows: "Love in its essence is spiritual fire. This is why fire in the Word's spiritual sense means love. This is why priests pray in church for heavenly fire to fill their hearts—they mean love. In the tabernacle among the Israelites, the fire on the altar and the fire of the lampstand represented divine love. The heat in blood, which is vital to us and to many animals as well, comes solely from the love that makes up our life. This is why we 'catch fire,' 'heat up,' and 'become inflamed' when our love becomes impassioned or bursts into anger and blazing rage. From the fact that spiritual heat, which is love, produces physical heat in us even to the point that our faces and limbs become hot and inflamed, it stands to reason that the fire of the physical sun came into being from no other source than the fire of the spiritual sun, which is divine love.

[13] "To sum up: As we just said, the center is the origin of the expanse, and not the reverse. The center of life, which is the sun of the angelic heaven, is divine love most closely radiating from God, who is within that sun. The expanse around that center, called the spiritual world, is from that sun. The earth's sun is also from that sun, and the expanse called the physical world is from the earth's sun. From all these points it is clear that the universe was created by God."

After that we went away, and he came with us beyond the entrance to his lecture hall, speaking to us about heaven and hell and God's guidance with a new keenness of mind.

The Essence of God: Divine Love and Wisdom

36 I have drawn a distinction between God's underlying reality and God's essence because there is a difference between God's infinity and God's love. Infinity pertains to God's underlying reality; love pertains to God's essence. As I said above [§§18, 21], God's underlying reality is more universal than God's essence. Likewise, God's infinity is more universal than God's love. "Infinite" is an adjective modifying God's attributes and the components of God's essence. All these are said to be infinite. In the same way, divine love is said to be infinite, and so are divine wisdom and divine power. I do not mean that God's underlying reality came about before God's essence, but rather that it is an ingredient or component of that essence that is connected with that essence, that gives that essence direction, and that forms and also elevates that essence.

This part of this chapter, like the parts that went before, will be divided into points, as follows:

1. God is love itself and wisdom itself. These two constitute his essence.
2. Because goodness comes from love and truth comes from wisdom, God is goodness itself and truth itself.
3. Love itself and wisdom itself are life itself, or life in itself.
4. Love and wisdom are united in God.

5. The essence of love is loving others who are outside of oneself, wanting to be one with them, and blessing them from oneself.

6. These essential characteristics of divine love were the reason the universe was created, and they are the reason it is maintained.

I will take up these points one by one.

1. *God is love itself and wisdom itself. These two constitute his essence.* All the infinite things in God and all the infinite things radiating from him relate to two essentials: love and wisdom. Our earliest ancestors saw this relationship. In the sequence of ages that then followed, however, people removed their minds from heaven, so to speak, and plunged them into worldly and bodily preoccupations, with the result that people became unable to see this relationship. They began not to know what love is in its essence, and therefore what wisdom is in its essence. They forgot that without a form there is no love, because love operates in forms and through them.

37

God is substance itself and form itself, and is therefore the first and only substance and form, whose essence is love and wisdom. All things that were made, were made by God [John 1:3]. It follows, therefore, that it was from love by means of wisdom that God created the universe and each and every thing in it. As a result, divine love together with divine wisdom is present in every single entity that has been created. Furthermore, love is the essence that not only forms all things but also bonds and unites them to each other; therefore love is the force that holds all things in connection.

[2] Countless things in the world could be used to illustrate this. For example, there are two essential and universal things through which each and every thing on earth comes into existence and continues to exist: *the heat and the light* of the sun. They are present in the world because they correspond to divine love and wisdom. The heat that radiates from the sun in the spiritual world is in fact essentially love, and its light is essentially wisdom.

As further illustration, take the two essential and universal things through which human minds come into existence and continue to exist: *the will and the intellect.* The mind of each of us consists of these two things. They are present and operative in each and every detail of the mind. This is because the will is a vessel and a dwelling place for love, and the intellect is a vessel and a dwelling place for wisdom. Will and intellect therefore correspond to the divine love and the divine wisdom from which they originate.

For another illustration I could use the two essential and universal things through which human bodies come into existence and continue to exist: *the heart and the lungs,* or the systolic and diastolic motions of the heart and the respiration of the lungs. It is a known fact that these two pairs of motions are at work in each and every detail of our bodies. This happens because the heart corresponds to love and the lungs to wisdom, a correspondence that is fully demonstrated in *Angelic Wisdom about Divine Love and Wisdom* [371–431], published in Amsterdam.

[3] Countless examples in both worlds, spiritual and physical, can convince us that love produces or begets all forms like a bridegroom and husband, by means of wisdom as a bride and wife.[144] For now I will mention this example alone: the whole angelic heaven is arranged into the form it takes, and is kept in it, by divine love acting through divine wisdom.

People who attribute the creation of the world to any other force than divine love acting through divine wisdom, and who do not realize that these two qualities constitute the essence of God, descend from the sight of reason to the mere sight of the eye. They embrace nature as the creator of the universe; as a result they conceive monsters and give birth to phantoms. The thoughts they have are false, they use them as the basis of their reasoning, and the conclusions they reach are eggs with night birds inside.[145] People like this cannot be called minds; they are eyes and ears without an intellect, or thoughts without a soul. They speak of colors as if they could exist without light; of trees as if they could exist without having been seeds; of all things on earth as if they could exist without the sun. Such people designate things begun as beginnings, and things caused as causes. They turn everything upside down, put their reason to sleep, and see dreams.

38　　2. *Because goodness comes from love and truth comes from wisdom, God is goodness itself and truth itself.* Everyone knows that all things relate to goodness and truth (which is an indication that all things come from love and wisdom). Everything derived from love is called good. It feels good. Love reveals itself in pleasure, and pleasure feels good to everyone. Everything derived from wisdom is called true. Wisdom, which consists of nothing but truths, casts its subjects in a delightful light. When we perceive that delight, something true is coming from something good.

Love is all things that are good combined, and wisdom is all things that are true combined. Both sets of things are from God, who is love itself and therefore goodness itself, and wisdom itself and therefore truth itself.

As a result, there are two things that are essential to the church, called goodwill and faith. Each and every thing in the church consists of these two; in fact, these two have to be in each and every aspect of the church. The reason for this is that all good things related to the church have to do with goodwill and are called goodwill; and all true things related to the church have to do with faith and are called faith. It is our pleasure in love, which is the same as our pleasure in goodwill, that makes us call love good. It is our delight in wisdom, which is the same as our delight in having faith, that makes us call a true thing true. This pleasure and this delight bring those qualities to life; without any life coming from pleasure or delight, goodness and truth are more or less dead, and are in fact sterile.

[2] There are actually two kinds of pleasure having to do with love, and two kinds of delight that seem related to wisdom: the pleasure of a good kind of love or the pleasure of an evil kind of love; and a delight in true faith or a delight in false faith. People call the pleasure from each kind of love a good thing when they feel it; they also call the delight from each kind of faith a good thing when they perceive it, although because it is in the intellect it is actually true rather than good. Yet the two kinds are opposite to each other. When we feel good from the one type of love, it is actually good, but from the other type, it is actually evil. When we see truth in the one type of faith it is actually true, but in the other type, it is false.

The love in which we feel a genuinely good pleasure is comparable to the type of heat from the sun that makes plants fruitful and thriving, and causes fertile soil, and productive trees and grains. Where this type of heat is in effect, the land becomes like a paradise, a garden of Jehovah, or the [biblical] land of Canaan.[146] The delight we feel in the truth related to this love is like the sunlight in spring, or like a ray of light shining on a crystal vase of gorgeous flowers, causing them to open and give off a sweet fragrance.

The love in which we feel an evil pleasure is comparable to the type of heat from the sun that makes plants dry and withered, and causes sterile soil and harmful plants like thorns and brambles. Where this type of heat is in effect, the land becomes an Arabian desert with serpents, hydras, and presters.[147] The delight we feel in the falsity related to this love is like sunlight in winter, or like a ray of light shining on a jar of maggots and stinkbugs swimming in vinegar.

[3] It is important to realize that everything good structures itself, and also envelops itself, with things that are true. This is how it differentiates itself from other types of good. Furthermore, types of good from

the same "family" join together to form bundles, and also envelop their bundles, in order to differentiate themselves from other types of good. This method of formation is clear from all parts of the human body, large and small.[148]

A similar thing happens in the human mind, as should be inferable from the constant correspondence of all things related to the mind with all things related to the body. It follows that on the inside the human mind is constructed of spiritual substances, and on the outside, of earthly substances and finally physical materials. The mind that feels a good kind of pleasure from love is inwardly made of spiritual substances like those in heaven. The mind that feels an evil kind of pleasure from love is inwardly made of spiritual substances like those in hell. The evil things in the latter mind are in bundles tied with falsities. The good things in the former mind are in bundles tied with truths. Since this is how good things are bound together, and evil things as well, the Lord says that "the tares need to be gathered into bundles for burning, and so do all things that offend" (Matthew 13:30, 40, 41; John 15:6).

39
3. *Because God is love itself and wisdom itself, he is life itself, or life in itself.* The Gospel of John says, "The Word was with God, and the Word was God. In it there was life, and that life was the light for humankind" (John 1:1, 4). "God" in this case means divine love, and "the Word" means divine wisdom. Divine wisdom is actually life, and life is actually the light that radiates from the sun in the spiritual world—the sun that surrounds Jehovah God.

Divine love produces life the way fire produces light. Fire has two qualities: burning and shining. Its burning radiates heat and its shining radiates light. Likewise love has two qualities. The burning quality of fire corresponds to one of them; it is something that affects our will at the deepest level. The shining quality of fire corresponds to the other; it is something that affects our intellect at the deepest level. This is where our love and intelligence come from, because, as I have said several times now, the heat that radiates from the sun in the spiritual world is essentially love, and its light is essentially wisdom. That love and that wisdom flow into each and every thing in the universe and affect them at the deepest level. In us, they flow into our will and intellect; both were created as vessels to receive what flows in, the will as a vessel for love and the intellect as a vessel for wisdom.

From all this three points emerge: that our life finds its home in our intellect; that that life is only as good as our wisdom; and that that life is modified by the love in our will.

We also read in John, "As the Father has life in himself, so he also **40** granted the Son to have life in himself" (John 5:26). This means that as the Divine itself that has existed from eternity is alive in itself, so also the human aspect that it acquired in time is alive in itself. "Life in itself" means the absolute and only life from which all angels and people on earth are alive.

Our reason is capable of seeing this in relation to the light that radiates from the sun in the physical world. That light cannot be created, but the forms for receiving it can. Our eyes are forms tuned to receive that light. When the light flows in from the sun, we see. It is similar with life. Life, as I just pointed out [§39], is light radiating from the sun in the spiritual world. That light too cannot be created, but it is at all times flowing in. As it enlightens our intellect, it also brings it to life. Because light, life, and wisdom are one, wisdom cannot be created either, nor can faith, truth, love, goodwill, or goodness; but forms for receiving those things have been created. They are human and angelic minds.

Be very careful, then, not to convince yourself that you are alive from yourself—do not think you are wise, have faith, are loving, perceive truth, or will or do what is good from yourself. As people do convince themselves of these things, they cast their mind down from heaven to earth and change from being spiritual to being oriented to nature, their own senses, and their own body. They close the higher regions of their mind. Doing so blinds them to everything having to do with God, heaven, or the church. Then whatever they happen to think, reason, or say on these subjects is ridiculous, because they are in the dark. At the same time, ironically, they gain greater confidence in the wisdom of their perspective. Since the higher regions of their mind are closed, where the true light of life makes its home, a lower region of their mind opens up that is attuned only to the glimmer of the world. That glimmer, devoid of light from the higher regions, is faint and deceptive.[149] In it, false things seem true and true things false; argumentation on false premises seems like wisdom, and on true premises seems like madness. People like this truly believe they have the visual powers of an eagle, when in fact they cannot see what comes from wisdom any more than a bat can see in broad daylight.

4. *Love and wisdom are united in God.* All the goodness of love and **41** goodwill comes from God, and so does all the truth of wisdom and of faith, as any wise person in the church knows. In fact, all human reason is capable of seeing that this is true, once it is aware that love and wisdom originate in the sun that surrounds Jehovah God in the spiritual world;

or to put it another way, once it is aware that love and wisdom come from Jehovah God through the sun that surrounds him. The heat radiating from that sun is essentially love, and the light radiating from it is essentially wisdom. From this it becomes as clear as day that love and wisdom are united at their source—namely, God, who is the origin of that sun.

This point can be visualized [by thinking] of the sun in the physical world. It is nothing but fire. Heat radiates from its fieriness; light radiates from the glow of its fieriness. At the outset, then, heat and light are one. [2] As they radiate, however, they are separated, as you can tell from the fact that some objects they strike take in more heat and some more light. A more extreme separation occurs in us. With us, the light of life (intelligence) and the heat of life (love) are distinct. This separation exists because we need to be reformed and regenerated,[150] and this will not happen unless the light of life, or intelligence, teaches us what we should want and what we should love.

It is important to know that God is continually building a partnership between love and wisdom in us, but if we are not facing God and believing in him, we ourselves are constantly separating the two.

The greater the partnership within us, then, between these two things—the goodness of love or of goodwill and the truth of wisdom or of faith—the more we become an image of God and are raised toward heaven and even into heaven where the angels are. On the other hand, the more these two things are separated in us, the more we become an image of Lucifer and of the dragon[151] and are cast down from heaven to earth and then below the earth into hell.

When love and wisdom have a partnership in us, we become like a tree in springtime, when heat joins equally with light to make the tree bud, flower, and bear fruit. On the other hand, when love and wisdom are separated in us we become like a tree in winter, when heat withdraws from light, making the tree bare and bald of all its foliage.

[3] When spiritual heat, or love, withdraws from spiritual light, or wisdom, or equally when goodwill withdraws from faith, we become like humus that rots and becomes acidic—worms breed in it, and if seedlings come up at all, their leaves are covered with little leaf-eating grubs. Then enticements to love evil, which are really cravings, burst forth in us. Rather than controlling and restraining them, our intelligence loves them, takes care of them, and feeds them.

In a word, to separate love and wisdom or goodwill and faith—two things God is constantly trying to bring together—is comparable to taking all the redness out of a face so that it becomes as pale as death, or taking all the whiteness away from the redness so that the face becomes as inflamed as a firebrand.

Separating love and wisdom is also comparable to breaking a couple's marriage bond and turning the wife into a prostitute and the husband into an adulterer. Love is like a husband, and so is goodwill; wisdom is like a wife, and so is faith. Their being separated causes spiritual prostitution and whoring, in the form of falsifying what is true and contaminating what is good.

It is also important to know that there are three levels of love and wisdom, and therefore there are three levels of life. The human mind is formed into areas that go with these levels. The life in the highest area of the mind is the highest level of life. The life in the middle area of the mind is a lesser level of life. The life in the lowest area of the mind is the lowest level of life.

These areas in us are opened one after the other. The lowest area of the mind, where there is the lowest level of life, is opened during childhood and adolescence, by means of factual information. The second area of the mind, where there is a greater level of life, is opened during adolescence and early adulthood, by means of thought that builds on factual information.[152] The highest area of the mind, where there is the highest level of life, is opened during early adulthood, middle age, and beyond, by means of perceiving both moral and spiritual truths.

Another important thing to know is that life in its greatest perfection is not thinking; it is perceiving truth in the light of truth. The level of this perception in people can be used to determine what level of life they have. For example, there are people who, immediately upon hearing something true, perceive the truth of it. In the spiritual world they are represented as eagles. Then there are people who do not perceive what is true, but they do arrive at truth from argumentation based on other things that are apparent. They are represented as songbirds. There are people who believe something to be true because it was decreed by a man in authority. They are represented as jays or magpies.

There are also some who are unwilling and others who are unable to perceive what is true; they can perceive only what is false. The reason is that the light they are in is faint and deceptive. In that light what is false seems true, and what is true seems like something hidden in a thick cloud overhead or like a shooting star; or else it just seems false. Such people's thoughts are represented as night birds, and their speaking as screech owls. Those among them who have become adamant in their own false impressions cannot stand to hear things that are true. As soon as anything true reaches the outermost part of their ear, they reject it in disgust much the way a nauseous stomach distended with bile will regurgitate food.

43 5. *The essence of love is loving others who are outside oneself, wanting to be one with them, and blessing them from oneself.* Two things—love and wisdom—constitute the essence of God; but three things constitute the essence of God's love: his loving others who are outside of himself, his wanting to be one with them, and his blessing them from himself. The same three constitute the essence of his wisdom because in God love and wisdom are united, as was just explained. It is love that wants those three things, however, and wisdom that brings them about.

[2] The first essential, *God's loving others outside himself,* is recognizable in God's love for the entire human race. And as those who love the purpose also love the means, God also loves all the other things he created, because they are the means.

All people and all things in the universe are outside God, in that they are finite and God is infinite. God's love goes out and extends not only to good people and good things but also to evil people and evil things. It goes not only to the people and things that are in heaven but also to those that are in hell—not only to Michael and Gabriel but also to the Devil and Satan, for God is the same everywhere from eternity to eternity.[153] As he says, "He makes his sun rise on good people and evil people, and sends rain on the just and on the unjust" (Matthew 5:45).

Despite this, evil people and things are still evil. This is a result of what is in the people and the objects[154] themselves. Evil people and things do not receive the love of God as it truly and most profoundly is; they receive the love of God according to their own nature, much the way thorns and nettles receive the heat from the sun and the rain from the sky.

[3] The second essential of God's love, *his wanting to be one with others,* is recognizable in his partnership with the angelic heaven, with the church on earth, with everyone in the church, and with everything good and true that forms and constitutes an individual and a church. In fact, seen in its own right, love is nothing but an effort to forge a partnership.

In order to fulfill the purpose intended by the essence of his love, God created human beings in his own image and likeness—characteristics with which he could forge a partnership.

Divine love constantly aims to forge a partnership with us, as is clear from the Lord's saying that he wants to be one with people, he in them and they in him, and he wants the love of God to be in them (John 17:21, 22, 23, 26).

[4] The third essential of God's love, *his blessing others from himself,* is recognizable in eternal life, which is the unending blessedness, good fortune, and happiness that God gives to those who let his love in. As God is love itself, he is also blessedness itself; and as every love exudes pleasure, so divine love eternally exudes blessedness itself, good fortune itself, and happiness itself. God gives these blessings to angels and people after death through his partnership with them.

The true nature of divine love is recognizable from its sphere, which pervades the universe and affects each of us in different ways depending on our state. That sphere of divine love has a special influence on parents. Because of it, they tenderly love their children (who are outside themselves), they want to be one with them, and they want to bless them from themselves. The sphere of divine love affects not only the good but also the evil, and not only people but also animals and birds of every kind.

Surely in the course of giving birth every mother's only thought is of bonding with and caring for her offspring. Every bird hatching chicks from eggs thinks only of cherishing them under her wings and putting food in their mouths with kisses.[155] Even poisonous snakes and vipers love their offspring, as is commonly known.

This universal sphere has a special influence on those who let God's love in—those who believe in God and love their neighbor. The goodwill that is in them is an image of God's love.

Even among people who are not good, friendship emulates this love. At her or his own table, the host will give the guest the better food. Friends will kiss, hug, and join hands, and promise each other help and support. This love is also the sole origin of alliances and the tendency for like-minded and compatible people to form partnerships.

Even in inanimate things like trees and plants that same divine sphere is at work, although in this case it operates through the sun in this world, and its heat and light. Heat comes from the outside into trees and plants and becomes a part of them, causing them to sprout and then

44

develop flowers and fruit, which are in turn blessings to animals. Physical heat has this effect because it corresponds to spiritual heat, which is love.

In fact, even among various substances of the mineral kingdom there are representations of divine love at work. Allegories of divine love appear in the processes for refining these substances to increase their usefulness and value.

45 From this description of divine love's essence, you can also see what the essence of diabolical love is like; it becomes visible by contrast.

Diabolical love is a love for oneself. This is called love, but seen in its own right it is really hatred. It does not love anyone outside itself. It does not want to form a partnership with others in order to bless them; it wants to bless only itself. From deep inside, it constantly strives to dominate all others and to own the good things they have.

Eventually it wants to be adored as God. This is why those who are in hell do not acknowledge God. Instead they acknowledge as gods those who have power over others. From hell's point of view, then, there are lower and higher gods, or lesser and greater gods, according to the reach of each one's power. Because all who are in hell carry love for themselves in their heart, they burn with hatred against their "god."

The "gods" in turn burn with hatred against all who are under their thumb; they think of them as vile slaves. They manage to speak softly to them as long as their followers keep showing adoration. They openly rage against all others. Inwardly or at heart, they rage against their followers as well.

Love for oneself is the same love you see among thieves, who kiss each other when they are on a job together, but later each burn with a desire to kill the others and take their share.

In hell, love for oneself is the dominant force. It causes the people there and their selfish lusts to appear at a distance as various species of wild animal. Some people there look like foxes and leopards, some like wolves and tigers, some like crocodiles and venomous snakes. Their love for themselves also causes the deserts they live in to consist of mere piles of stones and bare gravel, with swamps here and there that contain croaking frogs. Over their huts fly miserable screeching birds.[156] These animals and birds are the same as the owls, the wild beasts of the desert, and the jackals mentioned in the prophetical books of the Word in reference to the love of dominating that comes from love for oneself (Isaiah 13:21; Jeremiah 50:39; Psalms 74:14).

6. These essentials of divine love were the reason the universe was created, and they are the reason it is maintained. By examining and scrutinizing the three essentials of divine love, one can come to see that they were the reason for creation. The first essential, *loving others outside of himself,* was a reason for creation in that the universe is outside God (just as the world is outside the sun). The universe is something to which God could extend his love and in which he could put his love into action and so find rest. We read that after God had created heaven and earth he rested; and that he made the Sabbath day for that reason (Genesis 2:2–3).

You can see that the second essential, *God's wanting to be one with others,* was also a reason for creation from the fact that people were created in the image and likeness of God. The "image" and the "likeness" mean that we were made as forms that are receptive to love and wisdom from God— forms that God could be one with, and on whose account he could be one with all the other things in the universe, which are all nothing but means. A connection with the final cause is also a connection with the intermediate causes.[157] Genesis, the Book of Creation, makes it clear that all things were created for the sake of humankind (Genesis 1:28–30).

That the third essential, *God's blessing others from himself,* is a reason for creation you can see from the fact that the angelic heaven was provided for everyone who has let God's love in, a place where the blessings of all come from God alone.

The three essentials of God's love are the reason the universe is maintained as well, because maintaining is an ongoing creation, just as continuing to exist is the same as perpetually coming into being. Divine love is the same from eternity to eternity. The nature God's love has now and will have in the future is the same nature it had when creating the world.

If you understand all this in the right way, you will be able to see the universe as a coherent work from beginning to end, a work holding purposes, means, and results in indissoluble connection.

Every love has a purpose. All wisdom moves toward fulfilling that purpose by intermediate means, using those means to achieve effective, useful results. Therefore it follows that the universe is a work that embodies divine love, divine wisdom, and usefulness of all kinds. In every conceivable way, then, it is a coherent work from beginning to end.

The fact that the universe consists of constant useful functions produced by wisdom under love's initiative is something all wise people can contemplate as if they were seeing it in a mirror. Once they acquire a general picture of how the universe was created, they can focus on the details. This is because parts adapt to the whole, and the whole places the parts in a harmonious arrangement. In what follows, the truth of this will come to light in many ways.

48　To these points I will add the following memorable occurrence.

Once I had a conversation with two angels, one of whom came from a heaven in the east and the other from a heaven in the south.[158] When these angels realized that I was meditating on secrets of wisdom having to do with love, they said, "Are you not aware of the wisdom games that take place in our world?"

"Not yet," I said.

"There are lots of them," they said. They explained that spirits who love truth in a spiritual way (loving it because it is true and because it leads to wisdom) gather together on receiving a sign; these spirits then debate issues that require deep understanding, and draw conclusions.

The angels took me by the hand, saying to me, "Come with us and you will see and hear. We received the sign that a gathering is happening today."

They led me across a large flat area of land to a hill. I was surprised to see here a covered walkway or colonnade formed entirely of living palm trees. It began at the bottom of the hill and continued to the top. We went into it and made our way up the hill. At the hill's highest point a stand of trees came into view. Within this stand of trees, earth had been built up in such a way as to form an arena. In the arena there was a level area paved with pebbles of different colors. Around the paved part, on all four sides, there were chairs set up on which the lovers of wisdom were sitting. At the center of the whole arena there was a table. On it lay a document sealed with a signet ring.

[2] The people sitting on the chairs invited us to take some unoccupied seats, but I replied, "I was brought here by these two angels not to sit, but to watch and to listen."

Then the two angels went to the table in the middle of the paved area and broke the seal on the document. To the seated participants they read what was written in the document—mysteries of wisdom that the crowd was to discuss and unfold. These mysteries had been written by angels of the third heaven and sent down to that table.

There were three mysteries. First, human beings were created in the image and the likeness of God [Genesis 1:26]; what is that image and what is that likeness? Second, animals and birds, whether noble or not,[159] are born with knowledge that relates to every drive or love they have; why then are human beings born without any knowledge that relates to any drive or love they have? Third, what does the tree of life mean, what does the tree of the knowledge of good and evil mean, and what does eating from them mean [Genesis 2:9, 16–17; 3:6]? Below these points it said, "Connect these three into a single statement, write it on a new sheet of paper, put it on this table, and we will look at it. If on balance your statement seems well considered and accurate, each of you will be given a prize for your wisdom."

After they had read this aloud the two angels walked away and were lifted up into their respective heavens. Then the people on the chairs began to discuss the mysteries set before them and to unravel them. They took turns speaking. Those sitting on the north side went first, then those sitting on the west side, then those sitting on the south side, and finally those sitting on the east side.

The group took up the first topic for discussion: "Human beings were created in the image and the likeness of God; what is that image and what is that likeness?" First the following verses from the Book of Creation were read before the whole group:

> God said, "Let us make human beings in *our image,* according to *our likeness."* And God created human beings in *his own image;* in *the likeness of God* he made them. (Genesis 1:26–27)

> On the day that God created human beings, he made them in *the likeness of God.* (Genesis 5:1)

[3] Those sitting on the north side spoke first. They said, "The image of God and the likeness of God are the two kinds of life that God has breathed into us all: the life in our will and the life in our intellect. We read, 'Jehovah God breathed a soul *of lives* into Adam's nostrils, and the human being turned into a living soul' (Genesis 2:7). We believe this means that willing what is good and perceiving what is true were breathed into Adam—this is how he received 'a soul of lives.' Because the life breathed into Adam came from God, the image and the likeness mean a purity of love and wisdom, and of justice and judgment, in Adam."

Those sitting on the west side agreed, but added that the pure state God breathed into Adam is something God has been continually breathing into everyone else ever since. That pure state, then, is present in human beings inasmuch as they are vessels that receive it. Their capacity as receiving vessels makes human beings images and likenesses of God.

[4] Those sitting on the south side were the third to take a turn. They said, "The image of God and the likeness of God are two different things, although they have been united in human beings ever since creation. From some kind of inner light we see that we all have the power to destroy the image of God in ourselves, but not the likeness of God. We can glimpse this as though through a veil from the fact that Adam kept the likeness of God after he lost the image of God. After the curse it says, 'See how this human being knows good and evil, like one of us' (Genesis 3:22); and later on, Adam is called the likeness of God, but not the image of God (Genesis 5:1). We will leave it, however, to our friends sitting on the east side, who therefore have better light, to say what the image of God and the likeness of God really are."

[5] When it had grown quiet, those sitting on the east side rose from their chairs and looked up toward the Lord. Then they sat back down and said, "An image of God is a vessel for God. God is love itself and wisdom itself; therefore the image of God is our openness to love and wisdom from God. The likeness of God, on the other hand, is the perfect likeness and the full appearance that love and wisdom are in us as if they were completely our own. We all utterly feel as if we have love and wisdom on our own, as if we intend what is good and understand what is true by ourselves. In reality, though, not a bit of it comes from us; it is from God. God alone has love and wisdom on his own, because God is love itself and wisdom itself. The likeness or the appearance that love and wisdom or goodness and truth are in us as our very own makes us human and enables us to have a partnership with God and therefore to live to eternity. It flows from this that what makes us human is our ability on the one hand to intend what is good and understand what is true completely as if we were on our own, and our capacity on the other hand for knowing and believing that we are doing this with God's help. As we come to know and believe that we are getting help from God, God puts his image in us. God does not put his image in us, however, if we believe that we are doing it on our own without God's help."

[6] When they had said this, a passion from their love for truth came over them, which led them to say the following: "How could any

of us receive, retain, or pass on any love or wisdom if we did not experience it as our own? How could we have a partnership with God through love and wisdom if we had no way of doing our part to form that partnership? There is no such thing as a partnership without mutuality. What makes the partnership mutual is that we love God and we act on what we receive from God, doing so as if we were on our own but trusting that we have God's help. How could we live to eternity if we had no partnership with the eternal God? How then would we be human if that likeness were not in us?"

[7] All agreed with this and said, "We need to draw a conclusion from all this." They came to the following: "We are vessels to receive God. A vessel to receive God is an image of God. Because God is love itself and wisdom itself, we are vessels to receive love and wisdom; our vessel becomes an image of God as we actually do receive love and wisdom. We are a likeness of God because we experience things from God in ourselves as if they were our own. We go from being a likeness to being an image of God to the extent that we acknowledge that the love and wisdom or goodness and truth in us are not ours and did not originate in us; they exist solely in God and they come exclusively from God."

[8] Next the group took up the second topic for discussion: "Animals and birds, whether noble or not, are born with knowledge that relates to every drive or love they have; why then are human beings born without any knowledge that relates to any drive or love they have?"

The participants began by verifying the truth of the premise in various ways, particularly the notion that human beings have no innate knowledge or instinct, not even in relation to marriage love. They made inquiries and heard from researchers[160] that newborns lack even an innate knowledge or instinct for recognizing their mother's breast; newborns learn to nurse only when their mother or whoever is nursing them gives them her breast. Newborns know only how to suck, an instinct they gained from sucking all the time while in their mother's womb. Shortly after birth, they do not know how to walk or how to shape sound into any human word, or even how to use different sounds to express their love and emotions the way animals do. Unlike animals, they have no idea what food would be good for them—they seize anything at hand, clean or dirty, and put it in their mouths. The researchers also said that without instruction people have absolutely no idea how to make love to the opposite sex. Not even young men and women know how without learning about it from others. In a nutshell, we are born as mindlessly physical[161] as a worm and remain that way unless we learn from others how to know, understand, and grow wise.

[9] Next the participants verified that animals, whether noble or not, are born with all the knowledge related to the various drives or loves that affect their lives. This is true of land animals, birds that fly in the sky, reptiles, fish, and even the little creatures known as insects. They all know everything that is good for them to eat, everything about how to make a home for themselves, and everything about how to mate and how to produce and raise their offspring. The participants verified these facts by recalling the astounding things they had seen, heard, and read in the physical world where they used to live, in which animals are real rather than symbolic.[162]

Once the truth of the premise was proven in this way, the participants turned their minds to hunting for and finding a means of unfolding and uncovering this mystery. They all said that these phenomena must come about as a result of divine wisdom intentionally making humans human and animals animal, and creating the circumstance that our imperfection at birth becomes our perfection, while an animal's perfection at birth becomes its imperfection.

[10] Then the people on the north side went first in giving their opinion. They said, "We are born without knowledge so that we can be open to all knowledge. If we had been born with knowledge, we would not have been open to any concepts except those we were born with; nor would we have been capable of acquiring any further knowledge."

They illustrated this with an analogy: "When first born we are like ground in which no seeds have been planted, but which has the capacity to take in any and all seeds and help them grow and bear fruit. An animal is like ground that is already sown and is full of grasses and small plants. The seeds already sown in that ground fill it to capacity. If more seeds are planted, they are choked out. This is why we take so many years to grow up. In our growing years we are like ground that can be cultivated to yield crops, flowers, and trees of all kinds. Animals grow up in just a few years, and in their growing years they cannot be cultivated beyond their innate potential."

[11] The people on the west side spoke next. They said, "It is true that unlike animals we are born without knowledge. We are, however, born with a capacity and a tendency—a capacity for knowing and a tendency to love. We have an inborn ability to love not only things that have to do with ourselves and the world but also things that have to do with God

and heaven. At birth our physical senses are scarcely alive except in a dim way and our inner senses are not alive at all—a situation that allows us progressively to come to life and become human. First we become earthly, and then rational, and finally spiritual. This would not happen if we were born like animals with various types of knowledge and love already in place. Knowledge and feelings of love that are inborn limit the progression; but capacities and tendencies that are inborn do not limit it at all. Human beings are therefore capable of being perfected in knowledge, intelligence, and wisdom to eternity."

[12] The people on the south side then took their turn in giving their opinion. They said, "It is impossible for human beings to learn anything from themselves. Since they have no innate knowledge, they have to learn it all from others. Because they cannot acquire any knowledge from themselves, they cannot acquire any love from themselves either, since where there is no knowledge there is no love. Knowledge and love are partners that are no more separable than the will and the intellect or feelings and thoughts, or essence and form for that matter. Therefore as we pick up knowledge from others, love accompanies it. The universal love that attaches to knowledge is love for knowing, and later it becomes love for understanding and growing wise. These types of love are found only in human beings, never in animals; they flow in from God.

[13] "We stand in agreement with our colleagues on the west side on the point that we are all born without love and therefore without knowledge; we are born only with a tendency to love and a resulting capacity for acquiring knowledge. We acquire knowledge from others, not from ourselves. Actually this happens *through* others, in the sense that they did not receive the knowledge from themselves either—it all comes originally from God.

"We also agree with our colleagues on the north side on the point that when first born we are all like ground in which no seeds have yet been planted, but in which all seeds, whether noble or not, can be planted. This is why 'human' is related to 'humus,' and 'Adam' to *adama,* or 'soil.'[163] We would like to add to these points that animals are born with earthly loves and with the knowledge that goes with these loves. Nevertheless the knowledge animals possess does not lead them to know, think, understand, or be wise about anything. Their loves lead them to knowledge much the way guide dogs lead the blind through streets. Animals are blind in intellect. Or better yet, they are like sleepwalkers who do what they do from blind knowledge while their intellect sleeps."

[14] The last to speak were the people on the east side. They said, "We agree with what our friends have said. We humans learn from and through others, not from ourselves. Therefore we need to recognize and acknowledge that everything we know, understand, and have wisdom about comes from God. There is no other way for us to be born or generated by God and become an image and a likeness of him. An image of God is what we become by acknowledging and believing that all the goodness of love and goodwill and all the truth of wisdom and faith that we have received and are still receiving come from God, and none comes from ourselves. A likeness of God is what we are as a result of experiencing these things in ourselves as if they were our own. We experience them in this way because rather than being born with knowledge, we acquire it as we go along. Our acquiring of knowledge seems to us to be something we do ourselves. God grants us this experience so that we may be human rather than animal. Our seeming autonomy in intending, thinking, loving, knowing, understanding, and becoming wise allows us to acquire knowledge, elevate it to an understanding, and turn it into wisdom as we put it to use. This is how God unites us to himself, and how we unite ourselves to God. None of this could take place unless God had provided for us to be born in total ignorance."

[15] After this statement the whole group wanted to form a conclusion from their discussion. Their conclusion was, "We are born without any knowledge so that we can come into all knowledge, make progress in understanding, and move onward into wisdom. We are born without any love so that by intelligently applying what we learn we can come into all love, can come to love God through loving our neighbor, and can thereby develop a partnership with God that makes us truly human and allows us to live forever."

[16] Then the participants picked up the document and read the third topic for discussion: "What does the tree of life mean, what does the tree of the knowledge of good and evil mean, and what does eating from them mean?"

They all asked the group on the east side to unravel this mystery, "since," they said, "it is a matter of deeper understanding and you who are from the east have a blazing light, meaning that you have a wisdom that comes from love. This kind of wisdom is in fact what the garden of Eden means, where the two trees were situated."

The people on the east side replied, "We will give an answer, yet because human beings receive everything from God and nothing from themselves, we will give an answer from him, although we will still give it as if it were our own.

"A tree means a human being," they said. "Its fruit means the good done by that human being's life. Therefore the tree of life means someone who lives from God. Because love and wisdom, along with goodwill and faith—or rather, goodness and truth—are God's life in us, the tree of life means people who have those things from God and who have eternal life as a result. Much the same thing is meant by the tree of life from which people were allowed to eat (Revelation 2:7; 22:2, 14).

[17] "The tree of the knowledge of good and evil means those who believe that they live on their own rather than from God—that the love and wisdom and the goodwill and faith—or again, the goodness and truth—that are in them are their own and not God's. They believe this because the likeness and appearance of their thinking, intending, speaking, and acting on their own is completely convincing. Because they use this appearance to convince themselves that they are in fact God, therefore the serpent said, 'God knows that on the day you eat some of the fruit of that tree, your eyes will be opened and you will be like God, knowing good and evil' (Genesis 3:5).

[18] "Eating from those trees means accepting and internalizing. Eating from the tree of life means accepting eternal life. Eating from the tree of the knowledge of good and evil means accepting damnation. The serpent means the Devil, which is loving ourselves and having pride in our own intelligence. Love for ourselves owns the latter tree. If we have pride because we love ourselves, we are trees of the knowledge of good and evil.

"It is horrendously wrong, then, to believe that Adam was wise and did what was good on his own, and that this was what was pure about his state. Adam himself was in fact cursed because of that very belief. That is what it means to eat from the tree of the knowledge of good and evil, and that is why Adam fell at that time. His earlier state had been pure because then he believed he was wise and was doing what was good with God's help and in absolutely no respect on his own. This is what it means to eat from the tree of life. The only person who ever became wise on his own and did what was good on his own was the Lord while he was in the world, because divinity itself was in him and was his from birth. That is how he became the Redeemer and Savior by his own power."

[19] From these points the participants drew the following conclusion: "The meaning of the tree of life, the tree of the knowledge of good and evil, and eating from those trees is as follows: Our life is God in us. With

God in us we have heaven and eternal life. Our death, on the other hand, is the conviction and belief that our life is we ourselves and not God. This attitude brings us hell and eternal death, meaning damnation."

[20] After this they checked over the document that the angels had left on the table. They saw written at the bottom, "Connect these three into a single statement."

They brought them together and found that the three connected to form a single chain. The chain, their statement, was this: "We human beings have been created to receive love and wisdom from God and yet to experience them completely as if they came from ourselves, for the sake of our receiving them and forming a partnership with God. For this reason we are not born with any love, any knowledge, or any capability whatever for loving or becoming wise on our own. If we attribute all the goodness of love and all the truth of wisdom to God, we become living human beings. If we attribute them to ourselves, we become dead human beings."

They wrote this on a new sheet of paper and placed it on the table. Suddenly angels were present in a shining white cloud. They took the document to heaven. After it was read there, the people sitting on the chairs heard voices from heaven saying, "Good! . . . Good! . . . Good!"

Immediately someone came into view, flying down from above. He had two wings attached to his ankles and two more attached to his temples.[164] He was carrying prizes—robes, hats, and laurel wreaths. He landed on the ground, then gave opalescent robes to the people sitting on the north side. To the people sitting on the west side he gave scarlet robes. To the people sitting on the south side he gave hats whose rims were decorated with bands of gold and bands of pearls, and whose raised left sides were decorated with diamonds cut in the shape of flowers. To the people sitting on the east side, however, he gave laurel wreaths with rubies and sapphires in them. Decorated with these prizes from their wisdom games, they all went joyfully home.

God's Omnipotence, Omniscience, and Omnipresence

49 We have discussed divine love and wisdom and have shown that these two qualities make up the divine essence. We turn next to God's omnipotence, omniscience, and omnipresence because these three attributes come from divine love and divine wisdom much the way the sun's power and presence everywhere on earth come from the sun's heat and light. In fact, the heat of the sun in the spiritual world (the sun that surrounds Jehovah God) is essentially divine love, and its light is essentially divine wisdom. Clearly then, omnipotence, omniscience, and omnipresence are attributes of the divine *essence* the way infinity, immensity, and eternity are attributes of the underlying divine *reality*.

Up until now these three universal attributes of divine essence have not been understood, because it has not been known that they keep to their own pathways, meaning the laws of the divine design.[165] Therefore these attributes need to be elucidated in an examination of the following points:

1. It is divine wisdom, acting on behalf of divine love, that has omnipotence, omniscience, and omnipresence.
2. We cannot comprehend God's omnipotence, omniscience, and omnipresence unless we know what the divine design is, and unless we learn that God is the divine design, and that he imposed that design on the universe as a whole and on everything in it as he created it.
3. In the universe and everything in it, God's omnipotence follows and works through the laws of its design.
4. God is omniscient; that is, he is aware of, sees, and knows everything down to the least detail that happens in keeping with the divine design, and by contrast is aware of, sees, and knows what goes against the divine design.
5. God is omnipresent in his design from beginning to end.
6. Human beings were created as forms of the divine design.
7. The more we follow the divine design in the way we live, the more we receive power against evil and falsity from God's omnipotence, receive wisdom about goodness and truth from God's omniscience, and are in God because of God's omnipresence.

These points need to be unfolded one by one.

1. *It is divine wisdom, acting on behalf of divine love, that has omnipotence, omniscience, and omnipresence.* Omnipotence, omniscience, and omnipresence belong to divine wisdom acting on behalf of divine love, not to divine love acting through divine wisdom. This is a secret from heaven that has never yet dawned on anyone's understanding, because before this no one has known what love is in its essence, or what wisdom is in its essence, much less how the one flows into the other. Love, with everything that belongs to it, flows into wisdom and takes up residence there like a monarch of a realm or a head of a household. The actual

50

administration of justice is something love leaves to wisdom's judgment; and since justice relates to love and judgment to wisdom, this means that love leaves the administration of love to its [partner,] wisdom. More light will be shed on this secret in what follows. For now, the statement above will have to serve as a general rule.

The following words in John mean that God is omnipotent, omniscient, and omnipresent through the wisdom of his love:

> In the beginning was the Word, and the Word was with God, and the Word was God. All things were made by it, and nothing that was made came about without it. In it there was life, and that life was the light for humankind. And the world was made by it; and the Word became flesh. (John 1:1, 3, 4, 10, 14)

In this passage "the Word" means divine truth or, what amounts to the same thing, divine wisdom. This is why the Word is also called "life" and "light," since life and light are nothing but wisdom.

51 In the Word, "justice" is associated with love and "judgment" with wisdom. For this reason I will present some passages to the effect that God governs the world with these two qualities.

> *Jehovah, justice and judgment* are the support of your throne. (Psalms 89:14)

> Those who wish to glory should glory in this, that *Jehovah* creates *judgment* and *justice* on earth. (Jeremiah 9:24)

> *Jehovah* should be exalted because he filled the earth with *judgment* and *justice.* (Isaiah 33:5)

> *Judgment* will flow like water and *justice* like a mighty stream. (Amos 5:24)

> *Jehovah, your justice* is like the mountains of God; *your judgments* are like a great deep. (Psalms 36:6)

> *Jehovah* will bring out his *justice* like a light, and [his] *judgment* like noonday. (Psalms 37:6)

> *Jehovah* will judge his people in *justice* and his poor ones in *judgment.* (Psalms 72:2)

> When I learn the *judgments* of your *justice,* seven times a day I praise you for the *judgments* of your *justice.* (Psalms 119:7, 164)

> I will betroth myself to you in *justice* and *judgment.* (Hosea 2:19)

Zion will be redeemed with *justice,* and its returned exiles with *judgment.* (Isaiah 1:27)

He will sit on the throne of David and over his kingdom, to establish it with *judgment* and *justice.* (Isaiah 9:7)

I will raise up for David a righteous offshoot who will reign as king and execute *judgment* and *justice* on earth. (Jeremiah 23:5; 33:15)

Elsewhere we read that we ought to practice justice and judgment, as in Isaiah 1:21; 5:16; 58:2; Jeremiah 4:2; 22:3, 13, 15; Ezekiel 18:5; 33:14, 16, 19; Amos 6:12; Micah 7:9; Deuteronomy 33:21; and John 16:8, 10, 11.

2. *We cannot comprehend God's omnipotence, omniscience, and omnipresence unless we know what the divine design is, and unless we learn that God is the divine design and that he imposed that design on the universe as a whole and on everything in it as he created it.* Astounding quantities and varieties of folly have crept into human minds and slithered into the church through the heads of its founders as a result of their not understanding the design that God built into the universe and everything in it. A mere list of these foolish notions, which appears below [§§56–58], will make this clear.

For now let me open a discussion of the divine design with a general definition: *A "design" is the quality of arrangement, boundaries, and interaction among parts, substances, or entities that together make up a form. This quality results in a state—a state that is perfect when produced by wisdom acting on the basis of love, and imperfect when spawned by unsound reasoning acting on the basis of mere desire.*

This definition uses the terms substance, form, and state. By substance we mean form as well, because every substance is a form, and the quality of that form is its state. The perfection or imperfection of that state is a result of the design it has.

Because these points are metaphysical, though, they are unavoidably cloaked in thick darkness; but in the ensuing discussion, application of these terms in illustrative examples will dispel this darkness.

God is the divine design because he is substance itself and form itself. He is substance because from him come all things that subsist,[166] that came into existence in the past, and that are coming into existence now. He is form because every quality of [these] substances arose and arises from him. Quality comes from no other source than form.

Now, because God is the absolute, the first, and the only substance and form and is also the absolute and only love and the absolute and only wisdom, and because wisdom produces form on the basis of love, and the state and quality of the form depend on its design, it follows that God is the design itself. It also follows that from himself God imposed a design on the universe and on every single thing in it, and the design imposed was absolutely perfect because all that he created was good, as we read in Genesis, the Book of Creation.

(In its own place we will show that evil of every kind and hell itself came into existence *after* creation.)[167]

Now we turn to thoughts that are more accessible to, clearer for, and gentler on the mind.

54 Explaining the type of design that was built into the universe at creation would take many volumes. (A little sketch of it will appear under the next subheading, on creation [§§75–80]).

One point that needs to be understood is this: Each and every thing in the universe was created with its own design so that it would continue to exist on its own. This happened from the very beginning so that each thing could become part of the overall design of the universe. The purpose is that the individual designs shall continue to exist within the universal design so that all are one.

Now for some examples. The human being was created with a design of its own, and also each individual part of a human being was created with a design of its own. The head has its own design, the body has its. The heart, the lungs, the liver, the pancreas, and the stomach have their own designs. Every organ of motion called a muscle has its own design. Every organ of sensation, such as the eye, the ear, and the tongue, has its own design. In fact, there is not a capillary or a fibril in the human body that lacks its own design. Yet all these countless parts connect with the overall design and join up with it in such a way that together they form one overall design.

The same applies to all other things. A mere list of them is enough for illustration. Every animal on land, every bird in the sky, every fish in the sea, every reptile, in fact, every insect even down to a grub has its own design built in from creation. Likewise every tree, shrub, bush, and vegetable has its own design. Furthermore, every stone and every mineral, even down to every type of dust on the earth has its own design.

55 As everyone can see, all well-established empires, countries, counties, republics, cities, and homes have laws that constitute the design and form of their government. In each of those arenas, the laws of justice are at the top, political laws are in second place, and business laws are in third place. If these laws are compared with a human being, the laws of

justice constitute the head, political laws the body, and business laws the clothes. This is why business laws can be changed like clothes.[168]

As for the design that God incorporated into the church, it is that God is part of every aspect of the church, and so is our neighbor, for whose sake we are to follow the design. There are as many laws of the design belonging to the church as there are truths in the Word. Laws related to God are to constitute its head, laws related to our neighbor its body, and rituals its clothing.

If the church's higher laws were not embodied in its rituals, the church would be like a body stripped naked, exposed to the heat in summer and the cold in winter. This would be like taking the walls and vaulted ceilings away from a church building so that the sanctuary, altar, and pulpit stood in the open air exposed to violent forces of different kinds.

3. *In the universe and everything in it, God's omnipotence follows and works through the laws of its design.* God is omnipotent, because he has all power from himself. All others have power from him. God's power and his will are one. Because he wills nothing but what is good, he cannot do anything but what is good. In the spiritual world no one can do anything against his or her will—a condition there that comes from God, from the fact that his power and his will are one. God is in fact goodness itself. When he does something good, he is in himself. He cannot walk away from himself.

Clearly then, his omnipotence fills, and works within, the sphere of the extension of goodness, a sphere that is infinite. At a deep level, this sphere pervades the universe and everything in it. At a deep level, this sphere also governs things outside of itself to the extent that they become part of it through their own design. If things do not become part of that sphere, it still sustains them. It tries in every way to bring them back to a design in harmony with the universal design that God inhabits with his omnipotence and follows in his actions. If things against the design are not brought back into the design, they are cast out of God; but there he still sustains them from deep within.

From all this you can see that divine omnipotence cannot move outside itself into contact with any evil, nor can it move evil away from itself. Evil turns itself away, which is how it ends up being completely separated from God and thrown into hell. Between heaven, where God is, and hell, there is a huge chasm.

From these few points you can see how insane people are who think that God can condemn anyone, curse anyone, throw anyone into hell, predestine anyone's soul to eternal death, avenge wrongs, or rage against

56

or punish anyone. People are even more insane if they actually believe this, let alone teach it. In reality, God cannot turn away from us or even look at us with a frown. To do any such thing would be against his essence, and what is against his essence is against himself.

57 The dominant opinion nowadays is that the omnipotence of God is like the absolute power of a monarch in the world, who can do whatever she or he wishes on a whim: absolve and condemn at will, make the guilty innocent, declare the unfaithful to be faithful, promote undeserving and unworthy people above those who are worthy and deserving. Under any pretext whatever, he or she can even seize citizens' assets, sentence them to death, and so on.

Through this ridiculous opinion, belief, and teaching about divine omnipotence, the same number of falsities, errors, and fabled monsters have poured into the church as there are movements, branches, and new sects of the faith. There is still room for more—as many more as the jars you could fill with water from a great lake, or as many as the snakes in an Arabian desert that could crawl out of their caves to enjoy basking in the sunshine. All you would need [to start a new movement, branch, or sect] are those two little words, "omnipotence" and "faith," and a program to spread enough conjectures, fables, and blithering to be physically stimulating.

Each of those two words pushes reason aside. Once our reason is disengaged, our thought process is no better than that of a bird flying overhead. What then becomes of the spiritual aspect that we have but animals lack? It becomes like the smell in a zoo: it suits the wild animals that are there but does not suit people unless they are particularly beastly.

If divine omnipotence extended to doing evil as well as good, what difference would there be between God and the Devil? They would be no different than two rulers, one of whom is a monarch and also a tyrant, while the other is a tyrant whose power has been curtailed so that he or she cannot be called a monarch anymore. They would be no different than a shepherd who is allowed to keep a sheep and a leopard, and another shepherd who is not allowed to do the same. Surely anyone can see that good and evil are opposites, and that if God by his omnipotence were able to will and do both good and evil, he could do absolutely nothing. He would have no power at all, much less omnipotence.

This situation would be much like the way two wheels going in opposite directions act against one another, causing each wheel to come to a stop. It would be like a ship whose course ran against a strong current in the opposite direction. If the ship did not drop anchor and stay still, it would be carried off to its doom. It would be like a human being with two wills that disagreed with each other. When one of them acted, the other would have to be still. Otherwise, if both acted at once, a dizzying madness would assault the mind.

If, as the modern-day belief goes, God's omnipotence was as absolute for doing evil as it is for doing good, surely it would be possible, even easy, for God to lift the whole of hell to heaven. He could turn devils and satans into angels. In a moment he could take all the ungodly people on earth, purify them from sin, make them new, holy, and reborn, and justify them, turning them from children of wrath into children of grace [Ephesians 2:3–8] solely by assigning and attributing to them the justice of his Son.[169]

God cannot do this with his omnipotence. It is against the laws of his design for the universe. It is also against the laws of his design for human beings, which dictate that the individual and God have to form a mutual partnership. (From later sections in this book [§§89, 99, 100, 110:4–6, 368–372] you will see that this is the case.)

The ridiculous modern-day belief about God's omnipotence would mean that God could turn all goat people into sheep people and move them at will from his left side to his right [Matthew 25:31–46]. He could transform the dragon's spirits into Michael's angels [Revelation 12:7]. He could give the sight of an eagle to someone with an intellect like a mole. In a word, he could make a dove person out of an owl person.[170]

God cannot do these things, because doing so is against the laws of his design, although he never stops wanting to or trying. If he could have done things like this he would not have let Adam listen to the serpent, pluck a piece of fruit from the tree of the knowledge of good and evil, and bring it to his mouth. If God could have avoided it, he would not have let Cain kill his brother. He would not have let David take a census of the people; he would not have let Solomon build shrines for idols, or let the kings of Judah and Israel desecrate the Temple, which they did a number of times. Indeed if he could have, he would have saved the whole human race without exception through his Son's redemption and would have uprooted hell in its entirety.[171]

Ancient gentiles[172] ascribed this kind of omnipotence to their gods and goddesses, as you can see from their myths. For example, in the story of Deucalion and Pyrrha, the stones they throw behind their backs become people; in another story Apollo turns Daphne into a laurel tree; in another, Diana turns a hunter into a deer. And there is a myth that one of their gods turned the young maidens of Parnassus into magpies.[173]

The belief about divine omnipotence today is similar to these ancient myths. In every region where there is religion many fanatical and heretical ideas have been brought into the world as a result.

59   4. *God is omniscient; that is, he is aware of, sees, and knows everything down to the least detail that happens in keeping with the divine design, and by contrast is aware of, sees, and knows what goes against the divine design.* God is omniscient, that is, he is aware of, sees, and knows all things, because he is wisdom itself and light itself. Wisdom itself is aware of all things. Light itself sees all things.

We showed above [§37] that God is wisdom itself. He is light itself because he is the sun of the angelic heaven that enlightens the intellect of all, both angels and people. As our eye is illuminated by the light of the physical sun, so our intellect is illuminated by the light of the spiritual sun—not only illuminated, but also filled with intelligence (depending on how much we love receiving it), since spiritual light is essentially wisdom.

This is why it says in David that God dwells in inaccessible light [Psalms 104:2; see also 1 Timothy 6:16]; and why it says in the Book of Revelation that in the New Jerusalem they do not need lamps because the Lord God enlightens them [Revelation 21:23]; and why it says in John that the Word that was with God and was God is the light that enlightens everyone who comes into the world [John 1:1, 9]. The "Word" in this last reference means divine wisdom. This is why the more wisdom angels have, the brighter a light they are in; and why when "light" is mentioned in the Word it means wisdom.

60   God is aware of, sees, and knows everything down to the least detail that happens in keeping with the divine design because it is a universal design that encompasses the smallest individual designs. (Individual things taken collectively are called universal, just as particular instances are collectively called something common or general.)

The universal design with [all] its individual designs is a masterwork so well connected together into one thing that you cannot touch or affect one part without something of a sensation flowing back to the others. Every created thing in this world has something comparable to this quality of the divine design in the universe.

Comparisons with observable phenomena will shed light on this. Throughout a human being, there are connective membranes and individual parts. The membranes enclose the individual parts, creating such a thorough connection that they become part of each other. This is accomplished through a common membrane around every unit in the body. This membrane wraps around the individual parts inside so that they act in a unified way to do whatever function or service that unit provides.

For example, the membrane around each muscle extends between individual motor fibers and wraps them with itself. The membrane around the liver, the membrane around the pancreas, and the membrane around the spleen also extend into the smaller parts inside these organs. The membrane around the lungs, called the pleura, extends in a similar way into the individual parts inside the lungs, as the pericardium also extends into each and every part of the heart. Likewise the peritoneum in general goes through anastomoses [points of communication] to join with all the membranes around individual organs. The same is also true of the meninges, the membranes around the brain. Using projecting filaments, these membranes extend into all the glands[174] below, and extend through the glands into fibers, and through the fibers into every single thing in the body. This is how the head uses the brains to control everything under its power.

The sole purpose in mentioning these examples is to show you observable phenomena, so that you may have some idea of how God is aware of, sees, and knows everything down to the least detail that happens in keeping with the divine design.

From what occurs in keeping with the divine design, God is aware of, knows, and sees everything down to the least detail that is done against the divine design.

When people are involved in evil, God does not hold them there; he holds them back from evil. He does not lead them; he struggles against them. He perceives the quantity and quality of evil and falsity from their constant wrestling, striving, struggling, fighting, and pushing back against his own good and truth, and therefore against himself. This comes from God's omnipresence in everything of his own design as well as his complete knowledge of everything in that design.

By analogy, when your ear focuses on harmony and on sounds that are in tune, and then something discordant or out of tune occurs, you notice precisely how wrong and how far off it is. A similar awareness occurs when you focus on some pleasure and then some unpleasant sensation interrupts.

By the same token, when your sight focuses on something beautiful, your appreciation of it is heightened if there is something misshapen beside it; this is why painters often place an unpleasant face next to a beautiful one. The same thing happens with goodness and truth. When evil and falsity struggle against good and truth, we perceive the evil and the falsity distinctly by contrast.

Everyone who focuses on goodness can sense evil, and everyone who focuses on truth can see falsity. The reason is that goodness is actually in the warmth of heaven and truth is in its light, while evil is in the coldness of hell and falsity is in its darkness. An illustration of this is that the angels of heaven are capable of seeing what goes on in hell and what type of monsters are there; but the spirits of hell are completely unable to see what goes on in heaven. They cannot see the angels any more than a blind person could, or more than an eye would see something by looking into empty air or ether.

Those who have the light of wisdom in their intellects are like people standing on a mountain in the middle of the day clearly seeing everything below. Those who have an even higher light are like people with telescopes who can see things off in the distance or far below as if they were close at hand. Those, however, who have defended falsities and are therefore in the faint, deceptive light of hell are like people on the same mountain at night with oil lamps in their hands who can see only what is nearby and even then can barely make out vague shapes or tell colors apart.

Some people have some light of truth but still have evil in their lives. As they go on loving and enjoying their particular evil, at first they view things that are true more or less the way a bat views towels on a clothesline in a garden—it flies to them as a safe haven. Later on these people become like night birds, and then at length like horned owls. Then they become like a chimneysweep stuck in a dark chimney; when he raises his eyes, he sees the sky through the smoke; when he looks down he sees the hearth from which the smoke ascends.

62   Keep in mind, however, that it is one thing to sense things that are opposite and another to sense things that are related. Opposites are things that stand outside and against the things that are inside. Something opposite first arises where one thing completely stops being anything and something else then arises that tries to act against the first thing, like one gear that opposes another gear, or a current that goes against another current. Related things, however, have to do with the arrangement of many different elements into a design so that they work together in harmony—for example, the gems of different colors in the sash across a queen's chest, or the multicolored flowers used in a garland to please the eye. Each side, then, contains things that are related to each other. The side of good contains things that are related to each other, and so does the side of evil; the side of truth contains things that are related to each other, and so does the side of falsity. Things related to each other exist in heaven and they exist in hell, but the things related to each other in hell are all opposite to the things related to each other in heaven.

Now, because God is aware of, sees, and knows all related things in heaven based on the divine design in which he himself is, and as a result he is aware of, sees, and knows all the opposing related things in hell, as follows from what was just said, therefore it is clear that God is just as omniscient in hell as he is in heaven. He also has full knowledge of people in the world. He is aware of, sees, and knows our evils and falsities from the goodness and truth that he is in and that are essentially him. As the Word says, "If I ascend into the heavens, you are there. If I lie down in hell, behold, you are there" (Psalms 139:8). Elsewhere it says, "If they dig through into hell, from there my hand will take them" (Amos 9:2).

5. *God is omnipresent in his design from beginning to end.* God's omnipresence in his design from beginning to end is a function of the heat and light from the sun that surrounds God in the spiritual world. The divine design was created through this sun. From it God sends forth a heat and a light that pervade the universe from beginning to end. That heat and that light give life to humankind and to every animal. They also produce the plant soul[175] that every plant in the world possesses. The two flow into every single thing and cause it to live and grow according to the design assigned to it upon creation.

Because God is not extended[176] and yet fills all things throughout the universe that are extended, he is omnipresent. I have shown elsewhere that God is in all space independently of space, and in all time independently of time [§30], and therefore the universe in its essence and design *is* the fullness of God.[177] Therefore he senses all things through his omnipresence, he provides all things through his omniscience, and he produces all things through his omnipotence. Clearly then, omnipresence, omniscience, and omnipotence are one; each presupposes the next. Therefore they cannot be separated.

63

64 The divine omnipresence can be illustrated by the amazing way angels and spirits become present to each other in the spiritual world. Because there is no [physical] space in that world—there is only apparent space—an angel or a spirit can be visibly present with another in a moment, provided she or he comes into the same state of love and thought [as that other], since love and thought create the appearance of space.

All who are in the spiritual world have this way of becoming present. This became clear to me from the fact that I was able to see people from Africa and India nearby in that world, although we were many thousands of miles apart on earth. In fact, I was able to become visibly present with people on planets in this solar system and even with people on planets in other solar systems beyond this one.[178]

Through this method of being present not in a place but in the appearance of a place, I have spoken with apostles, and with deceased popes, emperors, and monarchs; with Luther, Calvin, and Melanchthon, the founders of the modern-day church;[179] and with others from distant regions. If angels and spirits have such a method of being present, surely an infinite divine presence exists throughout the universe.

The reason angels and spirits have this method of being present is that every feeling of love and every resulting thought in the intellect is in space independently of space and in time independently of time. Any one of us can think about a sibling, a relative, or a friend who is in the Indies, and then focus on those people as if they were present with us. We can also feel love for them on the basis of our memories. These phenomena, which are known to us, illustrate the divine omnipresence to some extent.

The divine omnipresence can also be illustrated by human thoughts. When we call to mind things we saw at this or that place while traveling, it is as if we are present in those places again.

Indeed, our physical eyesight emulates this presence. It is unaware of an object's distance except through things in between that provide a means of measuring. In fact, the sun itself would seem to be near to or even in our eye if things between us and the sun did not indicate that it is very far distant. People who have written on optics have recorded this phenomenon in their books.[180]

The reason why our minds as well as our bodies have vision that can be present in this way is that our spirit sees through our spiritual eyes. Animals do not have a similar mental presence, however, since they have no spiritual sight.

From all this it stands to reason that God is omnipresent in his design from beginning to end. That he is also omnipresent in hell was shown in the point before this one [§§61–62].

6. *Human beings were created as forms of the divine design.* We have been created as forms of the divine design because we have been created as images and likenesses of God, and since God is the design itself, we have therefore been created as images and likenesses of that design.

65

The divine design originally took shape, and it continues to exist, from two sources: divine love and divine wisdom. We human beings have been created as vessels for these two things. Therefore the design that divine love and wisdom follow in acting upon the universe, and especially upon the angelic heaven, has been built into us.

As a result, heaven in its entirety is a form of the divine design in its largest possible manifestation. In the sight of God, heaven is like one human being. The correspondence between heaven and a human being is in fact complete. There are no communities in heaven that do not answer to some part, some internal or external organ, of the human body. For this reason a given community in heaven is said to be in the province of the liver, the pancreas, the spleen, the stomach, the eye, the ear, or the tongue, and so on. In fact, the angels themselves know which specific area within a given part of the human body they inhabit. I was given an opportunity to learn about this from living experience. I saw a community of several thousand angels together in the form of one human being. From that experience it became clear to me that heaven as a whole is an image of God, and an image of God is a form of the divine design.

It is important to know that everything that radiates from the sun around Jehovah God in the spiritual world relates to humanness. Therefore all things that take shape in that world combine to make a human form, and at their deepest level present that form themselves. As a result, all the objects that take shape there before the eyes are symbolic of a human being.

66

There are animals of every kind in that world. They are likenesses of the feelings of love and the resulting thoughts that angels have. The same goes for the tree gardens, flower gardens, and lawns and meadows there. The angels are also given insights about what feeling this or that object represents. Surprisingly, when their inner sight is opened up they recognize an image of themselves in the things around them. This happens because all people are their own love and their own thought. In everyone there are a variety and multiplicity of feelings and thoughts, some of which relate to the feeling embodied in one animal, and some to the feeling embodied in another. Therefore images of the angels' feelings take shape in that way. There will be more on this topic in the part of this chapter on creation [§§75–80].

From all this the truth becomes clear that the purpose of creation was [to provide for] an angelic heaven from the human race—humankind as a resting place for God to inhabit. And this is why human beings were created as forms of the divine design.

67 Before creation, God was love itself and wisdom itself. That love and that wisdom had a drive to be useful. Without usefulness, love and wisdom are only fleeting abstract entities, and they do indeed fly away if they do not move in the direction of usefulness. The two prior things without the third [love and wisdom without usefulness] are like birds flying across a great ocean that eventually become worn out, fall into the ocean, and drown.

God created the universe so that usefulness could exist. Therefore the universe could be called a theater of useful functions. Because we, the human race, are the principal reason for creation, it follows that absolutely everything else was created for our sake. All aspects of the divine design have been brought together and concentrated in us so that God can perform the highest forms of useful service through us.

Without usefulness as a third party, love and wisdom would be as unreal as the heat and light of the sun would be if they had no effect on people, animals, and plants. That heat and that light become real by flowing into things and having an effect on them.

Another set of three things that follow in order is purpose, means, and result. The learned world knows that a purpose is nothing unless it has reference to an efficient cause or means;[181] and the purpose and the means are nothing unless there is a result. We can of course contemplate a purpose and the means of accomplishing it purely in our minds, but we still do so only for the sake of the result that the purpose intends and that the means make possible.

Likewise with love, wisdom, and useful service. Useful service is what love intends and what it occasions through the means. When useful service results, love and wisdom take on a real existence. In that useful service, they set up a place for themselves to live and stay, and there they rest as if they were at home. We are that way ourselves when God's love and wisdom are in us and we do something useful. The reason we were created images and likenesses of God, or forms of the divine design, was so that we would be able to do God's useful services.

7. *The more we follow the divine design in the way we live, the more we*   **68**
receive power against evil and falsity from God's omnipotence, receive wisdom about goodness and truth from God's omniscience, and are in God because of God's omnipresence. The more we follow the divine design in the way we live, the more power we receive from God's omnipotence to fight against forms of evil and falsity, because no one can resist evils or the falsities that go with them except God alone. All forms of evil and falsity are from hell. There they stick together as one thing, exactly the same way all forms of goodness and truth do in heaven.

As we said above [§65], to God the totality of heaven is like one human being. On the other hand, hell is like one giant monster. Going against one evil and its falsity is going against that whole giant monster of hell—no one can do it except God, because he is omnipotent.

Clearly then, unless we seek help from God Almighty we have no more power of our own against evil and falsity than a fish has against the ocean, or a gnat against a whale, or a piece of dust against a mountain that is falling on it. On our own, the power we have against evil is much smaller than the power a locust has against an elephant or a fly against a camel. Furthermore, our power against evil and falsity is even weaker because we are born into evil. Evil cannot act against itself.

Therefore we have to follow the divine design in the way we live. We have to acknowledge God, his omnipotence, and our resulting safety from hell, and do our part to fight against the evil that is with us; this acknowledgment and this fighting go together as part of the divine design. Otherwise we cannot help being plunged into hell and swallowed up; and once there, we cannot help being driven by evils, one after the other, like a little rowboat on the sea being pushed around by storms.

The more we follow the divine design in the way we live, the more wis-   **69**
dom about goodness and truth we receive from God's omniscience. This is because all love for goodness and all wisdom about truth come from God. To put it another way, all the goodness of love and all the truth belonging to wisdom come from God—all the churches in the Christian world profess that it is so. Therefore we cannot inwardly have any true wisdom except from God, because God has omniscience, that is, infinite wisdom.

The human mind is divided into three levels, just as the angelic heaven is. The mind has the capability of being raised to a higher level and to another level higher still. Then again the mind can be brought down to a lower level and to another level lower still. As our minds are raised to the higher levels, we come into wisdom, because we come into the light of heaven. The mind cannot be raised except by God. The more our minds are raised to heaven, the more human we are. The more our minds are brought down to the lower levels, the more we come into the faint, deceptive light of hell. There we are not human, we are animals. (This is why people stand upright on their feet and look with their faces toward the sky, and are even capable of looking directly overhead. Animals, however, stand on their feet with their bodies parallel to the ground, looking down to the ground with their whole head, and only with difficulty can they raise their heads toward the sky.)

[2] If we lift our minds to God and acknowledge that all true wisdom comes from him, and we also follow the divine design in the way we live, we are like someone standing at the top of a tall building, who looks out on a crowded city below and watches what is happening in the streets. If, however, we are utterly convinced that all true wisdom comes from ourselves, from our own earthly light, we are like someone at the bottom of that same tall building who lurks in a room below ground looking at the same city through little holes in the wall, able to see the wall of only one of the houses in the city and to examine how its bricks are mortared.

When God is the source we draw on for wisdom, we are like a bird flying high, looking around at everything in the gardens, forests, and villages, and flying toward whatever we need. When we ourselves are the source we draw on for things related to wisdom without believing that those things actually come from God, we are like a hornet that flies near the ground and, on seeing a dunghill, lands there and enjoys the stench.

As long as we are living in the world, we all walk midway between heaven and hell. Therefore we are in an equilibrium. We can freely choose to look either upward to God or downward to hell. If we look upward to God, we recognize that all wisdom is from God and that in our spirits we are actually with angels in heaven. If we look downward (as we inevitably do if we have false thinking from an evil heart), in our spirits we are actually with devils in hell.

70 The more we follow the divine design in the way we live, the more fully we are in God because of God's omnipresence. Because God is omnipresent he is intrinsically present, so to speak, everywhere in his divine design, in the sense that he is the divine design, as we showed above [§§52–53]. Now, because we have been created as forms of the

divine design, God is in us. But this is true only to the extent that we fully follow the divine design in the way we live. When we do not follow that design in the way we live, God is still in us, but is only in the highest parts of us, making it possible for us to understand what is true and intend what is good. That is, he gives us a capacity to understand and an inclination to love. The more we go against the divine design in the way we live, however, the more we bar the lower levels of our minds or spirits and prevent God from descending into them and filling them with his presence. As a result, God is in us but we are not in God.

There is a common saying in heaven: God is in all of us, the evil as well as the good, but we are not in God unless we follow the divine design in the way we live. The Lord says that he wants us to be in him and him to be in us (John 15:4).

[2] When we follow the divine design in the way we live we are in God, because God is omnipresent in the universe and in everything within it *at the inmost level,* since things on the inmost level are in the divine design. Things that go against the divine design are all outside that inmost level. On the outer levels God's omnipresence takes the form of an ongoing struggle with things that are against the divine design, and a constant effort to restore them to the divine design. The more we allow ourselves to be restored to the divine design, the more thoroughly present God is in each of us; consequently to a greater extent God is in us and we are in God.

It is no more possible for God to be absent from us than it is for the sun (through its heat and light) to be absent from our earth. The living things on earth, however, do not always feel the sun's power. To feel it, they have to receive both the heat and the light that radiate from the sun, as they do in spring and summer. [3] This situation is applicable to God's omnipresence as well. The more we are in harmony with the divine design, the more spiritual heat and light, or to put it another way, the more of love's goodness and wisdom's true perspective we have.

Spiritual heat and light are not, however, like physical heat and light. During the winters, the amount of physical heat available to the world and the objects in it diminishes. During the nights, the amount of light diminishes. This happens because the earth makes units of time with its rotations and its orbit. Spiritual heat and light do not behave the same way. Through his sun and its heat and light God is always present and does not go through changes the way the sun of our solar system appears to do. We ourselves turn away from God much the way the earth turns away from the sun. When we turn away from wisdom's true perspective we are like the earth turning away from the sun by night. When we turn away from the goodness of love we are like the earth turning away from the sun in winter. The useful effects of the sun in the physical world correspond in this way to the useful effects of the sun in the spiritual world.

71   To these points I will add three memorable occurrences.

The first memorable occurrence. Once I heard beneath me the sound of ocean waves. I asked what it was. Someone told me it was a riot that had broken out among the people gathered in the lower earth, a place just above hell.[182] Soon the ground under our feet, which served as a roof over the people there, began to yawn wide. Then I was stunned to see huge flocks of night birds soaring out of the chasm. As they flew on they fanned out to the left. Immediately after them, locusts sprang up onto the grass and turned it all into a desert. A little later I began to hear night birds screeching back and forth to one another, and over to the side an incoherent wailing as if there were ghosts in the woods.

Afterward I saw beautiful birds from heaven fanning out to the right. The distinguishing features of those birds were their golden wings, which were irregularly streaked and spotted with something like silver. On the heads of some were crown-shaped crests.

As I was watching all this with amazement, suddenly a spirit flew up from the lower earth where the riot was going on. He possessed the power to change his form into that of an angel of light.[183] He was shouting, "Where is the person who is talking and writing about the design God Almighty restricted himself to in relation to humankind? Down below we heard these things through the roof."

When he reached the ground he hurried along a paved road. As at last he drew near me, he suddenly disguised himself as an angel of heaven.

Addressing me in a tone that was not his own he said, "Are you the one who is thinking and talking about the divine design? Tell me briefly what the divine design is, and say a few things about it."

[2] "I'll give you a summary," I answered, "but I won't go into details, because you wouldn't understand."

Then I said, "One: God is the divine design itself. Two: He created humankind on the basis of his design and in keeping with it, and built that design into us. Three: He created our rational minds in imitation of the divine design in the whole spiritual world, and our bodies in imitation of the divine design in the whole physical world. This is why the ancients called a person both a heaven in miniature and a world in miniature.[184] Four: As a result, it is a law of the divine design that we are to rule our microcosm or physical-world-in-miniature from our microheaven or spiritual-world-in-miniature, just as God rules everything about the macrocosm or physical world from his macroheaven or spiritual world. Five: A law of the divine design following from this is that we are to bring ourselves into a state of faith by means of truths from the Word and bring ourselves into a state of goodwill by means of good actions; and this is how we reform and regenerate ourselves. Six: It is a law of the divine design that we are to use our own power and do our own work to purify ourselves from sins; we do not stand in impotent faith and wait for God miraculously to wipe them away. Seven: It is also a law of the divine design that we are to love God with all our soul and with all our heart, and to love our neighbor as ourselves. We are not to hang around and wait for God miraculously to put each love into our minds and hearts like putting bread from the baker in our mouths."

I said other things like that as well.

[3] To this the satan replied in a soothing voice that had pride behind it, "What are you saying? That on the basis of our own power we need to bring ourselves into the divine design by practicing its rules? Don't you know that we are not under the law but under grace? All things are given for free. We cannot take anything for ourselves unless it is given to us from heaven. In the spiritual arena we have no more ability to act on our own than Lot's wife, the statue; or Dagon, the idol of the Philistines in Ekron.[185] It is impossible for us to grant ourselves justification;[186] justification can be achieved only through faith and goodwill."

To the things he said I made only this one reply: "It is also a law of the divine design that by our own work and power we are to gain faith for ourselves by means of truths from the Word, yet we are to believe that our faith comes from God and not a grain of it from ourselves. Likewise, by our own work and power we are to become justified, yet we are to believe that our justification comes from God and not even a jot[187] of it from ourselves. We have been commanded to believe in God, to love God with all our strength, and to love our neighbor as ourselves. Think about it and tell me how God could command these things if we had no ability to obey and do them?"

[4] At that the satan's face changed. It went from white to a sickly yellow; then it soon turned completely black, and with a pitch-black mouth he said, "You're speaking paradoxes against our paradoxes!"

Then he immediately sank down toward his own people and disappeared. The birds on the left and the ghosts made strange sounds and then threw themselves into the sea that people there call the Reed Sea.[188] The locusts hopped along after them. The air and the land were cleansed of those wild things, and the riot below came to a stop. All became calm and serene.

72 *The second memorable occurrence.* Once I heard a strange murmur from far away. In my spirit I followed the path of the sound and moved closer to its source. When I reached it, to my surprise it was a group of spirits debating predestination and the [divine] assignment of spiritual credit or blame. They were Dutch and English, with a few spirits from other countries.[189] At the end of each piece of reasoning they were shouting, "We're amazed! We're amazed!"

The topic of the debate was this: "Why doesn't God assign his Son's merit and justice to all the people he has created and treat them all as redeemed? He is omnipotent. If he wants, can't he make Lucifer, the dragon, and all the goats into archangels?[190] He is omnipotent. Why does he let the Devil's injustice and ungodliness triumph over his Son's justice and the piety of those who worship God? It would be very easy for God to see all people as worthy of faith and therefore salvation. What would it take except a little word to that effect? If he doesn't do this, isn't he acting against his own words, which are that he wants the salvation of all and the death of none [Ezekiel 33:11]? Tell us, then: Where and what is the cause of damnation for those who perish?"

Then some Dutch person who believed in predestination, including the predestination of the fall of Adam [Genesis 3], said, "That decision is simply up to the Omnipotent One. Does the clay complain to the potter when he makes a chamber pot out of it?"

Another one said, "The decision regarding everyone's salvation is in God's hand, as a pair of scales is in the hand of someone weighing something."

[2] At the sides stood a number of people who were simple in faith and upright at heart. Some of these bystanders had bloodshot eyes, some seemed stunned, some seemed drunk, and some seemed to be suffocating. They were muttering to each other, "What have we to do with all this deliriousness? They believe that God the Father attributes his Son's

justice to whomever he wants, whenever he wants, and sends his Holy Spirit to give the rewards of that justice. This belief has made them stupid. To them it seems that in order to avoid claiming for ourselves even a speck of contribution to our own salvation, we must act in every way like a stone when we undertake to become justified, and like a piece of dead wood[191] in matters spiritual."

Then one of these bystanders pushed his way into the group and said in a loud voice, "Oh, you demented people! You are debating about goat's wool![192] Obviously you don't realize that God Almighty is the divine design itself and that the laws of the divine design are countless. Their number, of course, is the number of truths in the Word. God cannot act against those laws, because acting against them would be acting against himself. It would be acting not only against justice but also against his own omnipotence."

[3] The bystander looked over to the right and saw in the distance what looked like a sheep and a lamb, as well as a dove in flight. To the left he saw a goat, a wolf, and a vulture. He said, "You believe that God in his omnipotence could turn that goat into a sheep, that wolf into a lamb, and that vulture into a dove, or the reverse. Not so. Doing that is against the laws of his divine design, of which not even the tip of one letter[193] can fall to the ground, according to his own words [Luke 16:17]. How then could God put the justice of his Son's redemption into someone who is rebelling against the laws of his justice? How can justice itself commit the injustice of predestining anyone to hell, and throwing anyone into the fire beside which the Devil stands, lighting the torches that he holds? Oh, you demented people, empty of spirit! Your faith has led you astray. In your hands faith is like a trap for catching doves."

When he finished saying this, some sorcerer of the opposite belief made a kind of trap. He hung it in a tree and said, "Watch me catch that dove!"

Soon a hawk flew to the trap, stuck its neck in, and hung limp. The dove saw the hawk and flew away. The bystanders were amazed and shouted, "That *is* impressive—a just reward!"

The next day some people from the main group came to me—the group that believed in predestination and God's assigning of spiritual credit or blame. They said, "We are drunk in a way, not on wine but on the things that man said yesterday. He spoke about omnipotence and also about the divine design. He concluded that the design is as divine as omnipotence is. He even said that God himself is the divine design. He said that there are as many laws of the divine design as there are truths in the Word—not just thousands but millions—and that God is bound by

73

his laws in the Word as we are bound by ours. But what does that make divine omnipotence, if it is restricted by laws? It takes all the absoluteness out of omnipotence. Isn't God's power then less than the power of a monarch on a worldly throne? Monarchs can turn the laws of justice in another direction as easily as they turn the palms of their hands. They can have the absolute power of an Octavian Augustus; they can also have the absolute power of a Nero.[194] After we thought for a while about omnipotence bound by laws, we felt drunk and likely to lose consciousness if we didn't find some remedy very quickly.

"Our prayers have been said on the basis of our faith. We have prayed for God our Father to have mercy for the sake of his Son, believing that he could have mercy on whomever he wished, forgive the sins of whomever he pleased, and save whomever he wanted to. We wouldn't have dared take away in the least from his omnipotence. Therefore binding God with the chains of some of his own laws seems unspeakable to us, because it goes against his omnipotence."

[2] When they finished they looked at me and I looked at them. They appeared thunderstruck. I said, "I will take an appeal to the Lord and bring back a remedy to enlighten the issue. In the meanwhile, though, I'll resort to some examples.

"God Almighty created the world from the design in himself," I said. "The divine design in which he is and which he follows as he rules is something he built into the world. He endowed the universe and everything in it with its own design. Human beings have theirs, animals theirs, birds and fish theirs, insects theirs; every species of tree, even every type of grass has its own design.

"As examples to provide enlightenment, I'll briefly give the following. There are laws of the divine design imposed on human beings that indicate that we are to acquire truths from the Word for ourselves and that we are to base our thinking on them in an earthly way and, as much as we can, in a rational way. This is how we develop an earthly faith for ourselves. On God's side, there are laws of the divine design dictating that he is to come closer, fill those truths with his own divine light, take our earthly faith, which is only knowledge and persuasion, and fill it with a divine essence. This is the only way for faith to become capable of saving. There is a similar process for developing goodwill.

"Let's list some other points briefly. According to God's laws, he can forgive us our sins only to the extent that we follow our laws and stop doing them. God cannot regenerate us spiritually beyond the point to which we, following our laws, have regenerated ourselves in an earthly way. God makes an unceasing effort to regenerate us and save us, but he cannot do it unless we prepare ourselves as a vessel, leveling a pathway for God [Isaiah 40:3–4] and opening the door [Revelation 3:20]. A suitor cannot enter his beloved's bedroom before she becomes his bride—she locks the door and keeps the key with her. After she has become a bride, though, she gives her bridegroom the key. [3] Even for all God's omnipotence, he could not have redeemed humankind unless he had become human. He could not have made his human nature divine unless it was first like a human being as an infant and then like a human being as a child. Later his human nature also needed to form itself into a vessel and a dwelling place for his Father to enter, which he did by fulfilling everything in the Word, meaning all the laws of the divine design in it. The more he completed this process, the more he united himself to the Father and the Father united himself to him.

"However, these are just a few points I bring up for the sake of illustration, so that you can see that divine omnipotence exists within the divine design and follows that design in its governing called providence. Constantly and to eternity divine omnipotence acts in accordance with the laws of its own design. God cannot act against them or change even the tip of one letter of them, because he *is* the divine design along with all its laws."

[4] After I finished speaking, a bright, golden-colored light flowed in through the roof and formed angel guardians[195] flying in the air. The redness in the light lit up the temples of some of the people, but only toward the backs of their heads, not yet near their foreheads, because they were muttering, "We still don't know what omnipotence is."

"It will be revealed," I said, "but only after the things I have already said gain more light in you."

The third memorable occurrence. Far away I saw a large crowd of people wearing hats. Some had hats covered in silk; they belonged to the ecclesiastical class. Some had hats whose rims were decorated with golden bands; they belonged to the class of ordinary citizens. Both groups were educated and scholarly. I also saw some people wearing caps; they were uneducated.[196]

I moved in the direction of these people and heard them talking with each other about limitless divine power. They were saying, "If divine power followed laws that were created as part of the divine design, it would be limited, not unlimited. It would be power, but not all power. Anyone can see that no compulsion by law could force omnipotence to act this way and not that way. When we think about omnipotence and at the same time about laws of the divine design that omnipotence would be obliged to follow, our preconceived ideas about omnipotence are jarred, like a hand on a broken walking stick."

[2] When the crowd noticed me nearby, some members of it hurried over and asked me quite forcefully, "Are you the one who has confined God in laws like chains? The outrage! You have ripped apart the belief on which we base our salvation. At the heart of our belief we place the justice of the Redeemer. On top of that is the omnipotence of God the Father. As an appendix we add the actions of the Holy Spirit and its effectiveness in the spiritual arena, where we are completely powerless. It is enough, then, to mention the absolute justification that our faith entails because God is omnipotent. I[197] have heard, though, that you see emptiness in our belief because you see nothing of the divine design for human response in it."

When they finished I opened my mouth and spoke in a loud voice, saying, "Learn what the laws of the divine design are, and then investigate the full ramifications of your belief. You will see a great wasteland and a long, twisted leviathan[198] there with nets wrapped around it in an inextricable knot. Do what we read Alexander did when he saw the Gordian knot. To undo its bends, he drew his sword, cut the knot in two, threw it on the ground, and crushed its fibers with his heel."[199]

[3] When the people in the crowd heard this, they were biting their tongues. They wanted to give me a tongue-lashing, but they did not dare, because they saw heaven open above me and heard a voice out of it that said, "First control yourselves and learn about the divine design and the laws of that design that God Almighty follows in his actions. God created the universe from himself as the design; he created it according to the design, for the sake of the design. He created human beings in a similar way and built the laws of his divine design into us. Because of those laws we were created as images and likenesses of God. In brief, the laws are that we must believe in God and love our neighbor. The more we do these two things with our earthly power, the more we make ourselves a vessel for the divine omnipotence, and God connects himself to us and us to himself. As a result, our faith becomes living and effective for our salvation. Our action becomes goodwill, again in a form living and effective for our salvation.

"It is important to know, though," the voice continued, "that God is always present, constantly at work and making an effort in us. He even influences our free choice. He never violates it, however, because if he did, we would lose our dwelling in God; there would remain only a dwelling for God in us, as there is for all things on earth, all things in heaven, and even for the things that are in hell. From God we get our power, our will, and our ability to understand. There is no reciprocal dwelling for us in God, though, unless we live by the laws of the divine design given in the Word. Then we become images and likenesses of him; then paradise is given to us for a possession, and the fruit of the tree of life for food.

"The rest of us gather around the tree of the knowledge of good and evil, speak with the serpent there, and eat. Later we are expelled from paradise. Nevertheless God does not abandon us; we abandon God."

[4] The people in hats understood this and gave their approval, but the people in caps denied it;[200] they said, "In that case wouldn't omnipotence be limited? But limited omnipotence is a contradiction."

I replied, "There is no contradiction in acting all-powerfully with judgment in following the laws of justice, or the laws of wisdom inscribed on love. The contradiction arises when you think God can act against the laws of his own justice and love, which would not be acting with judgment or with wisdom. Your belief entails a contradiction like that: on the basis of grace alone, God can justify unjust people and bestow on them all the gifts of salvation and all the rewards of life.

"I will briefly state what God's omnipotence is. God used his omnipotence to create the universe. As he did so, he built his own design into each and every thing. God also uses his omnipotence to maintain the universe. He forever guards its design and its laws. When anything falls away from his design, he brings it back into the design and reintegrates it.

"God also used his omnipotence to establish the church. He revealed the laws of its design in the Word. When the church slipped away from the divine design, he restored it. When it fell completely out of the divine design, he came down into the world. Through the human manifestation that he took on, he clothed himself with omnipotence and reestablished the church.

[5] "God uses his omnipotence and also his omniscience to examine us all after death. He prepares the just, the sheep, for their places in heaven; by assigning them places he builds heaven. He prepares the unjust, the goats, for their places in hell; by assigning them places he builds hell.[201] He arranges heaven into communities and hell into hordes according to all the different loves their inhabitants have. In heaven there are as many varieties of love as there are stars in the sky above the earth.

He unites the communities of heaven so that they are like one person before him. Likewise he brings the hordes of hell together so they are like one devil. He separates hell from heaven with a great chasm, so that hell will not inflict violence on heaven and heaven will not inflict torment on hell. (The more heaven flows in, the more those in hell are tormented.) If God were not using his omnipotence in every moment to do all the above, so much wildness would come over people that they could never be restrained by the laws of any design and the human race would perish. This and more would happen if God were not the divine design and were not omnipotent in his design."

When they heard this, the people who had been wearing hats left with them under their arms, praising God.

In the spiritual world the intelligent wear hats. The unintelligent wear caps because they are bald; their baldness means that they are dense. The people with caps went away to the left, but the people with hats went to the right.

The Creation of the Universe

75 Because this first chapter is on God the Creator, there should also be some mention of his creation of the universe, just as the next chapter on the Lord the Redeemer also needs to address redemption. We cannot, however, get a fair idea of the creation of the universe unless some preliminary global concepts first bring our intellect into a state of perception. These global concepts are as follows:

[2] (1) There are two worlds: a spiritual world where there are angels and spirits, and a physical world where there are people.

(2) Both worlds have suns. The sun in the spiritual world is pure love from Jehovah God, who is within that sun. The spiritual sun radiates heat and light. The essence of the heat it radiates is love, and the essence of the light is wisdom. That heat and that light have an effect on people's wills and intellects. The heat affects the will; the light affects the intellect.

The sun in the physical world is pure fire. As a result, the heat and the light from it are dead. Physical heat and light serve as a clothing for spiritual heat and light and as a device through which spiritual heat and light reach people.

[3] (3) In the spiritual world both the heat and the light that radiate from the sun are substantial and are called spiritual. So are all the things in that world that come about from that heat and light.

In the physical world, these two comparable things, the heat and the light, that radiate from this sun are material and are called physical. So are all the things in this world that come about from this heat and light.

[4] (4) In both worlds there are three levels. They are called vertical levels. These result in the three areas where the three angelic heavens are set up. They also result in the three levels of the human mind, which correspond to the three angelic heavens. Everything else both here and there also has three levels.

[5] (5) There is a correspondence between things in the spiritual world and things in the physical world.

[6] (6) There is a design that has been built into each and every thing in each world.

[7] (7) First we need to get an overall idea about the above. Otherwise the human mind, in its utter ignorance of all this, easily slips into the idea that the universe was created by nature; and only out of respect for the authority of the church will it say that nature was created by God. If people do not know how God created nature, when they take a deep look at the subject they slip headfirst into a materialist philosophy that denies God.

Now, because it would take a large volume to lay out and properly demonstrate these seven points one by one, and because a section on that topic would not be integral to the theological system laid out in this book, I want to present only some memorable occurrences.[202] From these an idea of how God created the universe can be conceived, and after conception some offspring representing that idea can be born.

The first memorable occurrence. One day I was in a meditation on the creation of the universe. Angels who were above me to the right noticed my meditation. Their region had had a number of meditations and debates on that same subject. Therefore one of them came down and invited me to join them. I came into my spirit[203] and accompanied the angel.

After I entered their community I was brought to its leader. In the leader's court I saw a gathering of about a hundred, with the leader in the middle. One of them said, "We became aware up here that you were meditating on the creation of the universe. A number of times we have been in similar meditations, but were unable to come to a conclusion. This was because there was an idea stuck in our minds—an idea of chaos as a great egg from which everything in the universe hatched in

76

sequence.[204] Now, however, we see that the universe is too large to have hatched in this way. There was another idea stuck in our minds as well: that God created everything out of nothing.[205] Now we realize that nothing is made of nothing. Nevertheless our thinking has not yet been able to evolve far enough beyond these two ideas to see with any illumination how creation actually came about. For that reason we called you away from where you were in hopes that you would disclose your meditation on the subject."

[2] Hearing that, I replied, "I will indeed.

"For a long time I meditated on this without success," I went on.[206] "Later, when the Lord sent me into your world,[207] I became aware of the futility of drawing any conclusions about the creation of the universe without first knowing several facts: There are two worlds: the one in which there are angels, and the other in which there are people. Through death people cross over from their own world into the other world. Then I also saw that there are two suns.[208] All spiritual things flow forth from one of them; all physical things from the other. The sun that all spiritual things flow from consists of pure love from Jehovah God; he is within that sun. The sun that all physical things flow from consists of pure fire.

"After I realized this, on one occasion when I was in a state of enlightenment I was granted the insight that the universe was created by Jehovah God through the sun that surrounds him. Because love does not exist apart from wisdom, I could also see that the universe was created by Jehovah God from his love through his wisdom. Since then, everything I have seen in the world where you are and everything I have seen in the world where I am in my body convinces me of the truth of this.

[3] "It would take too long to lay out the way creation progressed from the very beginning; but when I was in a state of enlightenment I saw that there were spiritual atmospheres that were created by means of the heat and light from the sun in your world. At their core those atmospheres are substantial. Each one led to the next. Because there were three of these atmospheres, and therefore three levels of them, three heavens were made—one for angels who are at the highest level of love and wisdom, another for angels at the second level, and a third for angels at the lowest level.

"This spiritual universe could not exist, however, without a physical universe in which it could accomplish its useful effects. Therefore at the same time a sun was created as the source of all things physical. Through this sun by means of its heat and light three atmospheres were created to surround those prior atmospheres the way a nutshell surrounds a kernel or the inner bark of a tree surrounds the wood. Finally, through these atmospheres the globe of lands and seas was created. Here people, animals, and fish, and trees, bushes, and plants were created out of earthly materials consisting of soils, stones, and minerals.

[4] "This is only a very general sketch of creation and its stages. The particular and individual stages could not be explained without filling volumes of books. They would all come to the following conclusion, though: that God did not create the universe out of nothing. As you said, nothing is made out of nothing. God created the universe through the sun in the angelic heaven—a sun that comes from his underlying reality and is therefore pure love together with wisdom. The universe, meaning both worlds (the spiritual and the physical), was created out of divine love through divine wisdom, as every single thing in it witnesses and attests. If you consider phenomena in the universe in a coherent and sequential way and set them in the light you already possess in your intellectual perceptions, you will see this clearly.

"You must keep in mind, though, that the love and the wisdom that become one in God are not love and wisdom in the abstract. Think of them as a substance in him. God is the absolute, the first, and the only substance or essence that exists in itself and subsists of itself.

[5] "That everything is created out of divine love and wisdom is the meaning of the following words in John: 'The Word was with God, and the Word was God. All things were made by it, and the world was made by it' (John 1:1, 3, 10). God there means divine love and the Word means divine truth or divine wisdom. In that passage the Word is called light. Light, when it is said of God, means divine wisdom."

After this, as I was saying goodbye, sparkles of light from the sun in that world came down through the angelic heavens into their eyes, and passed through their eyes into the dwellings of their minds. Enlightened in this way, they expressed agreement with what I had said. Afterward they accompanied me out to the entrance. My companion from before journeyed with me to the house where I was,[209] and then went back up to his community.

The second memorable occurrence. Early one day, after I had emerged from sleep but was still not fully awake, I was meditating in the light of the cloudless morning, when through the window I saw something like lightning flashing and heard something like a peal of thunder.[210] As I was wondering what was going on, I heard from heaven that there were some not far from me who were aggressively debating about God and nature. The flashes of light like lightning and the rumble in the air like thunder were correspondences manifesting the conflict and clashing of the arguments. One side was for God, the other for nature.

This spiritual confrontation arose in the following way. Some satans in hell had said to each other, "I wish we could talk to angels from heaven. We could fully and completely demonstrate to them that what they call God, the source of all things, is actually nature. God is only a word, unless it means nature."

Because the satans believed this with all their heart and soul, and because they longed to talk with angels from heaven, they were given permission to come up from the mud and darkness of hell and speak with two angels who were just then coming down from heaven. [2] The satans were in the world of spirits, which is midway between heaven and hell.[211] Once they spotted the angels, the satans hurried rapidly toward them.

With voices full of rage the satans began shouting, "Are you the angels of heaven we are allowed to meet face to face to debate God and nature? They call you wise for acknowledging God, but actually you are complete idiots. Who has seen God? Who understands what God is? Who grasps the idea that God rules and has power over the universe and everything in it? Only the lower classes would acknowledge something they don't see or understand. What is more obvious than the fact that nature is the all in all? What eye has seen anything but nature? What ear has heard anything but nature? What nose has smelled anything but nature? What tongue has tasted anything but nature? What hand or body has felt anything but nature? Our physical senses are our witnesses to truth. We swear on the testimony of our senses. Our breathing is another witness—the respiration that keeps our body alive. What do we breathe but nature? Our heads and yours are in nature. Where does the inflow into the thoughts in our heads come from if not from nature? If nature were taken away, could you think at all?" And many other arguments made out of the same ingredients.

[3] After the satans finished, the angels answered, "You speak that way because you trust your senses alone. All the spirits in hell enmesh their thinking in their physical senses. They cannot lift their minds above their senses. So we forgive you. A life of evil and a belief in falsity have closed off the inner realms of your minds so completely that you cannot be lifted above sensory input—unless you happen to be in a state that is remote from the evils in your life and the falsities in your belief. A

satan who hears the truth can in fact understand it as well as an angel can; but the satan does not retain it, because evil erases truth and introduces falsity. We are aware, though, that you are in a remote state now and are able to understand the truth we are telling you. Pay attention, then, to what we are about to say.

"You used to be in the physical world," the angels continued. "You left that place and now you are in the spiritual world. Before now, did you know anything about life after death? You previously denied that there was a life after death. You put yourselves on a par with animals. Did you know anything before about heaven and hell? Did you know anything about the light and heat in this world? Do you realize that you are now above the realm of nature and no longer in it? This world is spiritual, and so is everything in it. Spiritual things are so far beyond physical things that not even the least bit of the nature where you used to be can flow into this world.

"Because you viewed nature as some god or goddess, you still view the light and heat of this world as nature's light and heat, although they do not belong to nature at all; in fact, what is light and warm in nature is dark and cold here.

"Did you know anything before about the sun in this world that provides our light and heat? Were you aware that this sun is pure love, while the sun in the physical world is pure fire? You realized that the sun of pure fire in the physical world was the origin and sustainer of nature. Did you realize that the sun of pure love in heaven is the origin and sustainer of life itself (which is love together with wisdom)? Nature, then, which you made into a god or a goddess, is clearly dead.

[4] "If you were granted protection, you could ascend with us into heaven. If we were granted protection, we could descend with you into hell. In heaven you would see magnificent and dazzling things. In hell we would see hideous and filthy things. This difference between heaven and hell exists because all who are in heaven worship God, while all who are in hell worship nature. The magnificent and dazzling things in the heavens correspond to feelings of love for good and truth. The hideous and filthy things in the hells correspond to feelings of love for evil and falsity. From all that we have said, then, make up your minds now about whether God or nature is the all in all."

The satans replied to this, "In our current state, from what we have heard we are able to conclude that there is a God; but when our enjoyment of evil preoccupies our minds we see nothing but nature."

[5] I could see and hear the two angels and the satans because they were standing not far from me. To my surprise, around them I saw many who had been famous scholars when they were in the physical world. I was amazed to notice that at one moment the scholars would stand beside the angels and the next moment beside the satans; they agreed with whomever they were standing beside.

I was told, "The changes in place the scholars make are actually the changes of state in their mind as they agree first with one side and then with the next. They are chameleons in their beliefs. What's more, we'll tell you a mystery. We have looked down into the world at famous scholars and have found that six hundred out of a thousand are for nature and the rest are for God. Furthermore, we found that the only reason there were even that many for God was that they often made statements based not on any comprehension but merely on their having heard that nature comes from God. Repeated statements based on something remembered give the impression of belief even when there is no thought or understanding there."

[6] Afterward the satans were granted protection and went up with the two angels into heaven. They did indeed see magnificent and dazzling things. Enlightened in the light of heaven there, they acknowledged that there is a God, that nature was created to serve the life that comes from God, and that nature of itself is dead. It activates nothing on its own; instead it is activated by life.

When they had seen and learned these things they went back down. As they went down, their love for evil returned. It closed off their intellect at the top and opened it up at the bottom; above it there appeared a dark shadow flashing with hellfire. The instant they set foot on the ground it opened up under them[212] and they fell back down to their own people.

78 *The third memorable occurrence.* The next day an angel from some community in heaven came to me and said, "In our community we heard that you were summoned to a community close to ours because you were meditating on the creation of the universe and that you talked to them about creation. At the time they agreed with what you told them; later it also made them very happy. Now I will show you[213] how God produced animals and plants of every kind."

The angel took me down to a huge green meadow and said, "Look around."

I looked around and I saw birds of gorgeous colors. Some were flying, some were sitting on trees, and some were down in the meadow plucking the petals off roses. Among the birds there were also doves and swans.

These things vanished from my sight and then I saw not far from me flocks of sheep and lambs and of kids and nanny goats. Around the flocks I saw herds of cattle and calves, as well as camels and mules. In a grove I saw deer with tall antlers and also unicorns.

After I had seen that, the angel said, "Turn your face to the east."

I saw a garden with fruit trees—orange trees, lemon trees, olive trees, grapevines, fig trees, pomegranate trees—and also shrubs with berries.

Then the angel said, "Now look to the south."

I saw crops of various kinds—wheat, millet, barley, and beans. Around them I saw flowerbeds of roses with beautifully varied colors. To the north, however, I saw woods full of chestnut trees, palms, linden trees, sycamores, and other leafy trees.

[2] When I had seen that, the angel said, "All the things you saw correspond to different feelings of love felt by the angels who are nearby."

He listed the feeling each thing corresponded to.

"In fact," he went on, "those things are not the only correspondences. Everything else that takes a visible form before our eyes is also a correspondence: our homes, the useful things in them, the tables and food, the clothing, and even the gold and silver coins. Likewise the diamonds and other jewels that adorn married and unmarried women in the heavens. From all the above we become aware of the quality of love and wisdom in each person. The things that are in our homes and support our usefulness there stay the same; but for people who wander from community to community, things like this change as the people's relationships change.

[3] "The purpose of showing you these things was for you to be able to see the whole of creation from a particular instance. God is absolute love and absolute wisdom. His love includes an infinite number of feelings. His wisdom includes an infinite number of perceptions. The correspondences of those feelings and perceptions are all the things that appear on earth. This is where the birds and animals come from. This is where the trees and shrubs come from. This is where the grains and crops come from. This is where the plants and grasses come from.

"God is not extended[214] but he is everywhere in what is extended. He is in the universe from beginning to end. Because he is omnipresent, correspondences of the qualities of his love and wisdom are found everywhere in the physical world. In our world, called the spiritual world, there are similar correspondences surrounding those who receive feelings and perceptions from God. The difference is that in our world God creates things of this kind in a moment to match the feelings of angels, while in your world things like this were originally created in a similar way but there was a provision for their perennial renewal from generation to generation; and so creation goes on.

[4] "The reason why there is instantaneous creation in our world while in yours there is a creation that continues across generations is that the atmospheres and soils in our world are spiritual while those in your world are physical. Physical things were created to cover spiritual things the way animal or human skin covers the body, inner and outer bark cover tree trunks and branches, membranes and meninges cover brains, sheaths cover nerves, coatings cover nerve fibers, and so on. For this reason all things in your world have constancy and perennially return."

Then the angel added, "Pass on what you have seen and heard here to the inhabitants of your world. Until now they have been in total ignorance about the spiritual world. Yet without being notified of it no one could even guess, let alone know, that in our world creation is still going on and that when God first created the universe something very similar to this happened in your world."

[5] After that we talked about a number of different things, eventually including hell. None of the things seen in heaven is seen in hell. Hell has only their opposites, because the feelings of love there, which are yearnings for evil, are opposite to the feelings of love the angels have. Around individuals in hell, and generally in the deserts there, there appear flying creatures of the night such as bats, screech owls, and other owls. There are also wolves, leopards, tigers, rats, and mice. There are poisonous snakes of all kinds, as well as dragons and crocodiles. Where there is any vegetation, brambles, stinging nettles, thorns, thistles, and certain poisonous plants spring up. Alternately the vegetation disappears and you see only stones in piles and swamps where frogs croak.

All the above are also correspondences, but correspondences to the feelings of love in hell, which as I said before are yearnings for evil.

These things in hell are not created by God. Where things like this exist in the physical world, they were not created by God either—all the things that God created and creates were and are good. As hell came into existence, hellish things came into existence on earth. Hell consists of people who turned away from God and became devils and satans after death.

But talking about horrible things began to hurt our ears, so we turned our thoughts away from them and recalled again what we had seen in the heavens.

The fourth memorable occurrence. Once when I was thinking about the creation of the universe, some spirits from the Christian world came up to me. Among philosophers of their day, they had been some of the most famous and were esteemed the wisest of all.[215]

"We noticed that you were thinking about creation," they said. "Tell us what your thinking is about that."

But I replied, "Tell me first what *your* thinking is."

One of them said, "My thinking is that creation comes from nature. Nature created itself. It existed from eternity, since there is no such thing as a vacuum—a vacuum is impossible.[216] What else except nature do we see with our eyes, hear with our ears, smell with our noses, or breathe with our chests? Because nature is outside us it is also inside us."

[2] When another philosopher heard this he said, "You mention nature and you make it the creator of the universe, but you don't know how nature produced the universe. I'll tell you. It rolled itself into vortices. They collided with each other much the way clouds do, or the way houses do when they collapse in an earthquake. As a result of that collision, denser substances gathered together to form the earth while more fluid substances separated from the denser material and came together to form oceans. Lighter substances separated out from the oceans to become ether and air, and the lightest of these was the sun. Haven't you noticed that when you mix oil, water, and dirt together they spontaneously separate and form layers one above the other?"

[3] On hearing this, another philosopher said, "You made that up! Everyone knows that the real origin of all things was a chaos that filled a quarter of the universe. In the middle of the chaos there was fire; around the fire was ether; around the ether was matter. The chaos developed cracks, and fire erupted through them like Etna and Vesuvius.[217] This resulted in the sun. Then the ether rolled out and poured all around. This resulted in the atmosphere. Finally the remaining matter formed a ball. This resulted in the earth.

"As for the stars, they are just light sources in the expanse of the universe. They arose from the sun and its fire and light. At first, you see, the sun was like an ocean of fire. In order not to set fire to the earth it pulled little shining flames out of itself and allotted them a place in the surrounding space. This completed the universe and produced its firmament."

[4] Then one person who was there stood up and said, "You are all wrong. You seem wise to yourselves and I seem simple to you, but in my simplicity I have believed and I still believe that God created the universe. Since nature is part of the universe, God then was also the Creator of all nature. If nature had created itself, would it have existed from eternity? What madness!"

As he was speaking, one of the so-called wise philosophers urgently pushed closer and closer to him. The philosopher brought his left ear right up to the speaker's mouth; his right ear was stuffed with a piece of cotton. He asked him what he had said, so the speaker repeated it again. Then the philosopher who had hurried forward looked around to see if there was a priest nearby; he noticed one beside the speaker. So the philosopher turned around and said, "I too confess that all nature is from God, but . . ." Then he left; and speaking in a whisper to his friends, he told them, "I said that because there was a priest nearby. You and I know that nature is from nature. That makes nature God, so that is why I said all nature is from God, but . . ."

[5] The priest heard what they whispered and said, "Your wisdom, which is purely philosophical, has led you astray. It has closed the inner realms of your minds so tightly that no light from God or his heaven can flow in and enlighten you. You have extinguished that light." Then he added, "Hold a debate and figure out among yourselves where your immortal souls come from. Do they come from nature? Were they together in that great chaos?"

So then the philosopher went to his colleagues and asked them to join him in unraveling this knotty question.

They concluded that the human soul is nothing but ether. Thought, they decided, is nothing but a modification in the ether caused by the light of the sun, and the ether is part of nature.

They said, "Everyone knows that we use air to speak. What is thought except speech in a still purer air called the ether? This is how thought and speech become one thing. We see this in human children. First they learn to talk. In the next phase they learn to talk to themselves, which is thinking. What else is thought, then, but a modification of the ether? What else is the sound of speech but a modulation of thought? On the basis of all this we conclude that the soul, where thinking happens, is part of nature."

[6] Other philosophers among them did not disagree but shed further light on the issue by saying, "Souls came into being when the ether in the great chaos formed a ball. In the highest realm the ether divided into countless individual forms. These forms pour down into people when they begin to think on a level that is purer than air. These forms are then called souls."

Another philosopher said, "I'll grant you that the individual forms made out of ether in the highest realm were countless. Nevertheless the number of people born since the world was created has exceeded the number of forms. How then could there be enough of these ethereal forms? So I thought to myself that the souls that go out through people's mouths when they die[218] come back to the same people after several thousand years. The people go back, therefore, and live a similar life to the one they had before. As we know, many of the wise believe in reincarnation and things like that."[219]

Other conjectures besides these were tossed out by the rest, but they were too insane for me to even mention.

[7] A few minutes later the priest came back. The philosopher who had previously said that God created the universe now told the priest what the group had decided about the soul.

In response the priest told them, "What you have said is exactly what you thought in the world. You don't even realize that you're not in that world—you are in another one called the spiritual world! All whose positions in favor of nature have limited them to their bodies and senses are unaware that they are not in the same world where they were born and raised. There they were in a body made of physical matter; here they are in a body made of spiritual substance. People made of spiritual substance see themselves and others around them in exactly the same way that people made of physical matter see themselves and others around them. This is because substance comes before matter.

"Since you think, speak, see, smell, and taste things in much the same way as you did in the physical world, you believe that nature is the same here. Nature in this world, though, is just as different and distant from the nature in that world as spiritual substance is from physical matter or something primary is from something secondary. As the nature in the world where you used to live is comparatively dead, so the positions you have taken in favor of nature have more or less killed you, at least in areas related to God, heaven, and the church, as well as in the realm of your own souls.

"Nevertheless the intellects of all people, the evil as well as the good, can rise all the way to the light where the angels of heaven are. There they can all see that there is a God and a life after death. They can see that our souls are not ethereal; they are not made out of the nature of the physical world; they are spiritual and therefore will live forever. Our intellects are capable of being in that angelic light as long as our physical loves[220] are removed—loves that belong to the physical world and favor it and its nature, and loves that belong to the body and favor it and its sense of self."

[8] At that point the Lord instantly removed loves like that from the philosophers, and they were allowed to talk with angels. From their conversation in that state they became aware that there is a God and that they were living after death in another world. They blushed with complete embarrassment and cried, "We have been insane! We have been insane!"

This was not, however, their own state, so after a few minutes it became tiresome and unwelcome to them. They turned their backs on the priest, not wanting to hear him talking anymore, and returned to their former loves, which were merely material, worldly, and bodily.

They headed off to the left, wandering from community to community. Eventually they came to a road where they felt a breeze that brought them pleasure in things they loved the most, so they said, "Let's take this road."

They took it and went downward. Eventually they came to spirits who felt pleasure in the same kinds of love and worse. Since those philosophers felt pleasure in doing evil things, and had in fact done evil things to many along the way, they were imprisoned and became demons. Then their pleasure turned into torment. Punishments and fear of punishment restrained them and reined them in from the former pleasure that constituted their nature.

They asked people who were in the same prison, "Are we going to live like this forever?"

Some answered, "We've been here for a number of centuries, and we'll be here forever and ever. The nature we developed in the world cannot be changed. Not even punishments can drive this nature out of us—if they do succeed in driving it out, after a little while it comes rushing back in again."

80 *The fifth memorable occurrence.* On one occasion a satan was allowed to come up from hell. A woman came with him. He came to the house where I was. When I saw them I closed the window, but I did talk to them through the glass. I asked the satan where he came from. He said he came from a group of his own people. I asked him where the woman was from. He gave the same answer.

She was part of a gang of sirens.[221] They have the ability to project images. They can give themselves looks, clothing, and accessories of any kind. On one occasion they give themselves the body of Venus; on another, they give themselves a gorgeous face, as if they were one of the Muses; on yet another, they array themselves as queens with crowns and robes and stride majestically, holding a silver staff. These are the characteristics of sirens in the world of spirits—they are whores who specialize in fantasy.

They project these images by thinking with the senses and shutting off any deeper level of thought.

I asked the satan whether this woman was his wife. He answered, "What is a wife? I don't know what that is. My community doesn't know what that is. She is my whore."

Then she aroused her man's lust—another thing sirens are very good at. So he gave her a kiss and said, "Ah, my female Adonis."[222]

[2] But now to something more serious. I asked the satan what his job was. He said, "My job is to be learned. Don't you see the laurel wreath on my head?" His Adonis used her skills to conjure up a laurel wreath, which she put on him from behind.[223]

"Since there is formal education in the community you come from," I said, "tell me what you believe, and what your colleagues believe, about God."

He replied, "Our God is the universe, which we also call nature. Our simple folk call the universe 'the atmosphere,' which they think of as the air. Our experts also call it 'the atmosphere,' but they include the ether in that. As for God, heaven, angels, and the like—many people in this world have much nonsense to say about them, but they are empty words. Those are imaginary things triggered by unusual weather phenomena and things in the sky that trick the eyes of many people here.

"All the things that are visible on earth were created by the sun. Winged and wingless insects are born every time the sun returns in spring. Because of the sun's heat, birds come together in love and reproduce. Because of the sun's heat, warm earth turns seeds into shoots and then into offspring in the form of fruit. Doesn't this mean that the universe is God? Surely then nature is a goddess, the universe's spouse, who conceives, bears, raises, and feeds all the things I just mentioned."

[3] I went on to ask what his community believes, and what he believes, about religion. He replied, "Because we are more learned than the average person, religion to us is nothing but an evil spell cast on the multitudes. To average people, religion is like an atmosphere surrounding their senses and imaginations. Pious images fly in that atmosphere like butterflies in the air. Their faith hooks these images together into a chain like a silkworm building a cocoon, from which it will then emerge as the king of the butterflies. The ignorant crowd loves images that transcend what can be sensed or thought. Why? Because they wish they themselves could fly. With religion they make themselves wings so they can rise up like eagles and boast to the inhabitants of earth, saying, 'Look at me!' We, on the other hand, believe what we can actually see and love what we can actually touch."

At that point he touched his whore and said, "I believe in this because I see it and I touch it. Those other charades we toss out our front windows, and we blow them away with our raucous laughter."

[4] Afterward I asked him what he and his colleagues believe about heaven and hell. With a loud, mocking laugh he replied, "What is heaven but the ethereal firmament at its highest points? What are the angels there but the spots that wander around the sun? What are the archangels but comets with a long tail on which a whole gang of them lives? What is hell but the swamps where people imagine the frogs and crocodiles to be devils? Anything beyond these ideas of heaven and hell is garbage introduced by some church leader to win glory from the ignorant population."

Now, the satan said all these things just as he had thought them in the world. He was unaware that he was living after death; he had forgotten everything he had heard when he first entered the world of spirits. So when he was asked about life after death he answered, "It is an imaginary thing. Perhaps some vapor rising off a cadaver in a grave in a kind of human shape, or else the idea of ghosts that people make up stories about—something like that brought the idea of life after death into the human imagination."

At that point I could no longer keep myself from bursting into laughter. I said, "Satan, you are beyond insane! What are you now? You are human in form. You can talk, see, hear, and walk. Call to mind that you once lived in another world that you have forgotten, and that you are now living after death. Recall that the way you talked just now was exactly the way you used to talk."

He was given recollection and he remembered. Then he felt ashamed and shouted, "I am insane! I saw heaven above and heard angels saying ineffable things, but it happened when I had just arrived here. Now I am going to remember this and go tell it to the colleagues I left behind. Perhaps they will be as embarrassed as I was."

He kept saying over and over that he would call his colleagues insane, but as he went down, oblivion drove the memory away. When he arrived below he became as insane as they were, and called what he had heard from me insanity.

This shows how satans think and talk after death. People who have made falsity so strong in themselves that it becomes their belief are called "satans." People who have made evil strong in themselves by living it are called "devils."

Chapter 2

The Lord the Redeemer

81 THE previous chapter was on God the Creator, and also included material on creation. This chapter is on the Lord the Redeemer, and also includes material on redemption. The following chapter is on the Holy Spirit, and will also include material on divine action.

By "the Lord, the Redeemer" we mean Jehovah in his human manifestation. In what follows, we will show that Jehovah himself came down and took on a human manifestation for the purpose of redeeming.

We speak of "the Lord" rather than "Jehovah" because Jehovah of the Old Testament is called "the Lord" in the New, as you can see from the following passages. In Moses it says, "Hear, O Israel, *Jehovah* your *God, Jehovah* is one. You are to love *Jehovah God* with all your heart and with all your soul" (Deuteronomy 6:4–5); but in Mark it says, "*The Lord* your *God* is one *Lord.* You are to love *the Lord* your *God* with all your heart and with all your soul" (Mark 12:29–30). Likewise in Isaiah it says, "Prepare a way for *Jehovah;* make a level pathway in the solitude for our God" (Isaiah 40:3); but in Luke it says, "I will go before the face of *the Lord* to prepare the way for him" (Luke 1:76). There are other instances elsewhere.

Furthermore, the Lord commanded his disciples to call him Lord [John 13:13]. Therefore this is what he was called by the apostles in their letters, and afterward what he was called in the apostolic church, as is clear from its creed, called the Apostles' Creed.[224]

One reason for this change of names was that the Jews did not dare to say the name Jehovah, because of its holiness. Another reason is that "Jehovah" means the underlying divine reality,[225] which existed from eternity; but the human aspect that he took on in time was not that underlying reality. The nature of the underlying divine reality or Jehovah was shown in the previous chapter, §§18–26, 27–35.

228

Because of this, here and in what follows when we say "the Lord" we mean Jehovah in his human manifestation.

The concept of the Lord has an excellence that surpasses all other concepts that exist in the church or even in heaven. Therefore we need to adhere to an orderly sequence, as in the following, to make this concept clear:

1. Jehovah, the Creator of the universe, came down and took on a human manifestation in order to redeem people and save them.
2. He came down as the divine truth, which is the Word; but he did not separate the divine goodness from it.
3. In the process of taking on a human manifestation, he followed his own divine design.
4. The human manifestation in which he sent himself into the world is what is called "the Son of God."
5. Through acts of redemption the Lord became justice.
6. Through these same acts he united himself to the Father[226] and the Father united himself to him, again following the divine design.
7. Through this process God became human and a human became God in one person.
8. When he was being emptied out he was in a state of progress toward union; when he was being glorified he was in a state of union itself.[227]
9. From now on, no Christians will go to heaven unless they believe in the Lord God the Savior and turn to him alone.

I need to address these statements one by one.

1. *Jehovah God came down and took on a human manifestation in order to redeem people and save them.* The belief among Christian churches nowadays is that God, the Creator of the universe, procreated a Son from eternity. That Son came down and took on a human manifestation in order to redeem people and save them. This belief is wrong, however. It spontaneously falls apart as long as our thinking focuses on the fact that there is one God. To sound reason it is worse than nonsense to think that the one God procreated some Son from eternity and that God the Father together with the Son and the Holy Spirit, each of whom is individually God, together make one God. This fiction completely vanishes like a shooting star in the air when the Word is quoted to show (a) that Jehovah God himself came down and became human and (b) that Jehovah God also became the Redeemer.

[2] As for the first point, the following passages show that Jehovah God himself came down and became human:

Behold, a virgin will conceive and bear a Son, who will be called *God with us.* (Isaiah 7:14; Matthew 1:23)

A Child is born to us; a Son is given to us. Authority will rest on his shoulder, and his name will be called Wonderful, *God,* Hero, *Father of Eternity,* Prince of Peace. (Isaiah 9:6)

It will be said in that day, "Behold, this is our God. We have waited for him to free us. This is Jehovah whom we have waited for. Let us rejoice and be glad in his salvation." (Isaiah 25:9)

The voice of one crying in the desert, "Prepare a way for *Jehovah;* make a level pathway in the solitude for *our God.* And all flesh will see it together." (Isaiah 40:3, 5)

Behold, the *Lord Jehovih*[228] is coming with strength, and *his* arm will rule *for him.* Behold, *his* reward is with *him;* like a *shepherd* he will feed his flock. (Isaiah 40:10–11)

Jehovah said, "Rejoice and be glad, daughter of Zion. Behold, I am coming to live in your midst." Then many peoples will cling to *Jehovah* in that day. (Zechariah 2:10–11)

I, Jehovah, have called you in justice; I will give you as a covenant to the people. *I am Jehovah. This is my name. I will not give my glory to another.* (Isaiah 42:6, 8)

Behold, the days are coming when I will raise up for David a righteous offshoot who will reign as king and execute judgment and justice on the earth. And this is his name: *Jehovah our Justice.* (Jeremiah 23:5–6; 33:15–16)

Then there are the passages where the coming of the Lord is called "the day of Jehovah," such as Isaiah 13:6, 9, 13, 22; Ezekiel 31:15; Joel 1:15; 2:1, 2, 11, 29, 31; 3:1, 14, 18; Amos 5:13, 18, 20; Zephaniah 1:7–18; Zechariah 14:1, 4–21; and elsewhere.

[3] That Jehovah himself was the one who came down and took on a human manifestation is clearly established in Luke, when it says, "Mary said to the angel, 'How will this take place, since I have not had intercourse?'[229] The angel replied to her, '*The Holy Spirit will descend upon you, and the power of the Highest will cover you;* therefore the *Holy One* that is born from you will be called *the Son of God*'" (Luke 1:34–35). In

Matthew it says that in a dream an angel told Joseph, who was betrothed to Mary, that the child that had been conceived in her was from the Holy Spirit. And Joseph did not have intercourse with her until she gave birth to a Son and called his name Jesus (Matthew 1:20, 25). The "Holy Spirit" means the divine power that radiates from Jehovah God, as we will see in the third chapter of this work [§§138–188].

Everyone knows that an offspring's soul and life come from its father, and the body comes from that soul.[230] To state it very openly, then, the Lord's soul and life came from Jehovah God; and because divinity cannot be divided, the Lord's soul and life was the Father's divinity itself. This is why the Lord frequently called Jehovah God his Father, and Jehovah God called the Lord his Son. What would be more absurd to hear therefore than the idea that the soul of our Lord came from Mary his mother? Yet this is the very thing that both Roman Catholics and Protestants are dreaming today,[231] and they have not been awakened by the Word yet.

The idea that it was some eternally begotten Son who came down and took on a human manifestation turns out to be utterly wrong, collapses, and vanishes in the face of passages in the Word like the following, where Jehovah himself says that he is the Savior and Redeemer:

83

> Am not *I Jehovah?* And there is no other God except me. I am a just God, and *there is no Savior except me.* (Isaiah 45:21–22)
>
> *I am Jehovah, and there is no Savior except me.* (Isaiah 43:11)
>
> *I am Jehovah, your God,* and you are not to acknowledge a God except me. *There is no Savior except me.* (Hosea 13:4)
>
> So that all flesh may know that *I, Jehovah, am your Savior and your Redeemer.* (Isaiah 49:26; 60:16)
>
> As for *our Redeemer, Jehovah Sabaoth*[232] *is his name.* (Isaiah 47:4)
>
> *Their Redeemer is strong; Jehovah Sabaoth is his name.* (Jeremiah 50:34)
>
> Jehovah, my rock and my Redeemer. (Psalms 19:14)
>
> Thus says *Jehovah, your Redeemer,* the Holy One of Israel: "I am *Jehovah, your God.*" (Isaiah 48:17; 43:14; 49:7)
>
> Thus said *Jehovah, your Redeemer:* "I, *Jehovah,* am the maker of all things. I alone [stretch out the heavens. I extend the earth] by myself." (Isaiah 44:24)

Thus said *Jehovah,* the King of Israel, and *its Redeemer, Jehovah Sabaoth:* "I am the First and the Last, and there is no God except me." (Isaiah 44:6)

You, Jehovah, are our Father; *our Redeemer* from everlasting is your name. (Isaiah 63:16)

"With the compassion of eternity I will have mercy." So says *your Redeemer, Jehovah.* (Isaiah 54:8)

You have redeemed me, *Jehovah of truth.* (Psalms 31:6)

Israel should hope in *Jehovah,* because with *Jehovah* there is compassion; with him there is the most *redemption.* He will *redeem* Israel from all its forms of wickedness. (Psalms 130:7–8)

Jehovah God and *your Redeemer,* the Holy One of Israel, *will be called God of all the earth.* (Isaiah 54:5)

From these passages and very many others, all who have eyes and open minds can see that God, who is one, came down and became human for the purpose of redeeming people. Anyone who pays attention to the divine sayings just quoted can see this as clearly as something in the morning light.

There are people, though, who are in the dark of night because they have convinced themselves that there was another god, eternally begotten, who came down and redeemed humankind. These people close their eyes to these divine sayings, and consider with eyes shut how to twist the sayings and apply them to their false beliefs.

84 God could not have redeemed people, that is, rescued them from damnation and hell, without first taking on a human manifestation.[233] There are many reasons for this; they will be disclosed step by step in what follows. Redemption was a matter of gaining control of the hells, restructuring the heavens, and then establishing a church. Despite his omnipotence, God could not accomplish these things except through his human manifestation, as one cannot do work without arms. In fact, in the Word his human manifestation is called the arm of Jehovah (Isaiah 40:10; 53:1). By analogy, one cannot attack a fortified city and destroy the temples of idols there without powerful means.

The Word as well makes it clear that having a human manifestation gave God the omnipotence to do this divine work. God is in the inmost and purest realms. There was no other way he could cross over to the lowest levels where the hells exist and where people were at that time, just as a soul cannot do anything without a body. By analogy, there is no way to overpower enemies who are not in sight and whom we cannot get close to with weapons such as spears, shields, or guns.

To redeem people without a human manifestation would have been as impossible for God as it would be for someone [outside India] to take control of people in India without sending in troops on ships.[234] It would be as impossible as growing trees on heat and light alone if air had not been created as a medium through which they travel and earth had not been created in which the trees could grow. In fact, it would be as impossible as catching fish by throwing a net in the air and not in the water.

Given Jehovah's inherent nature, despite his omnipotence he could not touch any individual devils in hell or any individual devils on earth and control them or their rage or tame their violence unless he could be as present in the farthest realms as he is in those closest to him. In his human manifestation he is in fact present in the farthest realms. This is why the Word refers to him as the First and the Last, the Alpha and the Omega, the Beginning and the End [Revelation 1:8, 11; 21:6; 22:13].

2. Jehovah God came down as the divine truth, which is the Word; but he did not separate the divine goodness from it. Two things constitute the essence of God: divine love and divine wisdom; or, what is the same, divine goodness and divine truth. (Above at §§36–48 we showed that these two constitute the essence of God.) The expression "Jehovah God"[235] in the Word means these two qualities. "Jehovah" means divine love or divine goodness; "God" means divine wisdom or divine truth. This is why these names occur in various ways in the Word. At times just Jehovah is named; at other times, just God. When the subject is divine goodness he is called Jehovah. When the subject is divine truth he is called God. When both are involved he is called Jehovah God.

It is clear from John that Jehovah God came down as divine truth, which is the Word:

> In the beginning was the Word, and the Word was with God, and the Word was God. All things were made by it, and nothing that was made came about without it. And the Word became flesh and lived among us. (John 1:1, 3, 14)

"The Word" in this passage means divine truth because the Word that exists in the church is divine truth itself. The Word was dictated by Jehovah himself, and what Jehovah dictates is pure divine truth—it cannot be anything else. [2] Nevertheless, because it passed all the way through the heavens into the world, it became adapted to angels in heaven and also to people in the world. As a result, in the Word there is a spiritual meaning in which divine truth is in the light and there is an earthly meaning in which divine truth is in shadow. The divine truth in this Word is what was meant in John.

This is clearer still from the fact that the Lord came into the world to fulfill all the things in the Word. This is why it says many times that this or that happened to him in order to fulfill Scripture [see §262]. Divine truth is precisely what "the Messiah" and "Christ" mean, what "the Son of Humankind" means, and what "the Comforter, the Holy Spirit" that the Lord sent after his death means. During his transfiguration on the mountain before his three disciples (Matthew 17[:1–13]; Mark 9[:2–13]; Luke 9[:28–36]) and also during his transfiguration before John in Revelation 1:12–16, the Lord represented himself as the Word, as we will see in the chapter below on Sacred Scripture [§222].

[3] From the Lord's own words it is clear that he was present in the world as divine truth: "I am the way, *the truth,* and the life" (John 14:6). This is also clear from these words: "We know that the Son of God came and gave us understanding so that we would know *the truth.* And we are *in the truth in the Son of God, Jesus Christ.* He is the true God and eternal life" (1 John 5:20).

This becomes still clearer from the fact that he is called the light, as in these passages:

He was *the true light* that enlightens everyone who comes into the world. (John 1:9)

Jesus said, "For a brief time *the light* is still *with you.* Walk while you have *the light* so the darkness will not overtake you. While you have *the light,* believe in *the light* so that you may become *children of the light."* (John 12:35, 36)

I am the light of the world. (John 9:5)

Simeon said, "My eyes have seen your salvation, *a light* of revelation to the nations." (Luke 2:30, 32)

This is the judgment, that *the light has come into the world. Those who do the truth come toward the light.* (John 3:19, 21)

There are other such passages as well. "The light" means divine truth.

86 Jehovah God came into the world as divine truth for the purpose of redeeming people. Redemption was a matter of gaining control of the hells, restructuring the heavens, and then establishing a church. Divine goodness does not have the power to do these things, but divine truth that comes from divine goodness does. In and of itself, divine goodness is like the round butt of a sword, like a blunted piece of wood, or like a bow by itself. Divine truth that comes from divine goodness is like a sharp sword, like a sharpened wooden spear, and like a bow with arrows, all three of which are effective weapons against enemies. In fact, swords, spears, and bows in the spiritual sense of the Word mean truths for battle (see *Revelation Unveiled* 52, 299, 436).

Nothing but divine truth from the Word could attack, conquer, and bring under control the falsities and evils that the entirety of hell possessed then and still possesses now. Nothing else could found, build, and organize a new heaven—another thing God did at the time. Nothing else could establish a new church on earth. Besides, all God's strength, force, and power belong to the divine truth that comes from divine goodness. This was why Jehovah God came down as divine truth, which is the Word.

This is why it says in David, "Gird your sword upon your thigh, O *Mighty One,* and in your honor arise, *ride on the word of truth.* Your right hand will teach you amazing things. Your arrows are sharp. Your enemies will fall beneath you" (Psalms 45:3–5). These statements concern the Lord, his battles with the hells, and his conquests of them.

Human beings provide an obvious example of the nature of goodness without truth as opposed to the nature of truth that is connected with goodness. All our goodness resides in our will; all our truth resides in our intellect. For all its goodness, our will cannot accomplish anything whatever without our intellect. It cannot function; it cannot talk; it cannot sense. All its force and power comes through our intellect, that is, through our truth, since the intellect is truth's vessel and its dwelling place.

The situation with our will and our intellect is similar to the functioning of the heart and the lungs in our bodies. When the lungs are not breathing, the heart is incapable of producing any bodily movement or sensation. What produces movement and sensation is the breathing of the lungs in connection with the heart. A proof of this is the loss of consciousness experienced by people who suffocate or fall in the water, when their breathing stops but the systolic activity of their heart continues. As we know, they lose sensation and the ability to move. Their condition is similar to embryos in mothers' wombs. The reason for it is that the heart corresponds to the will and its goodness, while the lungs correspond to the intellect and its truths.[236]

The power of truth is perfectly obvious in the spiritual world. Individual angels who have divine truths from the Lord, even if their physique is as feeble as that of a baby, can take on a whole squadron of infernal spirits that look like giants, like the Anakim and the Nephilim.[237] One angel can force such spirits to flee, chase them to hell, and push them down into underground caves there. Whenever those spirits come out of the caves they do not dare come near the angel.

In that world those who have divine truths from the Lord are like lions, even if in physique they are no stronger than sheep. Even in this world the same is true for people in relation to evils and falsities. People who have divine truths from the Lord have the power to fight devils who are in full battle formation. Essentially those devils are nothing but evils and falsities.

Divine truth has this kind of strength because God is absolute goodness and absolute truth. He created the universe by means of divine truth, and all the laws of the divine design through which he preserves the universe are truths. This is why it says in John, "All things were made by the Word, and nothing that was made was made without it" (John 1:3, 10); and in David, "By the Word of Jehovah the heavens were made, and all the host of them by the breath of his mouth" (Psalms 33:6).

88 Although God came down as divine truth, he did not separate the divine goodness from it. This becomes clear from his conception, about which we read that the power of the Highest covered Mary (Luke 1:35). "The power of the Highest" means the divine goodness.

This also becomes clear from the passages where the Lord says that the Father is in him and he is in the Father, that all things belonging to the Father are his, and that the Father and he are one, and so on. "The Father" means the divine goodness.[238]

89 3. *In the process of taking on a human manifestation, God followed his own divine design.* In the section on divine omnipotence and omniscience we showed that in the act of creating, God introduced his design into the universe as a whole and into each and every thing in it. Therefore in the universe and in all its parts God's omnipotence follows and works according to the laws of his own design. The treatment of those laws runs from §§49 to 74.

Now, because God came down, and because he is the design (as was also shown in that section), there was no other way for him to become an actual human being than to be conceived, to be carried in the womb, to be born, to be brought up, and to acquire more and more knowledge so as to become intelligent and wise. Therefore in his human manifestation he was an infant like any infant, a child like any child, and so on with just one difference: he completed the process more quickly, more fully, and more perfectly than the rest of us do.

This statement in Luke shows that he followed the divine design in his progress: "The child Jesus grew and became strong in spirit, and he advanced in wisdom, age, and grace with God and with humankind" (Luke 2:40, 52). Other statements about the Lord in the same Gospel make it clear that he grew up more quickly, more fully, and more perfectly than the rest of us; for example, when he was "a child of twelve, he sat and taught in the Temple in the midst of the scholars, and all who heard him were astounded at his insightful answers" (Luke 2:46–47). Likewise later on; see Luke 4:16–22, 32.

The Lord's life followed this path because the divine design is for people to prepare themselves to accept God; and as they prepare themselves, God enters them as if he were coming into his own dwelling and his own home. The preparation entails developing a concept of God and of the spiritual things related to the church—that is, developing intelligence and wisdom.

It is a law of the divine design that the closer and closer we come to God, which is something we have to do as if we were completely on our own, the closer and closer God comes to us. When we meet, God forms a partnership with us. The Lord followed this design even to the point of union with his Father, as we will show later on [§§97–99, 105–106].

People who do not know that the divine omnipotence follows and works according to the divine design are capable of hatching many concepts from their own imaginations that contradict and oppose sound reason. For example, they might wonder why God did not instantly take on a human manifestation without going through life stages. They might wonder why he did not create or assemble a body for himself from substances from all four directions of the world. If he had, he could have presented himself as a human God before the Jewish people and in fact before the entire world. Or if he had especially wanted to go through the birth process, why did he not pour his whole divinity into that embryo, or else into himself as a baby? Or right after he was born why did he not expand himself to the size of an adult and immediately start speaking divine wisdom? People who think of divine omnipotence without thinking of the

90

divine design are capable of conceiving and giving birth to these thoughts and others like them, and filling the church with craziness and garbage—which, of course, has actually happened.

Take for example the idea that God could procreate a Son from eternity and could arrange that a third God would then emanate from himself and his Son. Or the idea that God could be enraged at the human race and schedule it for destruction, but then be willing to be brought back to compassion by the Son through the Son's intercession and the Father's recollection of the cross. Not only that, but God could put his Son's justice into people and insert it into their hearts like Wolff's "simple substance," in which, as that author himself says, everything of the Son's merit exists, even though that substance cannot be divided, since divided it would collapse into nothing.[239] Then there is the idea that through a Papal bull God could forgive the sins of anyone he felt like forgiving and could purify utterly godless people of their black sins, thereby making dark devils shine like angels of light, while the godless people changed and developed no more than a stone would, but instead stayed as still as a statue or an idol.

People who fixate on divine, absolute power without recognizing or acknowledging any divine design are capable of scattering abroad these and many other insane ideas the way a winnower scatters chaff on the wind. On spiritual topics having to do with heaven, the church, and eternal life, people like this are prone to wander far from divine truths like a blind man in a forest who one moment trips over stones, the next knocks his head against a tree, and the next catches his hair in the branches.

91 The divine miracles followed the divine design as well; they followed the design of inflow from the spiritual world into the physical one. Until now no one has known anything about this design, however, because no one has known anything about the spiritual world. The nature of this design will be revealed in its own time, when I come to the discussion of divine miracles as opposed to magical miracles.[240]

92 4. *The "Son of God" is the human manifestation in which God sent himself into the world.* The Lord frequently says that the Father "sent" him, or that he "was sent" by the Father (for example, Matthew 10:40; 15:24; John 3:17, 34; 5:23, 24, 36, 37, 38; 6:29, 39, 40, 44, 57; 7:16, 18, 28, 29; 8:16, 18, 29, 42; 9:4; and very often elsewhere). The Lord says this because "being sent into the world" means coming down among people, which he did through the human manifestation he took on through the Virgin Mary.

The human manifestation really is the Son of God, in that he was conceived by Jehovah God as the Father, as it says in Luke 1:32, 35.

He is called "the Son of God," "the Son of Humankind," and "the Son of Mary." "The Son of God" means Jehovah God in his human manifestation. "The Son of Humankind" means the Lord in his role as the Word. "The Son of Mary" properly means the human manifestation he took on. Just below we will show that "the Son of God" and "the Son of Humankind" have the meanings just mentioned. As for "the Son of Mary" meaning just the human manifestation, this is obvious from human reproduction. The soul comes from the father, the body from the mother. The soul is in the father's semen; it is clothed with a body in the mother. To put it another way, everything we have that is spiritual comes from our father; everything physical comes from our mother.[241]

In the Lord's case, the divine nature he had came from Jehovah his Father; the human nature he had came from his mother. These two natures united together are "the Son of God." The truth of this is clearly substantiated by the Lord's birth, as recorded in Luke: "The angel Gabriel said to Mary, 'The Holy Spirit will descend upon you and the power of the Highest will cover you; therefore the Holy One that is born from you will be called the Son of God'" (Luke 1:35).

Another reason why the Lord described himself as "sent" by the Father is that "someone who has been sent" has a similar meaning to "an angel." The word "angel" in the original language[242] means "one who has been sent." [The Lord] is said to be [an angel] in Isaiah, "*The Angel of the Faces*[243] *of Jehovah* has freed them. Because of his love and his mercy he redeemed them" (Isaiah 63:9); and in Malachi, "Suddenly *the Lord* will come to his temple—the One you seek, *the Angel of the Covenant,* whom you desire" (Malachi 3:1); besides other passages.

Where we discuss the divine Trinity below in chapter 3 of this work [§§163–188] it will become clear that the divine Trinity—God the Father, the Son, and the Holy Spirit—exists within the Lord; the Father in him is the divinity he draws on, the Son is his divine human manifestation, and the Holy Spirit is the divine power that radiates [from him].

Since the angel Gabriel said to Mary, "The *Holy One* that will be born from you will be called the Son of God," I will now quote passages from the Word to show that the Lord in his human manifestation is called "the Holy One of Israel":

93

> I was seeing in visions, behold a Wakeful and *Holy One* coming down from heaven. (Daniel 4:13, 23)

> God will come from Teman, and *the Holy One* from Mount Paran. (Habakkuk 3:3)

I, Jehovah, am *holy*, the Creator of Israel, *your Holy One*. (Isaiah 43:15)

Thus said Jehovah, the Redeemer of Israel, *its Holy One*. (Isaiah 49:7)

I am Jehovah your God, *the Holy One of Israel, your Savior*. (Isaiah 43:1, 3)

As for our *Redeemer*, Jehovah Sabaoth is his name, *the Holy One of Israel*. (Isaiah 47:4)

Thus says Jehovah, your *Redeemer, the Holy One of Israel*. (Isaiah 43:14; 48:17)

Jehovah Sabaoth is his name, and *your Redeemer, the Holy One of Israel*. (Isaiah 54:5)

They challenged God and *the Holy One of Israel*. (Psalms 78:41)

They have abandoned Jehovah and provoked *the Holy One of Israel*. (Isaiah 1:4)

They said, "Cause *the Holy One of Israel* to cease from our faces." Therefore thus said *the Holy One of Israel*. (Isaiah 30:11, 12)

Those who say, "His work should go quickly so we may see it; and the counsel of *the Holy One of Israel* should approach and come." (Isaiah 5:19)

In that day they will depend on Jehovah, *on the Holy One of Israel*, in truth. (Isaiah 10:20)

Shout and rejoice, daughter of Zion, because great in your midst is *the Holy One of Israel*. (Isaiah 12:6)

A saying of the God of Israel: "In that day his eyes will look toward *the Holy One of Israel*." (Isaiah 17:7)

The poor among people will rejoice in *the Holy One of Israel*. (Isaiah 29:19; 41:16)

The earth is full of guilt against the Holy One of Israel. (Jeremiah 50:29)

Also see Isaiah 55:5; 60:9; and elsewhere.

"The Holy One of Israel" means the Lord in his divine human manifestation, for the angel says to Mary, "*The Holy One* that will be born from you will be called *the Son of God*" (Luke 1:35).

From the passages just cited that describe Jehovah as the Holy One of Israel, you can see that although the names are different, "Jehovah" and "the Holy One of Israel" are one.

Many, many passages show that the Lord is called "the God of Israel," such as Isaiah 17:6; 21:10, 17; 24:15; 29:23; Jeremiah 7:3; 9:15; 11:3; 13:12; 16:9; 19:3, 15; 23:2; 24:5; 25:15, 27; 29:4, 8, 21, 25; 30:2; 31:23; 32:14, 15, 36; 33:4; 34:2, 13; 35:13, 17, 18, 19; 37:7; 38:17; 39:16; 42:9, 15, 18; 43:10; 44:2, 7, 11, 25; 48:1; 50:18; 51:33; Ezekiel 8:4; 9:3; 10:19, 20; 11:22; 43:2; 44:2; Zephaniah 2:9; and Psalms 41:13; 59:5; 68:8.

In the Christian churches of today it is common to call the Lord our Savior "the Son of Mary"; it is rare for people to call him "the Son of God" unless they mean the eternally begotten Son of God. This is a result of Roman Catholics putting Mother Mary's sainthood above the rest and setting her up as the goddess or queen of all their saints.[244]

Yet in fact, in the process of being glorified the Lord put off everything from his mother and put on everything from his Father, as we will fully demonstrate later on in this work [§§102–103]. Because the phrase "the Son of Mary" has become a common expression on everyone's lips, many horrendous things have poured into the church. This is especially true of those who have not taken into consideration things said in the Word about the Lord—for example, that the Father and he are one, that he is in the Father and the Father is in him, that all things belonging to the Father are his, that he called Jehovah his Father, and that Jehovah the Father called him his Son.

The horrendous things that have poured into the church from our calling him "the Son of Mary" instead of "the Son of God" are that we lose the idea of the Lord's divinity and we lose everything in the Word that is said about him as the Son of God. Furthermore, this concept lets in Judaism, Arianism, Socinianism, Calvinism in its original form, and finally materialist philosophy.[245] Materialist philosophy brings with it the extreme position that the Son of Mary was Joseph's child, or that his soul came from his mother, and as a result he is called "the Son of God," but truly he is not. All people, both clergy and laity, should check to see whether the idea they have spawned and nurtured of the Lord as "the Son of Mary" is any different from the idea of him as a mere human being.

Already by the third century a concept like this was becoming prevalent among Christians, as the Arians were on the rise. To salvage divinity for the Lord, the Council of Nicaea[246] made up "the eternally begotten Son of God." Although it was a fiction, this concept did succeed at the time in elevating the Lord's human nature to something divine; and it still works for many even today. It does not work, however, for those who see the hypostatic union[247] as a union of two separate entities, one of whom is superior to the other.

94

What other outcome could this concept have but the destruction of the entire Christian church? The church is based entirely on worshiping Jehovah in human form; it is based on the Human God. The Lord states in many places that no one can see the Father, recognize him, come to him, or believe in him except through his human manifestation.[248]

If people do not do this, all the church's precious seeds turn into seeds of little value.[249] Olive seeds turn into pine seeds; seeds from an orange, a lemon, an apple, and a pear turn into seeds from a willow, an elm, a linden, and a holly; seeds from a grapevine turn into seeds from a swamp rush; and wheat and barley turn into chaff. In fact, all forms of spiritual food become like the dust that snakes eat. Our spiritual light then becomes nature's light; and in the long run it becomes the light of our physical senses, which is in reality a faint, deceptive light. Then we become like a bird that used to fly high but then its wings were cut off and it fell to earth; now as it walks around it does not see more than what lies at its own feet. Then when we think about the church's spiritual teachings that are necessary for our eternal life, our thoughts about them are no more than the thoughts of a jester. All this is what happens when we regard the Lord God, the Redeemer and Savior, as no more than the Son of Mary, a mere human being.

95 5. *Through acts of redemption the Lord became justice.* Christian churches nowadays say and believe that merit and justice belong to the Lord alone because of the obedience he gave in this world to God the Father and especially because of his suffering on the cross. They suppose, however, that the Lord's suffering on the cross was the act of redemption itself.[250] That was not in fact an act of redemption; it was an act of glorification of his human nature (see the discussion of redemption under the next subheading [§§114–137]). The acts of redemption through which the Lord made himself justice were these: carrying out the Last Judgment, which he did in the spiritual world; separating the evil from the good and the goats from the sheep;[251] driving out of heaven those who had joined the beasts that served the dragon [Revelation 13]; assembling a new heaven of the deserving and a new hell of the undeserving; bringing both heaven and hell back into the divine design; and establishing a new church. These acts were the acts of redemption through which the Lord became justice. Justice is following the divine design in all that one does, and bringing back into the divine design things that have fallen away from that design. Justice is the divine design itself.

These acts are meant by the following words of the Lord: "It is fitting for me to fulfill *all the justice of God*" (Matthew 3:15); also by these words in the Old Testament:

> Behold, the days are coming when I will raise up for David a *righteous* offshoot who will reign as king and execute *justice on earth*. And this is his name: *Jehovah is our Justice*. (Jeremiah 23:5–6; 33:15–16)

> I speak with *justice;* I am great in order to save. (Isaiah 63:1)

> He will sit on the throne of David to establish it with *judgment and justice*. (Isaiah 9:7)

> Zion will be redeemed with *justice*. (Isaiah 1:27)

Our contemporaries who hold high offices in the church describe the Lord's justice in a completely different way. In fact, they say that what renders the faith capable of saving is that the Lord's justice is written into us.[252] The truth is this: because of its nature and origin, and because in and of itself it is purely divine, the Lord's justice could not become part of anyone or produce any salvation any more than the divine life could, which is divine love and divine wisdom. The Lord does come into every one of us bringing his love and wisdom; but unless we are following the divine design in our lives, that life, although it may indeed be in us, makes no contribution whatever to our salvation. It gives us only the ability to understand what is true and do what is good.

Following the divine design in the way we live is following God's commandments. When we live and function in this way, then we acquire justice for ourselves; but we do not gain the justice of the Lord's redemption, we gain the Lord himself as justice. This is what the following passages mean: "Unless *your justice* is more abundant than that of the scribes and Pharisees,[253] you will not enter the kingdom of the heavens" (Matthew 5:20). "Blessed are those who suffer persecution for the sake of *justice,* for theirs is the kingdom of the heavens" (Matthew 5:10). "At the close of the age angels will go out and separate the evil from among *the just*" (Matthew 13:49), and elsewhere. Because the divine design is justice, "the just" in the Word means those who have followed the divine design in their lives.

The justice itself that the Lord became through acts of redemption cannot be ascribed to us, written into us, fitted into or united with us any

96

more than light can belong to the eye, sound can belong to the ear, will can belong to the muscles that act, thought can belong to the lips that speak, air can belong to the lungs that breathe, or heat can belong to the blood, and so on. These elements all flow in and work with our body parts but do not become part of them, as everyone intuitively knows.

We acquire justice the more we practice it. We practice justice the more our interaction with our neighbor is motivated by a love for justice and truth.

Justice dwells in the goodness itself or the useful functions themselves that we do. The Lord says that every tree is recognized by its fruit. Surely we get to know other people well through paying attention not only to what they do but also to what outcome they want—what they are intending and why. All angels pay attention to these things, as do all wise people in our world.

Everything that grows and flourishes in the ground is identified by its flowers and seeds and by what it is good for. All types of metal are differentiated by their usefulness, all types of stone by their properties. Every piece of land is assessed on the basis of its features, as is every type of food, and even every animal on land and every bird in the sky. Why not us?

The factors that give our actions their quality will be disclosed in the chapter on faith [see especially §§373–377].

97 6. *Through those same acts the Lord united himself to the Father and the Father united himself to him.* Acts of redemption brought about this union because the Lord performed these acts in his human manifestation. As he performed them, the Divine meant by "the Father" came closer to him, helped him, and cooperated with him. At last they forged so close a partnership that they were not two but one. This union is the "glorification" referred to in what follows.

98 The idea that the Father and the Son, meaning the divine nature and the human nature, are united in the Lord like a soul and a body is part of the modern-day church's belief and is based on the Word. Nevertheless barely five out of a hundred or fifty out of a thousand know it. The culprit is the doctrine of justification by faith alone.[254] Many clergy who seek a scholarly reputation to advance their careers and financial situations are focusing all their effort on this doctrine, to the point where nowadays it occupies and obsesses every square inch of their mind. This doctrine has intoxicated their thinking as if it were alcohol. Like drunks, then, they miss the most crucial element in the church, which is that Jehovah God came down and took on a human manifestation. Yet our partnership with God is possible only through this union [of Father and Son]; and our salvation is possible only through our partnership with God. Anyone who takes into consideration that God is everything to all heaven, everything to all the church, and therefore everything to all theology can see that salvation depends on our recognition and acknowledgment of God.

First we will show that the union of the Father and the Son, or the divine nature and the human nature in the Lord, is like the union of a soul and a body. Next we will show that that union is reciprocal.

The concept of a union like the one between a soul and a body was established in the Athanasian Creed—a creed accepted by the entire Christian world as its position on God. There we read, "Our Lord Jesus Christ is both God and a human being. Yet although he is both God and a human being, still he is one Christ, not two. He is one because the divine nature took on a human nature for itself. In fact, he is completely one; he is one person. As a soul and a body is one human being, so God and a human being is one Christ."[255]

Admittedly, people take this to be a union between an eternally begotten Son of God and a Son born in time; but God is one, not three. Therefore when this is taken to be a union with the one God from eternity then the position in the Athanasian Creed agrees with the Word.[256]

In the Word we read that the Son was conceived by Jehovah the Father (Luke 1:34–35). Since this was the origin of his soul and life, it says that he and the Father are one (John 10:30), and that those who see and know him see and know the Father (John 14:9). "If you had known me you would have known my Father also" (John 8:19). "Those who receive me receive the One who sent me" (John 13:20). The Word also says that he is close to the Father's heart (John 1:18), that absolutely everything the Father has belongs to him (John 16:15), that he himself is called Father of Eternity (Isaiah 9:6), and that he has power over all flesh (John 17:2) and all power in heaven and on earth (Matthew 28:18).

From these and many other passages in the Word we can clearly see that the union of the Father and the Son is like the union of a soul and a body. For this reason even in the Old Testament he is often named Jehovah, Jehovah Sabaoth, and Jehovah the Redeemer (see §83 above).

99　This union is also reciprocal, as the following passages in the Word clearly show:

> Philip, do you not believe that I am in the Father and the Father is in me? Believe me that I am in the Father and the Father is in me. (John 14:10, 11)

> So that you will know and believe that the Father is in me and I am in the Father. (John 10:38)

> So that all may be one as you, Father, are in me and I am in you. (John 17:21)

> Father, all that is mine is yours, and all that is yours is mine. (John 17:10)

The union is reciprocal because no union or partnership between two exists unless each party moves closer to the other. Every partnership in the entirety of heaven, in all world, and throughout the human form is the result of two parties moving into a closer relationship with each other until both parties intend the same things. This leads to a similarity, harmony, unanimity, and agreement in every detail between the parties.

This is how our soul and our body form a partnership with each other. This is how our spirit forms a partnership with the sensory and motor organs of our body. This is how our heart and our lungs form a partnership. This is how our will and our intellect form a partnership. This is how all our parts and organs form partnerships, both within themselves and with each other. This is how the minds of people who deeply love each other form a partnership. It is an integral part of all love and friendship. Love wants to love and it wants to be loved.

In the world, too, all things that are inseparably linked to each other have a reciprocal interaction. There is an interaction like this between the heat of the sun and the heat in a piece of wood or a rock, and in living things between their vital heat and the heat in all their tissues. There is a similar interaction between the earth[257] and a root, through the root with the tree, and through the tree with the fruit. Also like this is the relationship of a magnet to a piece of iron, and so on.

If a given partnership is not the result of two things moving closer to each other in a mutual and reciprocal way, then a partnership develops that is only superficial rather than deep. In time, the partners in a superficial relationship drift away from each other, sometimes so far that they no longer recognize each other.

100　A real partnership is not possible unless it happens mutually and reciprocally. Therefore the Lord's partnership with us is mutual and reciprocal, as is obvious from the following passages: "Those who eat my flesh and drink my blood *live in me and I in them*" (John 6:56). *"Live in me and I [shall live] in you. Those who live in me and I in them* bear much fruit" (John 15:4, 5). "If any open the door, I will come in and *will dine with them and they with me*" (Revelation 3:20); and other passages as well. This partnership comes about as we move closer to the Lord and the Lord moves closer to us; for it is a fixed and unchangeable law that the closer we move toward the Lord, the closer the Lord moves toward us. (For more on this, see the chapters on goodwill and faith [§§336–462].)

7. *Through this process God became human and a human became God* ▪▪▪▪
in one person. From all the previous sections in this chapter it follows that Jehovah God became human and a human became God in one person. It especially follows from two of those sections: "Jehovah, the Creator of the universe, came down and took on a human manifestation in order to redeem people and save them" (§§82–84); and "Through acts of redemption the Lord united himself to the Father and the Father united himself to him mutually and reciprocally" (§§97–100). From the reciprocal nature of that union it is obvious that God became human and a human became God in one person. The same thing also follows from the fact that their union was like the one between a soul and a body. This fits with the modern-day church's belief based on the Athanasian Creed (see §98 above). It also fits with the Lutheran belief expressed in the section called the Formula of Concord in the volumes containing the Lutheran orthodoxy.[258] There it is strongly established from both Sacred Scripture and the church fathers, as well as through argumentation, that Christ's human nature was raised to divine majesty, omnipotence, and omnipresence; and that in Christ, God is human and a human is God; see pages 607 and 765.[259] That section also offers convincing proof that the Word refers to Jehovah God's human manifestation as "Jehovah," "Jehovah God," "Jehovah Sabaoth," and "the God of Israel."

Paul says, "All the fullness of divinity dwells physically in Jesus Christ" (Colossians 2:9). John says that Jesus Christ, the Son of God, is the true God and eternal life (1 John 5:20). We showed above (§§92–93) that the phrase "the Son of God" properly refers to his human manifestation. For another thing, Jehovah God calls both himself and his human aspect "Lord." We read, "*The Lord* said to my *Lord,* 'Sit at my right hand'" (Psalms 110:1). In Isaiah we read, "A Child is born to us, a Son is given to us, whose name is *God, Father of Eternity*" (Isaiah 9:6).

In David the word "Son" also refers to the Lord in his human manifestation: "I will announce a decision. Jehovah said, '*You are my Son.*

Today I fathered you.' Kiss *the Son* or he will be angry and you will perish on the way" (Psalms 2:7, 12). This does not mean an eternally begotten Son; it means the Son born in the world. It is a prophecy of the Lord to come. That is why it is called a decision that Jehovah is announcing to David. In the same Psalm it says before that, "I have anointed my King over Zion" (Psalms 2:6); and afterward it says, "I will give him the nations as an inheritance" (Psalms 2:8). Therefore "today" in this passage means "in time," not "from eternity." To Jehovah the future is present.

102　There is a belief that the Lord in his human manifestation not only was but still is the Son of Mary. This is a blunder, though, on the part of the Christian world. It is true that he was the Son of Mary; it is not true that he still is. As the Lord carried out the acts of redemption, he put off the human nature from his mother and put on a human nature from his Father. This is how it came about that the Lord's human nature is divine and that in him God is human and a human is God. The fact that he put off the human nature from his mother and put on a divine nature from his father—a divine human nature—can be seen from his never referring to Mary as his mother, as the following passages show: "The mother of Jesus said to him, 'They have no wine.' Jesus said to her, 'What do I have to do with you, *woman?* My hour has not yet come'" (John 2:3–4). Elsewhere it says, "Jesus on the cross saw his mother and the disciple he loved standing next to her. He said to his mother, '*Woman,* behold your son.' Then he said to the disciple, 'Behold your mother'" (John 19:26, 27). On one occasion he did not acknowledge her: "There was a message for Jesus from people who said, 'Your mother and your brothers are standing outside, and they want to see you.' Jesus said in reply, 'My mother and my brothers are these people who are hearing the Word of God and doing it'" (Luke 8:20, 21; Matthew 12:46–49; Mark 3:31–35). So the Lord called her "woman," not "mother," and gave her to John to be his mother. In other passages she is called his mother, but not by the Lord himself.

[2] Another piece of supporting evidence is that the Lord did not acknowledge himself to be the son of David. In the Gospels we read,

> Jesus asked the Pharisees, saying, "What do you think about the Christ? Whose son is he?" They say, "David's." He said to them, "Why then does David in the spirit call him his Lord when he says, '*The Lord* said to *my Lord,* "Sit at my right hand until I place your enemies as a footstool

for your feet"'? If David calls him Lord, how is he his son?" And no one could answer him a word. (Matthew 22:41–46; Mark 12:35, 36, 37; Luke 20:41–44; Psalms 110:1)

[3] Here I will add something previously unknown. On one occasion I was given an opportunity to talk to Mother Mary. She happened past, and I saw her in heaven over my head in white clothing apparently made of silk. Then, stopping for a while, she said that she had been the Lord's mother in the sense that he was born from her, but by the time he became God he had put off everything human that came from her. Therefore she adores him as her God and does not want anyone to see him as her son, because everything in him is divine.[260]

From the points above another truth now becomes manifest: Jehovah is as human in what is first as he is in what is last, as the following passages indicate: "I am the Alpha and the Omega, the Beginning and the End, the One who is, who was, and who is to come, the Almighty" (Revelation 1:8, 11). When John saw the Son of Humankind in the middle of seven lampstands, he fell at his feet as if dead; but the Son of Humankind laid his right hand on John and said, "I am the First and the Last" (Revelation 1:13, 17; 21:6). "Behold, I am coming quickly to give to all according to their work. I am the Alpha and the Omega, the Beginning and the End, the First and the Last" (Revelation 22:12, 13). And in Isaiah, "Thus said Jehovah, the King of Israel and its Redeemer, Jehovah Sabaoth: 'I am the First and the Last'" (Isaiah 44:6; 48:12).

To these points I will attach the following secret.

103

The soul we get from our father is our true self. The body we get from our mother is part of us but is not our true self. It is only something that clothes us, woven out of substances belonging to the physical world. Our soul is woven out of substances belonging to the spiritual world. After death we put off the physical component we acquired from our mother but keep the spiritual component we acquired from our father, along with a border[261] around it made of the finest substances in nature. For those of us who go to heaven this border is at the bottom and the spiritual part of us is above it. For those of us who go to hell the border is at the top and the spiritual part of us is below it. This border allows angelic people to speak from heaven and say what is good and true. It allows devilish people to speak from hell when they speak from their hearts, and to seem to speak from heaven when they speak with their lips, the latter being what they do in public and the former what they do at home.

[2] Our soul is our true self and is spiritual in origin. It is clear then why it is that a father's higher mind, lower mind, character, tendencies, and feelings of love live on in one descendant after the other. They return and surface noticeably in generation after generation. As a result, many families, and in fact whole nations, resemble their first father. A common image manifests itself in the individual faces of successive generations.

That image does not change unless the spiritual realities of the church come into play. The reason why the general image of Jacob and Judah still remains in their descendants and they are differentiated from others by that image is that even to the present they have stuck firmly to their religious position.[262]

In the sperm that conceives each one of us, there is a whole graft or offshoot of our father's soul that is wrapped in substances from nature. Our body is formed by means of this in our mother's womb. The formation of our body may lean toward a likeness of our father or a likeness of our mother, but the image of our father remains inside and constantly tries to assert itself. If it cannot manifest itself in the first child, it successfully manifests itself in the younger children.[263]

[3] In sperm there is a whole image of the father because, as I say, the soul is spiritual in origin. What is spiritual has nothing in common with space; therefore it is the same in something small as it is in something large.

As for the Lord, by acts of redemption while he was in the world he put off everything human that came from his mother and put on a human nature that came from his Father—a divine human nature. As a result, in him a human is God and God is human.

104 8. *When the Lord was being emptied out he was in a state of progress toward union; when he was being glorified he was in a state of union itself.* The church recognizes that the Lord had two states while he was in the world: one called being emptied out; the other called glorification.[264]

The prior state, being emptied out, is described in many passages in the Word, especially in the Psalms of David, but also in the Prophets. There is even one passage in Isaiah 53 where it says, "He emptied out his soul even to death" (Isaiah 53:12). This same state also entailed the Lord's being humbled before the Father. In this state he prayed to the Father. In this state he says that he is doing the Father's will and attributes everything he has done and said to the Father.

The following passages show that he prayed to the Father: Matthew 26:36–44; Mark 1:35; 6:46; 14:32–39; Luke 5:16; 6:12; 22:41–44; John 17:9, 15, 20. The following show that he did the Father's will: John 4:34; 5:30.

The following show that he attributed everything he had done and said to the Father: John 8:26, 27, 28; 12:49, 50; 14:10.

In fact, he cried out on the cross, "My God, my God, why have you abandoned me?" (Matthew 27:46; Mark 15:34). Furthermore, without this state it would have been impossible to crucify him.

The state of being glorified is also a state of union. The Lord was in this state when he was transfigured before three of his disciples. He was in it when he performed miracles. He was in it as often as he said that the Father and he were one, that the Father was in him and he was in the Father, and that all things belonging to the Father were his. After complete union he said he had power over all flesh (John 17:2) and all power in heaven and on earth (Matthew 28:18). There are also other such passages.

The reason why the Lord experienced these two states, the state of being emptied out and the state of being glorified, is that no other method of achieving union could possibly exist. Only this method follows the divine design, and the divine design cannot be changed.

105

The divine design is that we arrange ourselves for receiving God and prepare ourselves as a vessel and a dwelling place where God can enter and live as if we were his own temple. We have to do this preparation by ourselves, yet we have to acknowledge that the preparation comes from God. This acknowledgment is needed because we do not feel the presence or the actions of God, even though God is in fact intimately present and brings about every good love and every true belief we have. This is the divine design we follow, and have to follow, to go from being earthly to being spiritual.

The Lord had to go through the same process to make his earthly human manifestation divine. This is why he prayed to the Father. This is why he did the Father's will. This is why he attributed everything he did and said to the Father. This is why he said on the cross, "My God, my God, why have you abandoned me?" [Matthew 27:46; Mark 15:34]. In this state God appears to be absent.

After this state comes a second one, the state of being in a partnership with God. In this second state we do basically the same things, but now we do them with God. We no longer need to attribute to God everything good that we intend and do and everything true that we think and say in the same way as we used to, because now this acknowledgment is written on our heart. It is inside everything we do and everything we say.

In this same way, the Lord united himself to his Father and the Father united himself to the Lord. In a nutshell, the Lord glorified his human nature (meaning that he made it divine) in the same way that he regenerates us (meaning that he makes us spiritual).

The chapters on free choice [§§463–508], goodwill [§§392–462], faith [§§336–391], and reformation and regeneration [§§571–625] below will fully demonstrate three things: that all people who go from being earthly to being spiritual go through these two states; that they are brought to the second state through the first; and that this is how they move from this world to heaven. Here I will say only that in the first state, [also] called the state of being reformed, we have complete freedom to direct our actions with the faculty of reasoning that we have in our intellect. In the second state, the state of being regenerated, we have the same freedom but we intend, act, think, and speak with a new love and a new intelligence that come from the Lord.

In the first state our intellect plays the lead role while our will plays a supporting role. In the second state our will plays the leading role while our intellect plays a supporting role, although it is still the intellect that acts in connection with the will, not the will that acts through the intellect.

The same process applies to the joining of goodness and truth, the joining of goodwill and faith, and the joining of the inner and the outer self.

106 Because these two states follow the divine design, and the divine design fills everything large and small down to the least detail in the universe, therefore there are a number of different things in the universe that represent these two states.

The first state is represented by the stages we all go through from infancy to childhood and into our teenage years, our twenties, and our thirties.²⁶⁵ These stages entail our being deferential and obedient to our parents, and learning from teachers and ministers.

The second state, however, is represented by our stages later on when we are responsible for ourselves and our own choices, when we have our own will and our own understanding, and have authority in our own home.

The first state, then, is represented by the situation of a prince, the son of a king, or else a son of a duke, before he becomes the king or the duke himself; or by the situation of any citizens before they become civic leaders; or of any royal subjects before they take government positions; or of any students studying for the ministry before they become priests. The same applies to the situation of those priests before they become rectors, and of those rectors before they become deans. The same also applies to the situation of any young women before they marry; or to the situation of any female servants before they become heads of households. This is generally the situation of apprentices before they go into business for themselves, of soldiers before they become ranking officers, and of male servants before they become heads of households. The first state in every case is a kind of slavery while the second state belongs to our own will and intellect.

These two states are also represented by various things in the animal kingdom. The first state is represented by animals and birds as long as they are still with their mothers and fathers, when they follow them around constantly and are fed and raised by them. The second state is represented when they leave their parents and take care of themselves.

Caterpillars are another example. They represent the first state when they inch along and eat leaves; the second, when they shed their old form and become butterflies.

These two states are also represented by members of the plant kingdom. The first state is represented when a plant grows from a seed and is decked out with branches, boughs, and leaves; the second is represented when the plant produces fruit and generates new seeds. This sequence is equivalent to the way truth and goodness join together, in that all parts of a tree correspond to kinds of truth, and pieces of fruit correspond to good things [that result].

If we stay in the first state and do not go on to the second we are like a tree that produces only leaves but no fruit. It says in the Word that this type of tree has to be uprooted and thrown into the fire (Matthew [7:19]; 21:19; Luke 3:9; 13:6–9; John 15:5, 6). This is also like a slave who does not want to be free. There used to be a law that slaves like this had to be taken to a door or a post and have their ears pierced with an awl (Exodus 21:6). "Slaves" are people who have no partnership with the Lord. "The free" are people who have such a partnership; for the Lord says, "If the Son makes you free, you are truly free" (John 8:36).

9. *From now on, no Christians will go to heaven unless they believe in the Lord God the Savior and turn to him alone.* We read in Isaiah, "Behold, I am creating a new heaven and a new earth, and the earlier heaven and earth will not be remembered or overwhelm the heart. Behold, I am going to make Jerusalem a rejoicing and its people a joy" (Isaiah 65:17). In the Book of Revelation we read, "I saw a new heaven and a new earth, and I saw the holy Jerusalem coming down from God out of heaven, prepared like a bride for her husband. And the One sitting on the throne

107

said, 'Behold, I will make all things new'" (Revelation 21:1, 2, 5). A number of times we read that no one can come into heaven except the people who have been written in the Lamb's book of life (Revelation 13:8; 17:8; 20:12, 15; 21:27). "Heaven" in these passages does not mean the visible heaven or sky that is before our eyes; it means the angelic heaven. "Jerusalem" does not mean some city from the sky; it means the church that will descend out of the angelic heaven from the Lord. "The Lamb's book of life" does not mean a book written in heaven that will be opened; it means the Word, which is from the Lord and is about him.

In fact, the reason why Jehovah God, who is called "the Creator" and "the Father," came down and took on a human manifestation was so that we could turn to him and form a partnership with him, a point I have supported, proven, and established with the previous statements in this chapter.

When we go to see someone, we do not go to the person's soul. Who would be able to go to someone's soul? No, we go to the actual person. We see the person eye to eye and talk with the person face to face. It is the same with God the Father and the Son because God the Father is present in the Son the way a soul is present in its body.

[2] The following passages in the Word teach that we have to believe in the Lord God the Savior:

> God so loved the world that he gave his only begotten Son so that everyone who believes in him would not perish but would have eternal life. (John 3:16)

> Those who *believe in the Son* are not judged; but those who *do not believe* have already been judged because they have not believed in the name of the only begotten Son of God. (John 3:18)

> Those who *believe in the Son* have eternal life. Those who *do not believe in the Son* will not see life; instead God's anger will remain upon them. (John 3:36)

> The bread of God is the One who comes down from heaven and gives life to the world. Those who come to me will never hunger and those who *believe in me* will never thirst. (John 6:33, 35)

> This is the will of the One who sent me, that all who see the Son and *believe in him* should have eternal life, and I will revive them on the last day. (John 6:40)

They said to Jesus, "What shall we do to perform the works of God?" Jesus answered, "This is God's work, to *believe in the One* whom the Father sent." (John 6:28, 29)

Truly I say to you, those who *believe in me* have eternal life. (John 6:47)

Jesus cried out, saying, "If any are thirsty, they must come to me and drink. *If any believe in me,* rivers of living water will flow out of their bellies." (John 7:37, 38)

Unless *you have believed* that I am [he], you will die in your sins. (John 8:24)

Jesus said, "I am the resurrection and the life. Those who *believe in me,* even if they die they will live. And everyone who lives and *believes in me* will never die." (John 11:25, 26)

Jesus said, "I have come into the world as a light so that all who *believe in me* will not remain in darkness." (John 12:46; 8:12)

As long as you have the light, *believe in the light* so that you may be children of the light. (John 12:36)

People will live in the Lord and the Lord in them (John 14:20; 15:1–5; 17:23), a situation that is brought about by faith.

To both Jews and Greeks Paul proclaimed repentance before God and *belief in our Lord Jesus Christ.* (Acts 20:21)

I am the way, the truth, and the life. No one comes to the Father except through me. (John 14:6)

[3] Those who believe in the Son believe in the Father, since as we said above, the Father is in the Son like a soul in a body. The following passages make this clear:

If you had known me you would have known my Father also. (John 8:19; 14:7)

Those who see me see the One who sent me. (John 12:45)

Those who receive me receive the One who sent me. (John 13:20)

This is because no one can see the Father and live (Exodus 33:20), which is why the Lord says,

No one has ever seen God. The only begotten Son, who is close to the Father's heart, has made him visible. (John 1:18)

No one has seen the Father except the One who is with the Father. He has seen the Father. (John 6:46)

You have never heard the voice of the Father or seen what he looks like. (John 5:37)

There are those of course who know nothing about the Lord, such as most people who are in those two great parts of the world called Asia and Africa, as well as in the Indies, for example. If they believe in one God and follow the principles of their religion in their lives they are saved by their faith and by their life.[266] Spiritual credit or blame applies only to those who know; it does not apply to those who do not. We do not blame the blind for tripping. As the Lord says, "If you had been blind you would have had no sin; but now that you say you see, your sin remains" (John 9:41).

108 To further support this point I will relate some things that I know and can testify to because I have seen them.

Today a new angelic heaven is being built by the Lord. It is being made up of those who believe in the Lord God the Savior and who go directly to him; the rest are rejected. From now on if any from the Christian world come into the spiritual world (as happens to us all after we die) and they do not believe in the Lord, do not turn to him alone, and are unable at that point to change in this regard because they have lived in evil ways or have convinced themselves of falsities, when they take their first step toward heaven they are pushed back. Their face is turned away from heaven toward the lower earth.[267] They go off in that direction and join up with spirits in the lower earth who are meant by the dragon and the false prophet in the Book of Revelation.

From now on all people from Christian areas who do not believe in the Lord are not going to be listened to, either. In heaven their prayers are like foul smells and like belches from damaged lungs. If people like that think their own prayer is like burning frankincense, nevertheless it does not reach the angelic heaven any more effectively than would the smoke from a fire that was blown back into their eyes by a storm coming down. Or their praying is like burning incense in a censer under a monk's robe.

This is what is going to happen from this time on with all piety that is directed to a separated Trinity rather than a united one.

The main point of this book is that the divine Trinity is united in the Lord.

Here I will add something previously unknown. Several months ago the Lord called together the twelve apostles and sent them out into the whole spiritual world just as they had been sent out before to the physical world. Their assignment was to preach this gospel. Each apostle was assigned a territory to cover. They are carrying out their assignment with complete enthusiasm and energy.

These topics will be specifically covered in the last chapter of this book on the close of the age, the Coming of the Lord, and the New Church [§§753–791].

A Supplement

All the churches that existed before the Lord's coming were symbolic churches.[268] They could see divine truths only in shadow. After the Lord's coming into the world a church was instituted by him that saw divine truths—or rather was able to see divine truths—in full light. The difference between these churches is like the difference between evening and morning. In fact, in the Word the state of the church before the Lord's coming is called "evening" and the state of the church after his coming is called "morning."

    109

Before his coming into the world the Lord was of course present with people in the church, but only indirectly through angels who represented him. Since his coming he is now directly present with people in the church. In the world he added on a divine physical form that enables him to be present with people in the church.

The Lord's process of glorification was a transformation of the human nature that he took on in the world. The transformed human nature of the Lord is the divine physical form. A proof of this is that the Lord rose from the tomb with the whole body he had had in the world. Nothing was left in the tomb. Therefore he took with him from the tomb every aspect of his earthly human form. This is why after the resurrection he said to disciples who thought they were seeing a spirit, "See my hands and my feet, that it is I myself. Feel me and see; for a spirit does not have flesh and bones as you see I have" (Luke 24:37, 39). From these words it is clear that through the process of glorification his physical body became divine. Therefore Paul says, "All the fullness of divinity dwells physically in Christ" (Colossians 2:9); and John says that the Son of God, Jesus Christ, is the true God (1 John 5:20). From these teachings angels know that in all the spiritual world, only the Lord is a complete human being.

[2] The church recognizes that all the worship among the ancient Israelite and Jewish people was purely external and that it foreshadowed the inner worship the Lord initiated later on. It is recognized, then, that before the Lord's coming, worship was based on emblems and allegories that represented true worship in its proper form.

Now, the Lord was indeed seen among the ancients, for he says to the Jews, "Your father Abraham rejoiced that he would see my day, and he did see it and was glad. I tell you, I existed before Abraham did" (John 8:56, 58). But that was only a representation of the Lord, which involved angels, and therefore everything having to do with the church among the ancients became symbolic. After the Lord came into the world those symbolic representations disappeared. The inner reason for this is that through the divine physical form the Lord added on in the world, he enlightens not only our inner spiritual self but also our outer physical self. If both of these are not enlightened at the same time, we are in shadow, but when they are both enlightened at once we are in daylight.

If just our inner self is enlightened but not our outer self, or if just our outer self is enlightened but not our inner self, we are like people who are asleep and dreaming; soon after they wake up they remember their dream and make various false inferences based on it. We are also like sleepwalkers who think the things they see are in broad daylight.

[3] The difference between the state of the church before the Lord's coming and after it is like one person reading in moonlight and starlight and another person reading in sunlight. Obviously, the eye makes mistakes in that first type of light, a mere white light, but it does not make mistakes in the other type of light, which includes the colors of flame.

For this reason it is said of the Lord, "The God of Israel spoke, the Rock of Israel said to me, 'He was like a morning light when the sun arises, a morning without clouds'" (2 Samuel 23:3, 4). "The God of Israel" and "the Rock of Israel" are the Lord. Elsewhere it says, "The light of the moon will be like the light of the sun, and the light of the sun will be seven times as strong, like the light of seven days, on the day when Jehovah will bind up the brokenness of his people" (Isaiah 30:26). These words refer to the state of the church after the Lord's coming.

In brief, the state of the church before the Lord's coming was like an old woman with makeup on her face, who looks beautiful to herself because of the warm color of the makeup. The state of the church after the Lord's coming is like a young woman who is beautiful because of the blush of her own natural complexion.

The state of the church before the Lord's coming is like the skin from a piece of fruit—like an orange, an apple, a pear, or a grape—and like the taste of that skin. The state of the church after his coming is like the flesh of those types of fruit and like the taste of that flesh. And so on.

This is because ever since the Lord added on a divine physical form, he enlightens our inner spiritual self and our outer earthly self at the same time. When just our inner self is enlightened but not our outer self, a shadow is cast. The same is true when our outer self is enlightened but not our inner self.

Here I will add the following memorable occurrences.

The first memorable occurrence. In the spiritual world I once saw a strange light[269] in the [night] sky that fell slowly down to the earth. It had a glow around it. It was a strange aerial phenomenon that the local population called "the dragon." I made a note of the place where it landed; but in the early dawn as the sun was first coming up it disappeared, as all strange lights at night do.

Later in the morning I went to the place where I had seen it fall in the night. To my surprise, the ground there was a mixture of sulfur, iron filings, and white clay. Then I suddenly noticed two tents, one directly over the spot and the other beside it to the south. I looked up and I saw a spirit falling down from heaven like a thunderbolt. He was hurled right onto the tent that stood directly over the spot where the strange aerial phenomenon had come down. I was in the other tent that was next to it to the south. I stood up in the doorway of my tent, and I saw that the spirit, too, was standing in the doorway of his tent.

I asked him why he had fallen out of heaven like that. He answered that Michael's angels had thrown him down as an angel of the dragon.[270]

"It was because I voiced some of the beliefs I had convinced myself of in the world," he said. "Among them was this one: God the Father and God the Son are not one; they are two. As it turns out, though, all who are in the heavens today believe that God the Father and God the Son are one like a soul and a body. Any statement to the contrary is like a stinging irritation up their noses or like an awl piercing their ears. They become disturbed and pained by it, so they order anyone voicing opposition to leave, and if you resist, they throw you out."

[2] So I asked him, "Why don't you believe what they believe?"

He replied that after leaving the world, people are unable to believe anything else except the convictions they have already adopted. These beliefs remain entrenched in people and cannot be pulled out—especially not personal convictions about God. In the heavens everyone's location depends on his or her idea of God.

I also asked what evidence he had used to convince himself that the Father and the Son were two. He said, "It is the fact that in the Word the Son prays to the Father not only before suffering on the cross but even during it; and also that he humbles himself before his Father. How then can they be one like a soul and a body are one in us? Do we pretend to address a prayer to someone else or pretend to humble ourselves to someone else when we are actually that other person? No one does that—certainly not the Son of God. For another thing, in my day the entire Christian church had split the Divinity into persons, each person being one entity on its own. *'Person' is defined as something that exists and subsists on its own.*"[271]

[3] When I heard that I replied, "I gather from what you said that you are totally ignorant of how God the Father and the Son are one. Because you don't know that, you have convinced yourself of false beliefs that the church still has about God.

"Surely you know that when the Lord was in the world he had a soul like every other human being. Where would his soul have come from but God the Father? That God the Father is its origin is abundantly clear in the Word of the Gospel writers. What then is that entity called the Son except a human manifestation conceived by the divine nature of the Father and given birth to by the Virgin Mary?

"A mother cannot conceive a soul. That idea completely contradicts the divine design that governs the birth of every human being. Neither could God the Father have given a soul from himself and then withdrawn, the way every father in the world does. God is his own divine essence, an essence that is single and undivided; and since it is undivided it is God himself. This is why the Lord says that the Father and he are one, and that the Father is in him and he is in the Father, as well as other things like that.

"The people who drafted the Athanasian Creed had a distant glimpse of this. Even after splitting God into three persons they wrote that in Christ, God and a human being, that is, the divine nature and the human nature, are not two; they are one like the soul and the body in one human being.

[4] "The Lord's praying to the Father while in the world as if the Father were someone else and humbling himself before the Father as if the Father were someone else followed the unchangeable divine design established from the time of creation, which everyone has to follow in order to form a partnership with God. That design is that as we forge our connection with God by living according to the laws of the divine design, which are God's commandments, God forges his connection with us and turns us from earthly people into spiritual people.

"The Lord united himself to his Father and God the Father united himself to the Lord in the same way. When the Lord was an infant, he was like an infant. When he was a child, he was like a child. We read that he advanced in wisdom and grace, and later on asked the Father to glorify his name, meaning his human nature. (To glorify is to make divine through union with God himself.) When the Lord prayed to the Father, then, he was clearly in a state of being emptied out, which was his state of progress toward union.

[5] "That same design has been built into every one of us from creation. Of course, it all depends on how we prepare our intellect with truths from the Word and adapt it to receive faith from God, and how we prepare our will with acts of goodwill and adjust it to receive love from God. In a similar way, depending on how jewelers cut a diamond they can adapt it to receive and transmit the brilliance of the light, and so on.

"We prepare ourselves to receive God and to forge a partnership with him by following the divine design in our lives. The laws of that design are all God's commandments. In the case of the Lord, he fulfilled all these laws down to the finest details. By so doing he made himself a vessel for divinity in all its fullness. This is why Paul says that all the fullness of divinity dwells physically in Jesus Christ, and why the Lord himself says that all things belonging to the Father are his.

[6] "Furthermore, we must keep in mind that only the Lord is actually active in us. On our own we are completely passive. Thanks to life inflowing from the Lord we too can be active. Because of the constant inflow from the Lord it seems to us as though we are active on our own.

Because of this inflow we have free choice, which is given to us so we can prepare ourselves to receive the Lord and forge a partnership with him. Forging a partnership cannot happen unless that partnership is reciprocal. It becomes reciprocal when we act with our own freedom, and yet on the basis of faith we attribute all our action to the Lord."

[7] Next I asked whether he, like his colleagues, confessed that there is one God. He replied that he did. Then I said, "I am afraid, though, that the confession of your heart is that there is no God. What the mouth says emanates from what the mind thinks, does it not? The confession of your lips that there is one God will therefore tend to drive out of your mind the thought that there are three, and in turn your mind's thought will tend to drive away from your lips the confession that there is one. Surely this will eventually culminate in denial of God. The position that there is no God would eliminate the whole discrepancy between your mind and your lips. About God, then, your mind will surely conclude that nature is God. About the Lord, it will conclude that his soul was either from his mother or from Joseph. Yet all the angels in heaven turn away from these two conclusions as something horrible and detestable."

After I said that, the spirit was sent off into the great pit referred to in Revelation 9:2–3 where the dragon's angels debate the mysteries of their faith.

[8] The next day when I looked out at the spot, in place of the tents I saw two statues that looked like human beings. They were made out of dust from the ground, which as I say was a mixture of sulfur, iron, and clay. One statue looked as though it had a scepter in its left hand, a crown on its head, and a book in its right hand, as well as a bodice held in place by a diagonal sash covered with gems, and a robe with a train that flowed out behind it toward the other statue. These features, however, had been put on the statue through someone's power to project images.

Then I heard a voice there from some follower of the dragon: "This statue portrays our faith as a queen. The statue behind it portrays goodwill as faith's maidservant."

The other statue was made out of the same mixture of different types of dust. It was placed just beyond the edge of the robe flowing down off the queen's back. The second statue held a sheet of paper in its hand with writing on it that said, "Warning: don't come too close or touch the robe."

Then suddenly a rain shower fell from heaven, drenching each statue. They began to fizz because they were made out of that mixture of sulfur, iron, and clay. (A mixture of those substances in powdered form tends to effervesce when water is added to it.)[272] An internal fire then melted them into piles that stood thereafter like burial mounds on that piece of ground.

The second memorable occurrence. In our earthly world we have two types of thought, inner thought and outer thought, and because of that we have two modes of verbal communication. We are able to talk on the basis of both our inner and outer thought at the same time, and we are able to talk on the basis of our outer thought separate from our inner thought. In fact, we can say the opposite of what we think inside, which is something we do to put on appearances, insincerely agree with people, and play the hypocrite.

In the spiritual world, though, our thought process is single, not dual. There we say what we think. If we do not, we emit a horrible sound that hurts people's ears. Nevertheless we have the option of being silent and not publicizing the thoughts in our mind. So when hypocrites come among the wise they either leave right away or throw themselves into a corner of the room, make themselves inconspicuous, and sit in silence.

[2] Once there was a large conference in the world of spirits. This was the very topic they were discussing with each other. The participants were saying that it is a hardship for spirits who have had unacceptable thoughts about God and the Lord not to be able to say what they think when they come into the company of the good.

In the center of the participants there was a group of Protestants, many of them clergy, and next to them a group of Roman Catholics including monks.[273] Both the Protestants and the Catholics were saying at first that it is not hard. "Why not say what we think?" they maintained. "If we happen not to think the right things, we can always close our mouths and keep quiet."

The clergy said, "Who doesn't have the right thoughts about God and the Lord?"

So some participants in the conference said to each other, "Let's test these Protestants and Catholics!"

Some [in the central groups] were convinced that there is a trinity of persons in God. The participants told them to say and think "One God." They were unable to. They twisted and puckered their lips into all sorts of shapes but they still could not articulate the sound of any words but those in harmony with their thoughts and mental images, which were of three persons and therefore three gods.

[3] Some [in the central groups] were convinced that faith should be separate from goodwill. They were told to say the name "Jesus." They

could not, although they could all say "Christ" and also "God the Father." [The participants] were amazed at this and wanted to know why. The reason, they discovered, was that those people had prayed to God the Father for the sake of the Son, but had not prayed to Jesus as their Savior, and "Jesus" means Savior.

[4] Then they were told to think about the Lord's human nature and say "divine-human." No Protestant clergy person who was there could do it, but some Protestant lay people could. At that point they gave the discussion some structure.

1. The following passages from the Gospels were read out loud to [the Protestant clergy]: "The Father has given all things into the hand of the Son" (John 3:35). The Father has given the Son power over all flesh (John 17:2). "All things have been handed to me by the Father" (Matthew 11:27). "All power in heaven and on earth has been given to me" (Matthew 28:18). They were told, "On the basis of these passages, hold it in your mind that Christ in both his divine nature and his human nature is the God of heaven and earth. Then say 'divine-human.'" They still could not say it. They reported that on the basis of those passages they were able to hold some thoughts in their minds about it, but they could not hold any acknowledgment, so they were unable to say it.

[5] 2. Then Luke 1 verses 32, 34, and 35 were read to them, showing that the Lord's human manifestation was the Son of Jehovah God. It was pointed out that in those passages he is called "the Son of the Highest" and everywhere else he is called "the Son of God," and also "the only begotten One." The participants asked [the Protestant clergy] to hold this in their thoughts and also to consider that an only begotten Son of God born in the world could not possibly be anything other than God, just as the Father is God, and then say "divine-human."

"We can't," they said. "Our spiritual thinking, which goes on very deep inside us, does not allow incompatible ideas access to the thought processes located near speech."

They said they were realizing that they could not now divide their thinking the way they had been able to in the physical world.

[6] 3. Then the Lord's words to Philip were read to them: "Philip said, 'Lord, show us the Father.' And the Lord said, 'Those who see me see the Father. Do you not believe that I am in the Father and the Father is in me?'" (John 14:8–11). Other passages that say that the Father and the Son are one were also read, such as John 10:30. [The Protestant clergy] were told to hold this in their thinking and say "divine-human." Since

that thought was not rooted in any acknowledgment that even in his human manifestation the Lord is God, they contorted and twisted their lips to the point of exasperation and tried to force their mouth to enunciate the words, but they did not have the power; because all who are in the spiritual world find that the words they speak match the ideas that arise from the things they have acknowledged. If those ideas do not exist, the words are impossible, because speech is ideas turned into words.

[7] 4. Then the following passage was read to [the Protestant clergy] from teachings that are accepted in the entire Christian world: "The divine nature and the human nature in the Lord are not two but one. In fact, they are one person, united like the soul and the body in one human being." This is part of the belief that was stated in the Athanasian Creed and ratified by councils. They were told, "From this passage you had every opportunity to form and acknowledge an idea that the Lord's human nature is divine because his soul is divine, for this is part of the church teachings you acknowledged in the world. Furthermore, the soul is the very essence of a person and the body is the person's form, and essence and form are one, like underlying reality and manifestation, or like the cause that produces an effect and the effect produced."

[The Protestant clergy] held on to that idea and tried on that basis to say "divine-human," but they could not. Their inner idea of the Lord's human nature expelled and destroyed this new "supplemental" idea, as they were calling it.

[8] 5. There was a further reading to them from John: "The Word was with God, and the Word was God. And the Word became flesh" (John 1:1, 14). And this: "Jesus Christ is the true God and eternal life" (1 John 5:20). Also a passage from Paul: "All the fullness of divinity dwells physically in Christ Jesus" (Colossians 2:9).

They were told to think like this, meaning to think that God who was the Word became human, that he is the true God, and that all the fullness of divinity dwells physically in him. This they did, but only in their outer thought. A resistance in their inner thought made it impossible for them to say "divine-human." They openly stated that "divine-human" was an idea they could not have. "God is God," they said, "and human is human. God is a spirit, and a spirit to our thinking is no different from wind or ether."

[9] 6. Finally they were asked, "Don't you know that the Lord said, 'Live in me and I [shall live] in you. Those who live in me and I in them bear much fruit, because without me you cannot do anything' (John 15:4, 5)?"

Because some of them were Anglican clergy, a passage stated at their Holy Communion was read to them: "For when we spiritually eat the flesh of Christ and drink the blood, then we dwell in Christ, and Christ in us."[274] They were told, "If you now think that this situation could not occur unless the Lord's human manifestation was divine, then say 'divine-human' from this acknowledgment in your thought."

They still could not say it. The idea had been too deeply impressed on them that what was divine could not be human and what was human could not be divine, and so too had the idea that his divine nature came from the divinity of the eternally begotten Son, and that his human nature was just like anyone else's.

They were asked, "How can you think that way? Can a rational mind really think that some Son was born from God from eternity?"

[10] 7. Next the participants focused on the Lutheran Protestants. They said to them that the Augsburg Confession and Luther himself taught the following:[275]

> The Son of God and the Son of Humankind are one person in Christ. Even his human manifestation is omnipotent and omnipresent. It sits at the right hand of God the Father and rules all things in the heavens and on earth, fills all things, is with us, and dwells and is at work in us. His human manifestation deserves no different adoration, because through his human manifestation, which is perceptible, we adore the Divinity that is not perceptible. In Christ, God is human, and a human is God.

To this they replied, "Is that so?" They looked around. Soon they said, "We didn't know these things before, so we can't say 'divine-human.'"

Nevertheless first one, then another, said, "We read that text and we even wrote some of it, but still when we thought about it they were only words. We did not have the inner idea that goes with them."

[11] 8. Finally the participants turned to focus on the Catholics and said, "Perhaps *you* are able to pronounce 'divine-human,' since you believe that in your Eucharist Christ is fully present in the bread and wine, in each and every part of them. You adore Christ as the most holy God when you display and convey the host. Since you call Mary 'the Bearer of God' or 'the one who gave birth to God,' you therefore acknowledge that she bore God, that is, the Divine-Human Being."

They then tried to say it, but they could not. What came to their minds was a physical idea of Christ's body and blood, as well as the belief that his humanity is separable from his divinity, and is actually separated in the case of the pope, to whom only Christ's human power, not his divine power, had been transferred.

Then a monk stood up and said that he could think of the Holy Virgin Mary and also the saint of his monastery as divine-human.

Another monk came forward and said, "With the idea I have of the holy pope—an idea I have come to cherish—I can more easily speak of the holy pope than of Christ as divine-human."

Some other Catholics, however, pulled him back and said, "Shame on you!"

[12] After this heaven seemed to open and tongues like little flames seemed to come down and flow into some people.[276] They began praising the Lord's divine humanity and saying, "Remove the idea of three gods. Believe that all the fullness of divinity dwells physically in the Lord. Believe that the Father and he are one as the soul and the body are one. Believe that God is a human being, not wind or ether. Then you will be connected to heaven, and from the Lord you will be able to name Jesus and say 'divine-human.'"

The third memorable occurrence. Once I woke up just after first light. I went out into the garden in front of my house and watched the sun rising in its splendor. There was a halo around it, at first very subtle, but later on more definite, shining as though it was made of gold. Beneath the sun's rim I saw a cloud rising up. Mirroring the flame of the sun, it gleamed like a ruby.

At that point I fell into a meditation based on the myths of the most ancients, reflecting on how they pictured Aurora, the Dawn, as having silver wings and carrying gold in her mouth.[277] Mentally taking great pleasure in these sights, I came into my spirit.

I heard some spirits in a discussion saying, "I would love an opportunity to talk to that innovator who has tossed an apple of discord[278] among the leaders of the church. Many lay people have rushed to that apple, picked it up, and set it before our eyes."

The "apple" they meant was the little volume titled *Survey of Teachings for the New Church.*[279]

"It is something genuinely schismatic that no one has thought of before," they said.

I heard one of them cry out, "Schismatic? It's heretical!"

Some by his side retorted, "Be quiet! It isn't heretical. It cites many statements from the Word that the strangers in our midst (meaning our lay people) pay attention to and support."

[2] When I had heard all that, I went to them (since I was in my spirit) and said, "Here I am. What's your concern?"

One of them—I heard later that he was a German, a native of Saxony—speaking with the tone of authority, immediately said, "Where did you get the audacity to overturn the worship that has been established in the Christian world for so many centuries, the practice of calling on God the Father as Creator of the universe, his Son as its Mediator, and the Holy Spirit as its Effecter? You remove the first and the last God from our concept of personhood. Yet the Lord himself says, 'When you pray, pray like this: "Our Father who is in the heavens, your name must be kept holy; your kingdom must come."' We are commanded then to call on God the Father."

After he had spoken it became quiet. All who sided with him stood like mighty soldiers on warships who have spotted the enemy fleet and are about to shout, "Now to battle! The victory is sure!"

[3] Then I stood up to speak. "Surely you are all aware," I said, "that God came down from heaven and became a human being. We read, 'The Word was with God and the Word was God, and the Word became flesh.' Again, surely you all know"—and I looked at the Lutherans, including the tyrant who had just spoken to me—"that in Christ, who was born of the Virgin Mary, God is human and a human is God."

The crowd objected loudly to this, so I said, "Don't you know this? It accords with the point of view in your confession called the Formula of Concord, where this statement is made and extensively supported."

The tyrant turned to the crowd and asked whether they had known this. They replied, "We haven't paid much attention to what that book says about the person of Christ, but we have sweated over the article there on justification by faith alone. Still, if that is what it says, we will grant you that."

Then one of them remembered and said, "It does say that. It goes on to say that Christ's human nature was raised to divine majesty and all the attributes that go with it, and that Christ in his human nature sits at the right hand of his Father."[280]

[4] When they heard that they kept quiet. With that point resolved, I spoke again and said, "Since that is so, is the Father then anything other than the Son, and is the Son anything other than the Father?"

Because this too sounded harsh to their ears, I went on to say, "Hear the actual words the Lord said. If you haven't paid attention to them before, pay attention to them now. He said, 'The Father and I are one. The Father is in me and I am in the Father. Father, all that is mine is yours, and all that is yours is mine. Those who see me see the Father.' What else do these words mean except that the Father is in the Son and the Son is in the Father, and they are one like the soul and the body in a human being, so they are one person? This has to be part of your faith if you believe the Athanasian Creed, where statements just like this occur.

"Of the passages I quoted, just take this saying of the Lord's: 'Father, all that is mine is yours, and all that is yours is mine.' Surely this means that the Father's divine nature belongs to the Son's human nature and the Son's human nature belongs to the Father's divine nature; and therefore in Christ God is human and a human is God and they are one as the soul and the body are one.

[5] "We can all say the same thing of our own soul and body: 'All that is yours is mine and all that is mine is yours. You are in me and I am in you. Those who see me see you. We are one individual and we have one life.' Why? Because the soul exists throughout us and in every part of us. Our soul's life is the life in our body. It is something the soul and the body share.

"Clearly then, the divine nature of the Father is the Son's soul, and the human nature of the Son is the Father's body. Where does a son's soul come from except from his father? Where does his body come from except from his mother? When I say 'the divine nature of the Father' what I mean is 'the Father himself,' since he is the same as his nature; his nature is one undivided thing.

"The truth of this is clear from the angel Gabriel's words to Mary: 'The power of the Highest will cover you, and the Holy Spirit will descend upon you; and the Holy One that will be born from you will be called the Son of God' [Luke 1:35]. Just before that the Lord is called 'the Son of the Highest' [Luke 1:32], and elsewhere he is called 'the only begotten Son' [John 3:16, 18; 1 John 4:9].

"Those of you, however, who call him only 'the Son of Mary' lose the idea of his divinity. The only people who lose that, though, are learned clergy and scholarly laity whose only goal in lifting their thoughts above their physical senses is to gain glory for their own reputation; but that glory does not merely overshadow, it actually extinguishes, the light that brings the glory of God.

[6] "Let's go back to the Lord's prayer. There it says, 'Our Father who is[281] in the heavens, your name must be kept holy; your kingdom must come' [Matthew 6:9–10]. You who are here understand these words as referring solely to the Father in his divine nature. I, however, understand them as referring to the Father in his human manifestation, which is in fact the Father's name. The Lord said, 'Father, glorify your name' [John 12:28], that is, your human manifestation. When this takes place, then God's kingdom comes. This prayer was commanded for this time, that is, when people are going to God the Father through his human manifestation.

"In fact, the Lord says, 'No one comes to the Father except through me' [John 14:6]. And in the prophet, 'A Child is born to us, a Son is given to us, whose name is *God,* Hero, *Father of Eternity*' [Isaiah 9:6]. Elsewhere it says, 'You, Jehovah, are our Father; our Redeemer from everlasting is your name' [Isaiah 63:16]. There are also a thousand other passages where the Lord our Savior is called Jehovah. This is the true interpretation of the words of that prayer."

[7] After I had said all that I looked at them. I noticed that their faces changed as they changed their minds. Some were agreeing with me and looking at me; some were disagreeing and turning away from me.

Then to the right I saw a cloud the color of an opal, and to the left a dark cloud, and precipitation below each of them. Under the dark cloud the precipitation was like a hard rain in late fall; under the opalescent cloud it was like dew falling at the beginning of spring.

Suddenly I came from my spirit into my body and returned from the spiritual world to the physical one.

113 *The fourth memorable occurrence.* I looked out across the world of spirits and saw an army on red horses and black horses. The riders looked like monkeys. They were turned around with their faces and chests facing the horses' backs and tails, while the riders' backs and the backs of their heads faced the horses' necks and heads. The reins were hanging around the riders' necks. They were uttering [battle] cries at some riders on white horses and plying the reins with both hands, yet in fact they were reining in their horses from battle. This went on and on.[282]

Then two angels descended from heaven, and came over to me and said, "What do you see?"[283]

I told them how I was watching a very entertaining cavalry. I asked what was going on and who they were.

"Those people are from the place that is called Armageddon in Revelation 16:16," the angels replied. "As many as several thousand have gathered there with the purpose of fighting those who are from the Lord's new church that is called the New Jerusalem.

"At that spot they have been discussing the church and religion, although they have no church, because they have no spiritual truth, and they have no religion, because they have no spiritual goodness. They have been discussing the church and religion with their mouths and lips, but only with the purpose of using the church and religion to dominate [others].

[2] "In early adulthood they learned to sanction faith alone and learned something about God. When they were promoted to higher-ranking positions in the church, they held on to what they had learned for a while. Then they gradually ceased thinking about God or heaven, and instead began thinking about themselves and the world. They did not think about blessedness or happiness in eternity; they thought about prominence and wealth in time. They moved the teachings they had been attracted to in early adulthood out of the inner realms of their rational mind—realms that communicate with heaven and are in heaven's light. They drove them instead into the outer realms of their rational mind— realms that communicate with the world and are in the world's light. In the final stage they pushed those teachings down to the realm of their physical senses. For them the teachings of the church became the exclusive property of their lips; those teachings were no longer part of their thinking on the basis of reason, let alone part of their feelings of love. As a result, they do not now let in any divine truth that is part of the church or any genuine goodness that is part of religion.

"The inner realms of their mind have become like beakers full of iron filings mixed with powdered sulfur. If water is poured in the beakers, first there is increasing heat and then there is fire, which breaks the beakers.[284] Likewise, when they hear living water, which is the genuine truth in the Word, and it goes into their ears, they burst violently into flames and expel it as something that is about to break their heads.

[3] "These are the people who looked to you like monkeys riding backward on red horses and black horses with the reins around their own necks. Those who have no love for the truth or the goodness from the Word that belong to the church want to see the back, not the front, of a horse. A horse means one's understanding of the Word. A red horse means an understanding of the Word that has lost its goodness. A black horse means an understanding of the Word that has lost its truth. Those people were uttering battle cries against riders on white horses because a white

horse means an understanding of the Word's truth and goodness. They appeared to drag their horses backward by the neck because they themselves were afraid to fight, fearing that the truth of the Word would reach many people and would come to light that way. This is the interpretation."

[4] The angels went on to say, "We are from the community in heaven that is called Michael. The Lord commanded us to come down to the place called Armageddon where the cavalry you saw was on the attack. To us in heaven Armageddon means the mindset that fights, using falsified truths[285] as weapons—a mindset that originates in a love for dominating and being superior to all. We sense your desire to know about that battle, so we will tell you something about it.

"After we came down from heaven we went to the place called Armageddon. We saw as many as several thousand who had gathered there, but we did not go into the crowd. Off to the south side of that area there were some houses where there were children and teachers. We went there, and they kindly took us in. We enjoyed their company. Their faces were all good-looking as a result of their lively eyes and their impassioned way of speaking. What made their eyes lively was their awareness of what is true, and what made their talk impassioned was their passion for what is good. So we presented a gift to them of hats whose rims were decorated with bands made of golden threads with pearls woven in, as well as clothing of white and blue.

"We asked them whether they had looked at the neighboring area called Armageddon. They said they had looked out a window just under the roof of the house. They had seen a gathering there, but those gathering changed shapes, at one point looking like nobility, at another not even seeming to be human; they looked like statues and carved idols with a crowd around them on their knees. We too had seen that group in different forms. Some looked like people, some like leopards, some like goats. The goats had horns that curved downward; they were digging up the ground with them. We explained those metamorphoses—whom they portrayed and what they meant.

[5] "But back to the main point. When the people who had gathered heard that we had gone into those houses, they said to each other, 'What do they want with those children? We should send some from our crowd over there to throw them out.' And so they did.

"When their envoys arrived they said to us, 'Why did you go into those houses? Where are you from? With full authority we order you to leave.'

"We replied, 'That is not an order you can give with any authority. Admittedly, in your own eyes you are like the Anakim, and the people who are here are like dwarves. But nonetheless you have no power or jurisdiction here except by fraud, and that is not valid. Tell your people that we have been sent here from heaven to assess whether religion exists among you or not. If it doesn't, you will be thrown out of the place. Propose the following to your people, therefore—a point in which lies the essence of the church and religion. How do they understand the following words in the Lord's prayer: "Our Father, you who are in the heavens, your name must be kept holy; your kingdom must come" [Matthew 6:9–10]?'

"When the others heard this, at first they said, 'What is this?' But then they said they would propose it. They left and conveyed this proposition to their people.

"Their people replied, 'What kind of a proposition is that?' But they understood the hidden agenda. They thought, 'They want to know whether these words support the orientation of our faith to God the Father.' So they said, 'The words are clear that we must pray to God the Father, and because Christ is our Mediator, we must pray to God the Father for the Son's sake.'

"Soon in their indignation they decided to come over to us in person and tell us this. In fact, they said that they were going to twist our ears. They left that place and came to a stand of trees that was near the houses where the children and their teachers were. In the middle of the trees there was a raised level area like a natural stage. They went onto that stage hand in hand. We were there waiting for them. There were piles of sod on the ground there. They sat on these piles, because they had said to each other, 'We are not going to stand up in front of them; we'll sit down.'

"One of them who was able to make himself appear to be an angel of light had been ordered by the rest to speak to us. He said, 'You have proposed to us that we reveal our opinions on the first words of the Lord's prayer and how we understand them. Therefore I am telling you that we understand those words to mean that we have to pray to God the Father. Because Christ is our Mediator and we are saved by his merit, we have to pray to God the Father with a belief in Christ's merit.'

[6] "We said to them, 'We are from the community in heaven called Michael. We have been sent to assess and investigate whether you who have gathered in that place have any religion or not. The idea of God permeates every aspect of religion. Through that idea a partnership [with

God] is forged, and through that partnership comes salvation. In heaven we recite the Lord's prayer every day just as people on earth do. When we do so we don't think of God the Father, because he cannot be seen. We think of him in his divine-human manifestation, because in that he can be seen.[286] In that human manifestation he is called Christ by you, but the Lord by us. To us the Lord is our Father in the heavens.

"'The Lord taught that he and the Father are one, that the Father is in him and he is in the Father, and that those who see him see the Father. He also taught that no one comes to the Father except through him, and that the will of the Father is that people should believe in the Son. Those who do not believe in the Son do not see life; in fact, God's anger remains on them. From these teachings it is clear that access to the Father is gained through the Lord and in him. Because that is true, the Lord also taught that all power in heaven and on earth was given to him.

"'In the prayer it says, "Your name must be kept holy; your kingdom must come." We have demonstrated from the Word that his divine-human manifestation *is* the name of the Father; and that the Father's kingdom exists when the Lord is directly approached, but does not exist at all when God the Father is directly approached. That is why the Lord commanded the disciples to preach the kingdom of God. This is the kingdom of God.'

[7] "When they heard that, our opponents said, 'You are citing many passages from the Word. We may have read things like that there, but we don't remember. Open the Word before us and read those things from it, especially that point about the kingdom of the Father coming when the Lord's kingdom comes.'

"Then they said to the children, 'Bring the Word,' so the children brought it.

"From it we read the following: 'As he preached the gospel of the kingdom, John[287] said, "The time has been completed. *The kingdom of God* has come near" (Mark 1:14, 15; Matthew 3:2). Jesus himself preached the gospel of the kingdom and that *the kingdom of God* was coming near (Matthew 4:17, 23; 9:35). Jesus commanded his disciples to preach and evangelize *the kingdom of God* (Mark 16:15; Luke 8:1; 9:60); he gave a similar command to the seventy he sent out (Luke 10:9, 11).' We also read passages such as Matthew 11:5; 16:27, 28; Mark 8:35; 9:1, 47; 10:29, 30; 11:10; and Luke 1:19; 2:10, 11; 4:43; 7:22; 21:30, 31; 22:18.

"We said, 'The following passages make clear that the kingdom of God that was evangelized was the Lord's kingdom and at the same time the Father's kingdom:

> The Father has given all things into the hand of the Son. (John 3:35)

> The Father has given the Son power over all flesh. (John 17:2)

> All things have been handed to me by the Father. (Matthew 11:27)

> All power in heaven and on earth has been given to me. (Matthew 28:18)

And also these passages:

> Jehovah Sabaoth is his name, and he will be called the Redeemer, the Holy One of Israel, God of all the earth. (Isaiah 54:5)

> I saw and behold, there was someone like *the Son of Humankind.* He was given dominion, glory, and a kingdom. All people and nations will worship him. His dominion is a dominion of an age that will not pass, and his kingdom is one that will not perish. (Daniel 7:13, 14)

> When the seventh angel sounded, great voices rang out in the heavens saying, "The kingdoms of the world have become kingdoms of our Lord and his Christ, and he will reign forever and ever." (Revelation 11:15; 12:10)

[8] "We also used the Word to teach them that the Lord came into the world not only to redeem angels and people but also to unite them to God the Father through himself and in himself. He taught that if people believe in him, he is in them and they are in him (John 6:56; 14:20; 15:4, 5).

"Upon hearing that they asked, 'Then how can your Lord be called Father?'

"We said, 'That is based on the passages we already read to you, and also on the following passages: "A Child is born to us, a Son is given to us, whose name is *God,* Hero, *Father of Eternity*" (Isaiah 9:6). "You are our Father. Abraham did not know us and Israel did not acknowledge us. You, *Jehovah, are our Father; our Redeemer from everlasting is your name*" (Isaiah 63:16). When Philip wanted to see the Father, Jesus said, "Have you not known me, Philip? Those who see me see the Father" (John 14:9; 12:45). Who else then is the Father except the One whom Philip was seeing with his eyes?

"'And let's add this as well. Throughout the whole Christian world there is a saying that those who are part of the church form the body of Christ and are in his body. How then can people who belong to the church go to God the Father without going through the One whose body they are in? Otherwise they would have to go completely outside that body to go to the Father.'

"Finally, we informed them, 'Today the Lord is establishing the new church meant by the New Jerusalem in the Book of Revelation [Revelation 3:12; 21:2, 10]. In it there will be worship of the Lord alone, as there is in heaven. *This is fulfilling everything contained in the Lord's prayer from beginning to end.*'

"To support all these points we used the Word in the Gospels and in the Prophets, and we quoted so much from the Book of Revelation, which from beginning to end is about this church, that they became tired of hearing it.

[9] "Annoyed at all this, those Armageddonites wanted to interrupt our diatribe now and then. Finally they broke in and shouted, 'You have spoken against the doctrine of our church, which teaches us to go directly to God the Father and believe in him. You have made yourselves guilty of violating our faith. Therefore go away from here. If you don't, you will be thrown out.'

"Their minds became inflamed with their own threats and soon turned toward action, but then by a power given to us we struck them with a blindness. Because they couldn't see us, as they went on the attack they ran off in the wrong direction. Some fell down into the great pit mentioned in Revelation 9:2, which is now on the eastern side of the southern region. The spirits there support a belief in justification by faith alone. The people there who are using the Word to support that belief are now being sent into a desert in which they are taken all the way to the farthest edge of the Christian world. There they are being integrated among pagans."

Redemption

114 It is known in the church that the Lord has two roles, a *priestly* one and a *royal* one. Few know, however, what each role consists of; therefore they will be described. In his priestly role the Lord is called Jesus; in his royal role he is called Christ. In the Word, in his priestly role he is called Jehovah and the Lord; in his royal role he is called God and the Holy One of Israel, as well as King.[288]

The two roles are differentiated from each other, just as love and wisdom are, or their equivalents, goodness and truth. Therefore whatever the Lord did from divine love or divine goodness, he did from his priestly position. On the other hand, whatever the Lord did from divine wisdom or divine truth, he did from his royal position. In fact, in the Word "priest" and "priesthood" mean divine goodness, and "king" and "royal" mean divine truth. The priests and kings in the Israelite church represented these two roles.

As for redemption, it relates to both roles. Which aspect of it relates to which role will be disclosed in what follows. In order that the details may be clearly perceived, the explanation will be broken up into topics or points. They will be the following:

1. Redemption was actually a matter of gaining control of the hells, restructuring the heavens, and by so doing preparing for a new spiritual church.

2. Without this redemption no human being could have been saved and no angels could have continued to exist in their state of integrity.

3. The Lord therefore redeemed not only people but also angels.

4. Redemption was something only the Divine could bring about.

5. This true redemption could not have happened if God had not come in the flesh.

6. Suffering on the cross was the final trial the Lord underwent as the greatest prophet. It was a means of glorifying his human nature, that is, of uniting that nature to his Father's divine nature. It was not redemption.

7. Believing that the Lord's suffering on the cross was redemption itself is a fundamental error on the part of the church. That error, along with the error about three divine Persons from eternity, has ruined the whole church to the point that there is nothing spiritual left in it anymore.

I will discuss these matters point by point.

1. *Redemption was actually a matter of gaining control of the hells, restructuring the heavens, and by so doing preparing for a new spiritual church.* I can say with absolute certainty that these three actions are redemption, because

115

the Lord is bringing about redemption again today. This new redemption began in the year 1757 along with a Last Judgment that happened at that time. The redemption has continued from then until now. The reason is that today is the Second Coming of the Lord. A new church is being instituted that could not have been instituted unless first the hells were brought under control and the heavens were restructured.

Because I have been allowed to see it all I could describe how the hells were brought under control and how the new heaven was built and put into the divine design, but that would be the subject of a whole work. In a little work published in London in 1758 I did lay out how the Last Judgment was carried out.[289]

Gaining control over the hells, restructuring the heavens, and establishing a new church was redemption because without those actions no human being could have been saved. In fact, they follow in a sequence. The hells had to be controlled first before a new angelic heaven could be formed, and that heaven had to be formed before the new church on earth could be instituted, because people in the world are so closely connected to angels from heaven and spirits from hell that at the level of the inner mind they are one. This point will be taken up in the last chapter of this book, which specifically covers the close of the age, the Coming of the Lord, and the New Church [§§753–791].

116 Many passages in the Word make it clear that while he was in the world the Lord fought battles against the hells, conquered them, brought them under control, and made them obedient to himself. I will extract just a few.

In Isaiah:

> Who is this who comes from Edom, from Bozrah with his clothes spattered, this one honorable in his clothing, walking in the magnitude of his strength?
>
> "It is I who speak with justice, great in order to give salvation."
>
> Why are your clothes reddish? Why are your clothes like those of someone trampling in a winepress?
>
> "I trampled the winepress alone. There was no man from the people with me. Because I trampled people in my anger and stamped on them in my rage, their victory was spattered on my clothes. For the day of revenge was in my heart and the year of my redeemed had come. My arm performed salvation for me. I made the enemies' victory go down into the ground."
>
> He said, "Behold those others are my people, my children."

That is why he became their Savior. Because of his love and his mercy he redeemed them. (Isaiah 63:1–9)

These words are about the Lord's battles against the hells. The clothes in which he was honorable and which were reddish mean the Word, to which the Jewish people had done violence. The combat itself against the hells and victory over them is described by his trampling people in his anger and stamping on them in his rage. The fact that he was alone and fought from his own power is described by these phrases: "there was no man from the people with me"; "my arm performed salvation for me"; and "I made the enemies' victory go down into the ground." His bringing salvation and redemption as a result is described by these phrases: "That is why he became their Savior"; and "because of his love and mercy he redeemed them." The fact that this was the reason for his coming is meant by these phrases: "the day of revenge was in my heart and the year of my redeemed had come."

[2] Also in Isaiah:

He saw that there was no one and was astounded that there was no one interceding. Therefore his own arm performed salvation for him and justice made him stand up. Then he put on justice like a breastplate and a helmet of salvation on his head. He put on the clothes of vengeance and covered himself with zeal like a cloak. Then the Redeemer came to Zion. (Isaiah 59:16, 17, 20)

In Jeremiah:

They were terrified; their mighty ones were broken. They fled in flight and did not look back. That day belonged to the Lord Jehovih Sabaoth, a day of retribution for him to take revenge on his enemies, for the sword to eat and be satisfied. (Jeremiah 46:5, 10)

These last two passages are about the Lord's combat against the hells and victory over them.

In David:

Strap the sword on your thigh, Powerful One. Your arrows are sharp. Populations fall beneath you—enemies of the king at heart. Your throne is for an age and forever. You have loved justice. God anointed you for this. (Psalms 45:3, 5–7)

There are also many other relevant passages in the Psalms.

[3] Because the Lord conquered the hells alone with no help from any angel he is called Hero[290] and a Man of Wars (Isaiah 42:13; 9:6), the King of Glory, Jehovah the Mighty, a Hero of war (Psalms 14:8, 10), the Mighty One of Jacob (Psalms 132:2), and in many passages "Jehovah Sabaoth," that is, "Jehovah of Armies." For the same reason his coming is called *the terrible day of Jehovah; a cruel day; a day of indignation, rage, anger, revenge, destruction, and war; a day of the trumpet, of the call to arms, of uproar;* and so on.

In the Gospel writers we read the following:

> Now is the judgment of the world; the Prince of This World is cast to the outside. (John 12:31)

> The Prince of This World has been judged. (John 16:11)

> Have confidence; I have overcome the world. (John 16:33)

> I saw Satan falling like a thunderbolt out of heaven. (Luke 10:18)

In these passages "the world," "the Prince of This World," "Satan," and "the Devil" mean hell.

[4] In addition, the Book of Revelation from beginning to end describes the condition of the Christian church today and the fact that the Lord is going to come again, take control of the hells, make a new angelic heaven, and then establish a new church on earth. All this is foretold there but it has not been disclosed before today. The reason is that the Book of Revelation, like all the prophetic portions of the Word, was written in pure correspondences. If the correspondences had not been disclosed by the Lord, hardly anyone could have correctly understood a single verse there.

Now, for the sake of the new church, everything in the Book of Revelation has been disclosed in *Revelation Unveiled,* published in Amsterdam, 1766. Some will see those things—those who believe the Word of the Lord in Matthew 24 about the state of the church today and about his coming. In fact, the only people who are still ambivalent are those who have planted two of the modern-day church's beliefs so deeply in their own hearts that those beliefs cannot be uprooted: the belief in three divine Persons from eternity; and the belief that the suffering on the cross was the actual redemption. As noted in the memorable occurrence above at §113[:2], these people are like beakers full of iron filings and powdered sulfur. If water is poured in the beakers, first there is increasing heat and then there is fire, which breaks the beakers. Likewise, when these people hear some living water, which is the genuine truth in the

Word, and it goes into their eyes or ears, they burst violently into flames and expel it as something that is about to break their heads.

Gaining control of the hells, restructuring the heavens, and then establishing a church can be illustrated by various comparisons.   **117**

They can be illustrated by a comparison with an army of looters or rebels who invade a country or a city, set fire to the houses, plunder the citizens' goods, and divide the spoils among themselves, enjoying and glorifying themselves because of it. Redemption itself can be illustrated by a comparison with an upright monarch who attacks these invaders with an army, puts some of them to the sword, imprisons the rest in labor camps, takes the stolen goods away from them to give back to the citizens, and then restructures the country and gives it protection against attack by similar assailants in the future.

It could also be illustrated by a comparison with wild animals that have formed packs and are charging out of the forest attacking flocks and herds and even people. The people do not dare to go outside the walls of the city and cultivate the land, so the fields are becoming deserts and the people in the city are about to die of hunger. Redemption could be illustrated by analogy with killing some of the wild animals, driving away the others, and protecting the fields and plains from any further attack of the kind.

It could also be illustrated by locusts that are consuming every green thing in the ground and then by the means of stopping them from going any farther. Also by caterpillars at the beginning of summer that strip the leaves off the trees (thus preventing the fruit from coming) so that the trees stand as naked as in midwinter; and then by the act of shaking the caterpillars off and restoring the garden to flowering and fruit-bearing.

The church would have been in a comparable situation unless the Lord through redemption had separated the good from the evil, had cast the evil into hell, and had lifted the good to heaven.

What would it be like in an empire or a country that knew no justice or judgment? Justice and judgment take evil people away from the company of the good; they protect good people from being violated so that they may live safely in their own homes and, as it says in the Word, sit in serenity under their own fig tree and their own vine [1 Kings 4:25; Micah 4:4].

2. *Without that redemption no human being could have been saved and no angels could have continued to exist in their state of integrity.* First I need   **118** to say what redemption is. To redeem means to free the captive and the bound from damnation, to rescue them from everlasting death, to snatch them from hell, and to carry them away from the hand of the

Devil. The Lord did this by gaining control over the hells and establishing a new heaven.

Otherwise we could not have been saved, because the spiritual world is so closely connected to the earthly world that they are inseparable. The main connection between the two worlds is through our inner levels—our souls and our minds. For good people, that connection is with the souls and minds of angels; for evil people it is with the souls and minds of hellish spirits. We are so united to the angels or the hellish spirits that if they were taken away from us we would fall down as dead as a piece of wood. Neither could the angels or the hellish spirits continue to exist if we were taken away from them. This makes it clear why redemption was brought about in the *spiritual* world and why heaven and hell had to be restructured before a church could be established on earth. This sequence is clear in the Book of Revelation: after the new heaven was made, the New Jerusalem, which is the new church, came down from that heaven (Revelation 21:1, 2).

119 If the Lord had not brought about redemption, angels could not have continued to exist in a state of integrity either. To the Lord, the entire angelic heaven along with the church on earth is like a single human being. The angelic heaven constitutes the inner level of that person; the church constitutes the outer level.

To be more specific, the highest heaven forms the head of that person; the second and the lowest heavens form the chest and the midsection of that person's body; and the church on earth constitutes the person's body from below the waist to the feet. The Lord himself is the soul and life of the whole person.

If the Lord had not brought about redemption, that person would have been destroyed. The loss of the church on earth destroys that body from the waist down; the loss of the lowest heaven destroys the digestive area; the loss of the second heaven destroys the thorax. Then the head loses consciousness because it has no relationship with the body.

[2] Analogies will illustrate this. It is like someone's feet becoming gangrenous and the gangrene climbing progressively higher, reaching the genitals and then the abdominal organs, and finally attacking the region of the heart. As we know, at that point the person succumbs to death.

This can also be illustrated by analogy with diseases of the internal organs below the diaphragm. When they fail, the heart begins to palpitate and the lungs begin to heave desperately. In the end the heart and lungs stop functioning.

This can also be illustrated by analogy with our higher and lower self. The higher self is strong as long as the lower self is obediently fulfilling its obligations; but if the lower self is resistant rather than obedient, and worse yet if it attacks the higher self, the higher self eventually becomes weak and finally gets carried away by the lower self's pleasures until the higher self agrees and goes along with the lower self.

This can also be illustrated by comparison with people standing on a mountain who notice that the land below is flooded and the water is rising higher and higher. When it reaches the level where they are standing, unless they can ensure their own safety by getting on some life raft washed to them on the floodwaters, they too are submerged.

Likewise when people on a mountain see a thick fog rising higher and higher above the ground, covering the fields, villages, and cities. Finally, when the fog reaches them, they do not see a thing—not even in the spot where they themselves are standing.

[3] It is like this for angels. When the church on earth dies, the lower heavens also disintegrate. The reason is that the heavens consist of people from the world. When there is nothing good left in the human heart and no truth from the Word, the heavens are flooded with evils that rise up; they are choked by them as by the waters of the Styx.[291] Nevertheless the Lord hides [good spirits] somewhere else and preserves them till the day of the Last Judgment, then lifts them into a new heaven.

The Book of Revelation refers to these good spirits in the following statements:

> I saw under the altar the souls of those who had been killed for the sake of God's word and for the testimony that they had given. They were shouting with a loud voice saying, "How long, Lord, you who are holy and true, will you refrain from judging and avenging our blood on those who live on earth?" They were given white robes and were told that they should rest a little longer until they were all together, they and their fellow slaves, and their brothers and sisters who were going to be killed as they had been. (Revelation 6:9, 10, 11)

If there had been no redemption by the Lord, injustice and malice would have spread throughout the Christian realm in both worlds (the earthly and the spiritual).

120

There are many reasons for this. One is that all human beings after death come into the world of spirits. They are exactly the same then as they were before. When they first enter that world, none of them can be prevented from interacting with parents, siblings, relatives, and friends who have died.[292] At that time every husband first looks for his wife and every wife looks for her husband. Their spouses as well as their family and friends introduce them into various social groups that include people who are outwardly like sheep but are inwardly like wolves. The newcomers are corrupted by these wolves—even the newcomers who have been particularly devoted to religion. Because of this, and also because of horrible practices that are unknown in the physical world, that world is as full of malicious people as a pond is green with frogs' eggs.

[2] Interaction with evil people there has this contagious effect, as you can clearly see from the following similar situations: As you spend time with thieves or pirates[293] you eventually become like them. As you live among adulterous men and promiscuous women, eventually you think nothing of adultery. If you join a rebel group, eventually you think nothing of doing violence to anyone.

All evils are contagious. They are like a plague you become infected with just by breathing in and out. They are like cancer and gangrene that spread and corrupt nearby areas, then more and more remote areas, until the whole body dies.

The cause: from birth we all enjoy evil.

[3] From the points made just now it can be clear that if the Lord had not brought about redemption, no human being could have been saved and no angels could have continued to exist in their state of integrity.

The sole and only direction in which to run for refuge is to the Lord, or else we perish. He says,

> Live in me and I [shall live] in you. Just as a branch cannot bear fruit by itself unless it lives in the vine, the same goes for you unless you live in me. I am the vine. You are the branches. Those who live in me and I in them bear much fruit. For without me you can do nothing. If any do not live in me, they are cast out. Once dried they are thrown into the fire and burned. (John 15:4, 5, 6)

121 3. *The Lord therefore redeemed not only people but also angels.* This follows from something stated in the previous point: no angels could have continued to exist without being redeemed by the Lord. The following reasons supplement those already given.

The first reason: At the time of the Lord's First Coming the hells had risen so high that they filled the entire world of spirits that is midway between heaven and hell. They not only wrecked the heaven called the lowest heaven, they also attacked the middle heaven and harassed it in a thousand ways. If the Lord had not preserved it, it would have been destroyed.

This kind of attack by the hells is meant by the tower built in the land of Shinar whose top reached all the way to heaven. The confusion of their languages thwarted those people's efforts; they were scattered and the city was called Babel (Genesis 11:1–9). The meaning of the tower and of the confusion of their languages is explained in *Secrets of Heaven,* published in London.[294]

[2] The reason why the hells had risen so high was that by the time the Lord came into the world the whole planet had completely alienated itself from God by worshiping idols and practicing sorcery; and the church that had existed among the children of Israel and later among the Jews had been utterly destroyed by their falsifying and contaminating the Word.

After death both of the above groups arrived in the world of spirits. Over time they grew in numbers there to such an extent that they could not have been driven out thereafter if God himself had not come down and used the power of his divine arm to deal with them. The Lord in fact did so, as I have described in *Last Judgment,* a little work published in London in 1758. While the Lord was in the world, he accomplished their overthrow.

The Lord is again doing something similar today since, as I said, today is his Second Coming, an event foretold throughout the Book of Revelation and in Matthew 24:3, 30; Mark 13:26; Luke 21:27; and Acts 1:11, as well as other places.

A difference is that during his First Coming the hells were swollen with idol-worshipers, sorcerers, and falsifiers of the Word. During this Second Coming the hells are swollen with so-called Christians—some who are steeped in materialist philosophy, and others who have falsified the Word by using it to sanction their made-up faith about three divine persons from eternity and about the Lord's suffering as the true redemption. The dragon and his two beasts in Revelation 12 and 13 mean the so-called Christians just mentioned.

[3] The second reason why the Lord's redemption affected angels as well is that the Lord restrains not only all people but also all angels from evil, and keeps them focused instead on what is good. No angels or people are good on their own. Everything good comes from the Lord. When the angels' footstool (meaning the world of spirits) was stolen, it was as if the platform under someone's chair was suddenly removed.

The angels are not pure before God. This is something the Prophets and also Job make clear. This is also clear from the fact that there is no such thing as an angel who was not previously a human being. These points support what was said at the beginning of this work under the headings "the faith of the new heaven and the new church in a universal form" and "in a specific form":

> The Lord came into the world to separate hell from the human race. He accomplished this by repeatedly doing battle with hell and conquering it. In this way he gained control over it and forced it to obey him. (§2)

Also these words there:

> Jehovah God came down and took on a human manifestation for the purpose of forcing everything in heaven and everything in the church back into the divine design. For at that time the power of the Devil, that is, hell, was stronger than the power of heaven, and on earth the power of evil was stronger than the power of goodness; therefore a total damnation stood at the door and threatened. By means of his human manifestation Jehovah God lifted this pending damnation and redeemed both people and angels. From all this it is clear that if the Lord had not come, no one could have been saved. The situation today is similar. If the Lord does not come into the world again, no one can be saved. (§3)[295]

122　　The Lord rescued the spiritual world from universal damnation, and through the spiritual world he is going to rescue the church from universal damnation.

This rescue can be illustrated by comparing it with a king whose children have been captured by an enemy, locked in prisons, and bound with chains; by a series of victories over that enemy the king frees the children and brings them back to his court.

The divine rescue would also be comparable to a shepherd, like Samson or David, snatching sheep from the jaws of a lion or a bear. Or it would be comparable to a shepherd who drives away lions and bears that have rushed out of a forest into the pastures, chases those wild animals to the farthest borders, finally pushes them back into wetlands or deserts, and then returns to the sheep, pastures them in safety, and quenches their thirst with clear spring water.

This divine rescue can also be illustrated by comparing it with a person who notices a snake that is coiled up on the road with the intention of striking the heel of a passerby, catches the snake by the head, carries it home (although the snake is wrapping itself around the person's arm), and there cuts off its head and throws the rest into the fire.

This divine rescue can also be illustrated by a bridegroom or husband who sees an adulterer attempting to rape his bride or wife. He attacks the rapist and either wounds the rapist's hand with a sword, or assaults the rapist's legs and groin with punches, or instructs his servants to throw the rapist out into the street and to brandish their clubs while they follow the rapist all the way to his home. When the bride or wife has been freed the bridegroom escorts her to their bedroom. In fact, in the Word a bride and wife mean the Lord's church and adulterers mean those who violate the church, that is, those who contaminate his Word. Because the Jews had done this the Lord called them an adulterous generation [Matthew 12:39; 16:4; Mark 8:38].

4. *Redemption was something only the Divine could bring about.* If you knew what hell is like, and you knew how high it swelled and how it flooded the entire world of spirits at the time of the Lord's coming, and you saw the great power with which the Lord cast hell down and scattered it and then restructured both it and heaven in accordance with the divine design, you could not help being stunned and exclaiming that all of it was something only the Divine could do.

First, *what hell is like.* It consists of millions, since it consists of all from the creation of the world who have alienated themselves from God through their evil lives and false beliefs.

Second, *how high hell swelled and how it flooded the entire world of spirits at the time of the Lord's coming.* This has been somewhat explained in the earlier points [§§115–122]. No one knows the situation at the time of the *First* Coming, because it has not been revealed in the literal sense of the Word. I have been allowed to see with my own eyes the situation at the time of the Lord's *Second* Coming. One can draw conclusions about the earlier situation from that. I described this situation in the little work *Last Judgment,* published in London in 1758.

That little work also covers *the great power with which the Lord cast hell down and scattered it.* My eyewitness accounts appear in that little work, but copying them here would be a pointless exercise because it is in print and there are still many copies available at the printer's in London.[296]

Everyone who reads it can clearly see that the Last Judgment was the work of Almighty God.

[2] The fourth point, *how the Lord then restructured everything in heaven and in hell in accordance with the divine design,* I have not yet described, because the restructuring of the heavens and the hells has been going on since the day of the Last Judgment until the present time and is still going on. Nevertheless, after I have published this book, if further information is desired, I will present it to the public.[297]

If I may add a personal comment on this topic: I see the face, so to speak, of the Lord's divine omnipotence every day.

Strictly speaking, this restructuring of the spiritual world has to do with *redemption,* whereas the stages before it had to do with *the Last Judgment.* People who keep redemption and the Last Judgment separate are capable of seeing many things in prophetical passages in the Word. These things, though hidden in allegories there, still give clear descriptions— provided that their correspondences are explained in such a way as to allow the light of the intellect to fall on them.

[3] Redemption and the Last Judgment can be illustrated only with comparisons, and even these are inadequate.

They could be illustrated by comparison with a battle against the armies of every nation in the entire world, armed with spears, shields, swords, guns, and cannons, under generals and officers who are cunning, experienced strategists. (I say this last part because many spirits in hell are skilled in practices unknown in our world, which they rehearse on each other—ways of stalking those who are from heaven, and ambushing, setting siege to, and attacking them.)

[4] The Lord's battle with hell can also be compared, although inadequately, with someone fighting against all the wild animals in the world, slaughtering or taming them until not one animal would dare to go out and attack any human being who is with the Lord. Then if any wild animal so much as put on a menacing look, it would suddenly stop itself as if it felt a vulture deep inside its chest trying to pierce it to the very heart.

In fact, the wild animals in the Word depict hellish spirits. The wild animals with which the Lord spent forty days (Mark 1:13) also mean hellish spirits.

[5] The Last Judgment and redemption could also be compared to resisting the whole ocean after dikes have broken and waves are pounding cities and the countryside.

In fact, when the Lord controls the sea by saying "Peace, be still" (Mark 4:38, 39; Matthew 8:26; Luke 8:23, 24), it means the Lord's process of gaining control over the hells. There and in many other passages the sea means hell.

[6] The Lord uses the same divine power today to fight against hell in every one of us who is being regenerated. Hell attacks us all with diabolical fury. If the Lord did not counter hell and control it, we could not help succumbing. Hell is like one monstrous human being or a massive lion; in fact, it is compared to a lion in the Word. The Lord has to chain the forelegs and shackle the hind legs of that lion, that monster. Otherwise the only possible outcome would be that once we were rescued from one evil we would spontaneously fall into the next, and in fact into many others.

5. This true redemption could not have happened if God had not come in the flesh. The preceding point showed that redemption was something only the Divine could bring about—for anyone other than God Almighty it would have been impossible. Furthermore, God could not have brought about this redemption if he had not taken on flesh (that is, become human), because in his infinite essence Jehovah God could not come near hell, let alone enter it. He exists in what is first and most pure. If Jehovah God as he is in himself were only to breathe on those who are in hell he would instantly kill them all. When Moses wanted to see him he said, "You cannot see my faces,[298] because no human being will see me and stay alive" (Exodus 33:20). If Moses could not do this, still less could those who are in hell, where everyone exists in what is lowest, densest, and farthest away [from God]. Those who are earthly are the lowest. Therefore if Jehovah God had not taken on a human manifestation, clothing himself with a body that is on the lowest level, his undertaking any act of redemption would have been a waste of time.

We could not attack an enemy without being armed for battle and coming within range. We could not destroy or drive away the dragons, hydras, and basilisks[299] in some desert without putting a breastplate on our body, a helmet on our head, and a spear in our hand. We could not catch whales at sea without a ship and whaling equipment. These examples are not actual parallels, but they do illustrate the fact that God Almighty could not have even attempted to battle hell without first putting on a human manifestation.

[2] It is important to know, however, that the Lord's battle with the hells was not some verbal to and fro like a philosophical debate or a legal battle. That kind of battle has no effect whatever on hell. It was a spiritual battle using the divine truth connected with divine good—the very vitality of the Lord. When this truth visibly flows in, no one in the hells is able to oppose it. There is so much power in it that when demons from

124

hell merely sense that it might be present they run away, throw themselves down into deep places, and squeeze into underground shelters to hide. This phenomenon is the same thing described by Isaiah: "They will go into caverns in the rocks and into crevices in the dust, dreading Jehovah, when he rises to terrify the earth" (Isaiah 2:19); and in the Book of Revelation: "They will all hide themselves in caves in the rocks and in the rocks on the mountains, and they will say to the mountains and the rocks, 'Fall on us and hide us from the face of the One sitting on the throne and from the anger of the Lamb'" (Revelation 6:15, 16, 17).

[3] How much power the Lord exercised from divine goodness when he carried out the Last Judgment in 1757 is clear from the descriptions in the little work *Last Judgment.* For example, in the world of spirits there were mountains and hills occupied by hellish spirits that the Lord ripped from their moorings and moved far away; some he flattened. He flooded their cities, villages, and fields, and turned their land upside down. He threw those mountains and hills and their inhabitants into quagmires, ponds, and swamps; and more. The Lord alone accomplished all this using the power of divine truth connected with divine goodness.

125 Jehovah God could not have taken these actions and made them effective without a human manifestation, as various comparisons can illustrate.

An invisible person cannot shake hands or talk with a visible one. In fact, angels and spirits cannot shake hands or talk with us even when they are standing right next to our bodies or in front of our faces. No one's soul can talk, or do things, with anyone else except through its own body. The sun cannot convey its light and heat into any human, animal, or tree, unless it first enters the air and acts through that. It cannot convey its light and heat to any fish unless it passes through the water. It has to act through the element the entity is in. None of us could scale a fish with a knife or pluck a raven's feathers if we had no fingers. We cannot go to the bottom of a deep lake without a diving bell.[300] In a word, one thing needs to be adapted to another before the two can communicate and work with or against each other.

126 6. *Suffering on the cross was the final trial the Lord underwent as the greatest prophet. It was a means of glorifying his human nature, that is, of uniting that nature to his Father's divine nature. It was not redemption.* There are two things for which the Lord came into the world and through which he saved people and angels: redemption, and the glorification of his human aspect. These two things are distinct from each other, but they become one in contributing to salvation.

In the preceding points we have shown what *redemption* was: battling the hells, gaining control over them, and then restructuring the heavens. *Glorification,* however, was the uniting of the Lord's human nature with the divine nature of his Father. This process occurred in successive stages and was completed by the suffering on the cross.[301]

All of us have to do our part and move closer to God. The closer we come to God, the more God enters us, which is his part. It is similar with a house of worship: first it has to be built by human hands; then it has to be dedicated; and finally prayers are said for God to be present and unite himself to the church that gathers there.

The union itself [between the Lord's divine and human natures] was completed by the suffering on the cross, because this suffering was the final spiritual test that the Lord went through in the world. Spiritual tests lead to a partnership [with God]. During our spiritual tests, we are apparently left completely alone, although in fact we are not alone—at those times God is most intimately present at our deepest level giving us support. Because of that inner presence, when any of us have success in a spiritual test we form a partnership with God at the deepest level. In the Lord's case, he was then united to God, his Father, at the deepest level.

The Lord was left to himself during the suffering on the cross, as is clear from his crying out on the cross: "God, why have you abandoned me?" [Matthew 27:46]. This is also clear from the following words spoken by the Lord: "No one is taking my life away from me—I am laying it down by myself. I have the power to lay it down and I have the power to take it up again. I received this command from my Father" (John 10:18).

From the points just made it is clear that it was not the Lord's divine nature that suffered, it was his human nature; and then the deepest union, a complete union, took place.

An illustration of this is that when we suffer physically, our soul does not suffer, it merely feels distress. After victory, God relieves that distress and washes it away like tears from our eyes.

Redemption and the suffering on the cross must be seen as separate. Otherwise the human mind gets wrecked as a ship does on sandbars or rocks, causing the loss of the ship, the helmsman, the captain, and the sailors. It goes astray in everything having to do with salvation by the Lord. If we lack separate ideas of these two things we are in a

127

kind of dream; we see images that are unreal and we make conjectures based on them that we think are real but are just made up. We are like someone walking out [to a tryst] at night, who, thinking that the leaves of a tree within his grasp are human tresses, sidles closer, only to entangle his own hair in them.

Although redemption and the suffering on the cross are two different things, nevertheless they become one in contributing to salvation. When the Lord became united to his Father, which happened through the suffering on the cross, he became the Redeemer forever.

128 The suffering on the cross completed the process of *glorification*[302] (meaning the uniting of the Lord's divine-human nature to the divine nature of the Father). The Lord himself says so in the Gospels: "After Judas left, Jesus said, 'Now the Son of Humankind is glorified, and God is glorified in him. If God is glorified in him, God will also glorify him in himself and glorify him immediately'" (John 13:31, 32). Here glorification refers to both God the Father and the Son; it says "God is glorified in him and will glorify him in himself." Clearly this means that they became united.

"Father, the hour has come. Glorify your Son so that your Son may also glorify you" (John 17:1, 5). This form of expression occurs here because the uniting was reciprocal. As it says, the Father was in him and he was in the Father.

Jesus said, "'Now my soul is disturbed.' And he said, 'Father, glorify your name.' And a voice came out of heaven, 'I both have glorified it and will glorify it again'" (John 12:27, 28). It says this because the uniting occurred in successive stages.

"Was it not fitting for Christ to suffer and enter into his glory?" (Luke 24:26). In the Word when "glory" is related to the Lord it means the divine truth united to divine goodness.

From these passages it is very clear that the Lord's human manifestation is divine.

129 The Lord was willing to undergo spiritual tests, including even the suffering on the cross, because he was the ultimate prophet. The prophets stood for the church's teachings from the Word. As a result they represented the nature of the church in various ways—even by doing unjust, harsh, and wicked things that God commanded them to do. In the Lord's case, however, he was the Word itself. During his suffering on the cross he was the ultimate prophet, representing the way the Jewish church had desecrated the Word.

An additional reason why the Lord was willing to suffer on the cross was that by doing so he would come to be acknowledged in the heavens as the Savior of both worlds. Every aspect of his suffering meant something related to the desecration of the Word. When people in the church understand these aspects in physical terms, angels understand them in spiritual terms.

The following passages make it clear that the Lord was the ultimate prophet: "The Lord said, '*A prophet* is nowhere less honored than in his own country and in his own house'" (Matthew 13:57; Mark 6:4; Luke 4:24). "Jesus said, 'It is not right for *a prophet* to die away from Jerusalem'" (Luke 13:33). "Fear took hold of them all. They were praising God and saying that *a great prophet* had risen among them" (Luke 7:16). They called Jesus "*that prophet* from Nazareth" (Matthew 21:11; John 7:40, 41). It says in Deuteronomy that a *prophet* would be raised up from among his brothers and sisters, and they would obey his words (Deuteronomy 18:15–19).

The prophets represented their church's condition relative to its teachings from the Word and its life according to them, as the following stories from the Word make clear:

130

Isaiah the prophet was commanded to take the sackcloth off below his waist and the sandals off his feet and go naked and barefoot for three years as a sign and a wonder (Isaiah 20:2, 3).

Ezekiel the prophet was commanded to represent the state of the church by making travel bags, moving to another place before the eyes of the children of Israel, taking out his bags from time to time, going out in the evening through a hole in the wall, and covering his face so he could not see the ground. In this way he would be a wonder to the house of Israel. He was told to say, "Behold, I am your wonder. As I have done, so it will be for you" (Ezekiel 12:3–7, 11).

Hosea the prophet was commanded to represent the church's condition by marrying a promiscuous partner, which he did. She bore him three sons, one of whom he called Jezreel, the second No Mercy, and the third Not My People. At another point he was commanded to go love a woman who already had a lover and who was committing adultery, and buy her for himself (Hosea 1:2–9; 3:1, 2).

One prophet was commanded to put ashes over his eyes and let himself be beaten and whipped (1 Kings 20:35, 38).

Ezekiel the prophet was commanded to represent the condition of the church by taking a brick and sculpting Jerusalem on it, laying siege to it, building a rampart and a mound against it, putting an iron frying pan between himself and the "city," and sleeping on his left side and then on his right side. He also had to take wheat, barley, lentils, millet, and spelt and make bread out of them. He also had to make a cake of barley with human excrement; but because he begged not to have to do that, he was allowed to make it with cow dung instead. He was told,

> Lie on your left side and put *the injustice done by the house of Israel* on it. For the number of days during which you sleep on that side *you will carry their injustice.* For I will give you the years of their injustice according to the number of days, 390 days *for you to carry the injustice done by the house of Israel.* But when you have finished them, you will lie again on your right side to *carry the injustice done by the house of Judah.* (Ezekiel 4:1–15)

[2] By these actions the prophet Ezekiel carried the injustices done by the house of Israel and the house of Judah; but he did not take away those injustices or atone for them, he only represented them and made them visible. This is clear from the following verses in the same chapter:

> "Like this," says Jehovah, "will the children of Israel eat their unclean bread. Behold I am breaking the staff of bread so that they lack bread and water. A man and his brother will become desolate and will waste away because of their injustice." (Ezekiel 4:13, 16, 17)

The same thing is meant by the statement about the Lord that says, "He bore our diseases, he *carried* our pains. Jehovah put on him the injustices committed by us all. Through his knowledge he justified many as *he himself carried their injustices"* (Isaiah 53:4, 6, 11). This whole chapter in Isaiah is about the Lord's suffering.

[3] The following details of the Lord's suffering make it clear that he was the ultimate prophet, embodying the Jewish church's treatment of the Word:[303] *He was betrayed by Judas. The chief priests and the elders arrested him and condemned him. They hit him repeatedly. They beat his head with a cane. They put a crown of thorns on him. They tore up his clothes and cast lots for his undergarment. They crucified him. They gave him vinegar to drink. They pierced his side. He was buried, and on the third day he rose.*

His betrayal by Judas meant his betrayal by the Jewish nation, among whom the Word existed at that time. Judas represented that nation. The chief priests and the elders who arrested and condemned him meant that whole church. Their punching him repeatedly, spitting in his face, whipping him, and beating his head with a cane meant that they had done the same to the divine truths in the Word. Their putting a crown of thorns on him meant that they had falsified and contaminated those divine truths. Their tearing up his clothes and casting lots for his undergarment meant that they had split apart all the truths of the Word but they had not split apart its spiritual meaning, which was symbolized by the Lord's undergarment. Their crucifying him meant that they had desecrated and destroyed the entire Word. Their offering him vinegar to drink meant that everything they offered him had been completely falsified; therefore he did not drink it. Their piercing his side meant that they had completely annihilated everything true and everything good in the Word. His being buried meant his casting off what was left from his mother. His rising on the third day meant the glorification, the union of his human nature with the divine nature of the Father.

From all this it is clear that "carrying injustices" does not mean taking them away; it means representing the desecration of the Word's truth.

This point can also be illustrated by comparisons. (I make comparisons for the sake of ordinary people, who see more in a comparison than they do in a deductive analysis based on the Word and on reason.)

131

When any citizens or subjects obey the commands and orders of their king, they are united to him. If they endure oppressive circumstances for him, they are more deeply united to him. If they suffer death for him, as happens in battles and wars, they are still more deeply united to him.

In the same way, doing the other person's will is how a friend is united to a friend, a child to a parent, or a servant to the head of the household. If the friend, child, and servant defend their superiors against enemies they are more deeply united to them. If they fight for their superiors' honor they are even more deeply united to them.

Take for example a young man and the young woman he hopes to marry. When he confronts people who are destroying her reputation, surely he becomes more united to her. What about when he is injured fighting a rival? It is a law inscribed on nature that under these circumstances the couple will become more deeply united.

The Lord says, "I am the good shepherd. The good shepherd lays down his life for the sheep. For this reason the Father loves me" (John 10:11, 17).

132 *7. Believing that the Lord's suffering on the cross was redemption itself is a fundamental error on the part of the church. That error, along with the error about three divine Persons from eternity, has ruined the whole church to the point that there is nothing spiritual left in it anymore.* There is no topic that fills more books by orthodox[304] theologians today, that is more intensely taught and aired in lecture halls, or that is more frequently preached and pronounced from the pulpit than the following: *God the Father was angry at the human race, so he not only moved us all away from himself but locked us into a universal damnation and cut off communication with us. Nevertheless, because he is gracious, he either convinced or goaded his Son to come down to take a limited damnation on himself and ritually purge the Father's anger. This was the only way the Father could look on the human race with any favor. So this was in fact done by the Son. For example, in taking on our damnation, the Son let the Jews whip him, spit in his face, and then crucify him like someone accursed of God (Deuteronomy 21:23). After that happened the Father was appeased, and out of love for his Son he retracted the damnation, but only from those for whom the Son would intercede. Therefore the Son became a Mediator to the Father for all time.*[305]

[2] These ideas, and others like them, resound in churches today and reverberate off the walls like an echo from a forest, filling the ears of all who are there. Surely, though, everyone with decent reasoning enlightened by the Word can see that God is compassion and mercy itself. He is absolute love and absolute goodness—these qualities are his essence. It is a contradiction to say that compassion itself or absolute goodness could look at the human race with anger and lock us all into damnation, and still keep its divine essence. Attitudes and actions of that kind belong to a wicked person, not a virtuous one. They belong to a spirit from hell, not an angel of heaven. It is horrendous to attribute them to God.

[3] If you investigate what caused these ideas, you find this: People have taken the suffering on the cross to be redemption itself. The ideas above have flowed from this idea the way one falsity flows from another in an unbroken chain. All you get from a vinegar bottle is vinegar. All you get from an insane mind is insanity.

Any inference leads to a series of related propositions. These are latent within the original inference and come forth from it, one after the other. This idea, that the suffering on the cross was redemption, has the capacity to yield more and more ideas that are offensive and disgraceful to God, until Isaiah's prophecy comes to pass:

> The priest and the prophet have gone astray because of beer; they stagger in their judgment. All the tables are full of the vomit they cast forth. (Isaiah 28:7, 8)

This idea of God and redemption has turned the entire theology from something spiritual into something earthly of the lowest kind. This is because mere earthly characteristics have been attributed to God. Yet everything about the church hinges on its concept of God and its view of redemption (which is the same as its view of salvation).[306] The concept of God and redemption is like a head: every part of the body is connected to it. When the concept is spiritual, everything about the church becomes spiritual; when it is earthly, everything about the church becomes earthly. Because the church's concept of God and redemption became merely earthly (meaning that it was down on the level of our bodies and senses), all the dogmatic ideas expressed since then by the church's heads and members have been merely earthly. Further ideas that hatch from these ideas will inevitably be false, because our earthly self constantly opposes our spiritual self; our earthly self sees spiritual things as phantoms and apparitions in the air.

This materialistic idea of redemption and of God has allowed thieves and robbers, so to speak (John 10:1, 8, 9), to take over the roads that lead in the direction of heaven and the Lord God the Savior. The main doors have been torn off the churches and now dragons, screech owls, wild beasts of the desert, and jackals have come in and are singing together out of tune.

This idea of redemption and God has been injected into the modern-day belief about prayer, as we know. We are supposed to ask God the Father to forgive our offenses for the sake of the cross and his Son's blood; we are supposed to ask God the Son to pray and intercede for us; and we are supposed to ask God the Holy Spirit to justify us and sanctify us.[307] Is this any different from praying to three gods, one after the other? Under this system, what differentiates divine governance from an aristocratic or hierarchical government? Or even the triumvirate that once occurred in Rome?[308] Instead of a "triumvirate," this should be called a "triumpersonate."

Under this belief, it would be easy for the Devil to "divide and conquer," as the saying goes—that is, to cause a division of minds and incite

133

rebel movements, now against one god, now against another (as people have been doing since the time of Arius[309] up to the present). The Devil would then be able to dethrone the Lord God the Savior, who has all power in heaven and on earth (Matthew 28:18), put some puppet of his own there, and either redirect worship to the puppet or reduce the amount of worship to both.

134 Here I will add the following memorable occurrences.

The first memorable occurrence. Once I went to a church in the world of spirits. Many people had gathered there. Before the service, they were debating back and forth about redemption.

The church was a square building. It had no windows in the walls, but there was a large opening overhead in the center of the roof. Light from heaven came in through that opening and provided more illumination inside than would have been supplied by windows in the walls.

As the people were talking back and forth about redemption, all of a sudden a pitch-black cloud sailing in from the north covered the opening. It became so dark inside that the people could not see each other at all and could scarcely see their own hands. While they were standing there stunned by this, the black cloud split down the middle. Through the gap the people saw angels coming down from heaven. The angels drove away the clouds on either side so that it became light again in the church.

Then the angels sent one of their own down to the church. At the request of the other angels, that angel asked the people what topic they were arguing about that so dark a cloud should come over them, taking away their light and plunging them in darkness.

They answered that the topic was redemption: "We were saying that the Son of God redeemed us all by suffering on the cross. By suffering he ritually purged and freed the human race from damnation and eternal death."

The angel who had been sent down said, "Why by the suffering on the cross? Explain why that was redemptive."

[2] At that point the priest came in and said, "I will lay out in sequence the things we know and believe. God the Father was angry at the human race. He damned it, excluded it from his mercy, declared us all detestable and accursed, and assigned us all to hell. He wanted his Son

to take that damnation on himself. The Son agreed. For this purpose the Son came down, took on a human manifestation, and let himself be crucified, thereby transferring the damnation of the human race to himself. For we read, 'Accursed is everyone who hangs on the wood of the cross' [Deuteronomy 21:22–23; Galatians 3:13]. By interceding and mediating like this, the Son appeased the Father. Then, moved with love for the Son and affected by the wretched state he saw him in on the wood of the cross, the Father proclaimed that he would give pardons, 'But only,' he said, 'for those to whom I attribute your justice. These children born of anger and a curse I will turn into children born of grace and a blessing. I will justify them and save them. The rest remain, as I proclaimed them before, children born of anger.' This is our faith; and that is the justice, added by God the Father to our faith, that enables this faith alone to justify us and save us."

[3] After the angel heard this he was silent for a long time; he could not help feeling stunned. Eventually he broke his silence and said the following:

"How can the Christian world be that insane? How can it wander that far from sound reason toward derangement? How can it base its fundamental dogma of salvation on paradoxes of this kind?[310]

"Surely anyone can see that those ideas are totally opposite to the divine essence, meaning the Lord's divine love and divine wisdom, as well as his omnipotence and omnipresence. No decent master could treat his servants that way. Not even a wild animal would treat its offspring or its young that way. That's horrible!

"To stop calling out to every member of the human race would go against the divine essence. It would go against the divine essence to change the divine design that has been established from eternity—the principle that all are judged by their own lives. It would go against the divine essence to take love or mercy away from anyone, let alone from the whole human race. It would go against the divine essence for the Father to be brought back to mercy by seeing the Son feeling wretched. Wouldn't that be the same as the Father's being brought back to his own essence, since mercy is the very essence of God? It is horrendous to think that he ever left it. From eternity to eternity, he *is* mercy.

[4] "Surely it is also impossible to transfer the justice of redemption to any entity (as you believe). This justice belongs to divine omnipotence. It is impossible to attribute and assign this justice to people, and pronounce them just, pure, and holy in the absence of any other means.

It is impossible to forgive people's sins and renew, regenerate, and save people just by giving them credit they do not deserve.

"Is it that easy to turn injustice into justice or a curse into a blessing? Couldn't God in that case turn hell into heaven and heaven into hell? Couldn't he turn the dragon into Michael and Michael into the dragon to break up their fight? What else would he need to do then but take away the faith that had been credited to one person and credit it to another? If that were possible, we in heaven would spend eternity shaking with fear!

"It is not consistent with justice or judgment for anyone who committed a crime to become guiltless, or for the crime to be wiped away, by someone else's taking it on. Surely this goes against all justice, both divine and human.

"The Christian world is still ignorant that the divine design exists. It is especially ignorant of the design that God built into the world at creation. God cannot go against that design—that would be going against himself, for God is the divine design itself."

[5] The priest understood what the angel had said, because the angels above were pouring down light from heaven. The priest groaned and said, "What can we do? Everyone today preaches this, prays it, believes it. All mouths are saying, 'Good Father, have mercy on us and forgive us our sins for the sake of the blood that your Son shed on the cross for us.' To Christ they all say, 'Lord, intercede for us.' We priests add, 'Send us the Holy Spirit.'"

The angel said, "I have watched priests make salves from a shallow understanding of the Word and smear those salves on eyes that have been blinded by their faith. Either that or from the same source they make medicated bandages to put on the wounds inflicted by their own dogmas; but the wounds don't heal. They are chronic.

"Therefore go to the person who is standing there"—and he pointed to me with his finger. "On behalf of the Lord he will teach you that the suffering on the cross was not redemption. It was the uniting of the Lord's humanity with the Father's divinity. Redemption, on the other hand, was gaining control over the hells and restructuring the heavens. Without these achievements, carried out while the Lord was in the world, no one on earth or in heaven would have attained salvation. That man will also tell you the divine design that was set up at creation for people to follow in their lives in order to be saved. Those who live by that design are numbered among the redeemed and are called the chosen."

After the angel said that, windows formed on the sides of the church. Light flowed in through them from the four directions of that world. Angel guardians appeared, flying in a brilliant light. The angel was taken up to his companion angels above the opening in the roof; and we left feeling happy.

The second memorable occurrence. One morning after I woke up, the sun in the spiritual world appeared to me in its splendor. Beneath it I saw the heavens as far away from that sun as our earth is from our sun. Then from the heavens I heard individual words that would be impossible for me to convey, which came together to form a statement that could be expressed as follows: *There is one God, he is human, and his dwelling place is in that sun.* This utterance came down through the middle heavens to the lowest one. From there it came into the world of spirits, where I was.

The angels' idea of one God gradually turned into an idea of three gods as it came down—I could sense it. So I went over to speak with spirits who were thinking three gods.

"What a heinous idea!" I said. "Why did it ever occur to you?"

"We are thinking *three* from our mental image of a triune God," they answered, "but this does not come down into words when we speak. Out loud we always say that God is one. If there is a different idea in our minds, so be it, as long as it does not flow down and break up the oneness of God in what we say. From time to time, though, our idea does in fact flow down, because it is there inside us. If we happened to speak at that point we would be saying three gods; but we are careful not to say that so that we are not laughed at by people who hear us."

[2] Then they openly voiced their real thinking and said, "Aren't there three gods, though? There are three divine persons, each of whom is God. What else can we think when the leader of our church, drawing on the treasury of the church's sacred dogmas, ascribes creation to one divine person, redemption to another, and sanctification to the third? Worse yet, when our leader assigns them activities, he gives each person its own activity and says that that activity cannot be shared by the other persons. The activities are not only creating, redeeming, and sanctifying, but also assigning spiritual credit or blame, mediating, and putting things into effect. In that case surely there is one who created us, who also assigns us credit or blame; a second who redeemed us, who also mediates for us; and a third who gives us our assigned and mediated credit or blame, who also sanctifies us.

"Everyone knows that the Son of God was sent into the world by God the Father to redeem the human race. That's why he became the

One who purges, mediates, appeases, and intercedes. Because he is the same as the Son of God from eternity, there are two persons that are distinct from each other. And because the two of them are in heaven, the one sitting on the other's right-hand side, there has to be a third who carries out in the world the decisions the other two made in heaven."

[3] When they finished I kept quiet, but I was thinking to myself, "What idiocy! They have no idea what the Word means by mediation."[311]

Then the Lord commanded three angels to come down from heaven and become connected to me so that I could draw on deep perception as I talked to the spirits who had the idea of three gods, particularly on the topics of mediation, intercession, appeasement, and ritual purging. The spirits I was talking to attribute those activities to the second person, the Son, but only after he became human. Yet he became human many ages after creation. In the meantime those four means of salvation did not exist: God the Father had not been appeased, the human race had not been ritually purged, and no one had been sent from heaven to intercede or mediate.

[4] Then I spoke to them from the inspiration that came over me at that point. I said, "Come near, all who are able, and hear what the Word means by mediation, intercession, ritual purging, and appeasement. They are four activities attributed to the grace of the one God in his human manifestation.

"No human being can ever get close to God the Father. Neither can God the Father get close to any human being. He is infinite. He is in his underlying reality, which is Jehovah. If he came close to any of us with that underlying reality he would consume us the way fire consumes a piece of wood and leaves nothing but ashes. This is clear from what God said to Moses when Moses wanted to see him: God said that no one can see him and live (Exodus 33:20). The Lord says, 'No one has ever seen God except the Son, who is close to the Father's heart' (John 1:18; Matthew 11:27). The Lord also says, 'No one has heard the voice of the Father or seen what he looks like' (John 5:37).

"Admittedly, we read that Moses saw Jehovah eye to eye and spoke with him face to face [Exodus 33:11; Deuteronomy 34:10]; but an angel was involved as an intermediary. The same with Abraham and Gideon.

"Now, because this is the true nature of God the Father, it pleased him to take on a human manifestation and give people access through it so that he could hear them and talk to them. This human manifestation is what is called the Son of God. This is what mediates, intercedes, appeases, and ritually purges.

"Let me, therefore, give the meaning of these four activities carried out by God the Father's human manifestation:

[5] "*Mediation* refers to his human manifestation as the medium through which we can get closer to God the Father, and God the Father can get closer to us and teach and lead us so as to save us. This is why the Son of God, meaning the human manifestation of God the Father, is called the Savior, and in the world was called Jesus, which means salvation.

"*Intercession* refers to ongoing mediation. Absolute love, with its mercy, forgiveness, and grace, constantly intercedes; that is, it mediates for the people who do its commandments, the people it loves.

"*Ritual purging* refers to the removal of the sins that we would quickly fall into if we turned to Jehovah without mediation.

"*Appeasement* refers to the actions of mercy and grace that prevent us from causing our own damnation through sin and also protect us from desecrating what is holy. This has the same meaning as the mercy seat over the ark in the tabernacle.[312]

[6] "It is known that God uses appearances when he speaks in the Word: for example, the appearance that he is angry, takes revenge, tests people, punishes them, throws them into hell, and damns them. Indeed, the appearance is that he does evil. Nevertheless, he is angry at no one, does not take revenge on, test, or punish anyone, throw anyone into hell, or damn anyone. To do this would be as far from God as hell is from heaven—in fact, infinitely farther. Therefore these are expressions of an appearance. In a sense, *ritual purging, appeasement, interceding,* and *mediating* are also expressions of an appearance. They mean activities through God's human manifestation that provide us access to God, and to grace from God.

"Because people have not understood these qualities they have divided God into three and have founded every teaching in the church on these three. By doing so they have falsified the Word. The result is *the abomination of desolation* foretold by the Lord in Daniel [11:31; 12:11], and later on in Matthew chapter 24[:15]."

After I had spoken, the group of spirits withdrew from around me. I noticed that the spirits who were still thinking three gods were looking down toward hell. The spirits who were thinking that there is one God within whom there is a divine Trinity and that the Trinity is in the Lord God the Savior were looking toward heaven. To the latter group the sun in heaven appeared, where Jehovah exists in his human manifestation.

136　　*The third memorable occurrence.* From far away I saw five halls.[313] Each one was surrounded with light from heaven. The first hall was surrounded with crimson light like the light in the clouds just before sunrise on earth. The second hall was surrounded with a yellow light like the light of the dawn after the sun has come up. The third hall was surrounded with a bright white light like the light in our world at midday. The fourth hall was surrounded with a half light as when daylight begins to mix with evening shadows. The fifth hall stood in the shadow of evening itself.

These halls in the world of spirits are buildings where educated people meet to discuss various deep questions that serve to develop their knowledge, intelligence, and wisdom.

Once I spotted these halls, a strong desire to go to one of them came over me. I went in my spirit to the one that was surrounded with a half light. I entered the hall and saw a group of educated people who had gathered. They were discussing with each other the implications of the statement that since being taken up into heaven the Lord sits at the right hand of God (Mark 16:19).

[2] Many of the participants said that it should be taken to mean just what it says—the Son sits next to the Father. When they were asked why, some said that the Father placed the Son on his right side because of the redemption that the Son had brought about. Some said that the Son sits there because of love. Some said that he sits there because he is the Father's adviser and the angels honor him. Others said that he sits there because the Father had allowed him to rule in his place—the Word says that he was given all power in heaven and on earth. A large part of the group, however, said he sits there so that he can hear the people on the right[314] for whom he intercedes; all people in the church today go to God the Father and pray that he may have mercy for the sake of his Son; this has the effect that the Father turns to the Son to receive the Son's mediation. Some others said that it is only the Son of God from eternity who sits to the right of the Father. He sits there in order to share his divinity with the Son of Humankind born in the world.

[3] On hearing these statements, I felt utterly astounded that these well-educated people were still so ignorant about heaven, even though they had already spent some time in the spiritual world. I became aware of the reason, though: because of their confidence in their own intelligence, they had not let themselves be taught by the wise.

So that they would no longer remain in ignorance about the Son sitting at the right hand of the Father, I raised my hand and asked that the participants lend their ears to a few things I desired to say on the subject.

Because they agreed, I said, "Don't you know from the Word that the Father and the Son are one, and that the Father is in the Son and the Son in the Father? The Lord openly says so in John chapter 10, verse 30, and chapter 14, verses 10 and 11. If you don't believe these statements you divide God into two. Once you have done that, you cannot help thinking about God in a way that is earthly, limited to your senses, and even materialistic. This type of thinking has been occurring in the world ever since the Council of Nicaea, which introduced the idea of three divine persons from eternity. With that idea, the Council turned the church into a stage with painted drop curtains where actors perform new plays.

"Surely everyone knows and acknowledges, however, that there is one God. If you acknowledge this in your heart and your spirit, all the ideas you uttered a moment ago will spontaneously disperse and bounce off you into the air like nonsense off the ear of a wise person."

[4] Many of them blazed with anger when they heard that. They had a burning desire to twist my ears and demand silence from me. Instead the leader of the gathering said indignantly, "This is not a discussion about unity and plurality in God. We believe in both. This discussion concerns the meaning of the fact that the Son sits at the right hand of his Father. If you know anything about this, say it."

"I will," I answered, "but please stop all the noise. *Sitting at the right hand* doesn't mean literally sitting at the right hand! It means the omnipotence God has through the human manifestation he took on in the world. Through that human manifestation God became the same on the lowest level as he is on the highest.[315] Through that human manifestation he entered the hells, dismantled them, and gained control over them. Through that human manifestation he restructured the heavens. It was through that human manifestation, then, that he redeemed both people and angels, a redemption that will last forever.

"If you consult the Word, and you are in a condition that allows for enlightenment, you are going to perceive that *the right hand* there means omnipotence. For instance in [Isaiah and] David:[316] '*My hand founded* the earth, and *my right hand* hammered out the heavens' (Isaiah 48:13). 'God has sworn by *his right hand* and by the arm of his strength' (Isaiah 62:8). '*Your right hand* sustains me' (Psalms 18:35). 'Pay attention to the

Son whom you have strengthened for yourself. *Your hand* is for *the man on your right.* You have strengthened yourself for the Son of Humankind' (Psalms 80:15, 17).

"From these passages it is clear how we should understand another passage: 'Jehovah said to my Lord, "Sit at *my right hand* until I place your enemies as a footstool for your feet." Jehovah will send the rod of your strength out of Zion to rule in the midst of your enemies' (Psalms 110:1, 2). The whole of Psalm 110 is about the Lord's battle with the hells and the process of gaining control over them. Because the right hand of God means omnipotence, the Lord says that he is going to sit at *the right hand of power* (Matthew 26:63, 64), and at *the right hand of God's strength* (Luke 22:69)."

[5] The group shouted disapproval; but I said, "Be careful now. Perhaps the hand[317] will appear from heaven. When it appears—and I myself have seen it—it strikes unbelievable terror into you because of its power. That hand convinced me that the right hand of God means omnipotence."

No sooner had I said this than the hand appeared in the sky just above us. It was huge. When they saw it, it struck so much terror into them that they rushed in throngs to the doors. Some ran to the windows to throw themselves out. Some collapsed, fainting because they could not breathe. I was not terrified, though. I walked out slowly behind them.

When I was at a distance I turned around and saw the hall covered in a dark cloud. Word came to me from heaven that the cloud was there now because the participants had been speaking from a belief in three gods; but the light that had been around the hall before would return when saner people were meeting there.

137 *The fourth memorable occurrence.*[318] I heard that a council had been summoned that was made up of those who were famous for writing and research on the modern-day faith and on the justification of the elect by that faith.[319]

This was in the world of spirits. I was allowed to attend in spirit. I saw that the participants were from the clergy. There were some who agreed and some who disagreed. To the right stood people who in the world had been called the apostolic fathers, who had lived in the centuries before the Council of Nicaea. To the left stood men from after those centuries who were well known for their printed works or works their followers had copied in manuscript form. Many in the latter group had clean-shaven faces and wore curled wigs of women's hair. Some of them had collars with ruffs; some had collars with bands.[320] The former group, however, were bearded and wore no wigs.

Before both groups stood a man who had been a judge and critic of the writers of this century. With the staff in his hand, this chairman banged on the floor and brought about silence. He stepped up onto the dais where the central chair was and uttered a groan. After groaning he intended to shout out loud, but the breath expended in groaning made the shout catch in his throat.

[2] Finally, when he was able to speak, he said, "Friends, what times we live in! Someone has risen out of the herd of the laity. He has no gown, no cap, no laurel.[321] Yet he has pulled our faith down from heaven and thrown it into the river Styx. What a crime! Yet that faith is our only star. It shines like Orion during the night and like Lucifer in the morning.[322] That man, although well advanced in years, remains completely blind to the mysteries of our faith because he has not opened our faith and seen in it the justice of the Lord our Savior, as well as the Lord's mediation and appeasement. And since he hasn't seen these aspects of our faith, he has also missed the wonders of justification by that faith. These wonders are the forgiving of sins, regeneration, sanctification, and salvation.

"Instead of accepting our faith, which is supremely effective for one's salvation because it is a faith in three divine persons and therefore in the whole of God, this man has redirected belief toward the second Person— in fact, not even the whole second Person, but just his human manifestation. That human manifestation we do indeed call divine, because it was the incarnation of the Son from eternity; but who thinks of it as anything other than something merely human? What faith can we have in that except one that gushes materialist philosophy like a fountain? Since that kind of faith is not spiritual, it is virtually the same as faith in a substitute or a saint. You all know what Calvin said in his day about worship from a faith like that.[323] Any one of you, tell us, please, where faith comes from. Doesn't it come directly from God? That is why it contains all the means of salvation."

[3] At that the chairman's colleagues on the left side (the men with clean-shaven faces, curly wigs, and ruffs around their necks) burst into applause and shouted, "Very wisely said! We know that we cannot receive anything that is not given us from heaven!"

[Then the chairman continued,][324] "That prophet should tell us where faith comes from and what faith is if it isn't this. It is impossible for faith to be different or to come from any other source. Revealing another true faith besides this one is as impossible as riding a horse to some constellation in the sky, grabbing one of its stars, hiding it in your coat pocket, and bringing it back with you!"

He included this last comment to make his friends laugh at any new faith.

[4] The men on the right side, though, who were bearded and wore no wigs, were upset when they heard this. One of them, an old man, stood up. (Later, however, he looked like a young adult, because he was an angel from heaven, where people of every stage of life become young adults.)[325]

The old man said, "I have heard the nature of the faith you all have—the faith the chairman praised just now. But that faith is nothing but the tomb of our Lord after the resurrection, locked up again by Pilate's soldiers. I have opened that faith but found nothing inside it except magicians' wands used by the sorcerers in Egypt for doing miracles. To your eyes, your faith looks like a treasure chest made of gold and encrusted with precious stones; but when it is opened, the chest is empty, except perhaps for some dust from papal relics[326] left in the corners. Papists have the same faith, you see, except that they are hiding it now behind external acts of piety.[327]

"To use a simile, your faith is also like the Vestal virgin in ancient times who was buried alive for extinguishing the sacred fire.[328] In fact, I can state it directly: to my eyes your faith looks just like the golden calf around which the children of Israel danced after Moses had left to go up to Jehovah on Mount Sinai [Exodus 32:1–20]. [5] Don't be surprised that I have spoken about your faith in these analogies—this is the way we who are in heaven speak about it.

"Our faith, on the other hand, is, was, and will be to eternity a belief in the Lord God the Savior, whose humanity is divine and whose divinity is human. It is a faith, then, that is adapted for reception. It is a faith that unites what is divine and spiritual to what is human and earthly. It becomes a spiritual faith on an earthly plane. What is earthly then becomes transparent from the spiritual light of our faith.

"The truths that constitute our faith are as many as the verses in the sacred tome.[329] These truths are all like stars, whose light reveals, and shows the shape of, our faith. People acquire this faith from the Word by means of their earthly light—the light of knowledge, thought, and persuasion; but if people believe in the Lord, he turns this faith into conviction, trust, and confidence. Through this process their faith comes to be spiritual as well as earthly, and enlivened by goodwill. To us this faith is like a queen decorated with as many precious stones as could be seen in the wall of the Holy Jerusalem (Revelation 21:17–20).

[6] "So that you won't think the words I am saying are exaggerated and discount them as a result, I will read you something from the Holy Word that will make it clear that our faith is not faith in a human being, as you think it is; it is faith in the true God in whom everything divine exists. John says, 'Jesus Christ is the true God and eternal life' (1 John 5:20). Paul says, 'All the fullness of divinity dwells physically in Christ' (Colossians 2:9). In the Acts of the Apostles it says of Paul, 'To both Jews and Greeks he preached repentance before God and faith in our Lord Jesus Christ' (Acts 20:21). The Lord himself says that all power in heaven and on earth has been given to him (Matthew 28:18); but these are just a few passages."

[7] After that the angel looked at me and said, "You know what the beliefs of the so-called Evangelicals[330] are or should be about the Lord the Savior. Recite a few of them so that we may know whether they foolishly believe that the Lord's human manifestation is merely human, or whether they ascribe anything of divinity to that human manifestation, and if so, how."

I then read out loud excerpts from the book of Evangelical orthodoxy called the *Formula of Concord,* printed in Leipzig in 1756.[331] I read the following: "In Christ the divine nature and the human nature are so united that they are one Person" (pages 606, 762).[332] "Christ is truly God and a human being in an individual Person; he remains so to eternity" (pages 609, 673, 762).[333] "In Christ God is human and a human is God" (pages 607, 765).[334] "Christ's human nature has been exalted to all divine majesty" (with quotes from many of the apostolic fathers, pages 844–852, 860–865, 869–878).[335] "In his human nature Christ is omnipresent and fills all things" (pages 768, 783, 784, 785).[336] "In his human nature Christ has been given all power in heaven and on earth" (pages 775, 776, 780).[337] "In his human nature Christ sits at the right hand of the Father" (pages 608, 764).[338] "We are to call on Christ in his human nature" (page 226; this statement is supported there by Scriptural passages).[339] The Augsberg Confession completely supports this worship (page 19).[340]

[8] After I read these things out loud, I turned to the chairman and said, "I know that all who are here are associated with people on earth who are like them. Tell me, if you would: do you know whom you are associated with?"

He answered in a solemn tone, "I do know. I am associated with a famous man, a commander of battalions in the church's army of the enlightened."[341]

Because he answered in such a solemn tone, I said, "Forgive my asking if you know where that famous commander lives."

"I do know," he said. "He lives not far from where Luther is buried."

Smiling at this I said, "Why do you say *where Luther is buried?* Don't you know that Luther has risen, and that he has now recanted his errors regarding justification by faith in three divine Persons from eternity? Surely you know that because of this he has been transferred to join the blessed in the new heaven, and that he laughs when he looks upon his insane followers."[342]

"I know," he retorted, "but what difference does that make to me?"

Then in the same tone he had used, I addressed him and said, "Pass on to the famous person you are associated with that I am concerned that on a recent occasion he went against the orthodoxy of his own church and took away the Lord's divinity. He let his pen plow a furrow and carelessly sowed materialist philosophy in it when he wrote against the worship of our Lord the Savior."

"I can't do that," the chairman replied, "because on this topic he and I are more or less of one mind. Besides, he doesn't understand the things I tell him, although all the things he tells me I understand very clearly. The spiritual world enters the material world and perceives the thoughts of people there, but it doesn't work the other way around. These are the present conditions of interaction between spirits and people."

[9] Since the chairman and I were already conversing, I added: "If possible I'd like to digress to some other questions. Do you know that the orthodoxy of the Evangelicals, presented in their church handbook called the *Formula of Concord,* teaches that in Christ, God is human and a human is God and that his divinity and humanity exist in one individual person and remain so to eternity? If so, how then could he, and how can you, befoul the worship of the Lord with materialist philosophy?"

To that he replied, "Do I know that? Yes and no."

Therefore I went on to say, "I ask your associate, although he is absent, or else you in his place: where did the soul of the Lord our Savior come from? If you say it came from Mary, you are insane. If you say it came from Joseph, you desecrate the Word. But if you say it came from the Holy Spirit you have the right answer, provided that by the Holy Spirit you mean the Divinity emanating and having an effect, which means that the Lord is the Son of Jehovah God.

[10] "Again I ask, what is the hypostatic union[343] [in the Lord our Savior]? If you reply that it is a union between two entities, one above and the other below, you are insane, because in that case you could view God our Savior as two entities just as you have viewed the Godhead as three entities. If you say that it is a personal union like the partnership between the soul and the body, you have the right answer. This follows your doctrine and the doctrine of the church fathers. See the *Formula of Concord* pages 765 to 768.[344]

"Also check the Athanasian Creed where it says, 'Proper faith is for us to believe and confess that our Lord Jesus Christ is both God and a human being. Yet although he is both God and a human being, still he is one Christ, not two. He is one in every way, not by a mixing of substance but by a oneness of person. For as the rational soul and the flesh is one human being, so God and a human being is one Christ.'[345]

[11] "Still further I ask, what was the damnable heresy of Arius that caused Emperor Constantine the Great to call the Council of Nicaea?[346] Wasn't it the denial of the divinity of the Lord's human manifestation?

"For another thing, tell me whom you see as the subject of the following words in Jeremiah: 'Behold, the days are coming when I will raise up for David a righteous offshoot who will rule as king; and this is his name: Jehovah is our Justice' (Jeremiah 23:5, 6; 33:15, 16). If you say 'the Son from eternity,' you are insane. He was not the Redeemer. If you say 'the Son born in time, who was "the only begotten Son of God"' (John 1:18; 3:16), you have the right answer. By redeeming us, he became the justice on which you base your faith. Also read Isaiah 9:6 and the other passages predicting that Jehovah himself was going to come into the world."

At this the chairman looked away in silence.

[12] The presiding officer then wanted to end the council with a prayer but suddenly a man in the left-hand group interrupted. He had a cloth head-covering on with a hat on top of it. He touched his hat with one finger and said, "I too am associated with a man in your world. He has been appointed to a highly exalted position. I know this because I speak on his behalf as on my own."

I asked him where that eminent man lives. He answered, "In Göteborg. From him I once got the impression that your new doctrine smacks of Muhammadanism."[347]

I saw that all the spirits on the right where the apostolic fathers were standing were shocked when they heard that word, and their faces fell. I heard them crying, both in thought and out loud, "What an outrage! What times we live in!"

To calm their understandable wrath I lifted my hand and asked for their attention. When they gave it to me, I said, "I am aware that a man of stature wrote some such accusation in a letter; later the letter was printed. If he had known at that point, however, what blasphemy it was, he would surely have torn it to pieces with his own fingers and given it to Vulcan to consume.[348] The Lord responded to a similar attack when the Jews said that Christ was doing miracles with something other than divine power (Matthew 12:22–32). Among other things, the Lord says in that response, 'Whoever is not with me is against me. Whoever is not gathering with me is scattering' (Matthew 12:30)."

At this, the chairman, his ally, lowered his face. Soon, however, he lifted it again and said, "Now I have heard harder things than ever from you!"

I countered, "There are two doctrines behind these proceedings: materialist philosophy and Muhammadanism—lies invented by treachery, two deadly stabs aimed at turning and deterring the human will from the holy worship of the Lord."[349]

I turned to the man from the left-hand group and said, "Tell your man in Göteborg, if you can, to read what the Lord has said in Revelation 3:18 and also in Revelation 2:16."[350]

[13] When I said that, a riot broke out, but it was calmed by light sent down from heaven. As a result of the light, many on the left crossed over to join those on the right. Two groups who stayed on the left were those spirits whose thoughts were without purpose and who would therefore hang on the sayings of any authority, and those spirits who saw the Lord as only a human being. The light sent down from heaven seemed to be repelled by these latter two groups, but it seemed to flow into the spirits who crossed from left to right.

Chapter 3

The Holy Spirit and the Divine Action

UPON entering the spiritual world, which generally happens on the third day after death,[351] all members of the Sacred Order[352] who have developed a just idea of the Lord our Savior are first taught about the divine Trinity. They are specifically taught that the Holy Spirit is not a separate God; the Word uses the phrase to mean the divine action that radiates from the one omnipresent God. They are specifically taught about the Holy Spirit because after death many fanatics who have believed they were divinely inspired[353] fall into the mad delusion that they themselves are the Holy Spirit. There are many church people who believed while they were in the world that the Holy Spirit spoke through them. They terrify others with the Lord's statement in Matthew that it is an unforgivable sin to speak against what the Holy Spirit has inspired in them (Matthew 12:31, 32).

After all are taught, any who abandon their belief that the Holy Spirit is a separate God are later informed about the unity of God. They are told that that unity has not been partitioned into three Persons, each of whom is God and Lord (as the Athanasian Creed would have it). Instead the divine Trinity exists within the Lord the Savior like the soul, the body, and the radiating effect of any human being.

Then they undergo preparations to accept the faith of the new heaven. After their preparation is complete, a road opens up for them to a community in heaven where that same faith exists. They are given a place to live among their companions. There they live in eternal bliss.

Because we have covered God the Creator and the Lord the Redeemer, we need to cover the Holy Spirit as well. This treatment, like the rest, will be divided into separate points. They are as follows:

1. The Holy Spirit is the divine truth and also the divine action and effect that radiate from the one God, in whom the divine Trinity exists: the Lord God the Savior.

2. Generally speaking, the divine actions and powerful effects meant by the Holy Spirit are the acts of reforming and regenerating us. Depending on the outcome of this reformation and regeneration, the divine actions and powerful effects also include the acts of renewing us, bringing us to life, sanctifying us, and making us just; and depending on the outcome of these in turn, the divine actions and powerful effects also include the acts of purifying us from evils, forgiving our sins, and ultimately saving us.354

3. In respect to the clergy, the divine actions and powerful effects meant by "the sending of the Holy Spirit" are the acts of enlightening and teaching.

4. The Lord has these powerful effects on those who believe in him.

5. The Lord takes these actions on his own initiative on behalf of the Father, not the other way around.

6. Our spirits are our minds and whatever comes from them.

139   1. *The Holy Spirit is the divine truth and also the divine action and effect that radiate from the one God, in whom the divine Trinity exists: the Lord God the Savior.* The Holy Spirit really means the divine truth; therefore it also means the Word. In this sense, the Lord himself is in fact the Holy Spirit. Nevertheless, because the church nowadays characterizes the Holy Spirit as the divine action (meaning that part of the Divine that actually justifies us), therefore the divine action is what we mean by "the Holy Spirit" in the discussion here. For another thing, divine action takes place through the divine truth that radiates from the Lord. Whatever radiates out has one and the same essence as the source it radiates from. Take for example someone's soul, someone's body, and someone's effect: these three together share one essence. In us that essence is merely human. In the Lord there was a divine essence and also a human one. After the Lord's glorification these two essences were as completely united as a cause is with its effect or an essence with its form. Therefore three essential components, called the Father, the Son, and the Holy Spirit, are one in the Lord.

[2] I have already demonstrated that the Lord is divine trueness or truth [see §85:3]. As for the Holy Spirit being divine truth, the following passages make this clear:

> A branch will come out of the trunk of Jesse. The spirit of Jehovah will rest upon him, the spirit of wisdom and intelligence, the spirit of counsel and strength. He will strike the earth with the rod of his mouth, and

with the spirit of his lips he will kill the ungodly. Justice will be his loincloth, and the truth will wrap his thighs. (Isaiah 11:1, 2, 4, 5)

He will arrive like a narrow river; the spirit of Jehovah will lift up a standard against him. Then the Redeemer will come to Zion. (Isaiah 59:19, 20)

The spirit of the Lord Jehovih is upon me. Jehovah has anointed me. He has sent me to proclaim the good news to the poor. (Isaiah 61:1; Luke 4:18)

This is my covenant. My spirit that is upon you, my words, will not leave your mouth from now on forevermore. (Isaiah 59:21)

[3] Since the Lord is absolute truth, everything that radiates from him is truth. All this truth is known as the Comforter, which is also called the Spirit of Truth and the Holy Spirit, as the following passages clearly show:

I tell you *the truth:* it is better for you that I go away, because if I do not go away the Comforter will not come to you; but if I do go away I will send him to you. (John 16:7)

When *the Spirit of Truth* comes, he will lead you into *all truth.* He will not speak on his own; rather, whatever he hears he will say. (John 16:13)

[The Comforter] will glorify me because he will take *from what is mine* and will make it known to you. Everything the Father has is *mine.* This is why I said that [the Comforter] will take from *what is mine* and will make it known to you. (John 16:14, 15)

I will ask the Father to give another Comforter to you, *the Spirit of Truth.* The world cannot accept him because it does not see him or recognize him; but you know him because he dwells among you and will be in you. I will not leave you orphans; I am coming to you and you will see me. (John 14:16, 17, 18)

When the Comforter comes—*the Spirit of Truth* whom I am going to send you from the Father—he will testify about me. (John 15:26)

The Comforter is called "the Holy Spirit" (John 14:26).

[4] In mentioning the Comforter and the Holy Spirit, the Lord was referring to himself. This is clear from these words of his: "the world would not recognize him *but you know him;*" "I will not leave you

orphans, *I am coming to you; you will see me.*" And elsewhere, "Behold I am with you every day, even to the close of the age" (Matthew 28:20). Also from the Lord's saying, "He will not speak from himself; instead he will take from what is mine."

140   Now, because the Holy Spirit means divine truth and this was in the Lord and was the Lord himself (John 14:6), and the Holy Spirit could not come from anywhere else, therefore the Word says, "The Holy Spirit was not yet in existence, because Jesus was not glorified yet" (John 7:39); and after he was glorified, "He breathed on his disciples and said, 'Receive the Holy Spirit'" (John 20:22). The Lord breathed on his disciples and said this because breathing on someone is an outward representation of divine inspiration. To be inspired is in fact to be inserted into angelic communities.

From these points the intellect can grasp what the angel Gabriel said about the Lord's conception: "The Holy Spirit will descend upon you and the power of the Highest will cover you; therefore the Holy One that is born from you will be called the Son of God" (Luke 1:35). Likewise, "The angel of the Lord said to Joseph in a dream, 'Do not be afraid to accept Mary as your bride, for the Child that is conceived in her is from the Holy Spirit.' And Joseph did not touch her until she bore her first-born Son" (Matthew 1:20, 25). The "Holy Spirit" in this passage is the divine truth that radiates from Jehovah the Father. This emanation was the power of the Highest that covered Mary then. This view is therefore in alignment with the following statement in John: "The Word was with God, and the Word was God. And the Word became flesh" (John 1:1, 14). The Word there means divine truth, as you can see above under the heading "the faith of the new church," §3.

141   We have already shown that the divine Trinity exists within the Lord. This will be shown further in the following sections where we will need to deal with this point explicitly. Here I will only add something to show the absurdity of dividing the Trinity into persons.

It would be like a minister in the church teaching from the pulpit what people should believe and practice while another minister stands next to him and whispers in his ear, "You are saying the right thing; say some more about that." The two of them tell a third minister standing on the pulpit stairs[355] to go down into the church, open the congregation's ears, and pour these things into their hearts; the third minister is also told to make the people pure and holy—living examples of justice.

The divine Trinity divided into persons, each of whom is individually God and Lord, is like three suns over one solar system—one sun beside another high up, and a third sun lower down that bathes angels and people and brings the heat, the light, and all the power of the first two suns into human minds, hearts, and bodies and refines them the way fire under a retort sharpens, clarifies, and sublimates substances. If this were the reality, surely we would all be burned to ashes.

A governance in heaven by three divine persons would be like a government of three monarchs in one country. It would be like a leadership of three equally powerful generals over one army. It would be much like the Roman government before the times of the Caesars when there was a consul, a senate, and a tribune for the common people.[356] Power was indeed divided between them, but the ultimate power was held by them all together.

Anyone can see that it would be ridiculous, preposterous, and insane to impose a government like that over heaven. Yet that kind of government would be imposed if power like the supreme consul's were given to God the Father, power like the senate's to the Son, and power like the tribune's to the Holy Spirit. This is what is involved in attributing to each person a function of his own, especially if you add that these activities cannot be shared.

2. *Generally speaking, the divine actions and powerful effects meant by the Holy Spirit are the acts of reforming and regenerating us. Depending on the outcome of this reformation and regeneration, the divine actions and powerful effects also include the acts of renewing us, bringing us to life, sanctifying us, and making us just; and depending on the outcome of these in turn, the divine actions and powerful effects also include the acts of purifying us from evils, forgiving our sins, and ultimately saving us.*[357] These are the powerful effects, one after the other, that the Lord has on people who believe in him and who adapt and modify themselves in order to welcome him and invite him to stay. Divine truth has these effects. Among Christians the Word has these effects because the Word is the only means by which Christians can go to the Lord and the Lord can come to them. As I said before, the Lord is absolute divine truth; so is everything that emanates from him. It is important to take this to mean the divine truth *in connection with goodness,* which is the same as faith in connection with goodwill; faith is nothing but truth, and goodwill is nothing but goodness.

The divine truth in connection with goodness, that is, faith in connection with goodwill, is the force that reforms and regenerates us; then renews us, brings us to life, sanctifies us, and justifies us; and, depending on our level of growth and forward movement, purifies us from evils. (Being purified from our evils is the same as having our sins forgiven.)

142

All these actions of the Lord cannot be explained here one by one, however. Each one would need its own analysis with support from the Word and illustrative reasoning. This is not the place for that. The reader [who wishes to know more about them] should turn instead to the topics that come later in the book: goodwill [§§392–462], faith [§§336–391], free choice [§§463–508], repentance [§§509–570], and reformation and regeneration [§§571–625].

It is important to know that the Lord is carrying out these salvation processes in every single one of us all the time. They are the steps to heaven. The Lord wants to save everyone; his purpose is to save all people. Anyone who has a purpose desires the means to achieve it. The Lord's coming, his redeeming humankind, and his suffering on the cross were for the sake of our salvation (Matthew 18:11; Luke 19:10). Because saving people was his purpose and is his purpose forever, it follows that having the powerful effects on us that were just listed is his intermediate purpose, and saving us is his ultimate purpose.

143 The producing of these powerful effects is the "Holy Spirit" that the Lord sends to those who believe in him and who modify themselves to receive him. The producing of these powerful effects is also meant by "the spirit" in the following passages:

> I will give a new heart and *a new spirit.* I will put *my spirit* within you and I will make you walk the path of salvation. (Ezekiel 36:26, 27; 11:19)

> Create a clean heart in us, O God, and renew *a firm spirit* within me. Restore to me the joy of your salvation, and let *a willing spirit* sustain me. (Psalms 51:10, 12)

> Jehovah forms *the human spirit* within us. (Zechariah 12:1)

> In my soul I awaited you at night. *In my spirit,* which is within me, I awaited you in the morning. (Isaiah 26:9)

> Make yourselves a new heart and a new spirit. Why should you die, O house of Israel? (Ezekiel 18:31)

And so on.

In these passages, "a new heart" means wanting what is good and "a new spirit" means understanding what is true. The reference to God's giving a soul to those who walk the path of salvation makes it clear that the Lord has these powerful effects on those who do what is good and believe what is true—those who have a faith that is connected with goodwill. This is also clear from the mention of a "willing spirit." The necessity for us to do our part of the work is clear from the following words: "Make yourselves a new heart and a new spirit. Why should you die, O house of Israel?" [Ezekiel 18:31].

We read that when Jesus was baptized the heavens opened and John **144** saw the Holy Spirit coming down like a dove (Matthew 3:16; Mark 1:10; Luke 3:22; John 1:32, 33). This happened because baptism means regeneration and purification, and so does a dove.

Surely anyone can see that that dove was not the Holy Spirit and that the Holy Spirit was not in the dove. In heaven doves appear quite often. Every time they appear, the angels know that they correspond to feelings and thoughts in other angels nearby about regeneration and purification. As soon as the angels go to those other angels and start a conversation on a different subject than the one being pondered when the doves appeared, the doves immediately vanish.

The situation is similar with many things the prophets saw. John, for example, saw a lamb on Mount Zion (Revelation 14:1 and elsewhere). Surely everyone realizes that the Lord was not that lamb and was not in that lamb. The lamb was instead a representation of the Lord's innocence. This highlights the error of those who deduce the existence of three persons in the Trinity from the dove seen above the Lord when he was baptized and the voice heard from heaven saying, "This is my beloved Son" [Matthew 3:16, 17].

The Lord uses faith and goodwill to regenerate us. This is the meaning of John the Baptist's saying, "I baptize you for repentance with water, but the one who is coming after me will baptize you with *the Holy Spirit* and with fire" (Matthew 3:11; Mark 1:8; Luke 3:16). Baptizing with the Holy Spirit and with fire means regenerating through the divine truth that is in faith and the divine goodness that is in goodwill. The following words of the Lord also mean the same thing: "Unless you have been born of water and spirit you cannot enter the kingdom of God" (John 3:5). "Water" in this passage, and elsewhere in the Word, means truth in our earthly or outer self, while "spirit" means truth connected with goodness in our spiritual or inner self.

Now, the Lord is absolute divine truth from divine goodness—this is **145** his very essence. We all do what we do because of our essence. It is clear then that the Lord constantly tries (and cannot help trying) to implant truth and goodness, or faith and goodwill, in everyone.

Many things in the world could be used to illustrate this [connection between essence and action]. For one thing, we all will and think, and as much as possible speak and act, on the basis of our essence.

Faithful people, for example, have faithful thoughts and intentions. People who are honorable, honest, godly, and religious have thoughts and intentions that are honorable, honest, godly, and religious. On the other hand, people who are arrogant, cunning, deceitful, and greedy have thoughts and intentions that are one with their essence. Jokers want only to joke around, and fools want only to babble their opposition to anything wise. In a word, an angel focuses and works only on what is heavenly, and a devil only on what is hellish.

As this is true of every bird, animal, fish, and winged or wingless insect, so it is true of every creature in the animal kingdom down to the lowest level: everything is known by its essence or nature. Every creature has its instincts accordingly.

Likewise in the plant kingdom, every tree, every bush, and every plant is known by its fruit and its seed. Its essence is bred into its fruit and its seed. It cannot produce anything that is unlike itself and its own kind. In fact, every type of soil or clay, every type of stone both precious and common, and every type of mineral and metal is recognized by its essence.

146　　*3. In respect to the clergy, the divine actions and powerful effects meant by "the sending of the Holy Spirit" are the acts of enlightening and teaching.* The actions of the Lord listed in the preceding point—reforming, regenerating, renewing, bringing to life, sanctifying, justifying, purifying, forgiving sins, and finally saving—flow from the Lord into both clergy and lay people. These actions are accepted by those who are in the Lord and in whom the Lord is (John 6:56; 14:20; 15:4, 5).

In the case of the clergy, however, there are other actions of the Lord as well: enlightening and teaching. The reason is that for ministers, being enlightened and taught is a part of their jobs that comes with their inauguration into the ministry.

Also, when ministers preach with passion they believe they are inspired, just like the Lord's disciples on whom the Lord breathed and said, "Receive the Holy Spirit" (John 20:22; see also what Mark 13:11 says). Some ministers even maintain that they have felt an inflow.[358]

Ministers have to be very careful, though, not to convince themselves that the passion that comes over many of them when they preach is God at work in their hearts. The same level of passion and an even more ardent one is found in fanatics who believe they are divinely inspired, in people who have the falsest teachings, and even in people who see no value in the Word and worship nature as their god, who toss faith and goodwill into packs on their backs.[359] When they preach and teach they hang these packs in front of their faces like some ruminatory stomach, squeezing and regurgitating out of them things they know will feed their listeners.

Passion in preaching is just an intensity in the earthly self. If passion has a love for truth inside it, then it is like the sacred fire that flowed into the apostles, about which it says in Acts:

> There appeared to them divided tongues as of fire, and one rested on each one of them. As a result they were all filled with the Holy Spirit. (Acts 2:3, 4)

If, on the other hand, there is a love for falsity inside that passion or intensity, then it is like fire smoldering inside a piece of wood that bursts into flame and burns the house down.

You who deny that the Word is holy and the Lord divine, please take your pack off your back and open it (as you freely do when you are at home). You will see.

When they enter the church, and even more when they climb the stairs into the pulpit, I know that the people meant by Lucifer in Isaiah—the people of Babylon, especially those who named themselves the Society of Jesus[360]—are overcome with passion. For many of them that passion comes from a hellish love. They raise their voices more vehemently and draw sighs from their chests more deeply than those whose passion comes from a heavenly love.

There are also two other spiritual actions of the Lord in members of the clergy; see §155 below.

The church is still hardly aware that in all our desire, thought, action, and speech, there is an inside and an outside. From early childhood we are taught to speak from the outside, no matter how the inside disagrees, which leads to pretense, flattery, and hypocrisy. People are double. The only simple people are those whose outer selves think and speak, and desire and act, from their inner selves. These people are in fact referred to as "simple" in the Word; for example, Luke 8:15, 11:34,[361] and elsewhere, even though they are wiser than double people.

Every created thing has two-fold and three-fold design, as the human body shows. Every nerve in the body is made of fibers, and every fiber is made of fibrils. Every muscle consists of bundles of fibers, and each bundle consists of individual motor fibers. Every artery consists of three layers of sheaths. It is the same in the human mind—its spiritual organic structure is the same. As I said before [§§34, 42, 69], the structure of the human mind is divided into three different levels. The highest or inmost

147

of these is called the heavenly level, the middle is called the spiritual level, and the lowest is called the earthly level.

There are people who deny that the Word is holy and that the Lord is divine; in every case their minds think at the lowest level. Nevertheless, because these people have learned the church's spiritual teachings from early childhood, they accept them, but they put them down below earthly preoccupations, which are various things having to do with academics, politics, and the civic and moral arena. Because these preoccupations sit at the lowest level of their mind, the level that is closest to speech, these people draw on the church's spiritual teachings when they speak in church and at public gatherings. Astoundingly, at the time they do not even realize that they are speaking and teaching something they do not believe. Nevertheless, when they are at home and feeling free, the door that had closed off their inner mind opens up and then they laugh at their own talk to the crowd. They say in their hearts that theological teachings are attractive traps for catching doves.

148　The inner and outer selves of people like that are like poisons with a coating of sugar, and like the wild gourds that the servants of the prophets gathered and put into a stew, but shouted when they ate it, "There is death in the pot!" (2 Kings 4:38–41). These people can also be likened to the beast from the earth that had two horns like the Lamb but spoke like a dragon (Revelation 13:11). Later in the Book of Revelation that beast is called the false prophet.

These people are like robbers spending time in a city where upright citizens live. The robbers behave morally and speak rationally while they are in town, but when they return to the woods they are wild animals. Or they are like pirates who are humans on land but crocodiles at sea. The pirates on land and the robbers in the city go around like panthers wearing sheepskins.

These people are like monkeys dressed in human clothing, with a mask of a human face in front of their own face. They can be likened to a woman preparing to go out, who puts on perfume, makeup, and a white silk dress embroidered with flowers; but when she comes home again, she strips for several lovers and gives them her disease.

This is the nature of those who take holiness away from the Word and divinity away from the Lord in their hearts, as years of experience in the spiritual world have allowed me to know. In that world all are kept at first in their outer selves; but afterward their outer selves are removed and they shift to their inner selves. At that point their comedy becomes a tragedy.

4. *The Lord has these powerful effects on those who believe in him.* The Lord has the powerful effects meant by the sending of the Holy Spirit on those who believe in him; that is, these are the people he reforms, regenerates, renews, brings to life, sanctifies, justifies, purifies from evils, and finally saves. This is clear from all the passages in the Word that establish that salvation and eternal life come to those who believe in the Lord (see the passages quoted in §107 above). The following passage makes the same point:

> Jesus said, "Any who *believe in me*—as Scripture says, rivers of living water will flow out of their bellies." This he said of *the Spirit* that *those who believe in him* are going to receive. (John 7:38, 39)

Also this passage:

> *The testimony of Jesus is the spirit of prophecy.* (Revelation 19:10)

The "spirit of prophecy" means a true doctrinal perspective from the Word. "Prophecy" has no other meaning except a doctrinal perspective. To prophesy means to teach that perspective. The testimony of Jesus means confessing faith in him. The testimony of Jesus also has this meaning in the following passage:

> Michael's angels conquered the dragon using the blood of the Lamb and the Word *of his testimony.* The dragon went away to make war on the rest of his seed, who were keeping God's commandments and who have the testimony of Jesus Christ. (Revelation 12:11, 17)

The people who are going to receive the powerful spiritual effects listed above [§142] are those who believe in the Lord Jesus Christ. He *is* salvation and eternal life. He is salvation because he is the Savior—this is the meaning of his name, Jesus. He is eternal life because those in whom he is and who are in him have eternal life. He is even called "eternal life" in 1 John 5:20.

Now, because the Lord is salvation and eternal life, it follows that he is also everything that enables us to gain salvation and eternal life. Therefore he is every part of reforming, regenerating, renewing, bringing to life, sanctifying, justifying, purifying from evils, and finally saving. The Lord is carrying out these processes in all of us, meaning that he is trying to have these effects on us; and when we adapt and modify ourselves to receive them, he actually carries them out in us. (Even the acts of adapting and modifying ourselves are actually from the Lord.) If we do not accept the Lord's processes with a willing spirit, he cannot carry them out in us, but his desire to do so remains constant.

151 Believing in the Lord is not only acknowledging him but also doing what he commands. Merely acknowledging him is just a matter of thought in our intellect. Doing what he commands also entails an acknowledgment in our will. The human mind consists of an intellect and a will. Thinking belongs to our intellect; doing belongs to our will. Therefore when we make a mere acknowledgment based on thinking in our intellect, we move toward the Lord with only half our mind. When we act, however, then we move toward the Lord with our whole mind; and this is believing.

The alternative to true belief is to divide our hearts, forcing our gaze upward while our flesh turns to face the ground. Then we fly like an eagle between heaven and hell. We do not follow our line of sight, however; we follow the pleasures of our flesh. Because our pleasures lie in hell, we fly down there. After indulging in our pleasures there and pouring out a libation of new wine to the demons, we develop a polite affectation and a sparkle in our eye; and so we masquerade as an angel of light.

These are the kind of satans[362] that we become after death if we acknowledge the Lord but do not do what he commands.

152 In a previous section [§142] we showed that the Lord's first and last purpose is for people to have salvation and eternal life. Since first and last purposes include all intermediate purposes as well, it follows that all the spiritual processes listed above [§142] are present in the Lord at the same time. In fact, the Lord brings all these processes to us at the same time, but they nonetheless take effect one after the other.

Our human body grows; so does our human mind. Our body grows in stature; our mind in wisdom. Furthermore, our mind rises up from one level to another. It goes from being earthly to being spiritual, and from being spiritual to being heavenly. At the lowest level we are knowledgeable; at the middle level we have understanding; at the highest level we are wise. This rising of the mind, though, happens only over the course of time; it takes place as we acquire truths for ourselves and connect them to something good.

This process is much like building a house. First we get ourselves the materials for it—the bricks, the shingles, the beams, the boards. Then we lay the foundation, put up the outside walls, frame out the rooms, hang the doors, install the windows in the walls, and build the stairs from one level to the next. All these stages and features are together at once in our goal, however, which is the comfortable and respectable living space we planned and provided for.

It is the same with a church building. As it is being constructed, all stages and features of it share one goal: the worship of God. The same goes for everything else—for example, horticulture and farming. It is also the same with management and business: the goal itself leads to the equipment and preparations necessary to meet that goal.

5. *The Lord takes these actions on his own initiative on behalf of the Father, not the other way around.* The reference to "taking actions" in this opening sentence means the same thing as "sending the Holy Spirit," since the processes listed above—reforming, regenerating, renewing, bringing to life, sanctifying, justifying, [purifying] from evils, and forgiving sins—which are attributed these days to the Holy Spirit as a God by himself, are actually processes carried out by the Lord.

153

As for the point that these processes are carried out by the Lord on behalf of the Father and not the other way around, I will first support this from the Word and then illustrate it with parallels.

Support from the Word occurs in the following passages:

> When the Comforter comes, *whom I am going to send from the Father*—the Spirit of Truth that goes out from the Father—he will testify about me. (John 15:26)

> If I do not go away, the Comforter will not come to you; but if I do go away, *I will send him to you.* (John 16:7)

> The Comforter, the Spirit of Truth, will not speak to you on his own; *he will take from what is mine* and make it known to you. All things whatever that the Father has *are mine.* This is why I said that he will take *from what is mine* and make it known to you. (John 16:13, 14, 15)

> The Holy Spirit was not yet in existence, because Jesus was not glorified yet. (John 7:39)

> Jesus breathed on the disciples and said, "Receive the Holy Spirit." (John 20:22)

> Whatever you ask in my name, *I will do it,* so that the Father is glorified in the Son. If you ask anything in my name, *I myself will do it.* (John 14:13, 14)

[2] From these passages it is perfectly obvious that the Lord "sends the Holy Spirit," that is, carries out those processes that are ascribed nowadays to the Holy Spirit as a God by himself. The Lord said that he was going to send the Holy Spirit from the Father; he was going to send

the Holy Spirit "to you." Furthermore, the Holy Spirit was not yet in existence, because Jesus was not glorified yet; and after Jesus was glorified he breathed on the disciples and said, "Receive the Holy Spirit." The Lord also said "Whatever you ask in my name, I myself will do it"; and said that the Comforter was going to take "from what is mine" that which he was to make known. (For evidence that the Comforter is the same as the Holy Spirit, see John 14:26.)

It is not that God the Father carries out those processes on his own initiative through the Son, but rather that the Son carries them out on his own initiative on behalf of the Father, as the following passages clearly show: "No one has ever seen God. The only begotten Son, who is close to the Father's heart, has made him visible" (John 1:18 and elsewhere). "You have never heard the voice of the Father or seen what he looks like" (John 5:37). [3] From these passages it follows that God the Father works *on* and *in* the Son but not *through* him. Instead, the Lord works on his own initiative on behalf of his Father. For he says, "Everything the Father has is mine" (John 16:15). "The Father has given all things into the hand of the Son" (John 3:35). Also, "as the Father has life in himself, so he has given the Son to have life in himself" (John 5:26). And "the words that I speak are spirit and are life" (John 6:63).

Admittedly, the Lord does say that the Spirit of Truth goes out from the Father (John 15:26).[363] The reason he says this, however, is that the Spirit of Truth goes out from God the Father into the Son, and it goes out from the Son on behalf of the Father. This is why it says, "In that day you will recognize that the Father is in me and I am in the Father, and you are in me and I am in you" (John 14:11, 20).

The Lord's clear statements reveal as blatantly incorrect the Christian world's belief that God the Father sends the Holy Spirit to us. The Greek Church,[364] as well, is wrong to believe that God the Father sends the Holy Spirit directly.

The concept that the Lord sends the Holy Spirit on his own initiative on behalf of God the Father, not the other way around, comes from heaven. Angels call it a secret that has not yet been discovered in the world.

154

This point can also be illustrated by a number of parallels.

We all know that after the Lord bestowed the Holy Spirit on the apostles, they preached the good news across much of the world and publicized it through speaking and writing. They did this on their own initiative on behalf of the Lord. Peter wrote and taught one way, James another way, John a third, and Paul a fourth. Each of them used their own intelligence. The Lord filled them all with his spirit, but they each took a portion of it that depended on the quality of their perception, and they each exercised that portion depending on the quality of their own ability.

All the angels in the heavens are filled with the Lord—they are in the Lord and the Lord is in them. Yet for each of them, the speech and action depends on the quality of the mind. Some speak and act simply, and some wisely, with infinite variety. They all speak on their own initiative on behalf of the Lord.

[2] The same goes for all ministers in the church—those with false beliefs as well as those with true beliefs. They each have their own voice and their own intelligence. They each speak on the basis of their own mind, meaning the spirit inside them.

Consider the situation of all Protestants, whether they happen to be called Evangelical or Reformed. Once they have been taught the theological system handed down by Luther, Melanchthon, or Calvin, it is not that Luther, Melanchthon, and Calvin, or the theologies themselves, speak on their own initiative through the Protestants' mouths.[365] Instead, the Protestants speak on their own initiative on behalf of their church founders.

Every dogma can be explained in a thousand different ways. It is like a horn of plenty. People take out of the dogma whatever is matched and suited to their character, and use their particular gifts to explain it.

[3] This point can also be illustrated by the action of the heart on and in the lungs, and the lungs' reaction on their own initiative on behalf of the heart. These are two distinct things, yet they are reciprocally united. The lungs breathe on their own initiative on behalf of the heart. The heart, however, does not breathe through the lungs. If it did they would both stop functioning.

The same applies to the heart's action on and in every internal organ in the body. The heart sends blood out in all directions. The internal organs draw on that blood. Each organ takes whatever it needs depending on how vital a service it provides. Its level of service also determines how it functions; different organs function in different ways.

[4] The same point can be illustrated by the following parallels as well. The evil we get from our parents, called hereditary evil, acts on us and in us. So does goodness from the Lord. Goodness comes from above or within; evil from below or outside. If evil were to act through us we could not be reformed, but we would not be responsible either. By the same token, if goodness from the Lord acted through us we

could not be reformed. Because good and evil are a matter of our free choice[366] we become guilty when we act on our own initiative on behalf of evil, and innocent when we act on our own initiative on behalf of goodness. Because evil is the Devil and goodness is the Lord, we become guilty if we act on behalf of the Devil, and innocent if we act on behalf of the Lord. The free choice that we all have makes it possible for us to be reformed.

[5] The same situation exists for all of us with our inner and outer selves. These selves are two distinct things, yet they are reciprocally united. Our inner self acts on and in our outer self, but not through it. Our inner self contains thousands of things. Our outer self takes from our inner self only what is suited for some useful purpose. In our inner self, the part of our mind that enables us to have volition and perception,[367] there are arrays of concepts in enormous quantities. If these concepts flowed out through our mouths they would be like a blast of air from an industrial bellows. Our inner self, with its universe of contents, is comparable to an ocean, a large flower garden, or a park. The outer self takes from it just as much as it needs to get something done.

When the Lord's Word is quite thoroughly present in our inner self it too is comparable to an ocean, a large flower garden, or a park. In that case we speak and act on our own initiative on behalf of the Word. The Word does not act through us. The same is true in regard to the Lord, because he is the Word, that is, the divine truth and the divine goodness in it. The Lord acts on his own (or from the Word) on us and in us, but not through us, because we act and speak freely on the Lord's behalf when we act and speak from the Word.

[6] The point here can be more accurately illustrated by the mutual interaction between soul[368] and body. The soul and the body are two distinct things, yet they are reciprocally united. The soul acts on and in the body but not through it. Instead, the body acts on its own initiative on behalf of the soul.

The soul does not act through the body in that the soul and the body do not consult and engage in decision making with each other. The soul does not command or request the body to do this or that, or say this or that with its mouth. The body does not call for or petition the soul to give it, or supply it with, something. Everything belonging to the soul belongs to the body, mutually and reciprocally.

The same is true for the divine and the human natures in the Lord. The Father's divine nature is the soul of his human nature, and the human nature is his body. The human nature does not ask its divine nature to tell it what to say or do. This is why the Lord says, "In that day you will ask in my name. And I will not tell you that I am going to petition the Father on your behalf, for the Father himself loves you, because you have loved me" (John 16:26, 27). "In that day" means after glorification, that is, after complete and absolute union with the Father.

The Lord himself is divulging this secret for those who will be part of his new church.

It was shown above, in point 3 of this part of the chapter [§146], that the divine effects (which are meant by the actions of the Holy Spirit) that specifically apply to the clergy are the processes of enlightening and teaching them. There are, however, two intermediate processes to add to the two just mentioned: their perceiving and shaping [what they are learning]. For the clergy, then, there are four processes that follow in sequence: becoming enlightened; perceiving; shaping; and being instructed.

The *enlightening* is done by the Lord.

The process of *perceiving* takes place in the individuals. It is affected by the quality of mind they have developed as a result of doctrinal teachings. If these doctrinal teachings are true, the light that enlightens them clarifies their perception. If these doctrinal teachings are false, their perception becomes obscured. It may still seem clear [to the ministers], however, because of other teachings that lend confirmation. The apparent clarity is caused by a faint, deceptive light that to mere earthly vision seems clear.

The process of *shaping* depends on the type of love that exists in the minister's will. The enjoyment related to that love actually does the shaping. If the minister has enjoyment in an evil love and the false perspective that goes with it, that enjoyment generates a passion that is outwardly rough, prickly, intense, and fire-belching; inside the passion there is anger, rage, and lack of compassion. If, however, the minister has enjoyment in a good love and the truth that goes with it, the passion is outwardly even, smooth, thundering, and blazing; inside the passion there is goodwill, grace, and compassion.

The process of *being instructed* follows as an effect from the other three processes as causes.

Therefore the enlightening that comes from the Lord is turned into different types of light and heat in individual ministers depending on the quality of each individual's mind.

155

156   6. *Our spirits are our minds and whatever comes from them.* Our "spirit" really means nothing else but our mind. Our mind is what lives on after death. It is then called a spirit. If it is good, it is called an angelic spirit and later on an angel. If it is evil, it is called a satanic spirit and later on a satan.[369] For each one of us, our mind is our inner self, our true self. It lives inside our outer self that constitutes our body. When our body is cast aside, which death does for us, we are in a complete human form.

People are wrong, then, to believe that our mind exists only in our head. Our mind is present in our head only in its primary structures. Everything that we think with our intellect and do from our will first emanates from these primary structures. In the rest of our body, our mind is present in extensions of these primary structures[370] that have been designed to allow us sensation and action. Because our mind is inwardly connected to the parts of our body, our mind supplies those parts with sensation and motion and also inspires awareness as if our body thought and acted on its own, although every wise person knows this is not how it is.

Now, because our spirit thinks with its intellect and acts with its will, and our body thinks and acts not on its own but with the help of our spirit, it follows that our "spirit" means our intelligence and our type of love, as well as whatever emanates from our love and intelligence and has an effect.

Many passages in the Word make clear that our "spirit" means the nature of our mind. When I quote only a few of these passages, anyone will be able to see that this is exactly what "spirit" means. The following are just a few of the many:

> And Bezaleel was filled with the spirit of wisdom, intelligence, and knowledge. (Exodus 31:3)

Nebuchadnezzar said of Daniel that there was "an excellent spirit" of knowledge, intelligence, and wisdom in him (Daniel 5:12).

> Joshua was filled with the spirit of wisdom. (Deuteronomy 34:9)

> Make yourselves a new heart and a new spirit. (Ezekiel 18:31)

> Blessed are the poor in spirit, because the kingdom of the heavens consists of such people. (Matthew 5:3)

> I live among people with a beaten and humble spirit so that I may revive the spirit of the lowly. (Isaiah 57:15)

The sacrifices of God are a broken spirit. (Psalms 51:17)

I will give a cloak of praise to replace a constricted spirit. (Isaiah 61:3)

And so on.

"Spirit" can also mean the nature of a corrupt and unjust mind, as the following passages make clear:

He spoke to the foolish prophets who follow their own spirit. (Ezekiel 13:3)

Conceive garbage, give birth to stubble; in your spirit, fire will consume you. (Isaiah 33:11)

A man who is a wanderer in his spirit and who babbles a lie. (Micah 2:11)

A generation whose spirit was not steadfast with God. (Psalms 78:8)

A spirit of promiscuity. (Hosea 5:4; 4:12)

To melt every heart and constrict every spirit. (Ezekiel 21:7)

What has come up in your spirit will never be done. (Ezekiel 20:32)

Provided there is no guile in their spirit. (Psalms 32:2)

The spirit of Pharaoh was disturbed. (Genesis 41:8)

Likewise the spirit of Nebuchadnezzar (Daniel 2:3). These and many other passages make it obvious that our "spirit" means our mind and its characteristics.

Since our spirit means our mind, therefore "being in the spirit," as the Word sometimes says, refers to the state of our mind when it is separated from our body. In this state the prophets saw the sort of things that exist in the spiritual world; therefore this state is called "a vision of God." At those times, the prophets' state was like the state of spirits and angels in the spiritual world. In this state our spirit can move from place to place while our body stays where it is (as is also true of our mind's eye).

This is the state I myself have been in now for twenty-six years, with the difference that I am in my spirit and my body at the same time, and only sometimes out of my body.[371]

Ezekiel, Zechariah, Daniel, and John (when he wrote the Book of Revelation) were in this state, as is clear from the following passages: Ezekiel said, "The spirit lifted me up and led me into Chaldea to the captivity in *the vision of God,* in *the spirit of God.* In this way *the vision* that I

157

saw came over me" (Ezekiel 11:1, 24). The spirit lifted Ezekiel up and he heard the earth tremble behind him (Ezekiel 3:12, 14). The spirit lifted him up between earth and heaven, and led him away to Jerusalem where he saw abominable things (Ezekiel 8:3–4). He saw four creatures that were angel guardians and various details about them (Ezekiel 1 and 10). Then he saw a new earth in the form of a new temple, and an angel measuring the temple (Ezekiel 40–48). At that time he was in a vision and in the spirit (Ezekiel 40:2; 43:5).

[2] The same thing happened to Zechariah when an angel was with him and he saw a man riding among the myrtle trees (Zechariah 1:8–9); when he saw four horns and a man who had a string in his hand for measuring (Zechariah 1:18; 2:1–2); when he saw Joshua the high priest (Zechariah 3:1, 6); and when he saw four chariots with horses headed off between two mountains (Zechariah 6:1–3).

Daniel was in the same state when he saw four beasts rising up out of the sea, and many details about them (Daniel 7:1–8); and when he saw battles between a ram and a goat (Daniel 8:1–14). He was in a vision when he saw those things (Daniel 7:1, 2, 7, 13; 8:2; 10:1, 7, 8). In a vision he saw the angel Gabriel and spoke with him [Daniel 8:15–27].

[3] The same thing happened to John when he wrote the Book of Revelation. He said he was *in the spirit* on the Lord's day (Revelation 1:10); he was carried off into the wilderness *in the spirit* (Revelation 17:3); and he was on a high mountain *in the spirit* (Revelation 21:10). He was seeing things *in a vision* (Revelation 9:17).

Elsewhere [in the Book of Revelation] he says that he *saw* the things he described. For example, he saw the Son of Humankind in the middle of seven lampstands. He saw a tabernacle, a temple, an ark, and an altar in heaven; a book sealed with seven seals and horses that came out of it; four creatures around a throne; twelve thousand chosen people, some from every tribe; a lamb on Mount Zion; locusts rising up from an abyss; a dragon and its war with Michael; a woman giving birth to a male child and running away into a desert because of the dragon; two beasts, one rising up out of the sea and another out of the land; a woman sitting on a scarlet beast; a dragon thrown into a lake of fire and sulfur; a white horse and a great supper; the holy city Jerusalem coming down, with details of its entrances, its wall, and the wall's foundations; a river of living water; and trees of life producing different types of fruit every month; and so on.[372]

Peter, James, and John were in the same state when they saw Jesus transfigured, as was Paul when he heard ineffable things from heaven.

A Supplement

Since the Holy Spirit is the subject of this chapter, it is very worthwhile to point out that nowhere in the Word of the Old Testament is the Holy Spirit mentioned. The "spirit of holiness" occurs in three passages, once in David (Psalms 51:11), and twice in Isaiah (Isaiah 63:10, 11). The Holy Spirit is of course frequently mentioned in the Word of the New Testament, both in the Gospels and in the Acts of the Apostles and their Epistles. The reason for this is that the Holy Spirit first came into existence when the Lord had come into the world. The Holy Spirit emanates from him on behalf of the Father. The Lord alone is holy (Revelation 15:4). This is why the angel Gabriel mentioned to Mother Mary "the *Holy One* that will be born from you" (Luke 1:35).

Now, it says, "The Holy Spirit was not yet in existence, because Jesus was not glorified yet" (John 7:39), and yet before that it says that the Holy Spirit filled Elizabeth (Luke 1:41) and Zechariah (Luke 1:67), and also Simeon (Luke 2:25). The reason for this is that the spirit of Jehovah the Father filled them, and this is called "the Holy Spirit" because of the Lord, who was already in the world.

This is why no passage in the Word of the Old Testament says that the prophets spoke on behalf of the Holy Spirit; they spoke on behalf of Jehovah. It constantly says *Jehovah spoke to me, the word of Jehovah came to me, Jehovah said, says Jehovah.* So that no one will doubt the truth of this, I want to list the references in Jeremiah alone where these expressions occur:

Jeremiah 1:4, 7, 11, 12, 13, 14, 19; 2:1, 2, 3, 4, 5, 9, 19, 22, 29, 31; 3:1, 6, 10, 12, 14, 16; 4:1, 3, 9, 17, 27; 5:11, 14, 18, 22, 29; 6:6, 9, 12, 15, 16, 21, 22; 7:1, 3, 11, 13, 19, 20, 21; 8:1, 3, 12, 13; 9:3, 7, 9, 13, 15, 17, 22, 24, 25; 10:1, 2, 18; 11:1, 6, 9, 11, 17, 18, 21, 22; 12:14, 17; 13:1, 6, 9, 11, 12, 13, 14, 15, 25; 14:1, 10, 14, 15; 15:1, 2, 3, 6, 11, 19, 20; 16:1, 3, 5, 9, 14, 16; 17:5, 15, 19, 20, 21, 24; 18:1, 5, 6, 11, 13; 19:1, 3, 6, 12, 15; 20:4; 21:1, 4, 7, 8, 11, 12; 22:2, 5, 6, 11, 18, 24, 29, 30; 23:2, 5, 7, 12, 15, 24, 29, 31, 38; 24:3, 5, 8; 25:1, 3, 7, 8, 9, 15, 27, 28, 29, 32; 26:1, 2, 18; 27:1, 2, 4, 8, 11, 16, 19, 21, 22; 28:2, 12, 14, 16; 29:4, 8, 9, 16, 19, 20, 21, 25, 30, 31, 32; 30:1, 2, 3, 4, 5, 8, 10, 11, 12, 17, 18; 31:1, 2, 7, 10, 15, 16, 17, 23, 27, 28, 31, 32, 33, 34, 35, 36, 37, 38; 32:1, 6, 14, 15, 25, 26, 28, 30, 36, 42; 33:1, 2, 4, 10, 12, 13, 17, 19, 20, 23, 25; 34:1, 2, 4, 8, 12, 13, 17, 22; 35:1, 13, 17, 18, 19; 36:1, 6, 27, 29, 30; 37:6, 7, 9; 38:2, 3, 17; 39:15, 16, 17, 18; 40:1; 42:7, 9, 15, 18, 19; 43:8, 10; 44:1, 2, 7, 11, 24, 25, 26, 30; 45:2, 5;

46:1, 23, 25, 28; 47:2; 48:1, 8, 12, 30, 35, 38, 40, 43, 44, 47; 49:2, 5, 6, 7, 12, 13, 16, 18, 26, 28, 30, 32, 35, 37, 38, 39; 50:1, 4, 10, 18, 20, 21, 30, 31, 33, 35, 40; 51:25, 33, 36, 39, 52, 58.

These are just the passages in Jeremiah. It says the same thing in all the other prophets. It does not say that the Holy Spirit spoke; and it does not say that Jehovah spoke to them through the Holy Spirit.

159 To these points I will add the following memorable occurrences.

The first memorable occurrence. Once when I was spending some time with angels in heaven, in the distance below I saw a huge cloud of smoke with flames shooting out of it periodically. I said to the angels who were talking with me at that moment, "Although few up here know it, the origin of the smoke that one sees in hell is the hellish spirits' use of reasoning to support things that aren't true; and the origin of the fire seen in hell is their blowing up at others who speak against them.

"It is equally unknown in this spiritual world as it is in the world where I am physically alive that flame is nothing but smoke that is on fire," I added. "I have often observed this myself. I have watched the plumes of smoke rising from the logs in the fireplace. When I set fire to them with a match, I have seen that the plumes of smoke become flames. The flames have the same shape as the plumes of smoke had. The individual particles of smoke become little sparks that burn together. (The same thing happens when you set fire to gunpowder.) The situation is similar in the case of the smoke that we are seeing down below us now. It consists of a great number of things that aren't true. The flame shooting out of it is the intense passion the hellish spirits have to defend the things that aren't true."

[2] The angels said to me, "Let's pray to the Lord to be allowed to go down and get near them in order to learn what their false beliefs are that are smoking and burning like that."

It was granted. A column of light appeared around us that went all the way down to that place.

Once down there, we saw four sets of spirits in ranks. They were adamantly defending the idea that one must turn to God the Father and worship him, because he cannot be seen; one must not turn to his Son born in the world and worship him, because he is human and can be seen.

When I looked to the sides, to the left I saw learned clergy, and behind them regular clergy. To the right I saw educated laity, and behind them, uneducated laity. Between us, though, there was a gaping void that could not be crossed.

[3] We turned our eyes and ears to the left where the learned clergy were, with the regular clergy behind them. We heard them reasoning about God in the following way: "On the basis of the doctrine of our church—the single view of God shared by the entire European world—we know that we have to turn to God the Father, because he cannot be seen. By so doing we also turn to God the Son and God the Holy Spirit, who likewise cannot be seen because they are coeternal with the Father. Because God the Father is the Creator of the universe and is therefore in the universe, wherever we turn our eyes he is present. When we pray to him he graciously hears us. After accepting the Son's mediation, the Father sends the Holy Spirit, who carries the glory of the Son's justice into our hearts and blesses us.

"Created as we were to be teachers of the church, when preaching we have felt in our chests the holy effect of that sending and we have inhaled a devoutness from its presence in our minds. We have been affected in this way because we have directed all our senses to a God who cannot be seen, who works not in a particular way in the sight of our intellect but in a universal way throughout the whole system of our mind and body through his emissary Spirit. Worshiping a God who can be seen, a God whom our minds can picture as a human being, would not yield such good results."

[4] The regular clergy who were behind them applauded these points and added, "Where does holiness come from if not from a Divinity who is beyond our ability to picture or perceive? On first hearing even a mention of such a Divinity, our faces light up and broaden into a smile. Like the caress of some sweet-smelling breeze, the thought exhilarates us and we thump our chests with vigor. To the mention of a Divinity who is within our ability to picture and perceive, we react completely differently. When this comes within earshot it translates into something merely earthly and not divine.

"For the same reason the Roman Catholics conduct their mass in the Latin idiom; from the sanctuary of the altar they take the host, about which they utter divine and mystical things, and display it, and the people fall to their knees, as before the greatest of mysteries, and breathe in the holiness."

[5] After that we turned to the right where the educated laity were, and behind them the uneducated laity. We heard the following statements coming from the educated laity.

"We know that the wisest people among the ancients worshiped a God who was beyond their power to picture, whom they called Jehovah. Later on in the age that followed, however, people deified their deceased rulers, among whom were Saturn, Jupiter, Neptune, Pluto, Apollo, and Minerva, Diana, Venus, and Themis.373 People built temples for them and worshiped them as divinities. As the times worsened, that worship led to idolatry and eventually made the whole world insane. With unanimous consent, therefore, we agree with our priests and elders that there are three divine persons from eternity, each of whom was and is God. We are satisfied that these three are beyond our power to picture."

The uneducated laity behind them added, "We agree. God is one thing and a human being is another. We are aware, though, that if someone proposes the existence of a human God, the common people with their sensory concept of God are going to welcome the idea."

[6] Then the spirits' eyes were opened and they saw us nearby. Annoyed that we had heard them, they immediately stopped talking. The angels, with a power that had been given them, closed the outer or lower levels of the spirits' thought, which were the source of the statements they had just made. The angels opened instead the inner or higher levels of the spirits' thought and compelled them to speak about God from those levels.

The spirits then spoke and said, "What is God? We haven't seen the way he looks or heard his voice. What then is God except nature with all its levels? Nature we have seen, because it shines in our eyes. Nature we have heard, because it sounds in our ears."

On hearing that, we asked them, "Have you ever seen Socinus, who acknowledged only God the Father, or Arius, who denied the divinity of the Lord the Savior, or any of their followers?"374

"No, we haven't seen them," they answered.

"They are deep beneath you," we said.

Soon we summoned some of the spirits from down there and asked them about God. They said the same type of things as these spirits had been saying. The spirits from below also said, "What is God? We can make as many gods as we want."

[7] We said, "It is pointless to talk to you about the Son of God born into the world, but we are going to do it nonetheless.

"Faith is like a bubble in the air. It was beautifully colored in the first and second ages,[375] but was in danger of bursting in the third and following ages because no one saw God. Therefore to preserve our faith about him, faith in him, and faith from him, it pleased Jehovah God to come down and take on a human manifestation. He did this to bring himself into view and to convince us that God is not a figment of our imagination; he is the absolute being who was and is and will be from eternity to eternity. God is not a three-letter word; he is everything real from alpha to omega.[376] Therefore he is the life and salvation of all who believe in him as a God who can be seen, although he is not the life and salvation of those who say they believe in a God who cannot be seen, because believing, seeing, and recognizing are one. This is why the Lord said to Philip, 'Those who see and recognize me, see and recognize the Father.' This is also why the Lord says elsewhere, 'The Father's will is for them to believe in the Son. Those who believe in the Son have eternal life. Those who do not believe in the Son will not see life; in fact, God's anger remains upon them.'" (These words occur in John 3:15, 16, 36; 14:6–15.)

On hearing this, many in the four sets of spirits became so enraged that smoke and flame came out of their nostrils; so we went away. After the angels accompanied me to my home, they went back up to their heaven.

The second memorable occurrence. Once I was out on a walk with some angels. We were walking in the world of spirits, which is midway between heaven and hell, the place where all of us first go after we die. There we are prepared, if we are good, for heaven; if we are evil, for hell. I was speaking with them about many different things, among which was the following.

160

"In the world where I am currently living in my body, countless stars appear at night, large and small. They are all suns that transmit just their light to our solar system. When I noticed that there are also visible stars in your world, I reckoned that there are the same number here as in the world where I live."

Delighted by this topic of conversation, the angels said, "There could well be the same number. Every community in heaven at times shines like a star to those who are below heaven. There are countless communities in heaven, all arranged according to different feelings of love for what is good. These feelings are infinite *in* God; therefore there are countless feelings *from* him. Since these heavenly communities were foreseen before creation, I suppose that the stars were provided in the same amount, meaning that an equal number of stars was created for the world where people with a physical earthly body were going to live."

[2] While we were having that conversation, I noticed a paved road to the north. It was so crowded with spirits that there was scarcely a foot of space between each spirit.

I said to the angels, "I have seen that road before, with spirits on it like the rank and file of armies. I have heard that this is the road traveled by all who are leaving the physical world. The road is covered with that many spirits because tens of thousands of people die every week, and they all migrate to this world after death."377

The angels added, "The road comes to an end in the middle of the world of spirits, where we are now. It stops here because on the side toward the east there are communities that love God and their neighbor; to the left toward the west there are communities that are against those loves; and in front in the south378 there are communities of spirits who are more intelligent than others. This is why those who have recently left the physical world arrive here first. Once they are here, they are at first in their outer selves, the parts of themselves they had been closest to in their prior world. Later on, they come more and more into their inner selves. Then their true quality is investigated. Once this is discovered, the good are brought to their places in heaven, and the evil to their places in hell."

[3] We stopped walking in the middle area where the road for arrivals came to an end. We said, "Let's spend a little time here and talk to some of the new arrivals." We chose twelve of them. Since they had just arrived from the physical world they did not realize they were not still in that world. We asked them what they believed about heaven and hell and life after death.

One of them replied, "Our Sacred Order379 impressed on me the belief that we are going to live after death, and that there is a heaven and a hell. As a result I came to believe that all who live morally go to heaven; and since everyone lives morally, no one goes to hell. Therefore hell is a myth made up by the clergy to prevent us from living evil lives. What difference does it make if I think about God this way or that way? Thought is only foam on the water that bursts and disappears."

Another near the first said, "My belief is that heaven and hell exist. God rules heaven, and the Devil rules hell. Because they are enemies and are opposed to each other, one calls evil what the other calls good. Moral people are phonies who can make evil look good and good look evil. They stand on both sides. What is the difference then whether I am with one Lord or the other, provided he likes me? People enjoy good and evil equally."

[4] A third person at the side of the second said, "What difference does it make to my situation if I believe that heaven and hell exist? Who has come from there and told us?[380] If everyone lives after death, why hasn't one person out of that great multitude come back to tell us about it?"

The fourth person, next to the third, said, "I'll tell you why no one has come back to tell us about it. The reason is that when we breathe our souls out, we are in fact dead. Then we become a ghost and we are dissipated, or we are like the breath in someone's mouth, which is only blowing air. How can something like that come back and talk to anyone?"

A fifth person went next and said, "Friends, wait for the day of the Last Judgment. Then all will return to their bodies, and you will see them and talk with them. Each one will tell his or her fate to the next."

[5] The sixth, standing on the other side, started laughing and said, "How could a spirit, which is blown air, come back into a body that has been consumed by worms and into a skeleton that has been burnt in the sun and has crumbled to dust? How can an Egyptian who was turned into a mummy and who has since been mixed by an apothecary into extracts, powders, ointments, and pills[381] come back and tell anyone anything? Wait for that last day, if you have the faith; but you are going to wait for ever and ever for nothing."

After that the seventh one said, "If I believed in heaven and hell and life after death, I would also believe that birds and animals are going to live on as well, since some of them are just as moral and rational as we are. People say animals don't live on, so I say people don't either. It is a fair piece of reasoning—the one point follows from the other. What are we except animals?"[382]

The eighth one, standing behind the seventh one's back, came forward and said, "Believe in heaven if you want, but I don't believe in hell. God is omnipotent. He can save everyone."

[6] The ninth shook the eighth one's hand and said, "God is not only omnipotent but also gracious. He couldn't throw anyone into eternal fire. If any were already in the fire, he would set them free and take them away from there."

The tenth rushed from the line into the middle and said, "I don't believe in hell either. God sent us his Son, and the Son bore the sins of the whole world and purged them. What is the Devil capable of doing against that? Since he can't do anything, what then is hell?"

The eleventh, who was a priest, became very angry when he heard that and said, "The people who are saved are those who have acquired the faith on which Christ's merit has been inscribed. Those whom God has chosen acquire that faith. It is up to the Almighty and his judgment to choose who is worthy. Who could argue against *that?*"

The twelfth, who was in politics, remained silent. Asked to give the final response, he said, "I will not express from my heart anything about heaven, hell, or the life after death. No one knows anything about them. Nonetheless, provided the priests do not insult anyone, let them preach those things, because commoners are then held mentally bound to laws and to leaders by an invisible chain. Public safety depends on this, does it not?"[383]

[7] We were stunned to hear their points of view. We said to each other, "Although these people are called Christians, they are neither human nor animal. They are human animals."

Nevertheless, to rouse them from their sleep we said, "Heaven and hell do exist, as does the life after death. You'll be convinced of this by the time we drive away your unawareness about the state of life you are now in. During the first days after they die, all people fail to realize they are not still alive in the same world they were in before. The intervening time is like a period of sleep. When they wake up from it they feel as though they are just where they used to be. The same goes for you today. That's why you just said the same things you thought in your former world."

Then the angels shook away the people's unawareness. The people saw that they were in a different world with other people they did not recognize. They shouted, "Hey, where are we?"

"Not in the physical world anymore," we said. "Now you are in the spiritual world, and we are angels."

As they woke up they said, "If you are angels, then show us heaven."

"Stay here for a little while," we replied. "We'll be back."

When we returned half an hour later we found them waiting for us. "Follow us into heaven," we said.

They came and we went up with them. Because we were with them, the guards opened the door and let them in. To the angels who received newcomers at the threshold, we said, "Examine them."

The examiners turned the people around and noticed that the backs of their heads were badly hollowed out. The examiners said, "Go away from here. You enjoy doing evil, and therefore you have no connection to heaven. In your hearts you have denied the existence of God and have despised religion."

We then told the people, "Don't delay leaving, or you'll be *thrown* out." They hurried down and went away.

[8] On the way home we discussed why people who enjoy doing evil would have heads that in this world look hollowed out at the back. I gave a reason: We have two brains, one at the back of our head called the cerebellum, and the other in our forehead called the cerebrum. The love in our will resides in the cerebellum. The thought in our intellect resides in our cerebrum. When the thought in our intellect fails to guide the love in our will, the inmost structures of the cerebellum, which are actually heavenly, collapse, causing this hollowness.

The third memorable occurrence. In the spiritual world I once heard the sound of a mill. It was in the northern area. At first I wondered what it was, but then I remembered that a mill and grinding grain mean research in the Word to support a particular doctrinal perspective.

I went to the place where I had heard the sound coming from. As I came near, the sound disappeared. Then I saw an arched roof just above the ground. To enter the place you had to go through a cave, so I went down and in. To my surprise, there was a room there where I saw an old man sitting among books, holding the Word in front of him. He was searching through it for anything that would serve his doctrinal perspective. Little slips of paper were lying all around him on which he had written applicable quotations. In the next room over there were copyists who were collecting the slips of paper and committing what was written on them to a full sheet of paper.

First I asked the man about the books around him. He said, "They all deal with the topic of the faith that justifies us.[384] The works from Sweden and Denmark deal with it in depth; the work from Germany in greater depth; the works from Britain in even greater depth; but the profoundest of them all come from Holland."[385]

"They disagree in various other ways," he added, "but on the point that we are justified and saved by faith alone they all agree."

Then he said that he was at that time collecting passages from the Word on the crux of the faith that justifies us. "The crux," he said, "is that God the Father lapsed from an attitude of grace toward the human race because of its wrongdoing. Therefore in order to save the human race there was a divine necessity for someone to provide satisfaction, reconciliation,

161

appeasement, and mediation. This someone needed to bear the damnation that justice required; and no one could bear this except God's only Son. After this was accomplished, access opened up to God the Father on account of the Son, for we say, 'Father, have mercy on us on account of your Son.'"

He added, "I continue, as always, to perceive this point of view as in accord with reason and Scripture. How else could God the Father be approached except through our faith in the Son's merit?"

[2] As I heard this, I felt astounded that he would say it accords with reason and Scripture when in reality it goes against reason and Scripture. In fact, I candidly told him so.

With sudden anger he countered, "How can you say that?"

So I opened my mind to him and said, "Surely it goes against reason to think that God the Father lapsed from an attitude of grace toward the human race, rejected us, and cut off communication with us. Isn't divine grace an attribute of the divine essence? If so, then to lapse from an attitude of grace would be to lapse from the divine essence, and lapsing from the divine essence would mean that God wouldn't be God anymore. Can God be alienated from himself? Believe me, as grace on God's part is infinite, it is also eternal. (We are capable, of course, of losing God's grace if we don't accept it.) If grace were to leave God, that would be the end of all heaven and the whole human race. That is why grace on God's part goes on forever, a grace not only toward angels and people but also toward devils in hell. Since what I have said accords with reason, how can you say our only access to God the Father is through faith in the merit of his Son, when there is perpetual access through grace?

[3] "And why do you speak of access to God the Father *on account of* the Son? Why not *through* the Son? Isn't the Son the Mediator and Savior? Why wouldn't you go to the Mediator and Savior himself? He is both God and human. Does anyone on earth go straight to some czar, monarch, or member of the royal family? You need a liaison to introduce you. The Lord came into the world to introduce us to the Father. There is no access except through the Lord. The access is perpetual when you go directly to the Lord himself, since he is in the Father and the Father is in him. Search in Scripture now and you'll see that this accords with it, while your way to the Father goes against Scripture as it also goes against reason. I'll also tell you that it is outrageous to climb up to God the Father instead of going through the One who is close to the Father's heart and who alone is with him. Haven't you read John 14:6?"[386]

On hearing this the old man became so angry that he jumped out of his chair and shouted to his copyists to throw me out. When I walked out right away on my own, he picked up a book that happened to be at hand and threw it at me from the doorway. The book was the Word.

The fourth memorable occurrence. A dispute came up among spirits about whether any of us can see any theological or doctrinal truth in the Word unless we have help from the Lord. All agreed on one point: none of us can see truth in the Word unless we have help from God, because "we cannot receive anything unless it is given to us from heaven" (John 3:27). Therefore the topic of debate was whether any of us can see truth in the Word without going directly to the Lord. One side said that we have to go directly to the Lord because he *is* the Word. The other side said that we also see doctrinal truth when we go straight to God the Father.

162

A side topic came up for discussion: whether it is acceptable for any Christian to circumvent the Lord and go directly to God the Father. Someone asked, "Isn't that an improper, dangerous, insolent, and outrageous thing to do, since the Lord says that no one comes to the Father except through him (John 14:6)?"

So the spirits left this point alone. Next they said that we can all see doctrinal truth from the Word in our own earthly light. That was rejected. They insisted nonetheless that we can see truth if we pray to God the Father.

Something from the Word was read to them. They prayed on their knees for God the Father to enlighten them. In reference to the things that had been read to them from the Word, they stated that this or that point there was true, although it was really false. The experiment was repeated several times to the point where it became tiresome. They finally admitted that they could not do it.

Spirits on the side that went directly to the Lord, however, saw things that were true and taught the others.

[2] After the debate had been settled that way, up came some spirits from the abyss. They looked at first like locusts, then like little people. They were spirits who while in the world had prayed to God the Father and had convinced themselves that people are justified by faith alone. They were the same as the spirits depicted by Revelation 9:1–11.

They maintained that in a clear light and also on the basis of the Word they could see that we are justified by faith alone without having to do the works of the Law.[387] They were asked, "By which faith?"

"Faith in God the Father," they answered.

After they were examined, however, they received word from heaven that they did not know even one doctrinal truth from the Word. They countered that they were in fact able to see their own truths in the light. They were told that the light they see them in is faint and deceptive.

"What is faint, deceptive light?" they asked.

They were informed, "Faint, deceptive light is a light that reinforces what is false. It corresponds to the light that owls and bats have—for them darkness is light and light darkness."

This point was proven by the fact that when the spirits looked up to heaven, where true light exists, they saw darkness, and when they looked down to the abyss where they were from, they saw light.

[3] Irritated by this proof, they said that light and darkness do not really exist; they are just conditions of the eye. It is based only on conditions of the eye that we say light is light and darkness is darkness. It was demonstrated to them, however, that their light was faint and deceptive, a light that reinforced what is false. They were shown that their light was only an activity of their own mind that originated in the fire of their cravings, not unlike the light that cats have, whose eyes look like glowing candles when they are in pantries at night because of their burning appetite for mice.[388]

Angry at hearing this, they said they were not cats and were not like cats, because they could [see] if they wanted to; but they left, because they were afraid of being asked why they did not want to. They made their way down into their abyss. (Those who are down there and others like them the angels call owls and bats, and also locusts.)

[4] When they arrived among their own kind in the abyss and told them, "Angels said we don't know any doctrinal truths, not even one; they called us owls, bats, and locusts," then a riot broke out.

The spirits there then said, "Let's pray to God to be allowed to go up. We will clearly show we have many doctrinal truths that even the archangels themselves[389] will acknowledge."

Because they prayed to God, their request was granted. As many as three hundred came up. Once they appeared above the ground they said, "In the world we were famous, we were celebrities, because we knew and taught the secrets of justification by faith alone. On the basis of supporting evidence we saw not just light but a gleaming splendor. The same thing happens now in our little study areas. Yet we have heard from colleagues of ours who were with you that this light is not light but darkness, because according to you we don't have any doctrinal truths from the Word. We know that every truth in the Word shines. It has been our belief that this was the source of the gleaming when we were deeply meditating on our mysteries. Therefore we will demonstrate that we have truths from the Word in great abundance."

They said, "Don't we have this truth, that there is a Trinity—God the Father, the Son, and the Holy Spirit—and that we should all believe in the Trinity? Don't we have this truth, that Christ is our Redeemer and Savior? Don't we have this truth, that Christ alone is justice, and he alone has merit; and we are unjust and ungodly if we try to attribute any of his merit and justice to ourselves? Don't we have this truth, that no people alive can do anything spiritually good on their own, and everything that is truly good comes from God? Don't we have this truth, that there is such a thing as goodness done for reward, and also goodness that is hypocritical, and these types of goodness are actually evil? Don't we have this truth, that we nevertheless have to do good works? Don't we have this truth, that there is such a thing as faith, that we have to believe in God, and as we believe we have life? And many other things from the Word like that. Can any of you deny a single one of those truths? Yet you have said that in our debates there are no truths, not even one. Surely then your harsh statements against us are unwarranted."

[5] "All the things you listed are truths in themselves," the angels answered, "but among you they have been falsified. They became false because of a false premise.

"We'll give you visible proof of what we're asserting. There is a place not far from here where light flows straight in from heaven. In the middle of the place there is a table. When someone puts on the table a piece of paper that has a truth from the Word written on it, because of the truth written on it the piece of paper shines like a star. So write your truths on a piece of paper, allow it to be placed on the table, and you'll see."

They did. They gave the piece of paper to a guard, who put it on the table. The guard then said to them, "Stand back and look at the table."

They stood back and watched. Lo and behold, the piece of paper began to shine like a star.

Then the guard said, "You see that the statements you wrote on the piece of paper are true. Now come closer and stare at the piece of paper."

They did. Suddenly the light vanished and the piece of paper became as black as if it had been coated with soot from a furnace.

Then the guard said, "Touch the piece of paper with your hands, but be careful not to touch the writing."

When they did, the piece of paper burst into flames and burned up.

After they all saw that, they were told, "If you had touched the writing you would have heard roaring sounds and burned your fingers."

Some who were standing at the back then said, "Now you see that the truths you have misused to support the mysteries of your justification are true in themselves, but for you they are falsified truths."

The spirits glanced up at that point and heaven looked like blood to them, and then like thick darkness. To the eyes of angelic spirits some of the spirits from the abyss then looked like bats, some like night birds, some like horned owls. The spirits from the abyss ran off into their own darkness, which looked deceptively bright to their eyes.

[6] The angelic spirits who were there were amazed because they had not known anything about that place and the table there before. Then a voice came to them from the direction of the south saying, "Come here and you'll see something even more amazing."

So they went. They came into a room with walls that were shining as if made of gold. The angelic spirits saw another table there. On it, the Word lay closed, surrounded by precious stones arranged in a form like heaven.390

"When the Word is opened up," said the angel guard, "a light of inexpressible splendor shines out. At the same time, because of the precious stones, a kind of rainbow appears over and around the Word. When an angel from the third heaven comes here, the rainbow over and around the Word appears against a red background. When an angel from the second heaven comes here and looks, the rainbow appears against a sky blue background. When an angel from the lowest heaven comes here and looks, the rainbow appears against a shining white background. When a good spirit comes here and looks, a light appears that is varied like marble."

The guard visibly demonstrated to them that this was the case.

The angel guard also said, "If any come along who have falsified the Word, first the brightness goes down. If they come close and stare at the Word, something like blood appears around the Word. They are then warned to leave because of danger."

[7] Nevertheless, someone who had been a leading author in the world on the doctrine that we are justified by faith alone came boldly forward and said, "When I was in the world I didn't falsify the Word. I exalted goodwill along with faith. I taught that the Holy Spirit renews,

regenerates, and sanctifies people who are in an ongoing state of faith that leads them to perform acts of goodwill. I taught that faith does not exist by itself, meaning without good works, just as a tree is not good without fruit, the sun without light, or fire without heat. I brought accusations against people who said that good works were not necessary. In addition, I enlarged the role of the Ten Commandments and repentance as well. In an amazing way, then, I applied everything in the Word to the topic of faith. Nevertheless, I revealed and demonstrated that it is faith alone that brings salvation."

In complete confidence in his own assertion that he had not falsified the Word, he came up to the table. Despite a warning from the angel, he touched the Word. Flame and smoke suddenly shot out of the Word and there was an explosion with a loud bang that threw him into the corner of the room. For quite a few minutes he lay there as if he were dead.[391]

The angelic spirits were astonished by this. It was explained to them that beyond everyone else he had been the main promoter of acts of goodwill as extensions of faith. Nevertheless, by acts of goodwill he had merely meant political activity (also called civic and moral activity) because this needs doing for the sake of the world and our prosperity in it; in his view such activity was unnecessary for our salvation. He also speculated that there is invisible work done by the Holy Spirit—work of which we know nothing—that is instilled in [the activation][392] of faith in our state.

[8] After that the angelic spirits talked to each other about falsification of the Word. They agreed on the point that to falsify the Word is to take truths out of it and use them to reinforce falsities, which is dragging truths out of and away from the Word and killing them. An example would be taking all the truths listed before by the spirits from the abyss, applying them to the modern-day faith, and explaining them from that point of view. (I will show later [§178] that that faith is pregnant with falsities.)

Another example would be to take this truth from the Word: we have to live with goodwill and do what is good to our neighbor. We could reason that everything good that comes from ourselves is not really good since we hope to be rewarded for it, and on that basis convince ourselves that we ought to do what is good, but not for the sake of our salvation. If we adamantly espouse this point of view, however, we are dragging this truth out of and away from the Word and slaughtering it. In his Word, the Lord requires that all who want to be saved must love their neighbors and lovingly do them good.

The same goes for the rest of their list.

The Divine Trinity

163   We covered God the Creator and creation; then we covered the Lord the Redeemer and redemption; lastly we covered the Holy Spirit and the divine action. Because we have covered the triune God in this way, we need to cover the divine Trinity as well. The Trinity is well known to the Christian world, yet in other ways it is unknown. Only through understanding the Trinity can we gain a just idea of God; and in the church a just idea of God is like the sanctuary and the altar in a church building. It is like the crown on the head and the scepter in the hand of a monarch sitting on a throne. The entire body of theology depends on it the way a chain hangs from its hook. Believe it or not, we are even allotted our own place in heaven depending on our idea of God. It is like a touchstone for testing the quality of gold and silver,[393] that is, the goodness and truth in us. There exists no goodness in us that brings salvation except the goodness we have from God; and there exists no truth in us whose quality does not come from that core of goodness.

For us to see the nature of the divine Trinity in full perspective, the explanation of the Trinity needs to be divided into points as follows:

1. There is a divine Trinity, which is the Father, the Son, and the Holy Spirit.
2. These three, the Father, the Son, and the Holy Spirit, are three essential components of one God. They are one the way our soul, our body, and the things we do are one.
3. This Trinity did not exist before the world was created. It developed after the world was created, when God became flesh. It came into existence in the Lord God the Redeemer and Savior Jesus Christ.
4. At a conceptual level, the idea of a trinity of divine persons from eternity (meaning before the world was created) is a trinity of gods. This idea is impossible to wipe out just by orally confessing one God.
5. The apostolic church knew no trinity of persons. The idea was hatched by the Council of Nicaea. The council introduced the idea into the Roman Catholic church; and the Roman Catholic church introduced the idea into the churches that have since separated from it.
6. The Nicene and Athanasian views of the Trinity led to a faith that has perverted the whole Christian church.

7. The result is the abomination of desolation and the affliction such as has never existed before and will never exist again, which the Lord foretold in Daniel, the Gospels, and the Book of Revelation.

8. In fact, if the Lord were not building a new heaven and a new church, the human race would not be preserved.

9. Many absurd, alien, imaginary, and misshapen ideas of God have come into existence from the Athanasian Creed's assertion of a trinity of persons, each of whom is individually God.

Now these points will be elaborated one by one.

1. *There is a divine Trinity, which is the Father, the Son, and the Holy Spirit.* It is very obvious in the Word that there is a divine Trinity, which is the Father, the Son, and the Holy Spirit. Take the following passages for example:

164

> The angel Gabriel said to Mary, "The *Holy Spirit* will descend upon you and the *power of the Highest* will cover you; therefore the Holy One that is born from you will be called *the Son of God."* (Luke 1:35)

Here three are named: the Highest (who is God the Father), the Holy Spirit, and the Son of God.

> When Jesus was baptized, behold the heavens opened and John saw *the Holy Spirit* coming down like a dove upon him; and a voice from heaven said, "This is *my* beloved *Son,* in whom I am well pleased." (Matthew 3:16, 17; Mark 1:10, 11; John 1:32)

The Trinity is even more obvious from the Lord's words to his disciples:

> Go out and make disciples of all nations, baptizing them in the name of *the Father, the Son, and the Holy Spirit.* (Matthew 28:19)

The Trinity is also obvious from these words in John:

> There are three who testify in heaven: *the Father, the Word, and the Holy Spirit.* (1 John 5:7)

Further evidence besides these passages is that the Lord prayed to his Father and spoke about him and with him; and he said that he was going to send and had sent the Holy Spirit. Furthermore, in their letters the apostles frequently mention the Father, the Son, and the Holy Spirit. These sources clearly show that there is a divine Trinity, which is the Father, the Son, and the Holy Spirit.

165 Nonetheless, left to itself reason is utterly unable to see this Trinity. How are we to understand its three parts? Are they three gods who are one God in essence and name? Are they three distinct qualities of one underlying material, meaning that they are just qualities or attributes of a single God that have names? Or is there some other alternative?

The only good advice tells us to turn to the Lord God our Savior and read the Word under his supervision (since he is the God of the Word). Then we will be enlightened and see truths that even reason will acknowledge.

If you do not turn to the Lord, even if you read the Word a thousand times and see a divine trinity and a divine unity there, the only understanding you will get will be that there are three divine persons, each of whom is individually God; and therefore there are three gods. The common sense of all in the whole world finds this conclusion repulsive, however. Therefore to avoid being abused, people have come up with a strange compromise: although there are in fact three gods, the faith insists that we not say three gods; instead we must say there is one God. Furthermore, if we do not wish to undergo a barrage of verbal hostility, our intellect has to be especially imprisoned in this regard and held in chains under obedience to faith—from now on, according to the Christian leadership in the Christian church, this has to be the holy way.

[2] Such is the paralyzed offspring that was born as a result of not reading the Word under the Lord's supervision. Any of us who do not read the Word under the Lord's supervision read it under the supervision of our own intelligence; but when it comes to objects in spiritual light, such as all the essential teachings of the church, our intelligence is [as blind] as an owl [in daylight]. In that case, when we read about the Trinity in the Word and we get the impression that although there are three, still they are one, it seems to us like a response from an oracle. Since we do not understand it, we chew on it, because if we put it straight in front of our eyes it would be a puzzle. The harder we worked to solve the puzzle, the more we would entangle ourselves in darkness, until we began to set our intellect aside as we thought about it, which is like setting our eyes aside in the act of seeing.

To put it briefly, when we read the Word under the supervision of our own intelligence (which we all do if we do not acknowledge that the Lord is the God of heaven and earth, and turn to him and worship him alone), we are like children playing a game of blindfolding their eyes and trying to walk in a straight line. They believe they are walking straight, although step by step they turn increasingly to one side, till they come around to the opposite direction, bump into a stone, and fall over.

[3] If we read the Word with our own intelligence, we are like sailors navigating without a compass, who steer their ship onto the rocks and perish. We are like someone out walking through a large field in a thick fog who sees a scorpion but thinks it is a bird; in trying to catch it and pick it up, the person is fatally stung. We are like a seagull or an osprey that sees a tiny part of the back of a huge fish under the water, so it flies down and attacks, but its beak becomes stuck and it is dragged underwater and drowns. We are like someone who goes into a labyrinth without a guide or a spool of thread; the deeper we go in, the more we forget the way out.

If we read the Word under the supervision of our own intelligence rather than under the Lord's supervision, we think we are as keen-sighted as Lynceus and have more eyes than Argus,[394] when nevertheless inwardly everything we see is false and nothing true. As we convince ourselves of this falsity, it looks to us like the North Star, and we point all the sails of our thought toward it. By then our eyesight for truths is no better than a mole's: if we see truths at all, we bend them to favor things we ourselves made up—we distort and falsify the holy contents of the Word.

2. *These three, the Father, the Son, and the Holy Spirit, are three essential components of one God. They are one the way our soul, our body, and the things we do are one.* In any given thing there are general essential components and there are also specific essential components. The general and specific components combine to make one essence.

166

In our case, our general essential components are our soul, our body, and the things we do. These three components combine to make one essence, as you can see from the fact that one component comes from and exists for the other in an unbroken chain. We begin from our soul. The soul is the essence of the semen that originates us. Our soul not only initiates but also sequentially produces the features of our body. Then there are the things we do, which come from both our soul and our body. Because one of these components produces another, and therefore the subsequent components are grafted onto and connected to those that came before them, it follows that these three components share one essence. This is why they are called the three essential components.

The same three essential components—soul, body, and action—existed and still exist in the Lord God the Savior, as everyone acknowledges. The concept that the Lord's soul came from Jehovah the Father is something

167

only the Antichrist could deny, since the Word of both testaments calls him the Son of Jehovah, the Son of God the Highest, and the only begotten One. The Lord's primary essential component, then, is the Father's divinity, like the soul in us. It follows that the Son whom Mary bore is the body of that divine soul; for what develops in the mother's womb is the body that was conceived by and derived from the soul. This, then, is the second essential component. Actions make a third essential component because they come from both the soul and the body; for things produced have the same essence as the things that produce them.

The three essential components that are Father, Son, and Holy Spirit are one in the Lord as our soul, our body, and our actions [are one in us]. This is clear and obvious from the Lord's statement that the Father and he are one, and that the Father is in him and he is in the Father. The Lord is also one with the Holy Spirit because the Holy Spirit is divinity radiating from the Lord on behalf of the Father, as I have fully shown from the Word in §§153 and 154 above. To demonstrate this point again would therefore be an extra serving—it would be burdening the table with food after people are already full.

168   When told that the Father, the Son, and the Holy Spirit are the three essential components of the one God as our soul, our body, and our actions [are the essential components of a human being], the human mind may still think that three persons play the roles of these three essential components, when in fact there could not be three separate persons. When, however, we see the Father's divinity as the soul, the Son's divinity as the body, and the Holy Spirit's divinity (or divinity emanating) as action, and we see them as three essential components of one single God, then they become understandable. For the Father has his own divinity; the Son derives his divinity from the Father; and the Holy Spirit derives its divinity from them both. Since they share the same soul and essence, they constitute one God.

If we called these three divine components persons, however, and assigned each one its own responsibility—if we saw the Father as assigning spiritual credit or blame, the Son as mediating, and the Holy Spirit as putting things into effect—then we would be splitting a divine essence that is actually unified and indivisible. We would have made none of the three fully God; we would have given each one only a third of the power—an arrangement that a sound intellect has no choice but to reject.

169   We are all capable of using the trinity within each of us to picture the Trinity in the Lord. In every one of us there is a soul, a body, and our actions. It is the same in the Lord. According to Paul's letter to the Colossians, "All the fullness of divinity dwells physically" in the Lord (Colossians 2:9). Therefore there is a divine trinity in the Lord and a human one in us. It is a mysterious concept that there are three divine persons and yet there is one God, and that although there is one God, he is not one person. Surely reason has nothing in common with this idea. It puts our reason to sleep and makes our mouths speak like a parrot. When our reason is asleep, everything our mouths utter is without life. When our mouths say things that our reason diverges from and disagrees with, our statements are bound to be foolish.

Nowadays human reason has been restricted in regard to the divine Trinity like someone chained hand and foot in a prison. Our reasoning power is like a Vestal virgin buried in the ground for extinguishing the sacred fire.[395] Yet the divine Trinity ought to shine like a lighthouse in the minds of people in the church, since God with his trinity and with the unity in his trinity is essential to all that is holy in heaven and in the church. Making the soul one God, the body another, and the actions a third would be exactly like turning the three essential components in us into three separate entities. Does this not amount to mutilating and killing us?

3. *This Trinity did not exist before the world was created. It developed after the world was created, when God became flesh. It came into existence in the Lord God the Redeemer and Savior Jesus Christ.* Nowadays the Christian church asserts that the divine Trinity came into existence before the world was created: Before time, Jehovah God bore a Son. Then the Holy Spirit went out from them both. Each of the three is a God all by himself, in that each is a single self-sufficient person.

Because this concept does not square with any type of reasoning, it is called a mystery. The only way to grasp the concept is to think that the three share one divine essence—an essential eternity, immensity, and omnipotence and therefore equal divinity, glory, and majesty.

I will show in the sections to come, however, that such a concept becomes a trinity of gods and is therefore not a divine Trinity. On the other hand, from everything I have already said it is evident that a trinity of Father, Son, and Holy Spirit that developed after God became flesh, and therefore after the world was created, is a real divine trinity because it is a trinity in one God. This divine trinity exists in the Lord God the Redeemer and Savior Jesus Christ because the three essential components of the one God that go together to form one essence exist within him.

Paul's point that all the fullness of divinity dwells in Christ is clearly paralleled in the Lord's own statements that all things belonging to the Father are his and that the Holy Spirit speaks from him, not on its own. Furthermore, when the Lord rose from the tomb, he took along his entire human body, including its flesh and bones (Matthew 28:1–8; Mark 16:5, 6; Luke 24:1, 2, 3; John 20:11–15). He did this in a way that no other human being does. He himself gave experiential proof of this to the disciples when he said,

> See my hands and my feet—that it is I myself. Touch me and see. For a spirit does not have flesh and bones as you see I have. (Luke 24:39)

This statement has the power to convince any open-minded person that the Lord's human manifestation is divine, and therefore that in him God is human and a human is God.

171 The Trinity that the modern-day Christian church has embraced and integrated into its faith is that God the Father bore a Son from eternity, and the Holy Spirit came forth from them both. Each one is a god all by himself.

The only way the human mind can grasp this trinity is to view it as a "triarchy," like a government of three monarchs in one country, three generals over one army, or three heads in one household, each of whom has equal power. What other outcome could such a situation have except destruction? Any of us who try to picture or sketch that triarchy in our mind's eye, with its unity in mind as well, can view it only as a person with three heads on one body or three bodies with one head. This deformed image of the Trinity is bound to show up in those who believe in three divine persons, each of whom is God in his own right—those who connect them into one God while denying that "one God" means one person.

The concept of an eternally begotten Son of God who later comes down and takes on a human manifestation is like the ancient nonsense about human souls created at the beginning of the world that enter bodies and become people. It is also like the absurd notion that someone's soul can cross over into someone else's.[396] Many in the Jewish church used to believe this. They thought that the soul of Elijah was in the body of John the Baptist and that David was going to return in his own body or someone else's to reign over Israel and Judah, because it says in Ezekiel, "I will raise up one shepherd over them, who will feed them—my servant David. He will be their shepherd. And I, Jehovah, will be their God and

David will be a prince in their midst" (Ezekiel 34:23, 24, 25; there are other such references as well). They did not realize that "David" there means the Lord.

4. *At a conceptual level, the idea of a trinity of divine persons from eternity (meaning before the world was created) is a trinity of gods. This idea is impossible to wipe out just by orally confessing one God.* The following words in the Athanasian Creed make it very obvious that a trinity of divine persons from eternity is a trinity of gods: "The Father is one person, the Son another, and the Holy Spirit another. The Father is God and Lord, the Son is God and Lord, and the Holy Spirit is God and Lord. Nevertheless there are not three gods and lords; there is one God and Lord. Just as Christian truth compels us to confess each person individually as God and Lord, so the catholic religion forbids us to say three gods or three lords."

This creed has been accepted by the entire Christian church as ecumenical or universal. Today everything known and acknowledged about God comes from it. Those who took part in the Council of Nicaea that gave birth to this posthumous child[397] called the Athanasian Creed had no other concept of the Trinity except a trinity of gods, as any can see who merely keep their eyes open as they read it. Since then they have not been the only people thinking in terms of a trinity of gods; the Christian world thinks in terms of no other Trinity because its whole concept of God comes from that creed and everyone now lives in a faith based on those words.

[2] I submit it as a challenge to everyone—both laity and clergy, laureled professors and doctors as well as consecrated bishops and archbishops, even cardinals robed in scarlet and in fact the Roman pope himself—that the Christian world nowadays thinks of no other Trinity except a trinity of gods. You should all examine yourselves and then speak on the basis of the images in your mind.

The words of this creed—the universally accepted teaching about God—make it as clear and obvious as water in a crystal bowl. For example, the creed says that there are three persons, each of whom is God and Lord. It also says that because of Christian *truth,* people ought to confess or acknowledge that each person is individually God and Lord, but that the catholic or Christian *religion* or *faith* forbids us to say three gods or lords. This would mean that truth and religion, or truth and faith, are not the same thing; they are at odds with each other.

172

The writers of the creed added the point that there is one God and Lord, not three gods and lords, so that they would not be exposed to ridicule before the whole world. Who would not laugh at three gods? On the other hand, though, anyone can see the contradiction in the phrase they added.

[3] If instead they had said that the Father has a divine essence, the Son has a divine essence, and the Holy Spirit has a divine essence, but nevertheless there are not three divine essences, there is one indivisible essence, then that mystery would be explainable. That is, "the Father" means the divine nature as an origin, "the Son" means the divine-human nature that came from that origin, and "the Holy Spirit" means the divine influence that radiates out. These are three aspects of one God. Another way of putting it is that the Father's divinity means something like the soul in us, the divine-human manifestation means something like our body, which comes from our soul, and the Holy Spirit means something like our actions, which come from both our body and our soul. Then we see three essences that belong to one and the same person. Together they form one indivisible essence.

173 The idea of three gods is impossible to wipe out just by orally confessing one God, because it has been planted in our memory since childhood. We all think on the basis of what is in our memory.

The human memory is like the rumen that some birds and animals have. As these creatures go through the process of getting nourishment from their food, they first put their food in the rumen. They take it back out several times, and then put it in the main area of their stomach, where the food is digested and dispensed to serve all their body's functions. The human intellect is like the main area of the stomach; the human memory is like the rumen.[398]

Anyone can see that the idea of three divine persons who existed from eternity, which is the same as the idea of three gods, cannot be wiped out just by orally confessing one God. Just look at the following piece of evidence: it has not been wiped out yet. There are famous people who do not want it to be wiped out, who insist that the three divine persons are one God but stubbornly deny that because God is one, he is also one person. Surely all wise people, though, think to themselves that "person" here does not mean person at all. It means the attribution of some quality. Which quality exactly, we do not know. Because we do not know, the concept of three gods stays sown in our memory from childhood like the root of a tree in the ground. If the tree is cut down, a new shoot appears.

[2] My friend, do not just cut down that tree; dig out the root as well. Then plant your garden with trees that bear good fruit. Make sure the idea of three gods is not stuck in your mind as your mouth says "one God" without any accompanying mental picture. If the intellect above your memory is thinking three gods at the same time as the intellect below your memory is making your mouth say "one God," your intellect is like some clown on a stage who can play two parts at once. He switches from one part to the other, saying something in one role and contradicting it in the other, and in the argument calling his one self wise and his other self demented. Eventually he will stand in the middle looking both ways and thinking neither of them is anything. Likewise, if there is not one God and there are not three, then there is no God. This is the sole source of the materialist philosophy predominant today.

In heaven no one can even mention a trinity of persons, each of whom is individually God. The heavenly atmosphere itself in which thoughts travel in waves, as sound travels through air, works against it. Only hypocrites there can get away with it, but in the atmosphere of heaven their speaking has a bad sound like grinding teeth, or it squawks like a crow trying to sing like a songbird.

In fact, I have heard from heaven that using oral confession of one God to wipe out a belief in a trinity of gods (when that belief has been planted in the mind with supporting evidence) is as impossible as it would be to pass a whole tree through its own seed or to pass a man's whole chin through a single hair of his beard.

5. *The apostolic church knew no trinity of persons. This idea was first developed by the Council of Nicaea. The council introduced the idea into the Roman Catholic church; and it in turn introduced the idea into the churches that have since separated from it.* By "the apostolic church" I mean not only the church that existed in various places in the time of the apostles but also the church that existed over the two or three centuries after their time. Eventually, however, people started to tear the door to the house of worship off its hinges and break into the sanctuary like thieves. By the house of worship I mean Christianity; by the door I mean the Lord God the Redeemer; and by the sanctuary I mean his divinity. Jesus said, "*Truly I say* to you, those who do not enter through the door to the sheepfold but instead *climb up some other way* are thieves

174

and robbers. I am the door. Anyone who enters through me will be saved" [John 10:1, 9].

The crime just mentioned was committed by Arius and his followers. [2] Therefore Constantine the Great called a council in Nicaea, a city in Bithynia.[399] The people who had been called there to throw out Arius's damaging heresy invented, defended, and gave sanction to the idea that three divine persons—the Father, the Son, and the Holy Spirit—had existed from eternity, each with a personality, a reality, and a continued existence of his own. They also concluded that the second person, the Son, came down, took on a human manifestation, and brought about redemption; and that his human nature was divine because of a hypostatic union.[400] Through this union he had a close relationship with God the Father.

From that time on, balls of atrocious heresies relating to God and the person of Christ began to roll out across the globe, raising the head of the Antichrist, dividing God into three and the Lord the Savior into two, and destroying the temple that the Lord had erected through his apostles to the point where not one stone was left attached to another, as the Lord said (Matthew 24:2, where "the temple" means not only the Temple in Jerusalem but also the church, on whose close or end that whole chapter focuses).

[3] What else could be expected from the Council of Nicaea? What else could be expected from subsequent councils that likewise split divinity into three parts and placed the incarnate God beneath all three, on their footstool? These councils removed the church's head from its body by "climbing up some other way," that is, bypassing the Lord and going up to God the Father as some other god. They kept just the phrase "the merit of Christ" in their mouths, wishing for God the Father to have mercy on its account and hoping that justification would thereby flow in directly with its whole entourage: the forgiving of sins, renewal, sanctification, regeneration, and salvation—all without any participation from the individual.

175 It is very obvious from the creed of what is known as the apostolic church[401] that it had no awareness at all of any trinity of persons or of three persons from eternity. There the following words occur: "I believe in God, the Father Almighty, Creator of heaven and earth. I believe in Jesus Christ, his only begotten Son, our Lord, who was conceived of the Holy Spirit and born of the Virgin Mary. And I believe in the Holy Spirit."

There is no mention here of any "Son from eternity." The Son mentioned here was conceived of the Holy Spirit and born of the Virgin Mary. From the writings of the apostles the people of that church knew that Jesus Christ was the true God (1 John 5:20); that all the fullness of divinity dwelt physically in him (Colossians 2:9); that the apostles preached faith in him (Acts 20:21); and that all power in heaven and on earth had been given to him (Matthew 28:18).

How much trust should we put in councils when they do not go directly to the God of the church? The church is the body of the Lord. He is its head. What good is a body without a head? What kind of a body has three heads, under whose direction the people constituting that body develop plans and make decisions? Enlightenment is spiritual when it comes from the Lord alone, who is the God of heaven and the church, and who is also the God of the Word. When councils do not go directly to God, enlightenment becomes more and more earthly and even mindlessly physical. Then if we catch a whiff of any genuine theological truth in its inner form we immediately reject it from the thinking of our rational mind like chaff tossed into the air from a winnowing basket. In that case, false perspectives come in to replace the truth, and darkness comes in instead of rays of light. Then we are standing in a cave with glasses on our nose, candle in hand, closing our eyes to spiritual truths that are in the light of heaven and opening them to input from the faint, deceptive light of our physical senses. Later a similar thing happens when we read the Word: our mind falls asleep to what is true and wakes up to what is false. We become like the description of the beast from the sea: we develop the mouth of a lion, the body of a leopard, and the feet of a bear (Revelation 13:2).

There is a saying in heaven that when the Council of Nicaea finished, the followings things happened that the Lord had predicted to his disciples:

> The sun will be darkened and the moon will not give its light; the stars will fall from heaven, and the powers of the heavens will be shaken. (Matthew 24:29)

In fact, the apostolic church had been like a new star appearing in the sky. The church after the two Nicene councils was like the same star dimming and disappearing (a phenomenon that has in fact happened several times in the physical world, according to astronomers' observations).[402]

176

We read in the Word that Jehovah God dwells in inaccessible light [1 Timothy 6:16]. Who then could turn to him unless he dwelt in *accessible* light, that is, unless he came down, took on a human manifestation, and in it became the Light of the world (John 1:9; 12:46)? Surely anyone can see that turning to Jehovah the Father in his own light is as impossible as taking Dawn's wings from her and using them to fly to the sun, or feeding off the sun's rays instead of proper food. It would be like a bird flying in the ether or a deer running through the air.[403]

177 6. *The Nicene and Athanasian views of the Trinity led to a faith that has perverted the whole Christian church.* On the Nicene and Athanasian Trinity being a trinity of gods, see the evidence from those creeds given above at §172. Those creeds gave rise to the faith in the modern-day church, which is a faith in God the Father, God the Son, and God the Holy Spirit. The faith in God the Father is that he assigns and ascribes to us the justice of his Son the Savior. The faith in God the Son is that he intercedes and bargains for us. The faith in the Holy Spirit is that he actually instills the justice of the Son that has been assigned to us and seals it as an established fact by justifying us, sanctifying us, and regenerating us. This is the modern faith, which is enough evidence all by itself to prove that the church acknowledges and worships a trinity of gods.

[2] In any church, not only all its worship but also all its dogma ultimately go back to that church's faith. You could say, then, that the nature of a church's faith determines the nature of its teachings. It follows that the faith in question, because it is a faith in three gods, has perverted every aspect of the church. Faith is an origin; teachings are derived from it. What is derived receives its essence from its origin.

If you carefully examine the church's individual teachings—for example, on God, the person of Christ, goodwill, repentance, regeneration, free choice, the selection of the chosen people, the purpose of the sacraments of baptism and the Holy Supper[404]—you will clearly see that there is a trinity of gods in each one of them. If some teaching does not make the Trinity completely apparent, it still flows from the Trinity the way water flows from a spring.

I cannot present an examination of this kind here, but it would be worth presenting at some point, to open people's eyes to the relationship between teachings and faith. Therefore I will show this relationship in an appendix to this work.[405]

[3] The church's faith in God is like a body's soul. The church's teachings are like the body's limbs.

Faith in God is also like a queen, and dogmatic teachings are like her court officials. Just as the officials hang on the queen's every word, so dogmatic teachings depend on the stated faith.

One can judge solely from its faith how a given church understands the Word. A faith adapts the Word to itself. As if the faith had ropes, it pulls whatever it can get from the Word in its own direction.

If a faith is false, it commits prostitution with every truth in the Word, dragging that truth into perversion and falsifying it. A false faith drives us spiritually insane. If a faith is true, it agrees with the whole Word. The God of the Word, who is the Lord God the Savior, then pours light into that faith, blesses it with his divine assent, and makes us wise.

[4] The modern-day faith (which in its inner form is a faith in three gods, although in its outer form it is a faith in one God) has extinguished the light in the Word and has removed the Lord from the church. It has quickly turned the church's morning into night. (This point too will be seen in the appendix.) The changes in the faith were made by heretics before the Council of Nicaea as well as heretics at the council and after it.

How much trust should we put in councils when they do not use the door to enter the sheepfold? Instead they "climb up some other way," as the Lord says in John 10:1, 9. The debating at those councils was like the walking of a blind person by day or a sighted person by night, each of whom fails to see a great pit before falling into it.

For example, how much trust should we put in councils when they have established the notions of viewing the pope as Christ's representative, deifying dead people, calling on them as supernatural powers, venerating their images, authorizing indulgences, splitting the Eucharist, and more?[406] How much trust should we put in the council that established the horrendous idea of predestination and erected it as a religious icon in front of all church buildings?[407]

Instead, my friend, as you approach the Word, go to the God of the Word and enter the sheepfold of the church through the Door. Then you will be enlightened. Then, as if you were on a mountain top, you will see the earlier tracks and mistaken turns in the dark forest at the foot of the mountain—not only those of many other people, but also your own.

The faith of any church is like a seed from which all its dogmas grow. **178** It is like the seed of a tree that generates all the tree's features including its fruit. It is like human seed that generates descendants and families one after the other.

If you know a church's primary faith—the one they say is so crucial that it will bring you salvation—then you comprehend the nature of that church.

The following example may illustrate this point: Imagine a faith or belief that says nature created the universe. From that belief come many other beliefs: what we call God is really the universe; nature is its essence; the ether is the highest god the ancients called Jupiter; the air is the goddess the ancients called Juno, the one they made into a spouse for Jupiter; the ocean is a god below the others whom we, like the ancients, could call Neptune; and because nature's divinity extends even to the center of the earth, there is a god there whom we, like the ancients, could call Pluto; the sun is a royal hall for all the gods to meet in when Jupiter calls a council;[408] fire is life from God; birds fly in God, animals walk on God, fish swim in God; thoughts are only modifications in the ether,[409] just as speaking those thoughts involves modulations in the air; and different types of love are just incidental changes in our mental condition caused by the rays of the sun flowing into them. Among these beliefs there is also the view that life after death, heaven, and hell are myths made up by the clergy to win honor and wealth; but although they are myths, they are nevertheless useful and should not be openly ridiculed, because they serve the public by putting simple minds on a leash so that they obey their civic leaders. Still, those who are captivated by religion are unrealistic people, their thoughts are delusions, their actions are amusing, and they are subservient to the clergy in that they believe in things they do not see and see things that lie outside their mental range.[410]

These derivative beliefs and many others like them are contained in the original belief that nature created the universe. They come out when the full implications of that belief are explored.

I have listed all this so you may know that the modern-day church's faith (which in its inner form is a faith in three gods, but in its outer form is a faith in one God) has squadrons of falsities inside it. There are as many falsities to be brought out as there are baby spiders in the egg case produced by a mother spider.

Anyone with a mind made truly rational by light from the Lord sees this. No others are going to see it, though, when the door to that faith and its offspring has been bolted shut by the principle that it is wrong for reason to examine its mysteries.[411]

179   *7. The result is the abomination of desolation and the affliction such as has never existed before and will never exist again, which the Lord foretold in*

Daniel, the Gospels, and the Book of Revelation. In Daniel we read the following words:

> In the end desolation [will fly in] on a bird of abominations; even to the close and the cutting down, it will drip steadily upon the devastation. (Daniel 9:27)

In the Gospel of Matthew the Lord says these words:

> Then many false prophets will rise up and lead many astray. Therefore when you see that the abomination of desolation foretold by the prophet Daniel is standing in the holy place, let those who read note it well. (Matthew 24:11, 15)

Later in the same chapter we read,

> Then there will be a great affliction such as has never existed since the world began until now and will never exist again. (Matthew 24:21)

This affliction and abomination are dealt with in seven chapters in the Book of Revelation.[412] They are meant by the black horse and the pale horse that came out of the book whose seal the Lamb had opened (Revelation 6:5–8). They are meant by the beast that came up from the abyss and made war on the two witnesses and killed them (Revelation 11:7–10). They are meant by the dragon that stood by the woman who was about to give birth, that intended to devour her child, and that pursued her into the desert and cast water like a river out of its mouth to swallow her up (Revelation 12). Also by the beasts of the dragon, one from the sea and the other from the land (Revelation 13); and by the three spirits like frogs that came out of the mouth of the dragon, the mouth of the beast, and the mouth of the false prophet (Revelation 16:13).

In addition, the affliction and abomination are meant by these events: the seven angels poured out the bowls of God's anger that contained the seven last plagues, pouring them onto the earth, into the sea, into springs and rivers, onto the sun, onto the throne of the beast, into the river Euphrates, and finally into the air, and then a tremendous earthquake occurred unlike any that had happened since the creation of humankind (Revelation 16). An earthquake means the act of turning the church upside-down, which was caused by falsities and by falsified truths—this meaning parallels the meaning of the great affliction such as has never existed since the world began (Matthew 24:21).

The following words have a similar meaning:

> The angel sent a sickle to harvest the vineyard of the earth and throw it into the great winepress of God's anger. The winepress was trampled and blood went out; sixteen hundred stadia[413] away it was as high as a horse's bridle. (Revelation 14:19, 20)

Blood means falsified truth. There are many other examples in those seven chapters.

180   The Gospel writers described the stages of decline and corruption that the Christian church would undergo (Matthew 24; Mark 13; Luke 21). Their reference to "a great affliction such as has never existed since the world began and will never exist again" [Matthew 24:21] means an attack by falsities against the truth until there is no truth left that has not been falsified and finished off. ("Affliction" has the same meaning in other passages in the Word as well.)

Their reference to "the abomination of desolation" means the same thing, as does "the desolation [flying] on a bird of abominations" and "the close and the cutting down" in Daniel [9:27]. The events in the Book of Revelation listed in the previous section [§179] also describe the same attack.

This attack came because the church saw God's unity in the Trinity and his Trinity in the unity in three persons instead of one. The church has been mentally based on picturing three gods and vocally based on confessing one God. People in the church have separated themselves from the Lord, even to the point where they no longer have any concept of divinity in relation to his human nature. Yet he is in fact God the Father in human form, which is why he is called "Father of Eternity" (Isaiah 9:6) and why he says to Philip, "Those who have seen me have seen the Father" (John 14:7, 9).

181   You may well ask what the source is that yields the abomination of desolation that Daniel describes (Daniel 9:27) and the affliction such as has never existed before and will never exist again (Matthew 24:21). The answer you will find is the faith itself that is universal to the Christian world, together with the now traditional concepts of how that faith flows into us, acts on us, and is assigned to us. Astoundingly, the position that that faith is the only thing that justifies us (although that belief is really a fairy tale, not a faith) occupies every square inch of the Christian churches. In the Sacred Order,[414] it rules as virtually the only theology. This position is what all candidates for the ministry eagerly learn,

consume, and absorb in college. Then, as if they were people inspired with heavenly wisdom, they teach that position in churches and publish it in books. Through it they pursue and achieve the name, reputation, and glory of having superior erudition. Because of it they are given diplomas, fellowships, and awards.

All this goes on despite the fact that nowadays this faith alone has darkened the sun, deprived the moon of its light, caused the stars of heaven to fall, and shaken the powers of the heavens, as the Lord foretold in Matthew 24:29. I have been given absolute proof that this faith has so blinded human minds today that they do not want, and therefore are virtually unable, to see any divine truth inwardly [as if it were] in the light of either the sun or the moon. They can see it only [as if it were] reflected superficially off some rough surface in firelight at night. I can therefore make this assertion: If divine truths about the true partnership between goodwill and faith, about heaven and hell, about the Lord, about life after death, and about eternal happiness were to be written in silver letters[415] and sent down from heaven, people who believe that we are sanctified and justified by faith alone would not even consider them worth reading. At the other extreme, though, if a paper asserting that faith alone makes us just were to be sent up from the hells, the same people would seize it, kiss it, and hold it close to their heart as they carried it home.

8. *In fact, if the Lord were not building a new heaven and a new church, the human race would not be preserved.* We read in Matthew, **182**

> Then there will be a great affliction such as has never existed since the world began until now and will never exist again. In fact, unless those days were cut short no flesh would be preserved. (Matthew 24:21, 22)

This chapter in Matthew concerns "the close of the age," which means the end of the modern-day church. "Cutting those days short" means ending that church and starting a new one.

Surely everyone knows that unless the Lord had come into the world and redeemed us, we could not have been saved. "Redeeming us" means constructing a new heaven and a new church.

In the Gospels the Lord predicted that he was going to come into the world again (Matthew 24:30, 31; Mark 13:26; Luke 12:40; 21:27; see also the Book of Revelation, especially in the last chapter). As I have shown above in the second part of the last chapter, on redemption [§§114–137], today the Lord is again redeeming us, constructing a new heaven, and building a new church for the purpose of saving humankind.

[2] Here is the great secret as to why the human race could not be preserved if the Lord were not building a new church. As long as the dragon and its crew stay down in the world of spirits where they were thrown, no divine truth united to divine good can get across to people on earth without being perverted and falsified or ceasing to exist. This is what the Book of Revelation means when it says,

> The dragon was thrown down onto the earth and its angels were thrown with it. Woe to those who live on the earth and in the sea, because the Devil has come down to them in a giant rage. (Revelation 12:9, 12, 13)

It was after the dragon was thrown down into hell (Revelation 20:10) that John saw a new heaven and a new earth and saw the New Jerusalem coming down from God out of heaven (Revelation 21:1, 2). The "dragon" means those who share the belief of the church today.

[3] In the spiritual world I have talked several times with people who say faith alone makes us just. I said that their teaching is wrong and also absurd; it brings on spiritual complacency, blindness, sleep, and night; and it is eventually lethal to the soul. I urged them to give it up.

I received the response, "Why stop? This is the sole reason that the clergy can claim to be better educated than lay people."

I replied that in that case they must view a superior reputation as their goal, not the saving of souls. Since they have applied the truths in the Word to their own false principles, which means they have contaminated them, they are the angels of the abyss called Abaddons and Apollyons (Revelation 9:11; those names mean people who have destroyed the church by completely falsifying the Word).

They replied, "What? Since we know the mysteries of that faith, we are *oracles*. We give answers from that faith as if it were a sacred shrine. We are not Apollyons; we are Apollos."[416]

Irritated at that, I said, "If you are Apollos you are also leviathans.[417] The leaders among you are coiled leviathans, and the followers among you are uncoiled leviathans. God will visit you with his sword, great and strong (Isaiah 27:1)."

They just laughed at that.

183   9. *Many absurd, alien, imaginary, and misshapen ideas of God have come into existence from the Athanasian Creed's assertion of a trinity of persons, each of whom is individually God.* The teaching that there have been three divine persons from eternity—the chief of all teachings in Christian churches—has produced many unseemly ideas about God that are unsuitable for the Christian world, especially since that world could be and ought to be a light revealing God and his unity to all the peoples and nations in the four quarters of the earth.

All who live outside the Christian church, both Muslims and Jews, as well as other non-Christians with whatever kind of worship, have rejected Christianity solely because of its belief in three gods. Christian missionaries know this. They are extremely careful not to publicize the trinity of persons taught in the Nicene and Athanasian Creeds, because people would go away laughing.

[2] The teaching that there have been three divine persons from eternity has produced absurd, ludicrous, and silly mental images. In fact, these mental images keep coming up in any of us who continue to believe the words of this teaching. They rise up through our ears and eyes into the visualization in our thoughts.

The images are that God the Father sits high above our heads. The Son sits by his right hand. The Holy Spirit sits in front of them both, listening to them and then immediately running around the planet dispensing the gifts of justification according to their decision. The Holy Spirit instills those gifts, turning children of anger into children of grace and the damned into the chosen.

I challenge learned clergy and educated laity to check and see whether they harbor any other picture besides this one in their minds. This picture, you see, flows in spontaneously from this teaching (see the memorable occurrence above at §16).

[3] This teaching also leads people to conjecture what the three talked about before the world was created. Did they talk about creating the world? Did they talk about predestining people and justifying them, as the Supralapsarians[418] would have us believe? Did they talk about redemption? For that matter, what have they been saying to each other *since* the world was created? What is the Father saying, with his power and authority of assigning spiritual credit and blame? What is the Son saying, with his power of mediating? This teaching also leads some to conjecture that it belongs to the Son's mercy to assign people spiritual credit or blame, which is the same as choosing them for hell or heaven, since the Son generally intercedes for all people and specifically intercedes for some individuals. Toward these individuals the Father has an attitude of grace because he is moved with love for the Son, having seen the Son's anguish on the wood of the cross.

Anyone can see that these conjectures are a form of irrationality about God. Yet in the Christian churches they are sacred objects that we have to kiss with our lips. Nevertheless, we must not give them close mental attention, because they transcend rationality and will make us insane if they are raised from our memory into our intellect. This precaution, though, does not do away with our mental picture of three gods—it just gives us a stupid belief. Thoughts about God that are based on this faith resemble the footsteps of someone sleepwalking and dreaming in the dead of night, or the footsteps of someone born blind who is walking in the light of day.

184 You can clearly tell that a trinity of gods dwells in the minds of Christians—although out of shame they would never say so—by the way many of them ingeniously demonstrate that three are one and one is three. They use various phenomena in plane geometry, solid geometry, arithmetic, and physics, as well as folding pieces of clothing and pieces of paper.[419] Like a bunch of clowns, they horse around with the divine Trinity.

Their clowning is like people's eyesight when they have a fever: they see one object, be it a person, a table, or a candle, as three objects, or three objects as one. It is like the trick people play by softening wax in their fingers and pressing it into different shapes. First they make a three-sided shape to show the trinity; then they make a ball to show the unity, and they say, "Isn't the substance one and the same?"

Truly, though, the divine Trinity is like the pearl of great price [Matthew 13:46]. Dividing the Trinity into persons is like cutting a pearl into three parts: it completely destroys the pearl.

185 To these points I will add the following memorable occurrences.

The first memorable occurrence. The spiritual world has climatic zones just like the physical world—there is nothing in this world that is not also in that one. Yet the zones in each have different origins. In the physical world, climatic zones are determined by the distance of the sun from the equator. In the spiritual world, climatic zones are determined by how far the feelings in our will and the consequent thoughts in our intellect are from true love and true faith. All things in the spiritual world relate to love and faith.

In the frigid zones in the spiritual world you see the same type of conditions you see in the frigid zones in the physical world. In that part of the spiritual world you see ground that is frozen solid and bodies of water frozen solid, with snowdrifts on them. The people who move to that area are people who had put their intellect to sleep in this world by giving it no energy for spiritual thinking; as a result they had no energy for doing anything useful either. They are called the spirits of the north.

[2] On one occasion a longing came over me to see a region in the frigid zone where the spirits of the north live. Therefore I was led in the spirit to the north all the way to an area where the ground was completely covered in snow and all forms of water were frozen solid.

It was a Sunday. I noticed that the people (meaning spirits) were about as tall as people in the world. Because of the cold, they wore a lion's skin on their head with the lion's mouth over their mouth. They wore leopard skins over their bodies, front and back, down to their thighs. They wore a bearskin on their feet and lower legs.[420]

I saw many of them riding in carriages. Some were riding in carriages carved in the form of a dragon with horns sticking out in front. The carriages were being drawn by small horses whose tails were cut off. The horses were charging around like terrifying wild animals. The driver, holding the reins in his hands, was constantly goading and forcing the horses on their way.

After a while I saw that the crowds were flocking to a church that I had not noticed because it was buried in snow. The church caretakers were heaving the snow aside, digging out access for the arriving worshipers. The worshipers got out of their carriages and entered the church.

[3] I too was allowed to go in and see the church building from the inside. It was lit with a great many lamps and lanterns. The altar was made out of a hewn stone. Behind it hung a plaque with an inscription: *The divine Trinity, the Father, Son, and Holy Spirit, who are essentially one God but personally three.*

A priest was standing next to the altar. After kneeling three times before the plaque above it, he eventually ascended the stairs into the pulpit with a book in his hand.

The first topic of his sermon was the divine Trinity. He cried out, "What a great mystery! God most high bore a Son from eternity and through him brought forth the Holy Spirit. The three of them are connected by their essence but separate in their tasks: assigning, redeeming, and putting into effect. But if we let our reason examine these points, our sight will be blinded. We will develop a blind spot like people who stare straight at the naked sun. Therefore, my listeners, on these points we should hold our intellect under obedience to faith."

[4] Then he cried out again and said, "What a great mystery our holy faith is! We believe that God the Father assigns the Son's justice and sends the Holy Spirit, who then uses the assigned justice to work the benefits of justification, which are, briefly, forgiving sins, renewing, regenerating, and saving. Yet of the Holy Spirit's inflowing or action we have no more awareness than did Lot's wife after she turned into a statue of salt.[421] About its indwelling or condition we have no more awareness than a fish in the sea. My friends, a treasure lies in our faith, yet it is so well hidden that not a particle of it shows. Therefore in this respect also we should hold our intellect under obedience to faith."

[5] After sighing a few times, he cried out once more and said, "What a great mystery is the process of becoming chosen people! We become chosen when God assigns the faith to us. He assigns that faith with free choice and pure grace to whomever he wants whenever he wants to. We are like a log of wood as he pours it in, but we become like a tree afterward. Pieces of fruit, which are good works, do indeed hang from that tree (which is a symbol for our faith), but they are not integral to it. The value of the tree is not based on its fruit. My brothers and sisters, because this sounds like it contradicts our religion yet is a mystical truth, here again we should hold our intellect under obedience to faith."

[6] Then after quite a delay while he stood as if he were drawing some further point out of his memory, he went on to say, "From a mountain of mysteries I will choose just one more. Spiritually speaking we don't have a speck of free choice. As the top hierarchy and leaders of our order state in their handbooks of theological principles, we are unable to will, think, or understand anything in the arenas of faith and salvation, which are specifically labeled as spiritual. We are even incapable of adapting and applying ourselves to learning about faith and salvation. Therefore I myself would say that on our own we're incapable of drawing on reason to think about faith and salvation, and of drawing on thought to babble about it, except like a parrot, a magpie, or a raven. Spiritually speaking we are actually donkeys. Only physically are we human. But, my colleagues, before your reasoning faculty becomes uncomfortable, let's hold the intellect under obedience to faith as we've done in relation to other issues.

"Our theology, you see, is a bottomless pit. If you let your intellect look into it, you'll be shipwrecked and swallowed up, and you'll perish.

Now hear me well—we are still nonetheless in the very light of the Gospel that shines high above our heads. Watch out for the pain, though, [that the light can cause]! Thankfully, the hairs on our head and the bones in our skull block and prevent that light from penetrating the private space of our intellect."

[7] After he finished his remarks, he came down from the pulpit and offered votive prayers at the altar, and the worship service came to an end.

Afterward I went over to a group of people who were talking together. The priest was there also. The people standing there said to the priest, "We wish to express our undying gratitude to you for a sermon that was both magnificent and rich in wisdom."

I asked them, "Did you understand anything?"

"We took it all in with open ears," they answered. "But why do you ask whether we understood it? Isn't the intellect too stupid to understand these topics?"

To what they had said the priest added, "Because you heard and did not understand, you are blessed, since you have salvation as a result."

[8] Later on I talked to the priest. I asked whether he had a post-graduate degree. He answered, "I have a master's degree."

Then I said, "Sir, I heard you preaching mysteries. If you know of those mysteries but you don't know what they contain, you don't know anything. The mysteries are then just like a treasure chest bolted shut with three locks. Unless you open it up and look inside, which would require your intellect, you don't know whether the things inside are precious, worthless, or toxic. They could be the eggs of a poisonous snake and the webs of spiders, as Isaiah describes in chapter 59, verse 5."

At that, the priest glared at me severely.

The worshipers went out and climbed aboard their carriages, drunk on paradoxes, knocked senseless by meaningless expressions, and wrapped in darkness regarding all aspects of faith and the means of being saved.

The second memorable occurrence. On one occasion I was turning over in my thinking [the question of] what level of our mind theological issues occupy. Because they are spiritual and heavenly I started out thinking they must occupy the highest level in us. (The human mind is differentiated into three levels, like a three-story house. Similarly, the homelands of the angels are differentiated into three heavens.)

186

Then an angel appeared standing next to me and said, "In those who love the truth because it is true, theological issues rise even to the highest level. The heaven of such people is on that level, and they have the light that angels have. Moral issues that have been examined and seen in a theoretical way are located on the second level under theological issues, because moral issues communicate with spiritual issues. Political issues dwell on the first level, below moral issues. Academic subjects, which come in many different forms and can be broken into genera and species, form a doorway to all the higher issues.

"People who have spirituality, morality, politics, and academics prioritized like this think what they think and do what they do on the basis of justice and judgment. The reason for this is that the light of truth, which is also the light of heaven, radiates through their highest level and lights up what is lower down, just as the light from the sun passes through the upper atmospheres and eventually through the air to provide light for the eyesight of people, animals, and fish.

"Theological issues do not, however, occupy the same place in people who love the truth only for the sake of their own glorious reputations and not because it is true. In these people theological issues occupy the lowest level where academic subjects are considered. In some people, theology and scholarly study become intertwined, but in others they cannot become intertwined. Political issues occur on the same level beneath theological issues, and moral issues fall beneath them. In people like this, the two higher levels are not open on the right-hand side,[422] so these people have no inner reason that judges and they have no love for justice. Instead they have cleverness that enables them to talk about any subject as if they were intelligent and to support whatever comes to their mind as if they were rational. The topics that they love to reason about the most, though, are false because those topics are connected to lies told by their five senses.

"This is why there are so many people in the world who cannot see teachings that are true in the Word any more than someone born blind could. When they hear teachings that are true, they hold their noses so the smell will not upset or nauseate them. In the presence of falsities, they open all their senses and drink those falsities in the way a whale swallows water."

187 *The third memorable occurrence.* Once as I was meditating on the dragon, the beast, and the false prophet mentioned in the Book of Revelation, an angelic spirit appeared to me and asked what I was meditating on. I said, "The false prophet."

The angelic spirit said, "I will take you to the place where the spirits meant by the false prophet are." He added, "They are the same spirits portrayed in chapter 13 of the Book of Revelation as the beast from the earth who had two horns like a lamb, but who spoke like a dragon."

I followed the angelic spirit. To my surprise I saw a crowd with church leaders in the center of it. The leaders were teaching that nothing saves us except faith in Christ's merit and that works are good things to do, but not for our salvation. They were also proclaiming that works need to be taught from the Word so as to put lay people, especially simple ones, on a leash so that they obey their civic leaders and feel compelled from within by religion to practice moral goodwill.

[2] Then one of them saw me and said, "Do you want to see our shrine? It has a sculpture in it that portrays our faith."

I went and saw it. It was magnificent! In the center of the shrine there was a statue of a woman dressed in scarlet clothes. She had a gold coin in her right hand and a chain of pearls in her left.

Both the statue and the shrine, however, were projected images. Hellish spirits have the ability to portray magnificent things using projected images. They do it by closing off the inner levels of our mind and opening only its outer levels.

When I realized that the statue and the shrine were conjured up through sorcery I prayed to the Lord. Suddenly the inner levels of my mind were opened. Then instead of a magnificent shrine, I saw a house that was full of cracks from the roof all the way to the foundation. Nothing in it was solidly connected. Instead of the woman, I saw a dummy hanging in the house that had the head of a dragon, the body of a leopard, the feet of a bear, and the mouth of a lion. It was exactly like the beast from the sea described in Revelation 13:2. Instead of the floor, there was a swamp that contained thousands of frogs.[423] I was told that under the swamp there was a great hewn stone; and beneath it the Word lay deeply hidden.

Seeing this I said to the sorcerer, "Is this your shrine?"

"It is," the sorcerer said.

Just then, though, the sorcerer's inner sight opened up as well. The sorcerer saw the same things I was seeing and loudly shouted, "What is this? Where did this come from?"

"It came from the light of heaven," I said, "which has disclosed the true quality of each form here, including the quality of your faith, which has been separated from spiritual goodwill."

[3] Immediately the east wind[424] came up and blew away the shrine with the sculpture. It dried up the swamp and exposed the stone that had the Word lying underneath it.

Then a warm, springlike breeze blew in from heaven. To my surprise I then saw a tent in that same place, a very simple one in its outer form.

Angels who were with me said, "Look, it is Abraham's tent just as it was when the three angels came to him to announce that Isaac was going to be born [Genesis 18:1, 2, and following]. The tent looks simple to the eye, but as the light of heaven flows in, it becomes more and more magnificent."

The angels were then granted the ability to open the heaven where spiritual angels live—the angels who have wisdom. In the light that flowed in from that heaven, the tent looked like the Temple in Jerusalem. When I looked inside, I saw that the foundation stone under which the Word had been hidden was now covered in precious stones. From the precious stones a kind of lightning was flashing across to walls that had reliefs of angel guardians on them, giving the angel guardians beautifully different colors.

[4] As I was feeling awestruck by these sights, the angels said, "You are about to see things that are even more miraculous." They were then granted the ability to open the third heaven where heavenly angels live— the angels who have love. As a result of the blazing light that flowed in from that heaven, the entire temple disappeared. In its place I saw the Lord alone, standing on the foundation stone, which *was* the Word. He looked much the way he had when seen by John in Revelation chapter 1.

Yet because holiness then filled the inner realms of the angels' minds so that they felt an overwhelming urge to fall forward on their faces, suddenly the channel of light from the third heaven was closed by the Lord and the channel of light from the second heaven was reopened. As a result, the earlier appearance of a temple, and also a tent, returned. The tent was in the middle of the temple.

These experiences illustrated what Revelation 21 means when it says, "Behold, the tent[425] of God is with people, and he will dwell with them" (Revelation 21:3); and when it says, "I saw no temple in the New Jerusalem, because the Lord God Almighty is its Temple, and the Lamb" (Revelation 21:22).

188 *The fourth memorable occurrence.* Since the Lord has allowed me to see amazing things in the heavens and below them, I have been commanded and am obligated to pass on what I have seen.

I saw a magnificent palace that had a chapel in its center. In the middle of the chapel there was a golden table that had the Word on it. Two angels were standing next to the table. Around the table there were three rows of chairs. The chairs in the first row were covered in pure silk of a purple color, the chairs in the second row in pure silk of a sky blue color, and the chairs in the third row in white cloth. High above the table a canopy was suspended beneath the ceiling. It gleamed so brightly with precious stones that it created an effect like a glowing rainbow [that appears] when the sky begins to clear after a rain shower.

Suddenly members of the clergy appeared, occupying all the chairs. They were all wearing the robes of their priestly ministry.

To one side there was a cabinet with an angel guard standing nearby. Inside the cabinet there were shining pieces of clothing laid out in a beautiful array.

[2] It was a council that had been called by the Lord.426 I heard a voice from heaven that said, "Discuss."

The participants said, "About what?"

"About the Lord the Savior and about the Holy Spirit," the voice said.

When they began thinking about these topics they had no enlightenment, so they prayed. Then a light flowed down from heaven that first lit up the backs of their heads, then their temples, and finally their faces.

Then they began. They started where they had been told to, with the first topic, the Lord the Savior. The first issue to be discussed was, "Who took on a human manifestation in the Virgin Mary?"

An angel standing next to the table that had the Word on it read to them the following words in Luke:

> The angel said to Mary, "Behold, you will conceive in your womb and will bear a Son, and you will call his name Jesus. He will be great and will be called *the Son of the Highest.*" And Mary said to the angel, "How will this take place, since I have not had intercourse?"427 The angel replied and said to her, "*The Holy Spirit will descend upon you, and the power of the Highest will cover you;* therefore *the Holy One* that is born from you will be called the Son of God." (Luke 1:31, 32, 34, 35)

Then the angel read these words in Matthew:

> In a dream an angel told Joseph, "Joseph, descendant of David, do not be afraid to take Mary as your bride, *for the Child that has been conceived in her is from the Holy Spirit.*" And *Joseph did not have intercourse with her* until she gave birth to her firstborn Son and called his name *Jesus.* (Matthew 1:20, 25)

In addition to these passages, the angel read many things from the Gospels, such as Matthew 3:17; 17:5; John 1:18; 3:16; 20:31; and many other passages where the Lord in his human manifestation is referred to as the Son of God, and where from his human manifestation he calls Jehovah his Father. The angel also read from the Prophets where it is foretold that Jehovah himself is going to come into the world. Two of the latter passages were the following from Isaiah:

> It will be said in that day, "*Behold, this is our God.* We have waited for him to free us. This is *Jehovah whom we have waited for.* Let us rejoice and be glad in his salvation." (Isaiah 25:9)

> The voice of one crying in the desert, "Prepare a way for *Jehovah;* make a level pathway in the solitude for *our God.* For the glory of *Jehovah* will be revealed, and all flesh will see it together. Behold, *the Lord Jehovih is coming with strength;* like a *shepherd* he will feed his flock." (Isaiah 40:3, 5, 10, 11)

[3] The angel said, "Since Jehovah himself came into the world and took on a human manifestation, therefore in the Prophets Jehovah is called *the Savior* and *the Redeemer.*"

Then the angel read them the following passages:

> "The only *God* is among you; there is no other God." Surely you are the God who was hidden, *O God the Savior of Israel.* (Isaiah 45:14, 15)

> Am not I *Jehovah?* There is no other God except me. I am *a just God, and there is no Savior except me.* (Isaiah 45:21, 22)

> *I am Jehovah, and there is no Savior except me.* (Isaiah 43:11)

> I am Jehovah your God, and you are not to acknowledge a God except me. *There is no Savior except me.* (Hosea 13:4)

> So that all flesh may know that *I, Jehovah, am your Savior and your Redeemer.* (Isaiah 49:26; 60:16)

> *As for our Redeemer, Jehovah Sabaoth*[428] *is his name.* (Isaiah 47:4)

> *Their Redeemer is strong; Jehovah Sabaoth is his name.* (Jeremiah 50:34)

> *Jehovah,* my rock and *my Redeemer.* (Psalms 19:14)

> Thus says *Jehovah, your Redeemer,* the Holy One of Israel: "I am Jehovah, your God." (Isaiah 48:17; 43:14; 49:7; 54:8)

> You, *Jehovah,* are our Father; *our Redeemer* from everlasting is your name. (Isaiah 63:16)

Thus said *Jehovah, your Redeemer:* "I, Jehovah, am the maker of all things. I alone [stretch out the heavens. I extend the earth] by myself." (Isaiah 44:24)

Thus said Jehovah, the King of Israel and *its Redeemer, Jehovah Sabaoth:* "I am the First and the Last, and there is no God except me." (Isaiah 44:6)

Jehovah Sabaoth is his name, and *your Redeemer,* the Holy One of Israel. *He will be called God of all the earth.* (Isaiah 54:5)

Behold, the days are coming when I will raise up for David a righteous offshoot who will reign as king. And this is his name: *Jehovah is our Justice.* (Jeremiah 23:5–6; 33:15–16)

In that day, Jehovah will be king over the whole earth; *in that day there will be one Jehovah, and his name will be one.* (Zechariah 14:9)

[4] With the support of all these passages, the clergy sitting in the chairs unanimously stated that it was Jehovah himself who took on the human manifestation, and that he did so in order to redeem and save humankind.

At that point, though, we heard a voice from Roman Catholics who had hidden behind the altar.[429] The voice said, "How could Jehovah God become human? He is the Creator of the universe!"

One of the clergy sitting in the second row of chairs said, "Who then was the human manifestation?"

The man who had been behind the altar before, but was now standing beside it, said, "The Son from eternity."

He received this reply: "In your confession the eternally begotten Son is the same as the Creator of the universe. What is a Son and an eternally begotten God? How could the divine essence, which is one indivisible thing, be separated? How could one part of it come down and not the whole essence at once?"

[5] The second issue for discussion related to the Lord: "Surely then the Father and he are one as the soul and the body are one."

They said that this would follow, because his soul was from the Father.

Then one of the clergy sitting in the third row of chairs read the following words from the statement of faith known as the Athanasian Creed: "Our Lord Jesus Christ, the Son of God, is both God and a human being. Yet still he is one Christ, not two. In fact, he is completely one; *he is one person. As a soul and a body make one human being, so God and a human being is one Christ.*"

The reader said, "The creed that contains these words has been accepted by the entire Christian world including the Roman Catholics."

The participants said, "What more do we need? God the Father and he are one as the soul and the body are one."

They added, "Because this is so, we see that the Lord's human manifestation is divine because it is the human manifestation of Jehovah. We also see that we must seek help from the Lord's divine-human manifestation. Only in this way, not in any other, can we have access to the divine nature that is called the Father."

The angel supported their conclusion with more passages from the Word, among which were the following: "A Child is born to us; a Son is given to us. His name will be called Wonderful, Counselor, *God,* Hero, *Father of Eternity,* Prince of Peace" (Isaiah 9:6). "Abraham did not know us and Israel did not acknowledge us. You, *Jehovah,* are *our Father; our Redeemer from everlasting is your name*" (Isaiah 63:16). And in John, "Jesus said, 'Those who believe in me believe in the One who sent me. Those who see me see the One who sent me'" (John 12:44, 45). "Philip said to Jesus, 'Show us the Father.' Jesus said to him, *'Those who see me see the Father.* Why then are you saying, "Show us the Father"? Do you not believe that *I am in the Father and the Father* is in me? Believe me *that I am in the Father and the Father is in me*'" (John 14:8, 9, 10, 11). "Jesus said, *'I and my Father are one'*" (John 10:30). Also, "Everything the Father has is mine and everything I have is my Father's" (John 16:15; 17:10). And finally, "Jesus said, 'I am the way, the truth, and the life. No one comes to the Father except through me'" (John 14:6).

[6] The angel reading these quotations added that the same things the Lord says here about himself and his Father we could also say about ourselves and our soul.[430]

When the participants had heard this they all said with one voice and one heart, "The Lord's human manifestation is divine. For us to gain access to the Father we have to go to his human manifestation, since this is how Jehovah God put himself in the world and made himself visible to human eyes. Through this he became accessible. Jehovah God also made himself visible and therefore accessible in a human form to the ancients; but back then he used an angel. Because that human form was symbolic of the Lord who was to come, everything related to the church among the ancients was symbolic."

[7] The next discussion focused on *the Holy Spirit.* First there was a disclosure of the way many people picture God the Father, the Son, and the Holy Spirit. They picture God the Father sitting on high with the Son at his right hand. Both of them send out the Holy Spirit to enlighten people, teach them, justify them, and sanctify them.

Then a voice was heard out of heaven saying, "We do not support these mental images. Jehovah God is omnipresent. If we know and acknowledge this, we also acknowledge that Jehovah God is the one who enlightens us, teaches us, justifies us, and sanctifies us. There is no mediating God who is distinct from him like two separate people, let alone a God who is distinct from two other gods. That earlier meaningless picture needs to be removed and this proper picture needs to be accepted. Then you will see this point clearly."

[8] Then we heard a voice from the Roman Catholics. They were standing next to the altar in the chapel. The voice said, "What then is the Holy Spirit mentioned in the Word by the Gospel writers and Paul, by which so many learned clergy say they are led, especially in our denomination? Surely no one in the Christian world nowadays denies the existence of the Holy Spirit and its actions."

One of the clergy in the second row of chairs turned and said, "You are saying that the Holy Spirit is a person on its own and a God on its own; but what is a 'person' going out and emanating from a person if not an influence going out and emanating? A person cannot go out and emanate from another person, but an influence can. To put it another way, a god going out and emanating from a god is actually a divine influence going out and emanating. One god cannot go out and emanate from another through yet another, but a divine influence can go out and emanate from the one God."

[9] After hearing that, the clergy sitting in the chairs unanimously concluded that the Holy Spirit is not a person on its own or a god on its own; it is the holy divine influence that goes out and emanates from the unique and omnipresent God, who is the Lord.

The angels who were standing by the golden table that held the Word responded to that by saying, "Good! Nowhere in the Old Covenant[431] does it say that the prophets spoke the Word of the Holy Spirit. They spoke the Word of Jehovah. When the New Covenant speaks of the Holy Spirit, it means the divine influence that goes forth enlightening people, teaching them, bringing them to life, reforming them, and regenerating them."

[10] After that another issue related to the Holy Spirit came up: "From whom does the divine influence meant by the Holy Spirit emanate? From the Father or from the Lord?"

While they were discussing this a light shone down on them from heaven. In that light they saw that the holy divine influence meant by the Holy Spirit does not emanate from the Father through the Lord; it emanates from the Lord on behalf of the Father. It is comparable to the situation with human beings. Our actions do not emanate from our souls through our bodies; they emanate from our bodies on behalf of our souls.

An angel who was standing by the table supported this point with the following passages from the Word: "The One whom the Father sent speaks the words of God. Not in a measured way has he given him the spirit. The Father loves the Son and has given all things into his hand" (John 3:34, 35). "A branch will come out of the trunk of Jesse. The spirit of Jehovah will rest upon him, the spirit of wisdom and intelligence, the spirit of counsel and strength" (Isaiah 11:1, 2). The spirit of Jehovah has been granted to him and it is in him (Isaiah 42:1; 59:19, 20; 61:1; Luke 4:18). "When the Holy Spirit comes *whom I am going to send you from the Father*" (John 15:26). "He will glorify me *because he will take from what is mine* and will make it known to you. *Everything the Father has is mine. This is why I said that he will take from what is mine and will make it known to you*" (John 16:14, 15). "If I go away, *I will send the Comforter to you*" (John 16:7). The Comforter is the Holy Spirit (John 14:26). "*The Holy Spirit was not yet in existence, because Jesus was not glorified yet*" (John 7:39). After he was glorified, *Jesus breathed on his disciples and said, "Receive the Holy Spirit"* (John 20:22). And in the Book of Revelation, "Who will not glorify your name, O Lord? For you alone are holy" (Revelation 15:4).

[11] The angel continued, "Since the Holy Spirit means the Lord's divine influence that results from his divine omnipresence, when he told his disciples about the Holy Spirit that he was going to send to them from the Father he also said, 'I will not leave you orphans. *I am going away and coming [back] to you;* and in that day you will recognize that *I am in my Father and you are in me and I am in you*' (John 14:18, 20, 28). And just before he left the world he said, 'Behold I am with you every day, even to the close of the age' (Matthew 28:20)."

After reading these passages the angel said, "It is clear from these passages and many others in the Word that the divine influence called the Holy Spirit emanates from the Lord on behalf of the Father."

In response the clergy sitting in the chairs said, "This is divine truth!"

[12] At the end the participants produced the following declaration: "From the discussions in this council, we have come to see clearly and to acknowledge as the sacred truth that the divine Trinity exists in the Lord God the Savior Jesus Christ. The Trinity is made up of the divine nature as an origin called 'the Father,' the divine-human manifestation called 'the Son,' and the emanating divine influence called 'the Holy Spirit.' We proclaim then that 'all the fullness of divinity dwells physically in Christ' (Colossians 2:9). Therefore there is one God in the church."

[13] After the events of this magnificent council came to an end, the participants stood up. The angel guarding the cabinet came over and brought shining clothing to each one of those who had been sitting in the chairs. The clothing was interwoven here and there with golden threads. The angel said, "Please accept these wedding garments."[432]

The participants were led in glory to the new Christian heaven, which is going to be connected to the church of the Lord on earth, which is the New Jerusalem.

Chapter 4

Sacred Scripture, the Word of the Lord

I

Sacred Scripture, the Word, Is Divine Truth Itself

189 IT is on everyone's lips that the Word comes from God, is divinely inspired, and is therefore holy.[433] Nonetheless, until now we have not known where the divinity is in the Word. At the literal level the Word seems like poor writing in a strange style, lacking the sublime and lucid quality that modern works seem to have.

There are people who can easily fall into the wrong perspective on the Word and into contempt for it—people who respect nature more than God or as God and who therefore think under the influence of themselves and their own identity rather than the influence of heaven from the Lord. When people like this read the Word they are prone to say to themselves, "What is this? What is that? Is this divine? Would a God who had infinite wisdom be capable of talking this way? Where is its holiness? Where else could the holiness come from except [the reader's] religious attitudes and convictions?"

190 People who think this way are not keeping in mind that it was the Lord Jehovah, the God of heaven and earth, who spoke the Word through Moses and the prophets. The Word could not be anything but divine truth, for what the Lord Jehovah himself says is divine truth. They are also not keeping in mind that the Lord the Savior, who is the same as Jehovah, spoke the Word to the Gospel writers. Much of it came from his own mouth, and the rest came from the Spirit of his mouth (which is the Holy Spirit) through his twelve apostles.

This is why the Lord says that there is spirit and life in his words, that he is the light that enlightens, and that he is the truth, as the following passages clearly show:

> Jesus said, "The words that I speak to you are spirit and are life." (John 6:63)

> Jesus said to the woman by Jacob's well, "If you knew the gift of God and who it is who is saying to you, 'Give me something to drink,' you would ask him and he would give you living water. Those who drink some of the water that I will give will not become thirsty to eternity. The water that I will give will become in them a well of water gushing for eternal life." (John 4:6, 10, 14)

Here as in Deuteronomy 33:28, "Jacob's well" means the Word. The Lord sat at that location and spoke with the woman because he is the Word. The "living water" means the truth in the Word.

> Jesus said, "If any are thirsty, they must come to me and drink. If any believe in me, as Scripture says, rivers of living water will flow out of their bellies." (John 7:37, 38)

> Peter said to Jesus, "You have the words of eternal life." (John 6:68)

> Jesus said, "Heaven and earth will pass away; my words will not pass away." (Mark 13:31)

The Lord's words are truth and life because he himself is truth and life, as he teaches in John: "I am the way, the truth, and the life" (John 14:6). Also in John, "In the beginning was the Word, and the Word was with God, and the Word was God. In it there was life, and that life was the light for humankind" (John 1:1, 4). "The Word" means the Lord in his role as divine truth. He alone has life and light. This is why the Word, which is from the Lord and is the Lord, is called *the fountain of living waters* (Jeremiah 2:13; 17:13; 31:9); *the fountain of salvation* (Isaiah 12:3); *the fountain* (Zechariah 13:1); and *a river of water of life* (Revelation 22:1). This is why it says that the Lamb who is in the middle of the throne will shepherd people and lead them to living fountains of waters (Revelation 7:17). There are other passages where the Word is also called *the sanctuary* and *the tent* where the Lord dwells with humankind [Ezekiel 37:26–28; Revelation 21:3].

Our earthly self, however, is incapable of being convinced by these quotations that the Word is divine truth itself in which there is divine

191

wisdom and divine life. Our earthly self evaluates the Word on the basis of style and does not see those qualities in its style. Nevertheless, the style of the Word is the divine style itself. There is no comparison between it and all other styles, no matter how sublime and excellent they may seem. The nature of the Word's style is that it has holiness in every meaning and every word; in fact, in some passages there is holiness in the very letters. As a result, the Word connects us to the Lord and opens heaven.

There are two things that emanate from the Lord: divine love and divine wisdom (or what amounts to the same thing, divine goodness and divine truth). In its essence the Word is each of these. Because the Word connects us to the Lord and opens heaven, as I just said, therefore the Word fills us with love for what is good and wisdom about what is true. It fills our will with love for what is good and our intellect with wisdom about what is true. This is how we receive life through the Word.

It is very important to realize, however, that the only people who receive life from the Word are those who read it for two purposes: to draw divine truths from it because it is the fountain of truth; and to apply to their life the divine truths they have drawn. The opposite happens to people who read the Word only with the purpose of increasing their status and gaining the world [see Matthew 16:26; Mark 8:36; Luke 9:25].

192 Any of us who are unaware that the Word has a spiritual meaning, like a soul within its body, have nothing else to judge the Word by except its literal meaning. Yet the literal meaning is like a case that contains the precious objects of the spiritual meaning. When we are unaware of the spiritual meaning, we cannot judge the divine holiness of the Word any more than we could judge a precious stone on the basis of the ore that envelops it, which sometimes looks very ordinary. Or imagine a case made out of jasper, lapis lazuli, amianthus (also called mica), or agate that contains rows of diamonds, rubies, sardonyxes, oriental topazes, and so on. If we do not realize it contains gems, it is no wonder we do not value the case any more than the worth of the material it is visibly made of. It is the same with the Word's literal meaning.

Therefore to prevent people from doubting that the Word is divine and most holy, the Lord has revealed to me its inner meaning, a meaning that is essentially spiritual and exists within its outer, earthly meaning like a soul in a body. The inner meaning is the spirit that brings the letter to life. The inner meaning has the power to prove even to our earthly self that the Word is divine and holy—provided we are willing to be convinced.

2

The Word Has a Spiritual Meaning
That Has Not Been Known until Now

Because the Word is divine, it has a spiritual core. When we are told this, **193** surely we all acknowledge it and agree. Up until now, though, has anyone known what that spiritual core is and where it is hidden in the Word? What the spiritual core is, I will show in a memorable occurrence at the end of this chapter.[434] Where it lies hidden in the Word, I will explain now.

The Word has a spiritual core because it came down from the Lord Jehovah and passed through the angelic heavens. As the Word came down, the divinity itself, which was originally inexpressible and imperceptible, became adapted to the awareness of angels and, further on, to the awareness of human beings. As a result, the Word has a spiritual meaning that is present within its earthly meaning much the way our soul is present in us, the thoughts of our intellect are present in what we say, and the feelings of our will are present in what we do.

If I may make comparisons with things that appear before our eyes in the physical world, the spiritual meaning is contained in the earthly meaning the way the whole brain is wrapped in its meninges or membranes; or the way the branch of a tree is wrapped in its inner and outer bark; or the way everything necessary for a chick's development is contained within the shell of its egg; and so on.

Until now no one has divined that this type of relationship exists between the Word's spiritual meaning and its earthly meaning. Therefore this secret needs to be made clear to the intellect, because it takes fundamental precedence over all the other secrets I have disclosed until now. It will become clear if it is laid out in the following order:

1. What the spiritual meaning is.
2. There is a spiritual meaning throughout the Word and in every part of it.
3. It is the spiritual meaning that makes the Word divinely inspired and holy in every word.
4. The spiritual meaning has been unknown until now.

5. From this point on, the spiritual meaning will be given only to people who have genuine truths from the Lord.

6. The Word has amazing qualities because of its spiritual meaning.

These points will now be unfolded one by one.

194 1. *What the spiritual meaning is.* The spiritual meaning is not the meaning that comes to light from the Word's literal meaning when someone examines and explains the Word in order to support some dogma of the church. That meaning could be called "the literal and ecclesiastical" meaning of the Word. The spiritual meaning is not apparent in the literal meaning. It lies inside it the way our soul is in our body, or our intellect's thoughts are in our eyes, or our feelings of love are in our face.

The spiritual meaning is the primary thing that makes the Word spiritual, not only for people but also for angels. The Word communicates with the heavens through that meaning. Because the Word is inwardly spiritual, it was written entirely in correspondences. Anything that is written in correspondences has an outermost meaning that is written in a style like the one used by the prophets, by the Gospel writers, and in the Book of Revelation. Although that style appears poor, nevertheless it conceals within itself divine wisdom and all angelic wisdom.

For an explanation of correspondence, go to the work *Heaven and Hell,* published in London in 1758, and look at the treatment of the correspondence of everything in heaven with everything in the human being (§§87–102) and the correspondence of heaven with everything earthly (§§103–115). You will also be able to look more extensively at correspondences in the examples from the Word I am going to present below [§§196–199].

195 There is a heavenly divine influence, a spiritual divine influence, and an earthly divine influence that emanate from the Lord, one after the other. Whatever emanates from the Lord's divine love is called heavenly divine influence; all of it is good. Whatever emanates from his divine wisdom is called spiritual divine influence; all of it is true. His earthly divine influence comes from the other two influences; it is a combination of them on the lowest level.

The angels of the [Lord's] heavenly kingdom, who constitute the third or highest heaven, are bathed in the divine influence emanating from the Lord that is called heavenly, for they have a love for what is good from the Lord. The angels of the Lord's spiritual kingdom, who constitute the second or middle heaven, are in the divine influence emanating from the Lord that is called spiritual, for they have divine wisdom[435] from the Lord. The angels of the Lord's earthly kingdom, who constitute the first or lowest heaven, are in the divine influence emanating from the Lord that is called the divine earthly influence. They have a faith from the Lord that is connected to goodwill. People in the church, however, are in any one of the three kingdoms depending on the people's love, wisdom, or faith. Depending on which of these the people have, they come into that heaven after death.[436]

The Lord's Word is like heaven. In its outermost meaning it is earthly; in its inner meaning it is spiritual; in its inmost meaning it is heavenly. All three are divine. It has been adapted, then, to the angels of the three heavens and to people as well.

2. *There is a spiritual meaning throughout the Word and in every part of it.* The best way to see this is through examples as follows:

In the Book of Revelation John says,

> I saw heaven opened, and behold, a white horse. The One sitting on it was called faithful and true, who judges with justice and does battle. His eyes were like a flame of fire. On his head were many gems.[437] He had a name written that no one knew except him. He was dressed in bloodstained clothing. His name was *the Word of God.* His armies in heaven followed him on white horses; they were dressed in linen that was white and clean. On his clothing and on his thigh he had a name written: *King of Kings and Lord of Lords.* Then I saw an angel standing in the sun who was crying with a great voice, "Come and gather yourselves for the great feast, that you may eat the flesh of kings and the flesh of commanders, the flesh of the mighty, the flesh of horses and those who ride on them, and the flesh of all people, free and slaves, small and great." (Revelation 19:11–18)

No one can see what these words mean except from the Word's spiritual meaning. We cannot see the spiritual meaning unless we work with the study of correspondences. All these words are correspondences; not a word is pointless. The study of correspondences teaches the meaning of the white horse, the One sitting on it, the eyes like a flame of fire, the gems on his head, the blood-stained clothing, the white linen worn by the members of his army from heaven, the angel standing in the sun, the great feast to which people should come and gather themselves, and the flesh of kings and commanders and of many other people and things that they were supposed to eat.

196

[2] For what each detail means spiritually, see the explanations in *Revelation Unveiled* 820–838. See also the small work *White Horse.* Because of those treatments, I will forgo a detailed explanation here. There I have shown that this passage describes the Lord in his role as the Word. His eyes that were like a flame of fire mean the divine wisdom that comes from his divine love. The gems on his head and the name that no one knows except him mean the divine truths of the Word that come from him and the fact that no one sees the nature of the Word in its spiritual meaning except the Lord and anyone to whom he reveals it. The blood-stained clothing means the Word's earthly meaning, its literal meaning, that has had violence inflicted upon it.

It is obvious that the Word is being described, because it says, *"His name is the Word of God."* It is also obvious that the passage refers to the Lord, because it says that the name of the One sitting on the white horse was *King of Kings and Lord of Lords.* This is like Revelation 17:14, where it says, "The Lamb will conquer them because *he is Lord of Lords and King of Kings."*

[3] The necessity for the Word's spiritual aspect to be revealed when the church comes to an end—this is the inner meaning of what is said of the white horse and the One sitting on it. It is also the meaning of an angel standing in the sun, extending an invitation to all to come and eat the flesh of kings and commanders and so on. Eating these things means our incorporation into ourselves of everything that is good from the Lord.

All the expressions in this passage would be pointless words, words without life or spirit, if there were no spiritual meaning inside them like the soul in a body.

197　Revelation 21 gives the following description of the New Jerusalem: In it there was a light like a highly precious stone, such as a jasper stone, that looked like a dazzling crystal. The New Jerusalem had a wall that was great and high and had twelve gates and twelve angels by the gates, and the names of the twelve tribes of the children of Israel were written there. The wall was 144 cubits[438] high, which is the measure of a human being, that is, of an angel. The construction of the wall was of jasper, and its foundation was made of every precious stone: jasper, sapphire, chalcedony, emerald, sardonyx, sard, chrysolite, beryl, topaz, chrysoprase, jacinth, and amethyst. The gates were twelve pearls. The city itself was pure gold, like clear glass. It was square. Its length, width, and height were equal: twelve thousand stadia.[439] And so on.

All these details need to be understood spiritually, as we can see from the fact that the New Jerusalem means a new church that is going to be established by the Lord, as I showed in *Revelation Unveiled* 880.

Since "Jerusalem" here means a church, it follows that all the things that are said about it as a city—about its gates, wall, foundations under the wall, and their measurements—contain a spiritual meaning, since the attributes of a church are spiritual.

In *Revelation Unveiled* 896–925 I have shown what these things mean. It is unnecessary, therefore, to demonstrate their meaning once more. It is enough for us to know that there is a spiritual meaning within all the details of this description like a soul within a body. Without that meaning we would understand nothing about the church from the details written here: for example, the city being made of pure gold; its gates, of pearls; its wall, of jasper; the foundations of its wall, of precious stones; the wall being 144 cubits high, which is the measure of a human being, that is, of an angel; and the city being twelve thousand stadia[440] in length, width, and height; and so on.

People who know correspondences and who therefore recognize the spiritual meaning understand these details. For example, the wall and its foundations mean the teachings of that church that are based on the literal meaning of the Word; and the numbers 12, 144, and 12,000 mean everything about that church, that is, all that is good and true in it combined.

The Lord spoke to his disciples about the close of the age (or the last time of the church); at the end of his predictions about the stages and changes it would go through he said the following:

198

> Immediately after the affliction of those days the sun will be darkened and the moon will not give its light; the stars will fall from heaven and the powers of the heavens will be shaken. Then the sign of the Son of Humankind will appear in heaven and all the tribes of the earth will wail. They will see the Son of Humankind coming in the clouds of heaven with power and great glory. He will send out angels with a great sound of a trumpet, and they will gather his chosen people from the four winds, from one end of the heavens to the other. (Matthew 24:29, 30, 31)

In the spiritual meaning, these statements do not indicate that the sun and the moon will be darkened, the stars will fall from heaven, the sign of the Lord will appear in heaven, and people will see him in the clouds and see angels with trumpets. Instead, the individual words there have spiritual meanings that relate to the church. The details that are mentioned relate to the church's state at its end.

In the spiritual meaning, the sun that will be darkened means love for the Lord. The moon that will not give its light means faith in him. The stars that will fall from heaven mean concepts of goodness and truth. The sign of the Son of Humankind in heaven means the divine truth from him in the Word that will become apparent. The tribes of the earth that will wail mean the loss of all true belief and all good love. The Son of Humankind coming in the clouds of heaven with power and glory means the Lord's presence in the Word and his ability to give revelations through it. The clouds of heaven mean the Word's literal meaning; the glory means the Word's spiritual meaning. The angels sent out with a great sound of a trumpet mean heaven as a source of divine truth. Gathering the chosen people from the four winds from one end of the heavens to the other means building a new heaven and a new church that consists of people who have faith in the Lord and who live by his commandments.

It does not mean a darkening of the sun and moon and a falling of stars to earth. This is obvious from the prophets, who have similar things to say about the state of the church when the Lord would come into the world. For example in Isaiah,

> Behold the savage day of Jehovah will come, a day of the rage of his anger. The stars of the heavens and their constellations will not shed their light. The sun will be darkened in its rising, and the moon will not let its light shine. I will visit malice upon the globe. (Isaiah 13:9–11)

In Joel,

> The day of Jehovah is coming, a day of darkness and blackness. The sun and the moon will be blackened, and the stars will withdraw their splendor. (Joel 2:1, 2, 10; 3:15)

In Ezekiel,

> I will cover the heavens and blacken the stars. I will cover the sun with a cloud, and the moon will not make its light shine. All sources of light I will cover, and I will bring darkness on the earth. (Ezekiel 32:7, 8)

"The day of Jehovah" means the Lord's coming that was going to take place when there was no longer any good love or any true belief left in the church, or any knowledge of the Lord, which is why it is called a day of darkness and blackness.

The Lord spoke in correspondences when he was in the world. While he was talking in an earthly way, he was also talking in a spiritual way. This is clear from his parables. Every word of them has a spiritual meaning inside.

199

Take, for example, the parable of the ten young women.[441] He said,

> The kingdom of the heavens is like ten young women who took their lamps and went out to meet the bridegroom. Five of them were prudent and five were foolish. When the foolish women took their lamps, they did not take any oil. The prudent women took oil in their lamps. When the bridegroom was delayed, they all became drowsy and fell asleep. In the middle of the night there was a shout: "Behold, the bridegroom is coming! Go out to meet him." At that, all the women woke up and trimmed their lamps. The foolish women said to the prudent ones, "Give us some of your oil, because our lamps are going out." The prudent women replied, "There might not be enough for us all. Go instead to the sellers and buy yourselves some." But as they were going away to buy some, the bridegroom arrived and the women who were prepared walked in with him to the wedding and the door was closed. Later the other women came along and said, "Lord, Lord, open up for us." But he answered and said, "I tell you truly, I do not know you." (Matthew 25:1–12)

The only people who see that in each of these details there is a spiritual meaning and therefore something holy and divine are those who have a general awareness of the existence and nature of spiritual meaning.

In the spiritual meaning, the kingdom of the heavens means heaven and the church. The bridegroom means the Lord. The wedding means the Lord's marriage to heaven and the church through the good that love does and the truth that faith perceives. The young women mean people who are in the church. Ten means all. Five means a part. Lamps mean beliefs. Oil means loving what is good. Sleeping and awakening mean our life in the world, which is an earthly life, and our life after death, which is a spiritual life. Buying means acquiring for ourselves. Going to the sellers and buying oil means trying after we have died to acquire from others a love for what is good. Since we can no longer acquire a love for what is good after we die, therefore although they brought their lamps and the oil they had purchased to the door where the wedding was taking place, the bridegroom told them, "I do not know you." The reason is that after our life in the world, the way we have lived in the world remains.

This makes it clear that the Lord spoke entirely in correspondences because he spoke from the divine nature that was in him and was his.

Young women mean people who are in the church. This is why the prophetic Word says *the virgin* or *daughter of Zion, of Jerusalem, of Judah, of Israel* so many times. Oil means love for what is good. This is why all the church's sacred objects were anointed with oil.

This correspondent nature applies to all the other parables and all the other words that the Lord spoke. This is why the Lord says that his words are spirit and are life (John 6:63).

200   3. *It is the spiritual meaning that makes the Word divinely inspired and holy in every word.* People in the church say that the Word is holy because the Lord Jehovah spoke it. In the literal meaning by itself, however, the Word's holiness is not apparent. Therefore once people come to doubt its holiness, afterward when they read the Word they find many things in it that convince them to doubt further. They say to themselves, "Is this holy? Is this divine?" Thoughts like this, flowing into many people and growing stronger, create the risk that the Word may be rejected as a worthless document and that the Lord's connection to these people may come to an end. The Lord has chosen to reveal the Word's spiritual meaning now so as to prevent this, and so that people will know where in the Word the divine holiness lies.

Examples will illustrate: In one verse the Word will mention Egypt; in another, Assyria; in others, Edom, Moab, the children of Ammon, the Philistines, Tyre and Sidon, and Gog. If people do not realize that the names of these places and people mean aspects of heaven and the church, they could be misled to think that the Word has much to say about peoples and nations and only a little to say about heaven and the church; that it has much to say on worldly topics and little to say on heavenly topics. When people know what those places and their names mean, however, they can be brought back from their error to the truth.

[2] Likewise people see that the Word frequently mentions gardens, groves, and forests, as well as trees such as olives, grapevines, cedars, poplars, and oaks. It often mentions lambs, sheep, goats, calves, and oxen; and also mountains, hills, and valleys; and springs, rivers, bodies of water, and other such things. Those who know nothing about the Word's

spiritual meaning cannot help believing that those actual things are what is meant. They do not know that a garden, a grove, and a forest mean wisdom, intelligence, and knowledge; an olive, a grapevine, a cedar, a poplar, and an oak mean the heavenly, the spiritual, the rational, the earthly, and the sensory forms of good and truth in the church. A lamb, a sheep, a goat, a calf, and an ox mean innocence, goodwill, and earthly feelings.[442] Mountains, hills, and valleys mean the higher, the lower, and the lowest aspects of the church. [3] Egypt means scholarly study; Assyria, our rational faculty; Edom, our earthly aspect. Moab means the contamination of what is good; the children of Ammon mean the contamination of what is true. The Philistines mean faith without goodwill; Tyre and Sidon mean our concepts of goodness and truth; and Gog means external worship that lacks anything deeper. Generally speaking, Jacob in the Word means the earthly aspect of the church, Israel means the spiritual aspect of the church, and Judah means the heavenly aspect of the church.

When we know all this, we are able to think that the Word deals only with heavenly topics, and the worldly details in it are only outer things that have heavenly things inside them.

[4] Let us take an example from the Word as an illustration: We read in Isaiah,

> On that day there will be a pathway from Egypt into Assyria so that Assyria can go into Egypt and Egypt into Assyria. The Egyptians will serve with Assyria. On that day Israel will be part of a group of three with Egypt and Assyria, a blessing in the middle of the land. Jehovah Sabaoth will bless that group of three, saying, "Blessed be my people Egypt, and Assyria, the work of my hands, and Israel, my blessing." (Isaiah 19:23, 24, 25)

Spiritually these words mean that when the Lord's coming occurs, scholarly study, rationality, and spirituality are going to become one. Scholarly study will then serve rationality, and both of them will serve spirituality. (As I have said, Egypt means scholarly study, Assyria means rationality, and Israel means spirituality.) The "day" being named twice means the Lord's First Coming and his Second Coming.

4. *The spiritual meaning of the Word has been unknown until now.* All things that exist in the material world correspond to something spiritual; likewise all things that exist in the human body, as I have shown in the

201

work *Heaven and Hell,* §§87–115. No one has known until now, however, what *correspondence* is. In the earliest times, correspondence was very well known.[443] To the people who lived at that time the study of correspondences was the supreme field of study. It was so universal that the writing in all their books and codices displayed the use of correspondences. The Book of Job, a book of the early church, is full of correspondences. The Egyptian hieroglyphics[444] and the earliest myths were no different. All the early churches were churches that represented spiritual things in symbolic ways. Their worship was established with rituals and rules that consisted entirely of correspondences.

The same was true for all aspects of the church among the children of Israel: their burnt offerings, sacrifices, food offerings, and drink offerings were correspondences down to the last detail. So was the tabernacle and everything in it. So were their feast days—the Feast of Unleavened Bread, the Feast of Tabernacles, and the Feast of First Fruits.[445] So was the priestly role performed by Aaron and the Levites, as well as the clothing of their sacred office. (The specific spiritual things to which all the above correspond are shown in *Secrets of Heaven,* published in London.)[446] In addition, all the statutes and judgments that shaped their worship and their lives were correspondences.

Divine attributes present themselves in the world in the form of correspondences; therefore the Word was written entirely in correspondences. For the same reason, the Lord spoke in correspondences, since he spoke from what is divine.

Divinity is present in nature in the form of things that correspond to divine attributes and that have divine attributes known as heavenly and spiritual qualities hidden deep within them.

202 I have been taught that the people in the earliest church, which existed before the flood, had a nature so heavenly that they spoke with angels of heaven. The use of correspondences by these people enabled them to communicate with angels. As a result, the quality of their wisdom grew to the point where anything they saw on earth they thought about not only in an earthly way but also in a spiritual way; they and angels in heaven thought about it together.

I have also been taught that Enoch (who is mentioned in Genesis 5:21–24), along with friends of his, collected correspondences from the oral tradition of the earliest people and spread the study of correspondences to his descendants. As a result, the study of correspondences was not only known in many countries in the Middle East but was also further developed, especially in the land of Canaan, Egypt, Assyria, Chaldea, Syria, and Arabia; and in Tyre, Sidon, and Nineveh. From there it crossed into Greece, but turned into myths there, as you can see from the earliest Greek writings.

I wish to bring out an example from 1 Samuel chapters 5 and 6 so you can see that the study of correspondences was long preserved among the nations in the Middle East, particularly among those who were called the diviners and the wise ones, referred to by some as the magi.

203

This passage mentions that the ark containing the two tablets with the Ten Commandments written on them was captured by the Philistines. It was placed in the shrine of Dagon in Ashdod. On the first day, Dagon fell before it to the ground. On the next day, Dagon's head as well as the palms of its hands lay severed from its body across the threshold of the shrine. Because of the ark, as many as several thousand inhabitants of Ashdod and Ekron were afflicted with hemorrhoids and their land was devastated by rats. The Philistines therefore called together their provincial governors and diviners. To stave off impending death, they decided that they should make five hemorrhoids and five rats out of gold, and make a new cart and put the ark on it. They would send the ark back to the children of Israel on this cart, pulled by two cows that would bellow all the way, and the children of Israel would sacrifice the cows and the cart. If the Philistines accomplished this, the God of Israel would be appeased.

The meaning of these details clearly shows that everything the Philistine diviners thought of was a correspondence. The Philistines themselves meant people who have faith but lack goodwill. Dagon was a portrayal of their religion. The hemorrhoids that afflicted them meant earthly loves that become unclean when separated from spiritual love. The rats meant the devastation of the church by people falsifying the truth. The new cart meant the earthly teaching of the church. (A chariot or carriage in the Word means teachings that are based on spiritual truths.) The cows meant earthly feelings that are good. The hemorrhoids made of gold meant earthly loves that have been purified and have become good. The golden rats meant goodness remedying the devastation of the church, since gold in the Word means goodness. The bellowing of the cows along the way meant the difficulty of turning the lower self's cravings for evil into desires for goodness. The offering of the cows and the cart as a burnt offering meant that by these spiritual actions the God of Israel would be appeased.

All these actions that the Philistines undertook on the recommendation of their diviners were correspondences. This clearly shows that the study of correspondences was preserved for a long time among people outside the church.

204   Over the course of time, the early church's symbolic rituals, which were correspondences, began to turn into idolatry and even magic. Therefore in the Lord's divine providence the study of correspondences was gradually lost.

For the Israelite and Jewish nation, the study of correspondences was completely wiped out. Their worship did indeed consist entirely of correspondences and therefore it portrayed heavenly things, but they had no idea what anything in their worship meant. They were completely earthly people who did not want to know and could not know anything about what is spiritual and heavenly, or anything about correspondences for that matter, since correspondences are earthly symbols of spiritual and heavenly things.[447]

205   Among people outside the church in early times, the study of correspondences led to forms of idolatry because all things that are visible on earth have a correspondence—not only trees but also animals and birds of every kind, as well as fish, and everything else. Early people involved in the study of correspondences made images that corresponded to things in heaven. They enjoyed these images because the images stood for things related to heaven and the church. They placed these images not only in their temples but also in their homes, not in order to worship them but to be reminded of the heavenly things they meant. In Egypt and elsewhere there were images of calves, oxen, and snakes, as well as children, old people, and young women, because calves and oxen meant the emotions and forces in the earthly self; snakes meant prudence but also the deceitfulness of the senses; children meant innocence and goodwill; old people meant wisdom; and young women meant types of love for the truth; and so on.

When the study of correspondences was wiped out, later generations began worshiping the images and statues erected by the early people. They worshiped them first as sacred objects and then as deities, since they found them in and around temples.

Because of the study of correspondences, the early people had also worshiped in gardens and groves, depending on which species of trees were there. They also worshiped on mountains and hills. Gardens and groves meant wisdom and intelligence; and every tree meant some aspect of wisdom and intelligence. For example, an olive tree meant good actions that come from love, while a grapevine meant the true insights that come from those good actions. A cedar tree meant rational goodness and truth. A mountain meant the highest heaven, and a hill, a heaven below it.

The study of correspondences continued among many in the Middle East even to the time of the Lord's coming, as you can see from the wise ones from the Middle East who came to the Lord when he was born. Therefore a star went before them and they brought gifts with them: gold, frankincense, and myrrh (Matthew 2:1, 2, 9, 10, 11). The star that went before them meant knowledge from heaven. Gold meant the heavenly goodness; frankincense, the spiritual goodness; and myrrh, the earthly goodness that together form the source of all worship.

There was absolutely no study of correspondences among the Israelite and Jewish nation, although all the aspects of their worship, all the statutes and judgments given to them through Moses, and all the details throughout their Word were correspondences. The reason for this lack was that at heart the people were idolatrous. They had no desire at all to know that any aspect of their worship meant something heavenly or spiritual. They believed that all their rituals were intrinsically holy. If the heavenly and spiritual underpinnings had been revealed to them, they would have not only rejected those underpinnings but also desecrated them. As a result, heaven was so tightly closed to them that they were scarcely aware that eternal life existed.

The truth of this is very clear from the fact that the people did not acknowledge the Lord even though their entire Sacred Scripture had prophesied about him and foretold his coming. They rejected him for one single reason: he taught them about a heavenly kingdom, not an earthly one. They wanted a Messiah who would lift them above all the nations in the whole world, not some Messiah who was concerned with their eternal salvation.[448]

In the period of history that came next, the study of correspondences that yields the Word's spiritual meaning was not revealed, because at the time the Christian church began, Christians were so extremely simple that it was not possible to reveal this study to them. If it had been disclosed, it would have been of no use to them and they would not have understood it.

After that time, darkness came over the whole Christian world, first because of scattered heresies on many people's part, and soon afterward because of the Nicene Council's decisions and decrees about three divine persons from eternity and the person of Christ being the Son of Mary rather than the Son of Jehovah God. This led [in turn] to the modern-day faith that by going to three gods, one after the other, we are justified.[449] All aspects of the modern-day church depend on this faith the way our body parts depend on our head. Since people applied everything in the Word to this mistaken faith, its spiritual meaning could not be revealed. If it had been, they would have applied its meaning to their faith, and thereby desecrated the true holiness of the Word. By doing that they would have completely closed heaven to themselves and would have removed the Lord from the church.

207   The study of correspondences that yields the Word's spiritual meaning has been revealed today because now the divine truths of the church are coming forward into the light. These truths are what the Word's spiritual meaning consists of. When these truths are in us, the Word's literal meaning cannot be perverted. The Word's literal meaning is capable of being bent this way and that, but if it is bent in the direction of falsity, its inner holiness is destroyed, and so is its outer holiness. If it is bent in the direction of truth, it stays holy. (More will be said about this in what is to come [§§260, 508].)

The opening of the spiritual meaning at this day is what is meant by John's seeing heaven opened and seeing a white horse, and seeing and hearing an angel standing in the sun calling all people to a great feast (Revelation 19:11–18). The fact that the spiritual meaning would not be acknowledged for a long time, however, is what is meant by the beast and the kings of the earth who were going to make war against the One sitting on the white horse (Revelation 19:19) and by the dragon that first pursued the woman who had given birth to a son, then went out into the desert and cast water like a river out of its mouth to drown her (Revelation 12:13–17).

208   5. *From this point on, the spiritual meaning of the Word will be given only to people who have genuine truths from the Lord.* The reason for this is that none of us can see the spiritual meaning except with the help of the Lord alone, provided we have divine truths from him. The Word's spiritual meaning deals solely with the Lord and his kingdom. The spiritual meaning is the one with which his angels engage in heaven. It is his divine truth there.

It is possible for us to violate the Word's spiritual meaning if we are involved in the study of correspondences and we try to explore that meaning with our own intelligence. With just a few correspondences we know, we could pervert the spiritual meaning and even divert it to support something false. This would be a violent attack on divine truth, and so on heaven, where divine truth dwells. For this reason if any of us try on our own, without the Lord, to open the spiritual meaning, heaven closes and we either see nothing true or we become spiritually insane.

Another reason [why the spiritual meaning will be given only to people who have genuine truths from the Lord] is that the Lord teaches us all through the Word, using the concepts that we already have. He does not pour new concepts directly into us. Therefore if we do not already have divine truths, or we have only a few truths along with some falsities, we are capable of falsifying truths, much the way any heretic does with the Word's literal meaning. To prevent any of us from getting into the spiritual meaning and perverting the genuine truth that belongs to it, the Lord has placed safeguards on that meaning, which are referred to in the Word as angel guardians.[450]

6. *The Word has amazing qualities because of its spiritual meaning.* In the physical world, no amazing things happen because of the Word, since its spiritual meaning does not appear here and the true nature of that spiritual meaning is not being accepted at any deep level within us. In the spiritual world, however, amazing things do happen because of the Word, since all who are there are spiritual, and spiritual things affect spiritual people the way physical things affect physical people. There are many amazing things that happen in the spiritual world because of the Word; here I will mention just a few.   **209**

In the sanctuaries of church buildings in the spiritual world, the Word itself shines like a giant star before the eyes of the angels. Sometimes it shines like the sun. The glow around it causes exquisitely beautiful kinds of rainbows. This happens as soon as the sanctuary is opened.

[2] Each and every truth in the Word shines. This has been made clear to me by the fact that when anyone writes a verse from the Word on a piece of paper and throws it up in the air, the piece of paper generates a glowing form that takes the shape of the cut paper. As a result, spirits are able to use the Word to produce various light-emitting shapes such as birds and fish.

Something that is even more amazing is that when people rub the open Word—the writing itself—on their face or hands or the clothing they have on, their face, hands, or clothing shines as if they themselves were standing in a star and were surrounded by its light. I have very often seen this and I have been amazed. This made clear to me why Moses' face was shining when he carried the tablets of the covenant down from Mount Sinai [Exodus 34:29–30].

[3] In addition, there are many other amazing things that happen in the spiritual world because of the Word. For example, if people who have false beliefs look at the Word as it lies in its holy place, thick darkness overwhelms their eyesight, making the Word look black to them, sometimes as if it were coated with soot. If those same people touch the Word, there is an explosion with a loud bang, and they are thrown to the corner of the room and lie there as if dead for quite a while.[451]

If people who have false beliefs write something from the Word on a piece of paper and toss it up toward heaven, when it is in the air between their eye and heaven a similar explosion takes place. The piece of paper is blown to bits and disappears. The same thing happens if the piece of paper is thrown toward an angel who is standing nearby. I have often seen this.

[4] This has made it clear to me that people who have a body of false teaching have no communication with heaven by means of the Word. On the way to heaven, their reading of it blows apart and comes to an end like a firecracker lit and thrown in the air. The opposite happens to people who have a true perspective from the Lord through the Word. Their reading of the Word penetrates all the way into heaven and forms a connection with angels who are there.

When angels come down from heaven to carry out some task below, they look as if they are covered in little stars, especially around their heads. This is an indication that there are divine truths from the Word inside these angels.

[5] The same things that exist on earth exist in the spiritual world, except that there they have a spiritual origin. So gold and silver and all kinds of precious stones exist there. Their spiritual origin is the literal meaning of the Word. This is why the Book of Revelation describes the foundations of the New Jerusalem's wall as being twelve precious stones. The foundations of its wall stand for the beliefs of the new church that are based on the Word's literal meaning. This is also why there were twelve precious stones called the Urim and the Thummim[452] on Aaron's ephod. Answers from heaven came through these stones.

Many other amazing things happen with the Word in the spiritual world. They relate to the power of truth there, which is so immense that if I described it, it would exceed belief. The Word has so much power that it overturns mountains and hills there, moves them far away, throws them into the sea, and more. Briefly put, the power of the Lord that comes through the Word is infinite.

3

The Word's Literal Meaning Is the Foundation, the Container, and the Structural Support for Its Spiritual and Heavenly Meanings

In all that is divine there is a primary component, a middle component, and an outermost component. The primary component goes forth through the middle component to the outermost component; by doing so it takes on a form and a continued existence. As a result, the outermost component is a *foundation.* The primary component is also present in the middle component; and by means of the middle component it is present in the outermost component. Therefore the outermost component is also a *container.* Because the outermost component is both a container and a foundation, it is also a *structural support.*

The educated reader will understand that these three components could be called the purpose, the means, and the result; and also the being, the becoming, and the taking shape. The purpose is the being, the means is the becoming, and the result is the taking shape. Therefore in everything that is complete, there is a trine called the primary component, the middle component, and the outermost component, or the purpose, the means, and the result. People who understand this also understand that the outermost component of every divine work is complete and perfect; and everything is present in that outermost component because prior components are collectively present in it.

As a result of this, *three* in the Word has the spiritual meaning "being complete and perfect" and also "containing all aspects at once." Since the number three has these meanings, it comes into play in the Word whenever these qualities need to be designated. For example, Isaiah went around naked and barefoot for *three years* (Isaiah 20:3). Jehovah called Samuel *three times,* and *three times* Samuel ran to Eli. The *third time,* Eli understood (1 Samuel 3:1–8). Jonathan told David to hide himself in the field for *three days.* Jonathan shot *three arrows* to the side of a stone. Then David bowed down *three times* before Jonathan (1 Samuel 20:5, 12–42). Elijah stretched out on the widow's son *three times* (1 Kings 17:21). Elijah ordered people to pour water over the sacrifice *three times* (1 Kings 18:34). Jesus said that the kingdom of heaven is like leaven that a woman took and hid in *three measures* of meal until the whole amount was leavened (Matthew 13:33). Jesus said to Peter that Peter would deny him *three times* (Matthew 26:34). Jesus said to Peter *three times,* "Do you love me?" (John 21:15, 16, 17). Jonah was in the belly of the sea monster *for three days and three nights* (Jonah 1:17). Jesus said that he would demolish the temple, and rebuild it in *three days* (Matthew 26:61). In Gethsemane Jesus prayed *three times* (Matthew 26:39–44). Jesus rose *on the third day* (Matthew 28:1). There are many other passages as well where threes are mentioned. They are mentioned when the topic is a work that is finished and completed, since such is the meaning of that number.

212 There are three heavens: the highest, the middle, and the lowest. The highest heaven constitutes the Lord's heavenly kingdom; the middle heaven, his spiritual kingdom; and the lowest heaven, his earthly kingdom.[453] Just as there are three heavens, there are three layers of meaning in the Word: the heavenly meaning, the spiritual meaning, and the earthly meaning.

The points made above in §210 coincide with the points just made: the primary component is present in the middle component; and by means of the middle component it is also present in the outermost component. In exactly the same way, a purpose is present in the means; and through the means the purpose is present in the result.

This shows what the Word is like. Inside its literal meaning, which is earthly, there is an inner meaning that is spiritual; and inside the spiritual meaning there is an innermost meaning that is heavenly. The outermost meaning, which is earthly and is called the literal meaning, is a container for the two inner meanings. Therefore it is a foundation for them and also a structural support.

213 From the points just made it follows that without its literal meaning the Word would be like a palace without a foundation. It would be like a palace in the air, not on the ground, which would be only a shadow of a palace, and shadows disappear.

Without its literal meaning the Word would be like a church building that housed many sacred objects and had a sanctuary in the middle but lacked a roof or walls to contain them. If the roof and walls were lacking or taken away, the sacred objects would be stolen by thieves or violated by animals from the land and birds from the sky, causing the sacred objects to be lost.

It would be like the tabernacle of the children of Israel in the desert having the ark of the covenant in its innermost area, and the golden lampstand, the golden incense altar, and the table of showbread in its middle area, but lacking its outermost features—its curtains, veils, and pillars.[454]

In fact, without its literal meaning the Word would be like a human body without the coverings called the skin and membranes or the structural supports called the bones. Without these all the inner organs would fall apart.

It would be like the heart and the lungs in the thorax without the covering called the pleura and the structural supports called the ribs. It would be like the brain without the coverings called the dura and the pia mater and without the general covering, container, and structural support called the skull. This is how the Word would be without its literal meaning. Therefore it says in Isaiah, "Over all glory Jehovah creates a covering" (Isaiah 4:5).

4

In the Literal Meaning of the Word, Divine Truth Exists in Its Completeness, Holiness, and Power

In the literal meaning, the Word exists in its completeness, holiness, and power because, as I said above in §§210, 212, the two prior or deeper meanings called the spiritual and the heavenly meanings are together in the earthly or literal meaning. I will say some more about how they come together.

Both in heaven and on earth there is a sequential arrangement and there is a simultaneous arrangement. In a sequential arrangement, one thing comes after another from the highest level down to the lowest. In a simultaneous arrangement, however, one thing is beside another from inmost to outermost. A sequential arrangement is like a column with levels that form steps from top to bottom. A simultaneous arrangement is like a collapsed object with larger and larger cylinders from the center to the outermost surface.

Now I will say how a sequential arrangement turns eventually into a simultaneous arrangement. It happens in the following way: the highest parts of a sequential arrangement become the innermost parts of a simultaneous arrangement, and the lowest parts of a sequential arrangement become the outermost parts of a simultaneous arrangement. It is like the column of steps collapsing to become a coherent flat surface. This is how something simultaneous is formed out of a succession.[455]

214

This is how it is for everything in the physical world and everything in the spiritual world. Everywhere there is a primary component, a middle component, and an outermost component. The primary component extends and goes out through its middle component toward its outermost component. It is essential to understand, however, that there are different degrees of purity that affect how each arrangement comes about.

[2] Now for the Word. A heavenly influence, a spiritual influence, and an earthly influence emanate from the Lord in a sequential arrangement. On the outermost level, however, they are in a simultaneous arrangement, meaning that the Word's heavenly and spiritual meanings are together inside its earthly meaning. Once you comprehend this, you can see how the Word's earthly meaning is the foundation, container, and structural support for its spiritual and heavenly meanings. You can also see how divine goodness and divine truth have completeness, holiness, and power in the Word's literal meaning.

As all this makes clear, the Word in its literal meaning is truly the Word. Within it there is spirit and life. As the Lord says, "The words that I speak to you are spirit and are life" (John 6:63). The Lord spoke his words with an earthly meaning.

The heavenly and spiritual meanings are not the Word without the earthly meaning. They are like spirit and life without a body. As I said before (§213), they are also like a palace without a foundation.

215 Some of the truths in the Word's literal meaning are apparent truths rather than naked truths. They are like similes or comparisons taken from earthly situations, which are therefore accommodated and adapted to the grasp of people who are simple or young. Nevertheless, because they are correspondences they are still vessels and dwelling places for genuine truth. They are vessels that contain genuine truth the way a crystal goblet contains fine wine or a silver plate holds palatable food. They are like garments that clothe, like a baby's swaddling cloths or a young woman's beautiful clothing. They are like facts our earthly selves know that also involve our awareness and love of spiritual truth. The naked truths that are enclosed, contained, clothed, and involved are in the Word's spiritual meaning. There is also naked goodness in the Word's heavenly meaning.

Let me illustrate this from the Word:

[2] Jesus said, "Woe to you, scribes and Pharisees, because you clean the outside of your cup and plate, but the insides are full of plundering and

self-indulgence. Blind Pharisee! First clean the inside of your cup and plate, so that the outside may be clean as well." (Matthew 23:25, 26)

In saying this the Lord used similes and comparisons that are also correspondences. He mentioned a cup and a plate. A cup does not just *relate to* the truth in the Word; it also *means* that truth. A cup relates to wine, and wine means truth. A plate relates to food, and food means goodness. Therefore cleaning the inside of their cup and plate means using the Word to purify the inner things in their mind related to their will and thought. "So that the outside may be clean as well" means that by doing this, their outer aspects—their actions and conversations—would be purified, because the essence of actions and conversations comes from within.

[3] For another example,

Jesus said, "There was a rich person who wore purple and fine linen and indulged himself splendidly every day. And there was a poor person named Lazarus, covered with sores, who was put on his porch." (Luke 16:19, 20)

Here again, in saying this the Lord used similes and comparisons that were correspondences with spiritual content. The rich person means the Jewish nation. He is called rich because the Jewish nation had the Word, and the Word contains spiritual wealth. The purple and fine linen he wore mean the goodness and truth of the Word: the purple means the Word's goodness; the fine linen means its truth. "Indulging himself splendidly every day" refers to the delight that the Jews felt because they had the Word and heard many things from it in their temples and synagogues. Lazarus, the poor person, means the people outside the Jewish church, because they did not have the Word. Lazarus being put on the rich person's porch means that people outside the Jewish church were despised and rejected by the Jews. Lazarus's sores mean that people outside the church had many false beliefs because they did not know the truth.

[4] Lazarus means the people outside the Jewish church because the Lord loved the people outside the church just as he loved Lazarus (John 11:3, 5, 36), raised him from the dead, called him his friend (John 11:11), and gave him a place at his table (John 12:2).

As the two passages quoted just above make clear, things that are good and true in the Word's literal meaning are like vessels or clothing for the naked goodness and truth that lie hidden in the Word's spiritual and heavenly meanings.

[5] Since this is the nature of the Word in its literal meaning, it follows that if we have divine truths and we have faith that the Word is divinely holy at heart, and better still if we have faith that the Word is divinely holy because of its spiritual and heavenly meanings, then as we read the Word in enlightenment from the Lord we see divine truths in earthly light. The light of heaven in which the Word's spiritual meaning exists then flows into the earthly light in which the Word's literal meaning exists and lights up the intellectual faculty in us that is called rationality. It causes our rationality to see and acknowledge divine truths both where they stand out and where they are hidden. For some people, divine truths flow in with heaven's light even when they are not aware of it.

216 Because of its heavenly meaning, the Word at the inmost part of its core is like a gentle flame that kindles us. Because of its spiritual meaning, the Word at the mid-part of its core is like a light that enlightens. Because of its earthly meaning, then, the Word on the outermost level is like a translucent object that receives both of the above. The flame makes it fiery red and the light makes it shining white, like snow. Therefore it is either like a ruby or a diamond. Because of the heavenly flame it is like a ruby. Because of the spiritual light it is like a diamond.

Since this is the nature of the Word in its literal meaning, therefore the Word in this meaning is represented

1. by the precious stones that constituted the foundations of the New Jerusalem;
2. by the Urim and Thummim on Aaron's ephod;[456]
3. by the precious stones from the garden of Eden that the king of Tyre is said to have worn;
4. by the curtains, veils, and pillars in the tabernacle;
5. and by the exteriors of the Temple in Jerusalem.
6. When the Lord was transfigured he represented the Word in its glory.
7. The Nazirites represented the power of the Word in its outermost form.
8. The Word has indescribable power.

These points need individual explanations.

217 1. *The precious stones that constituted the foundations of the New Jerusalem (Revelation 21:17–21) mean the truths in the Word's literal meaning.* In §209 above I mentioned that precious stones exist in the spiritual world just as they do in the physical world; their spiritual origin is the truths in the Word's literal meaning. This seems unbelievable, but it is nevertheless the truth. As a result, whenever precious stones are named in the Word, in the spiritual meaning they stand for truths. We are told that the foundations of the wall around the city, the New Jerusalem, were constructed of precious stones. These stones mean the true teachings in the new church, since the New Jerusalem means the new church in relation to its teachings from the Word. Its wall and the foundations of its wall, then, can have no other meaning than the outside of the Word, its literal meaning. The literal meaning is the source of what is taught; and through its teachings the literal meaning is the source of the church. It is like a wall with foundations that surrounds and protects a city.

We read the following statements in the Book of Revelation about the New Jerusalem and its foundations:

> The angel measured the wall of the city of Jerusalem at 144 cubits, which was the measure of a human being, that is, of an angel. The wall had twelve foundations adorned with every precious stone. The first foundation was jasper, the second sapphire, the third chalcedony, the fourth emerald, the fifth sardonyx, the sixth sard, the seventh chrysolite, the eighth beryl, the ninth topaz, the tenth chrysoprase, the eleventh jacinth, the twelfth amethyst. (Revelation 21:17–20)

The twelve foundations of the wall were made of the same number of precious stones because the number twelve means everything true that comes from something good; therefore it also means all the church's teachings. For a detailed explanation of these verses (along with verses before and after them in that chapter) corroborated with parallels in the prophetic Word, see my *Revelation Unveiled* [909–915].

2. *The Urim and Thummim on Aaron's ephod mean the things that are good and true in the Word's literal meaning.* There were Urim and Thummim on Aaron's ephod. Aaron's priesthood represented the Lord's divine goodness and his efforts to save us. The clothes of Aaron's priesthood and sacred office represented divine truths from the Lord. The ephod represented divine truth in its outermost form, and therefore it represented the Word's literal meaning, since this is divine truth in its outermost form. The twelve precious stones called the Urim and Thummim alongside the names of the twelve tribes of Israel, then, represented all the divine truths combined that come from divine goodness.

218

In Moses we read the following about these stones:

> [The artisans] are to make an ephod out of [gold,] blue, and purple threads, interwoven with double-dyed scarlet and cotton threads. Then

they are to make a breastplate of judgment in the same fashion as the ephod. You will cover it with settings for stones. There will be four rows of stones: a ruby, a topaz, and an emerald in the first row; a chrysoprase, a sapphire, and a diamond in the second row; a lapis lazuli, an agate, and an amethyst in the third row; and an aquamarine, a sard, and a jasper in the fourth row. These stones will be next to the names of the sons of Israel. For the twelve tribes there will be engravings on a signet stone next to their names. Aaron will carry the Urim and Thummim on the breastplate of judgment. The Urim and Thummim should be over Aaron's heart when he walks before Jehovah. (Exodus 28:6, 15–21, 30)

The symbolic meanings of Aaron's clothes—his ephod, outer garment, inner garment, turban, and belt—have been given in *Secrets of Heaven,* published in London, in the treatment on this chapter [§§9834–9835, 9856–9878, 9905–9909]. There I showed that the ephod represents divine truth in its outermost form. Its precious stones represent truths made translucent by goodness. Twelve of them in four rows mean all truths of this kind from first to last. The twelve tribes mean every aspect of the church. The breastplate means the divine truth that comes from divine goodness in a universal sense. The Urim and Thummim mean the outermost radiance of the divine truth that comes from divine goodness. Urim means "shining fire." Thummim means "radiance" in angelic language and "wholeness" in Hebrew. I also mentioned there that answers came through variations of light and a quiet awareness or else by direct verbal communication, and so on.

All this makes it clear that these stones stood for the truths in the outermost meaning of the Word that come from goodness. No other truths give answers from heaven. The divine emanating influence is fully present in the Word's outermost meaning.

219   3. *The precious stones from the garden of Eden that the king of Tyre is said to have worn mean the same thing.* We read in Ezekiel,

> O king of Tyre, you who seal up your measurement, you were full of wisdom and perfect in beauty. You were in Eden, the garden of God. Every precious stone was your covering: ruby, topaz, and diamond; beryl, sardonyx, and jasper; sapphire, chrysoprase, and emerald; and gold. (Ezekiel 28:12, 13)

In the Word, "Tyre" means the church in relation to its concepts of goodness and truth. The "king" means the truth in the church. The garden of Eden means wisdom and intelligence gained from the Word. Precious stones mean truths made translucent by goodness, like the truths in the Word's literal meaning. Because these truths are meant by those precious stones, the stones are called his covering. On the literal meaning covering the insides of the Word, see §213 above.

4. *The curtains, veils, and pillars in the tabernacle represented the types of good and truth that exist in the Word's literal meaning.* The tabernacle that Moses built in the desert represented heaven and the church, which is why Jehovah revealed the form of it on Mount Sinai. All the objects inside the tabernacle—the lampstand, the golden incense altar, and the table for showbread—represented and meant what is holy in heaven and the church. The most holy place, which contained the ark of the covenant, represented and therefore meant the inmost aspect of heaven and the church. The law written on two tablets meant the Word. The angel guardians above it meant safeguards to prevent violation of the Word's holiness.[457]

Since outer things derive their essence from inner things, and outer and inner things together derive their essence from what is inmost, which in this case was the law, therefore all aspects of the tabernacle represented and meant the holy things in the Word.

It follows from this that the outermost features of the tabernacle—the curtains, veils, and pillars that were coverings, containers, and structural supports—meant the outermost aspects of the Word, which are the forms of truth and goodness in its literal meaning. Because this was their meaning, all the curtains and veils were made of cotton interwoven with blue and purple threads, and with double-dyed scarlet threads, depicting angel guardians (Exodus 26:1, 31, 36).

Where *Secrets of Heaven* deals with this chapter in Exodus [§§9592–9692], I have explained both generally and specifically what the tabernacle and its contents represented and meant. There I have shown that the curtains and veils represented outer aspects of heaven and the church, and therefore outer aspects of the Word as well. The cotton or linen meant truth from a spiritual origin. The blue threads meant truth from a heavenly origin. The purple threads meant heavenly goodness. The double-dyed cloth meant spiritual goodness. Angel guardians meant protection of the inner aspects of the Word.

5. *The exteriors of the Temple in Jerusalem, as well, represented the types of good and truth that exist in the Word's literal meaning.* The Temple represented heaven and the church just as the tabernacle did, although the Temple meant the heaven where the spiritual angels are,

220

221

while the tabernacle meant the heaven where the heavenly angels are. Spiritual angels have wisdom because of the Word. Heavenly angels have love because of the Word.

The Lord himself teaches in John that in its highest meaning the Temple at Jerusalem stood for the Lord's divine-human manifestation:

> "Break this temple in pieces and I will raise it in three days." He was speaking of *the temple of his body.* (John 2:19, 21)

When something means the Lord it also means the Word, because he is the Word.

Since the interiors of the Temple represented the inner parts of heaven and the church, and the inner parts of the Word as well, its exteriors in turn represented and meant the outer parts of heaven and the church, and the outer parts of the Word as well, which belong to its literal meaning. We read of the exteriors of the Temple that they were built of whole, uncut stone, with cedar on the inside face; all the walls were carved on the inside with angel guardians, palm trees, and open flowers; and the floor was overlaid with gold (1 Kings 6:7, 29, 30). All these details stand for the outer parts of the Word, which are holy aspects of its literal meaning.

222　　6. *When the Lord was transfigured, he represented the Word in its glory.* Of the Lord's transfiguration before Peter, James, and John, we read that his face shone like the sun; his clothing became like light; Moses and Elijah were seen speaking with him; a shining cloud came over the disciples; and from the cloud a voice was heard saying, "This is my beloved Son. Hear him" (Matthew 17:1–5).

I have been taught that in this instance the Lord represented the Word. His face shining like the sun represented the divine goodness of his divine love. The clothes that became like the light represented the divine truth of his divine wisdom. Moses and Elijah represented the historical Word and the prophetic Word.[458] Moses represented the Word that was written through him, and the historical Word in general. Elijah represented the whole prophetic Word. The shining cloud that covered the disciples represented the Word in its literal meaning. That is why a voice was heard coming from the cloud saying, "This is my beloved Son. Hear him."

All communications and answers from heaven come solely through outermost things like those in the Word's literal meaning. The Lord communicates in a complete way.

7. *The Nazirites represented the power of the Word in its outermost form.* **223**
In the book of Judges we read about Samson. He was a Nazirite from his
mother's womb. His hair was the source of his strength. A Nazirite and a
Naziriteship in fact mean "hair."[459] Samson himself showed that his hair
was the source of his strength when he said,

> No razor has come upon my head, because I am a Nazirite from my
> mother's womb. If I am shaved, my strength will leave me and I will
> become weak and be like any other person. (Judges 16:17)

Without knowing what a "head" means in the Word, we cannot
imagine why a Naziriteship that means "hair" would be instituted or why
Samson's hair would be the source of his strength. A head means the
intelligence that angels and people have from the Lord through divine
truth. Hair, then, means an intelligence because of divine truth on the
lowest or outermost level. Since this was the meaning of hair, it was a rule
for the Nazirites that they were not to shave the hair on their head,
because it was the Naziriteship of God on their head (Numbers 6:1–21).
There was also a rule that the high priest and his sons were not to shave
their heads, or they would die and wrath would come upon the entire
house of Israel (Leviticus 10:6). Hair was so holy because of its meaning
(which comes from its correspondence) that even the hair of the *Son of
Humankind* (that is, the Lord in his role as the Word) is described. It was
as shining white as wool, like snow (Revelation 1:14). The Ancient of
Days is described as having similar hair (Daniel 7:9).

Since hair means truth on the outermost levels and therefore means
the literal meaning of the Word, we become bald in the spiritual world if
we despise the Word. On the other hand, if we value the Word highly
and hold it as sacred, we will have good-looking hair in that world.

This correspondence is the reason why forty-two youths were torn
apart by two she-bears for calling Elisha bald (2 Kings 2:23, 24). Elisha
represented the church's teaching from the Word. The she-bears stood for
the power of truth on the outermost levels.

The power of divine truth or of the Word exists in its literal meaning
because at that level the Word is complete, and people and angels of each
of the Lord's kingdoms share in it together.

8. *The Word has indescribable power.* Nowadays scarcely anyone **224**
knows that there is any power in truths. People think that the truth is
just something spoken by someone in authority, so it needs to be done;
they think the truth is only like a breath from someone's mouth and a

sound in someone's ear. Actually, truth and goodness are the origin of all things in both worlds, the spiritual and the physical. Truth and goodness are the means by which the universe was created and by which it is preserved. They are the means by which people were created. The two of them are everything to all things.

The Gospel of John openly states that the universe was created by divine truth: "In the beginning was the Word, and the Word was God. All created things were made by it. The world was made by it" (John 1:1, 3, 10). David says, "The heavens were made by the Word of Jehovah" (Psalms 33:6). In each of these passages "the Word" means divine truth. Since the universe was created by divine truth, the universe is also preserved by divine truth, since preservation is an ongoing creation, just as continuing to exist is the same as perpetually coming into being.[460]

[2] We human beings were made by divine truth, because all aspects of us relate to intellect and to will. Our intellect is a vessel for divine truth just as our will is a vessel for divine goodness. Therefore the human mind, consisting as it does of these two primary faculties, is nothing less than a form of divine truth and divine goodness organized both spiritually and physically. The human cerebrum is that form. Since everything in human beings depends on their minds, all the things that constitute their bodies are just appendages that are activated and brought to life by these two primary faculties.

[3] These points make it clear why God came into the world as the Word and became a human being. He did so to redeem humankind. God took on all power through a human manifestation that was divine truth. He took the hells that had risen all the way up to the heavens where the angels were, and he threw them down, brought them under control, and forced them to obey him. This was not done by a *verbal* "word"; it was done by the *divine* Word, which is divine truth.

Then he opened a great chasm between the hells and the heavens so that no one from hell could cross. If any of them try, at the first step they feel tortured like a snake thrown on a sheet of red hot iron or on a swarm of ants. As soon as devils and satans catch a whiff of divine truth, they immediately dive headlong into the depths, hurl themselves into caves, and seal them up so completely that not a crack is left open. The reason is that their wills have evil desires and their intellects have false beliefs. They therefore have the opposites of divine goodness and divine truth. Because, as I say, everything in human beings depends on these two primary structures of life, divine truth affects devils and satans profoundly and violently from head to toe.

[4] You can see from this that the power of divine truth is indescribable. Since the Word that the Christian church has is a three-leveled container for divine truth, it is obvious that this Word is what is meant in John 1:3, 10.[461]

The power of the Word is indescribable. I could support this point with many pieces of evidence I have experienced in the spiritual world; but since these would stagger belief, I will forgo any listing of them here. You can see some of them mentioned in §209 above.

On the basis of the points just made, I will, however, make this assertion: A church that has divine truths from the Lord has power over the hells. This is the church the Lord was talking about when he said to Peter, "On this rock I will build my church, and the gates of hell will not prevail against it" (Matthew 16:18). The Lord said these words after Peter proclaimed that Christ was the Son of the living God (Matthew 16:16). The "rock" in this passage means this very truth. In fact, everywhere in the Word a "rock" means the Lord's divine truth.

5

The Church's Body of Teaching
Has to Be Drawn from the Word's Literal Meaning
and Supported by It

The preceding part of this chapter showed that the Word is complete, holy, and powerful in the literal meaning. Because the Lord is the Word and is the First and the Last, as he says in Revelation 1:17, it follows that the Lord is most present in the literal meaning. From it he teaches and enlightens us. These thoughts need to be put forward in the following sequence: **225**

1. The Word is not understandable without a body of teaching.[462]
2. A body of teaching has to be drawn from the Word's literal meaning.
3. Nevertheless, the divine truth needed for a body of teaching becomes manifest only to those who have enlightenment from the Lord.

1. *The Word is not understandable without a body of teaching,* because the Word's literal meaning consists entirely of correspondences whose function is to allow spiritual and heavenly things to coexist in it and every word to be a container and a support for these spiritual and heavenly **226**

contents. Therefore in the literal meaning divine truths are rarely naked; instead they are clothed and are called apparent truths. There are many things in the literal meaning that are adapted to the grasp of simple people who do not lift their thoughts above the kind of things they see before their eyes. Some things seem like contradictions, although when the Word is viewed in its own spiritual light there is no contradiction. Furthermore, in some passages in the Prophets there are collections of names of people and places from which no meaning can be extracted. Since this is the nature of the Word's literal meaning, it is clear that it cannot be understood without a body of teaching.

[2] Examples may illustrate. We read that Jehovah relents (Exodus 32:12, 14; Jonah 3:9; 4:2); and we also read that Jehovah does not relent (Numbers 23:19; 1 Samuel 15:29). These passages cannot be reconciled without a body of teaching. We read that Jehovah inflicts parents' sins on their children to the third and fourth generation (Numbers 14:18). Yet we also read that parents are not to die because of their children nor children because of their parents, but all die in their own sin (Deuteronomy 24:16). A body of teaching brings these passages out of disharmony into harmony.

[3] Jesus says, "Ask and it will be given to you; seek and you will find; if you keep knocking it will be opened" (Matthew 7:7, 8; 21:21, 22). Without a body of teaching, people might believe that we are all going to receive whatever we ask of anyone. On the basis of a body of teaching, however, we know that it is whatever we ask of the Lord that we will be given. The Lord in fact teaches this: "If you live in me and my words live in you, ask for whatever you want and it will be done for you" (John 15:7).

[4] The Lord says, "Blessed are the poor, for theirs is the kingdom of God" (Luke 6:20). Without a body of teaching, we might think that heaven is for the poor but not for the rich. A body of teaching instructs us that this means the poor *in spirit,* for the Lord says, "Blessed are the poor in spirit, for theirs is the kingdom of the heavens" (Matthew 5:3).

[5] Furthermore, the Lord says, "To avoid being judged, do not judge. The judgment you use to judge others will be used on you" (Matthew 7:1, 2; Luke 6:37). Without a body of teaching we could be convinced that we should not judge that an evil person is evil. On the basis of a body of teaching, however, we are allowed to judge as long as we do it justly. For the Lord says, "Judge with just judgment" (John 7:24).

[6] Jesus says, "Do not be called teacher, because your teacher is the One, the Christ. Do not call anyone on earth your father, for your father is the One in the heavens. Do not be called governors, for your governor

is the One, the Christ" (Matthew 23:8, 9, 10). Without a body of teaching we might think we were forbidden to call anyone teacher, father, or governor. From a body of teaching, however, we come to know that doing this is acceptable in its earthly meaning, although it is not acceptable in its spiritual meaning.

[7] Jesus said to his disciples, "When the Son of Humankind sits on the throne of his glory, you too will sit on twelve thrones judging the twelve tribes of Israel" (Matthew 19:28). On the basis of these words we might conclude that the Lord's disciples were going to judge people when in fact the disciples could not judge anyone. A body of teaching unveils the secret when it teaches that the Lord alone, who is omniscient and knows the hearts of all, is going to be the judge and is able to judge. His twelve disciples mean all the forms of goodness and truth that the church has received from the Lord through the Word. On this basis a body of teaching concludes that these forms of goodness and truth are going to judge everyone, as the Lord says in John 3:17, 18; 12:47, 48.

There are many other situations like these in the Word. From them it is perfectly obvious that the Word is not understandable without a body of teaching.

With the help of a body of teaching, the Word is not only understood, it shines in our intellect—it is like a lampstand with the lamps lit. Then we see much more than we had seen before and understand things we had not understood before. Things that are unclear or out of harmony we either pass by without noticing or we notice and explain in such a way that they harmonize with our body of teaching.

The Word is viewed on the basis of a given body of teaching and explained along its lines. Our experience of the Christian world testifies to this. All Protestants see the Word through their body of teaching and use it to explain the Word. So do all Roman Catholics. Jews do likewise. A body of false teaching yields false beliefs, and a body of true teaching yields true beliefs. Clearly then, a body of true teaching is like an oil lamp in the dark and a signpost on a roadway.

It stands to reason, then, that people who read the Word without a body of teaching are in the dark about every truth. Their mind is meandering and undecided, liable to go astray, and even susceptible to heresies. Such people will in fact embrace heresies if those heresies have gained any popularity or authority and their own reputation is therefore not in danger. To them the Word is like a lampstand that gives no light. In the shadows they think they see many things, but in fact what they see is practically nothing, because a body of teaching is the only oil lamp.

I have seen angels examining people like this and discovering that they were capable of using the Word to support whatever they wanted. The angels also discovered that these people do in fact support whatever they want, especially things that feed their love for themselves and for others they are partial to. I saw them stripped of their clothing, an indication that they had no truths.[463] In that world, clothes are truths.

229 2. *A body of teaching has to be drawn from the Word's literal meaning and supported by it.* The reason for this is that the Lord is present, teaching and enlightening, in the Word's literal meaning. The Lord never works in an incomplete or partial way, and the literal meaning is where the Word is complete, as I have shown before. As a result, a body of teaching has to be drawn from the Word's literal meaning.

You can draw a complete body of genuinely true teaching from the Word's literal meaning. In that meaning the Word is like a clothed person whose face, forearms, and hands are exposed. All the teachings that relate to our faith and life and therefore our salvation are exposed there. The other teachings are clothed. Even then, in many passages where the teachings are clothed they are still visible, as a woman with a thin piece of silk over her face can still see objects in front of her. In fact, as the truths in the Word are multiplied and organized by our love for them, they shine out and become more and more clearly evident.

230 You might think that we could gain a body of genuinely true teaching by exploring the Word's *spiritual* meaning through the study of correspondences. In fact, a body of teaching is not gained through that meaning; it is only enlightened and corroborated by that meaning, for, as I said before in §208, people who know a few correspondences are capable of falsifying the Word by connecting and applying correspondences to support some preconceived idea already lodged in their mind.

For another thing, no one is given the spiritual meaning except by the Lord alone. The Lord safeguards that meaning as he safeguards the angelic heaven, for heaven dwells in it.

231 3. *The genuine truth in the Word's literal meaning, the truth that is needed for a body of teaching, becomes manifest only to those who have enlightenment from the Lord.* Enlightenment comes from the Lord alone and affects people who love truths because they are true and who make them useful in their lives. Other people do not have enlightenment concerning the Word. Enlightenment comes from the Lord alone because the Word is from him, and therefore he is in it. Enlightenment comes to people who love truths because they are true and who make them useful in their lives, because these people are in the Lord and the Lord is in them. The Lord is truth itself, as I showed in the chapter on the Lord. Loving the Lord is living by his divine truths, that is, doing useful things with those truths, as we read in the following words in John:

> On that day you will recognize that you are in me and I am in you. The people who love me are the people who have my instructions and follow them. I will love them and will manifest myself to them. I will come to them and make a home with them. (John 14:20, 21, 23)

These are the people who are enlightened when they read the Word. For them the Word shines and becomes translucent.

The Word shines for these people and becomes translucent to them because the details in the Word have spiritual and heavenly meanings inside. These meanings are in the light of heaven. The Lord flows through these meanings and their light into the Word's earthly meaning and its light in the people. As a result of this light, the people first acknowledge the truth with deep perception and then see it in their own thought. This happens whenever people have a desire for truth because it is true. This desire, you see, leads to perception, and perception leads to thought. This process leads to the acknowledgment that is known as faith.

Something opposite to this happens to people who read the Word **232** under a false body of religious teaching, especially if they use the Word to support their body of teaching and are pursuing their own glory or the wealth of the world. Under these circumstances the truths in the Word seem to be in the shadows of night and things that are false seem to be in the light of day. Such people read truths but do not see them. If they see the shadow of truths, they falsify those truths. The Lord was referring to people like this when he said that they have eyes but they do not see; they have ears, but they do not understand (Matthew 13:14, 15). The light in which they view spiritual things related to the church becomes nothing but earthly as a result. The things their minds then see are like the ghosts people sometimes see when just waking up in bed, or like the mistaken impression sleepwalkers have that they are wide awake.

I have been given the opportunity to talk to many people after death **233** who believed that in heaven they were going to shine like stars because (so they said) they regarded the Word as holy, read it through many times over, and collected many passages from it that they used to support the dogmas of their faith. As a result, they became famous scholars and believed they were going to become Michaels and Raphaels.464 Many of them were examined to learn what love had driven them to study the Word. Some of them were motivated to study by love for themselves so that they could become respected leaders of the church. Others were motivated to study by love for the world so as to increase their wealth. When they were subjected to another examination to find out what they knew from the Word, it was discovered that their knowledge of it contained nothing genuinely true. All they knew was what is called *falsified truth that is actually putrid falsity,* so called because in heaven it smells like something that has gone bad. They were informed that this had happened to them because their objective in reading the Word was not to find a truth to believe or a good way to live but to reach some selfish or worldly goal. When people have themselves or something worldly as their objective, as they read the Word their mind is preoccupied with themselves or the world. As a result, they are constantly thinking of their own self-importance, and human self-importance is in pitch darkness when it comes to anything related to heaven and the church. People who are in this condition cannot be raised by the Lord into the light of heaven; they cannot accept any influence from the Lord through heaven.

I have seen these people let into heaven. When it was discovered there that they had no truths, they were thrown out. Nevertheless a misplaced pride and a feeling that they were deserving stayed with them.

There was an entirely different outcome for people who had been motivated to study the Word by a desire to know the truth because it is true and because it is helpful and useful not only for their own lives but also for their neighbors' lives. I have seen these people raised into heaven into the light of divine truth there and lifted into angelic wisdom and the happiness that heaven's angels enjoy.

6

The Word's Literal Meaning
Provides a Connection to the Lord
and Association with Angels

234 The Word provides a connection to the Lord because he is the Word; that is, he is the divine truth and the divine goodness within it. The literal meaning provides this connection because in this meaning the Word has its completeness, holiness, and power, as I have shown in the relevant

passage above [§§214–224]. The connection to the Lord is not apparent to us; it exists in our love for the truth and our perception of it.

The Word's literal meaning also provides association with angels in heaven because within the literal meaning there is a spiritual meaning and a heavenly meaning. The angels are in these higher meanings. Angels of the Lord's spiritual kingdom are in the Word's spiritual meaning, and angels of the Lord's heavenly kingdom are in the Word's heavenly meaning. These two meanings unfold out of the Word's earthly meaning when the Word is read by people who regard it as holy. The unfolding is instantaneous and the association forms immediately.

A number of experiences have made it obvious to me that spiritual angels are associated with the Word's spiritual meaning and heavenly angels are associated with the Word's heavenly meaning. I was allowed to perceive that a line of communication to the heavens opened up while I was reading the Word in its literal meaning—at one moment to one community, at another moment to another community. The things that I understood in the earthly meaning the spiritual angels understood in the spiritual meaning and the heavenly angels understood in the heavenly meaning. It was instantaneous. Having perceived this communication several thousand times, I have no room left for doubt about it. **235**

In fact, there are spirits below the heavens who abuse this communication. They recite some saying from the Word's literal meaning and immediately observe and record the community that it communicates with. This too I have often seen and heard.

I have been allowed to know through living experience, then, that the Word in its literal meaning is a divine medium for connecting us to the Lord and associating us with angels in heaven.

Examples will illustrate how spiritual angels receive their meaning and heavenly angels receive theirs from the earthly meaning when we read the Word. Four of the Ten Commandments will provide examples. **236**

Take the *fifth commandment*,[465] "You will not murder." We take this to mean not only murdering but also hating and longing for revenge even to the point of death. Spiritual angels take "murdering" to mean acting like a devil and killing someone's soul. Heavenly angels take "murdering" to mean hating the Lord and the Word.

[2] The *sixth commandment*, "You will not commit adultery." We take "committing adultery" to mean whoring, doing obscene things, saying lustful things, and having filthy thoughts. A spiritual angel takes

"committing adultery" to mean contaminating the good things taught by the Word and falsifying its truths. A heavenly angel takes "committing adultery" to mean denying the Lord's divinity and desecrating the Word.

[3] The *seventh commandment,* "You will not steal." We take "stealing" to mean stealing, cheating, and using any excuse to take our neighbor's possessions. A spiritual angel takes "stealing" to mean using things that are false and evil to deprive others of the true and good things in their faith. A heavenly angel takes "stealing" to mean attributing to ourselves what belongs to the Lord and claiming his justice and merit for ourselves.

[4] The *eighth commandment,* "You will not testify falsely." We take "testifying falsely" to include lying and libeling. A [spiritual] angel takes "testifying falsely" to mean saying and convincing people that falsity is truth and evil is good, and the reverse. A heavenly angel takes "testifying falsely" to mean slandering and blaspheming the Lord and the Word.

[5] This shows how spiritual and heavenly meanings are unfolded from and drawn out of the Word's earthly meaning, which contains them. An astounding thing is that the angels receive their meanings independently of their knowing what we are thinking. Yet the angels' thoughts and ours are united through correspondences like a purpose, its means, and its result. In fact, purposes actually exist in the heavenly kingdom, means actually exist in the spiritual kingdom, and results actually exist in the earthly kingdom. That is how we now associate with angels through the Word.

237 A spiritual angel draws out and extracts spiritual things from the Word's literal meaning, and a heavenly angel draws out and extracts heavenly things, because these things agree with their nature and are compatible with it. To illustrate the truth of this, I can use similar situations in nature's three kingdoms—animal, plant, and mineral. In the animal kingdom, when food has become chyle,[466] blood vessels draw out and extract their blood from it, nerve fibers derive their sap from it, and so do the structures from which the [nerve] fibers branch out. In the plant kingdom, a tree, including trunk, branches, leaves, and fruit, stands upon its root. Through the root it draws out of the ground and extracts a relatively crude sap for the trunk, branches, and leaves, a more refined sap for the flesh of the fruit, and a most refined sap for the seeds inside the fruit.[467] In the mineral kingdom, here and there in the womb of the earth there are raw minerals pregnant with gold, silver, copper, and iron. As a result of exhaled gases and the flow of liquid from the rocky substance, gold extracts its own irreducible element, silver its own, copper its own, and iron its own; and a watery effluvium conveys them from one place to another.[468]

In its letter the Word is like a case that has precious stones, pearls, and **238** gems laid out in a pattern inside. When we regard the Word as holy and read it in order to have a useful life, our minds have thoughts like a jewel case that someone takes hold of and sends up to heaven. As the jewel case rises, it opens, making the precious things inside accessible to the angels, who are profoundly delighted to see them and to hold them up to the light. The angels' pleasure is shared with us; this process brings angels into association with us and allows them to share with us not only that pleasure but also their perceptions.

The Holy Supper was established to allow us this kind of association with angels as well as a connection to the Lord. During the Holy Supper, in heaven *the bread* becomes divine goodness and *the wine* becomes divine truth, both of which are from the Lord. Ever since creation this correspondence has existed for two reasons: so the angelic heaven and the church on earth, or more generally the spiritual world and the physical world, could be one; and so the Lord could be connected to both of them at once.

Association with angels comes about through the Word's earthly or **239** literal meaning because three levels of life have been built into every one of us from creation: a heavenly level, a spiritual level, and an earthly level. As long as we are alive in the world we are conscious of the earthly level; during this time we are conscious of the spiritual angelic level only to the extent that we have genuine truths, and we are conscious of the heavenly level only to the extent that we live our lives by those truths. Even in that case, we do not come into full consciousness of what is spiritual or heavenly until after death, because what is spiritual or heavenly is locked and hidden inside our earthly ideas. When our earthly level passes away through death, the spiritual and heavenly levels remain and form the basis of the ideas in our thinking.

It stands to reason, then, that only the Word has spirit and life. As the Lord says,

> The words that I speak to you are spirit and are life. (John 6:63)

> The water that I will give you will become a fountain of water springing up to eternal life. (John 4:14)

> People do not live on bread alone, but on every word that comes from the mouth of God. (Matthew 4:4)

> Work for the food that remains for eternal life, which the Son of Humankind will give you. (John 6:27)

7

The Word Exists throughout the Heavens;
It Is the Source of Angelic Wisdom

240 Up until now people have not known that the Word exists in the heavens. They had no way of knowing this as long as the church remained unaware that angels and spirits are people who have faces and bodies just as people do in our world. Angels and spirits also have things that are like the things people have, with one difference: the things angels have are spiritual. All the things around them have a spiritual origin, while we here in the physical world, and all the things around us, have a physical origin. As long as this piece of information was still hidden there was no way to know that the Word does in fact exist in the heavens and that it is read by the angels there and by the spirits below the heavens.

To prevent this point from staying hidden forever, I have been allowed to have interaction with angels and spirits, to talk to them and see the things they have, and afterward to pass on many of the things I have heard and seen. This I have done in the work *Heaven and Hell,* published in London in 1758. That work shows that angels and spirits are people and that they have in great abundance all the things we have in this world. For angels and spirits being people, see §§73–77, 453–456 in that work. For their possession of things similar to those we have in this world, see §§170–190. For their having divine worship and sermons in church buildings, see §§221–227. For their possession of writing and books, see §§258–264. For their possession of the Word, see §259.

241 As for the Word in heaven, it has a spiritual style of writing that is completely different from our earthly style of writing. This spiritual writing style consists entirely of letters that have individual meanings. There are also little lines, curves, and dots above, between, and inside the letters to heighten the meaning.

Among angels in the spiritual kingdom, the lettering is like printed lettering in our world. Among angels in the heavenly kingdom, some copies of the Word have lettering like Arabic script, while others have lettering like the script of ancient Hebrew (except that the letters are curved at the top and bottom) with diacritical marks above, between, and inside the letters. Each mark contains an entire meaning of its own.

[2] Because the angels have writing like this, the names of people and places are replaced in their Word by special markings. From them the wise understand the spiritual or heavenly thing that each name means. For example, "Moses" means the Word of God that was written through Moses, and in a broader sense the historical Word. "Elijah" means the prophetic Word.[469] "Abraham," "Isaac," and "Jacob" mean the Lord's divine heavenly quality, his divine spiritual quality, and his divine earthly quality. "Aaron" means a priestly quality and "David" a royal one, both of which belong to the Lord. The names of the sons of Jacob or the twelve tribes of Israel mean different aspects of heaven and the church; the names of the Lord's twelve disciples have similar meanings. "Zion" and "Jerusalem" mean the church's body of teaching from the Word. "The land of Canaan" means the church itself. Places and cities on this and on that side of the Jordan mean different aspects of the church and its body of teaching.

It is the same with numbers. In the versions of the Word in heaven these too are absent. In their places are the things the numbers correspond to.

From all this it is clear that the Word in heaven is similar in its literal meaning to our Word, and it corresponds to it as well. Their Word and our Word are therefore one.

[3] It is amazing that the Word in the heavens has been written in such a way that the simple understand it simply and the wise understand it wisely. As I say, there are many curves and diacritical marks over the letters that heighten the meaning. Simple people pay no attention to them and do not know what they mean. Wise people pay more and more attention to them depending on how wise they are, right up to the highest level of wisdom.

In its sanctuary every larger community keeps a copy of the Word written out by angels who were inspired by the Lord, so that the Word elsewhere will not change in the least detail.

The Word that is in our world is like the Word in heaven in that the simple understand it simply and the wise wisely. The mechanism for this is different here, however.

On the point that the angels receive all their wisdom from the Word, **242** they themselves assert this. They have as much light as they have understanding of the Word. Heaven's light is divine wisdom; before angels' eyes this divine wisdom takes the form of light.

In the sanctuaries where their copies of the Word are kept, the light is fiery or shining white. There is more light in such places than anywhere else in heaven.

The wisdom of heavenly angels goes almost as far beyond the wisdom of spiritual angels as the wisdom of spiritual angels goes beyond our human wisdom. The reason for this is that heavenly angels have a love from the Lord for what is good, while spiritual angels have wisdom from the Lord about what is true. Where love for what is good exists, there dwells wisdom also. Where truths exist, there dwells only as much wisdom as there is love for what is good. This is why the Word is written one way in the Lord's heavenly kingdom and another in his spiritual kingdom. The heavenly kingdom's form of the Word expresses loving forms of goodness in letters and conveys the specific types of love with diacritical marks. The spiritual kingdom's form of the Word expresses truths of wisdom in letters and conveys inner perceptions of truth with diacritical marks.

From all this you can imagine what kind of wisdom lies hidden in the Word that we have in this world. Inside it there lies all angelic wisdom, which is inexpressible. If we are made angels by the Lord through the Word, we will come into that wisdom after death.

8

The Church Is Based on the Word; the Nature of the Church in Individuals Depends on Their Understanding of the Word

243 The church is unquestionably based on the Word—I have shown above that the Word is divine truth (§§189–192); that the church's body of teaching is based on the Word (§§225–233); and that we are connected to the Lord through the Word (§§234–239). The idea that the understanding of the Word shapes the church is something that could be called into question, however, since there are people who believe they are part of the church because they have the Word, because they read it or hear it from a preacher, and because they know something of its literal meaning, although they do not know how to understand this or that saying in the Word and some of them do not care. Therefore I will present support for two ideas: it is not the Word but the understanding of it that forms the church; and the quality of the church is determined by the way people in it understand the Word.

The church depends on its understanding of the Word because it **244** depends on true perceptions related to faith and good actions related to goodwill. These true perceptions and good actions are universal characteristics that not only spread out across the entire literal meaning of the Word but also lie hidden within it like valuables in a safe.

The features of the Word's literal meaning are apparent to all of us because they meet our eyes directly. The features that lie hidden in the spiritual meaning, however, are not apparent to any except those who love truths because they are true and who do good things because they are good things to do. The treasures that the literal meaning covers and guards are revealed to these people. These treasures are the things that essentially constitute the church.

As everyone knows, the church depends on its body of teaching and **245** its body of teaching is based on the Word. Nevertheless, it is not the body of teaching itself but its integrity and purity,[470] and therefore an understanding of the Word, that forms the church. The church in miniature that is in us as individuals is also formed and established not by a body of teaching but by our faith and by our living our faith. Likewise, what forms and establishes the church in miniature in any of us is not the Word; it is the faith based on true perceptions and the life based on good actions that we individually draw from the Word and apply to ourselves.

The Word is like a mine that has gold and silver deep down in great abundance; it is like a mine where the farther in we go, the more precious are the types of stone we find. Our understanding of the Word is what gives us access to these "mines." If we did not understand the Word's true nature as it is at its heart and in its depth, the Word would no more form the church in us than mines like these in the Middle East would make some person in Europe rich. It would be different, of course, if that person were one of the owners and operators of the mine.

For people who search the Word for truths to believe and good ways to live, the Word is like the treasures belonging to the ruler of Persia or the emperors of Mongolia and China, and the people in the church are like governors under those leaders who are allowed to take whatever they want for their own use. People who merely own the Word and read it but do not search it for genuine truths to believe and genuinely good ways to live are like people who know from reading newspapers that there are astounding treasures in those other lands, but they themselves do not get a penny from those treasures.

People who own the Word but do not receive from it any understanding of genuine truth or any willingness to do genuine good are like people who think they are rich because they have borrowed money from others or who think themselves well off because they include in their reckoning other people's properties, houses, and possessions, which as anyone can see is not their wealth. They are also like people who parade around in magnificent clothing and ride in gilded carriages with attendants on the back and sides, and with heralds running out in front, but not a bit of this magnificence belongs to them.

246　The Jewish nation used to be like this. Because it possessed the Word, the Lord compared it to a rich man who wore purple and fine linen and gloriously indulged himself every day, but did not get enough truth or good out of the Word even to show compassion to poor Lazarus, covered with sores, who was lying in front of his door [Luke 16:19, 20]. The members of that nation not only failed to assimilate any truths from the Word, but they assimilated falsities in such quantities that in the long run nothing true was apparent to them. Falsities do not simply cover up truths; they obliterate and annihilate them. This was why the Jews did not acknowledge the Messiah even though all the prophets had announced his coming.

247　Many passages in the Prophets show that the church among the Israelite and Jewish nation was completely destroyed and was no longer a church because its members had falsified the meaning, or their understanding, of the Word. Nothing else destroys a church.

In the Prophets, especially in Hosea, the name "Ephraim" stands for an understanding of the Word, whether true or false. Throughout the Word, in fact, "Ephraim" means the church's understanding of the Word. Because an understanding of the Word forms the church, Ephraim is called *a precious child* and *one born of delight* (Jeremiah 31:20); *a firstborn* (Jeremiah 31:9); *the strength of Jehovah's head* (Psalms 60:7; 108:8); *powerful* (Zechariah 10:7); and *someone outfitted with a bow* (Zechariah 9:13); and Ephraim's children are said to be *armed* and to *shoot with a bow* (Psalms 78:9). A "bow" means a body of teaching from the Word that fights against false ideas. For this reason Israel laid his right hand rather than his left on Ephraim and blessed him, and Ephraim took the place of Reuben (Genesis 48:5, 11, and following). For this reason during Moses' blessing of the children of Israel, Ephraim and his brother Manasseh were exalted above all the rest as part of Moses' blessing of their father, Joseph (Deuteronomy 33:1–17).

[2] The Prophets, especially Hosea, also describe as "Ephraim" what the church is like when it has lost its understanding of the Word. For example,

> Israel and Ephraim will collapse. Ephraim will be desolate. Ephraim will be oppressed and broken in judgment. (Hosea 5:5, 9, 11, 12, 13, 14)

> What will I do to you, Ephraim, since your holiness has gone away like a cloud at sunrise and like the dew that falls in the morning? (Hosea 6:4)

> They will not live on Jehovah's land. Ephraim will go back to Egypt and will eat what is unclean in Assyria. (Hosea 9:3)

"Jehovah's land" is the church; "Egypt" is scholarly study on the part of our earthly self; "Assyria" is reasoning based on that study. The latter two things together falsify our deeper understanding of the Word. This is why it says that Ephraim will go back to Egypt and eat what is unclean in Assyria.

> [3] Ephraim is feeding on the wind and pursuing the east wind. Every day he increases lying and devastation. He is making a pact with Assyria and oil is being carried down to Egypt. (Hosea 12:1)

"Feeding on the wind," "pursuing the east wind," and "increasing lying and devastation" means falsifying truths and thereby destroying the church.

Ephraim's whoring means the same thing, in that "whoring" in the following passages means falsifying an understanding of the Word and its genuine truth:

> I know that Ephraim has whored in every way and Israel has become defiled. (Hosea 5:3)

> In the house of Israel, I have seen a foul thing. Ephraim has whored there and Israel has become defiled. (Hosea 6:10)

"Israel" is the church itself; "Ephraim" is the understanding of the Word on which the church depends and is based. This is why it says that Ephraim whored and Israel became defiled.

[4] Since the church in the Israelite and Jewish nation was obviously destroyed by falsifying the Word, therefore we read of Ephraim,

> I will give you away, Ephraim. I will hand you over, Israel, like Admah, and I will make you like Zeboiim.[471] (Hosea 11:8)

Because the prophet Hosea from the first chapter to the last is about a genuine understanding of the Word becoming falsified and the church being destroyed by that, and because "whoring" there means falsifying the truth, therefore the prophet Hosea was commanded to represent the condition of the church by marrying a whore and having sons by her (Hosea 1); and later by marrying an adulterous woman (Hosea 3).

I have quoted these passages to make known, and to support the concept, that the quality of the church is the quality of its understanding of the Word. If its understanding is based on genuine truths from the Word, the church is excellent and highly valuable. If its understanding is based on falsified truths from the Word, the church is ruined and in fact becomes something foul.

9

There Is a Marriage between the Lord and the Church, and Therefore a Marriage between Goodness and Truth, in the Individual Details in the Word

248 Until now people have not seen that there is a marriage between the Lord and the church, and therefore a marriage between goodness and truth, in the individual details in the Word. It has been impossible for people to see this because the Word's spiritual meaning was not revealed before, and this marriage is visible only through the spiritual meaning.

There are two meanings in the Word that lie hidden inside its literal meaning. They are called the spiritual meaning and the heavenly meaning. The elements of the Word's spiritual meaning relate primarily to the church, and the elements of its heavenly meaning relate primarily to the Lord. The elements of the Word's spiritual meaning also relate to divine truth, while the elements of the heavenly meaning relate to divine goodness. These two come together in the marriage that exists in the Word.

This is not apparent, though, to any except those who know what the names and the words stand for in the Word's spiritual and heavenly meanings. Some words and names apply to something good, others to something true; some words and names apply to both goodness and truth. If we do not know this, we cannot see the marriage in the individual details in the Word; this secret has not been discovered before, because of this blindness.

Because this type of marriage exists in the individual details in the Word, there are often two-part expressions whose elements seem like repetitions of the same thing. These are not in fact repetitions. One element relates to goodness and the other to truth. Both of them taken together form a composite and become one thing. The divine holiness of the Word is a result of this also. In every divine work there is goodness united to truth and truth united to goodness.

The heading above states that in the individual details in the Word **249** there is a marriage between the Lord and the church and *therefore* a marriage between goodness and truth, because wherever there is a marriage between the Lord and the church a marriage between goodness and truth is also present, since the latter marriage comes from the former one.

When a whole church, or just an individual within a church, has truths, the Lord flows into these truths with goodness and brings them to life. To put it another way, when people who are part of a church understand something true, the Lord flows into their intellect and enlivens it by bringing goodwill into it.

We all have two faculties of life called the intellect and the will. Our intellect is a vessel for truth and therefore for wisdom; our will is a vessel for goodness and therefore for goodwill. For us to become part of the church, these two parts of us have to become one. The two parts do in fact become one when we build our intellect with genuine truths (which happens to all appearances as if we were doing the building ourselves) and our will is filled with goodness and love (which is done by the Lord). Then the life of truth and the life of goodness are in us—the life of truth in our intellect and the life of goodness in our will. When these two lives are united, they become one life, not two. This is the marriage between the Lord and the church; it is also the marriage between goodness and truth in us.

Readers who pay attention to it can see that the Word has two-part **250** expressions whose elements seem to be repetitions of the same thing. For example, brother and friend, the poor and the needy, wasteland and desert, emptiness and void, enemy and adversary, sin and wickedness, anger and wrath, nations and peoples, joy and gladness, grief and weeping, justice and judgment, and so on. These seem like synonyms when in fact they are not. Brother, the poor, wasteland, [emptiness,] enemy, sin, anger, nations, joy, grief, and justice apply to goodness or, in an opposite sense, to evil. Friend, the needy, desert, void, adversary, wickedness, wrath, peoples, gladness, weeping, and judgment apply to truth or, in an opposite sense, to falsity. Yet it seems to readers who do not know this secret that the poor and the needy, wasteland and desert, emptiness and void, and so on, are the same thing. They are not, in fact, although they combine to form one thing.

In the Word there are also many things that are paired, such as fire and flame, gold and silver, bronze and iron, wood and stone, [bread and water,][472] bread and wine, purple and fine linen, and so on. Again this is because fire, gold, bronze, wood, bread, and purple apply to goodness, while flame, silver, iron, stone, water, wine, and fine linen apply to truth.

Something similar occurs when the Word says we have to love God *with our whole heart and our whole soul,* and that God is going to create in us *a new heart and a new spirit.* "Heart" applies to the goodness of our love, while "soul" and "spirit" apply to the truth of our faith.

There are also words that share in both goodness and truth. They are therefore stated alone without a connection to other terms.

These and many other features, though, stand out only to angels and to people who are aware of both the earthly meaning and the spiritual meaning at the same time.

251　　To show from the Word that there are two-part expressions in it whose elements seem like repetitions of the same thing would take too long—it would fill pages and pages. To remove doubt, however, I wish to list passages that mention *nations* and *peoples* together, and others that mention *joy* and *gladness* together.

The following are passages that mention *nations* and *peoples* together:

Woe to a sinful *nation,* to a *people* heavy with wickedness. (Isaiah 1:4)

The *peoples* walking in darkness have seen a great light; you have increased the *nation.* (Isaiah 9:2, 3)

Assyria is the rod of my anger. I will send it against a hypocritical *nation;* I will command it to go against a *people* of my wrath. (Isaiah 10:5, 6)

It will happen in that day that the *nations* will seek the Root of Jesse, who stands as a banner for the *peoples.* (Isaiah 11:10)

Jehovah is striking the *peoples* with an incurable blow; he is ruling the *nations* with anger. (Isaiah 14:6)

In that day, a far-flung and shaven *people* will be brought out as a gift for Jehovah Sabaoth, a measured and trampled *nation*. (Isaiah 18:7)

A strong *people,* they will honor you; a city of powerful *nations* will fear you. (Isaiah 25:3)

Jehovah will swallow up the covering over all *peoples,* the veil over all *nations*. (Isaiah 25:7)

Approach, you *nations,* and hear, you *peoples*. (Isaiah 34:1)

I called you to be a covenant for the *people,* a light for the *nations*. (Isaiah 42:6)

All the *nations* should be gathered together and the *peoples* should convene. (Isaiah 43:9)

Behold, I will lift my hand toward the *nations* and my banner toward the *peoples*. (Isaiah 49:22)

I gave him as a witness for the *peoples,* a leader and a legislator for the *nations*. (Isaiah 55:4, 5)

Behold, a *people* is coming from a northern land, and a great *nation* from the sides of the earth. (Jeremiah 6:22, 23)

No longer will I let you hear the slander of the *nations;* you will not bear the insult of the *peoples* anymore. (Ezekiel 36:15)

All *peoples* and *nations* will worship him. (Daniel 7:14)

To prevent the *nations* from making cruel remarks about them and saying among the *peoples,* "Where is their God?" (Joel 2:7)

The remnants of my *people* will plunder them and the remainders of my *nation* will inherit them. (Zephaniah 2:9)

Many *peoples* will come, and numerous *nations,* to seek Jehovah in Jerusalem. (Zechariah 8:22)

My eyes have seen the salvation that you have prepared before the face of all *peoples,* a light of revelation to the *nations*. (Luke 2:30, 31, 32)

You have redeemed us in your blood, [some] from every *people* and *nation*. (Revelation 5:9)

You need to prophesy again upon *peoples* and *nations*. (Revelation 10:11)

You will put me as the head of the *nations;* a *people* whom I had not known will serve me. (Psalms 18:43)

Jehovah makes the counsel of the *nations* useless; he turns the thoughts of the *peoples* upside down. (Psalms 33:10)

You will make us a proverb among the *nations,* a shaking of the head among the *peoples.* (Psalms 44:14)

Jehovah will subdue the *peoples* under us, and the *nations* under our feet. Jehovah rules over the *nations;* the willing among the *peoples* have gathered. (Psalms 47:3, 8, 9)

The *peoples* will confess you and the *nations* will rejoice, because you are going to judge the *peoples* in uprightness and lead the *nations* on earth. (Psalms 67:3, 4, 5)

Remember me, Jehovah, with the good pleasure of your *people,* so that I may rejoice in the joy of your *nations.* (Psalms 106:4, 5)

There are more passages like this as well.

Both nations and peoples are mentioned because "nations" mean those who focus on goodness or, in an opposite sense, on evil; and "peoples" mean those who focus on truths or, in an opposite sense, on falsities. For this reason, those who belong to the Lord's spiritual kingdom are called "peoples" and those who belong to the Lord's heavenly kingdom are called "nations," since all who are in the spiritual kingdom focus on truths and therefore intelligence; and all who are in the heavenly kingdom focus on good actions and therefore wisdom.

252   The same is true of many other paired expressions. For instance, where the word "joy" occurs, the word "gladness" also occurs, as in the following examples:[473]

Behold, *joy* and *gladness,* killing an ox. (Isaiah 22:13)

Joy and *gladness* will be attained; *sadness* and moaning will flee. (Isaiah 35:10; 51:11)

Gladness and *joy* were cut off from the house of our God. (Joel 1:16)

The voice of *joy* and the voice of *gladness* will be done away with. (Jeremiah 7:34; 25:10)

The fast of the tenth will be *joy* and *gladness* for the house of Judah. (Zechariah 8:19)

Be glad about Jerusalem; *rejoice* in it. (Isaiah 66:10)

Rejoice and *be glad,* daughter of Edom. (Lamentations 4:21)

The heavens will *be glad* and the earth will *rejoice.* (Psalms 96:11)

They will make me hear *joy* and *gladness.* (Psalms 51:8)

Joy and *gladness* will be found in Zion, thanksgiving and the voice of singing. (Isaiah 51:3)

There will be *gladness,* and many will *rejoice* over his birth. (Luke 1:14)

I will stop the voice of *joy* and the voice of *gladness,* the voice of the groom and the voice of the bride. (Jeremiah 7:34; 16:9; 25:10)

In this place the voice of *joy* and the voice of *gladness* will be heard again, the voice of the groom and the voice of the bride. (Jeremiah 33:10, 11)

This pair of expressions also occurs elsewhere.

Both joy and gladness are mentioned because joy applies to goodness and gladness applies to truth. Joy relates to love; gladness relates to wisdom. Joy relates to the heart; gladness relates to the spirit. Joy relates to the will; gladness relates to the intellect.

The marriage between the Lord and the church is obviously meant here when it mentions the voice of joy and the voice of gladness, the voice of the groom and the voice of the bride (Jeremiah 7:34; 16:9; 25:10; 33:10, 11). The Lord is the bridegroom and the church is the bride. For the Lord as the bridegroom, see Matthew 9:15; Mark 2:19, 20; Luke 5:34, 35. For the church as the bride, see Revelation 21:2, 9; 22:17. Therefore John the Baptist said of Jesus, "The One who has the bride is the groom" (John 3:29).

Due to the marriage of divine goodness and divine truth in the individual details in the Word, many passages mention both "Jehovah" and "God," or both "Jehovah" and "the Holy One of Israel," as if they were two, when in fact they are one. "Jehovah" means the Lord's divine goodness that comes from divine love. "God" and "the Holy One of Israel"

253

mean the Lord's divine truth that comes from divine wisdom. For more on the point that "Jehovah" and "God," or "Jehovah" and "the Holy One of Israel" appear in many passages in the Word together and yet they mean One Being, see *Teachings on the Lord the Redeemer*.[474]

10

We May Derive Heretical Ideas from the Word's Literal Meaning, but We Are Condemned Only If We Become Adamant about Those Ideas

254 I have already shown [§§226–228] that the Word is impossible to understand without a body of teaching, and that a body of teaching is like an oil lamp for making genuine truths visible. This is because the Word was written entirely in correspondences. As a result, many things in the Word are apparent truths, not naked truths. Many things in it were written to be understood by people who are merely earthly. Yet these things were written in such a way that simple people can understand them simply, intelligent people intelligently, and wise people wisely.

Since the Word is like this, its apparent truths, which are clothed truths, can be taken for naked truths. If apparent truths become convictions, however, they turn into mistaken ideas that are actually false. In Christianity all the heresies that have existed and that are currently in existence were born as a result of apparent truths being taken for genuine truths and being reinforced as such.

Our heretical ideas themselves do not condemn us; but using the Word and reasoning from our own lower self to reinforce the false ideas in the heresy and living in evil ways do condemn us. We are all born into the religion of our country or our family. We are initiated into it from early childhood. We retain that religion and cannot rid ourselves of its falsities, because of our interactions in the world and also our own intellectual inability to scrutinize truths that we have inherited in this way. Living in evil ways does condemn us, however, and so does becoming adamant about falsities to the point of destroying genuine truth. If people stay in their religion and believe in God, or—if Christians—they believe in the Lord, regard the Word as holy, and follow the Ten Commandments for religious reasons, then they simply will not swear allegiance to things that are false. Therefore, when they hear truths and see them in their own way they are able to embrace those truths and be led away from false notions. This is not true of people who have become adamant about false teachings in their religion. A false teaching that is adamantly believed is permanent. It cannot be uprooted. A false concept that people have reinforced in themselves is like something they have sworn allegiance to, especially if it ties in with their love for themselves or their pride in their own intelligence.

In the spiritual world I have spoken with people who lived hundreds of years ago who had become adamantly devoted to false ideas in their religion. I learned that these people still consistently maintain these ideas. I have also spoken with people in the spiritual world who had belonged to the same religion and had had the same thoughts as these others but who had not become adamant about these false ideas inside themselves. I learned that when the latter people were taught by angels they rejected these false ideas and embraced true ones. They were saved, but the others were not. **255**

After we die we are all taught by angels. If we can see truths, and can see falsities in contrast to truths, we are accepted [into heaven]. The only people who are able to see truths, however, are those who have not reinforced false ideas in themselves. Those who have reinforced false ideas are unwilling to see truths. If they see truths, they turn away and either laugh at what they have seen or falsify it. The real reason for this is that becoming adamant enters the will, and the will is the real person. The will controls the intellect as it wishes. Merely knowing something enters only the intellect, and the intellect has no jurisdiction over the will. Knowledge, therefore, is not really inside us, just as someone who is standing on a porch or in an entrance is not really inside the house.

Let me illustrate this with an example. Many passages in the Word attribute anger, wrath, and revenge to God; many passages say that God punishes people, throws them into hell, tempts them, and many other things like that. People who believe this in a simple, childlike way, and who therefore fear God and take care not to sin against him, are not condemned for having this simple belief. People are condemned, however, if they reinforce this idea in themselves to the point of believing that God has anger, wrath, and revenge, and therefore has evil traits, and that God angrily, wrathfully, and vengefully punishes us and throws us into hell. The reason these people are condemned is that they have done away with the real truth, which is that God is absolute love, absolute mercy, and absolute goodness, and someone who is all these things cannot be **256** angry, wrathful, or vengeful. The Word attributes these qualities to God because this is the way it seems. Things like this are apparent truths.

257 Many things in the Word's literal meaning are apparent truths. Real truths lie hidden inside them. It is not a damning thing to think and say apparent truths in a simple way. It is damning, however, to become adamant about apparent truths, since our becoming adamant destroys the divine truth that lies hidden inside them.

An example from nature can illustrate this. I cite it because something from nature provides clearer illustration and teaching than something spiritual.

To our eyes it seems that the sun goes around the earth once a day, and also once a year. On this basis we say that the sun rises and sets, which makes morning, midday, evening, and night, and also affects our time of year—the spring, summer, fall, and winter; its "motion" shapes both days and years. Yet in fact the sun remains motionless. It is an ocean of fire. The earth spins every day, and orbits the sun every year. People who simply or ignorantly think that the sun is moving around the earth do not destroy an idea that is physically true, which is that the earth rotates on its axis and follows the ecliptic in its yearly orbit. If, however, people rigidly believe the appearance that the sun is moving and use the reasoning of their earthly self as reinforcement, and especially if they use the Word's statements that the sun rises and sets as reinforcement, they undermine and destroy the truth.[475] Afterward, they can scarcely see the true reality, even if you visibly demonstrate to them that the whole starry heaven seems to move daily and yearly in the same way as the sun and yet not a single star changes its location relative to another.[476]

The sun's movement is an apparent truth. Its lack of movement is a genuine truth. Yet we all speak according to the apparent truth when we say that the sun rises and sets. This is acceptable. How else would we say it? But adamant loyalty to the appearance in our thinking weakens and darkens our rational understanding.

258 Becoming adamant about apparent truths in the Word leads us to damnation because it takes those apparent truths in the wrong way and destroys the divine truth they have inside. The reason for this is that each and every thing in the Word's literal meaning communicates with heaven. As I have shown above [§§196–200, 248–253], within each and every detail of the literal meaning there is a spiritual meaning. The spiritual meaning opens as the literal meaning passes from us to heaven.

Everything in the spiritual meaning is genuinely true. For this reason, when we have false ideas and apply the literal meaning to them, then our reading becomes entangled in false ideas; and when false ideas come in, true ideas are lost along the way between us and heaven.

For an analogy to this interaction, imagine someone throwing a balloon full of bile toward you, but before it reaches you the balloon bursts in midair and the bile goes in all directions. Aware that there is bile in the air, you turn away and shut your mouth so the bile will not touch your tongue.

Or imagine traveling with a jar that is cushioned by boughs of cedar. Inside the jar there is vinegar that is full of worms. During the journey, the jar breaks. Another passenger catches a whiff of it and, feeling nauseous, immediately grabs something to fan the smell away before it becomes overwhelming.

Or imagine an almond shell that has a tiny newborn snake inside it instead of an almond. Someone breaks open the shell and the wind carries the tiny snake right toward your eyes.[477] Clearly, you would try to turn away before it hit you.

Similar things happen when the Word is read by people who have false ideas and who apply statements from the Word's literal meaning to those false ideas. En route to heaven, their reading is rejected to prevent it from flowing in and assaulting the angels. When falsity touches truth, it is like the point of a needle touching a fibril of your nervous system or the pupil of your eye. Science knows that the fibril of a nerve will immediately recoil and bunch up. In a similar way, as soon as something touches your eye, your eyelid closes. Clearly then, truth that has been falsified breaks and closes the channel of communication with heaven. This is why it is damning to become adamant about some heretical falsity.

The Word is like a garden—it ought to be called a heavenly paradise. In that garden there are delicacies and pleasures of every kind. There are delicacies made with the different kinds of fruit and pleasures to be had from the flowers. In the middle of the garden there are trees of life with fountains of living water next to them. Surrounding the garden are the trees of a forest.

259

People who have divine truths because they have a body of teaching are in the middle of the garden where the trees of life stand. These people actively enjoy the garden's delicacies and pleasures. People who have truths from the literal meaning but no body of teaching are in the surrounding area; all they see are the things in the forest. People whose body of religious teaching is false and who have become inwardly adamant about that falsity are not even in the forest; they are outside it on sand flats where not even grass will grow. In fact, this is the actual condition in which they find themselves after death, as the work *Heaven and Hell* has shown.[478]

260   It is important to know as well that the literal meaning is a protection to prevent harm to the genuine truths that lie inside it. The nature of this protection is that the literal meaning can be turned this way and that and explained to different levels of comprehension without damaging or violating what is inside. It does no harm if one person takes the literal meaning one way and another takes it another way. It *is* harmful, however, if people bring in false ideas that go against divine truths. Only people who are adamant about falsities do this. Doing so does violence to the Word. The literal meaning offers protection to prevent this from happening. It also offers protection to people who have been given false ideas by their religion but have not become adamant about them.

The angel guardians in the Word both stand for and portray the protecting role of the Word's literal meaning. This protection is the meaning of the angel guardians who were placed at the entrance of the garden of Eden after Adam was thrown out with his wife. About this we read,

> When Jehovah God expelled the human, he made *angel guardians* dwell on the east side of the garden of Eden and made the flame of a sword turning this way and that to guard the pathway to the tree of life. (Genesis 3:23, 24)

[2] No one could see what these details mean without knowing the meaning of "angel guardians," "the garden of Eden," the garden's "tree of life," and "the flame of a sword turning this way and that." These details have been explained in the relevant chapter of *Secrets of Heaven,* published in London [§§305–313]. To be specific, the "angel guardians" mean protection. The "pathway to the tree of life" means the access to the Lord available to people through the truths in the Word's spiritual meaning. The "flame of a sword turning" means divine truth on the outermost level, which is like the Word in its literal meaning; it is similarly capable of being turned this way and that.

The same thing is meant by the *angel guardians made of gold* that were placed on the two ends of the mercy seat that was on top of the ark in the tabernacle (Exodus 25:18–21). The "ark" meant the Word because the Ten Commandments are the most basic thing in the Word. The "angel guardians" meant protection, which is why the Lord spoke with Moses from between the angel guardians (Exodus 25:22; 37:9; Numbers 7:89). Further, the Lord spoke to Moses in the earthly meaning because he does not speak with us unless he speaks in a complete way, and divine truth has its complete form in the literal meaning (see §§214–224 above).

The *angel guardians* on the curtains and the veil in the tabernacle (Exodus 26:31) had a similar meaning. The curtains and the veil in the tabernacle meant the outermost aspects of heaven and the church; therefore they meant the outermost aspects of the Word as well (see §220 above).

The same applies to the *angel guardians* carved on the walls and doors of the Temple in Jerusalem (1 Kings 6:29, 32, 35); see §221 above. Likewise, the *angel guardians* in the new temple (Ezekiel 41:18, 19, 20).

[3] Angel guardians mean the protection that prevents people from going directly to the Lord, heaven, and the divine truth in the form it takes inside the Word, and steers them instead to go indirectly through the [Word's] outermost level. For this reason we read the following statements about the king of Tyre:

> You who seal up your measurement; full of wisdom and perfect in beauty, you were in the Garden of Eden. Every precious stone was your covering. You, *O angel guardian,* were the stretching out of a covering. I lost you, *O protecting angel guardian,* in the midst of the stones of fire. (Ezekiel 28:12, 13, 14, 16)

"Tyre" means the church's knowledge of goodness and truth. "The king of Tyre" means the Word where that knowledge exists and originates. The king clearly means the Word on its outermost level and the angel guardian means protection, because it says, "You who seal up your measurement," "every precious stone is your covering," "you, O angel guardian, were the stretching out of a covering," and "O protecting angel guardian." On the precious stones listed in that passage as referring to aspects of the literal meaning, see §§217, 218 above. Since "angel guardians" mean the Word at the outermost level and protection as well, therefore we read the following phrases in David:

> Jehovah bowed down the heavens and came down. He rode upon an angel guardian. (Psalms 18:9, 10)

Shine forth, O Shepherd of Israel who sits upon angel guardians. (Psalms 80:1)

Jehovah sitting upon angel guardians. (Psalms 99:1)

Riding and sitting "upon angel guardians" refers to the Word's outermost meaning.

The Word's divine truth and the qualities of that truth are portrayed by four creatures that are also called angel guardians (Ezekiel 1, 9, 10), and by four creatures in the middle of the throne and next to it (Revelation 4:6–7). See *Revelation Unveiled* (which I published in Amsterdam) §§239, 275, 314.

II

While in the World, the Lord Fulfilled Everything in the Word; by Doing So He Became the Word or Divine Truth Even on the Last or Outermost Level

261 The fact that in the world the Lord fulfilled everything in the Word, and by doing so became divine truth or the Word even on the last or outermost level,[479] is what the following words in John mean:

And the Word became flesh and lived among us; and we saw his glory, glory like that of the only begotten child of the Father. He was full of grace and truth. (John 1:14)

"Becoming flesh" means becoming the Word on the last or outermost level.

When the Lord was transfigured, he showed his disciples his qualities as the Word on the last or outermost level (Matthew 17:2 and following; Mark 9:2 and following; Luke 9:28 and following). There it says that Moses and Elijah appeared in glory. "Moses" means the Word that was written by Moses, and the historical Word in general. "Elijah" means the prophetical Word. The Lord was represented as the Word on the last or outermost level to John as well (Revelation 1:13–16). All the details of that description of the Lord mean the last or outermost features of divine truth or the Word.

The Lord was of course the Word or divine truth before he came, but only on the first or inmost level. We read, "In the beginning was the

Word, and the Word was with God, and *the Word was God"* (John 1:1, 2). When the Word became flesh, however, the Lord became the Word even on the last or outermost level. This is why the Lord is called *the First and the Last* (Revelation 1:8, 11, 17; 2:8; 21:6; 22:12, 13; Isaiah 44:6).

The fact that the Lord fulfilled everything in the Word is clear from passages where it says that he fulfilled the law and the Scripture, and completed all things. For example,

262

> Jesus said, "Do not think that I came to dissolve the Law and the Prophets. I did not come to dissolve them but to fulfill them." (Matthew 5:17, 18)

> Jesus went into the synagogue and stood up to read. He was handed the book of the prophet Isaiah. He unrolled the scroll and found the place where it was written, "The spirit of Jehovah is upon me; this is why he anointed me. He sent me to preach the good news to the poor, to heal the brokenhearted, to proclaim release for the bound and sight for the blind, to preach the welcomed year of the Lord." Afterward he rolled up the scroll and said, *"Today this Scripture has been fulfilled in your hearing."* (Luke 4:16–21)

> To *fulfill the Scripture* that said, "The one who eats bread with me has lifted up his heel against me." (John 13:18)

> Not one of them was lost except the son of perdition, so that *the Scripture would be fulfilled.* (John 17:12)

> To *fulfill the Word* that said, "Of those whom you gave me, I did not lose one." (John 18:19)

> Jesus said to Peter, "Put your sword away in its place. *How then would the Scripture* that this must occur *be fulfilled?* This has happened in order to *fulfill the Scripture."* (Matthew 26:52, 54, 56)

> The Son of Humankind is leaving as *it was written* of him, so that *the Scriptures would be fulfilled.* (Mark 14:21, 49)

> In this way *the Scripture was fulfilled* that said, "He was reckoned among the unholy." (Mark 15:28; Luke 22:37)

> They divided his clothes among themselves, so that *the Scripture would be fulfilled:* "On my inner garment they cast lots." (John 19:24)

> After this, Jesus knew that all things were now completed so that *the Scripture would be fulfilled.* (John 19:28)

When Jesus had received the vinegar he said, "It is *complete,*" that is, *fulfilled.* (John 19:30)

These things happened to *fulfill the Scripture* that "You will not break a bone in him"; and furthermore another line in *Scripture says,* "They will see the One whom they pierced." (John 19:36, 37)

Before the Lord left, he taught his disciples that the whole Word was written about him and that he had come into the world to fulfill it, as the following words indicate:

He said to them, "You are foolish and slow at heart to believe all the things that were spoken by the prophets. Was it not fitting for Christ to suffer and enter into glory?" Then beginning with *Moses and all the Prophets,* he interpreted [points] *regarding himself in all the Scriptures.* (Luke 24:25, 26, 27)

Further, Jesus said,

It was right for all the things written about me in the Law of Moses and the Prophets and Psalms to be fulfilled. (Luke 24:44, 45)

The following words of the Lord make it clear that in the world he fulfilled everything in the Word down to the least detail:

Truly I tell you, until heaven and earth pass away, *not one little letter or the tip of one letter*[480] *will pass from the law until all of it is fulfilled.* (Matthew 5:18)

From the statements just made you can now clearly see that the Lord's fulfilling everything in the law does not mean that he fulfilled everything in the Ten Commandments; it means that he fulfilled everything in the whole Word. You can see that "the law" means everything in the Word from the following passages: "Jesus said, 'Is it not written in *your law,* "I said, 'You are gods'"?'" (John 10:34; the passage quoted is written in Psalms 82:6). "The crowd replied, 'We have heard from the *law,* "Christ remains forever"'" (John 12:34; the passage quoted is written in Psalms 89:34–37; 110:4; and Daniel 7:14). "To fulfill the Word that is written in *their law,* 'They hated me for no reason'" (John 15:25; the passage quoted is written in Psalms 35:19). "It is easier for heaven and earth to pass away than for the tip of one letter of the law to fall" (Luke 16:17). The "law" in these passages means the whole of Sacred Scripture, as it does a number of times elsewhere.[481]

Few people understand how the Lord is the Word. People think that **263** the Lord is able to enlighten and teach us through the Word but that we could not call him the Word on that account.

We need to realize that we are all our own will and our own intellect. This is how one person is differentiated from another. Since the will is a vessel for love and for all the forms of goodness that relate to that love, and the intellect is a vessel for wisdom and for all the forms of truth that relate to that wisdom, it follows that we are all our own love and our own wisdom, or what is the same thing, our own goodness and our own truth. Humans are not human on any other basis; and nothing else in us is human.

In the Lord's case, he is love itself and wisdom itself, and therefore goodness itself and truth itself. He became all this through fulfilling all the goodness and all the truth in the Word. Someone who thinks and speaks only the truth becomes that truth. Someone who intends and does only what is good becomes that goodness. Because the Lord fulfilled all the divine truth and divine goodness that are in the Word—both the truth and goodness in its earthly meaning and the truth and goodness in its spiritual meaning—he became goodness itself and truth itself, and therefore became the Word.

12

Before the Word That Exists in the World Today,
There Was a Word That Has Been Lost

Before the Word existed that was given through Moses and the prophets **264** among the Israelite nation, people knew a form of worship through sacrifices, and their prophets spoke the word of Jehovah. This is clear from things mentioned in the books of Moses.

The following is evidence that *people knew a form of worship through sacrifices:* The children of Israel were commanded to overturn the altars of other nations, shatter their statues, and cut down their groves (Exodus 34:13; Deuteronomy 7:5; 12:3). "At Acacia, Israel began to commit harlotry with the daughters of Moab; they invited the people to *sacrifices* for their gods, and the people ate" (Numbers 25:1, 2, 3). Balaam, who was from Syria, built altars and sacrificed oxen and sheep (Numbers 22:40;

23:1, 2, 14, 29, 30). Balaam also *gave a prophecy about the Lord* saying, "A star will rise out of Jacob and a scepter out of Israel" (Numbers 24:17); and Balaam *spoke the word of Jehovah in prophecy* (Numbers 22:13, 18; 23:3, 5, 8, 16, 26; 24:1, 13).

The passages just given make it clear that a divine worship existed among other nations that was virtually the same as the worship instituted by Moses among the Israelite nation. From words in Moses (Deuteronomy 32:7, 8) it appears that this worship existed even before the time of Abraham. This is still clearer from Melchizedek, king of Salem, who brought out bread and wine and blessed Abram, and Abram in turn gave Melchizedek tithes of all he possessed (Genesis 14:18–20). Melchizedek represented the Lord—he is called a priest to God the Highest (Genesis 14:18). In David it says of the Lord, "You are a priest forever on the order of Melchizedek" (Psalms 110:4). This is why Melchizedek brought out bread and wine as the holiest things in the church, just as bread and wine are holy in the Holy Supper also. Besides many others, these things are outstanding indications that before the Israelite Word there was a Word that gave these revelations.

265   The works of Moses make it clear that there was a Word among earlier people.[482] Moses cites it and quotes something from it (Numbers 21:14, 15, 27–30). The historical part of that Word was called *The Wars of Jehovah,* and its prophetical part was called *The Pronouncements.*

From the *historical* part of that Word, Moses quoted the following:

> Therefore it says in the *Book of the Wars of Jehovah:* "I was going to Suphah and the brooks of the Arnon, and the channel of the rivers of water that sloped down where Ar is living and then appears by the border of Moab." (Numbers 21:14, 15)

The "wars of Jehovah" in that Word, like the wars in ours, meant and depicted the Lord's battles with the hells and victory over them when he would come into the world. The same battles are meant and depicted in the historical portions of our Word[483]—for example, Joshua's wars with the nations in the land of Canaan and the wars waged by the judges and the kings of Israel.

[2] The following is a quotation from the *prophetic* parts of that Word:

> Therefore the *Makers of Pronouncements*[484] say: "Walk to Heshbon. The city of Sihon will be built and reinforced. For a fire went out from Heshbon, a flame from the city of Sihon; it consumed Ar of Moab, the

possessors of the heights of the Arnon. Woe to you, Moab. You have perished, O people of Chemosh. He has given his sons as fugitives and his daughters into captivity to Sihon, king of the Amorites. We killed them with arrows. Heshbon has perished all the way to Dibon, and we devastated [it] all the way to Nophah, which [stretches] all the way to Medeba." (Numbers 21:27–30)

Translators have rendered the name here as "the Makers of Proverbs," but it ought to be "the Makers of Pronouncements" or "the Prophetic Pronouncements." This is clear from the meaning of the word *meshalim* in Hebrew: it means not only proverbs but also prophetic pronouncements. For example, in Numbers 23:7, 18 and 24:3, 15 it says that Balaam gave *his pronouncement,* which was in fact a prophecy about the Lord. His pronouncement is called a *mashal,* which is the singular.[485] For another thing, the material that Moses quotes from that Word is in fact prophecies, not proverbs.

[3] That Word was just as divinely inspired. This is clear from Jeremiah where we read almost identical words:

A fire went out from Heshbon and a flame from the midst of Sihon that consumed the corner of Moab and the top of the children of tumult. Woe to you, Moab. The people of Chemosh have perished. For they have taken your sons into captivity and your daughters into captivity. (Jeremiah 48:45, 46)

Both David and Joshua also mention a prophetic book of the ancient Word called the *Book of Jasher* ("Book of the Upright Person"). David refers to it thus:

David lamented over Saul and over Jonathan and wrote to teach the children of Judah the bow; look at what was written in the *Book of Jasher.* (2 Samuel 1:17, 18)

And Joshua refers to it thus:

Joshua said, "O sun, stand still in Gibeon. O moon, stand still in the valley of Aijalon. Is this not written in the *Book of Jasher?*" (Joshua 10:12)

Clearly then, there was an ancient Word on earth, especially in the Middle East, that predated the Israelite Word. This earlier Word is still extant in heaven among the angels who lived during those centuries. It is

266

also still extant today among the nations in Great Tartary, as you can see from the third memorable occurrence after this treatment on the Sacred Scripture [§279].

13

Because of the Word,
Even People Who Are outside the Church
and Who Do Not Have the Word
Have Light

267 No connection to heaven is possible unless somewhere on earth there is a church where the Word exists and where the Lord is known through that Word. This is because the Lord is the God of heaven and earth—without the Lord there is no salvation. (For the Word providing a connection to the Lord and association with angels, see §§234–239 above.) It is enough if there is one church where the Word exists. Even if this church consists of comparatively few people, still the Lord is present throughout the world by means of the Word, since heaven is connected to the human race through the Word.

268 Now to say how the Word allows people throughout all parts of the world to experience the presence of, and a connection to, the Lord and heaven. To the Lord the entire angelic heaven is like one person. The same is true for the church across the earth. (For heaven and the church actually appearing as a human, see *Heaven and Hell* 59–86). The church where the Word is read and where the Lord is therefore known is like the heart and the lungs in that human being. The Lord's heavenly kingdom is like the heart, and his spiritual kingdom is like the lungs. Just as all the other limbs, internal organs, and parts of the human body have life and continued existence because of these two fountains of life, so too all the people around the world who have a religion, worship one God, and live good lives have life and continued existence because the church is connected to the Lord and heaven through the Word. Non-Christians are in that human being and play the part of its limbs and internal organs outside the thorax that holds the heart and lungs. Non-Christians have life from the Lord through heaven because of the Word in the Christian church, just as the limbs and organs throughout the body have life because of the heart and lungs. There is also a similar exchange between them.

This is also the reason why Christians who read the Word make up the chest of that [giant] human being. They are in fact central among all people. Surrounding them are Catholics.[486] Surrounding the Catholics are Muslims who acknowledge the Lord as the greatest prophet or the Son of God.[487] Farther out than these are Africans. People and nations in the Middle East and the Indies make up the farthest circumference.

One can determine that the whole of heaven is like this from a similar situation that exists in every individual community in heaven. Every community is a heaven in a smaller form, but a form that is nonetheless human. (On this situation, see §§41–86 in the work *Heaven and Hell*.) In every community in heaven, angels who are at the center of the community similarly play the role of the heart and the lungs. They have the most light. That light and a resulting awareness of truth spread out toward the edges in every direction—to all who are in the community—and give them spiritual life. It was once demonstrated that when the angels at the center, who constitute the realm of the heart and the lungs and who have the most light, were taken away, the angels around them came into an intellectual shadow and into so little awareness of truth that they started lamenting. As soon as the central angels returned, however, the others saw the light again and had the awareness of truth they had had before.

You could draw a comparison with heat and light from the sun in our world. They give trees and shrubs the power to grow even if the sun is low or behind a cloud, provided it is above the horizon. It is the same for the light and heat of heaven that come from the Lord as the sun there. That light is essentially the divine truth, the source of all the intelligence and wisdom that angels and people have. This is why we read that the Word was with God and was God, that it enlightens everyone who comes into the world, and that this light shines even in the darkness (John 1:1, 5, 9). "The Word" here means the Lord in his role as divine truth.

You can see then that the Word that exists among Protestants and the Reformed enlightens all nations and peoples through a spiritual communication. You can also see that the Lord ensures that there is always a church on earth where the Word is being read and the Lord is becoming known through it. When the Word was virtually rejected by Catholics,[488] in the Lord's divine providence the Reformation took place. As a result, the Word was taken from its hiding places, so to speak, and put to use. In fact, when the Word among the Jewish nation had been thoroughly falsified and contaminated, and more or less ceased to be the Word, then the Lord chose to come down from heaven, become the Word, and fulfill it.[489] By doing this he put the Word back together and restored it, giving light once again to the inhabitants of our world, as the Lord himself says in these words: "The people sitting in darkness have seen a great light; on the people sitting in the realm and shadow of death the light has dawned" (Isaiah 9:2; Matthew 4:16).

271   It has been predicted that at the end of this church darkness will arise again through ignorance that the Lord is the God of heaven and earth and through separation of faith from goodwill. Therefore to prevent the loss of a genuine understanding of the Word and a consequent loss of the church, the Lord has now chosen to reveal the spiritual meaning of the Word. He has chosen to reveal the fact that in this meaning, and from it in the earthly meaning, the Word contains countless things for restoring the church's light of truth, which has almost gone out.

Many passages in the Book of Revelation predict that at the end of this church the light of truth will almost go out. This is also the meaning of the following words of the Lord:

> Immediately after the affliction of those days, the sun will be darkened and the moon will not give its light; the stars will fall from heaven and the powers of the heavens will be shaken. Then they will see the Son of Humankind coming in the clouds of heaven with glory and power. (Matthew 24:29, 30)

"The sun" here means love for the Lord, "the moon" means faith in the Lord, and "the stars" mean concepts of what is good and true. "The Son of Humankind" means the Lord in his role as the Word. "The cloud" means the Word's literal meaning, and "the glory" means the Word's spiritual meaning and the way it shines through the literal meaning. "The powers" mean the Word's power.

272   An abundance of experience has taught me that human beings have a communication with heaven through the Word. When I read the Word through from the first chapter in Isaiah to the last chapter in Malachi and the Psalms of David, and I kept thinking about their spiritual meaning, I was given a clear perception that every verse communicates with some community in heaven, and therefore the whole Word communicates with the entirety of heaven. This made it clear to me that as the Lord is the Word, heaven is also the Word, since heaven is heaven from the Lord, and by means of the Word the Lord is everything to all heaven.

14

If the Word Did Not Exist,
No One Would Know about God, Heaven, Hell,
or Life after Death,
Still Less about the Lord

There are people who put forward the idea (something they have become **273** inwardly adamant about) that without the Word people would still know of the existence of God and of heaven and hell, as well as the other things the Word teaches about.[490] You cannot deal with such people on the basis of the Word; you have to use the earthly light of reason, because they believe in themselves, not the Word.

Investigate by using the light of your reason and you will find that there are two faculties of life in us. They are called the intellect and the will. The intellect is subject to the will, but the will is not subject to the intellect. The intellect only teaches and points out what we should be wanting and doing. As a result, many people have sharp minds and understand life's morality better than others, and yet do not live by it. Things would be different if these people wanted to be moral. Investigate further and you will find that we identify with our will. From the day we are born, our will is evil, and that produces falsity in our intellect.

When you have found this out, you will see another thing: left on our own, we do not want to understand anything that does not come from the self that we experience in our own will. And if there were no other source of knowledge, we would have no desire to understand anything unrelated to ourselves or our world; everything beyond our world would be in pitch darkness. For example, when we saw the sun, the moon, and the stars, if we happened to think about their origin, we could not help thinking they originated from us. This thinking is no deeper than that of scholars in our world who acknowledge the existence of nature alone[491] even though they know from the Word that all things were created by God. What would they be thinking if they had known nothing from the Word?

Did the classical philosophers such as Aristotle, Cicero, Seneca,[492] and the others, who wrote about God and the immortality of the soul, originally derive those concepts from their own intellects? No, they derived them from others who passed them on from still others who first learned them from the ancient Word that we mentioned earlier [§§264–266]. The writers of natural theology,[493] too, derive none of this type of thought from themselves; they merely use their rationality to establish concepts they learned from their church, which has the Word. There may even be some among them who defend spiritual concepts and yet do not believe them themselves.

274 I have been given the opportunity to see people born on islands who were reasonable about civic issues but knew nothing at all about God. In the spiritual world they look like baboons. Because they have been born human and therefore have a capacity for receiving spiritual life, they are taught by angels and are brought to life by concepts of the Lord as a human being.

What human beings are like when left to themselves becomes obvious from the people who are in hell. Some such people are scholars and leaders of the church who do not want even to hear about God; they certainly cannot mention God themselves. I have seen people like this and have talked to them. I have also talked to people who would explode with rage and anger when they heard anyone talk about the Lord.

On this basis, then, consider what people would be like if they had never heard about God, when this is what some people are like even though they have spoken about God, written about God, and preached about God.

People are like this because of their wills, which are evil. Their wills, as I said before, control their intellects and take away the truth that is in them from the Word.

If people had the capability of knowing on their own that there is a God and a life after death, why would they not know that we live on as people after death? Why would they believe that our soul or spirit is like wind or ether? Why would they imagine the spirit to be something that has no eyes to see with, no ears to hear with, no mouth to speak with—at least not before it rejoins its corpse and skeleton?[494]

Imagine a body of teaching that was hatched solely by the light of our own reason. Would it not teach that the proper object of worship ought to be we ourselves? This has in fact been taught for centuries and is still being taught now by people who know from the Word that God alone is to be worshiped. No other form of worship generated by us is possible—not even worship of the sun or the moon.

275 Since the earliest times, religion has existed and the inhabitants of our planet have known about God and something about life after death. People did not receive this knowledge from themselves or their own

intelligence; they received it from the ancient Word discussed above (§§264–266). Later on people received this knowledge from the Israelite Word. From these two Words, religious concepts spread to the Indies and their islands; through Egypt and Ethiopia into the countries of Africa; and from the coastal regions of the Middle East into Greece and from there into Italy.

Because that Word could be written only in language that was highly symbolic, using things in the world that correspond to and therefore stand for things in heaven, the nations eventually turned its religious concepts into idolatrous concepts—in Greece into myths—and turned divine attributes and characteristics into as many gods. Over these gods they placed a supreme god whom they called Jove, perhaps from Jehovah.[495]

It is generally known that they had a concept of paradise, a flood, sacred fire, and four ages—starting with the golden age and ending with the iron age, as recorded in Daniel 2:31–35.[496]

People who think their own intelligence could develop concepts of God, heaven and hell, and the spiritual things that the church teaches do not realize that our earthly self is intrinsically opposed to our spiritual self. Our earthly self tries either to uproot any spiritual things that come in or else to cover them in false concepts that are like grubs that devour the roots of vegetables and grains. **276**

People like this could be compared to people who dream that they are sitting on eagles and soaring on high, or sitting on Pegasuses and flying over Mount Parnassus toward Mount Helicon,[497] while they are actually like Lucifers in hell who nevertheless still call themselves children of the dawn (Isaiah 14:12).

They are like the people of the valley in the land of Shinar who set out to build a tower[498] whose top would reach to heaven (Genesis 11:2, 4). They are as confident in themselves as Goliath, not foreseeing that they could be laid out, as he was, by a single stone driven by a sling into their forehead.[499]

I should say what outcome awaits them after death. They first become like drunks, then silly, and finally brainless, and they sit in the dark. Be wary therefore of insanity like this.

❧   ❧   ❧   ❧   ❧

To these points I will add the following memorable occurrences. **277**

The first memorable occurrence. One day in the spirit I was touring various sites in the spiritual world for the purpose of observing the symbolic depictions of heavenly things that are on display in many locations there. In one home where there were angels I saw two large purses in which was concealed a significant quantity of silver. Because these money bags had been opened I was aware that anyone could take out the silver that had been deposited in them and even make off with it; however, there were two young men sitting next to the money bags as guards. The place where the bags had been deposited looked like a manger in a stable. In the next room, I noticed some modest young women and a faithful wife. Two little children were standing just outside that room. I was told not to play in a childish way with them but to treat them wisely. Afterward a whore appeared, and a horse that was lying dead.

After I had seen these displays, I was told that what I had seen represented the Word's earthly meaning with its spiritual meaning inside it. The large purses full of silver meant true concepts in tremendous quantities. The fact that the bags had been opened but were guarded by young men meant that any of us can get true concepts from the Word, but we have to be careful to avoid violating the spiritual meaning, which contains truths and nothing else. The manger in a kind of stable meant spiritual nourishment for the intellect. Mangers have this meaning because the horses that eat from them mean the intellect. The modest young women seen in the next room meant different kinds of love for the truth, and the faithful wife meant the union of goodness and truth. The little children meant a wise kind of innocence—the angels of the highest heaven, who are the wisest angels, look like little children from a distance because of their innocence. The whore and the dead horse meant that many people are falsifying the truth nowadays, causing the loss of all understanding of truth. A whore means falsification, and a dead horse means no understanding of the truth.

278 *The second memorable occurrence.* Once a sheet of paper was sent down to me from heaven that was full of writing in Hebrew lettering, but written in the way the ancients used to write. Letters that today are largely straight were curved then and had little horns or tips[500] that turned upward. Angels who were with me at the time said they knew whole meanings just from the letters. They derived these meanings especially from the curvature of the lines and of the tips of the letters. They explained what these meant individually and in combination. They said that the letter "h," which was added to both Abram and Sarai's names, meant infinity and eternity. They also explained to me the meaning of Psalm 32:2[501] in the Word on the basis of the letters alone. Taken all together the meaning of the letters was that *the Lord is also compassionate to those who do evil.*

The angels told me that the writing in the third heaven consists of letters that are bent and curved in various ways, each of which contains some meaning. The vowels in that writing indicate sounds that correspond to different feelings of love. Angels in that heaven cannot pronounce the vowel sounds of "i" and "e," so instead they use "y" and "eu." They do use the vowel sounds of "a," "o," and "u" since these give a full sound. There are some consonantal letters that these angels pronounce as soft rather than hard. This is why some Hebrew letters have a dot inside them as a sign to pronounce them as [hard, and no dot as a sign to pronounce them as] soft.[502] They said that pronouncing these letters as hard was practiced in the spiritual heaven because the angels there focus on truths and truth allows for hardness. The goodness among angels in the Lord's heavenly kingdom (the third heaven) does not allow for hardness. The angels [with me] said that the written Word they have also has curved letters with meaningful horns or tips.

All this makes it clear what these sayings of the Lord's mean: "Not one little letter or the tip of one letter will pass from the law until all of it is fulfilled" (Matthew 5:18); and "It is easier for heaven and earth to pass away than for the tip of one letter of the law to fall" (Luke 16:17).

The third memorable occurrence. Seven years ago, when I was remembering that Moses mentions two books called *The Wars of Jehovah* and *The Pronouncements* (Numbers 21), some angels became present and said to me that these books were the ancient Word.[503] Its *historical portion* was called *The Wars of Jehovah* and its *prophetical portion* was called *The Pronouncements.* The angels said that that Word is still preserved in heaven and is used by ancient peoples there who had had that Word when they were in the world. Some of the ancient peoples who are still using that Word in heaven came from the land of Canaan and its neighbors, such as Syria, Mesopotamia, Arabia, Chaldea, Assyria; Egypt; and Sidon, Tyre, and Nineveh. The people in all these countries had symbolic worship and therefore studied correspondences. The wisdom of their times was in fact based on the study of correspondences. That study gave them inner awareness and communication with the heavens. The people who knew the correspondences in that Word were called "the wise" and "the intelligent." Later they were called "diviners" and "magi."

[2] Since that Word was full of correspondences that referred indirectly to heavenly and spiritual realities, and consequently many people

279

began to falsify its correspondences, by the Lord's divine providence that Word disappeared over the course of time.

Another Word, written in correspondences that were less indirect, was given through the prophets of the children of Israel. In it many of the names of places were retained—places not only in the land of Canaan but also in the surrounding areas in the Middle East. All these names referred to aspects and conditions of the church. Their meanings were taken over from the ancient Word. This is why Abram was commanded to go into that country and why his descendants through Jacob were established there.

[3] Here I am allowed to relate something previously unknown about the ancient Word that used to exist in the Middle East before the Israelite Word: it is still preserved among the peoples who live in Great Tartary.

I have spoken with spirits and angels in the spiritual world who were originally from that area. They said that they possessed this Word and had done so since ancient times; that they followed this Word in conducting their divine worship; and that their Word consisted entirely of correspondences.

They said that their Word included the *Book of Jasher* that is mentioned in Joshua 10:12, 13, and 2 Samuel 1:17, 18. Other books it contains are *The Wars of Jehovah* and *The Pronouncements,* which are mentioned by Moses (Numbers 21:14, 15, 27–30). When I read these people the words that Moses quoted from it, they looked up the passages to see whether the words were still in their text, and they found the passages. These events made it clear to me that the ancient Word still exists among them. During our conversation they said that they worship Jehovah. Some of them worship Jehovah as a God who can be seen, some as a God who cannot be seen.

[4] They went on to say that they do not let in foreign immigrants except the Chinese, with whom they have peaceful relations because the Chinese emperor is from their area. They also said that their territory is so heavily populated that they cannot imagine that any other part of the entire world is populated more heavily. This seems plausible given the many miles of the Great Wall that the Chinese once built to protect themselves from an invasion of these people.[504]

I have also heard from angels that the first chapters in Genesis, which deal with creation, Adam and Eve, the garden of Eden, their children and descendants right down to the flood, and also Noah and his children, are in that Word as well. Moses copied these stories from that Word.

The angels and spirits from Great Tartary are found in a southern region toward the east. They are separated from all others by their location on a high plateau. They do not let in people from the Christian world. If some manage to climb up to them, they put them under guard to keep them from leaving. The reason for this separation is that they have a different Word.

The fourth memorable occurrence. Once from far away I saw paths that lay between rows of trees. Young people were gathered there in discussion groups to talk about topics related to wisdom. (This was in the spiritual world.) I moved in their direction, and when I was close enough I saw that all the others revered one person as most important among them because he excelled the rest in wisdom.

280

When he saw me, he said, "I was astounded when I saw you coming along on the road, because one moment you would be in view and the next you would disappear. One moment I can see you, and then suddenly I cannot. You are definitely not in the same state of life as we are!"

Tickled by that, I said, "I am not a trickster or a magician, but I do come and go! One moment I am in the light for you, the next moment I am in the shade. In this world I am both a foreigner and a native."

The sage looked at me and said, "What you are saying is strange and amazing. Tell me who you are."

"I am in the world you used to live in and have now left," I said, "which is called the earthly or physical world. I am also in the world where you are now, called the spiritual world. As a result I am in an earthly state and a spiritual state at the same time. I am in an earthly state with people on earth and in a spiritual state with all of you. When I am in an earthly state, you do not see me. When I am in a spiritual state, you do see me. This circumstance of mine is a gift from the Lord.

"As an enlightened man, you know that people in the earthly world do not see people in the spiritual world or the reverse. Therefore when I put my spirit in my body, you do not see me, but when I take it out of my body, you do see me.[505] This happens because of the difference between what is spiritual and what is earthly."

[2] When he heard me mention the difference between what is spiritual and what is earthly, he asked, "What is the difference? Isn't it like the difference between something more pure and something less pure? What is something spiritual then, except something earthly that is just more pure?"

"That is not the nature of the difference," I replied. "No matter how subtle something earthly becomes, it will never get close to becoming something spiritual.⁵⁰⁶ The difference is like the difference between something on a prior level and something on a subsequent level—there is no finite ratio between them. The prior level is present in the subsequent level the way a cause is present in an effect; and something on a subsequent level is the result of something on a prior level the way an effect is the result of a cause. This is why the one does not appear to the other."

The wise person's response to that was, "I have meditated a great deal on this difference, but so far without results. I wish I could learn about the difference!"

I said, "Not only are you going to learn about the difference between what is spiritual and what is earthly; you will even see it for yourself."

Then I said, "You are in a spiritual state when you are with your people, but in an earthly state when you are with me. You talk to your people in a spiritual language that is shared by every spirit and angel, but you talk to me in my own vernacular. When any spirits or angels communicate with a person, they speak the person's language. With a French person, they speak French. With a Greek, they speak Greek. With an Arab they speak Arabic, and so on.

[3] "To see the difference between spiritual and earthly language, do this. Go over to your own group and say something to them. Hold on to the words, return with them in your memory, and pronounce them to me."

He did it. He returned to me with the words on his lips and pronounced them. They were totally foreign and bizarre words that do not exist in any language in the physical world. By repeating this experiment several times, it became obvious that all who are in the spiritual world have a spiritual language that has nothing in common with any earthly language, and that we all acquire that spiritual language spontaneously after we die. (On another occasion I learned that the very sound of spiritual language is so different from the sound of earthly language that no matter how loud it is, spiritual sound is completely inaudible to an earthly person, and so is earthly sound to a spiritual person.)

[4] Later on I asked the sage and the people around him to go back to their homes, write some sentence on a piece of paper, and then bring the piece of paper back to me and read it. They did so and came back with the piece of paper in hand; but when they tried to read it they could not, because the writing consisted of nothing but some letters of the alphabet with curved marks over them, each of which meant some aspect of the topic. (Because every letter of the alphabet has a meaning there, you can see why the Lord is called the Alpha and the Omega.)⁵⁰⁷

Again and again they went back home, wrote, and came back, until eventually they realized that their writing involves and contains countless things that no earthly writing could ever express. Someone said that this was the case because a spiritual person thinks things that are beyond an earthly person's words or comprehension; those things cannot be translated into any written or spoken language.

[5] At that point some of the people there were unwilling to comprehend that spiritual thinking goes so far beyond earthly thinking that it is inexpressible in comparison. For this reason I said to them, "Do an experiment. Go to your spiritual community and think about something, keep it fixed in your memory, and come back and express it to me."

They went home, had a thought, kept it fixed in their memory, and came back. When they tried to express what they had been thinking about, they could not do it. They could not find any idea in earthly thought that fit any idea in their purely spiritual thought; and because the ideas of thought become the words of language, they could find no words to express it.

By going home again and coming back again several times, they became convinced that spiritual ideas are supernatural, inexpressible, indescribable, and incomprehensible to an earthly person. Because spiritual ideas are this transcendent, the people said that spiritual ideas or thoughts, relative to earthly ones, are ideas beyond ideas and thoughts beyond thoughts, and they express qualities beyond qualities and feelings beyond feelings. Therefore spiritual thoughts are the initiation and origin of earthly thoughts. This made it clear that spiritual wisdom is wisdom beyond wisdom—it is inexpressible to any wise person in the physical world.

[6] Then a voice from a higher heaven said that there is a wisdom that is deeper or higher still, which is called heavenly wisdom. Its quality relative to spiritual wisdom is the same as spiritual wisdom's quality relative to earthly wisdom. These wisdoms flow in, heaven by heaven, from the Lord's divine wisdom, which is infinite.

At this the man who had been speaking to me said, "I now see that one earthly idea contains many spiritual ideas, and one spiritual idea contains many heavenly ideas. Another outcome of this is that something that is divided does not become simpler and simpler but instead more and more complex, because it comes closer and closer to the Infinite, in whom all things exist in an infinite way."

[7] Then I said to the people there, "On the basis of these three experimental proofs, you see the type of difference that exists between

what is spiritual and what is earthly. You also see the reason why an earthly person cannot be seen by a spiritual person or a spiritual person by an earthly person, despite the fact that all people of both kinds are in a complete human form. Because they have this form in common, it might seem that an earthly person would be able to see a spiritual person. Yet the factors that make up the form of spiritual people are inner things belonging to the mind; and the mind of spirits and angels is made of things that are spiritual, while the mind of people, as long as they are still alive in the world, is made of things that are earthly."

After that a voice was heard coming from a higher heaven saying to one of the people there, "Come up here." That person went up and came back and said that until then the angels had not known the differences between what is spiritual and what is earthly, because no one had had the opportunity to make the comparison by being in both worlds at once[508] and those differences cannot be known without comparison and contrast.

[8] Before we parted company, we discussed this topic some more. I said, "The differences we are discussing come solely from the fact that you who are in the spiritual world are essential and nonphysical. Essences are the roots of physical substances. What is matter but an aggregation of essences? Therefore you are involved in primary structures and individual essences, while we are involved in derivatives of primary structures and composites.[509] You are involved in what is particular; we are involved in what is general. Something general cannot climb onto the same level with something particular; therefore earthly things that are physical cannot climb onto the same level as spiritual things that are formed of essences any more than the cable that moors a ship could pass through the eye of a sewing needle, or any more than a nerve could fit inside one of the fibers that compose it. This then is the reason why a physical person cannot think or say what a spiritual person can. This is why Paul says that the things he heard in the third heaven were inexpressible [2 Corinthians 12:2–4].

[9] "Furthermore, to think in a spiritual way is to think apart from time and space, while to think in an earthly way is to think in terms of time and space. Every idea that comes out of earthly thinking has some aspect of time and space attached to it. This is not true, however, of spiritual ideas. The reason is that the spiritual world does not have time and space in the way the physical world does; instead the spiritual world has apparent time and space.[510]

"Thoughts and perceptions also share this difference. This is why you are capable of thinking about God's essence and omnipresence *from eternity,* meaning about God before he created the world. You think about God's essence apart from time, and you think about his omnipresence apart from space, and therefore you comprehend things that transcend earthly human ideas."

[10] At that point I related how I had once been thinking about God's essence and omnipresence from eternity, meaning that I was thinking about God before he created the world; and because I could not remove space and time from the thoughts I was having, I became distressed as I saw an idea of nature starting to replace my idea of God. Then I was told, "Remove the ideas of space and time and you will understand." I was allowed to remove them, and I understood. From that point on, I have been able to think about God from eternity, but not at all about nature from eternity. God exists in all time independently of time and in all space independently of space. Nature, on the other hand, exists in all time in time itself and in all space in space itself. Nature and its time and space had to have a beginning; God, who exists apart from time and space, did not. Nature therefore comes from God. Nature came into being in time (not from eternity) along with its own time and space.

The fifth memorable occurrence. The Lord has allowed me to be in the spiritual world and the physical world at the same time. As a result, I can talk with angels as I do with people, which has allowed me to know the states people go through as they arrive after death in that previously unknown world. I have spoken to all my friends and relatives and also to monarchs and dukes, as well as to scholars who had met their fate. I have done this continually now for twenty-seven years.[511] Therefore from my own life experiences I am able to describe the states people go through after death. I could tell you what they are like for people who have lived good lives and what they are like for people who have lived evil lives. Here I will limit myself to some facts about the states people go through if they used the Word to convince themselves of theological falsities, especially if they did so to support justification by faith alone. The successive states they go through are the following:

(1) When they have died and are spiritually coming back to their own life, which generally happens on the third day after their heart has stopped beating,[512] they seem to themselves to have the same body they had had in the world—so much so that they have no idea they are not

281

still alive in the former world. In fact, they no longer have a physical body; they now have an essential body, which seems to their senses to be physical, but it is not.

[2] (2) After several days they realize they are in a world where various different communities have been established. That world is called *the world of spirits*. It is midway between heaven and hell. All the communities there, which are beyond number, are arranged in an amazing way according to good or evil earthly desires. The communities that are arranged according to good earthly desires communicate with heaven; the communities arranged according to evil earthly desires communicate with hell.

[3] (3) The new spirits (or people who are no longer physical) are taken around and transferred to various different communities—both good and evil communities—and examined to see whether things that are good and true elicit a response in them, or things that are evil and false, and exactly what that response is.

[4] (4) If they respond to things that are good and true, they are led away from evil communities and brought into good ones, again into various different communities until they come into one that answers to their own earthly desire. There they enjoy the goodness that corresponds to that desire. This process lasts until they take off their earthly desire and put on a spiritual one. At that point they are raised up into heaven.

This is what happens to people who lived a life of goodwill in the world and a resulting life of faith—people who believed in the Lord and abstained from evil because it is sinful.

[5] (5) On the other hand, if people used reasoning to reinforce their own false convictions and beliefs—especially if they used the Word for such reinforcement—and on that basis lived a merely earthly, purely evil life (for falsities go with evils, and evils stick to falsities), they desire evil and falsity but not goodness or truth. Therefore they are led away from good communities and brought into evil communities, again into various different communities until they come to one that answers to their cravings.

[6] (6) Nevertheless, because they had outwardly pretended in the world to have good desires, even though inside they had only evil desires, or cravings, they are alternately put back into, and held in, their outer states.

The people who had been leaders of organizations in the world are given leadership roles in communities in the world of spirits. They are put in charge of larger or smaller areas depending on the breadth of the positions they had previously held. Because these people do not love truth or justice, though, and are incapable of being enlightened to the point of even knowing what truth and justice are, they are dismissed after a few days. I have seen some transferred from one community to another and given administrative responsibilities in each community, but in every case after a short while they are dismissed.

[7] (7) After being repeatedly forced out of office, some are too worn out to run for further offices, and others do not dare to do so because they are afraid of ruining their reputation; so they leave and sit around feeling depressed. Then they are taken out into the wilderness where there are shelters. They enter these shelters and are given work to do. If they do the work they get food. If they do not, they go hungry. But eventually their need for food forces them to work.

(Food there is like the food in our world, except that there it has a spiritual origin. The Lord gives food from heaven to all according to the useful things they do. None is given to idle people, because they are useless.)

[8] (8) After some time they get tired of working, so they leave the shelters. Those of them who were priests get the urge to build something. Immediately there appear heaps of hewn stones, bricks, and boards of various sizes, as well as piles of rushes, reeds, clay, plaster, and tar.

When they catch sight of these materials, they feel a burning desire to begin construction. They start constructing a building by taking a stone, then a piece of wood, then a reed, then some mortar, and they put one thing on top of another in no order, although in their sight it seems orderly. The things they build by day fall down overnight, so the next day they pick materials out of the fallen rubble and start building again. They keep doing this until they get completely tired of building.

(This happens because of a correspondence with the fact that they had piled passages from the Word together to support false beliefs. These false beliefs build the church in exactly the way just described.)

[9] (9) Afterward, feeling bored, they leave and sit idle and alone. Because, as I just mentioned, idle people get no food from heaven, they begin to starve and cannot think about anything else except how they are going to get food and satisfy their hunger.

When they are in this state, people come along, so they beg for a little money from the people. The people say, "Why are you sitting idly like this? Come with us to our homes. We'll give you work to do and we'll feed you." So they happily get up and go off to the people's homes. There they are given their own jobs to do and are given food in exchange for their work. The problem is that all people who have become adamant about false beliefs are unable to do work that is good and useful. They can only do work that is evil and harmful. They cannot work faithfully; they can work only fraudulently and unwillingly. Therefore they leave their work. The only things they love to do are socializing and talking, walking around, and sleeping. At that point their bosses can no longer induce them to work; therefore they are exiled as useless.

[10] (10) Once they have been exiled, their eyes open and they see a road that heads down to a cave. When they arrive at the cave, a door opens and they go in. They ask whether there is food there. When they receive a positive answer, they ask permission to stay and are told that they may. They are taken in and the door closes behind them.

Then the person in charge of the cave comes and says to them, "You can no longer leave. Look at your companions here. They all labor, and as they labor food is given to them from heaven. I'm telling you this so that you'll know what's going on."

Others add, "The person in charge of us knows what type of work each of us is well suited to do and orders us to do that daily work. On the days when you do your work, you get food. If you don't do your work, you don't get food or clothing. Anyone who does something evil to someone else is thrown into a corner of the cave onto a bed of accursed dust.[513] There the evildoer is horribly tormented until the person in charge sees some sign of repentance. At that point the evildoer is released and ordered back to work."

[11] The newcomers are also told that after their work they are each allowed to go for a walk or socialize, and later on to sleep. The newcomers are taken deeper into the cave where there are harlots. Each man is allowed to have one of them and call her his partner,[514] but he is forbidden by law to sleep with other partners.

Hell consists of caves like this that are nothing but eternal workhouses. I have been allowed into some of them to look around for the purpose of reporting on them.

All the people there seemed lower class. They did not know who they had been or what work they had done in the world. The angel who was with me, however, told me, "This one was a servant, this one a soldier, this one a general, this one a priest; this one held a high position; this one had wealth. Yet for all they know now, they were slaves and companions back then as well. This is because they were similar inside, although very different on the outside. It is the inner selves that associate people in the spiritual world."

[12] To speak more generally about the hells, they consist entirely of caves and workhouses like this; but they are different where there are satans as opposed to devils.[515] The spirits called satans focused on false beliefs and were evil as a result. The spirits called devils focused on evil and had false beliefs as a result. In the light of heaven, satans appear gray like corpses; some look as dark as mummies. In the light of heaven, devils, on the other hand, look as if they are darkly glowing; some look pitch black, as black as soot. All the above have the faces and bodies of monsters. Yet in their own light, which is like the light from glowing coals, they do not look like monsters; they look like people. This has been granted to them so that they can interact.

Chapter 5

The Catechism, or Ten Commandments, Explained in Both Its Outer and Its Inner Meanings

282 EVERY nation on the face of the earth knows that it is evil to murder, to commit adultery, to steal, and to bear false witness, and knows that any country, state, or civilized society that did not forbid these evils would be doomed. No one thinks the Israelite nation was stupider than other nations and did not know these things were evils. Anyone might be amazed, then, that these laws, universally recognized on earth as they are, were delivered on Mount Sinai in such a miraculous way by Jehovah himself.

I have been told, though, that they were delivered in this miraculous way so that people would know that these laws are not only civil and moral laws but divine laws as well. Therefore to act against them would be not only doing something evil to our neighbor (meaning our fellow citizen and our community) but also sinning against God. When they were delivered by Jehovah on Mount Sinai, therefore, these laws became laws of religion as well. It should be obvious that whatever Jehovah commands, he commands as an aspect of religion; therefore his commands are something we need to follow for the sake of our salvation. Before I explain the Commandments, though, I will give a prefatory statement about their holiness, to show that they have religious import.

The Ten Commandments Were the Holiest Thing in the Israelite Church

283 The Ten Commandments are the most important thing in the Word. As a result, they were the most important thing in the church that was

464

established in the Israelite nation. In a brief encapsulation they included all the elements of religion that provide for God's connection to us and our connection to God. Therefore the Ten Commandments were the holiest thing of all.

The following points show that the Ten Commandments were the holiest thing: Jehovah the Lord himself, together with angels, came down on Mount Sinai in fire and delivered the Ten Commandments by direct speech. The mountain was fenced all around so that no one would approach and die. Not even the priests or the elders were allowed to approach; only Moses. The commandments were written on two tablets of stone by the finger of God. When Moses carried the tablets down for the second time, his face was glowing.

Afterward, the tablets were stored in an ark that was at the heart of the tabernacle. There was a mercy seat on top of the ark with angel guardians made of gold over it. The inmost area in the tabernacle, where the ark was placed, was called the most holy place. Outside the veil behind which the ark stood there were several things that represented holy things in heaven and the church: a table overlaid with gold that had the showbread on it, a golden altar for burning incense, and a golden lampstand with seven lamps. There was also a curtain around the tabernacle made out of [threads of] fine linen and of purple and scarlet [yarn]. The holiness of the whole tabernacle came from no other source than the law that was inside the ark.

Because of the holiness of the tabernacle that came from the law in the ark, the entire Israelite population camped around the tabernacle, tribe by tribe, in an arrangement that was given by command. When they traveled, the tribes moved in a specific sequence behind the ark, and there was a cloud over the ark by day and a fire by night.

Because of the holiness of this law and Jehovah's presence in it, Jehovah spoke to Moses from over the mercy seat between the angel guardians. In fact, the ark was called "Jehovah" there. Aaron was not allowed inside the veil unless he offered sacrifices and burned incense, or else he would die.

Because of Jehovah's presence in this law and surrounding it, the ark containing the law performed miracles. For example, the waters of the Jordan were split apart, and as long as the ark was resting in the middle of the riverbed the people crossed on dry land. When the ark was carried around the walls of Jericho, the walls fell. Dagon, an idol of the Philistines, at first fell face down before the ark. Later, Dagon lay decapitated with the palms of its hands across the threshold of the shrine. Because of the ark, as many as several thousand inhabitants of Beth

Shemesh were struck down. Uzza died because he touched the ark. David brought the ark back into Zion with sacrifices and shouts of triumph. Later on Solomon brought the ark into the Temple in Jerusalem where he had made a sanctuary for it; and so on. All these things make it clear that the Ten Commandments were the holiest thing in the Israelite church.

284 The points just made about the delivery, holiness, and power of this law are found in the following passages in the Word: Jehovah came down on Mount Sinai in fire, and then the mountain smoked and quaked, and there was much thunder and lightning, a thick cloud, and the sound of a trumpet (Exodus 19:16–18; Deuteronomy 4:11; 5:22–26). Before Jehovah came down, the people prepared and sanctified themselves for three days (Exodus 19:10, 11, 15). The mountain was fenced all around to prevent anyone from dying as a result of approaching it. Not even priests went up; only Moses (Exodus 19:12, 13, 20–23; 24:1, 2). The law was delivered on Mount Sinai (Exodus 20:2–14; Deuteronomy 5:6–21). The law was engraved on two tablets of stone and was written by the finger of God (Exodus 31:18; 32:15, 16; Deuteronomy 9:10). When Moses carried the tablets down the mountain for the second time, his face was glowing so much that he covered it with a veil while he was speaking to the people (Exodus 34:29–35). The tablets were stored in the ark (Exodus 25:16; 40:20; Deuteronomy 10:5; 1 Kings 8:9). The mercy seat was placed on top of the ark, and angel guardians made of gold were placed on top of the mercy seat (Exodus 25:17–21). The ark with its mercy seat and angel guardians was put in the tabernacle and constituted the primary and inmost part of it. The table covered with gold for the showbread, the golden altar for incense, and the golden lampstand with its lamps constituted an outer part of the tabernacle. The ten curtains made of [threads of] fine linen and of purple and scarlet [yarn] constituted the tabernacle's outermost part (Exodus 25:1–40; 26:1–37; 40:17–28). The place where the ark was kept was called the most holy place (Exodus 26:33). The entire Israelite population camped around the tabernacle tribe by tribe in a specific arrangement and traveled in a specific sequence behind it (Numbers 2:1–34). At those times there was a cloud over the tabernacle by day and a fire by night (Exodus 40:38; Numbers 9:15, 16–23; 14:14; Deuteronomy 1:33). Jehovah spoke to Moses from a place on top of the ark between the angel guardians (Exodus 25:22; Numbers 7:89). Because of the law that was inside it, the ark was called "Jehovah" there. When the ark would set out, Moses would say, "Arise, Jehovah." When it would rest, he would say, "Return, Jehovah" (Numbers 10:35, 36; also 2 Samuel

6:2; Psalms 132:7, 8). Due to the holiness of this law, Aaron was not allowed to go behind the veil unless he offered sacrifices and burned incense (Leviticus 16:2–14 and following). The waters of the Jordan river were split by the presence of the Lord's power in the law that was inside the ark; and as long as the ark was resting in the middle of the riverbed, the people crossed on dry land (Joshua 3:1–17; 4:5–20). When the ark was carried around the walls of Jericho, they fell down (Joshua 6:1–20). Dagon, an idol of the Philistines, fell to the ground in front of the ark, and afterward lay on the threshold of the shrine decapitated, with the palms of its hands cut off (1 Samuel 5). Because of the ark, as many as several thousand inhabitants of Beth Shemesh were struck down (1 Samuel 5 and 6). Uzza died because he touched the ark (2 Samuel 6:7). David brought the ark back into Zion with sacrifices and shouts of triumph (2 Samuel 6:1–19). Solomon brought the ark into the Temple in Jerusalem where he had made a sanctuary for it (1 Kings 6:19 and following; 8:3–9).

Since this law provides for the Lord's partnership with us and our **285** partnership with the Lord, it is called *the covenant* and *the testimony*. It is called the covenant because it provides for partnership; it is called the testimony because it confirms the agreements in the covenant. In the Word a "covenant" means a partnership and "testimony" means something confirming and witnessing to its agreements. This is why there were two tablets, one for God and one for us.[516] The partnership comes from the Lord, but it comes when we do the things that have been written on our tablet. The Lord is constantly present and wanting to come in, but we have to use the freedom we have been given by the Lord to open the door. He says, "Behold! I am standing at the door and knocking. If any hear my voice and open the door, I will come in and will dine with them and they with me" (Revelation 3:20).

The stone tablets on which the law was engraved were called *the tablets of the covenant*. Because of them the ark was called *the ark of the covenant* and the law itself was called *the covenant* (see Numbers 10:33; Deuteronomy 4:13, 23; 5:2, 3; 9:9; Joshua 3:11; 1 Kings 8:21; Revelation 11:19; and elsewhere).

Because "covenant" means partnership, it is said of the Lord that he will be "a covenant for the people" (Isaiah 42:6; 49:9). He is also called the angel or messenger of the covenant (Malachi 3:1), and his blood is called the blood of the covenant (Matthew 26:28; Zechariah 9:11; Exodus 24:4–10). This is why the Word is called the Old Covenant and the New Covenant. Covenants are made for love, friendship, association, and partnership.

286 There was tremendous holiness and power in this law because it is a synopsis of all the elements of religion. It was engraved on two tablets, one of which contains a synopsis of all things related to God, and the other, a synopsis of all things related to us. For this reason the commandments of this law are called *the ten words*[517] (Exodus 34:28; Deuteronomy 4:13; 10:4). They are called this because "ten" means all and "words" mean truths. Of course, they contained more than ten words. For an explanation that "ten" means all, and that tithes were established because of that meaning, see *Revelation Unveiled* 101; on the point that this law is a synopsis of all aspects of religion, see below [§289].

In Their Literal Meaning, the Ten Commandments
Contain General Principles to Be Taught and Lived;
in Their Spiritual and Heavenly Meanings,
They Contain Absolutely Everything

287 It is generally recognized that the Ten Commandments in the Word are called the law in a supreme sense because they contain all the principles to be taught and lived. They contain not only all the principles related to God but also all the principles related to us. For this reason this law was engraved on two tablets, one of which relates to God and the other to us.

It is also generally recognized that all the principles to be taught and lived come down to loving God and loving our neighbor. The Ten Commandments contain all the teachings about these two kinds of love. The entire Word teaches nothing else, as the Lord's words make clear:

> Jesus said, "You are to love the Lord your God with all your heart, with all your soul, and with all your mind; and your neighbor as yourself. The Law and the Prophets hinge on these two commandments." (Matthew 22:37–40)

"The Law and the Prophets" means the entire Word.
Further,

> A lawyer tested Jesus by saying, "Master, what should I do to inherit eternal life?" Jesus said to him, "What has been written in the law? How do you read it?" He replied, "You are to love the Lord your God with all your heart, with all your soul, with all your strength, and with

all your mind, and your neighbor as yourself." And Jesus said, "Do this and you will live." (Luke 10:25–28)

Because everything in the Word is about loving God and loving our neighbor, and the first tablet of the Ten Commandments contains a summary of everything about loving God while the second tablet contains a summary of everything about loving our neighbor, it follows that the Ten Commandments contain everything to be taught and lived.

If you visualize the two tablets, it is clear how they are connected. God looks at us from his tablet and we look at God from ours. The two tablets are therefore turned toward each other. On God's side it never fails that he is looking at us and doing what has to be done for our salvation. If we accept and do the things on our tablet, a reciprocal partnership [with God] develops. What happens to us then is indicated by the Lord's words to the lawyer: "Do this and you will live."

The Word often mentions "the law." I will now say what that means **288** in a narrow sense, in a broader sense, and in the broadest sense. In a narrow sense, "the law" means the Ten Commandments. In a broader sense, "the law" means the rules that Moses gave to the children of Israel. In the broadest sense, "the law" means the entire Word.

People know that *in a narrow sense "the law" means the Ten Commandments.*

In a broader sense, "the law" means the rules that Moses gave to the children of Israel. This becomes clear from the individual rules laid out in Exodus—they are called "the law":

This is the law of the trespass offering. (Leviticus 7:1)

This is the law of the sacrifice of peace offerings. (Leviticus 7:11)

This is the law of the grain offering. (Leviticus 6:14 and following)

This is the law of the burnt offering, the grain offering, the sacrifices for sin and guilt, and the consecrations. (Leviticus 7:37)

This is the law of the animals and the birds. (Leviticus 11:46 and following)

This is the law for a woman who has given birth to a son or a daughter. (Leviticus 12:7)

This is the law of leprosy. (Leviticus 13:59; 14:2, 32, 54, 57)

This is the law for someone who has a discharge. (Leviticus 15:32)

This is the law of jealousy. (Numbers 5:29, 30)

This is the law of the Nazirite. (Numbers 6:13, 21)

This is the law of cleansing. (Numbers 19:14)

This is the law of the red heifer. (Numbers 19:2)

[This is] the law for a king. (Deuteronomy 17:15–19)

In fact, the entire five books of Moses are called "the Law" (Deuteronomy 31:9, 11, 12, 26). They are called this in the New Testament as well (Luke 2:22; 24:44; John 1:45; 7:22, 23; 8:5; and elsewhere).

When Paul says, "We are justified by faith apart from the works of the Law" (Romans 3:28), by "the works of the Law" he means the rules just mentioned. This is clear from the words that follow this passage in Romans, as well as from Paul's words to Peter chiding him for making others follow Jewish religious practices. In the latter context, Paul says three times in one verse, "No one is justified by the works of the Law" (Galatians 2:14, 16).

In the broadest sense, "the law" means the entire Word. This is clear from the following passages: "Jesus said, 'Is it not written *in your law,* "You are gods"?'" (John 10:34, referring to something written in Psalms 82:6). "The crowd answered, 'We have heard from *the law* that Christ remains forever'" (John 12:34, referring to something written in Psalms 89:29; 110:4; and Daniel 7:14). "This was to fulfill the Word that was written in *their law,* 'They hated me for no reason'" (John 15:25, referring to something written in Psalms 35:19). "The Pharisees said, 'Do any of the rulers believe in him? But the crowd does, who do not know *the law*'" (John 7:48, 49). "It is easier for heaven and earth to pass away than for *the tip of one letter of the law* to fall" (Luke 16:17). In these passages, "the law" means the entire Sacred Scripture. There are a thousand passages like this in [the Psalms of] David.

289 In their spiritual and heavenly meanings, the Ten Commandments contain absolutely all the instructions to be taught and lived—all aspects of faith and goodwill. This is because each and every thing on both a large and a small scale in the Word's literal meaning conceals two inner meanings. One inner meaning is called spiritual, and the other, heavenly. Divine truth exists in its own light and divine goodness exists in its own warmth within these meanings. Because the Word has these characteristics as a whole and in each of its parts, the Ten Commandments need to be explained in all three meanings, called the earthly meaning, the spiritual meaning, and the heavenly meaning. You can see that this is the nature of the Word from the things I have shown above in the chapter on Sacred Scripture, or the Word, §§193–208.

If people were not told what the Word is like, none of them could **290** have any idea that there is an infinity in the Word's least details, meaning that it contains things beyond number that not even the angels could ever fully draw out. Everything in it is comparable to a seed that has the capability of growing out of the ground to become a huge tree, which produces a tremendous number of seeds that are capable in turn of producing similar trees that together make up a whole grove, whose seeds in turn lead to many groves, and so on to infinity. This is the nature of the Lord's Word on a detailed level; it is especially true of the Ten Commandments. Because they teach love for God and love for our neighbor, they are a brief synopsis of the entire Word.

In fact, the Lord used a similar analogy to explain that this is the nature of the Word:

> The kingdom of God is like a grain of mustard seed that someone took and sowed in a field. It is the least of all seeds, but when it has grown, it is bigger than all other plants and becomes a tree so that the birds of the air come and nest in its branches. (Matthew 13:31, 32; Mark 4:31, 32; Luke 13:18, 19; compare also Ezekiel 17:2–8)

If you think about angelic wisdom, you can see that the Word has this infinity of spiritual seeds, or truths. All angelic wisdom comes from the Word and grows inside the angels to eternity. The wiser they become, the more clearly they see that wisdom has no end, and the more clearly they perceive that they themselves are only in its front hall; they could never in the least touch the Lord's divine wisdom, which they call a bottomless depth. Since the Word comes from this bottomless depth, in that it is from the Lord, clearly all its parts have a kind of infinity.

The First Commandment

There Is to Be No Other God before My Face

These are the words of the first commandment (Exodus 20:3; Deuteron- **291** omy 5:7). In their *earthly meaning,* which is their literal meaning, the most accessible sense is that we must not worship idols; for it goes on to say,

> You are not to make yourself a sculpture or any form that is in the heavens above or the earth below or in the waters under the earth. You are not to bow yourself down to them, and you are not to worship them, because *I, Jehovah your God, am a jealous God.* (Exodus 20:4, 5)

The most accessible meaning of this commandment is that we must not worship idols, because before the time [when this commandment was given] and after it right up to the coming of the Lord much of the Middle East had idolatrous worship. What caused the idolatrous worship was that all the churches before the Lord came were symbolic and emblematic. Their symbols and emblems were designed to present divine attributes in different forms and sculpted shapes. When the meanings of these forms were lost, common people began worshiping the forms as gods.

The Israelite nation had this kind of worship in Egypt, as you can see from the golden calf that they worshiped in the wilderness instead of worshiping Jehovah. That type of worship never became foreign to them, as you can see from many passages in both the historical and the prophetical parts of the Word.[518]

292 This commandment, "There is to be no other God before my face," also has an earthly meaning that we must not worship any person, dead or alive, as a god. Worshiping people as gods was another practice in the Middle East and in various surrounding areas. The many gods of the nations there were of this type, such as Baal, Ashtoreth, Chemosh, Milcom, and Beelzebub.[519] In Athens and Rome there were Saturn, Jupiter, Neptune, Pluto, Apollo, Athena,[520] and so on. People worshiped some of these at first as holy people, then as supernatural beings, and finally as gods. The fact that these nations also worshiped living people as gods can be seen from the edict of Darius the Mede that for a thirty-day period no one was to ask anything of God, only of the king, or be thrown into the lions' den (Daniel 6:8–28).

293 In the earthly meaning, which is the literal meaning, the first commandment also entails that we are to love above all else no one except God and nothing except what comes from God. This also accords with the Lord's words (Matthew 22:37–39; Luke 10:25–28). Someone we love above all else is a god to us; and something we love above all else is divine to us. For example, if we love ourselves above all else, or if we love the world above all else, to us we ourselves are our god, or else the world is. This explains why under these circumstances we do not believe at heart in any god;

because of this we are connected to people like ourselves in hell, where all are gathered who have loved themselves or the world above all else.

The spiritual meaning of this commandment is that we must worship no other God except the Lord Jesus Christ, because he is Jehovah, and he came into the world and brought about redemption. If he had not done so, not one person and not one angel could have been saved.

It is clear from the following passages in the Word that there is no other God except him:

> It will be said in that day, "Behold, this is our God. We have waited for him to free us. This is Jehovah whom we have waited for. Let us rejoice and be glad in his salvation." (Isaiah 25:9)

> The voice of one crying in the desert, "Prepare a way for Jehovah; make a level pathway in the solitude for our God. For the glory of Jehovah will be revealed, and all flesh will see it together. Behold, the Lord Jehovih is coming with strength; like a shepherd he will feed his flock." (Isaiah 40:3, 5, 11)

> "The only God is among you; there is no other God." Surely you are the God who was hidden, O God *the Savior* of Israel. (Isaiah 45:14, 15)

> Am not I Jehovah? There is no other God except me. I am a just God, and there is no *Savior* except me. (Isaiah 45:21, 22)

> I am Jehovah, and there is no *Savior* except me. (Isaiah 43:11; Hosea 13:4)

> So that all flesh may know that I, Jehovah, am *your Savior* and *your Redeemer.* (Isaiah 49:26; 60:16)

> As for *our Redeemer,* Jehovah Sabaoth is his name. (Isaiah 47:4; Jeremiah 50:34)

> Jehovah, my rock and *my Redeemer.* (Psalms 19:14)

> Thus says Jehovah, *your Redeemer,* the Holy One of Israel: "I am Jehovah, your God." (Isaiah 48:17; 43:14; 49:7; 54:8)

> Thus said Jehovah, your *Redeemer:* "I, Jehovah, am the maker of all things. I alone [stretch out the heavens. I extend the earth] by myself." (Isaiah 44:24)

> Thus said Jehovah, the King of Israel and its *Redeemer,* Jehovah Sabaoth: "I am the First and the Last, and there is no God except me." (Isaiah 44:6)

294

Jehovah Sabaoth is his name, *your Redeemer,* the Holy One of Israel. He will be called God of all the earth. (Isaiah 54:5)

Abraham did not know us and Israel did not acknowledge us. You, Jehovah, are our Father; our *Redeemer* from everlasting is your name. (Isaiah 63:16)

A Child is born to us; a Son is given to us. His name will be called Wonderful, Counselor, God, Hero, *Father of Eternity,* Prince of Peace. (Isaiah 9:6)

Behold, the days are coming when I will raise up for David a righteous offshoot who will reign as king; and this is his name: *Jehovah is our Justice.* (Jeremiah 23:5–6; 33:15–16)

Philip said to Jesus, "Show us the Father." Jesus said to him, "Those who see me see the Father. Do you not believe that I am in the Father and the Father is in me?" (John 14:8, 9, 10)

All the fullness of divinity dwells physically in Jesus Christ. (Colossians 2:9)

We are in the truth in Jesus Christ. He is the true God and eternal life. Little children, keep yourselves away from idols. (1 John 5:20, 21)

These passages make it very clear that the Lord our Savior is Jehovah himself, who is the Creator, the Redeemer, and the Regenerator in one. This is the spiritual meaning of this commandment.

295 *The heavenly meaning of this commandment* is that the Lord Jehovah is infinite, immeasurable, and eternal; and omnipotent, omniscient, and omnipresent. He is the First and the Last; the Beginning and the End; the One who was, is, and will be. He is love itself and wisdom itself, or goodness itself and truth itself. Therefore he is life itself. He is the sole being; all things come from him.

296 All people who acknowledge and worship another god besides the Lord the Savior Jesus Christ, who is Jehovah God himself in human form, sin against this first commandment. So do all those who convince themselves that there are three actually existing divine persons from eternity. As these people reinforce themselves in this mistake, they become more and more earthly and mindless. They cannot inwardly comprehend any divine truth. If they hear and accept divine truth, they nonetheless pollute it and wrap it in mistaken ideas. For this reason they can be compared to people who live on the lowest or underground level of a house—they do not hear any of the conversation of people on the second or third floors, because the ceiling over their heads stops the sound from getting through.

[2] The human mind is like a three-story house that contains people on the bottom floor who have convinced themselves that there have been three gods from eternity, while on the second and third floors there are people who acknowledge and believe in one God in a human form that can be seen—the Lord God the Savior.

People who are mindlessly physical and utterly earthly are actually complete animals; the only thing that differentiates them from true brute animals is their ability to speak and to make false inferences. They are like someone who lives at a zoo where there are wild animals of every kind, who plays the lion one day, the bear the next, the tiger the next, the leopard or the wolf the next, and could play a sheep but would be laughing inside.

[3] People who are merely earthly think about divine truths only on the basis of worldly phenomena and the mistaken impressions of their own senses. They cannot lift their minds above them. As a result, their body of religious teaching could be compared to a soup made of chaff that they eat as if it were the finest cuisine. Or their body of teaching could be compared to the loaf of bread and the cakes that Ezekiel the prophet was commanded to mix from wheat, barley, beans, lentils, spelt, and human excrement or cow dung in order to represent what the church was like in the Israelite nation (Ezekiel 4:9 and following). It is the same with the body of teaching of a church that is founded and built on the idea of three divine persons from eternity, each of whom is individually god.

[4] By picturing it mentally as it truly is, anyone can see the hideous wrongness of this faith. It is like three people standing next to each other in a row: the first person is distinguished by a crown and a scepter; the second person's right hand is holding a book, which is the Word, while his left hand holds a golden cross spattered in blood; and the third person has wings strapped on and stands on one foot in an effort to fly off and take action. Over the three there is an inscription: *These three people, each of whom is a god, are one God.* Any wise man would see this picture and say to himself, "That's ridiculously unrealistic!"[521]

He would say something very different if he saw a picture of one divine person whose head was surrounded with rays of heavenly light, with the inscription: *This is our God—our Creator, Redeemer, and Regenerator in one, and therefore our Savior.* He would kiss this picture and take it home next to his heart, and when he and his wife and their children and servants would look at it they would feel uplifted.

The Second Commandment

*You Are Not to Take the Name of Jehovah Your God
in Vain, Because Jehovah Will Not Hold Guiltless
Someone Who Takes His Name in Vain*

297 In its *earthly meaning,* which is the literal meaning, taking the name of Jehovah God in vain includes abusing his name in various types of talking, especially in lies and deceptions, in swearing and oath-taking for no reason or to avoid blame; and using his name with evil intent, which is cursing, or in sorcery and magic spells.

To swear by God or by his holiness, by the Word or by the Gospel during coronations, inaugurations into the priesthood, and confirmations of faith is not taking God's name in vain, unless the people who take the oath later reject their promises as impossible or pointless.

Furthermore, because it is holiness itself, the name of God is used constantly in the sacred activities of the church, such as in prayers, hymns, and all aspects of worship, as well as in sermons and books on church-related topics. The reason is that God is in every aspect of religion. When he is ritually called forth by his name, he is present and hears. In these activities the name of God is kept holy.

The name of Jehovah God is intrinsically holy, as you can see by the fact that after their earliest times the Jews did not dare, nor do they now dare, to say the name Jehovah.[522] Out of respect for the Jews, the Gospel writers and apostles did not want to say the name either. Instead of "Jehovah" they said "the Lord," as you can see from passages from the Old Testament that are quoted in the New Testament but use "the Lord" instead of "Jehovah," such as Matthew 22:37 and Luke 10:27 that quote Deuteronomy 6:5, and so on.

The name of Jesus is also holy, as people generally know because the apostle said that at that name knees bend and should bend in heaven and on earth [Philippians 2:10]. For another thing, no devil in hell can pronounce the name Jesus.[523]

There are many names for God that are not to be taken in vain: Jehovah, Jehovah God, Jehovah Sabaoth, the Holy One of Israel, Jesus, Christ, and the Holy Spirit.

298 In the *spiritual meaning,* the name of God stands for everything that the church teaches on the basis of the Word—everything through which the Lord is called on and worshiped. Taken together, all these are names for God. Taking God's name in vain, then, means misusing any of these things for idle chatter, lies, deceptions, curses, sorcery, or magic spells. This too is abusing and blaspheming God, and therefore his name.

From the following passages you can see that the Word and anything from it that is used in the church or in any worship is God's name:

> From the rising of the sun my name will be invoked. (Isaiah 41:25)

> From the rising of the sun to the setting of it, great is my name among the nations. In every place incense is offered to my name. But you desecrate my name when you say, "Jehovah's table is defiled." And you sneeze at my name when you bring offerings that are stolen, lame, and sick. (Malachi 1:11, 12, 13)

> All peoples walk in the name of their God; we walk in the name of Jehovah our God. (Micah 4:5)

> They are to worship Jehovah in one place, the place where he will put his name (Deuteronomy 12:5, 11, 13, 14, 18; 16:2, 6, 11, 15, 16),

that is, where Jehovah will locate their worship of him.

> Jesus said, "Where two or three are gathered together in my name, I am there in the midst of them." (Matthew 18:20)

> As many as received him, he gave them power to be children of God, if they believed in his name. (John 1:12)

> Those who do not believe have already been judged because they have not believed in the name of the only begotten Son of God. (John 3:18)

> Those who believe will have life in his name. (John 20:31)

> Jesus said, "I have revealed your name to people and have made your name known to them." (John 17:26)

> The Lord said, "You have a few names in Sardis." (Revelation 3:4)

There are also many passages similar to these in which the name of God means the divine quality which radiates from God and through which he is worshiped.

The name of Jesus Christ, however, means everything related to his redeeming humankind and everything related to his teaching, and therefore everything through which he saves. "Jesus" means all his efforts to save the human race through redemption; "Christ" means all his efforts to save the human race through teaching.

299 In the *heavenly meaning,* taking the Lord's name in vain parallels what the Lord said to the Pharisees:

> All sin and blasphemy is forgiven people, but blasphemy of the Spirit is not forgiven. (Matthew 12:31, 32)

"Blasphemy of the Spirit" means blasphemy against the divinity of the Lord's human manifestation and against the holiness of the Word.

In the highest or heavenly meaning, the "name of Jehovah God" stands for the Lord's divine-human manifestation, as the following passages make clear:

> Jesus said, "*Father, glorify your name.*" And a voice came out of heaven that said, "I both have glorified it and will glorify it again." (John 12:27, 28)

> Whatever you ask in my name, I will do it, so that the Father is glorified in the Son. If you ask anything in my name, I will do it. (John 14:13, 14)

In the heavenly sense the phrase in the Lord's prayer "Your name must be kept holy" [Matthew 6:9] has the same meaning, as does the word "name" in Exodus 23:21 and Isaiah 63:16.[524]

Since Matthew 12:31 and 32 says that "blasphemy of the Spirit" is not forgiven us, and this is what the heavenly meaning refers to, for this reason the following phrase is added to this commandment: "because Jehovah will not hold guiltless someone who takes his name in vain."

300 The nature of names in the spiritual world makes it clear that someone's "name" does not mean her or his name alone but also her or his full nature. In that world, people all stop using the names they were given in baptism in this world and the names they received from their parents or their family. All there are named for what they are like. Angels get a name that indicates the moral and spiritual life they have. In fact, the Lord was referring to angels in the following passage:

> Jesus said, "I am the good shepherd. The sheep hear the shepherd's voice and he calls his sheep by name and leads them out." (John 10:3, 11)

The same holds true in the following passage:

> I have a few names in Sardis who have not defiled their clothes. Upon the person who conquers I will write the name of the city New Jerusalem and my new name. (Revelation 3:4, 12)

"Gabriel" and "Michael" are not the names of two people in heaven— these names mean all the angels in heaven who have wisdom about the

Lord and who worship him. The names of people and places in the Word do not mean people and places either; they mean aspects of the church.

Even in our world a "name" means more than just a name—it also means what someone is like. People's natures get attached to their names. We often say, "They're doing it for their name" or "to make a name for themselves." "Those are big names" means that those people are famous for characteristics they possess, such as creativity, scholarship, achievements, or the like.

It is common knowledge that people who insult or libel other people's names are in fact insulting or libeling the actions of the other people's lives. The two are conceptually linked. Such attacks ruin the reputation of people's names. Likewise, someone who says the name of a monarch, a duke, or a great person with disrespect also dishonors the person's majesty and dignity. It is equally true that someone who mentions anyone's name with a tone of contempt also disparages the deeds of that person's life—this applies to everyone. Every country has laws that forbid us to abuse, attack, or insult anyone's name (meaning anyone's nature and reputation).

The Third Commandment

Remember the Sabbath Day in Order to Keep It Holy;
for Six Days You Will Labor and Do All Your Work,
but the Seventh Day Is the Sabbath for Jehovah Your God

This is the third commandment, as you can see in Exodus 20:8, 9, 10; and Deuteronomy 5:12, 13, 14. In the *earthly meaning,* which is the literal meaning, it indicates that there are six days that belong to us and our labors, and a seventh day that belongs to the Lord and to the peaceful rest that he gives us. In the original language "Sabbath" means rest.

301

The Sabbath was the holiest thing among the children of Israel because it represented the Lord. The six days represented his labors and battles with the hells. The seventh day represented his victory over the hells and the resulting rest. That day was holiness itself because it represented the completion of the Lord's entire redemption.

When the Lord came into the world, however, and therefore symbols representing him were no longer needed, the Sabbath day was turned into a day for instruction in divine things, for rest from labors, for meditating on things related to salvation and eternal life, and for loving our neighbor.

It is clear that the Sabbath became a day for instruction in divine things, because the Lord taught on the Sabbath day in the Temple and in synagogues (Mark 6:2; Luke 4:16, 31, 32; 13:10). On the Sabbath the Lord also said to a healed person, "Take up your bed and walk"; and he told the Pharisees that it was acceptable for the disciples to pick ears of corn and eat them on the Sabbath day (Matthew 12:1–9; Mark 2:23–28; Luke 6:1–6; John 5:9–19). In the spiritual meaning, these details all stand for being instructed in religious teachings.

The fact that the Sabbath day turned into a day for loving our neighbor is clear from the Lord's practice and teaching (Matthew 12:10–14; Mark 3:1–9; Luke 6:6–12; 13:10–18; 14:1–7; John 5:9–19; 7:22, 23; 9:14, 16).[525]

All these passages make it clear why the Lord said that he was in fact the Lord of the Sabbath (Matthew 12:8; Mark 2:28; Luke 6:5). It follows from this saying of his that [before he came] the Sabbath day used to represent him.

302 In the *spiritual meaning,* this commandment refers to our being reformed and regenerated by the Lord. The six days of labor mean battling against the flesh and its cravings and also against the evils and falsities that are in us from hell. The seventh day means our becoming connected to the Lord and our being regenerated as a result. As long as this battle continues, we have spiritual labor; but when we have been regenerated, we rest. This will become clear from the points that will be made below in the chapter on reformation and regeneration [§§571–625]—especially the following points that are discussed there: (1) *Regeneration progresses analogously to the way we are conceived, carried in the womb, born, and brought up.* (2) *The first phase in our being generated anew is called "reformation"; it has to do with our intellect. The second phase is called "regeneration"; it has to do with our will and then our intellect.* (3) *Our inner self has to be reformed first. Our outer self is then reformed through our inner self.* (4) *Then a battle develops between our inner and outer self. Whichever self wins, it will control the other.* (5) *When we have been regenerated, we have a new will and a new intellect.* And so on.

In the spiritual meaning, this commandment refers to our reformation and regeneration because these processes parallel the Lord's labors and battles against the hells, his victory over them, and then rest. The way he glorified his human manifestation and made it divine is the same way he reforms and regenerates us and makes us spiritual. This is what is meant by *following him.* The battles of the Lord are called labors, and were labors, as is clear from Isaiah 53 and 63. Similar things are called labors in us (Isaiah 65:23; Revelation 2:2, 3).

In the *heavenly meaning* this commandment refers to connecting to the Lord and having peace as a result, because we are then safe from hell. The Sabbath means "rest," and in the highest sense "peace." For this reason the Lord is called "the Prince of Peace," and also calls himself peace. See the following passages:

303

> A Child is born to us; a Son is given to us. Authority will rest on his shoulder, and his name will be called Wonderful, Counselor, God, Hero, Father of Eternity, *Prince of Peace.* There will be no end to the increase of his government and *peace.* (Isaiah 9:6, 7)

> Jesus said, "*Peace* I leave to you. *My peace* I give to you." (John 14:27)

> Jesus said, "I have spoken these things *so that you may have peace in me.*" (John 16:33)

> How pleasant on the mountains are the feet of the One *proclaiming* and making us hear *peace,* saying, "Your king reigns." (Isaiah 52:7)

> Jehovah will redeem my soul in peace. (Psalms 55:18)

> *The work of Jehovah is peace; the labor of justice is rest and safety forever so that they may live in a dwelling of peace, in tents of safety, and in tranquil rest.* (Isaiah 32:17, 18)

Jesus said to the seventy whom he sent out,

> Whatever home you come into, first say, "*The peace of the Lord,*"[526] and if the people are *children of peace* then your *peace* will rest on them. (Luke 10:5, 6; Matthew 10:12, 13, 14)

> Jehovah will speak *peace* to his people; *justice and peace* will kiss each other. (Psalms 85:8, 10)

When the Lord himself appeared to the disciples he said,

> *Peace to you.* (John 20:19, 21, 26)

Isaiah 65 and 66 and other passages treat further the state of peace that people can come into with the Lord's help. The people to be accepted into the new church that the Lord is now establishing are going to come into this peace. (For the essence of the peace that the angels of heaven and those who are in the Lord have, see the work *Heaven and Hell* 284–290.

These sections also make it clear why the Lord calls himself the Lord of the Sabbath, that is, the Lord of rest and peace.)

304   Heavenly peace is peace in relation to the hells—a peace because evils and falsities will not rise up from there and break in. Heavenly peace can be compared in many ways to earthly peace. For example, it can be compared to the peace after wars when all are living in safety from their enemies, protected in their own city, in their house, with their own land and garden. It is as the prophet says, who speaks of heavenly peace in earthly language:

> They will each sit under their own vine and their own fig tree; no one will frighten them. (Micah 4:4; Isaiah 65:21, 22, 23)

Heavenly peace can be compared to rest and recreation for the mind after working extremely hard, or to a mother's consolation after giving birth, when her instinctive parental love unveils its pleasures. It can be compared to the serenity after storms, black clouds, and thunder; or to the spring that follows a severe winter, with the uplifting effect of seedlings in the fields and blossoms in the gardens, meadows, and woods; or to the state of mind felt by survivors of storms or hostilities at sea who reach port and set their feet on longed-for solid ground.

The Fourth Commandment

Honor Your Father and Your Mother
So That Your Days Will Be Prolonged
and It Will Be Well with You on Earth

305   This commandment reads this way in Exodus 20:12 and Deuteronomy 5:16. Honoring your father and your mother in the *earthly meaning*, which is the literal meaning, includes honoring our parents, obeying them, being devoted to them, and thanking them for the benefits they have given us—for feeding and clothing us, introducing us into the world so that we may become civil and moral people within it, and introducing us into heaven through religious instruction. In this way our parents have cared for our prosperity in time and our happiness to eternity. They do all these things from a love they have from the Lord, whose role they have played. In a comparable sense, it also means that wards whose parents have died are to honor their guardians.

In a broader sense, this commandment means honoring our monarch and government officials because on everyone's behalf they provide in a general way the necessities that parents provide in an individual way. In the broadest sense, this commandment means loving our country because it nurtures and protects us—it is called our "fatherland" from the word "father." In fact, it is the parents themselves who need to give honor to the country and those who serve it, and to sow this habit in their children.

In the *spiritual meaning,* honoring your father and your mother refers to revering and loving God and the church. In this sense "father" means God—the Father of all—and "mother" means the church. In the heavens little children and angels know no other father or mother, since their rebirth in that world comes from the Lord through the church. This is why the Lord says, "Do not call anyone on earth your father, for your father is the One in the heavens" (Matthew 23:9). (These words apply to little children and angels in heaven, but not to little children and people on earth.) The Lord teaches something similar in the prayer that is shared by all Christian churches: "Our Father, who is in the heavens: your name must be kept holy." **306**

In the spiritual meaning, "mother" stands for the church because as mothers on earth nourish their children with physical food, so the church nourishes people with spiritual food. For this reason in various places in the Word the church is called "mother"; for example, in Hosea: "Bring charges against your mother. She is not my wife and I am not her husband" (Hosea 2:2, 5). In Isaiah: "Where is the certificate of your mother's divorce, whom I put away?" (Isaiah 50:1; Ezekiel 16:45; 19:10). In the Gospels: "Jesus reached his hand toward the disciples and said, 'My mother and my brothers and sisters are those who hear the Word of God and do it'" (Matthew 12:48, 49, 50; Mark 3:33, 34, 35; Luke 8:21; John 19:25, 26, 27).

In the *heavenly meaning,* "father" stands for our Lord Jesus Christ and "mother" stands for the communion of saints, meaning his church that is scattered throughout the entire world. The following passages show that the Lord is the "Father": **307**

A Child is born to us; a Son is given to us. His name will be called God, Hero, *Father of Eternity,* Prince of Peace. (Isaiah 9:6)

You are *our Father.* Abraham did not know us and Israel did not acknowledge us. *You are our Father;* our Redeemer from everlasting is your name. (Isaiah 63:16)

Philip said, "Show us the Father." Jesus says to him, "*Those who see me see the Father.* How then are you saying, 'Show us the Father'? Believe me that I am in the Father and the Father is in me." (John 14:7–11; 12:45)

The following passages show that in the heavenly meaning "mother" stands for the Lord's church:

I saw a city, the holy New Jerusalem, prepared as *a bride adorned for her husband.* (Revelation 21:2)

The angel said to John,

Come. I will show you *the bride, the wife of the Lamb,*

and he showed him the holy city Jerusalem (Revelation 21:9, 10).

The time for *the Lamb's wedding* has come; *his bride* has prepared herself. Blessed are those who are called to the *marriage supper of the Lamb.* (Revelation 19:7, 9; see also Matthew 9:15; Mark 2:19, 20; Luke 5:34, 35; John 3:29; 19:25, 26, 27)

"The New Jerusalem" means the new church that the Lord is establishing today (see *Revelation Unveiled* 880–881). This church, not the one before it, is the "wife" and "mother" in this sense. The spiritual offspring that are born from this marriage are acts of goodwill and true insights related to faith. The people who have these things from the Lord are called "the children of the wedding," "children of God," and "those who are born of him."[527]

308 An important idea to grasp is that a divine field of heavenly love constantly radiates from the Lord to all people who embrace the teaching of his church. Like little children in the world with their father and mother, these people obey the Lord, stay close to him, and want to be nourished, that is, instructed by him.

From this heavenly field an earthly field arises. It is a field of love for babies and children. It is absolutely universal. It affects not only people but also birds and animals, including even snakes. In fact, it affects not only animate things but also inanimate things. In order for the Lord to have an effect on inanimate things as he does on spiritual things, he created a sun that is like a father to the physical world and an earth that is like a mother to it.[528] The marriage of the sun as a father and the earth as a mother produces all the growth that adorns the surface of the planet.

The influence of this heavenly field on the physical world occasions the miraculous progression in plants from seed to fruit to new seeds. It also results in many types of plant that turn their faces, so to speak, toward the sun by day and bow them when the sun sets, and in flowers that open when the sun rises and close when it sets. It also induces the songbirds to sing sweetly first thing in the morning and again after they have been fed by their mother, the earth. In these ways all these creatures honor their father and their mother.

All these phenomena are proof that through the sun and the earth the Lord makes available all the necessities for both the living beings and the inanimate things in the physical world. Therefore we read in David,

> Praise Jehovah from the heavens. Praise him, sun and moon. Praise him from the earth, great sea creatures and the depths. Praise him, fruit trees and all cedars, the wild beast and every animal, creeping things and birds with wings, the kings of the earth and all peoples, young men and young women. (Psalms 147:7–12)

Also in Job:

> Please, ask the animals and they will teach you. Ask the birds of heaven and they will make it known to you. Ask the shrub of the earth and it will instruct you. The fish in the sea will tell you the story. Which of all these things does not know that the hand of Jehovah has done this? (Job 12:7, 8, 9)

"Ask and they will teach" means watch, pay attention, and judge from these things that the Lord Jehovih created them.

The Fifth Commandment

You Are Not to Kill

This commandment, "You are not to kill," in its *earthly meaning* means not killing people, inflicting on them any fatal wound, or mutilating their bodies. It also means not bringing any deadly evil against their names and reputations, since for many people their reputation and their life go hand in hand.

309

In a broader earthly meaning, murdering includes hostility, hatred, and revenge, which involve longing for someone's death. Murder lies hidden inside these feelings like an area that is still burning inside a piece of wood under the ashes. Hellfire is nothing else. This is why we say someone blazes with hatred or burns for revenge. These feelings are murders at the level of intent even if not in act. If fear of the law, retribution, or revenge were taken away, these feelings would burst into action, especially if the intent involved deception or savagery.

The following words of the Lord make it clear that hatred is murder:

> You have heard that it was said by ancient people, "You are not to kill; and whoever kills will be exposed to judgment." But I say to you that any who are angry with their brother or sister for no good reason will be exposed to hellfire. (Matthew 5:21, 22)

The reason is that everything we intend is something we want and something we inwardly do.

310 In the *spiritual meaning,* murders stand for all methods of killing and destroying people's souls. There are many different methods, such as turning people away from God, religion, and divine worship; setting up roadblocks against such things; and persuading people to turn away from and even feel aversion to such things. All the devils and satans in hell practice these methods. People in our world who violate and prostitute the holy things of the church are connected to these devils and satans.

The king of the abyss, who is called Abaddon or Apollyon (meaning the Destroyer, Revelation 9:11), stands for people who use falsities to destroy souls. The "killed" in the prophetic Word have the same meaning, as for example in the following passages:

> Jehovah God said, "Feed the sheep for slaughter whom their owners have killed." (Zechariah 11:4, 5, 7)

> We have been killed all day long; we are considered a flock for slaughter. (Psalms 44:22)

> He will cause those who are yet to come to take root in Jacob. Was he killed in the way that his henchmen would kill? (Isaiah 27:6, 7)

> A stranger comes only in order to steal and slaughter the sheep. I have come so that they may have life and abundance. (John 10:10; other such passages are Isaiah 14:21; 26:21; Ezekiel 37:9; Jeremiah 4:31; 12:3; Revelation 9:5; 11:7)

This is why the Devil is called "a murderer from the beginning" (John 8:44).

In the *heavenly meaning,* killing refers to being angry with the Lord **311** for no good reason, hating him, and wanting to get rid of his name. People with such feelings are said to crucify the Lord; if he were to come back into the world again, they would do much the same thing the Jews did.[529] This is the meaning of "the Lamb in a state as if killed" (Revelation 5:6; 13:8), and the meaning of "crucified" in Revelation 11:8; Hebrews 6:6; and Galatians 3:1.

Devils and satans in hell have made clear to me the inner quality of **312** people who have not been reformed by the Lord. Devils and satans constantly have it in mind to kill the Lord. Because they cannot achieve this, they try to kill people who are devoted to the Lord. Since they cannot accomplish this the way people in the world could, they attack people with every effort to destroy their souls, that is, to demolish the faith and goodwill they have. The actual hatred and desire for revenge inside these devils look like fires that are dark and fires that are bright. Their hatreds look like dark fires and their desires for revenge look like bright fires. These feelings are not in fact fires, but they look like fires.

One can sometimes glimpse the savagery of the devils' hearts in visual form in the air above those devils. It looks as if they are battling, slaughtering, and massacring angels. Their feelings of anger and hatred against heaven are the source of these dreadful daydreams.

For another thing, these devils and satans look at a distance like wild animals of every kind—tigers, leopards, wolves, foxes, dogs, crocodiles, and snakes of all kinds. When devils and satans see tame animals in symbolic forms, they imagine themselves attacking the animals and trying to slaughter them.

I have seen devils that looked like dragons and were standing next to women with babies whom the dragons were trying to devour, like the situation we find in Revelation 12. These portrayals represent the devils' hatred against the Lord and his new church.

People in the world who want to destroy the Lord's church are similar to these devils and satans, although it does not seem that way to others who know these people, because their bodies—the instruments with which they practice moral actions—absorb their desires and keep them hidden. To the angels, however, who look at their spirits, not their bodies, these people look like the devils just mentioned. Who could ever realize things like this if the Lord had not opened someone's sight with the gift of looking into the spiritual world? Otherwise these points, along with many other things eminently worth knowing, would have remained forever hidden from the human race.

The Sixth Commandment

You Are Not to Commit Adultery

313 In its *earthly meaning,* this commandment covers not only committing adultery but also wanting to do and doing things that are obscene, and also having wanton thoughts and expressing them. As the Lord's words make clear, craving to commit adultery is committing adultery:

> You have heard that it was said by the ancients, "You are not to commit adultery." But I say to you that if a man looks at someone else's wife in such a way that he craves her, he has already committed adultery with her in his heart. (Matthew 5:27, 28)

The reason is that craving becomes a virtual deed when it is in the will. An attraction enters only our intellect, but an intention enters our will; and an intention based on a craving is a deed.

On these topics, see many things in the work *Marriage Love and Promiscuous Love,* published in Amsterdam, 1768. There are treatments there on the opposite of marriage love, §§423–443; on promiscuity, §§444[b]–460; on different kinds and degrees of adultery, §§478–499; on obsession with defloration, §§501–505; on the craving for variety, §§506–510; on the craving for rape, §§511, 512; on obsession with seducing the innocent, §§513, 514; and on accountability for the love of infidelity and the love of marriage, §§523–531. All the above are covered by this commandment in its earthly meaning.

314 In the *spiritual meaning,* "committing adultery" refers to contaminating the good things taught by the Word and falsifying its truths. The fact that committing adultery refers to these things has not yet been known, because the Word's spiritual meaning has been hidden until now. In the following passages it is obvious, however, that "committing adultery," "being adulterous," and "being promiscuous" have no other meaning in the Word:

> Run here and there through the streets of Jerusalem and see if you can find a man who *makes judgment and seeks truth.* When I fed them to the full, *they became promiscuous.* (Jeremiah 5:1, 7)

> Among the prophets of Jerusalem I have seen horrendous stubbornness, *committing adultery and walking in a lie.* (Jeremiah 23:14)

They have acted foolishly in Israel. They have *been promiscuous, and have spoken my Word falsely.* (Jeremiah 29:23)

They were *promiscuous* because they had abandoned Jehovah. (Hosea 4:10)

I will cut off the soul that looks off in the direction of sorcerers and soothsayers *to be promiscuous with them.* (Leviticus 20:6)

They are not to make a covenant with the inhabitants of the land; this is to prevent them from *being promiscuous with* other *gods.* (Exodus 34:15)

Because Babylon[530] contaminates and falsifies the Word more than the rest do, it is called *the great whore,* and the following things are said of it in the Book of Revelation:

Babylon has made all the nations drink the wine of the wrath of her promiscuity. (Revelation 14:8)

The angel said, "I will show you the judgment of the great whore with whom the kings of the earth were promiscuous." (Revelation 17:1, 2)

He judged the great whore who had corrupted the earth with her promiscuity. (Revelation 19:2)

Because the Jewish nation had falsified the Word, the Lord called it "an adulterous generation" (Matthew 12:39; 16:4; Mark 8:38) and "the seed of an adulterer" (Isaiah 57:3). There are also many other passages where adultery and promiscuity mean contamination and falsification of the Word; for example, Jeremiah 3:6, 8; 13:27; Ezekiel 16:15, 16, 26, 28, 29, 32, 33; 23:2, 3, 5, 7, 11, 14, 16, 17; Hosea 5:3; 6:10; Nahum 3:1, 3, 4.

315　In the *heavenly meaning,* "committing adultery" refers to denying the Word's holiness and desecrating the Word. This meaning follows from the spiritual meaning, which is contaminating the good things in the Word and falsifying its truths. People who in their heart laugh at everything having to do with the church and religion are people who deny the Word's holiness and desecrate the Word—in the Christian world every aspect of the church and religion comes from the Word.

316　People can seem chaste not only to others but even to themselves and yet be completely unchaste. There are various causes that produce this effect. People do not know that a sexual craving in their will is a deed, and it cannot be removed except by the Lord after they have practiced repentance. Abstaining from doing something does not make us chaste.

What makes us chaste is abstaining from *wanting* to do something that we could in fact do, because doing it would be sinful.

For example, if a man abstains from adultery and promiscuity solely out of fear of civil law and its penalties; or out of fear that he will lose his reputation and respect; or out of fear of sexually transmitted disease; or out of fear of being harassed by his wife and having no peace at home; or out of a fear that the other woman's husband and relatives will avenge themselves on him, or that their servants will whip him; or out of miserliness; or out of lack of ability caused by disease, misuse,[531] old age, or some other cause of impotence—in fact, if he abstains from adultery and promiscuity in obedience to any earthly or moral law but not at the same time to spiritual law, he nevertheless remains inwardly an adulterer and a promiscuous person. He still believes that adultery and promiscuity are not sins. In his spirit he does not make them unlawful before God. Therefore in his spirit he commits them, even if he does not commit them before the world in the flesh. As a result, when he becomes a spirit after death, he openly speaks in favor of such acts.

Adulterers could be compared to treaty breakers who violate agreements, or to the satyrs and priapuses[532] of old who would wander in the woods and shout, "Where are virgins, brides, and wives to play with?" In fact, in the spiritual world, adulterers actually look like satyrs and priapuses. Adulterers could also be compared to goats that sniff for other goats, and dogs that run around in the streets looking and smelling for other dogs with which to have sex. And so on.

When adulterers get married, their sexual potency could be compared to the blooming of tulips in spring—in a month tulips lose their blossoms and wither away.

The Seventh Commandment

You Are Not to Steal

317 In the *earthly meaning,* this commandment literally covers not stealing, robbing, or privateering during a time of peace.[533] It generally means not using stealth or pretense of any kind to take away someone else's possessions. It also covers all swindling, and illegal ways to profit, earn interest, and collect funds; also fraud in paying taxes and fees and in repaying loans.

Workers transgress against this commandment when they do their work dishonestly and deceptively; retailers, when they mislead customers with their merchandise, weighing, measuring, and calculations; officers, when they dip into their soldiers' pay; judges, when they tilt their judgments toward friends or relatives, or for bribes or other inducements, and thus bias their judgments or investigations and deprive others of goods that belong to those others by law.

In the *spiritual meaning,* "stealing" refers to using false and heretical 318 ideas to deprive others of the truths of their faith. Priests are spiritual thieves if they minister only for financial benefit or status and they teach things that on the basis of the Word they see, or at least could see, are not true. They rob people of the means of salvation, which are the truths related to faith.

Priests like this are called thieves in the following passages in the Word:

> Those who do not enter through the door to the sheepfold but climb up some other way are thieves and robbers. Thieves do not come in except to steal, slaughter, and destroy. (John 10:1, 10)

> Store up treasures, not on earth but in heaven, where thieves do not come in and steal. (Matthew 6:19, 20)

> If thieves, if people who knock things over in the night, come to you, how might you be cut off? Are they not going to steal whatever satisfies them? (Obadiah, verse 5)

> They run here and there in the city, they run on the wall, they climb into houses, they come in through windows like a thief. (Joel 2:9)

> They made a lie; the thief comes in, and the crowd scatters outside. (Hosea 7:1)

In the *heavenly meaning,* thieves stand for people who take divine 319 power away from the Lord and people who claim the Lord's merit and justice for themselves. Even if these people worship God, they trust themselves, not him, and believe in themselves, not in him.

There are people who teach false and heretical things and convince 320 the public that these things are true and theologically correct, and yet they read the Word and are therefore able to know what is false and what is true. There are also people who use errors to support false religious beliefs and lead people astray.

These people can be compared to con artists who perpetrate acts of fraud of every kind. Because the things just mentioned are actually thefts in a spiritual sense, these people can be compared to con artists who mint counterfeit coins, gild them or color them gold, and trade them as pure. They can also be compared to people who know skillful ways to cut and polish rock crystals, harden them, and sell them as diamonds. They can also be compared to people who would dress baboons and apes in human clothing with veils over their simian faces and lead them through town on horses or mules, claiming that they are nobles of an old and distinguished family.

They are also like people who would put masks covered in makeup over their own natural faces to hide their good looks.[534] They are like people who would display selenite or mica, which gleam like gold and silver, and sell them as ore containing precious metals. They are like people who would put on theatrical performances to divert others from true divine worship and to lure those others away from church buildings to theaters.

People who support falsities of all kinds and care nothing for the truth, who play the part of priests solely for financial benefit or status and are therefore spiritual thieves, are like thieves who have master keys with which they can open the doors of any home. These people are also like leopards and eagles that look around with sharp eyes for areas that are rich in prey.

The Eighth Commandment

You Are Not to Bear False Witness against Your Neighbor

321 In its most accessible *earthly meaning,* [this commandment against] "bearing false witness against our neighbor" or testifying falsely includes not being a false witness before a judge, or before others outside of a courtroom, against someone who is wrongly accused of some evil. We are not to make such false assertions in the name of God or something sacred, or base them on our own authority or on some expertise for which we are well known.

In a broader earthly sense, this commandment applies to political lies and hypocrisies of every kind that have an evil intent, as well as disparagement and slander of our neighbors to undermine the status, name, and reputation on which their whole good character depends.

In the broadest earthly sense, this commandment includes plots, deceptions, and evil intent against anyone for a variety of motives such as hostility, hatred, desire for revenge, envy, rivalry, and so on. These evils have false witness hidden inside them.

In the *spiritual meaning,* testifying falsely refers to convincing people that a false belief is a true one and an evil life is a good one, and the reverse; but only if these things are done deliberately, not out of ignorance. Doing them deliberately is doing them after we know what truth and goodness are, not before. The Lord says, "If you were blind you would have no sin. But now that you say, 'We see,' your sin remains" (John 9:41).   **322**

This falseness is what is meant in the Word by "a lie" and this deliberateness is what is meant by "deceit" in the following passages:

> We are striking a pact with death; we are making an agreement with hell. We have put our trust in lying and have hidden ourselves with falsity. (Isaiah 28:15)

> They are a people of rebellion, lying children. They do not want to hear the law of Jehovah. (Isaiah 30:9)

> Everyone from prophet to priest is acting out a lie. (Jeremiah 8:10)

> The inhabitants speak a lie, and as for their tongue, deceit is in their mouths. (Micah 6:12)

> You are to destroy those who speak a lie. Jehovah loathes a man of deceit. (Psalms 5:6)

> They taught their tongue to tell a lie, to dwell in the midst of their deceit. (Jeremiah 9:5, 6)

Because "a lie" means a falsity, the Lord says, "The Devil speaks a lie from his own resources" (John 8:44). "A lie" also means falsity and deception in the following passages: Jeremiah 9:4; 23:14, 32; Ezekiel 13:15–19; 21:29; Hosea 7:1; 12:1; Nahum 3:1; Psalms 120:2, 3.

In the *heavenly meaning,* testifying falsely refers to blaspheming the Lord and the Word and driving the actual truth out of the church. The   **323**

Lord is truth itself, and so is the Word. On the other hand, in this sense "testifying" means speaking the truth and "testimony" means the truth itself. This is why the Ten Commandments are called the testimony (Exodus 25:16, 21, 22; 31:7, 18; 32:15, 16; 40:20; Leviticus 16:13; Numbers 17:4, 10). Since the Lord is truth itself, he says that he testifies concerning himself. For the Lord as the truth itself, see John 14:6; Revelation 3:7, 14; for his testifying and being a witness to himself, see John 3:11; 8:13–19; 15:26; 18:37, 38.

324　　There are people who say false, deliberately deceitful things and articulate them with a tone that emulates spiritual feeling. There are even some who cite truths from the Word as they do so, falsifying these truths in the process. The ancients had names for people like these: they called them magicians (see *Revelation Unveiled* 462) and also sorcerers, and snakes from the tree of the knowledge of good and evil.

These pretenders, liars, and deceivers are like people who talk in a pleasant and friendly way with their enemies, but while they are talking they have a dagger behind their back, ready to kill. They are like people who smear venom on their swords before attacking their enemies; or like people who put poison in a well and toxic substances in wine and pastries. They are like charming, attractive whores who carry a malignant sexually transmitted disease. They are like stinging plants that damage our olfactory nerves if we lift them to our noses to smell them. They are like sweetened poisons, or like dung dried out in the fall that gives off a pleasant aroma. In the Word they are described as leopards (see *Revelation Unveiled* 572).

The Ninth and Tenth Commandments

You Are Not to Covet Your Neighbor's Household; You Are Not to Covet Your Neighbor's Wife or His Servant or His Maid or His Ox or His Donkey or Anything That Is Your Neighbor's

325　　In the catechism that is circulated these days, these have been divided into two commandments. One of them is the ninth commandment: "You are not to covet your neighbor's household." The other is the tenth: "You are not to covet your neighbor's wife or his servant or his maid or his ox or his donkey or anything that is your neighbor's." Because these two commandments are united and form just a single verse in Exodus 20:17 and in Deuteronomy 5:21, I have taken them up together. It is not my intention, however, to connect them into one commandment. I want to keep them distinguished into two commandments as they have been, since all the commandments are referred to as the ten words (Exodus 34:28; Deuteronomy 4:13; 10:4).

These two commandments look back to all the commandments that precede them. They teach and enjoin that we are not to do evil and that we are also not to crave doing evil. Therefore the Ten Commandments are not only for the outer self but also for the inner self. Someone who does not do evil things but nevertheless craves doing them is still doing them. The Lord says,

> If some man craves someone else's wife, he has already committed adultery with her in his heart. (Matthew 5:27, 28)

Our outer self does not become internal or become one with our inner self until our cravings have been removed. The Lord teaches this as well, when he says,

> Woe to you, scribes and Pharisees,[535] because you clean the outside of your cup and plate, but the insides are full of plundering and self-indulgence. Blind Pharisee! First clean the inside of your cup and plate, so that the outside may be clean as well. (Matthew 23:25, 26)

The Lord says more on this in that whole chapter from beginning to end. The inner problems that are pharisaical are the cravings to do what the first, second, fifth, sixth, seventh, and eighth commandments say not to do.

It is generally known that while he was in the world, the Lord gave the church inner teachings. The inner teachings for the church tell us not to crave doing evil. He taught us this so that our inner and outer self would become one, which is the same as being born anew—something the Lord discussed with Nicodemus (John 3). Only through the Lord can we be born anew or regenerated, and therefore become inner people.

These two commandments look back to all the commandments that came before as things not to be coveted. Therefore the household is mentioned first; then the wife; then the servant, the maid, the ox, and the donkey; and finally everything that belongs to one's neighbor. The "household" comes before everything on the rest of the list, for the husband, the wife, the servant, the maid, the ox, and the donkey are all part

326

of it. The "wife," who is mentioned next, comes before everything on the rest of the list after that, for she is the woman in charge of the household, as her husband is the man in charge of it. The servant and the maid are under them, and the ox and the donkey are under the servant and the maid. Finally, everything below or beyond the servant and the maid is covered by the phrase "anything that is your neighbor's." This shows that generally and specifically, in both a broad and a narrow sense, these two commandments look back to all the prior commandments.

327   In the *spiritual meaning,* these commandments prohibit all the cravings that go against the spirit, that is, against the spiritual qualities taught by the church, which primarily relate to faith and goodwill. If our cravings were not tamed, our flesh would pursue its own freedom and would quickly fall into every kind of wickedness. From Paul we know that "The flesh has cravings that go against the spirit and the spirit has cravings that go against the flesh" (Galatians 5:17). From James we know that "All are tested by their own craving. When they become captivated, then after the craving conceives, it gives birth to sin, and sin, when it reaches its final stage, brings forth death" (James 1:14, 15). From Peter we know that "The Lord holds for the judgment day the unjust who are to be punished, especially those who walk according to the flesh in craving" (2 Peter 2:9, 10).

In brief, these two commandments taken in their spiritual meaning look back to the spiritual meaning of all the commandments previously given, adding that we are not to crave doing those evil things. The same goes for all the commandments previously given in the heavenly meaning, but there is no point in listing them all again.

328   The cravings of the flesh—of the eyes and the other senses—when separated from the cravings of the spirit (meaning its feelings, desires, and pleasures) are identical to the cravings animals have. On their own, therefore, the cravings of the flesh are beastly. The desires of the spirit are what angels have; they are to be called desires that are truly human. Therefore the more we become addicted to the cravings of the flesh, the more of a beast and a wild animal we become; the more we give the desires of our spirit their due, the more of a human being and an angel we become.

The cravings of the flesh could be compared to grapes that have been parched and burnt or to wild grapes, while the desires of the spirit could be compared to juicy, flavorful grapes and to the taste of wine that has been pressed from them.

The cravings of the flesh are like stables that hold donkeys, goats, and pigs, while the desires of the spirit are like stables that hold thoroughbred horses, as well as sheep and lambs. In fact, the cravings of the flesh differ from the desires of the spirit the way a donkey differs from a horse, a goat from a sheep, and a pig from a lamb. They differ as much as slag and gold, lime and silver, coral and a ruby, and so on.

A craving and a deed are as closely connected as blood and flesh or oil and flame. The craving is in the deed the same way air from our lungs is in our breath and speech; or the wind is in the sail when we are sailing; or the water is in the waterwheel, causing the machinery to move and act.

The Ten Commandments Contain Everything about How to Love God and How to Love Our Neighbor

Eight of the commandments—the first, second, fifth, sixth, seventh, eighth, ninth, and tenth—say nothing about loving God or loving our neighbor. They do not say that we must love God or we must keep God's name holy. They do not say that we must love our neighbor, or deal honestly and uprightly with our neighbor. They say only, "There is to be no other God before my face; you are not to take God's name in vain; you are not to kill; you are not to commit adultery; you are not to steal; you are not to testify falsely; and you are not to covet what your neighbor has." Briefly put, we are not to intend, think, or do evil against God or against our neighbor.

329

We are not commanded to do things that directly relate to goodwill; instead, we are commanded not to do things that are the opposite of goodwill. This is because the more we abstain from evils because they are sins, the more we want the goodness that relates to goodwill.

In loving God and our neighbor, the first step is not doing evil, and the second step is doing good, as you will see in the chapter on goodwill [§§435–438].

[2] There is a love of intending and doing good, and there is a love of intending and doing evil. These two loves are opposite to each other. The second is a hellish love and the first is a heavenly one. The entirety of hell loves doing evil and the entirety of heaven loves doing good.

We, the human race, have been born into evils of every kind. From birth onward we have tendencies toward things that come from hell. Unless we are born again or regenerated, we cannot come into heaven.

Therefore the evil attributes we have from hell have to be removed first before we are able to want good attributes that come from heaven. None of us can be adopted by the Lord before we have been separated from the Devil. How our evil actions are removed and how we are brought to do good things will be shown in two chapters below: the chapter on repentance [§§509–570]; and the chapter on reformation and regeneration [§§571–625].

[3] The Lord teaches in Isaiah that our evil actions have to be moved aside first before the good things we are doing become good before God:

> Wash yourselves; purify yourselves. Remove the evil of your actions from before my eyes. Learn to do what is good. Then, if your sins had been like scarlet, they will become as white as snow; if they had been red as crimson, they will be like wool. (Isaiah 1:16, 17, 18)

The following passage in Jeremiah is similar:

> Stand in the entrance to Jehovah's house and proclaim there this word. "Thus spoke Jehovah Sabaoth, the God of Israel: 'Make your ways and your works good. Do not put your trust in the words of a lie, saying, "The temple of Jehovah, the temple of Jehovah, the temple of Jehovah is here [that is, the church]."[536] When you steal, kill, commit adultery, and swear falsely, then do you come and stand before me in this house that carries my name? Do you say, "We were carried away," when you are committing all these abominations? Has this house become a den of thieves? Behold I, even I, have seen it,' says Jehovah." (Jeremiah 7:2, 3, 4, 9, 10, 11)

[4] We are also taught by Isaiah that before we are washed or purified from evil, our prayers to God are not heard:

> Jehovah says, "Woe to a sinful nation, to a people heavy with wickedness. They have moved themselves backward. Therefore when you spread out your hands, I hide my eyes from you. Even if you increase your praying, I do not hear it." (Isaiah 1:4, 15)

When someone puts the Ten Commandments into action by abstaining from evil, goodwill is the result. This is clear from the Lord's own words in John:

> Jesus said, "The people who love me are those who have my commandments and follow them. Those who love me will be loved by my Father,

and I will love them and manifest myself to them, and we will make a home with them." (John 14:21, 23)

The "commandments" mentioned here are specifically the Ten Commandments, which prescribe that we should not do, or crave to do, what is evil. If we do not do evil or crave to do evil, we love God and God loves us. This is the benefit we receive after something evil has been removed.

I have stated that the more we abstain from what is evil, the more we will and intend what is good, because evil and good are opposites. Evil comes from hell and good comes from heaven. Therefore the more hell—that is, evil—is removed, the closer we get to heaven and the more we focus on good.

The truth of this becomes obvious when we see eight of the Ten Commandments in this way. For example: (1) The less we worship other gods, the more we worship the true God. (2) The less we take the name of God in vain, the more we love the things that come from God. (3) The less we want to kill and to act on the basis of hatred and revenge, the more we want what is good for our neighbor. (4) The less we want to commit adultery, the more we want to live faithfully with our spouse. (5) The less we want to steal, the more we aim to be honest. (6) The less we want to testify falsely, the more we want to think and speak what is true. (7) and (8) The less we covet what our neighbors have, the more we want our neighbors to be doing well with what they have. From this it becomes clear that the Ten Commandments contain everything about how to love God and our neighbor. Therefore Paul says,

> Those who love others have fulfilled the law. "You are not to commit adultery, you are not to kill, you are not to steal, you are not to be a false witness, you are not to covet things," and if anything else is commanded, it is included in this saying: "You are to love your neighbor as yourself." Goodwill does no evil to our neighbor. Therefore the fulfillment of the law is goodwill. (Romans 13:8, 9, 10)

To the above list, two principles need to be added that will benefit the new church: (1) On our own, none of us can abstain from evils because they are sins or do good things that are good before God. The more we abstain from evils because they are sins, the more we do good things from the Lord instead of from ourselves. (2) We need to abstain from evils and fight against them as if we were acting on our own. If we abstain from evils for any other reason than because they are sins, we are not abstaining from them, but merely making them invisible to the world.[537]

331 Evil and good cannot coexist; the more evil is removed, the more good is focused on and felt. This is the case because all who are in the spiritual world have a field of their particular love emanating around them. This field spreads all around and has an effect on others. It creates feelings of harmony or antipathy. These fields separate the good from the evil.

The fact that evil has to be removed before goodness is recognized, perceived, and loved could be compared with many situations that are possible in our world; for example, the following: Suppose someone keeps a leopard and a panther in an apartment and, as the one who feeds them, is able to live safely with them. No one else can visit unless their owner first removes these wild animals.

[2] Guests invited to the table of the king and queen would not forget to wash their faces and hands before attending. No bridegroom goes into the bedroom with his bride after the wedding without first washing himself all over and putting on a wedding garment. Anyone must first purify ore with fire and remove slag before getting pure gold or silver. Everyone separates the tares or weeds from the harvested wheat before taking it into the barn. Everyone removes the beards[538] from harvested barley with threshing tools before bringing it home.

[3] Everyone cooks some of the juice out of raw meat before it becomes edible and is set on the table. Everyone knocks the grubs and caterpillars off the leaves of trees in the garden to prevent them from devouring the leaves and causing a loss of fruit. Everyone removes garbage from the house and the front entrance and cleans up those areas, especially when expecting a visit from a prince or the prince's daughter to whom one is engaged. Does any man love a young woman and propose to marry her if she is riddled with malignancies or covered all over with pustules and varicose veins, no matter how much she puts makeup on her face, wears gorgeous clothing, and makes an effort to be attractive by saying nice things and paying compliments?

[4] The need for us to purify ourselves from evils, and not to wait for the Lord to do it without our participation, is like a servant coming in with his face and clothes covered in soot and dung, approaching his master, and saying, "Lord, wash me." Surely his master would tell him, "You foolish servant! What are you saying? Look, there is the water, the soap, and a towel. Don't you have hands? Don't they work? Wash yourself!"

The Lord God is going to say, "The means of being purified come from me. Your willingness and your power come from me. Therefore use these gifts and endowments of mine as your own and you will be purified." And so on.

The need for the outer self to be cleansed, but to be cleansed through the inner self, is something that the Lord teaches in Matthew chapter 23 from beginning to end.

To these points I will add four memorable occurrences.

The first memorable occurrence. On one occasion I heard sounds of shouting that seemed as if they were bubbling up through water from below. One shout was to the left: "*They are so just!*" A second shout was to the right: "*They are so learned!*" A third shout was at the back: "*They are so wise!*" Because I was struck by the thought that there might be just, learned, and wise people in hell as well, I had a desire to see whether there were in fact people like that down there. From heaven I was told, "You will see and hear."

I left home in the spirit and saw an opening in front of me. I went over to it and looked down. There was a ladder! I climbed down it. When I was below, I saw plains that were covered in shrubs, with thorn bushes and stinging-nettles here and there. I asked whether it was hell. The people said that it was the lower earth,[539] which is the next level up from hell. I tracked down the uproars one at a time.

I went toward the first shout: "*They are so just!*" I saw a group of people who in the world had been judges who took bribes and showed favoritism. Then I went toward the second shout: "*They are so learned!*" I saw a group of people who had been debaters in the world. I went toward the third shout: "*They are so wise!*" I saw a group of people who in the world had been providers of arguments.[540] I turned away from this last group and headed back toward the first group, where there were judges who took bribes, showed favoritism, and were proclaimed just.

To one side I saw a kind of amphitheater made of bricks with a black-tiled roof. I was told that this was their courtroom. There were three doorways into it on the north side and three on the west side. There were no doorways on the south side or the east side. This was an indication that their judgments were arbitrary and had nothing to do with justice.

[2] In the middle of the amphitheater there was a fireplace. The keepers of the fire were throwing pitch-pine logs full of tar and sulfur into it. The light that these logs cast onto the plaster walls created colorful images of birds that come out only in the evening or the night. The fireplace and

332

the light cast from it that took the shape of these images were in fact symbolic of these people's judgments—they reflected the ability these people had to color the issues in any case and make the issues look a certain way, depending on the favor the judges would receive.

[3] After half an hour, I saw elders and youths coming in wearing robes and gowns. They took their hats off and sat down on chairs behind tables to hear cases.

I heard and sensed how, by way of looking out for their friends, the judges skillfully and ingeniously bent and inverted their decisions into something that seemed just. They were so effective that they themselves were not able to see their injustice as anything but just, and justice as unjust. Their conviction of this was apparent in their faces and audible in the sound of their voices.

At that point enlightenment from heaven was granted to me, which enabled me to perceive whether individual points were lawful or not. I saw how energetically these judges covered up injustice and overlaid it with an appearance of justice. Out of all laws they would pick one that was supportive and bend the central issue of the case in its direction, using skillful argumentation to set other laws aside.

After they arrived at their judgments, they handed down sentences in favor of their clients, friends, and supporters. To pay back the favor the judges had done them, the clients, friends, and supporters went all the way down a long road shouting, *"They are so just! They are so just!"*

[4] After that I talked to angels of heaven about these judges, recounting some of the things I had seen and heard. The angels said, "Judges like that seem to others as if they have the sharpest intellects, when in fact they do not see what is just and fair at all. If favoritism is not involved, they sit like statues during the trials and say only, 'I accede,' and 'I am willing to go along with this person or that person.' The reason is that all their judgments are prejudiced; prejudice and favoritism dog their cases from beginning to end. They see nothing but what would benefit their friends. They avoid looking directly at anything that would argue against their friends; they only glance at it out of the corner of their eyes. If they have to address it, they wrap it up in argumentation and devour it the way a spider wraps its prey in silken threads.

"Therefore if they are not following the web of their prejudice they see no law. In fact, they have been assessed to find out whether they could see the law; the finding was that they could not. The people who live in your world will find this incredible; but tell them that this is a truth discovered by angels of heaven. Because these judges do not see justice at all, we in heaven view them not as human beings but as monstrous human images: their heads are made of friendship, their chests are made of injustice, their arms and legs are made of supporting arguments, and the soles of their feet are made of justice. If a particular form of justice doesn't favor their friend, they remove it and trample it. [5] You are about to find out what they are truly like inside. Their end has come."

Then suddenly the ground split open. Tables crashed into tables. Along with the whole amphitheater, the people were swallowed up. They were thrown into caves and imprisoned.

Then I was asked, "Do you want to see them there?"

To my amazement I saw that their faces were like polished steel; from their necks to their groins their bodies were like statues clothed in leopard skins, and their legs were like snakes. I saw that the law books that they had set on their tables had turned into playing cards. Now instead of being judges, they were given the task of turning vermilion into makeup and applying it to the faces of promiscuous women to make them beautiful.

After seeing this I wanted to go to the other two groups, the one that consisted entirely of debaters and the other that consisted entirely of providers of arguments, but I was told, "Rest for a little while. You will be given angels from the community directly above those groups to accompany you. The Lord is going to give you light through these angels, and you are going to see amazing things."

The second memorable occurrence. After a time I heard again the voices from the lower earth that I had heard before: "*They are so learned! They are so learned!*"

I looked around to see who was beside me, and to my surprise there were angels from the heaven that was directly above the people who were shouting, "*They are so learned.*"

I talked to the angels about the shouting. They said, "These are the type of scholars who argue only about *whether something exists or not.*[541] They rarely think, *it does exist.* Therefore they are like the wind that blows and goes on by; they are like bark around a tree with nothing inside it; they are like almond shells without almonds; they are like skins empty of fruit. Their minds lack inner judgment and are connected only to their bodily senses. If their senses cannot discern something, they are unable to come to a conclusion about it. They are exclusively oriented to their senses. We call them *debaters* because they never come to a conclusion.

333

Whatever they hear about, they take up for discussion and dispute whether it exists. They always take a contrary position. The thing they love the most is to attack things that are true and tear those things apart by making them the subject of debate. These are people who believe they are more learned than anyone else in the world."

[2] Once I had heard that, I asked the angels to take me to them. The angels brought me to a little valley that had steps going down toward the lower earth. We went down the steps and followed the voices that were shouting, "*They are so learned.*"

We came upon several hundred people standing in one spot treading the ground. Amazed by this I asked, "Why are they standing and treading the ground with their feet like this?" I added, "If they keep it up they could dig a hole in the ground with their feet."

The angels smiled at this and said, "They seem to be standing in one place like this, because they never think that anything exists; they think only about whether it exists, and argue over it. Since their thinking never advances beyond this stage, they look as if they are treading and wearing down one patch of ground without moving forward."

The angels also said, "When people arrive in this world from the physical one and hear that they are in another world, they gather together in many places to form groups. They ask where heaven and hell are, and also where God is. After they have been taught, they start arguing, disputing, and fighting about whether God exists. This is a result of the great number of materialists in the physical world today. When the topic of religion comes up, materialists start to debate about it with one another and with other groups. The ensuing proposition and debate rarely results in an affirmation of the faith that God exists. Materialists associate more and more with the evil, because only from God can one do something good with a love for what is good."

[3] Then I was taken down into their gathering. To my surprise they looked to me like people with pleasant faces and good-looking clothes. "They look this way in their own light," the angels said, "but if light from heaven flows in, their faces and clothes change."

Then that happened. They looked as if they had dark faces and clothes made out of black sacks. Then the light from heaven was taken away and they looked the way they had before.

Soon I started speaking with some people from the group. I said, "I heard shouting from the crowd around you—'*They are so learned!*' Might I be allowed, therefore, to enter a discussion with you on points that are of the utmost scholarly importance?"

"Say whatever you wish," they replied, "and we will give it adequate attention."

I asked, "What does a religion need to be like in order to save people?"

They said, "We are going to divide this question into a number of subquestions. Before we have come to conclusions on these we will not be able to give a reply to your question. The points for discussion will be the following. (1) Is religion anything? (2) Does salvation exist or not? (3) Is one religion more effective than another? (4) Do heaven and hell exist? (5) Does everlasting life after death exist? And more as well."

I asked for the first question: "Is religion anything?" They began discussing this with a host of arguments. I asked them to refer the question to the audience.[542] They did so. The general response was that this question needed so much investigation that there was no way it could be finished by the end of the evening.

"Could you finish within a year?" I asked.

Someone answered that it could not be finished within a hundred years.

I said, "Meanwhile you have no religion; and because salvation depends on religion, you have no concept of, faith in, or hope of salvation."

The person replied, "Won't someone have to show first whether religion exists, then what it is, and if it is anything? If it is something, it must exist for the wise; if it is not, then it exists only for the general public. As we know, religion is called a restraint, but there is the question of whom it restrains. If it is only a restraint for the general public, then it is not really anything. But if it is also a restraint for the wise, then it is something."

[4] On hearing that I said, "You are all anything but learned, because you are incapable of any other thought except whether something exists, and you deflect this question into subquestions. Can anyone be learned without knowing something for certain? Only when something is established can we move forward with it, just as people walk, putting one foot in front of the other; then we advance gradually into wisdom. Otherwise, rather than touching truths with even the tip of your finger, you move them farther and farther out of sight. Reasoning solely about whether something exists is reasoning about a hat that you never put on, or about a shoe that you never wear. What comes of it except not knowing whether anything exists or is anything other than an idea? What comes of it but not knowing whether salvation exists, or whether there is eternal life after death, or whether one religion is better than another, or whether there is a heaven or a hell? You are incapable of having any thought on these issues as long as you are stuck on the first step, treading the sand

there, rather than lifting one foot after another and moving forward. While your minds are standing out in the open like this away from the shelter of a decision, watch out that your minds don't harden inside and become statues of salt."543

After I said this I left. They were considerably irritated and threw stones at me. At that point they looked to me like statues that had no human reason inside. I asked the angels about the final outcome of their lives. The angels said, "The lowest of them are sent down deep to a desert and are forced to carry loads. Because they cannot offer anything on the basis of reason, they blather and speak nonsense. From far away they look like donkeys carrying burdens."

334 *The third memorable occurrence.* Afterward one of the angels said, "Follow me to the place where people are shouting, '*They are so wise!*'" He added, "The people you are going to see are bizarre. You will see faces and bodies that make them look human, though they are not."

I said, "They are animals, then?"

He answered, "They are not true animals; they are human animals. They are completely unable to see whether a truth is true or not, yet they can take anything they want and make it appear to be true. We call them *providers of arguments.*"

We followed the sound of shouting and came to the place. There we found a group of men. The group was surrounded by a crowd of people, some of whom were of noble lineage. When the nobles heard that the men in the group were providing arguments to support everything the nobles had said and were favoring them with such obvious agreement, the nobles turned to one another and said, "*They are so wise!*"

[2] The angel said to me, "We should not go up to them; instead we should call one of them away from the group."

We called one away and left with him. We said various things and he provided arguments to support all the details to the point where what we had said seemed absolutely true. Then we asked him whether he could provide arguments to support points that were opposite to these. He said, "Just as well as I could for the first points."544

Then openly and from the heart he said, "What is truth? Does any truth exist in the nature of things beyond what people make out to be true? Say whatever you like and I will make out that it is true."

I said, "Make this true, that faith is the most important thing in the church."

He did this with such skill and ability that scholars who were nearby were amazed and burst into applause. Then I asked him to make it true that goodwill was the most important thing in the church. He did it. Then I asked him to make it true that goodwill has nothing to do with the church. In both cases he fleshed out and adorned his argument with seemingly good material to the point where others present looked at each other and said, "He *is* wise, isn't he!"

I said to him, "Don't you know that goodwill is living a good life and having faith is believing the right things? Isn't it true that people who live a good life have a good faith? Therefore having faith is part of goodwill, and goodwill is part of having faith. Don't you see that this is the truth?"

"I will make it true and then see," he replied. He did so and said, "Now I see it." Yet he soon made its opposite true and said, "I also see that this is true."

We laughed and said, "Aren't they opposites? How can you see two opposite things as both being true?"

Annoyed, he answered, "You're mistaken. They are in fact both true, since nothing is true except what people make out to be true."

[3] Standing near him there was someone who had been a high-ranking ambassador in the world. He was astounded at this and said to the provider of arguments, "I will admit that something similar goes on in the world, but you are nevertheless insane. If you can, make it true that light is darkness and darkness is light."

The provider of arguments replied, "I'll do it with ease! What is light and darkness other than a state of our eye? Doesn't light change into shadow when our eye comes out of the bright sun and also when we stare intently straight at the sun? We all know that the state of our eye then changes so that light looks like a shadow. And the reverse: when the state of our eye stabilizes, the shadow looks like light. Night birds see the darkness of night as the light of day and the light of day as the darkness of night, and the sun itself looks to them like nothing but a dark and dusky ball. If we had eyes like a night bird, which would we call light and which would we call darkness? What then is light but a state of our eye, and if it is only a state of our eye, isn't light darkness and darkness light? Therefore the first point is true and the second point is true."

[4] Because this argumentation was actually convincing to some people, I said, "I notice that the provider of arguments doesn't know there is such a thing as true light and deceptive light. Both of these types of light appear to be light, but faint, deceptive light is not a true light. Relative to true light it is darkness. Night birds function in faint, deceptive light. Inside their eyes there is an obsession to hunt and devour birds. This light enables their eyes to see at night. Similarly, cats'

eyes in basements look like candles[545] because of the faint, deceptive light inside their eyes from their obsession to hunt and devour rats and mice. Clearly then, the light of the sun is true light; the light of obsession is faint, deceptive light."

[5] After that the ambassador asked the provider of arguments to make it true that crows are white, not black. He responded, "This too I will do with ease."

"Take a needle or a razor," he said, "and cut open the feathers of a crow. Then pluck the feathers out and look at the crow's skin. Aren't they both white? What is the surrounding blackness then except a shadow that shouldn't be used as a basis for judging the color of the crow? Blackness is only a shadow, as people skilled in the science of optics will tell you. Or grind a black stone or a black piece of glass to a fine powder and you'll see that the powder is white."

The ambassador replied, "But in fact the crow looks black to our eyes."

The provider of arguments rejoined, "Are you, a human being, really sure you want to think about something on the basis of appearances? On that basis it is indeed acceptable to speak of crows as being black, but you cannot think it. For another example, on the basis of appearance it is fine to say that the sun rises and sets, but because you are human you cannot think that, because the sun stands still while the earth moves around it. It is the same with the crow. Appearance is appearance. Say whatever you want—crows are completely and utterly white. In fact, they become white as they age. I've seen it myself."

The people nearby turned to look at me, so I said, "It is true that the shafts of crows' feathers are whitish, as is their skin. This is true, however, not only of crows but also of all the birds in the universe; and we all distinguish birds on the appearance of their color. If this were not the case, we would say that every bird is white, which would be pointless and absurd."

[6] Then the ambassador asked him, "Can you make it true that you yourself are insane?"

The provider of arguments said, "I could, but I don't want to. Who isn't insane?"

Then people asked the provider of arguments to say from the heart whether he was joking or whether he really believed that there is no truth except what people make out to be true. He replied, "That is what I believe, I swear."

Afterward this provider of arguments that support all points of view was sent to angels who had the ability to assess his nature. After the assessment they said, "He does not possess even a speck of understanding. In his case, everything above his rational faculty is closed off; only what is below it is opened up. Above people's rational faculty there is spiritual light; below it there is earthly light. The nature of earthly light with people is that it can provide arguments to support whatever they want; but if no spiritual light flows into the earthly light, people cannot see whether anything true is true or not. They also cannot see whether anything false is false or not. Spiritual light flowing into earthly light is what allows us to see truth and falsity. Spiritual light comes from the God of heaven, who is the Lord. Therefore this provider of arguments to support all points of view is not a human being or an animal: he is a human animal."

[7] I asked the angels what happens in the long run to people like this: "Can they keep company with the living, given that human life comes from spiritual light and that it is spiritual light that gives us understanding?"

The angels said, "When they are alone, people like this cannot think or say anything. They stand like silent robots,[546] as if they were utterly unconscious. They wake up as soon as their ears catch any sound."

"It is people who are inwardly evil who become like this," the angels added. "Spiritual light cannot flow into them from above; they merely bring something spiritual from the world that gives them the ability to come up with supporting arguments."

[8] After that I heard the voice of one of the angels who had assessed the provider of arguments saying to me, "Draw a universal conclusion from what you have heard."

The conclusion I drew was the following: *Being able to provide arguments to support whatever you want is not intelligence; intelligence is being able to see that what is true is true and what is false is false and to provide arguments to support that.*

Afterward I looked over at the group where the providers of arguments were standing. The crowd around them was shouting, "*They are so wise!*" To my surprise, a dark cloud encompassed them. There were bats and screech owls flying around in the cloud.

I was told, "The bats and screech owls flying in the cloud are correspondences and manifestations of the thinking of the providers of arguments. In this world those who provide arguments to support falsities until they look like truths are represented in the form of night birds. The eyes of night birds are lit from inside by a faint, deceptive light that allows them to see objects in the dark as if they were in the light. People who provide arguments to support falsities until they look like truths and then believe they are true have a similar but spiritual form of faint, deceptive light. All of them have lower vision; none has higher sight."

335   *The fourth memorable occurrence.* Once when I woke up in the early light before dawn, I saw ghostly shapes of various kinds before my eyes. Later on, when it was morning, I saw a faint, deceptive light[547] taking various forms [in the sky]. Some of the forms were like sheets of parchment covered in writing that kept folding in on themselves until they looked like shooting stars falling through the air and disappearing. Others were like open books, some of which shone like little moons, while others burned like candles. Some of the books went higher and higher until they passed out of sight, while others fell down to the earth and smashed into powder. On the basis of these visions, I conjectured that there were people standing below these aerial phenomena and that the people were having a dispute over things that were figments of their imagination, but that they nevertheless thought were very important. In the spiritual world, phenomena like this appear in the atmospheres because of the false reasoning of the people standing below them.

Soon the sight of my spirit was opened[548] and I noticed a number of spirits whose heads were ringed with laurel leaves and who were wearing togas with a floral pattern—signs that they were spirits who had been famous scholars in our world. Because I was in the spirit, I went over and mingled with the group. I could hear then that they were having a sharp and ardent dispute about *innate ideas.*[549] At issue was whether people are born with innate ideas the way animals are. The spirits who thought that people are not born with innate ideas were turning away from the spirits who thought that people are. Eventually the two groups were squared off against each other like the ranks of two armies about to battle with swords, except that since they had no swords they were battling with sharply pointed words.

[2] At that point an angelic spirit suddenly stood among them and spoke out in a loud voice, saying, "From not too far away I could hear that you are having a blazing dispute with one another about innate ideas and whether people have them the way animals do; but I say to you, *People have no innate ideas, and animals have no ideas at all.* This means that what you are fighting about is actually nothing or, as the saying goes, goat's wool or beards in a clean-shaven age."[550]

When the spirits heard this, they were all outraged and shouted, "Throw him out! What he is saying goes against common sense."

When they tried to throw the angelic spirit out, however, they saw him surrounded with a heavenly light. Because he was an angelic spirit, they could not break through the light. They backed up and moved a little farther away from him.

After the light drew back, he said to them, "Why did you get angry? Hear me out first. Put together the reasons I am about to give; then you yourselves draw a conclusion based on them. I foresee that those of you who have outstanding judgment will accede, and the storms that have arisen in your minds will grow calm."

In response, although the spirits still sounded annoyed, they said, "Speak then, and we will hear you out."

[3] Then the angelic spirit rose to speak and said, "You believe that animals have innate ideas. You have drawn this conclusion from the fact that their actions seem to be based on thought. Yet they have no thought at all; and if they have no thought, they cannot be said to have ideas. A sign that thought processes are active is that people behave in one way or another for one reason or another.

"Ponder, then, whether a spider that is weaving a web with the utmost skill is thinking in its tiny head, 'I am going to lay out threads in this sequence and then stabilize them with perpendicular threads so that my web doesn't fall apart when the air shakes it violently. At the outermost ends of threads that run in to the center I will fashion a seat for myself. There I will sense if anything comes in and will hurry to the center. For example, if a fly flies in and gets caught, I will quickly go in and wrap it up and it will become my food.'

"Does a bee think in its tiny head, 'I am going to fly away. I know where the fields are that have flowers in them. There I will extract wax from some flowers and honey from others. With the wax I will build adjacent cells one after the other, laid out in such a way that my colleagues and I can easily get in and out on passageways. Later we will put lots of honey away in the cells so that there will be enough to prevent our death over the coming winter'? Not to mention other miraculous behaviors that not only emulate human political and economic prudence but even outdo it in some respects [see §12:7 above].[551]

[4] "Again, does a hornet think in its tiny head, 'My colleagues and I will build a little home out of thin paper. We will curve its inside walls into a labyrinth and fashion the heart of it into a gathering place with a way in and a way out so cleverly designed that no other living thing that is not part of our clan will be able to find the way to the center where we are gathered'?

"Again, is a silkworm during its caterpillar phase thinking in its tiny head, 'Now is the time for me to get ready to spin silk. My goal is that when I have finished spinning silk I will fly off, and in the air—a place I have never been able to reach before—I will play with my friends and ensure that I will have offspring'? The same with other caterpillars that crawl along walls and then become chrysalises, pupas, nymphs, and finally butterflies. Does a fly ever have an idea about breeding with another fly, that the breeding should take place here and not over there?

[5] "It is the same for creatures with larger bodies as it is for these insects—for example, when birds and winged creatures of all kinds mate, build nests, lay eggs in them, incubate the eggs, hatch young, give them food, raise them until they fly away, and then drive them from the birds' nests as if they weren't the birds' own offspring, not to mention countless other phenomena. It is the same for animals, snakes, and fish.

"From what I have said, you can all see that the spontaneous actions of living creatures do not flow from any thought, and that ideas come into play only where there is thought. The mistaken concept that animals have ideas comes solely from the false belief that animals think just as people do and only verbalization differentiates them."

[6] After that the angelic spirit looked around. Since he saw that the spirits were still undecided on the issue of whether animals think or not, he continued his speech and said, "I sense that you are still stuck with an imaginary idea about brute animals thinking, since they have actions that are similar to human actions. I will tell you then where animals' actions come from.

"Every animal, every bird, every fish, reptile, and insect has its own earthly, sensory, and physical love. These loves dwell in the brains inside their heads. The spiritual world flows directly through their brains into their physical senses and uses those senses to determine their actions. This is why their bodily senses are far more refined than human senses. This inflow from the spiritual world is what is known as instinct. It is called instinct because it comes about without the help of thought. Instinct is also supplemented by the development of habits.

"The love animals have is a love solely for nutrition and propagation. A determination to act comes from the spiritual world through that love. They have no love for knowledge, intelligence, or wisdom, which are the means of developing higher levels of love in human beings.

[7] "As for people having no innate ideas, this is obvious from the fact that people have no innate thinking. Where there is no thinking, there are no ideas, for thinking and ideas go hand in hand. This conclusion can be reached by studying newborn babies. They are unable to do anything

except nurse and breathe. They are able to nurse not from anything innate but from continually sucking while they are in their mother's womb. They are able to breathe because they are alive—breathing is universal to life. Their physical senses are in extreme darkness; by [encountering external] objects they climb out of that obscurity bit by bit. Similarly, their ability to move develops through habitual movement. As they learn to babble words and sound them out, at first without any idea, a dim form of visualization gradually arises. As this becomes clearer, a dim form of imagination develops, and this leads to a dim form of thought. As this state gradually develops, ideas develop, which as I said go hand in hand with thought. Thought grows out of no thought as a result of education. This is how people have ideas. Ideas are formed; they are not innate. From these ideas flow people's words and actions."

On the point that people have nothing else innate except a faculty for knowing, understanding, and becoming wise, as well as a tendency to love not only knowledge, understanding, and wisdom but also their neighbor and their God, see above in the memorable occurrence at §48, and also a memorable occurrence below [§692].

After that I looked around and saw Leibniz and Wolff nearby.[552] They were paying close attention to the reasoning put forward by the angelic spirit. Leibniz then acceded and expressed his agreement, but Wolff went away both denying it and affirming it. Wolff's inner judgment was not as well developed as Leibniz's.

Chapter 6

Faith

336 FROM the wisdom of the ancients[553] came the following teaching: the universe, and each and every thing in it, relates to goodness and truth. Therefore all aspects of the church relate to love or goodwill[554] and faith, since everything that is called good flows from love or goodwill and everything called truth flows from faith.

Now, goodwill and faith are two distinct things, yet they become one in us and make us people of the church—they cause the church to exist within us. For this reason, among the ancients it was a matter of contention and dispute which of the two should be primary and rightly be called the firstborn. Some of them said it was truth and therefore faith. Others said it was goodness and therefore goodwill. Some people observed that soon after we are born we learn to talk and think; then talking and thinking lead to the development of our intellect through study, that is, through learning and understanding what is true. Then we use these means to learn and understand what is good. First, therefore, we learn what faith is, and afterward what goodwill is. The people who adopted this point of view considered true faith to be the firstborn and goodwill to be born later. For this reason they accorded faith the rights and privileges of the firstborn.

They overwhelmed their own intellect, however, with an abundance of arguments in favor of faith to the point where they did not see that faith is not truly faith unless it is connected to goodwill, and neither is goodwill truly goodwill unless it is connected to faith. The two unite. If the two do not unite, neither of them amounts to anything in the church. Below I will show that they are completely united.

[2] Now, in this introduction to the chapter I will just take a few words to disclose how the two unite or in what way, since this will help shed light on what follows.

From the standpoint of time, faith (meaning truth as well) is primary, but from the standpoint of purpose, goodwill (meaning goodness as

514

well) is primary. Whatever the primary purpose is, that is the element that is truly primary because it is of prime importance and is the real firstborn. Whatever is primary in time is only apparently primary, not truly primary.

So that this may be clearly understood I will illustrate it with analogous situations that occur in constructing a church building or a house, developing a fruit garden, and preparing a field. *Constructing a church building:* From the standpoint of time, the primary thing is to lay the foundation, raise the walls, put on the roof, and then put in an altar and build the pulpit. From the standpoint of purpose, however, the primary thing is to worship God in the building, which is why these other steps were taken. *Constructing a house:* From the standpoint of time, the primary thing is to build the outside of our house and then build inside it the various things that we need. From the standpoint of purpose, however, the primary thing is to have a comfortable place for us and the others in our household to live. *Developing a fruit garden:* From the standpoint of time, the primary thing is to level the ground, prepare the soil, plant the trees, and sow other plants that will be beneficial. From the standpoint of purpose, however, the primary thing is to use the fruit from the trees. *Preparing a field:* From the standpoint of time, the primary thing is to level the earth, plow it, harrow it, and then plant the seeds. From the standpoint of purpose, however, the primary thing is the harvest and the use of the crops.

On the basis of these analogies, anyone can conclude what is truly primary. Whether we are building a church or a house or developing a fruit garden or working to prepare a field, our primary intention is always the use of it. This is what we continually keep uppermost in our minds as we acquire the means of achieving our goal. We can conclude therefore that from the standpoint of time the primary thing is true understanding that comes from faith, but from the standpoint of purpose the primary thing is good action that comes from goodwill. Since the latter is truly primary, it is actually the firstborn in our mind.[555]

[3] It is important, however, to know what faith and goodwill are, each in its own essence, and this cannot be known unless each is divided up point by point—into points about faith and points about goodwill.

The points about faith are the following:

1. The faith that saves us is faith in the Lord God our Savior Jesus Christ.
2. Briefly put, faith is believing that people who live good lives and believe the right things are saved by the Lord.
3. The way we receive faith is by turning to the Lord, learning truths from the Word, and living by those truths.

4. Having a quantity of truths that are bound together like strands in a cable elevates and improves our faith.

5. Faith without goodwill is not faith. Goodwill without faith is not goodwill. Neither of them is living unless it comes from the Lord.

6. The Lord, goodwill, and faith form a unity in the same way our life, our will, and our intellect form a unity. If we separate them, each one crumbles like a pearl that is crushed to powder.

7. The Lord is goodwill and faith within us. We are goodwill and faith within the Lord.

8. Goodwill and faith come together in good actions.

9. There is faith that is true, faith that is illegitimate, and faith that is hypocritical.

10. Evil people have no faith.

Now these points need to be explained one by one.

I

The Faith That Saves Us
Is Faith in the Lord God Our Savior Jesus Christ

337 The faith that saves is faith in God our Savior, because he is divine and human. He is in the Father and the Father is in him; therefore they are one. If we turn to him, we are turning to the Father as well—to the one only God. Faith in any other god does not save us.

We are to believe or have faith in *the Son of God,* the Redeemer and Savior, conceived by Jehovah and born from the Virgin Mary, who is named *Jesus Christ.* This is clear from commands that he, and later his apostles, frequently repeated.

The following passages make it clear that he himself commanded us to have faith in him:

Jesus said, "This is the will of the Father who sent me, that all who see the Son and *believe in him* should have eternal life, and I will revive them on the last day." (John 6:40)

Those who believe in the Son have eternal life. Those who do not believe in the Son will not see life; instead God's anger will remain upon them. (John 3:36)

So that all who *believe in the Son* would not perish but would have eternal life. For God so loved the world that he gave his only begotten Son so that *everyone who believes in him* would not perish but would have eternal life. (John 3:15, 16)

Jesus said, "I am the resurrection and the life. *Those who believe in me* will never die." (John 11:25, 26)

Truly, truly I say to you, *those who believe in me* have eternal life. I am the bread of life. (John 6:47, 48)

I am the bread of life. *Those who come to me* will never hunger and those *who believe in me* will never thirst. (John 6:35)

Jesus cried out, saying, "If any are thirsty, they must come to me and drink. *If any believe in me,* as the Scripture says, rivers of living water will flow out of their bellies." (John 7:37, 38)

They said to Jesus, "What shall we do to perform the works of God?" Jesus answered, "This is God's work, *to believe in the One whom the Father sent."* (John 6:28, 29)

As long as you have the light, *believe in the light* so that you may be children of the light. (John 12:36)

Those who *believe in the Son of God* are not judged; but *those who do not believe* have already been judged *because they have not believed* in the name of the only begotten Son of God. (John 3:18)

These things have been written so that you may believe that Jesus is the Son of God and through believing may have life in his name. (John 20:31)

Unless you have believed that I am [he], you will die in your sins. (John 8:24)

Jesus said, "When the Comforter, the Spirit of Truth, has come, it will convict the world of sin, of justice, and of judgment: of sin, because they do not believe in me." (John 16:8, 9)

The faith that the apostles had was a faith in the Lord Jesus Christ, as many passages in their Epistles make clear. I will quote only the following: **338**

I myself am no longer alive; instead Christ is living in me. I am indeed alive in the flesh, but *with a living faith that is a faith in the Son of God.* (Galatians 2:20)

To both Jews and Greeks, Paul proclaimed repentance before God and *faith in our Lord Jesus Christ.* (Acts 20:21)

The one who took Paul outside said, "What must I do to be saved?" Paul said, "*Believe in the Lord Jesus Christ.* Then you and your household will be saved." (Acts 16:30, 31)

Those who have the Son have life. Those who do not have the Son of God, do not have life. I have written these things to you who believe in the name of the Son of God that you may know that you have eternal life and that you may believe in the name of the Son of God. (1 John 5:12, 13)

We are Jews by nature, not sinners from the nations. Since we know that people are not justified by the works of the Law but *by the faith of Jesus Christ, we* too *have come to believe in Jesus Christ.* (Galatians 2:15, 16)

Because their faith was a faith in Jesus Christ and also a faith that came from him, the apostles called it "the faith of Jesus Christ," as just above in Galatians 2:16, and also in the following passages: "Through *the faith of Jesus Christ,* God's justice is in and upon all who have come to believe, to justify those who have *the faith of Jesus*" (Romans 3:22, 26). Paul wished to "have the justice that comes *from the faith of Christ,* the justice that comes *from the God of faith*" (Philippians 3:9). "These are the people who keep the commandments of God and *the faith of Jesus Christ*" (Revelation 14:12). [Paul mentions salvation] "through *faith* that is in Christ Jesus" (2 Timothy 3:15). "In *Jesus Christ there is faith working through goodwill*" (Galatians 5:6).

The passages just quoted clarify which faith Paul meant in the wellworn phrase in the church today: "Therefore we conclude that people are justified by faith apart from the works of the Law" (Romans 3:28). It does not mean faith in God the Father; it means faith in his Son. Still less does it mean faith in three gods in a row, one from whom, a second for whom, and a third through whom [we have faith].

The reason the church today believes that Paul's saying refers to its own faith in three divine Persons is that for fourteen centuries, since the Council of Nicaea, the church has not recognized any other faith than this. As a result, it has not known any other faith, believing that this was the only faith and that no other faith was possible. Therefore everywhere that the Word of the New Testament says "faith," people have believed that this was the faith the Word meant. They have applied everything said about faith to this faith. Consequently, the only faith that saves—faith in God our Savior—has perished. Their position caused many mistakes to creep into their teachings, as well as many paradoxes that go against sound reason. In a church, every teaching that aims to teach and show the way to heaven and salvation depends on its faith. Since, as I say, many mistakes and paradoxes crept into their faith, it became necessary for them to proclaim the dogma that the intellect has to be kept under obedience to faith.

In Paul's words in Romans 3:28, "faith" does not mean faith in God the Father, it means faith in his Son, and "the works of the Law" do not mean the works of the law of the Ten Commandments, they mean the works of the Mosaic Law for the Jews (as you can see from the verses that follow Romans 3:28, as well as from similar words in Paul's Epistle to the Galatians 2:14, 15). The foundation stone of the modern-day church crumbles, then, and so does the shrine built on it, like a house sinking into the ground until only the top of the roof remains visible.

We are to believe or have faith in God our Savior Jesus Christ because this is believing in a God who can be seen, in whom is what cannot be seen. Faith in a God who can be seen—who is both human and divine at the same time—goes deep within us. Although faith is earthly in its form, it is spiritual in its essence. Within us faith becomes both spiritual and earthly, in that everything spiritual has to be received in what is earthly to become anything to us. Something purely spiritual does indeed enter us but we do not accept it. It is like the ether[556] that flows in and out of us without having any effect. For something to have an effect, we have to be mentally aware of it and open to it. We have no such awareness or openness unless something affects our earthly self.

On the other hand, faith that is entirely earthly, meaning faith that is deprived of its spiritual essence, is a mere persuasion or knowledge, not faith. A persuasion outwardly imitates faith, but because there is nothing spiritual inside it, there is nothing in it that saves. This is the type of faith possessed by all people who deny that the Lord's human manifestation is divine. This is what the Arian faith was like and what the Socinian faith is like. Both of these faiths rejected the Lord's divinity.[557]

What is a faith that is not directed toward some object? It is like our eyesight directed into deep space, which falls into a void and perishes. It is like a bird flying beyond the atmosphere into space, where it dies for lack of breath as if it were in a vacuum pump.[558]

This type of faith lives in the human mind the way the winds live in the halls of Aeolus,[559] or the way light lives in a shooting star: it rises into view like a comet with a long tail, but it also goes by like a comet and disappears.

[2] To put it briefly, faith in a God who cannot be seen is actually blind faith, because the human mind that has this type of faith does not see its God. Because the light of this faith is not both spiritual and earthly, it is a faint, deceptive light. Its light is like the light of a firefly, the light at night over swamps and marshes that contain sulfur, or the light in rotting wood. Nothing stands out in this light except imaginary things that you think you see, but they do not exist.

Faith in a God who cannot be seen gives no light, especially when people think of God as a spirit, and think of a spirit as being like the ether. People then view God the way they view the ether. They look for him in the universe, and when they do not find him there, they believe that nature is the god of the universe. This is the origin of the materialist philosophy[560] that is prevalent these days.

Yet the Lord said that no one has ever heard the voice of the Father or seen what he looks like (John 5:37). He also said, "No one has ever seen God; the only begotten Son, who is close to the Father's heart, has revealed him" (John 1:18). "No one has seen the Father except the One who is with the Father. He has seen the Father" (John 6:46). Also, no one comes to the Father except through him (John 14:6). And furthermore, if we see and recognize him, we see and recognize the Father (John 14:7 and following).

[3] Faith in the Lord God our Savior is a different kind of faith. Because he is both divine and human, we can turn to him and see him in our thoughts. This is not a faith with no object. It has an object from whom and in whom we have faith. If we have seen an emperor or a monarch, every time we remember that person an image of him or her comes to mind; in the same way, once we accept this faith it remains.

The gaze of this faith can be compared to looking at a shining white cloud with an angel in its midst who is inviting us to enter it and be raised into heaven. This is how the Lord looks to people who have faith in him. The Lord comes closer to us all as we recognize and acknowledge him. This occurs as we come to know and follow his principles, which are to abstain from evil things and do good things. At last he comes into our house and makes a home in us along with the Father who is in him, as the following words in John indicate:

> Jesus said, "The people who love me are those who have my commandments and follow them. Those who love me will be loved by my Father,

and I will love them and manifest myself to them. We will come to them and make a home with them." (John 14:21, 23)

These sentences were written in the presence of the Lord's twelve apostles. While I was writing them, the Lord sent the apostles to me.[561]

2

Briefly Put, Faith Is Believing That People Who Live Good Lives and Believe the Right Things Are Saved by the Lord

We are created for eternal life. All of us are capable of inheriting it, provided we use in our lives the means of salvation that have been prescribed for us in the Word. On these points all Christians agree, as do all non-Christians who have religion and sound reason. **340**

There are indeed many means of being saved, but each and every one of them relates to living a good life and believing the right things. Therefore they all relate to goodwill and faith, for goodwill is living a good life and faith is believing the right things. These two universal categories of means of being saved—goodwill and faith—are not just prescribed for us in the Word, they are commanded.

From the fact that they are commanded it follows that goodwill and faith give us the capacity of providing ourselves with eternal life through a power that is assigned and given to us by God. The more we use that power and look to God, the more God increases the power until he turns every aspect of our earthly goodwill into spiritual goodwill and every aspect of our earthly faith into spiritual faith. In this way God brings dead goodwill and faith to life, and brings us to life as well.

[2] Two things have to come together before we can be said to be living a good life and believing the right things. In the church these two things are called our inner self and our outer self. When our inner self has good intentions and our outer self has good actions, then the two unite. Our outer self acts from our inner self, and our inner self acts through our outer self; we act from God and God acts through us. On the other hand, if our inner self has evil intentions, but our outer self still has good actions, nonetheless both are acting from hell. Our intentions come from hell and our actions are hypocritical. Our hellish intentions are

inside every hypocritical thing we do, like a snake inside a plant or a grub inside a flower.

[3] If people know not only that we have an inner and an outer self but also what they are and that the two can work together either actually or seemingly, and also that our inner self lives on after death but our outer self is buried, they have access to an abundance of secrets about heaven and the world. People who unite these two in themselves for a good purpose become happy forever, but people who divide them, or worse yet if they unite them for an evil purpose, are unhappy forever.

341 If people who lived good lives and believed the right things were *not* saved, and God could freely save or condemn on a whim anyone he wanted to, people who perished could justly accuse God of lacking mercy and compassion or even of being vicious. Indeed they could deny that God is God. Furthermore they could argue that God said pointless things in his Word and gave principles that were worthless and ridiculous. For another thing, if people who lived good lives and believed the right things were not saved, they could accuse God of violating the covenant that he made on Mount Sinai and wrote with his own finger on the two tablets.

From the Lord's words in John 14:21–24 it is clear that God cannot avoid saving people who live by his principles and have faith in him. Everyone who has religion and sound reason can provide arguments to support this by considering that God, who is constantly with us and gives us life and the faculties of understanding and loving, cannot help loving us and being united to us in love if we live good lives and believe the right things. God has built this into every human being and every creature. Can a father and mother reject their babies? Can a bird reject its chicks? Can an animal reject its young? Not even tigers, panthers, or snakes are able to do this. Doing otherwise would be going against the design in which God exists and through which he acts, and going against the design he built into us at creation.

Now, as it is impossible on the one hand for God to condemn anyone who has lived a good life and has believed the right things, it is impossible on the other hand for God to save anyone who has lived an evil life and has therefore believed the wrong things. This too would go against the divine design and therefore against God's omnipotence, which cannot follow any other path than the path of justice. The laws of justice are truths that cannot be changed, for the Lord says, "It is easier for heaven and earth to pass away than for the tip of one letter of the law to fall" (Luke 16:17).

Everyone who knows anything about the essence of God and human free choice is able to perceive this. For example, Adam had the freedom to eat fruit from the tree of life and fruit from the tree of the knowledge of good and evil. If he had eaten fruit only from the tree (or trees) of life, would it have been possible for God to expel him from the garden? I think not. On the other hand, after he ate fruit from the tree of the knowledge of good and evil, would it have been possible for God to keep him in the garden? Again, I think not. Likewise, once an angel has been accepted into heaven, God cannot throw that angel into hell; and once a devil has been judged, God cannot move him to heaven. For God's inability to do either of these things despite his omnipotence, see the part on the divine omnipotence in the first chapter, §§49–70.

The preceding part of this chapter (§§337–339) showed that the faith that saves us is faith in the Lord God our Savior Jesus Christ. The question is, what is the first step toward faith in him? The answer is acknowledging that he is the Son of God. This was the first step toward faith that the Lord revealed and proclaimed when he came into the world. If people had not started by acknowledging that he was the Son of God, and therefore God from God, it would have been pointless for him, and later for his apostles, to have preached faith in him.

342

There is in fact something like this today among people whose thoughts are based on their own self-importance, that is, on their outer, earthly selves alone. They say to themselves, "How could Jehovah God conceive a son? How could a human being be God?" Therefore it is necessary to use the Word to establish and support this first step into faith; the following passages are offered for this purpose:

"The angel said to Mary, 'You will conceive in your womb and give birth, and you will call his name *Jesus. He will be great and will be called the Son of the Highest.'* And Mary said to the angel, 'How will this take place, since I have not had intercourse?'[562] The angel answered, 'The Holy Spirit will descend upon you, and *the power of the Highest* will cover you; therefore *the Holy One* that is born from you will be called *the Son of God*'" (Luke 1:31, 32, 34, 35). When Jesus was baptized, a voice came from heaven saying, "*This is my beloved Son,* in whom I am well pleased" (Matthew 3:16, 17; Mark 1:10, 11; Luke 3:21, 22). Furthermore, when Jesus was transfigured, a voice came from heaven saying, "*This is my beloved Son,* in whom I am well pleased. Hear him" (Matthew 17:5; Mark 9:7; Luke 9:35). [2] "Jesus asked his disciples, 'Who do people say I am?' Peter answered, '*You are the Christ, the Son of the living God.*' Jesus said, 'You are blessed, Simon, son of Jonah. I say to you, on this rock I will build my church'" (Matthew 16:13, 16, 17, 18).

The Lord said, then, that he would build his church on this rock, that is, on the truth and the confession that he is the Son of God. In fact, a "rock" means a truth, and also the Lord's divine truth. The church does not exist in someone who does not confess the truth that Jesus is the Son of God. That is why I said just above that this is the first step into faith in Jesus Christ—this is faith at its very outset.

John the Baptist saw and testified that Jesus is *the Son of God* (John 1:34). The disciple Nathaniel said to Jesus, "*You are the Son of God. You are the King of Israel*" (John 1:49). The twelve disciples said, "We have come to believe that *you are the Christ, the Son of the living God*" (John 6:69). Jesus is called *the only begotten Son of God* and *the only begotten from the Father*, who is close to the Father's heart (John 1:14, 18; 3:16). Jesus himself confessed before the high priest that he was the Son of God (Matthew 26:63, 64; 27:43; Mark 14:41, 42; Luke 22:70). "Those who were in the boat came and worshiped Jesus saying, '*Truly you are the Son of God*'" (Matthew 14:33). The eunuch who wanted to be baptized said to Philip, "*I believe that Jesus Christ is the Son of God*" (Acts 8:37). After Paul was converted, he preached that Jesus *is the Son of God* (Acts 9:20). Jesus said, "The hour is coming when the dead will hear *the voice of the Son of God*, and those who hear will live" (John 5:25). "Those who do not believe have already been judged because they have not believed in *the name of the only begotten Son of God*" (John 3:18). "These things have been written so that you may believe that *Jesus is the Christ, the Son of God*, and by believing may have life in his name" (John 20:31). "I have written these things to you who believe in *the name of the Son of God* so that you may know that you have eternal life and so that you may believe in *the name of the Son of God*" (1 John 5:13). "We know that *the Son of God* came and enabled us to know the truth. We are in the truth in *the Son of God, Jesus Christ*. He is the true God and eternal life" (1 John 5:20). "If any confess that *Jesus is the Son of God*, God lives in them, and they live in God" (1 John 4:15). Also elsewhere, as in Matthew 8:29; 27:40, 43, 54; Mark 1:1; 3:11; 15:39; Luke 8:28; John 9:35; 10:36; 11:4, 27; 19:7; Romans 1:4; 2 Corinthians 1:19; Galatians 2:20; Ephesians 4:13; Hebrews 4:14; 6:6; 7:3; 10:29; 1 John 3:8; 5:10; Revelation 2:18.

There are many other passages in which Jehovah mentions his Son and the Son himself calls Jehovah God his Father, as in the following: "Whatever the *Father* does, the *Son* does. As the *Father* raises the dead and brings them to life, so does the *Son*. As the *Father* has life in himself, so he has given the *Son* to have life in himself," therefore all should honor the *Son* as they honor the *Father* (John 5:19–27). This also happens in many other passages, including David: "I will announce this decision:

Jehovah said to me, '*You are my Son. Today I fathered you.*' Kiss the *Son* or he will be angry and you will perish on the way because he will flare up with his brief anger. *Blessed are all those who trust in him*" (Psalms 2:7, 12).

[3] On the basis of these passages, we can now draw the conclusion that everyone who wants to be a true Christian and be saved by Christ has to believe that *Jesus is the Son of the living God.*

Those who do not believe this and think of Jesus as only the Son of Mary implant in themselves various ideas about him that are damaging and destructive to their salvation (see above, §§90, 94, 102). One could say the same thing about them as about the Jews[563]—instead of a royal crown, they put a crown of thorns on Jesus' head, give him vinegar to drink, and shout, "If you are the Son of God, come down from the cross" [see Matthew 27:40]. Or else they say what the devil who tempted him said: "If you are the Son of God, tell these stones to become bread," or, "If you are the Son of God, throw yourself down [from the Temple roof]" (Matthew 4:3, 6).

People like this desecrate the Lord's church and his house of worship. They make it a den of thieves. They are the people who turn devotion to the Lord into something like devotion to Muhammad.[564] They do not distinguish between true Christianity, which is worship of the Lord, and materialist philosophy. They could be compared to people riding in a carriage or a wagon on thin ice, and the ice breaks under them, and they sink, and they and their horses and carriage disappear into the icy water. They could also be compared to people who weave a life raft out of rushes and reeds, using tar to glue it together; and they set out onto the great expanse of the ocean, but out there the tar glue dissolves; and choked by the brine, they are swallowed up and buried in the depths of the sea.

3

The Way We Receive Faith Is by Turning to the Lord,
Learning Truths from the Word,
and Living by Those Truths

Before I begin demonstrating *how faith arises* (which occurs when we turn to the Lord, learn truths from the Word, and live by those truths) and before we move into individual aspects of faith, I first need to present

343

categories of faith to give you an overview. This will help you understand more clearly not only things in this chapter on faith, but also points made in chapters to come on goodwill [§§392–462], free choice [§§463–508], repentance [§§509–570], reformation and regeneration [§§571–625], and the assignment of spiritual credit or blame [§§626–666]. Faith runs through each and every part of a systematic theology the way blood runs through the body's limbs, bringing them to life.

What the church today has to say about faith is generally known in the Christian world and specifically known among those in its religious hierarchy. Books only about faith and about faith alone fill the libraries of the church's theologians. In fact, hardly anything other than faith is considered to be a valid theological topic these days. Before taking what the church is saying nowadays about its faith and examining it in an appendix,[565] I will first list the general points that the new church teaches about its faith. They are as follows:

344   *The underlying reality of the faith of the new church* is (1) trust in the Lord God our Savior Jesus Christ; (2) confidence that he saves those who live good lives and believe the right things.

The essence of the faith of the new church is truth from the Word.

The manifestations of the faith of the new church are (1) spiritual sight; (2) harmony among truths; (3) conviction; (4) acknowledgment engraved on the mind.

The states of the faith of the new church are (1) a newborn faith, a growing faith, a mature faith; (2) faith based on genuine truth, and faith based on things that seem true; (3) faith based on memory, faith based on reason, faith based on light; (4) earthly faith, spiritual faith, heavenly faith; (5) faith based on life experiences, and faith based on miracles; (6) faith that is free and faith that is coerced.

For a universal idea and a specific idea of the form itself of the faith of the new church, see above, §§2 and 3.

345   Since I have just given a brief list of types of spiritual faith, I will also give a brief list of types of merely earthly faith. Such faith is actually a persuasion that pretends to be faith. It is a false persuasion. It is called heretical faith. Its categories are (1) illegitimate faith, in which false beliefs have been mixed with true ones; (2) promiscuous faith based on truths that have been falsified, and adulterous faith based on good things that have been contaminated; (3) closed or blind faith, which is a faith in mystical things that we believe in, although we do not know whether they are true or false, beyond reason or contrary to it; (4) wandering faith, which is faith in many gods; (5) half-blind faith, which is faith in some other god besides the true one, or among Christians, faith in someone else besides the Lord God our Savior; (6) hypocritical or pharisaical faith, which is faith of the mouth but not of the heart; and (7) imaginary and backwards faith, which presents falsity as truth and bolsters it with clever argumentation.[566]

As I said above, faith takes the form of spiritual sight in us. Since spiritual sight (the sight of the intellect and therefore the mind) and physical sight (the sight of the eye and therefore the body) correspond to each other, every state of faith is comparable to a state of the eye and its sight. The states of true faith are comparable to all the healthy states of eyesight. The states of false faith are comparable to all the unhealthy states of eyesight.

Let us compare the correspondences of these two kinds of sight, the mental and the physical, in each one's unhealthy states. *Illegitimate faith,* in which false beliefs have been mixed with true ones, is comparable to the disease of the eye and therefore of eyesight called a white macula or spot on the cornea, which obscures vision. *Promiscuous faith* based on truths that have been falsified and *adulterous faith* based on good things that have been contaminated are comparable to the eye disease and visual problem called a cataract—a drying and hardening of the crystalline fluid [of the lens]. *Closed* or *blind faith,* which is a faith in mystical things that we believe in, although we do not know whether they are true or false, beyond reason or contrary to it, is comparable to the eye disease called *gutta serena* or amaurosis—loss of sight because of blockage of the optical nerve, although the eye still looks as though it is functioning and healthy. *Wandering faith,* which is faith in many gods, is comparable to the disease of the eye that involves a loss of transparency in the anterior chamber, that is, a loss of vision resulting from an obstruction between the sclerotic tunic and the uvea. *Half-blind faith,* which is faith in some other god besides the true one, or among Christians, faith in someone else besides the Lord God our Savior, is comparable to the disease of the eye called strabismus. *Hypocritical* or *pharisaical faith,* which is faith of the mouth but not of the heart, is comparable to atrophy of the eye that causes loss of sight. *Imaginary and backwards faith,* which presents falsity as truth and bolsters it with clever argumentation, is comparable to the disease of the eye called nyctalopia, or night blindness, which is [poor] vision in the faint, deceptive light that occurs in the nighttime.[567]

346

347 As for *the manner in which faith is formed,* this happens by our turning to the Lord, learning truths from the Word, and living by those truths.

First of all, *faith is formed by our turning to the Lord,* because faith that is real, that is, faith that brings salvation, is faith from the Lord and faith in the Lord. It is clear from the Lord's words to the disciples that faith is *from* him: "Live in me and I [shall live] in you, because without me you cannot do anything" (John 15:4, 5). As for faith being a faith *in* the Lord, see the many passages cited above, §§337–338, which show that we have to believe in the Son. Given that faith is faith from the Lord and faith in the Lord, you could say that the Lord is faith itself, for its life and essence exist in the Lord and come from him.

[2] *Second, faith is formed by our learning truths from the Word,* because faith in its essence is truth. All the elements that constitute faith are truths. Faith, then, is nothing but an array of truths shining in our mind. Truths teach not only that we need to have beliefs but also in whom to believe and what to believe.

Truths need to be taken from the Word, because all the truths that make a contribution to our salvation are there. These truths are genuinely effective because they have been given by the Lord and have been engraved on the entire angelic heaven. As a result, when we learn truths from the Word, without our knowing it we come into contact and association with angels.

Faith without truths is like a seed without a kernel. If you grind it, you get nothing but chaff. Faith made of truths is like a seed from the harvest. If you grind it, you get flour. To put it briefly, truths are essential components of faith. If faith does not contain truths, it is merely like the sound of idle whistling. When faith contains truths, it is like the sound of the call to our salvation.

[3] *Third, faith is formed by our living by those truths,* because a spiritual life is a life that follows truths. Truths are not actually alive before they exist in actions. Truths dissociated from actions are just thoughts. If they do not become part of our will, they are not inside us; they are only on our threshold. Our will is our true self. Our thinking reflects our true self only to the extent that it is connected to our will.

People who learn truths and do not live by them are like people who scatter seeds on top of a field but do not plow them under—the seeds become swollen by the rain and split into empty husks. People who learn truths and do them are like people who sow and plow the seeds under.

With the benefit of rain, the seeds then grow into a harvest and become useful for nutrition. The Lord says, "If you know these things, you are happy if you do them" (John 13:17). And elsewhere, "Those who received seed in good ground are people who hear the Word and pay attention to it, and therefore bear fruit and become productive" (Matthew 13:23). Also, "Everyone who hears my words and does them I will compare to a prudent man who built his house on a rock. But everyone who hears my words and does not do them will be compared to a foolish man who built his house on sand" (Matthew 7:24, 26). *All* the words of the Lord are truths.

From what I have said just above it is clear that there are three things **348** that form faith in us: first, turning to the Lord; second, learning truths from the Word; and third, living by those truths. Now, because there are three parts to the formation of faith and each one is not the same as the others, it follows that they are separable. People could turn to the Lord and not know any truths about God and the Lord except things they had been told in the past. People could also know a great many truths from the Word and still not live by them. People for whom these three things are separated, meaning that they have one but not another, do not have a faith that will save them. A faith begins to have saving power when these elements are connected. The quality of the faith depends on what kind of connection the three have.

Where these three elements are kept separate, the faith there is like a sterile seed planted in the ground that breaks down into dust. Where these three elements are interconnected, the faith there is like a seed in the ground that grows into a tree whose fruit reflects the nature of their connection. Where these three elements are kept separate, the faith is like an unfertilized egg. Where they are interconnected, the faith is like a fertilized egg from a beautiful bird.

The faith of people who keep these three elements separate is like the eye of a fish or a crab that has been cooked. The faith of people who interconnect these three elements is like an eye that is clear right through from the vitreous fluid to the pupil's uvea. Faith in which these elements are kept separate is like a painting done with dark colors on a black stone. Faith in which these elements are connected is like a painting done with beautiful colors on a clear crystal.

The light from a faith in which these elements are kept separate is like the light of a glowing coal in the hand of a traveler at night, while the light from a faith in which these elements are connected is like the light of a blazing torch that makes each step clear as it is moved back and forth.

Faith without truths is like a vine that bears a few wild grapes. Faith made of truths is like a vine that bears bunches of high-quality grapes that yield excellent wine.

A faith in the Lord that lacks truths is like a new star that appears in the sky but then dims after a while.[568] A faith in the Lord that has truths is like a fixed star that endures forever.

Truth is the essence of faith. Therefore the quality of the truth determines the quality of the faith. Without truths, faith wanders around; with them, it stays in one place. In fact, a faith made of truths shines in heaven like a star.

4

Having a Quantity of Truths
That Are Bound Together like Strands in a Cable
Elevates and Improves Our Faith

349 If all we had was an awareness of the faith that exists nowadays, it would be impossible for us to know that in its proper surroundings faith is an array of truths; still less could we see from today's faith that we are capable of doing something to acquire faith for ourselves. Yet faith in its essence is truth. Faith is truth in its own light. Therefore as truth is something that we can acquire, so is faith. We can all turn to the Lord if we want to. We can all gather truths from the Word if we want to. Every truth that is in the Word, or from the Word, shines; and faith is truth in light.

The Lord, who is light itself, flows into us all. If we have truths from the Word, he makes them shine in us and become part of our faith. This is what the Lord is saying in John, that we live in the Lord and his words live in us (John 15:7). The Lord's words are truths.

To correctly understand this statement—that having a quantity of truths that are bound together like strands in a cable elevates and improves our faith—the discussion needs to be broken into the following points:

a. Truths of faith can be multiplied to infinity.
b. Truths of faith come together to form structures that are like fascicles of nerves.
c. Our faith improves depending on the quantity of truths we have and how well they fit together.

   d. However numerous these truths are and however divergent they appear, they are united by the Lord who is the Word; the God of heaven and earth; the God of all flesh; the God of the vineyard, or the church; the God of faith; the light itself; the truth itself; and eternal life.

[a] *The truths of faith can be multiplied to infinity.* This is clear from the wisdom of the angels of heaven, which grows forever. In fact, the angels say that there is never an end to wisdom. Wisdom has no other source except divine truths that have been analytically divided into forms by means of light flowing in from the Lord. Human intelligence that is truly intelligent has the same source.   **350**

Divine truth can be multiplied to infinity because the Lord is divine truth itself, or truth in its infinity. He attracts all people toward himself, but because they are finite, angels and people are unable to follow that current of attraction except to a limited extent. The force of attraction toward infinity persists all the same.

The Lord's Word is an ocean of truths, vast and deep, from which all angelic wisdom comes, although to those of us who do not know about its spiritual and heavenly meanings the Word appears to hold no more than a jug of water.

The multiplication of truths to infinity is like human sperm, one of which can lead to whole extended families that exist for tens of thousands of years. The proliferation of the truths of faith is like the proliferation of seeds in fields and gardens—they are capable of generating hundreds of millions of plants and continuing without end. In the Word, "seed" has no other meaning than truth, "field" means a body of teaching, and "garden" means wisdom.

The human mind is like soil in which both spiritual and earthly truths can be planted like seeds and can multiply without end. We derive this attribute from the infinity of God. He is constantly present in us with his light and warmth and his generative ability.

[b] *Truths of faith come together to form structures that are like fascicles of nerves.* People are still not aware of this. They do not know about it, because the spiritual truths that form the whole fabric of the Word have been invisible as a consequence of the mystical and enigmatic faith that takes up every square inch of modern-day theology. The result is that spiritual truths have sunk into the ground like old barns.   **351**

So that you will know what I mean by "structures" that are like "fascicles of nerves," I offer this explanation. The first chapter of this book, which is on God the Creator, has parts that form its structure. The first part of that chapter is on the oneness of God, the second on the underlying divine reality or Jehovah, the third on the infinity of God, the fourth on the essence of God, which is divine love and wisdom, the fifth on God's omnipotence, and the sixth on creation. Each of these parts is further subdivided into points that form its structure. These points wrap up the teachings they contain and form something like sheaves. These structures, on both the larger and the smaller scale, both jointly and separately, contain truths that elevate and improve our faith depending on the quantity of truths we have and on the bonds that exist between these truths.

[2] The human mind is structured. It is a spiritual organism that terminates in a physical organism in which and according to which the mind thinks or produces its ideas. People who do not know this cannot help thinking that perceptions, thoughts, and ideas are just rays and variations of light flowing into their heads and creating forms that they see and recognize as the thought process.[569] This is ridiculous. As everyone knows, our heads are full of brains, our brains are structured, our minds live in them, and our ideas become fixed and permanent there as we receive and reinforce these ideas.

The next question is, how is the mind organized? The answer is that all its parts are arranged to form structures that are like fascicles of nerves. The truths that constitute faith are also arranged this way in the human mind.

The truth of this can be illustrated by the following observations. [3] The cerebrum consists of two substances. One of them is glandular;[570] it is called the cortex or gray-matter. The other is made of fibrils and is called the medullary substance. The first of these two, the glandular substance, is arranged in clusters like grapes on a vine. These clusters, then, constitute the structure of the glandular substance. The other substance, the medullary one, consists of common bundles of fascicles of individual nerve fibrils that come from the glands of the first substance. These common bundles of nerve fascicles, then, constitute the structure of the medullary substance.

All the nerves that come from the brain and go down into the body to perform various functions there are nothing but sheaves and fascicles of fibers. So are all muscles, and all the internal organs and other organs of the body. All these parts have this form because they correspond to the structures of the organism of the mind.

[4] Furthermore, absolutely everything in the whole of nature has a structure that consists of common bundles of fascicles of fibers. Every tree,

shrub, bush, and vegetable—in fact, every type of grass and herb—has this characteristic in whole and in part. The overall cause of this is that divine truths are shaped this way. We read that all things were created by the Word, that is, by divine truth; and also that the world was made by the Word (John 1:1 and following). From all this you can see that if the human mind lacked a comparable organization of its substances, we would lack the analytical reasoning power that we all have. This reasoning power depends on how organized our minds are; that is, it depends on our having a quantity of truths that are bound together like strands in a cable. The level of organization in our minds in turn depends on our use of reason in freedom.

[c] *Our faith improves depending on the quantity of truths we have and how well they fit together.* This follows from what I said before. Furthermore, it is revealed to anyone who methodically investigates how complex structures function when they are interwoven as one thing: each part strengthens and supports the next; together they make one form; and when that form becomes active, its parts accomplish one action.

352

Since faith in its essence is truth, our faith becomes more spiritual, and more perfectly spiritual, depending on the quantity of truths we have and how well they fit together. That is, our faith becomes less and less sense-oriented and earthly, because it then rises up into a higher region of our mind. From that perspective it sees below itself a host of things in the nature of the world that strengthen and support it. True faith, achieved through a quantity of truths that fit together like strands in a cable, also becomes more enlightening, perceivable, obvious, and clear. True faith also becomes more easily united with acts of goodwill, and therefore more alienated from evils and progressively more remote from the enticements of the eye and the cravings of the flesh. Therefore faith becomes more truly happy. Above all, it becomes more powerful against evils and falsities, and therefore more and more living and empowered to save.

Just above I made the statement that every truth shines in heaven, and as a result, faith in its essence is truth shining [§§348, 349]. When the truths of this faith are multiplied, their shining light gives faith a beauty and attractiveness like that of forms, objects, and works of art whose colors harmonize well. It is like the precious stones of different colors on Aaron's breastplate that were collectively called the Urim and Thummim. It is also like the precious stones that the foundations of the wall of the New Jerusalem were made of (Revelation 21); and also like precious stones of different colors in a royal crown. In fact, precious

353

stones mean the truths that constitute faith. One could also draw a comparison with the beauty of a rainbow, and with the beauty of a field full of flowers or a garden in bloom during early spring.

Faith that is composed of a quantity of truths takes on a light and a glory that are like the lighting of church buildings with more and more candles, of homes with more and more lamps, and of streets with more and more streetlamps.

The elevation of faith through a quantity of truths can be compared to the increase in volume and the heightened musical effect that occurs when many instruments play together; also, the increase in fragrance that comes from putting together a whole garland of sweet-smelling flowers; and so on.

The power that faith acquires from a plurality of truths assembled to combat things that are false and evil can be compared to the solidity that a church building gains from well-crafted stonework and from columns that buttress its walls and support its vaulted ceilings. That power can also be compared to a squadron in a square formation in which the soldiers stand side to side and thus form, and move as, a single force. That power can also be compared to the muscles all over our body: although there are many of them and some are far apart, they still make one power in our actions; and so on.

354 [d] *However numerous these truths of faith are and however divergent they appear, they are united by the Lord who is the Word; the God of heaven and earth; the God of all flesh; the God of the vineyard, or the church; the God of faith; the light itself; the truth itself; and eternal life.* The truths of faith are various, and appear divergent to us. For example, some are about God the Creator, some are about the Lord the Redeemer, some are about the Holy Spirit and the divine action, some are about faith and about goodwill, some are about free choice, repentance, reformation, regeneration, the assignment of spiritual credit and blame, and so on.[571] Yet they are united in the Lord, and the Lord unites them in us, the way one vine unites many branches (John 5:1 and following). The Lord connects scattered and divided truths into one form so that they present one picture and form one action.

This can be illustrated by a comparison with the limbs, internal organs, and other organs in one body. Although they are different from each other and appear to our sight to be distinct, the human being composed of them does not feel like more than one entity. When a human being uses them all to act, he or she performs that action as if all these components constituted a single entity.

The same is true of heaven. Although it is divided into countless communities, before the Lord it nevertheless looks like one thing—in fact, like one human being, as I have shown above [§§65, 119:1, 268; compare §74:5]. The same thing is true of a country. Although it is broken up into many jurisdictions, provinces, and cities, it is united under a monarch who exercises justice and judgment. It is the same with the truths of faith that the Lord uses to make the church a church. This is because the Lord is the Word; the God of heaven and earth; the God of all flesh; the God of the vineyard, or the church; the God of faith; the light itself; the truth itself; and eternal life.

[2] It is clear from John that the Lord is the Word and is therefore all the truth in heaven and the church: "The Word was with God, and the Word was God. And the Word became flesh" (John 1:1, 14).

It is clear from Matthew that the Lord is the God of heaven and earth: "Jesus said, 'All power in heaven and on earth has been given to me'" (Matthew 28:18).

It is clear from John that the Lord is the God of all flesh: The Father has given the Son power over all flesh (John 17:2).

It is clear from Isaiah and from John that the Lord is the God of the vineyard, or the church: "My beloved had a vineyard" (Isaiah 5:1, 2); "I am the vine; you are the branches" (John 15:5).

It is clear from Paul that the Lord is the God of faith: "You have the justice that comes from faith in Christ, from the God of faith" (Philippians 3:9).

It is clear from John that the Lord is the light itself: "He was the true light that enlightens everyone who comes into the world" (John 1:9). In another passage Jesus said, "I have come into the world as a light so that all who believe in me would not remain in darkness" (John 12:46).

It is clear from John that the Lord is the truth itself: "Jesus said, 'I am the way, the truth, and the life.'" (John 14:6).

It is clear from John that the Lord is eternal life: "We know that the Son of God came into the world so that we would know the truth. We are in the truth in Jesus Christ. He is the true God and eternal life" (1 John 5:20).

[3] To these things I should add that because people are busy in this world, they cannot acquire for themselves more than a few truths of faith. Nevertheless, if they turn to the Lord and worship him alone, they gain the ability to recognize all truths. For this reason, as soon as all true worshipers of the Lord hear some truth of faith they had not known before, they immediately see it, acknowledge it, and accept it. The reason is that the Lord is in them and they are in the Lord. Therefore the light of

truth is in them and they are in the light of truth because, as I said before, the Lord is the light itself and the truth itself.

I can support this point from experience. I saw a spirit who seemed simple in his interaction with other spirits because he acknowledged the Lord alone as the God of heaven and earth, basing this faith of his on a few truths from the Word. He was taken up into heaven among the wiser angels. I was told that when he was there he was just as wise as they were. In fact, he uttered a great many truths, completely as if they were his own ideas, although he had known none of them before. [4] Those who come into the Lord's new church will experience the same state. This is the state that is described in Jeremiah:

> This will be the covenant that I will make with the house of Israel after these days. I will put my law inside them. I will write it on their hearts. No longer will people teach their friends, and brothers and sisters, saying "Know the Lord." They will all know me, from the least of them to the greatest of them. (Jeremiah 31:33, 34)

This state will also be like Isaiah's description:

> A branch will come out of the trunk of Jesse. The truth will wrap his thighs. Then the wolf will live with the lamb, and the leopard will lie down with the goat. A nursing child will play over a cobra's hole, and a weaned child will reach a hand over the den of a poisonous snake, because the earth will be full of the knowledge of Jehovah as the waters cover the sea. In that day the nations will seek the root of Jesse and glory will be his rest. (Isaiah 11:1, 5, 6–10)

5

Faith without Goodwill Is Not Faith;
Goodwill without Faith Is Not Goodwill;
and Neither of Them Is Living Unless It Comes from the Lord

355 The church today has separated faith from goodwill. The church says that faith alone apart from the works of the Law justifies us and saves us. It says that goodwill cannot be united to faith, because faith comes from God while goodwill (to the extent that it becomes actual in deeds) comes from ourselves.

These concepts, however, never entered the minds of any apostle, as their letters make obvious. This separation and division was introduced into the Christian church when the one God was partitioned into three persons and each was allotted equal divinity.

The next part of this chapter will illustrate that there is no faith without goodwill or goodwill without faith, and that neither of them has life except from the Lord. Here the following points need to be demonstrated in order to pave the way:

a. We are able to acquire faith for ourselves.
b. The same is true of goodwill.
c. The same is also true of the life within each of them.
d. Nevertheless, no faith, no goodwill, and none of the life within faith or goodwill comes from ourselves; instead they come from the Lord alone.

(a) *We are able to acquire faith for ourselves.* This was shown in the third part of this chapter above, §§343–348. This is also clear from the fact that faith in its essence is truth and any of us can acquire truths for ourselves from the Word. As we acquire truths and love them, we begin to acquire faith.

Furthermore, if we were unable to acquire faith for ourselves, all the passages in the Word that command faith would be pointless. For example, we read that it is the Father's will for us to believe in the Son. Those who believe in him have eternal life. Those who do not believe will not see life [John 3:36; 6:40]. We also read that Jesus will send the Comforter, who is going "to convict the world of sin" because it did not believe in him [John 16:8, 9], not to mention many other passages listed above in §§337, 338.

For another thing, all the apostles preached faith, specifically a faith in the Lord God our Savior Jesus Christ. What would be the point of all this if we were supposed to stand waiting for something to flow in, with our arms hanging down as if we were statues with movable limbs? In that case our limbs, unable to move themselves into a position to receive faith, might be moved from within toward something that was not faith.

Yet this is what is taught by the modern-day orthodoxy in the Christian world that separated from the Catholics:

> As far as goodness is concerned, we are so totally corrupt and dead that after the fall but before regeneration not even a spark of spiritual force remains extant in our nature that would enable us to prepare ourselves for the grace of God, or to take it if it were offered, or to be open to his

grace on our own and by ourselves, or in spiritual matters to have our own ability to understand, believe, embrace, think, will, start, finish, act, operate, co-operate, or adapt and accommodate ourselves to grace, or to have the power for a complete conversion or half a conversion or the least part of a conversion on our own. When it comes to spiritual things related to the salvation of our soul, we are like the statue of salt that Lot's wife became; we are like a log or a stone devoid of life, which lacks the benefit of eyes, or a mouth, or any senses. Nevertheless we have the ability to move and control our external limbs in order to go to public gatherings and hear the Word and the Gospel.

These statements appear in the book put out by the Lutheran church called the *Formula of Concord,* in the Leipzig edition of 1756, pages 656, 658, 661, 662, 663, 671, 672, 673.[572] When priests are inaugurated they swear on this book and therefore swear to this faith. Calvinists have a similar faith.

Anyone with reason and religion would hiss at these absurd and ridiculous statements. People would say to themselves, "If this were the case, what would be the point of the Word? What would be the point of religion? What would be the point of the priesthood? What would be the point of preaching? They would be pointless—they would be sounds that mean nothing."

Take some non-Christians who have good judgment whom you are hoping to convert and tell them that this is Christianity's approach to conversion and faith. Surely they will think of Christianity as a container with nothing inside it. If you take away all apparent human autonomy, how could they think of Christianity as anything else?

These points will be presented in clearer light in the chapter on free choice.

357　(b) *We are able to acquire goodwill for ourselves.* The situation here is the same as the situation with faith. What else does the Word teach except faith and goodwill? These two are essential for salvation. We read,

> You are to love the Lord with all your heart and with all your soul, and your neighbor as yourself. (Matthew 22:37–39)

> And Jesus said, "I give you a command to love each other. You will be recognized as disciples of mine by the fact that you love each other." (John 13:34, 35; see also 15:9; 16:27)[573]

There are also teachings to the effect that we need to bear fruit the way a good tree does and that those who do good things will be rewarded in the resurrection, not to mention many other teachings.

What would be the point of these teachings if we were unable to practice goodwill on our own or to acquire it for ourselves in any way? We are able to make charitable donations, to help the needy, to do good things in our home and in our work. We are able to live by the Ten Commandments. We have a soul that enables us to do these things, and a rational mind we can use to make ourselves move toward this or that goal. We are able to plan to put these actions into effect because they have been commanded in the Word, and therefore by God. No human being lacks this power. We all have it because God gives it to us all, and gives it as our own possession. As we practice acts of goodwill, surely we all feel that we are doing so on our own.

(c) *We are also able to acquire the life within faith and goodwill for ourselves.* The situation is again the same. We acquire this life as we go to the Lord, who is life itself. No one's access to him is blocked. He constantly invites every person to come toward him. He says,

> Those who come to me will not hunger; those who believe in me will never thirst. Those who come to me I will not throw out the door. (John 6:35, 37)

> Jesus stood and cried out, "If any are thirsty, they must come to me and drink." (John 7:37)

> The kingdom of the heavens is like someone who put on a wedding for his son and sent his servants to call those who had been invited. Finally he said, "Go to the ends of the streets[574] and invite any people you find to the wedding." (Matthew 22:1–9)

Surely everyone knows that the Lord's invitation or calling is universal. So is the grace to accept it.

By going to the Lord, we gain life because the Lord is life itself. He is not only the life within faith but also the life within goodwill. It is clear from the following passages that this life is the Lord and comes to us from the Lord:

> In the beginning was the Word. In it there was *life,* and that *life* was the light for humankind. (John 1:1, 4)

> Just as the Father raises the dead and brings them to life, so also the Son *brings to life* those whom he wishes to. (John 5:21)

> As the Father has life in himself, so he has given the Son *to have life in himself.* (John 5:26)

> The bread of God is he who comes down from heaven and gives *life* to the world. (John 6:33)

> The words that I speak to you are spirit and *are life.* (John 6:63)

Jesus said,

> Those who follow me will have *the light of life.* (John 8:12)

> I have come *so that they may have life* and abundance. (John 10:10)

> Those who believe in me, even if they die, *they will live.* (John 11:25)

> I am the way, the truth, and *the life.* (John 14:6)

> *Because I live, you too will live.* (John 14:19)

> These things have been written so that you may have *life* in his name. (John 20:31)

> He is *eternal life.* (1 John 5:20)

"The life within faith and goodwill" means the spiritual life the Lord gives people in their earthly lives.

359 (d) *Nevertheless, no faith, no goodwill, and none of the life within faith or goodwill comes from ourselves; instead they come from the Lord alone.* We read, "We cannot receive anything unless it is given to us from heaven" (John 3:27). And Jesus said, "Those who live in me and I in them bear much fruit, because without me you cannot do anything" (John 15:5). This has to be understood, however, in a particular way: On our own we cannot acquire any faith for ourselves except earthly faith, which is a persuasion that something is the case because a man[575] in authority said so. On our own we cannot acquire any goodwill for ourselves except earthly goodwill, which is our working to gain favor for the sake of some reward. In both of them the self is present, but life from the Lord is not present yet. Nevertheless, with this earthly faith and goodwill we are preparing ourselves to be a vessel for the Lord. As we are preparing ourselves, the Lord comes in and turns our earthly faith into spiritual faith, does the same with our goodwill, and brings them both to life. These things happen when we go to the Lord as the God of heaven and earth.

Because we have been created as images of God, we have been created as vessels for God. Therefore the Lord says, "The people who love me are those who have my commandments and follow them. I will love these people, come to them, and make a home with them" (John 14:21, 23).

Also, "Behold! I am standing at the door and knocking. If any hear my voice and open the door, I will come in and will dine with them and they with me" (Revelation 3:20).

In conclusion, as we prepare ourselves in an earthly way to receive the Lord, the Lord comes in and makes all the earthly things in us spiritual and therefore alive. On the other hand, however, the less we prepare ourselves, the more we distance the Lord from ourselves and do everything on our own; and what we do on our own has no life in it.

These points cannot be put in any clearer light before we come to the chapters on goodwill [§§392–462] and free choice [§§463–508]. Similar points will also appear later on in the chapter on reformation and regeneration [§§571–625].

In the preceding sections, I stated that our faith starts out as something earthly, but as we move toward the Lord it becomes spiritual; and the same applies to our goodwill. No one yet knows the difference, however, between earthly and spiritual faith and goodwill. This great mystery needs to be disclosed.

360

There are two worlds, the physical world and the spiritual world. Each world has a sun. From each sun emanates heat and light. The heat and light from the sun of the spiritual world have an intrinsic life in them from the Lord, who is within that sun. The heat and light from the sun of the physical world, on the other hand, have no intrinsic life in them. Instead they serve as vessels for the two higher forms of heat and light (as instrumental causes usually do for their principal causes)[576] and serve to convey that higher heat and light to people.

It is important to realize, therefore, that the heat and light from the sun in the spiritual world are the source of all that is spiritual. That heat and that light are themselves spiritual as well, because they have spirit and life within them. The heat and light from the sun in the physical world are the source of all physical things. Physical things in and of themselves have no spirit or life.

[2] Now, since faith relates to light and goodwill to heat, clearly if we are in the light and heat that emanate from the sun of the spiritual world, we have a faith and a goodwill that are spiritual. If we are limited to the heat and light that emanate from the sun of the physical world, we are limited to a faith and a goodwill that are earthly.

As spiritual light lies within physical light as if it was in its own vessel or container, and spiritual heat lies within physical heat in the same way, it follows that spiritual faith lies within earthly faith, and spiritual goodwill within earthly goodwill. The two come together with every step we take as we progress from the physical world into the spiritual world. We make this progress as we believe in the Lord, who is the light itself, the way, the truth, and the life, as he himself teaches.

[3] Since this is the case, when we have spiritual faith we clearly also have earthly faith, in that spiritual faith lies within earthly faith, as I just said. And because faith relates to light, it follows that when spiritual faith comes into us our earthly self becomes translucent, so to speak. Our earthly self also becomes beautifully colored, depending on how united our faith is to goodwill. The reason it takes on colors is that goodwill is a glowing red and faith is a shining white. Goodwill glows red with the flame of spiritual fire, and faith shines white with the brilliance of the light from that fire.

Just the opposite happens, however, if we do not have spirituality in our earthly self, but instead have something earthly in our spirituality. This is what happens to people who reject faith and goodwill. For these people, the inner level of the mind, where they go when they are left to their own thinking, is hellish. In fact, although they do not realize it, their thinking comes from hell. The outer level of their mind, from which they operate when they are talking to their friends in the world, may be spiritual in a way, but it is also riddled with things that are like the filthiness of hell. These people are in fact in hell, in the sense that they are in a state that is upside-down compared to the state of the people we were talking about before.

361 People who have faith in the Lord and goodwill toward their neighbor have spirituality within their earthly self, and as a result their earthly self becomes translucent. Once we realize this, we can see that the more translucent their earthly self becomes, the more wisdom they have about spiritual things. They also have more wisdom about earthly things, because as they are thinking, reading, or hearing about something, they see inside themselves whether it is true or not. This is an awareness they have from the Lord as spiritual light and heat flow down from him into the higher sphere of their intellect.

[2] The more spiritual our faith and our goodwill become, the more we are drawn away from our self-centeredness. We do not focus on ourselves, on payment, or on reward; we focus only on the pleasure of perceiving truths that relate to faith and doing good actions that relate to love. The more our spirituality increases, the more blissful that pleasure

becomes. This process is the source of our salvation, which is called eternal life.

This human state is comparable to the things that are most beautiful and most pleasant in our world. In fact, it is compared with them in the Word. It is compared to fruit-bearing trees, and the gardens in which they stand; flowering fields; precious stones; and exquisite food. This state is also compared to weddings and the festivities and celebrations that follow them.

[3] When this state is upside-down, however—that is, when an earthly self lies within our spirituality, and therefore we are inwardly devils although we are outwardly angels—then our state is comparable to a dead person in a coffin made out of precious, gilded wood. This state is also like a skeleton dressed up in someone's clothes riding around in a magnificent carriage. It is like a corpse in a tomb that is built like the temple of Diana.[577] Our inner self can be pictured as a mass of snakes in a cave, while our outer self is like butterflies whose wings are tinged with colors of every kind; yet these butterflies glue their polluted eggs to the leaves of productive trees, with the result that the fruit is consumed. In this state our inner self could be compared to a hawk, and our outer self to a dove: our faith and goodwill are like a hawk flying over a fleeing dove that eventually becomes worn out; then the hawk flies down and devours it.

6

The Lord, Goodwill, and Faith Form a Unity
in the Same Way Our Life, Our Will, and Our Intellect
Form a Unity; If We Separate Them, Each One Crumbles
like a Pearl That Is Crushed to Powder

First I must mention some things that till now have been unknown in the scholarly world and therefore also unknown to the clergy. These things have been as hidden, in fact, as things that are buried in the ground. Yet they are treasure chests full of wisdom. Unless they are dug up and presented to the public, people will struggle in vain to develop a just concept of God, faith, and goodwill; we will not know how we

362

ought to manage and prepare the state of our life now for the state of eternal life.

The things that have been unknown are these: We are nothing but an organ that receives life. Everything belonging to life flows into us from the God of heaven, who is the Lord. There are two faculties in us that receive life: they are called the will and the intellect. The will is a vessel for love and the intellect is a vessel for wisdom. Therefore the will is a vessel for goodwill and the intellect is a vessel for faith.

[2] All our willing and all our understanding flow in from outside us. The good impulses that relate to love and goodwill and the true insights that relate to wisdom and faith flow in from the Lord. All the things that oppose these flow in from hell. The Lord has provided that we feel inside us, as if they were our own, the things that flow in from outside. As a result, we produce from ourselves good impulses and true insights as if they were our own, although none of them is actually ours. They are nonetheless attributed to us as our own in order to give us free choice in willing and thinking, and to grant us concepts of what is good and what is true from which we can freely select whatever suits our temporal and eternal life.

[3] If you look askance or through squinting eyes at what I have just presented, you might draw many insane conclusions from it; but if you look at it squarely, you will be able to draw many wise conclusions from it. To help you look at it squarely, I needed first to present judgments and crucial teachings related to God and the divine Trinity. Later in the work I will lay out judgments and crucial teachings related to faith and goodwill, free choice, reformation and regeneration, and the assignment of spiritual credit or blame, as well as repentance, baptism, and the Holy Supper as means to an end.[578]

363   Now to the current point about faith—namely, that the Lord, goodwill, and faith form a unity in the same way our life, our will, and our intellect form a unity; and if we separate them, each one crumbles like a pearl that is crushed to powder. To see and acknowledge the truth of this, it is important to consider it in the following order:

     a. The Lord flows into everyone with all his divine love, all his divine wisdom, and all his divine life.

     b. Therefore the Lord flows into everyone with the entire essence of faith and goodwill.

     c. These qualities are received by us according to our form.

d. If we separate the Lord, goodwill, and faith, however, instead of being a form that accepts these qualities we are a form that destroys them.

(a) *The Lord flows into everyone with all his divine love, all his divine wisdom, and all his divine life.* In the Book of Creation, we read that we were created in the image of God and that God breathed the breath of life into our nostrils (Genesis 1:27; 2:7). This means that we are not life, we are merely organs that receive life. God could not create another being like himself. If he could have done so, there would be as many gods as there are people. God could not create life or light either. God could, however, create people as forms that receive life, just as he created the eye as a form that receives light. God could not and still cannot divide his own essence—it is an indivisible oneness. Therefore since God alone is life, it follows without a doubt that God uses his life to bring us all to life. Without being brought to life, we would all have flesh that was no more than a sponge and bones that were no more than a skeleton. We would have no more life than a clock that moves because of its pendulum and a weight or a spring. Given this fact, it also follows that God flows into every human being with all his divine life, that is, with all his divine love and divine wisdom. (For these two things constituting his divine life, see above, §§39, 40). Divinity is indivisible.

[2] Furthermore, we can understand how God flows in with all his divine life just as we understand that the sun in our world flows with all its essence (heat and light) into every tree, every bush, and every flower, and even into every stone, both precious and common. Every object draws its own share from the general inflow. The sun does not divide up its heat and light and give part of it to this thing and another part to that one.

The same thing is true of the sun in heaven—the source from which divine love emanates in the form of heat and divine wisdom in the form of light. Love and wisdom flow into human minds the way heat and light from the world's sun flow into bodies, bringing them to life depending on the quality of their form. Each form takes what it needs from the general inflow.

What the Lord says applies here:

Your Father makes his sun rise on the evil and on the good, and sends rain on the just and on the unjust. (Matthew 5:45)

[3] The Lord is omnipresent; and everywhere he is present, he is present with his entire essence. It is impossible for him to take out some of

his essence and give part of it to one person and another part to another. He gives it all. He also gives us the ability to adopt as much as we wish of it, whether a little or a lot. The Lord says that he has a home with those who do his commandments, and that the faithful are in him and he is in them. In a word, all things are full of God. We each take our own portion from that fullness.

This is true of atmospheres and oceans, and also of everything that is universal. The atmosphere is the same on a small and a large scale. It does not limit itself to giving one aspect of itself to someone who is breathing, a second aspect to a bird that is flying, a third aspect to the sails of a ship, and a fourth aspect to the vanes of a windmill. Instead, each thing draws on certain aspects of the atmosphere and applies to itself as much as it needs.

It is the same as a barn full of grain. The owners draw from it the provisions they need for a given day. The barn does not determine what they receive.

365   (b) *Therefore the Lord flows into everyone with the entire essence of faith and goodwill.* This follows from the previous point, since the essence of faith is life from divine wisdom and the essence of goodwill is life from divine love. Therefore, since the Lord is present along with these things that belong to him (namely, divine wisdom and divine love), he is also present along with all the true perceptions related to faith and all the good actions related to goodwill. "Faith" means all the truth from the Lord that we perceive, think, and speak. "Goodwill" means all the goodness from the Lord which moves us and which we then intend and do.

[2] As I said just above, the divine love that emanates from the Lord as a sun is perceived by the angels as heat, and the divine wisdom from that love is perceived as light. Someone who does not think beyond appearances might surmise that the heat I just mentioned is mere heat and that the light is mere light, like the heat and light that emanate from the sun in our world. In fact, the heat and light that emanate from the Lord as a sun hold in their core all the infinities that are in the Lord. That heat holds all the infinities of his love and that light holds all the infinities of his wisdom. Therefore they also hold an infinity that includes everything good related to goodwill and everything true related to faith. The reason for this is that the spiritual sun is present everywhere that its heat and light are present. That sun is a sphere that immediately surrounds the Lord, radiating from his divine love together with his divine wisdom. (As I have noted a number of times before [§§24, 29, 35, 39, 41, 49, 63, 66, 75, 76, 360], the Lord is within that sun.)

[3] These facts make it clear that nothing stands in the way of our being able to draw from the Lord everything good that relates to goodwill and everything true that relates to faith, since he is omnipresent. An example showing that nothing stands in the way is the love and the wisdom that heaven's angels have from the Lord. The angels' love and wisdom are beyond words and incomprehensible to our earthly self; they are also capable of increasing to eternity.

The fact that there are infinite things in the heat and light that emanate from the Lord, although they are perceived as simple heat and light, can be illustrated by various phenomena on earth. For example, we hear the tone of someone's voice in speech as a noncomposite sound, yet when angels hear it they perceive in it all that person's feelings, and can list and describe each one. We too can sense to some extent that there are qualities that lie within a voice when we listen to people talking to us. We can tell if there is contempt, ridicule, or hatred, or else goodwill, benevolence, cheerfulness, or other feelings behind what they say. Similar things lie hidden in the visual impression we receive when we look at someone.

[4] This phenomenon can also be illustrated by the fragrances in an ample garden or in a vast field full of flowers. The sweet smell given off by those plants consists of thousands and even tens of thousands of different elements; yet they are sensed as one impression. It is similar with many other things that appear on the outside as something uniform but are inwardly complex.

The source of human attraction and repulsion is feelings that emanate from people's minds. These feelings attract others who have similar feelings and repel others who do not. Although these emanations are countless and are not picked up by any physical sensation, they are perceived by the sensation of our soul as a single thing. In the spiritual world, all connections and associations are formed on the basis of them.

I have mentioned these things to illustrate what I said before about the spiritual light that emanates from the Lord. It contains all things related to wisdom and all things related to faith. It is this light that enables our intellect to see and perceive the objects of reason in an analytical way, just as our eye sees and perceives earthly objects in a proportional way.

(c) *The qualities that flow in from the Lord are received by us according to our form.* "Form" here means our state in regard to love and wisdom. Therefore it includes the state of our desires to do good out of goodwill and the state of our insights about the truths of faith.

366

God is one indivisible entity that is the same from eternity to eternity. He is not the same *simple* thing; he is the same *infinite* thing. All variation is supplied by the object in which it occurs, as I showed above [§364]. It is the receiving form or state that causes variations, as we can see from the life that is in little children, teenagers, young adults, middle-aged adults, and the elderly. Because we keep the same soul, we have the same life inside from infancy to old age; but as our state goes through life stages and different circumstances, we perceive the life inside us differently.

[2] God's life is present in all its fullness not only in people who are good and religious but also in people who are evil and ungodly. That life is the same in angels of heaven as it is in spirits of hell. The difference is that evil people block the road and shut the door to prevent God from coming down into the lower areas of their mind. Good people, on the other hand, smooth the road and open the door. They invite God to enter the lower areas of their mind since he already inhabits the highest areas of it. They change the state of their will so that love and goodwill may flow in, and change the state of their intellect so that wisdom and faith may flow in—they open themselves to God.

Evil people block that inflow with various bodily cravings and spiritual garbage that they spread around to prevent access. Nevertheless, God with all his divine essence still dwells in the highest parts of evil people and gives them the ability to will what is good and understand what is true. This ability is something that all human beings have, although it would not be theirs at all if life from God were not present in their soul. Many experiences have taught me that even the evil have this ability.[579]

[3] The way we individually receive life from God depends on our form. This can be illustrated with comparisons to every kind of plant. Every species of tree, every species of bush, every type of shrub, and every type of grass receives the inflowing heat and light according to its own form. This is true not only for plants that serve a good purpose but also for those that serve an evil purpose. The sun and its heat do not alter the form of the plants. Instead the forms themselves alter the effects of the sun.

The same is true for substances in the mineral kingdom. Every different substance, whether it has high quality or little value, receives what flows in according to the form of the structure of its component parts. No two types of stone, no two minerals, no two metals receive the inflowing heat and light in the same way. Some of them dapple themselves with exquisitely beautiful colors; some transmit light without altering it; some scramble the light inside themselves or suffocate it.

As you can see on the basis of these few examples, the sun in our world, along with its heat and light, is just as present in one object as it is in another, but the forms that receive it vary its effects; likewise the Lord is equally present to all, shining down from the sun in heaven, in whose midst he is, along with his heat (which is essentially love) and his light (which is essentially wisdom). It is our form as shaped by the state of our life that varies his effects. Therefore the Lord is not responsible for our failure to be reborn and saved; we ourselves are.

(d) *If we separate the Lord, goodwill, and faith, however, instead of being a form that accepts these qualities we are a form that destroys them.* If we separate the Lord from goodwill and faith, we separate the life from goodwill and faith. Then goodwill and faith either cease to exist or become deformed. (See above, §358, on the point that the Lord is life itself.) If we acknowledge the Lord but we leave out goodwill, we acknowledge the Lord only with our lips. Our acknowledgment and confession of him is something frozen that has no faith, because the spiritual essence of faith is lacking. Goodwill is the essence of faith. If we practice goodwill but do not acknowledge that the Lord is the God of heaven and earth and is one with the Father, as he himself teaches, then our practice of goodwill is only earthly and has no eternal life within it.

People in the church know that every good thing that is truly good is from God, and therefore from the Lord who is "the true God and eternal life" (1 John 5:20). The same is true of goodwill, because goodness and goodwill are one.

[2] Faith separated from goodwill is not faith, because faith is the light of human life and goodwill is its heat. Therefore if goodwill is separated from faith, the situation is the same as when heat is separated from light. Our state in that case is like the state of the world in winter when everything on earth dies away. For goodwill to be goodwill and faith to be faith, they cannot be separated any more than will and intellect can be separated. If will and intellect are separated, the intellect becomes nothing, and the will soon follows. The same is the case for goodwill and faith because goodwill dwells in the will and faith in the intellect.

[3] Separating goodwill and faith is like separating essence and form. The learned world knows that an essence without a form and a form without an essence are nothing. An essence has no quality without its form, and a form has no underlying reality without its essence. Therefore nothing can be attributed to either of them if they are separated from each other. Goodwill is the essence of faith and faith is the form of

goodwill, just as goodness is the essence of truth and truth is the form of goodness, as I said just above.

[4] These two things, goodness and truth, are in each and every thing that really exists. Goodwill relates to goodness and faith relates to truth. Therefore goodwill and faith can be illustrated by comparisons with many things in the human body and many things on earth.

A comparison with the respiration of the lungs and the systolic motion of the heart provides a perfect parallel. Goodwill cannot be taken away from faith any more than the heart can be taken away from the lungs. If the heartbeat stops, the lungs immediately stop breathing. On the other hand, if the lungs stop breathing, all sensation shuts down, all movement of muscles is lost, and soon the heart stops and the whole life comes to an end. This comparison provides a perfect parallel because the heart corresponds to the will and also to goodwill, while the breathing of the lungs corresponds to the intellect and also to faith, in that goodwill dwells in the will and faith dwells in the intellect, as I have said before. In the Word, "heart" and "spirit" have exactly these meanings.

[5] Separating goodwill and faith is also perfectly parallel to separating blood and flesh. When blood is separated from flesh it is gore at first and later becomes pus. Flesh that has been separated from blood progressively rots and breeds little worms.[580] In the spiritual meaning, "blood" means truth that is related to wisdom and faith, and "flesh" means goodness that is related to love and goodwill. This meaning of "blood" was demonstrated in *Revelation Unveiled* 379; this meaning of "flesh" was demonstrated in *Revelation Unveiled* 832.

[6] For both goodwill and faith to be anything, they cannot be separated any more than we can separate food and water or bread and wine. If we consume food or bread without water or wine, all they do is bloat our stomach. In the form of undigested lumps, they ruin our stomach and become like rotten, foul-smelling muck inside it. If we consume water or wine without food or bread, they too bloat our stomach and swell our blood-vessels and internal passages, which become so bereft of nutrition that they emaciate the body even to the point of death.[581] This comparison as well is a perfect parallel, since in the spiritual meaning "food" and "bread" mean goodness that relates to love and goodwill, and "water" and "wine" mean truth that relates to wisdom and faith (see *Revelation Unveiled* 50, 316, 778, 932).

[7] Goodwill that is connected to faith and faith that is reciprocally connected to goodwill could be likened to a lovely young woman whose facial color is beautiful because redness and whiteness are integrated in it.

This simile is also a perfect parallel because love, and therefore goodwill, glows red in the spiritual world due to the fire of the sun there, while truth, and therefore faith, shines white because of the light of that sun. Therefore goodwill that is separate from faith can be likened to a face that is blazing red with pimples, and faith that is separate from goodwill can be likened to the pale white face of a corpse.

Faith that is separate from goodwill can also be likened to the paralysis of one side of the body, or hemiplegia. As it progresses, people die from it. It can also be likened to Saint Vitus's or Saint Guy's dance, which befalls people who have been bitten by a tarantula.[582] These victims have a rationality comparable to that of people who have faith without goodwill. In both cases they dance with a fury and think of themselves as being alive, but in fact they have no more ability to focus their reasoning and think about spiritual truths than someone lying in bed being crushed by a suffocating nightmare.[583]

This provides adequate support for two of the topics in this chapter—the earlier one that *faith without goodwill is not faith; goodwill without faith is not goodwill;* and that *neither of them is living unless it comes from the Lord* [§§355–361]; and the current one, that *the Lord, goodwill, and faith form a unity in the same way our life, our will, and our intellect form a unity; if we separate them, each one crumbles like a pearl that is crushed to powder* [§§362–367].

7

The Lord Is Goodwill and Faith within Us;
We Are Goodwill and Faith within the Lord

People of the church are in the Lord and the Lord is in them. This is clear from the following passages in the Word: **368**

> Jesus said, "*Live in me and I [shall live] in you.* I am the vine and you are the branches. *Those who live in me and I in them* bear much fruit." (John 15:4, 5)

> Those who eat my flesh and drink my blood *live in me and I in them.* (John 6:56)

> On that day you will know that I am in my Father, and *you are in me and I am in you.* (John 14:20)

If any confess that Jesus is the Son of God, God lives in them, and they live in God. (1 John 4:15)

We ourselves cannot be in the Lord, but the goodwill and faith that are in us from the Lord can. These two make us essentially human.

We can shed some light on this mystery to disclose it to the intellect if we explore it in the following sequence:

a. Our partnership with God is what gives us salvation and eternal life.
b. It is impossible for us to have a partnership with God the Father. What is possible is a partnership with the Lord, and through the Lord, with God the Father.
c. Our partnership with the Lord is reciprocal: the Lord is in us and we are in the Lord.
d. This reciprocal partnership comes about through goodwill and faith.

The truth of these points will become clear from the following explanation.

369 (a) *Our partnership with God is what gives us salvation and eternal life.* Human beings were created with the capability of being in a partnership with God. We were created to be citizens of heaven and also citizens of the world. We are spiritual so we can be citizens of heaven and earthly so we can be citizens of the world. Our spiritual self is capable of thinking about God and perceiving things that relate to God. It is also capable of loving God and being moved by things that come from God. It follows that we are able to be in a partnership with God.

Our ability to think about God and to perceive things that come from God is completely beyond the reach of doubt. We are capable of thinking about God's unity; about God's underlying reality, which is Jehovah; about God's immensity and eternity; about the divine love and wisdom that constitute God's essence; and about God's omnipotence, omniscience, and omnipresence. We are capable of thinking about the Lord our Savior, his Son, and about his redemption and mediation. We can also think about the Holy Spirit and about the divine Trinity. All these things relate to God; in fact, they are God. Beyond this, we can think about God's influence, which primarily takes the form of faith and goodwill, not to mention many things that emanate from faith and goodwill.

[2] The fact that we are capable of not only thinking about God but also loving God is clear from the two commandments of God himself that read like this:

You are to love the Lord your God with all your heart and with all your soul. This is the first and great commandment. The second is like it:

you are to love your neighbor as yourself. (Matthew 22:37, 38, 39; Deuteronomy 6:5)

We are also capable of doing what God commands, which is the same as loving God and being loved by God, as the following words show:

> Jesus said, "The people who love me are those who have my commandments and follow them. Those who love me will be loved by my Father, and I will love them and manifest myself to them." (John 14:21)

[3] In fact, what else is faith but a partnership with God by means of truths that shape our understanding and thought? What else is love but a partnership with God through goodness that shapes our intentions and desires? God's connection to us is a spiritual connection that comes to an earthly plane; our connection to God is an earthly connection that comes from a spiritual plane.

The ultimate purpose in creating us citizens of heaven and also citizens of the world was this partnership. As citizens of heaven we are spiritual and as citizens of the world we are earthly. Therefore if we become spiritual-and-rational and also spiritual-and-moral, we forge a partnership with God. Through this partnership we have salvation and eternal life.

On the other hand, if we are only earthly-and-rational and earthly-and-moral, God is indeed connected to us but we are not connected to him. The result of this is spiritual death (which by definition is earthly life without spiritual life), because spirituality, in which the life of God exists, has been extinguished in us.

(b) *It is impossible for us to have a partnership with God the Father. What is possible is a partnership with the Lord, and through the Lord, with God the Father.* Scripture teaches this and reason sees it. Scripture teaches that God the Father never has been seen or heard, and never could be. As a result, nothing from him such as he is in his own essential underlying reality could have an effect on us. The Lord says,

370

> No one has seen God except the One who is with the Father. He has seen the Father. (John 6:46)

> No one knows the Father except the Son and those to whom the Son is willing to reveal him. (Matthew 11:27)

> You have never heard the voice of the Father or seen what he looks like. (John 5:37)

The reason for this is that God the Father is in the first principles and beginnings of all things. Therefore he transcends the entire reach of the human mind. He is in the first principles and beginnings of all things related to wisdom and all things related to love. No partnership is possible between those first principles and us. Therefore if he were to come near us or we were to go near him, we would be consumed and liquefied like a piece of wood at the focus of a huge burning mirror;[584] or better yet like a carved statue thrown into the sun itself. This is why Moses, who longed to see God, was told that we cannot see God and live (Exodus 33:20).

[2] The passages that I just quoted make it clear that we form a partnership with God the Father through the Lord. It was not the Father, it was the only begotten Son who is close to the Father's heart and has seen the Father, who disclosed and revealed the things that are of God and from God. The following passages also show that we form a partnership with God the Father through the Lord: "On that day you will know that I am in my Father, and you are in me and I am in you" (John 14:20). "The glory that you gave me, I have given them so that they may be one as we are one—I in them and you in me" (John 17:22, 23, 26). Jesus said, "I am the way, the truth, and the life. No one comes to the Father except through me." Then Philip wanted to see the Father, but the Lord replied, "Those who see me also see the Father, and those who know me also know the Father" (John 14:6, 7, and following). Elsewhere we read, "Those who see me see the One who sent me" (John 12:45).

In addition, the Lord says that he is the door, and that those who enter through him are saved, but those who climb up some other way are thieves and robbers (John 10:1, 9). He also says, "Those who do not live in me will be thrown out and put in the fire like a withered branch" (John 15:6).

[3] The reason is that the Lord our Savior is Jehovah the Father himself in human form. Jehovah came down and became human so that he could come close to us and we could come close to him, and a partnership could be forged, through which we could have salvation and eternal life. When God became human and then a human became God, he became able to draw near us in this adapted form and, as a human God and a divine Human, forge a partnership with us.

There are three stages to this that follow in sequence: adjusting to one another, coming closer together, and then forging a partnership. The adjustment has to happen before the two parties can come closer together, and both the adjustment and the coming closer have to happen before a partnership can be forged. The adjustment on God's part was to become human. God is perpetually coming closer to the extent that we are coming closer to him. And as this takes place, a partnership is forged. For each and every set of things that become one and share their existence, these three stages happen in this sequence and proceed in this order.

(c) *Our partnership with the Lord is reciprocal: the Lord is in us and we are in the Lord.* The partnership is reciprocal. Scripture teaches this and reason sees it. The Lord teaches that his partnership with his Father is reciprocal. He said to Philip, "Do you not believe that I am in the Father and the Father is in me? Believe me that I am in the Father and the Father is in me" (John 14:10, 11).

371

> So that you know and believe that the Father is in me and I am in the Father. (John 10:38)

> Jesus said, "Father, the hour has come. Glorify your Son, so that your Son will also glorify you." (John 17:1)

> Father, all that is mine is yours and all that is yours is mine. (John 17:10)

The Lord says something similar about his partnership with us, specifying that it is reciprocal. He says,

> Live in me and I [shall live] in you. Those who *live in me and I in them* bear much fruit. (John 15:4, 5)

> Those who eat my flesh and drink my blood *live in me and I in them.* (John 6:56)

> On that day you will know that I am in my Father, *and you are in me and I am in you.* (John 14:20)

> Those who do the commandments of Christ *live in him, and he lives in them.* (1 John 3:24; 4:13)

> If any confess that Christ is the Son of God, *God lives in them, and they live in God.* (1 John 4:15)

> If any hear my voice and open the door, I will come in and *will dine with them and they with me.* (Revelation 3:20)

[2] The very clear passages just quoted make it evident that the partnership between the Lord and us is reciprocal. Because the partnership is reciprocal, it obviously follows that we have to unite ourselves to the Lord so that the Lord will unite himself to us. Otherwise there will be a

parting and a separation rather than a partnership—not on the Lord's initiative but on our own.

To allow the partnership to be reciprocal, we have been given free choice. With it we can travel the road to heaven or the road to hell. Our ability to act reciprocally is a result of the freedom we have been given to unite ourselves to the Lord or unite ourselves to the Devil. (The nature of this freedom and the reasons we possess it will be illustrated later on in the text when we come to free choice [§§463–508], repentance [§§509–570], reformation and regeneration [§§571–625], and the assignment of spiritual credit or blame [§§626–666].)

[3] It is a lamentable thing that the reciprocal partnership between the Lord and us, even though it stands out so clearly in the Word, is still unknown to the Christian church. It is unknown because of theories about faith and free choice. The theory about faith holds that faith is granted without our contributing anything to acquiring it—we do not adjust ourselves to receive it or work on receiving it any more than would a log.[585] The theory about free choice holds that we do not have even a speck of free choice about spiritual things.

The salvation of the human race depends on the reciprocal partnership between the Lord and the individual. Therefore, to prevent this partnership from remaining unknown any longer, it is a necessity that it be disclosed. The most effective way to accomplish this is through examples, because they illustrate the partnership.

[4] There are two types of reciprocal partnership: one is *alternating;* the other is *mutual.* An *alternating* reciprocal cycle that results in a partnership can be illustrated by the lungs filling with air. We take in air, which expands our chest. Soon afterward we release the air we inhaled, which contracts our chest. This inhalation and consequent expansion are rendered possible by the air pressure in this column of air.[586] The releasing and contracting is accomplished by our own ribs as driven by our muscles. This shows the reciprocal partnership of the air and the lungs. The life of all our physical sensations and movements depends on this partnership, as we can tell from the fact that we lose both sensation and movement when we stop breathing.

[5] A reciprocal partnership that comes about through alternating cycles can also be illustrated by the partnership of the heart with the lungs and of the lungs with the heart. The heart moves blood from its right chamber into the lungs. The lungs return the blood to the left chamber of the heart. This is how the partnership on which the life of the whole body depends becomes reciprocal.

There is a similar partnership between the blood and the heart, and the reverse. Blood from the whole body flows through the veins into the heart, and flows out of the heart through the arteries to the whole body. Action and reaction forge this partnership.

A similar action and reaction between an embryo and its mother's womb allow their partnership to continue.

[6] The reciprocal partnership between the Lord and us, however, is not like this. It is a *mutual* partnership that is brought about by cooperation rather than action and reaction. The Lord acts. We receive the Lord's action. We then function as if we were on our own. In fact, we function on our own from the Lord. The things we do that are inspired by the Lord are credited to us as our own, since the Lord continually keeps us in free choice. The free choice we receive is an ability to will and think from the Lord, that is, from the Word, and also an ability to will and think from the Devil, that is, against the Lord and the Word. The Lord gives us this freedom so that we can forge a reciprocal partnership and be granted life and eternal blessedness as a result—something that would be impossible without a reciprocal partnership.

[7] A reciprocal partnership that is mutual can be illustrated by various things in us and in the world. The partnership between the soul and the body in everyone is this type of partnership. The partnership of our will and our action is of this type, as is the partnership of our thought and our speech. Other partnerships that work like this are the partnership of two eyes working together, and two ears, and two nostrils.

The optic nerve shows that our two eyes have this type of reciprocal partnership between them. In the optic nerve, fibers from both brains are intertwined, and they travel intertwined to each eye. The same is true for our two ears and our two nostrils.

[8] There is a similar mutual reciprocal partnership between light and the eyes, sound and the ears, odors and the nose, tastes and the tongue, and tactile sensations and the body. The eye is in light and light is in the eye. Sound is in the ear and the ear is in sound. Smells are in the nose, and the nose is in smells. Tastes are in the tongue and the tongue is in tastes. Tactile sensation is in the body and the body is in tactile sensation.

This kind of reciprocal partnership can also be compared to the partnership between a horse and a carriage; between an ox and a plow; between wheels and an engine; between sails and the wind; between a flute and the air. To sum up, the purpose and the means have this type of reciprocal partnership, as do the means and the result. But there is no room to explain the above examples one by one, because the explanation would fill many volumes.

372 (d) *This reciprocal partnership between the Lord and us comes about through goodwill and faith.* Today people know that the church constitutes the body of Christ. People also know that everyone who has the church inside is in some part of that body, as Paul says (Ephesians 1:23; 1 Corinthians 12:27; Romans 12:4, 5). Is the body of Christ anything except divine goodness and divine truth? This is what the Lord's words in John mean: "Those who eat my flesh and drink my blood live in me and I in them" (John 6:56). "The Lord's flesh" means divine goodness, as does "bread." "The Lord's blood" means divine truth, as does "wine." Below in the chapter on the Holy Supper you will see that these are their true meanings [§§702–709].

It follows that the more involved we are in acts of goodwill and in truths that relate to faith, the more we are in the Lord and the Lord is in us. Our partnership with the Lord is a spiritual partnership, and spiritual partnerships take place only through goodwill and faith.

I have shown in the chapter on Sacred Scripture that a partnership between the Lord and the church and thus a partnership between goodness and truth exists in every detail of the Word, §§248–253. Because goodwill is goodness and faith is truth, there is also a partnership between goodwill and faith throughout the Word.

From all this it now follows that *the Lord is goodwill and faith within us, and we are goodwill and faith within the Lord.* The Lord is spiritual goodwill and faith in our earthly goodwill and faith; and we are earthly goodwill and faith from the Lord's spiritual goodwill and faith. As the two types of goodwill and faith forge a partnership, they become a goodwill and a faith that are spiritual-and-earthly.

8

Goodwill and Faith Come Together in Good Actions

373 Every action that we take contains our whole self with the full measure and quality of our mind or our essential nature. Our "mind" means our love and our desire and the thoughts that come from them. These form our nature and our life in general. If we look at a person's actions in this way, they are like mirrors of the person.

This can be illustrated by a comparison with wild and domesticated animals. A wild animal is a wild animal, and a domesticated animal is a domesticated animal, in everything it does. A wolf is a wolf in everything it does. A tiger is a tiger in everything it does. A fox is a fox in everything it does. A lion is a lion in everything it does. The same goes for a sheep or a goat in all its actions. It is the same for us, except that our quality is determined by our inner self. If we are wolves or foxes inside, everything we do is inwardly wolfish or foxlike. The opposite is true if we are inwardly like a sheep or a lamb. Nevertheless, the inner quality that is present in everything we do is not necessarily apparent in our outer self, because our outer self can turn in different directions around our inner self, although our inner self remains nonetheless hidden within it. The Lord says, "Good people bring what is good out of the good treasure in their heart, and evil people bring what is evil out of the evil treasure in their heart" (Luke 6:45). He also says, "Every type of tree is known by its fruit. People do not pick figs from thorn bushes or gather grapes from a bramble bush" (Luke 6:44).

After we die it becomes very obvious to us that everything that comes from us has the nature of our inner self, since we are then living as our inner self and no longer as our outer self.

When the Lord, goodwill, and faith dwell in our inner self, then there is goodness within us, and all the work that comes from us is good. This point will be demonstrated in the following sequence.

a. "Goodwill" is benevolence toward others; "good works" are good actions that result from benevolence.
b. Goodwill and faith are transient and exist only in our minds unless, when an opportunity occurs, they culminate in actions and become embodied in them.
c. Goodwill alone does not produce good actions; even less does faith alone produce them. Good actions are produced by goodwill and faith together.

Now I will take up these points one by one.

(a) *"Goodwill" is benevolence toward others; "good works" are good actions that result from benevolence.* Goodwill and good works are two distinct things, just as will and action, or a mental impulse and a physical movement, are two distinct things. They are as distinct as our inner self and our outer self. Our inner self and our outer self are as distinct as a cause and an effect. The causes of all things are formed in our inner self, and all their

374

effects take place in our outer self. Therefore goodwill, because it belongs to our inner self, is intending benevolence to others, and good works, because they belong to our outer self, are good actions that result from that intention.

[2] Nevertheless there is an infinite difference between one person's benevolence and another's. Anything that someone does to please another is believed, or appears, to come from benevolence. It is hard to know, however, whether those good actions come from goodwill at all, let alone whether the goodwill they come from is genuine or illegitimate.

The infinite difference between one person's benevolence and another's originates in the individual's purpose, goal, and consequent plan. These lie hidden within the intention to do good things. They determine the quality of the individual's will.

In the intellect the will seeks ways and means of achieving its desired outcomes, which are results. In the intellect the will finds a light that enables it to see not only various options but also specifically when and how it must take action and thereby bring about its desired results, which are works. In the intellect the will also equips itself with the power to act. Therefore the works that result are in respect to their essence the result of the will, in respect to their form the result of the intellect, and in respect to their ultimate action the result of the body. This is how goodwill comes down into good works.

[3] This process can be illustrated by comparison with a tree. In many ways trees are like us. Hidden in their seeds lies a kind of purpose, goal, and plan of producing fruit. In these aspects the seeds correspond to the will in us, where our purpose, goal, and plan reside, as I said. Drawing on what is inside them, the seeds grow up out of the ground and clothe themselves with branches, boughs, and leaves. This is how they prepare the means of achieving their purpose, which is fruit. In these aspects the tree corresponds to our intellect. Finally, when the time is right and the opportunity for results exists, the tree blossoms and produces fruit. In these aspects the tree corresponds to our good works. It should be clear, then, that the pieces of fruit in respect to their essence are the result of the seed, in respect to their form are the result of the boughs and leaves, and in respect to their ultimate action are the result of the wood of the tree.

[4] This process can also be illustrated by comparing ourselves to a temple. According to Paul we are temples of God (1 Corinthians 3:16, 17; 2 Corinthians 6:16; Ephesians 2:21, 22). The purpose, goal, and plan for

us as temples of God is our salvation and eternal life. Salvation and eternal life relate to our will, where our purpose, goal, and plan reside. As we go along, we take in teachings about faith and goodwill from our parents, teachers, and preachers. When we come into our own judgment, we take in teachings about faith and goodwill from the Word and religious books. These are all means to an end. These means have to do with our intellect. Finally we end up being useful by following teachings as the means; this happens through the physical actions called good works. Therefore our purpose employs means to produce results that are in respect to their essence the result of our purpose, in respect to their form the result of the teachings of the church, and in respect to their ultimate action the result of our useful service. This is how we become temples of God.

(b) *Goodwill and faith are transient and exist only in our minds unless, when an opportunity occurs, they culminate in actions and become embodied in them.* We have both a head and a body. They are joined by the neck. The mind that wills and thinks is found in our head, and the power that acts and carries out is found in our body. If therefore we had only benevolence, or thoughts based on goodwill, but we did not do anything good or produce anything useful as a result, we would be like a head by itself or a mind by itself, which could not continue to exist on its own without a body. Surely everyone can see from this that goodwill and faith are not goodwill and faith when they are only in our head and our mind but not in our body.

Under those circumstances goodwill and faith are like birds flying in the sky that have no home of their own on the ground. They are like birds that are about to lay eggs but have no nests; the eggs slip out of the birds into the air or onto a twig of some tree and then fall and smash on the ground.

All things in our mind have a corresponding element in our body. The corresponding thing could be called an embodiment. Therefore when goodwill and faith are only in our mind, they are not embodied in us. Under those circumstances we could be compared to the airy human figures known as ghosts, as Fama was depicted by the ancients, with a laurel wreath on her head and a horn of plenty in her hand.[587] Because we would then be ghosts and yet would still be able to think, we could not help being constantly hounded by mental images (a problem also caused by false inferences based on various kinds of sophistry). We would be much like swamp reeds blown around by the wind that have shells at their base underwater and frogs croaking at the surface. Surely we can see

375

that things like this happen when people merely know some ideas from the Word about goodwill and faith but do not practice them.

In fact the Lord says, "*Everyone who hears my words and does them* I will compare to a prudent man who built his house on a rock. But *everyone who hears my words and does not do them* will be compared to a foolish man who built his house on the sand" or "on the ground without a foundation" (Matthew 7:24, 26; Luke 6:47, 48, 49). Goodwill and faith and made-up ideas about them, when we do not put them into practice, can also be compared to butterflies in the air that a sparrow sees, flies toward, and eats. Likewise, the Lord says, "A sower went out to sow. Some seeds fell on hard ground, and the birds came and ate them" (Matthew 13:3, 4).

376 Goodwill and faith do nothing for us when they are attached to only one part of our body (meaning our head) but are not anchored in actions. This is clear from a thousand passages in the Word, of which I will cite only the following here:

> Every tree that does not *bear good fruit* is cut down and thrown into the fire. (Matthew 7:19, 20, 21)

> "Those who are sown in good earth are people who hear the Word and pay attention, and *bear and produce fruit.*" When Jesus had said this he cried out, saying, "Those who have ears to hear must hear." (Matthew 13:3–9, 43)

> Jesus said, "My mother and my brothers and sisters are those who hear the Word of God and *do it.*" (Luke 8:21)

> We know that God does not hear sinners, but if people worship God and *do his will,* he hears them. (John 9:31)

> If you know these things, you are happy if *you do them.* (John 13:17)

> Those who have my commandments and *do them* are the people who love me. I will love them and will manifest myself to them. I will come to them and make my home with them. (John 14:15–21, 23)

> My Father is glorified by *your bearing much fruit.* (John 15:8)

> Hearers of the law are not justified by God, but doers of the law are. (Romans 2:13; James 1:22)

> In the day of anger and just judgment, God will repay all *according to their works.* (Romans 2:5, 6)

It is right for us all to appear before Christ's judgment seat, so that each of us may carry away *what we have done through our body in regard to those things,* whether good or evil. (2 Corinthians 5:10)

The Son of Humankind is going to come in the glory of his Father. Then *he will repay all according to their deeds.* (Matthew 16:27)

I heard a voice from heaven saying, "Blessed are the dead who die in the Lord from now on. The Spirit says that they will rest from their labors. *Their works follow them.*" (Revelation 14:13)

A book is opened, which is the book of life, and the dead are judged according to the things that are written in the book. *All are judged according to their works.* (Revelation 20:12, 13)

Behold, I am coming quickly, and my reward is with me to give to all *according to their work.* (Revelation 22:12)

Jehovah, whose eyes are open to all the ways of human beings, to give to them all according to their ways and *according to the fruit of their works.* (Jeremiah 32:19)

I will bring judgment upon them according to their ways and *will reward their works.* (Hosea 4:9)

Jehovah deals with us according to our ways and *according to our works.* (Zechariah 1:6)

There are thousands of other passages like these.

On this basis one can clearly see that goodwill and faith are not goodwill and faith before they exist in actions. If they exist only up in the sky or in the mind above actions, they are like images of a tabernacle or a church in the air that are just strange aerial phenomena that spontaneously disappear. They are like paintings on paper that bookworms are chewing through. They are like our living on a roof with no bed rather than in a house.

From all this you can see that goodwill and faith are transient entities when they are merely mental—unless, when there is an opportunity for us to do them, they culminate in actions and become embodied in them.

(c) *Goodwill alone does not produce good actions; even less does faith alone produce them. Good actions are produced by goodwill and faith together.* The reason for this is that goodwill without faith is not goodwill, and faith without goodwill is not faith, as I have shown above, §§355–358. Goodwill does not exist all alone by itself, and neither does faith. As a

377

result, it cannot be said that goodwill produces any good works on its own or that faith produces any good works on its own.

The situation is similar with the will and the intellect. There is no such thing as a will that exists all alone by itself; it would not produce anything. There is no such thing as an intellect that exists all alone by itself; it would not produce anything either. All productivity comes from both faculties working together; it comes from the intellect in connection with the will. This similarity exists because the will is the home of goodwill and the intellect is the home of faith.

I said, "even less does faith alone produce them," because faith is truth. To live our faith is to put truths into action. Truths enlighten goodwill and the practice of it. The Lord teaches that truths are enlightening when he says, "*Those who do the truth come to the light* so their works will be revealed, since those works were done in God" (John 3:21). Therefore when we follow truths in our doing of good works, we do good works "in the light," meaning intelligently and wisely.

The partnership between goodwill and faith is like the marriage between a husband and a wife. All their physical offspring are born to both the husband as their father and the wife as their mother. Likewise, all our spiritual offspring are born to goodwill as their father and faith as their mother.[588] Spiritual offspring are concepts of goodness and truth. These concepts allow us to recognize the lineage of whole spiritual families. In fact, in the Word's spiritual meaning "a husband" and "a father" refer to goodness related to goodwill, and "a wife" and "a mother" refer to truth related to faith.

From these parallels it is again clear that goodwill by itself or faith by itself could not produce good works, just as a husband by himself or a wife by herself could not produce children.

The truths that relate to faith not only enlighten goodwill, they also enhance its quality and even nourish it. Therefore if we have goodwill but we have no truths related to faith, we are like someone walking in a garden at night, plucking pieces of fruit from the trees without knowing whether they are beneficial or harmful to eat. Since the truths related to faith not only enlighten goodwill but also enhance its quality, as I said, it follows that goodwill without truths that are related to faith is like pieces of fruit without any juice in them, like parched figs or like grapes after the wine has been pressed out of them.

Since truths nourish faith, as I also said, it follows that if goodwill lacks truths that are related to faith, that goodwill has no more nourishment than we would have from eating a piece of burnt toast and drinking filthy water from a pond.

9

There Is Faith That Is True,
Faith That Is Illegitimate,
and Faith That Is Hypocritical

From its cradle, the Christian church was attacked and torn apart by schisms and heresies. As time went on, it was lacerated and butchered by them, much like the person we read about who went down from Jerusalem to Jericho and was surrounded by robbers; after they stripped him and beat him up, the robbers left him half-dead (Luke 10:30). **378**

The end result was what we read in Daniel about that church: "In the end desolation [will fly in] on a bird of abominations; even to the close and the cutting down, it will drip steadily upon the devastation" (Daniel 9:27); and the Lord's statement: "The end will come when you see the abomination of desolation that Daniel the prophet foretold" (Matthew 24:14, 15).

What happened to the church could be compared to a ship loaded down with merchandise of the highest quality. It was battered by storm winds immediately upon leaving port and a little later was wrecked at sea and sank. Some of its cargo was spoiled by water and some was carried off by fish.

[2] Church history makes it clear that from its infancy the Christian church was assaulted and torn apart. For example, even in the time of the apostles it was assaulted by Simon, who was a Samaritan by birth and a sorcerer by trade (see Acts 8:9 and following). It was also assaulted by Hymenaeus and Philetus, whom Paul mentions in his Epistle to Timothy [2 Timothy 2:17–18]; and by Nicolas, whose followers were the so-called Nicolaitans mentioned in Revelation 2:6 and Acts 6:5; not to mention Corinth.589

Just after the time of the apostles, many others went into revolt. For example, the Marcionites, the Noetians, the Valentinians, the Encratites, the Cataphrygians, the Quartodecimans, the Alogians, the Catharans, the Origenists or Adamantines, the Sabellians, the Samosatenians, the Manicheans, the Meletians, and finally the Arians.590

After that, armies of heretical movements invaded the church—the Donatinians, the Photinians, the Acatians or Semi-Arians, the Eunomians, the Macedonians, the Nestorians, the Predestinarians, the Papists, the Zwinglians, the Anabaptists, the Schwenkfeldians, the Synergists, the Socinians, the Antitrinitarians, the Quakers, the Herrnhuters, and many others.[591]

At length Luther, Melanchthon, and Calvin prevailed over them all. Their teachings are dominant today.[592]

[3] There are three main reasons why there were so many disputes and rebellions in the church: (1) the divine Trinity was misunderstood; (2) there was no just concept of the Lord; (3) the suffering on the cross was taken to be redemption itself.

The truth about these three things is essential to the faith the church is based on, the faith from which it is called a church. If people did not know the truth about these three things, it was inevitable that everything about the church would be dragged first off course and finally in the opposite direction. It was also inevitable that when the church arrived at that stage it would still believe that it had a true faith in God and a belief in all God's truths.

This situation among these people in the church is like people who put a blindfold over their eyes and believe they are walking in a straight line, although step after step they are actually veering off course and eventually heading in the opposite direction, where there is a pit into which they fall.

The only way the wandering people of the church can be redirected onto the road of truth is by their knowing what true faith is, what illegitimate faith is, and what hypocritical faith is. Therefore this will be demonstrated.

   a. There is only one true faith; it is faith in the Lord God our Savior Jesus Christ. It exists in people who believe that he is the Son of God, that he is the God of heaven and earth, and that he is one with the Father.

   b. Illegitimate faith is all faith that departs from the one and only true faith. Illegitimate faith exists in people who climb up some other way and view the Lord not as God but only as a human being.

   c. Hypocritical faith is no faith at all.

379   (a) *There is only one true faith; it is faith in the Lord God our Savior Jesus Christ. It exists in people who believe that he is the Son of God, that he is the God of heaven and earth, and that he is one with the Father.* There is only one true faith, because faith is truth. Truth cannot be split or cut in half in such a way that part of it heads left and part of it heads right, and maintain its trueness.

In a general sense, faith consists of countless truths. Faith is a combination of truths. Yet in a way the countless truths make one body. In the body of faith, there are truths that constitute its limbs: some make the limbs that are attached to the chest as its arms and hands; others are attached to the pelvis as its legs and feet. Inner truths constitute the head. The first truths derived from those inner truths constitute the sense organs that are in the face.

Inner truths constitute the head because saying "inner" also means "higher."[593] In the spiritual world, all things that are deeper within are also higher. This is true of the three heavens that are there.

The soul and life of this body and all its limbs is the Lord God our Savior. This is why Paul calls the church "the body of Christ" and says that people in the church constitute his limbs, depending on the state of their goodwill and faith [Romans 12:4–5; 1 Corinthians 12:12–31].

In the following words Paul also teaches that there is only one true faith:

> There is one body and one spirit, one Lord, *one faith,* one baptism, one God. He gave people the work of the ministry to build *the body of Christ* until we all come into *a unity of faith,* the knowledge of the Son of God, and a complete life to the measure of the stature of the fullness of Christ. (Ephesians 4:4, 5, 6, 12, 13)

[2] As for the one only true faith being a faith in the Lord God our Savior Jesus Christ, this was fully shown above, §§337, 338, 339.

The true faith exists in people who believe that the Lord is the Son of God, because they also believe that he is God. Faith is not faith if it is not faith in God.

Among all the truths that initiate faith and form it, the belief that the Lord is the Son of God is the first. This is clear from the Lord's reply to Peter when Peter said, "You are the Christ, the Son of the living God." Jesus said, "You are blessed, Simon. I say to you, on this rock I will build my church, and the gates of hell will not prevail against it" (Matthew 16:16, 17, 18). In this passage and elsewhere in the Word, the "rock" means the Lord in his role as divine truth as well as the divine truth that comes from the Lord. The truth that Peter stated is primary—it is the crown on the head and the scepter in the hand of Christ's body. This is clear from the Lord's saying that he is going to build his church on that rock and the gates of hell will not prevail against it. The following words in John show the nature of this point of faith: "If any confess that Jesus is the Son of God, God lives in them, and they live in God" (1 John 4:15).

[3] In addition to this sign that people have the one true faith, there is another: they believe that the Lord is the God of heaven and earth. This second sign follows from the previous one that the Lord is the Son of God. It also follows from the statements that all the fullness of divinity exists in him (Colossians 2:9); that he is the God of heaven and earth (Matthew 28:18); and that all things that belong to the Father are his (John 3:35; 16:15).

A third indication that people who believe in the Lord have an inner faith in him, and therefore have the one true faith, is that they believe the Lord is one with God the Father. The chapter on the Lord and redemption fully demonstrated that the Lord is one with God the Father and is the Father himself in human form. It is also obvious from the words of the Lord himself that he and the Father are one (John 10:30); that the Father is in him and he in the Father (John 10:38; 14:10, 11); that he said to his disciples that from then on they had seen and known the Father, and he looked at Philip and said that he was now seeing and knowing the Father (John 14:7 and following).

[4] These are the three definitive indications that people have faith in the Lord and that the faith they have is the one true faith. Not all who turn to the Lord have faith in him. True faith is an inner faith and an outer faith at the same time. People who have these three jewels of faith have both the inner aspects and the outer aspects of the faith. It is not only a treasure in their hearts but also a valuable asset to their lips.

People who do not acknowledge that the Lord is the God of heaven and earth, however, or that he is one with the Father, are inwardly looking toward other gods as well who have similar power. They see those other gods as having power that is to be used by the Son either as their representative or as someone who has earned the right through redemption to rule over the people he redeemed. People like this break true faith apart by dividing the unity of God. Once that unity is broken, faith no longer exists. Instead there is only a ghost of faith, which from an earthly perspective looks like an image of faith, but from a spiritual perspective looks like a monster from mythology.

Can anyone deny that true faith is faith in one God who is the God of heaven and earth—therefore a faith in God the Father in human form, a faith in the Lord?

[5] These three identifying signs, pieces of evidence, and indications that a given faith in the Lord is faith itself are like touchstones used for

identifying gold and silver.594 They are like stone markers or signposts along the road that show the way to the church building where the one true God is worshiped. They are like lighthouses on rocks by the sea that let sailors at night know where they are and which direction to steer their ships on the wind.

The first identifying sign of faith, which is the belief that the Lord is the Son of the living God, is like the morning star for all who are coming into his church.

(b) *Illegitimate faith is all faith that departs from the one and only true faith. Illegitimate faith exists in people who climb up some other way and view the Lord not as God but only as a human being.* All faith that departs from the one true faith is illegitimate. This is self-evident. Given that only one faith is true, it follows that any faith that departs from it is not true. The marriage between the Lord and the church generates everything that is good and that is true in the church. Everything that is essentially goodwill and essentially faith comes from that marriage. Any goodwill and faith that are not from that marriage come from an illegitimate bed, not a legitimate one. They come from either a polygamous marriage bed or an adulterous one. Every faith that acknowledges the Lord and yet adopts false and heretical beliefs comes from a polygamous bed.

380

A faith that acknowledges three lords over one church comes from an adulterous bed. It is like a single woman who is promiscuous; or like a married woman who has a husband but rents herself out overnight to two other men, and when she sleeps with them she calls each of them her husband. Therefore these types of faith are called illegitimate.

In many passages the Lord calls people with these types of belief "adulterers." He also means people like this when he mentions thieves and robbers in John:

> Truly I say to you, those who do not enter through the door to the sheep-fold *but instead climb up some other way* are thieves and robbers. I am the door. Anyone who enters through me will be saved. (John 10:1, 9)

Coming into "the sheepfold" is coming into the church and also coming into heaven. It means coming into heaven because heaven and the church are one. Nothing else constitutes heaven except the church in the spiritual world. Therefore just as the Lord is the bridegroom and husband of the church, he is also the bridegroom and husband of heaven.

[2] To test and find out whether a given faith is a legitimate or an illegitimate offspring, one can use the three indications presented just above:

acknowledgment that the Lord is the Son of God; acknowledgment that he is the God of heaven and earth; and acknowledgment that he is one with the Father. The more a given faith departs from these essentials, the more illegitimate it is.

People who view the Lord not as God but only as a human being have a faith that is both illegitimate and adulterous. This is obvious from two atrocious heresies, the Arian heresy and the Socinian heresy, which have been anathematized by and cut off from the Christian church because they deny the Lord's divinity and climb up another way. I am afraid that these abominations lie hidden in the general spirit of people in the church.

Astounding to say, the more that people believe they have better scholarship and judgment than others, the more readily they latch onto, and adopt as their own, ideas that the Lord is human but not divine and that because he is human he could not be divine. When people adopt these ideas as their own, they join the club of Arians and Socinians who in the spiritual world are in hell.[595]

[3] The reason for this general spirit among people in the church today is that all of us have a spirit who is allied with us. Without that spirit we could not think analytically, rationally, or spiritually. Without those types of thinking we would be brute animals, not human beings. We all invite to ourselves a spirit who is similar to the desire in our will and the consequent perception in our intellect. If we develop good desires through truths from the Word and through living by those truths, we connect an angel from heaven to ourselves. On the other hand, if we develop evil desires through convincing ourselves of false beliefs and through living an evil life, we connect spirits from hell to ourselves. Once these evil spirits are connected to us, we increasingly develop a kind of sibling relationship with satans. Then we become more and more convinced of falsities that are against the truths in the Word and more and more hardened in an Arian and Socinian loathing for the Lord, because no satan can stand to hear any truth from the Word or to say the name Jesus. If satans hear these things, they turn into furies running around and uttering blasphemy. Then if light from heaven flows in they throw themselves headfirst into caves, into their own pitch darkness. In those places they have a light like that of night birds in the dark or like that of cats in basements when they are chasing mice. This is how all people who deny the Lord's divinity and the Word's holiness in their heart and in their faith turn out after death.

Their inner self has this nature no matter how well their outer self does impressions and pretends to be Christian. I know this is true, because I have seen it and heard it.[596]

[4] There are people who honor the Lord as their Redeemer and Savior with their mouth and lips alone but view him in their heart and spirit as a mere human being. In every case, when these people speak and teach, their mouth is like a jar full of honey but their heart is like a jar full of bile. Their words are like pastries but their thoughts are like poisoned wine. They themselves are like cake rolls with little worms inside. If they are priests, they are like pirates at sea who fly the flag of a peaceful country, but when a nearby ship signals to them as allies, they replace that flag with a pirate flag and capture the ship and its passengers.[597]

They are also like serpents of the tree of the knowledge of good and evil who approach you as if they were angels of light. They hold apples in their hand from that tree that have been painted with deep red colors as if they were plucked from the tree of life. They offer them and say, "God knows that on the day you eat these, your eyes will be opened and you will be like God, knowing good and evil" (Genesis 3:5). When you eat, you follow the serpent into some underworld and you make your home with it. All around that underworld there are satans who ate the apples of Arius and Socinus.

People like this are also meant by the person who came [to the wedding] but was not dressed in a wedding garment and was thrown into outer darkness (Matthew 22:11, 12, 13). The wedding garment[598] is faith that the Lord is the Son of God, is the God of heaven and earth, and is one with the Father.

People who honor the Lord with only their mouth and their lips, while in heart and spirit they regard him as a mere human being, and who reveal their thoughts and convince others to believe those thoughts are spiritual murderers. The worst of them are spiritual cannibals. Human life comes from love and faith in the Lord. If this essential ingredient of faith and love is removed—the recognition that the Lord is the human God and the divine Human—our life becomes death; its removal kills and devours us the way a wolf kills and devours a lamb.

(c) *Hypocritical faith is no faith at all.* We become hypocrites when we think about ourselves a great deal and give precedence to ourselves rather than others. By doing this we focus the thoughts and feelings of our mind on our body and invest them there; we unite our thoughts and

381

feelings to our physical senses. This turns us into earthly, sense-oriented, and physical people. In this state, our mind cannot be disconnected from the flesh it is attached to; it cannot be lifted to God or see anything related to God in the light of heaven; it cannot see anything spiritual. Because we are then people of the flesh, any spiritual things that come through our hearing into our intellect seem to us like no more than ghosts or dust particles in the air; in fact, they seem like flies around the head of a running, sweating horse, so we mock them in our heart. It is common knowledge that the earthly self regards the things of the spirit or spiritual things as crazy.

[2] Of all earthly people, hypocrites are the lowest and most earthly. They are sense-oriented—their mind is tightly bound to their physical senses. They have no love for seeing anything except what their senses take in; and because the senses are in the material world, the senses force the mind to think about everything, including all aspects of faith, from the point of view of the material world.

If these hypocrites become preachers, they retain in their memory the types of things they heard said about faith when they were children, teenagers, and young adults. Yet since their words contain nothing spiritual, and all that their words do contain is merely earthly, when they speak before an assembled congregation, the words have no life in them at all. The words sound as if they have life in them, because hypocrites enjoy loving themselves and the world, a pleasure that leads them to hold forth eloquently and caress the ears of their listeners with sounds that are much like the melodies of a song.

[3] When hypocritical preachers go home after church, they laugh at all the things they have just said to the congregation about faith, and at the passages they have quoted from the Word. They might say to themselves, "I threw my net into the lake and caught some flatfish and shellfish," since that is how they picture anyone who has true faith.

Hypocrites are like a carved human figure with two heads, one inside the other. The inner head is attached to the figure's torso and body. The outer head is able to spin all the way around the inner head. The front of the outer head is painted with flesh colors to look like a human face, somewhat like the wooden heads that are set in the shop windows of wig-makers.

Hypocrites are like a ship that sailors can steer either with the wind or against it by adjusting the sail. Hypocrites give their approval to any who indulge them with what their flesh and their senses enjoy. That is how they set their sails.

[4] Ministers who are hypocrites are skilled comedians, impressionists, and actors who can impersonate royalty, military leaders, church leaders, and bishops; but shortly after they take off their costumes they go back to the whorehouse and live with the whores.

They are also like doors hanging on a revolving hinge that can be turned in two directions. Their mind is like this type of door: it can be opened in the direction of hell or in the direction of heaven. When it is opened in one direction it is closed in the other.[599]

It is astounding that when they are administering holy rituals and teaching truths from the Word, they actually do not realize that they do not believe those things. At that time they close their door toward hell. As soon as they go home, however, they do not believe a shred of it, because they then close their door toward heaven.

[5] The most completely hypocritical people have a deep-seated hatred of truly spiritual people—the same kind of hatred as satans have against the angels of heaven. The hypocritical people themselves do not feel this hatred while they are alive in the world. It surfaces after death when they lose the outer self in which they pretended to be spiritual. It is their inner self that is this kind of satan.

I should say what spiritual hypocrites look like to the angels of heaven—the kind of spiritual hypocrites who walk around in sheep's clothing but are inwardly as predatory as wolves (Matthew 7:15). In prayer, they look like acrobats walking on their hands. Their mouths call out from their hearts to demons and kiss them, but the sound they send toward God is that of their feet clapping in the air. When they stand on their feet, however, they have the eyes of a leopard, the gait of a wolf, the face of a fox, the teeth of a crocodile, and the faith of a vulture.

10

Evil People Have No Faith

All people who deny that God created the world, and who therefore deny the existence of God, are evil. They are atheistic materialists.[600] They are all evil, because everything good that is good not only in an earthly way but also in a spiritual way comes from God. Therefore people who deny the existence of God do not want to, and therefore cannot, accept anything good from any other source outside what is their own. What is

382

their own is the craving of their flesh. Anything that comes from that craving is spiritually evil, however good it may appear from an earthly perspective. People like this are evil in a theoretical way.

There are also people who are evil in a practical way. They are people who have no use for the divine precepts that are summed up in the Ten Commandments. These people live like outlaws. They too deny God at heart (although many of them confess him with their lips), because God and his commandments are united, which is why the Ten Commandments are called "Jehovah there" (Numbers 10:35, 36; Psalms 132:7, 8).

The following two propositions will make it more obvious that evil people have no faith:

a. Evil people have no faith, because evil relates to hell and faith relates to heaven.
b. All people in Christianity who are dismissive of the Lord and the Word have no faith, no matter how morally they behave or how rationally they speak, teach, or write, even if their subject is faith.

We will take these points up one at a time.

383   (a) *Evil people have no faith, because evil relates to hell and faith relates to heaven.* Evil relates to hell because everything evil comes from hell. Faith relates to heaven because everything true that is related to faith comes from heaven. As long as we are alive in the world, we are kept walking midway between heaven and hell in the spiritual equilibrium engendered by our own free choice. Hell is under our feet and heaven is over our head. Whatever comes up from hell is evil and false. Whatever comes down from heaven is good and true. Because we are between these two opposites and in spiritual equilibrium, we are freely able to choose, adopt, and incorporate into ourselves either the one or the other. If we choose evil and falsity, we unite ourselves to hell. If we choose goodness and truth, we unite ourselves to heaven.

The statements just made show not only that evil relates to hell and faith relates to heaven but also that evil and faith cannot be together in one object or one human being. If evil and faith were together, they would tear us apart as if we had been bound with two ropes, one of which was pulling us up and the other down. We would be like someone suspended in the air. We would be flying like a blackbird, now up, now down; when we were flying up, we would be worshiping God; when we were flying down, we would be worshiping the Devil. Anyone can see that this would be profane. No one can serve two lords without hating one and loving the other, as the Lord teaches in Matthew 6:24.

Various comparisons can illustrate the fact that there is no faith where evil exists. For example, evil is like fire. Hellfire is nothing but a love for evil. Evil consumes faith as if it were straw, and reduces it and everything related to it to ash.

Evil dwells in pitch darkness. Faith dwells in light. Evil uses falsities to extinguish faith, just as pitch darkness extinguishes light. Evil is as black as ink. Faith is as white as snow and as clear as water. Evil blackens faith the way ink blackens snow or water.

Here are other comparisons: evil cannot be united to truth that is related to faith any more than a rotten smell can be an ingredient in a sweet perfume, or urine can be an ingredient in a flavorful wine. Evil and faith cannot coexist any more than a reeking corpse and a living person can share the same bed. Evil and faith cannot live with each other any more than a wolf can live in a sheepfold, a hawk in a dovecote, or a fox in a henhouse.

(b) *All people in Christianity who are dismissive of the Lord and the Word have no faith, no matter how morally they behave or how rationally they speak, teach, or write, even if their subject is faith.* This follows as a conclusion from everything that has just been said: that the one only true faith is faith in the Lord, from the Lord; that any faith that is not faith in him and from him is earthly faith, not spiritual faith; and that faith that is merely earthly lacks the essence of faith inside it.

Faith comes from the Word. It has no other source, because the Word is from the Lord and therefore the Lord himself is in the Word. This is why the Lord says that he is the Word (John 1:1, 2). As a result, people who are dismissive of the Word are also dismissive of the Lord, for the two are connected as one thing. It also follows that those who are dismissive of either the Lord or the Word are dismissive of the church, since the church comes from the Lord through the Word.

Furthermore, those who are dismissive of the church are outside heaven, because the church is what brings people into heaven. People who are outside heaven are among the damned, and the damned have no faith.

People who are dismissive of the Lord and the Word have no faith no matter how morally they behave or how rationally they speak, teach, or write, even if their subject is faith, because they do not live a spiritual moral life and they do not have a spiritual rational mind. All they have is an earthly moral life and an earthly rational mind, and morality and rationality that are earthly are intrinsically dead. Because such people are dead, they have no faith.

People who are merely earthly and are dead in relation to faith are indeed able to speak and teach *about* faith, goodwill, and God, but they cannot speak and teach *from* faith, goodwill, and God.

The only people who have faith are those who believe in the Lord. Others have no faith, as is clear from the following passages: "Those who believe in the Son are not judged; but those who do not believe have already been judged because they have not believed in the name of the only begotten Son of God" (John 3:18). "Those who believe in the Son have eternal life. Those who do not believe in the Son will not see life; instead God's anger will remain upon them" (John 3:36). "Jesus said, 'When the Spirit of Truth has come, it will convict the world of sin because they do not believe in me'" (John 16:8, 9). And to the Jews the Lord said, "Unless you have believed that I am [he], you will die in your sins" (John 8:24). This is why David says, "I will announce a decision. Jehovah said, 'You are my Son. Today I fathered you.' Kiss the Son or he will be angry and you will perish on the way. Blessed are all those who trust in him" (Psalms 2:7, 12).

In the Gospels the Lord predicted that at the close of the age (meaning the last period of the church) there would be no faith because there would be no belief in the Lord as the Son of God, as the God of heaven and earth, and as someone who is one with the Father: "The abomination of desolation will come, and an affliction such as has never existed before and never will again. The sun will be darkened and the moon will not give its light; the stars will fall from heaven" (Matthew 24:15, 21, 29). And in the Book of Revelation: "Satan will be released from his prison. He will go out to lead astray the nations that are in the four corners of the earth, whose number is like the sand of the sea" (Revelation 20:7, 8). Because the Lord foresaw this, he also said, "But when the Son of Humankind comes, is he going to find faith on the earth?" (Luke 18:8).

385   To these points I will add these memorable occurrences.

The first memorable occurrence. Once an angel said to me, "Do you want to see clearly what faith and goodwill are, and therefore what faith separated from goodwill is, and what faith united to goodwill is? I will express it in visual terms for you."

"Please do!" I answered.

The angel said, "Instead of faith and goodwill, think of light and heat, and you will see them clearly. Faith in its essence is truth that relates to wisdom. Goodwill in its essence is affection that relates to love. In heaven, truth related to wisdom is light and affection related to love is heat. The light and heat that angels live in are, in essence, exactly this. As a result, you can clearly see what faith is when it is separated from goodwill and what it is when it is united to goodwill.

"When faith is separated from goodwill, it is like the light in winter. When faith is united to goodwill, it is like the light in spring. The light in winter, which is a light separated from heat, is united to coldness; therefore it completely strips trees of their leaves, kills grass, makes ground as hard as rock, and freezes water. Light in spring, which is a light united to heat, causes trees to grow, first producing leaves, then flowers, and finally fruit; it also unlocks and softens the ground so that it produces grass, plants, flowers, and shrubs; and it melts ice, so that water flows from its sources again.

[2] "The situation with faith and goodwill is absolutely identical. Faith separated from goodwill kills everything. Faith united to goodwill brings everything to life. This killing and this bringing to life are vividly visible in this spiritual world of ours, because here faith *is* light and goodwill *is* heat. Where faith has been united to goodwill there is a paradise of gardens, flower beds, and lawns; the more united faith and goodwill are, the more pleasing the gardens are. Where faith has been separated from goodwill, there is not even grass; the only greenness comes from thorns and brambles."

At that point there were some members of the clergy not far away. The angel called them "justifiers and sanctifiers of people through faith alone" and also "arcanists."[601] We said the same things to the members of the clergy and added enough proof that they could see that what we said was true. But when we asked them, "Isn't that so?" they turned away and said, "We didn't hear you." So we cried out to them and said, "Then keep listening to us," but they put both hands over their ears and shouted, "We don't *want* to hear you!"

[3] Afterward I spoke to the angel about faith alone. I said that living experience had led me to understand that faith alone is like the light in

winter. I told him that for several years spirits with various different types of faith had been walking past me. Every time people who had separated faith from goodwill came near me, such intense coldness would rise up my legs into my groin and finally into my chest that I almost thought the spark of my vitality had been extinguished. I would in fact have died if the Lord had not driven those spirits away and set me free.

Another thing seemed amazing to me: The spirits themselves did not feel any coldness within. They told me so. Therefore I compared those spirits to fish under ice that do not feel the cold because their life and their nature are intrinsically cold.

I was able to perceive at the time that their coldness emanated from the faint, deceptive light of their faith, much like the light that glows around swampy or sulfury places in midwinter after the sun has set. Travelers see that faint, deceptive, frigid light from time to time.

People who have separated faith from goodwill can be compared to mountains of pure ice that have been dislodged from their places in northern lands to drift here and there across the ocean. I have heard it said that when ships come near these icebergs, all who are on board shiver from the cold. Therefore groups of people who have separated faith from goodwill can be likened to icebergs, and even called icebergs if you wish.

People know from the Word that faith without goodwill is dead; but I will say where that death comes from. That death is from the cold. Faith dies of the cold like a bird in a severe winter: first its vision dies, then its ability to fly, and finally its breathing. Then it falls headfirst off its branch into the snow and is buried.

386 *The second memorable occurrence.* One morning after I woke up, I saw two angels coming down from heaven. One was coming from the southern part of heaven and the other from the eastern part. They were both in carriages drawn by white horses. The carriage that was carrying the angel from the southern part of heaven was shining like silver. The carriage that was carrying the angel from the eastern part of heaven was shining like gold. The reins the angels were holding in their hands were flashing with a fiery light like the rising sun. That is how the two angels looked from far away. When they came closer,[602] however, they no longer looked as though they were in carriages. They were simply in their own angelic form, which is human. The one who came from the eastern part of heaven was wearing shining clothes that were deep red. The one who came from the southern part of heaven was wearing clothes that were sky blue.

When they reached the lower regions below the heavens, they ran toward one another as if each were trying to be first [to reach the other].603 They hugged and kissed each other. I heard that when these two angels lived in the world they formed a bond of deep friendship. Yet now one was in the eastern part of heaven and the other was in the southern part. The eastern heaven holds angels who focus on love from the Lord; the southern heaven holds angels who focus on wisdom from the Lord.

After the angels spent a while talking about the magnificent things in their heavens, a question came up in their conversation about whether the essence of heaven is love or wisdom. They agreed right away that each one relates to the other; but they were discussing which one was the origin of the other.

[2] The angel from the heaven of wisdom asked the other angel, "What is love?"

The other angel replied, "The love that originates from the Lord as a sun is the vital heat that angels and people have—it is the underlying reality of their lives. The derivatives of love are called feelings. Feelings produce perceptions and therefore thoughts. It flows from this that wisdom starts out as love, and therefore thought starts out as the feeling related to that love. Looking at the derivatives in sequence makes it possible to see that thought is nothing but the form of the feeling. This is not generally known, because thoughts exist in light but feelings exist in heat, and therefore people reflect on their thoughts but not on their feelings.

"The fact that thought is nothing but the form of a feeling related to some love can be illustrated by the fact that speech is nothing but the form of sound. In fact, sound corresponds to feeling and speech corresponds to thought. Feelings make sounds, and thoughts speak.

"This point would become crystal clear if someone were to say, 'Take the sound out of your speech.' Would there be any speech left? Also, 'Take the feeling out of your thinking.' Would there be any thinking left?

"Clearly then, the most important ingredient in wisdom is love. Therefore the essence of the heavens is love and their form is wisdom. Or to put it another way, the heavens exist as the result of divine love and they take shape as the result of divine love acting through divine wisdom. Therefore, as we said before, each one does indeed relate to the other."

[3] At the time there was a spirit with me who had recently arrived [in the spiritual world], who heard all this and asked, "Is it the same for goodwill and faith, since goodwill relates to feeling and faith relates to thinking?"

"It is absolutely the same," the angel replied. "Faith is nothing but a formation of goodwill, exactly as speech is nothing but a formation of sound. In fact, faith is formed from goodwill in the same way that speech is formed from sound. Up in heaven we even know the mode of formation, but there is no time to lay that out now."

The angel added, "When I say 'faith,' I mean a spiritual faith whose life and spirit come solely from the Lord by way of goodwill, since goodwill is spiritual, and faith is spiritual through goodwill. Faith without goodwill, then, is a mere earthly faith, and mere earthly faith is dead; it unites itself to mere earthly feelings, which are nothing but cravings."

[4] The angels expressed these thoughts in a spiritual way. Spiritual speech includes thousands of nuances that earthly language cannot express. In fact, surprising to say, those nuances are not even thinkable with the ideas of earthly thought.

After the angels had said all this they left. As they were going back to their own heavens, stars appeared around their heads. When they got farther away from me, they looked as though they were in carriages again, as before.

387 *The third memorable occurrence.* After those two angels passed out of my sight, I noticed a garden to my right. It had olive trees, fig trees, laurels, and palm trees planted in an arrangement based on their correspondences. I looked into the garden and saw angels and spirits walking and talking among the trees.

Just then an angelic spirit looked back at me. ("Angelic spirits" is the term for people in the world of spirits who are being prepared for heaven.) The angelic spirit left the garden, walked up to me, and said, "Do you want to come with me into our paradise? You will see and hear amazing things!"

I went along. The angelic spirit said to me, "The people you see here"—and there were many of them—"all have a love for truth and have the light of wisdom as a result. There is a magnificent building here that we call the Temple of Wisdom. Yet people are unable to see it if they believe they have a significant amount of wisdom; they are even less able to see it if they believe they have a sufficient amount of wisdom; and they are the least able to see it if they believe their wisdom originates in themselves.

"The reason is that people like this lack the love for real wisdom that would make them receptive to the light of heaven. Real wisdom consists in our seeing in the light of heaven that what we know, understand, and have wisdom about is like a drop compared to the ocean of what we do not know, do not understand, and are not wise about. It is hardly anything at all.[604]

"All the people in this garden paradise who acknowledge on the basis of inner perception and vision that they have relatively little wisdom can see the Temple of Wisdom. The human mind's inner light lets people see it; but the mind's outer light without any inner light does not."

[2] I had often thought about this myself. At first through book-learning, later through my own perception of it, and finally because I saw it in an inner light, I had come to acknowledge that we have very little wisdom. Therefore I was granted ability to see the temple.

It had an amazing form: it stood extremely high above the earth; square; walls made of crystal; a roof made of translucent jasper elegantly arched; a foundation made of different types of precious stone.[605] There were steps of polished alabaster so that people could go up into the temple. At the sides of the steps there were images of lions with their cubs.

Then I asked whether it was all right to go in. I was told that it was all right, so I went up the stairs. As I went in, I saw something like angel guardians flying near the ceiling, but they soon disappeared. The floor I was walking on was made of cedar. With its translucent roof and walls, the whole temple was built to be a form of light.

[3] The angelic spirit came in with me. I mentioned what I had heard from the two angels about *love* and *wisdom,* and goodwill and faith. The angelic spirit said, "Did they not also mention a third element?"

"What third element?" I asked.

The angelic spirit answered, "Good, useful action. Love and wisdom without good, useful action are nothing. They are only conceptual entities. They do not become real until they exist in usefulness.

"Love, wisdom, and usefulness are three things that cannot be separated. If they are separated, none of them is anything. Love is nothing without wisdom, but in wisdom it is formed for something; the something that love is formed for is usefulness. Therefore when love exists in usefulness through the help of wisdom, it really exists, because it becomes actual.

"These three are just like purpose, means, and result. The purpose is nothing unless means exist to bring about results. If one of the three dissipates, each of the others dissipates and becomes more or less nothing.

[4] "The same is true for goodwill, faith, and good actions. Goodwill is nothing without faith. Faith is nothing without goodwill. Goodwill and faith are nothing without good actions, but in the form of good actions they become something, depending on how useful those good actions are.

"The same is true for feeling, thought, and work; and also for will, intellect, and action. The will without the intellect is like an eye that cannot see. The will and the intellect together without action are like a mind without a body.

"The truth of this is clearly visible in this temple, because the light we are in enlightens the inner realms of the mind.

[5] "Geometry, too, teaches that nothing is whole and complete unless it has a threefold nature. A line is nothing unless it becomes an area, and an area is nothing unless it becomes a three-dimensional body. Therefore the first dimension is expanded into the second in order to exist, and the two become embodied in the third dimension.

"This same principle applies to each and every created thing. All of them culminate in a third stage. This is why 'three' in the Word means whole and complete.

"For this reason I cannot help feeling amazed that some people claim they believe in faith alone, others in goodwill alone, and still others in good actions alone. Yet the first element is nothing without the second, and both of these are nothing without the third."

[6] Then I asked, "Isn't it possible for people to have goodwill and faith and yet not have good actions? Isn't it possible for people to have a desire and a thought, and yet do nothing?"

"That could happen only in theory," the angel answered. "It could not happen in reality. For these things to exist even theoretically, the people would have to maintain a drive or a will to do something. Will or drive is actually a form of action, since it is a constant striving to act, which under the right circumstances becomes an external action. Therefore all wise people take the internal actions of a drive or will to be entirely the same as external actions (because that is how God takes them), provided the drive or will continues when an opportunity to act presents itself."

388   *The fourth memorable occurrence.* I was talking with some of the people meant by "the dragon" in the Book of Revelation.[606] One of them said, "Come with me. I'll show you what entertains our eyes and hearts." He led me through a dark forest onto a hill from which I could watch the dragons' form of entertainment. I saw an amphitheater built in the round with seating rising at an angle in every direction, on which the spectators were sitting. The spectators sitting in the front row looked to me at a distance like satyrs and priapuses,[607] some with a loincloth covering their genitals and some who were completely naked. Sitting in the seats behind them there were promiscuous men and women. (Their movements suggested to me that that is what they were.)

Then the dragon said to me, "Now you are going to see our form of entertainment."

I saw what looked like bull calves, rams, sheep, goats, and lambs released into the arena. After they had all come in, a gate opened up and what looked like young lions, panthers, tigers, and wolves came rushing in. These animals attacked the others in a rage, tore them to pieces, and slaughtered them. After the gory slaughter, satyrs went out and sprinkled sand over the area where the kill had taken place.

[2] Then the dragon said to me, "This is our entertainment. It gives our minds great satisfaction."

I said, "Go away, you demon! It won't be long before you see this amphitheater turned into a lake of fire and sulfur."

He laughed at what I had said and went away.

Afterward, I was wondering to myself why the Lord allows things like that. In my heart I received an answer. Events like that are allowed as long as those people are in the world of spirits.[608] After their time in that world is finished, theatrical displays like that are turned into dreadful, hellish scenes.

[3] The whole spectacle had been conjured up by the dragon's ability to project images. The bull calves, rams, sheep, goats, and lambs did not in fact exist. The dragon spirits had taken all the genuinely good and true things about the church that they hate and made them look like those animals. The lions, panthers, tigers, and wolves were manifestations of the lusts of the people who looked like satyrs and priapuses. The spirits who wore nothing over their genitals believed that their evil is not apparent before God. The spirits who wore a loincloth believed that their evil is apparent but that they are not damned by it, provided they have faith. The promiscuous men and women were people who falsify the truths of the Word. (Promiscuity stands for falsification of truth.)

Everything in the spiritual world, when seen from a distance, has an external appearance that is based on correspondences. When these correspondences assume particular forms, they are called *representations of spiritual things in objects like those in the material world.*

[4] Later on I saw the spirits leaving the forest. The dragon left among the satyrs and priapuses. Their servants and lackeys, who were the promiscuous men and women, went along behind them. The crowd became larger as it went along.

At that point I could hear what they were saying to each other—that they had seen a flock of sheep and lambs in a meadow. This was a sign that they were near one of the many Jerusalem cities where goodwill is primary.

They said, "Let's go capture the city, drive out its inhabitants, and loot their possessions."

They came closer to the city, but there was a wall around it, with angel guards on the wall. So they said, "Let's use deceit to capture it. Let's send in someone who is skilled in double-talk,[609] who can whiten what is black, blacken what is white, and color the reality of any subject."

They managed to find someone who was an expert in theoretical philosophy. He could turn concepts based on reality into mere terminology, hide realities behind formulas, and then fly away like a hawk with its prey beneath its wings. They taught him how he should address the people in the city. He should say that his companions were the citizens' allies in religion and should be allowed in.

He came to the gate of the city and knocked. When the gate opened, he said that he wanted to speak to the wisest person in the city. He was allowed to enter and was taken to someone in the city.

In speaking to the wise person, he said, "My people are outside the city. They are asking to be let in. They are your allies in religion. Both you and we consider faith and goodwill the two essentials of religion. The only difference between us is that you say goodwill is primary and faith comes from it, while we say faith is primary and goodwill comes from it. What difference does it make if this or that is labeled primary, as long as we all believe in them both?"

[5] The wise person from the city replied, "You and I shouldn't discuss this alone. We should discuss it before a number of people acting as referees and judges. Otherwise we couldn't come to a decision."

Soon the referees and judges were summoned, and the dragon spirit addressed them using much the same language he had used before. Then the wise man from the city replied, "You have stated that it makes no difference whether goodwill or faith is taken to be primary in the church as long as there is agreement that both constitute the church and its religion.

"But it does make a difference—as much of a difference as there is between what is prior and what is posterior, between cause and effect, between something principal and something instrumental, and between something essential and something merely formal.[610] I frame it in these philosophical terms because I am aware that you are an expert in the theoretical philosophy that we call 'double-talk' and others call 'incantation.'

"But let's leave philosophical terminology aside. There is as much difference between considering faith primary and considering goodwill primary as there is between something superior and something inferior. In fact, if you are willing to believe it, there is as much difference as there is between the minds of spirits who live up high in this world and the minds of spirits who live down low.

"What is primary constitutes the head and the torso, so to speak. What comes from it constitutes the legs down to the soles of the feet.

"First of all, however, we should define goodwill and faith. Goodwill is a loving desire to do what is good for our neighbor on account of God, salvation, and eternal life. Faith is thought that is based on confidence in God, salvation, and eternal life."

[6] "I grant you your definition of faith," the delegate said, "and I also grant that goodwill is that loving desire to act on account of God, because it is acting on account of his commandments; but it is not acting on account of salvation and eternal life."

After this agreement and disagreement, the wise man from the city said, "Surely desire or love is primary, and thought comes from it."

The dragon's delegate said, "I deny that."

The wise man replied, "You cannot deny it! People do their thinking based on some love. Take away the love: can they think anything at all? It is exactly the same as taking the sound out of speech. If you take away the sound, can you say anything at all? In fact, sound comes from a desire related to some love, and speech comes from thought, since love makes the sound, and thought speaks.

"Another example is a flame and light. If you take away the flame, the light ceases to exist. It is the same with goodwill and faith, since goodwill relates to love and faith relates to thought. Surely you can understand, then, that the primary thing is the most important ingredient of the secondary thing, as in the case of flame and light.

"It is clear from this that if you don't make the primary element primary, you don't have the secondary element either. If you take faith, which belongs in the second place, and put it in the first place, in heaven you will look just like someone upside down, whose legs are up in the air and whose head is down below, like acrobats that walk on the palms of their hands.[611] And since that is how you appear in heaven, your good actions, your acts of goodwill, are like the kinds of things acrobats do with their feet because their hands are not available. Your goodwill is earthly, not spiritual, because it is upside-down."

[7] The delegate comprehended this—all devils can understand truth when they hear it. They just cannot retain it, because their desire for evil,

which is actually a craving belonging to their flesh, comes back into play and thrusts out any thought of the truth.

Afterward, the wise man of the city used many examples to show what faith is like when it is taken to be the primary thing: "It is merely earthly. It is a conviction without any spiritual life. Therefore it is not faith. I could almost say that there is no more spirituality in your faith than there would be in a faith that consisted of thinking about the country of Mongolia, a diamond mine there, and the royal treasure of the Mongolian emperor."

Angry at hearing this, the dragon spirit went away. He reported back to his people outside the city. When they heard that someone had defined goodwill as a desire to do good to one's neighbor on account of salvation and eternal life, they all shouted, "That's a lie!"

The dragon himself said, "It is criminal! Surely when people perform acts of goodwill for the sake of their own salvation they are hoping to earn merit."

[8] Then they said to each other, "We should call together even more of our people, besiege this city, and throw these 'goodwills' out."

Yet as they were working on this, fire appeared to come down from heaven and devour them! The fire was in fact a manifestation of their own rage and hatred against the people in the city for demoting faith from first place to second, placing it far beneath goodwill, and saying otherwise it would not be faith. It looked like they were devoured by fire, because hell opened under their feet and swallowed them up.

Things like this happened in many places at the time of the Last Judgment. These events were also meant by the following passage in the Book of Revelation:

> The dragon will go out to lead astray the nations that are in the four corners of the earth to gather them for war. They climbed up onto the plain of the earth and surrounded the camp of the saints and the beloved city, but fire came down from God out of heaven and devoured them. (Revelation 20:8, 9)

389 *The fifth memorable occurrence.* On one occasion I saw a document being sent down from heaven to a community in the world of spirits. In that community there were two people who governed the church. They had ministers and elders under them. The document strongly urged the people there to acknowledge the Lord Jesus Christ as the God of heaven and earth, as he himself taught (Matthew 28:18), and to give up the teaching that faith justifies people without the works of the Law, because that teaching is wrong.

This document was read and copied by many people. Many of them were using their own judgment in thinking and speaking about what was in the document. After they had accepted what the document said, however, they said to each other, "We should hear what our governors have to say about it." They did hear their governors, but the governors spoke against the document and expressed disapproval of it. The governors of that community were in fact hard-hearted because of falsities they had absorbed in the previous world. Therefore after a brief meeting with each other, the governors sent the document back to heaven where it had come from.

After that happened there was some muttering, but many lay people ended up changing their minds. Then the light of judgment about spiritual things that those lay people had had, which had been brilliant up until then, suddenly went out.

After they were warned again, but to no avail, I saw the community sinking down. I did not see how far down it went. It was taken out of sight of those who worship the Lord alone and who reject faith alone as the means of justification.

[2] Several days later, however, I saw about a hundred people coming up from the lower earth, where that little community had sunk. The group came over to me.

One of them spoke and said, "Do you want to hear something amazing? When we sank down, we were in a place that looked like a pond. Soon, however, it looked like dry ground. Afterward it became a little town where many of us had homes.

"A day later we discussed among ourselves what to do. Many said that we should go to the two governors of the church and politely point out that their sending the document back to heaven where it had come from caused all this to happen to us."

They did in fact choose some people who went to the governors. The person who was talking to me said that he had been part of that delegation.

"Then," he continued, "someone among us who was very skillful and wise spoke to the governors and said, 'We believed that the church and religion existed among us more than among others, because we had been told that we have the supreme light of the gospel. But some of us have been granted enlightenment from heaven; and with that enlightenment has come the perception that the church doesn't even exist in the Christian world anymore, because there is no religion there anymore.'

[3] "The governors said, 'What are you saying? Doesn't the church exist wherever the Word exists, Christ the Savior is known, and the sacraments are performed?'

"Our spokesperson replied, 'Those things are part of the church in the sense that they promote it, but they promote it within each of us, not outside of us.'

"Our spokesperson went on to say, 'Can the church exist where three gods are worshiped? Can the church exist where its entire body of teaching is based on a single statement by Paul that has been falsely interpreted, rather than on the Word? Can the church exist when people do not go to the Savior of the world, who is the God of the church?

"'Surely religion is abstaining from evil and doing good. Does a true religion hold that faith alone saves and not goodwill as well? Does a true religion hold that the goodwill that comes from people is only moral and civic? There is no religion in that kind of goodwill, as anyone can see. In faith alone there is no action or work. And yet religion consists in doing. All non-Christian nations in the world believe that acts of goodwill, or good works, have power to save. The whole of religion consists in good actions, and the whole of the church consists in a body of teaching that proclaims truths and uses those truths to teach good actions. Glorious things might have happened to us if we had only accepted the message of the document sent from heaven!'

[4] "Then one of the governors said, 'Your argument aims too high. The church is about the activation of faith. This is the kind of faith that fully justifies us and saves us. Religion is about an ongoing state of faith, which is the kind of faith that emanates from God and perfects us.[612] Take this in, my children.'

"But our wise spokesperson said, '*You* listen, O Fathers. According to your dogma, people have no more ability to activate their faith than a piece of dead wood. Can a piece of wood be brought to life and become part of the church? Surely your idea of the ongoing state of faith is a continuation and progression of the activation of faith. Since, according to your dogma, faith has all power to save, and there is no such power in acts of goodwill that people perform, where does religion come in?'

"Then the church leaders said, 'Friend, you say things like that because you don't know the secrets of justification by faith alone. People who don't know those secrets don't know the path of salvation from within. Your path to salvation is external and common. Travel it if you want, but you should keep in mind that everything good comes from God and nothing from human beings; and therefore people have no power of their own in spiritual matters. How then can people do something good that is spiritually good by themselves?'

[5] "When he heard that, our spokesperson was outraged and said, 'I am more familiar with your supposed revelations on justification than you are! And I will tell you bluntly that I have explored those supposed revelations and have found nothing but phantoms in them. Surely religion is a matter of acknowledging God and avoiding and hating the Devil. God is goodness itself. "The Devil" is evil itself. Every religious person in the world knows that. Acknowledging and loving God is a matter of doing what is good, because what is good belongs to God and comes from God. Avoiding and hating the Devil is a matter of not doing what is evil, because what is evil belongs to the Devil and comes from the Devil. But does your view of the activation of faith (which you label as a faith that fully justifies people and saves them) or rather, your view that we become just through faith alone, teach us to do anything good (keeping in mind that what is good belongs to God and comes from God)? Does it teach us to abstain from any evil (keeping in mind that what is evil belongs to the Devil and comes from the Devil)? Absolutely not, because you have decided that there is no salvation in either of these actions.

"'What is this *ongoing state of faith* you are talking about, which you just called a faith that emanates from God and perfects us? Isn't it exactly the same thing as your *activation of faith?* How can this faith be perfected if you exclude from it any good that human beings do as if they are acting on their own?

"'In your supposed revelations you say, "How can people be saved by any goodness that comes from themselves when in fact salvation costs them nothing? What good can people do without hoping to earn merit, when in fact all merit belongs to Christ? Doing something good for the sake of salvation would therefore be equivalent to attributing to ourselves what belongs to Christ alone. This would be trying to grant ourselves justification and save ourselves. Also how can people do any good work when the Holy Spirit does all the work without any help from us? What need would there be then for any additional goodness from us, since anything good that comes from us is not intrinsically good?" And so on.

[6] "'Aren't these your supposed revelations? To my eyes, however, they look like mere sophistry and trickery aimed at doing away with good works, which are acts of goodwill, in an effort to establish your

faith alone. Your views on faith and on everything spiritual that relates to the church and religion cause you to see people as logs. You see them as some inanimate sculpture and not as people created in the image of God who have been given, and are continually given, the ability to understand and will, to believe and love, and to speak and act completely as if they were on their own, especially in relation to spiritual things, because these are the things that make human beings human.

"'If people had no ability to think or act in spiritual ways as if they were acting on their own, what would be the point of the Word? What would be the point of the church and religion? What would be the point of worship? You know that doing good to your neighbor from love is goodwill, but you don't know what goodwill is. Yet goodwill is the soul and the essence of faith. And since goodwill is the soul and the essence of faith, what is faith when you remove goodwill? It is a dead thing. And a dead faith is nothing but a phantom. I call it a phantom because James says that faith without good works is not only dead but also diabolical' [James 2:14–26; 3:13–15].

[7] "When he heard his faith called dead, diabolical, and phantasmic, one of the governors became so enraged that he tore the miter⁶¹³ off his head, threw it on the table, and said, 'I will not put this back on until I have taken revenge on the enemies of the faith of our church.' Then shaking his head he muttered, 'That James! That James!'

"On the front of the miter there was a thin metal plate with an inscription: *Faith Alone Makes Us Just.*

"Then suddenly a monster with seven heads appeared, rising out of the ground. It had the feet of a bear, the body of a leopard, and the face of a lion, just like the beast described in Revelation 13:1, 2. We read that people made an image of that beast and worshiped it (Revelation 13:14, 15).

"The ghostly monster snatched the miter from the table, stretched the brim, and put the miter on its seven heads. Then the ground yawned open under its feet and it sank back down.

"When he saw this, the governor shouted, 'We're being attacked! We're being attacked!'

"Then we left. To our surprise, steps appeared before our eyes. We climbed them. They took us back to the earth, where we had been before, with its view of heaven."

The spirit who had come up with a hundred others from the lower earth told me all this.

390 *The sixth memorable occurrence.* In the northern region of the spiritual world I heard something like a roaring sound of water, so I went in that direction. As I came closer, the roaring stopped and I heard a noise like a crowd of people. Then I noticed a house full of holes; it had a wall around it. The noise was coming from the house.

I went up to the house. There was a doorkeeper there. I asked who was inside. The doorkeeper said the people inside were the wisest of the wise; they were having a debate on metaphysical topics. The doorkeeper said this out of a simple belief that it was true.

"Would it be all right if I went in?" I said.

The doorkeeper said, "Yes, as long as you don't speak—since I have permission to let [even] non-Christians in; they have to stand next to me here in the front hall."

I went inside. There I saw a circular area with a raised platform in the middle. A group of supposedly wise people was discussing the secrets of their faith.

Then a topic was proposed as a subject for discussion: the good that people do in *the ongoing state of being justified* by their faith or in their progression of faith after its *activation*—is that a religious good or not? They unanimously agreed that "religious good" means good that contributes to salvation.

[2] The point was sharply debated. The debaters who eventually won the upper hand were saying that the good things people do in their ongoing state of or progression in faith are only moral in nature. Those good actions are helpful for people's prosperity in the world but do nothing for their salvation. Only faith benefits their salvation.

They argued their point in the following way: "How could any good that people do voluntarily be united to something they get for free? Salvation is had for free. How could any good that people do be united to the merit of Christ? The merit of Christ is the sole source of salvation. And how could the work that people do be united to the work that the Holy Spirit does? It does everything without the help of humankind.

"Surely these, the only factors that save people, are present in the act of justification by faith alone; and these three sole things that bring salvation[614] become permanent in the ongoing state or progression of faith. Therefore additional good that people do could never be called religious good (or good that benefits their salvation, as we said). In fact, if people do good for the sake of salvation, their own will is in it. They cannot help hoping for some reward. Therefore it should be called religious *evil* instead!"

[3] There were two non-Christians standing next to the doorkeeper in the front hall. They heard these points and one said to the other, "These

people have no religion. Clearly, religion is doing good to our neighbor for the sake of God and therefore with God and from God."

The other one said, "Their faith has made them silly."

They both asked the doorkeeper who the people inside were. The doorkeeper said, "They are wise Christians."

The non-Christians said, "You're not making sense. You're trying to fool us. They are entertainers. At least that's how they sound."

At that point I left.

Because of the Lord's divine guidance, I came to that house, people were discussing those topics, and things unfolded as I have described.

391 *The seventh memorable occurrence.* Conversations with many lay people and many clergy in the spiritual world have taught me how barren of truth and how theologically emaciated the Christian world has become today.

Among the clergy there is so much spiritual poverty that they scarcely know anything. They know only that there is a trinity of Father, Son, and Holy Spirit and that faith alone saves. Of Christ the Lord, they know only some historical facts recorded in the Gospels. All the other things that the Word of both Testaments teaches about the Lord—for example, that the Father and he are one; that he is in the Father and the Father in him; that he has all power in heaven and on earth; that it is the Father's will that people should believe in the Son; and that people who believe in the Son have eternal life; and so on—are to them as unknown and buried as things on the bottom of the ocean or even in the center of the earth.

If things are read to them from the Word, they stand as if they were partly paying attention and partly not. The statements penetrate no more deeply into their minds than the whistle of the wind or the sound of a beaten drum.

From time to time, the Lord sends angels to examine the Christian communities in the world of spirits under heaven. The angels vehemently complain about these communities. They say that the level of stupid, empty discourse there about issues relating to salvation is almost on a par with the chattering of a parrot. In fact, they say that the learned Christian professors in those communities have no more understanding of divine and spiritual things than do statues.

[2] On one occasion an angel told me of conversations with two men from the clergy, one of whom had a faith that was separate from goodwill, and the other of whom had a faith that was not separate.

The conversation with the clergyman who had a faith that was separate from goodwill went like this:

The angel said, "Friend, who are you?"

"I am a Protestant Christian," he replied.

"What is your doctrinal point of view and your religion?"

"Faith."

"What is your faith?"

"My faith is that God the Father sent the Son to take the damnation of the human race on himself. We are saved by that."

The angel then asked, "What else do you know about salvation?"

"Salvation is accomplished through that faith alone."

"What do you know about redemption?"

"Redemption was brought about through the suffering on the cross. The Son's merit is assigned through that faith."

"What do you know about regeneration?"

"It happens through that faith."

"Tell me what you know about love and goodwill."

"They are that faith."

"Tell me what you think about the Ten Commandments and the other teachings in the Word."

"They are in that faith."

The angel then said, "Is there nothing for you to do?"

"What *should* I be doing? I can't do anything genuinely good on my own."

"Can you have faith on your own then?"

"I don't go into that. I must simply have faith."

Finally the angel said, "Is there anything else whatever that you know about salvation?"

"What else would there be, since salvation comes through that faith alone?"

Then the angel said, "You give answers like someone playing the same note again and again on a flute. I am not hearing anything but faith. If you know faith but you don't know anything else, you don't know anything. Go see your companions."

The clergyman then left. When he met his companions in the desert, the place was devoid of even as much as grass. Upon his inquiring why that was, they answered that inside themselves they had nothing related to the church.[615]

[3] The angel's conversation with the clergyman who had a faith that was united to goodwill went like this:

"Friend, who are you?"

"I am a Reformed Christian."[616]

"What is your doctrinal point of view and your religion?"

"Faith and goodwill."

"Those are *two* things."

"They can't be separated."

"What is faith?"

"Believing what the Word teaches."

"What is goodwill?"

"Doing what the Word teaches."

"Do you only believe that, or do you also practice it?"

"I also practice it."

The angel from heaven then looked at the clergyman and said, "My friend, come with me and live with us."

Chapter 7

Goodwill (or Loving Our Neighbor) and Good Actions

HAVING addressed faith, we now turn to goodwill, because faith and goodwill are united, just as truth and goodness are united. And truth and goodness are united like light and heat in springtime. I say this because spiritual light, which is the light that emanates from the sun in the spiritual world, is essentially truth. Therefore wherever the truth appears in that world it shines with a brightness that depends on how pure the truth is. The spiritual heat that emanates from that sun is essentially goodness. I state this because the same things apply to goodwill and faith that apply to good and truth. Goodwill is all the forms of good that we do for our neighbor combined. Faith is all the forms of truth that we think about God and about divine things combined.

[2] Since the truth that comes from faith is spiritual light and the goodness that comes from goodwill is spiritual heat, it follows that spiritual heat and light have properties similar to those of physical heat and light. Just as everything on earth blossoms when heat and light are united on earth, so everything in the human mind blossoms when heat and light are united in it. There is a difference, however: on earth the heat and light that cause blossoming are physical, but in the human mind the heat and light that cause blossoming are spiritual. Because the latter is a spiritual blossoming, it leads to wisdom and intelligence.

In addition to a similarity, there is also a correspondence between the two forms of heat and light. Therefore in the Word a human mind that contains goodwill united to faith and faith united to goodwill is compared to a garden. In fact, this is the meaning of the Garden of Eden (the truth of this has been fully shown in *Secrets of Heaven,* published in London).

[3] It is also important to realize that if there were no discussion of goodwill following the discussion of faith, the true nature of faith would

be incomprehensible since, as I have said and shown in the previous chapter, faith without goodwill is not faith; goodwill without faith is not goodwill; and neither of them is living unless it comes from the Lord, §§355–361. Also, the Lord, goodwill, and faith form a unity in the same way our life, our will, and our intellect form a unity; if we separate them, each one crumbles like a pearl that is crushed to powder, §§362–367. And furthermore, goodwill and faith come together in good actions, §§373 and following.

393 It is an abiding truth that faith and goodwill cannot be separated if we are to have a spiritual life and be saved. The truth of this is understandable to everyone, even people without the refinement of a costly education.[617]

Suppose someone says, "People who live good lives and have proper beliefs are saved." No one could hear that without seeing it with an inner perception and therefore agreeing to it intellectually. Suppose someone says, "People who believe the right things but do not live good lives are also saved." Any people who heard this statement would reject it from their intellect as they would remove a piece of dirt that had fallen in their eye. Their inner perception would immediately cause them to think, "People cannot have good beliefs when they do not live good lives. What would those beliefs be except a painted model of faith rather than a living image of it?"

Likewise, if people were to hear, "Those who live good lives but have no beliefs are saved," they would turn this over a few times and then perceive and think that this does not make sense either. They would think, "Every good thing that is truly and intrinsically good comes from God; therefore living a good life comes from God. A good life without beliefs, then, is like clay in a potter's hand that can be molded into forms that are only useful in the earthly kingdom, not in the spiritual kingdom." Besides, there is an obvious contradiction in these statements, especially if you put them side by side: people are saved if they have beliefs but do not live good lives, and people are saved if they live good lives but have no beliefs.

What it is to live well, which is an aspect of goodwill, is partly known, partly unknown these days—people know what it is to live a good earthly life but not what it is to live a good spiritual life. Therefore I need to cover this point, inasmuch as it is an aspect of goodwill. The discussion will be broken into a series of individual topics.

There Are Three Universal Categories of Love:
Love for Heaven; Love for the World; and Love for Ourselves

We are starting with these three categories of love because they are univer-   **394**
sal and fundamental to all types of love and because goodwill has something in common with each of the three.

Love for heaven means love for the Lord and also love for our neighbor. Love for heaven could be called love for usefulness, because both
love for the Lord and love for our neighbor have usefulness as their goal.

Love for the world is not only love for wealth and possessions but also
love for all the things that the world provides that please our physical
senses: beauty pleases our eye, harmony pleases our ear, fragrances please
our nose, excellent food pleases our palate, soft touches please our skin. It
also includes beautiful clothes, spacious accommodations, and social
groups to belong to—all the pleasures that we get from these and many
other things.

Love for ourselves is not only a love for respect, glory, fame, and status but also a love for seeking and getting high positions and becoming
a leader.

Goodwill has something in common with each of these categories
of love, because goodwill is by definition a love for usefulness of all
kinds. Goodwill wants to do what is good for our neighbor, and *goodness* is the same as *usefulness*. Each of the categories of love just mentioned have usefulness as their goal: love for heaven has the goal of
being useful in spiritual ways; love for the world has the goal of being
useful in earthly ways, which could also be called forms of civil service;
and love for ourselves has the goal of being useful in physical ways,
which could also be labeled benefits at home for ourselves and our
loved ones.

The next part of this discussion [§§403–405] will show that these   **395**
three categories of love are in each one of us from creation and by birth;
when they are prioritized in the right way they improve us, but when they
are not prioritized in the right way they damage us. At present it is enough
to mention that these three loves are prioritized in the right way when our
love for heaven plays the part of the head; our love for the world, the part
of the chest and abdomen; and our love for ourselves, the part of the lower
legs and feet.

As I have mentioned several times before [§§34, 42, 69, 147, 186, 296], the human mind is divided into three regions. From our highest region we focus on God; from our second or middle region we focus on the world; and from our third or lowest region we focus on ourselves. Because our mind has this structure, it can be lifted up or can lift itself up to focus on God and heaven; it can be spread out or spread itself out in every direction to focus on the world and its nature; and it can be lowered down or can lower itself down to focus on the earth and hell. In these respects physical sight emulates mental sight—physical sight too can look up, around, and down.

[2] The human mind is like a three-story house with stairs that provide transitions between levels. There are angels from heaven living on the top floor, people of the world on the middle floor, and demons on the bottom floor. People for whom these three categories of love have been prioritized in the right way can go up or down whenever they want. When they go up to the top floor, they are like angels among the angels there. When they go down to the middle floor, they are like angelic people with the people there. When they go even farther down, they are like worldly people with the demons there—they give the demons instructions, confront them, and tame them.

[3] When these three categories of love are properly prioritized in us, they are also coordinated in such a way that the highest love, our love for heaven, is present in the second love, our love for the world, and through that in the third or lowest love, our love for ourselves. In fact, the love that is inside steers the love that is outside wherever it wants. Therefore if a love for heaven is present in our love for the world and through that in our love for ourselves, with each type of love we accomplish useful things that are inspired by the God of heaven.

In operation these three loves function like the will, the intellect, and action: the will flows into the intellect, where it finds the means of producing action. There will be more on these last points in the next part of the discussion [§§403–405], which shows that if these three loves are prioritized in the right way, they improve us, but if they are not prioritized in the right way, they damage us and turn us upside down.

396 To present the points that follow in this chapter in such a way that they can be seen clearly (not to mention the points in chapters to follow on free choice [§§463–508], reformation and regeneration [§§571–625], and so on), I first need to present some points on *the will and the intellect;*

goodness and truth; love in general; love for the world and love for ourselves in specific; our outer and inner selves; and *people who are merely earthly and sense-oriented.*

These points will be brought to light so that when readers see the things that come later, their rational sight will not feel as if it were in a fog, rushing along city streets until it had no idea of the way home. What is theology without understanding or with an intellect that remains unenlightened while we read the Word? It is like having a lamp in our hand but not lighting the candle inside it, like the lamps held by the five foolish young women who had no oil.[618] Therefore these individual topics will be taken up in sequence.

1. *The will and the intellect.*

(a) There are two faculties that constitute our life. One is called the will, the other the intellect. They are distinct from each other, yet they were created to be one. When they are one, they are called "the mind." Therefore they are the human mind, where all of our life has its first beginnings, from which life then comes into our body.

(b) Just as everything in the universe—everything that is in the divine design—relates to goodness and truth, so everything in us relates to our will and our intellect. Goodness in us belongs to our will and truth in us belongs to our intellect. In fact, these two faculties or "lives" within us are vessels and abodes for goodness and truth. Our will is the vessel and abode for all things related to goodness, and our intellect is the vessel and abode for all things related to truth. Forms of good and truth exist nowhere else inside us. And since forms of good and truth exist nowhere else, love and faith do not exist anywhere else either, since love relates to goodness and goodness relates to love, and faith relates to truth and truth relates to faith.

(c) The will and the intellect also constitute our spirit. That is where our wisdom and intelligence, our love and goodwill, and our life in general reside. The body is merely an obedient servant.

(d) Nothing is more important to know than how the will and the intellect become a single mind. They become a single mind the way goodness and truth become one. The marriage between the will and the intellect is in fact similar to the marriage between goodness and truth. As will be shown in the next passage, which concerns goodness and truth, the nature of this marriage is that goodness is the underlying reality of a thing and truth is the resulting manifestation of the thing. Therefore in

397

us our will is the underlying reality of our life and our intellect is the resulting manifestation of our life, because the goodness in our will takes shape and presents itself to be seen in our intellect.

398

2. *Goodness and truth.*

(a) Everything in the universe that is in the divine design relates to goodness and truth. Nothing that exists in heaven or on earth does not relate to these two. The reason is that both goodness and truth emanate from God, the source of all things.

[2] (b) Clearly then it is necessary for people to know what goodness is, what truth is, how they relate to each other, and how the one is united to the other. This is especially necessary for the people of the church. As everything in heaven relates to goodness and truth, so does everything in the church, since the goodness and truth of heaven are also the goodness and truth of the church.

[3] (c) The divine design is that goodness and truth are to be united, not separated. They are to be one thing, not two. They are united when they emanate from God, and they are united in heaven. Therefore they should be united in the church. In heaven the union of goodness and truth is called "the heavenly marriage." All who are in heaven have this marriage. This is why heaven is compared to a marriage in the Word, and the Lord is called Bridegroom and Husband while heaven is called Bride and Wife, as is the church. Heaven and the church are called this because the people in heaven and in the church receive divine goodness in their truths.

[4] (d) All the intelligence and wisdom that angels have comes from this marriage. None of it comes from goodness that is separate from truth or truth that is separate from goodness. The same is true for people of the church as well.

[5] (e) Since the union of goodness and truth is like a marriage, goodness clearly loves truth and truth loves goodness in return. Each one desires to be united to the other. People of the church who do not have this love or desire do not have the heavenly marriage. The church is not yet in them, since a union of goodness and truth constitutes the church.

[6] (f) There are many kinds of goodness. In general there is goodness that is spiritual and goodness that is earthly. Both types come together in goodness that is genuinely moral. Just as there are different types of goodness, there are different types of truth, since truth belongs to goodness and is the form of goodness.

[7] (g) The situation with goodness and truth has an opposite in evil and falsity. As everything in the universe that is in the divine design

relates to goodness and truth, so everything that is against the divine design relates to evil and falsity. As goodness loves to be united to truth, so evil loves to be united to falsity and the reverse. As the union of goodness and truth gives birth to all intelligence and wisdom, the union of evil and falsity gives birth to all insanity and foolishness. If you look deeply at the union of evil and falsity, you will see that it is not a marriage but an act of adultery.

[8] (h) The fact that evil and falsity are the opposite of goodness and truth makes it clear that truth cannot be joined to evil and that goodness cannot be joined to the falsity that comes from evil. If truth is joined to evil it becomes false and no longer true because it has been falsified. If goodness is joined to the falsity that comes from evil the goodness becomes evil and no longer good because it has been contaminated. Falsity that does not come from evil, however, can be joined to goodness.

[9] (i) No people who are focused on evil and falsity as a result of their convictions and their lives are able to know what goodness and truth are, because they believe that their evil is good and their falsity is true. On the other hand, all who are focused on goodness and truth as a result of their convictions and their lives are able to know what evil and falsity are, because all goodness and truth are essentially heavenly, but all evil and falsity are essentially hellish; and everything heavenly is in the light but everything hellish is in the dark.

3. *Love in general.*

399

(a) Our love is our very life itself. The nature of our love determines the nature of our life and in fact our entire nature as a human being. Our dominant or leading love, however, is the love that constitutes us.[619]

Our dominant or leading love has many other loves; they are derived from it in a hierarchy beneath it. No matter how these other loves may look or seem, each one of them is part of our leading love. With it they make one government, so to speak. Our dominant love is like the monarch and leader of the rest: it guides our other loves and uses them as intermediate purposes through which it focuses on and aims for its goal. Both directly and indirectly, this goal is the primary and ultimate objective for them all.

[2] (b) The focus of our dominant love is what we love above all else. What we love above all else is constantly present in our thinking, because it is in our will and ultimately constitutes our life.

For example, if we love wealth above everything else, whether that means money or property, we are constantly contemplating how to get more. When we do get more we are profoundly overjoyed. When we lose wealth we are profoundly grief-stricken. Our heart is in it.

If we love ourselves above all else, we keep ourselves in mind at all times. We think about ourselves, talk about ourselves, and act for our own benefit, because our life is a life of self.

[3] (c) Our purpose is what we love above all else. We focus on it in each and every thing we do. It exists in our will like a hidden current in a river that moves and carries things along, even when we are doing something else, because it is what motivates us. It is the factor that people look for and identify in others; then they use it either to influence the others or to cooperate with them.

[4] (d) Our nature is completely shaped by the dominant force in our lives. That force is what differentiates us from other people. If we are good, our heaven is created to accord with it. If we are evil, our hell is created to accord with it. It is our will, our self, and our nature. It is the underlying reality of our life. It cannot be changed after we die, because it is our true self.

[5] (e) For each of us, all our pleasure, joy, and happiness comes from our dominant love and depends on it. This is because whatever we love we say is enjoyable, since we feel it that way. What we think about but we do not love we are also capable of calling enjoyable, but it is not the central enjoyment of our life. What our love enjoys we experience as good, and what our love does not enjoy we experience as evil.

[6] (f) There are two types of love that act as a source for all forms of goodness and truth. There are two types of love that act as a source for all forms of evil and falsity. The two loves that originate all forms of goodness and truth are love for the Lord and love for our neighbor. The two loves that originate all forms of evil and falsity are love for ourselves and love for the world. When the latter two loves are dominant, they are completely opposite to the former two loves.

[7] (g) Love for the Lord and love for our neighbor are the two loves that constitute heaven in us, as I said. They are the dominant types of love in heaven. Since they constitute heaven in us, they also constitute the church in us.

The two loves that originate all forms of evil and falsity, which as I said are love for ourselves and love for the world, constitute hell in us, since they are the dominant types of love in hell. Therefore they also destroy the church in us.

[8] (h) The two types of love that originate all forms of goodness and truth, which are the types of love in heaven, open and form our inner spiritual self, because that is where these loves reside. The two types of love that originate all forms of evil and falsity, which as I have said are the types of love in hell, close and destroy our inner spiritual self when they are dominant. They make us earthly and sense-oriented, depending on how extensively and powerfully dominant they are.

4. *Love for ourselves and love for the world in specific.*

400

(a) Love for ourselves is wanting good things for ourselves alone and not wanting good things for others unless we benefit—not even if the others are the church, our country, any human community, or other people who live in the area. Love for ourselves also entails doing something good for others only if it benefits our own reputation, honor, and glory. If we do not see these benefits in the good things we are doing for others, we say at heart, "What's the point? Why should I do this? What's in it for me?" and we no longer bother to do them. Clearly then, if we are wrapped up in loving ourselves we do not love the church, our country, our community, other people in our area, or anything else that is truly good. We love only ourselves and our own things.

[2] (b) When we are not focusing on our neighbor or the public in the things that we think about and do, let alone the Lord, we are wrapped up in loving ourselves. We are thinking only about ourselves and our own people. To put it another way, this is our nature when everything we do is for ourselves and our own people; if we do anything for the public, we do it only to look good; if we do anything for our neighbors, we do it only so they will like us.

[3] (c) I say "for ourselves *and our own people*" because if we love ourselves we also love our own people—specifically our own children and grandchildren, and generally all the people around us whom we call our own. Loving them is the same as loving ourselves, because we look at them as if we were looking at ourselves and we see them in relation to ourselves. "Our own people" also includes all the people who praise us, respect us, and look up to us. The rest may look human to our physical eyes, but with the eyes of our spirit we more or less see them as phantoms.

[4] (d) Love for ourselves is what we have if we despise our neighbors in comparison with ourselves. It is what we have if we think of people as our enemies because they do not favor, revere, or adore us. We are deeper in this love if we hate and persecute our neighbors for feeling that way. And

we are deeper still in this love if we have a burning desire for revenge against our neighbors and long for their destruction. If we have this nature, we eventually love to be savage.

[5] (e) We can see the nature of love for ourselves by comparing it with heavenly love. Heavenly love is a love for usefulness because it is useful; it is a love for the good things that we do for our church, our country, human society, and people in our area because they are good things to do. If, however, it is for our own sake that we love usefulness and good actions, we love them only as our drudges, because they serve us. Therefore if we love ourselves, we want our church, our country, human communities, and the people around us to serve us; we do not want to serve them. We place ourselves above them; we put them beneath ourselves.

[6] (f) Furthermore, the more we have a heavenly kind of love (we love actions that are useful and good and are moved with heartfelt pleasure when we do them), the more we are led by the Lord. This heavenly kind of love is the kind of love the Lord has; it is the kind of love that comes from him.

The more we love ourselves, the more we are led by ourselves and by our own self-centeredness. Our self-centeredness is nothing but evil. It is our hereditary evil. It is loving ourselves more than God and loving the world more than heaven.

[7] (g) The nature of love for ourselves is that the more the reins are let out—that is, the more its external constraints are removed, which are a fear of the law and its penalties and a fear of losing our reputation, respect, advantage, position, and life—the more our love for ourselves rushes on, until it wants to control not only the entire planet but also heaven and even God himself. It never has a limit or an end.

This limitless desire for control lies hidden within all people who are in love with themselves, although it is not visible to the world as long as the reins and constraints just mentioned hold them back. The nature of all people like this is that whenever further progress upward becomes impossible for them, they stay where they are until moving up becomes possible again. This explains why people who love themselves like this are unaware that there is an insane and limitless obsession hiding inside them.

No one can avoid seeing the truth of this, however, when looking at powerful people and monarchs—people who lack reins, constraints, and impossibilities. They rush on and overpower whole provinces and countries as long as they keep succeeding. They aspire to power and glory beyond all limits. This is particularly the case with people who extend their domain into heaven and transfer all the Lord's divine power to themselves. They always crave more.[620]

[8] (h) There are two kinds of ruling power: one comes from love for our neighbor; the other comes from love for ourselves. They are opposite to each other. If we have ruling power because we love our neighbors, we want what is good for all. We love nothing more than being useful and serving others. Serving others is doing good and useful things for them because we wish them well. This is what we love to do and what gives pleasure to our heart. In this case, the more we are promoted to high positions, the happier we are, not because of the high positions but because of the useful things we can then do with a wider scope and greater magnitude. This is the nature of ruling power in the heavens.

On the other hand, if we have ruling power because we love ourselves, we want what is good for no one except ourselves and our own. The useful things we do are for our own honor and glory. As far as we are concerned, honor and glory are the only really useful things. If we serve others, it is for the purpose of being served and honored and having power. We pursue high positions not for the good things we could do but to have importance and glory and the heartfelt pleasure they bring us.

[9] (i) The particular love for ruling power that people have had stays with them after their life in the world. People who had power because they loved their neighbor are entrusted with power in the heavens. In that situation, they do not have the power: the good and useful causes they love have the power. And when good and useful causes have the power, the Lord has the power.

People who had ruling power in the world because they loved themselves are thrown out of office after their life in the world comes to an end. They are then forced into slavery.

The points above make it now possible to recognize which people have love for themselves. It does not matter how they seem in outer form, whether haughty or obsequious. The attributes discussed above are in their inner selves, and the inner self is hidden from most other people. Their outer selves are taught to pretend to love the public and their neighbors—the opposite of what they feel. This too they do for their own sake. They are aware that loving the public and their neighbors deeply affects people and increases people's respect for them. This strategy works because heaven flows into a love for the public and for one's neighbor.

[10] (j) The evil qualities generally found in people who love themselves are contempt for others, jealousy, unfriendliness toward people who do not favor them; a resulting hostility; and various kinds of hatred, vengefulness, guile, deceit, ruthlessness, and cruelty. Where you find evils like this, you also find contempt for God and for the divine things that are the true insights and good actions taught by the church. If such people honor these things, their respect is only verbal, not heartfelt. Because evils like these are present, related falsities are also present, since falsities come from evils.

[11] (k) *Love for the world,* on the other hand, is wanting to redirect other people's wealth to ourselves with whatever skill we have. It is putting our heart in riches and letting the world distract us and steer us away from spiritual love (love for our neighbor) and heaven. We have a love for the world if we long to redirect other people's possessions to ourselves by various methods, especially if we use trickery and deception, and have no concern for how our neighbor is doing. If we have this type of love, we have a strong and growing craving for good things other people have. Provided we do not fear the law or losing our reputation, we take people's things away, and in fact rob people blind.

[12] (l) Yet love for the world is not as opposite to heavenly love as love for ourselves is—the evils hidden in it are not as enormous.

[13] (m) Love for the world takes many forms. It can be a love we have for wealth in order to be promoted to higher positions. It can be a love for honor and high position for the sake of increasing our wealth. It can be a love for wealth for the sake of various benefits that gratify us in the world. It can be a love for wealth for the sake of wealth itself: this kind is miserly. And so on. Our purpose in gaining the wealth is the use we hope to get out of it. This purpose or use determines the quality of the love. The nature of any love is the nature of the purpose it has; everything else about it serves as a means.

[14] (n) To summarize, love for ourselves and love for the world are completely opposite to love for the Lord and love for our neighbor. Therefore love for ourselves and love for the world, as I have just described them, are hellish loves. In fact, they rule in hell. They also create a hell in us.

Love for the Lord, however, and love for our neighbor are heavenly loves. In fact, they rule in heaven. They also create a heaven in us.

401

5. *Our inner and outer selves.*

(a) We have been created to be in the spiritual world and the physical world at the same time. The spiritual world is where angels are. The physical world is where people are. Because we have been created that way, we have been given an inner and an outer level: an inner level so we can be in the spiritual world and an outer level so we can be in the physical world. The inner level is called our inner self, and the outer level is called our outer self.

[2] (b) Everyone has an inner and an outer self, but they are different in good people than in evil people. The inner level of good people is in heaven and its light. Their outer level is in the world and its light; and the light of heaven within them illumines the light of the world. Their inner and outer levels are united like cause and effect or like something prior and something subsequent. With evil people, however, their inner level is in hell and its light. Compared to heaven's light, the light of hell is pitch darkness. The outer level of evil people can be in the same light that good people are in. Therefore they are upside-down. This explains how evil people are capable of speaking and teaching *about* faith, goodwill, and God, but not *from* faith, goodwill, and God the way good people can.

[3] (c) Our inner self is called our spiritual self because it is in the light of heaven, a light that is spiritual. Our outer self is called our earthly self because it is in the light of the world, a light that is earthly. People whose inner level is in the light of heaven and whose outer level is in the light of the world are spiritual on both levels, since spiritual light from within enlightens their earthly light and makes it its own. The reverse is true for evil people.

[4] (d) The inner self that is spiritual is actually an angel of heaven. Even while it is alive in our body, it is in a community with angels, although it does not realize that. After it is released from the body, it comes to live among those angels. The inner self among evil people, however, is a satan. Even while it is living in our body, it is in a community with satans.[621] After it is released from the body, it comes to live among those satans.

[5] (e) In people who are spiritual, the inner parts of their mind are actually raised up toward heaven, because heaven is their predominant focus. In people who are merely earthly, however, the inner parts of their mind are turned away from heaven toward the world, because the world is their predominant focus.

[6] (f) People who have only a general concept of the inner and outer self believe that the inner self is the part that thinks and wills while the outer self is the part that speaks and acts, since thinking and willing are internal while speaking and acting are external. One thing is important

to realize, however. When we are thinking and willing good things in relation to the Lord and all that is the Lord's, and when we are thinking and willing them in relation to our neighbor and all that is our neighbor's, then our thinking and willing are coming from an inner self that is spiritual. This is so because they are coming from true faith and a love for what is good. On the other hand, when we have evil thoughts about the Lord and our neighbor and evil intentions toward them, then our thinking and willing are coming from an inner self that is hellish, because they are coming from a false faith and a love for what is evil. Briefly put, the more we focus on loving the Lord and our neighbor, the more spiritual our inner self is. From that inner self we think and will, and from it we even speak and act as well. On the other hand, the more we focus on loving ourselves and the world, the more our thinking and willing come from hell, although we speak and act otherwise.

[7] (g) The Lord has provided and arranged that the more our thinking and willing come from heaven, the more our spiritual self opens and adapts. This opening is an opening to heaven, all the way to the Lord; and this adaptation is an adaptation to things that are in heaven.

On the other hand, the more our thinking and willing come from the world, not heaven, the more our inner spiritual self closes and our outer self opens and adapts. This opening is an opening to the world and this adaptation is an adaptation to the things that are in hell.

[8] (h) People whose inner spiritual selves have opened to heaven and the Lord are in the light of heaven. They have enlightenment from the Lord and a resulting intelligence and wisdom. They see truth from the light of truth. They sense what is good from a love for what is good.

People whose inner spiritual selves have closed, however, do not know what the inner self is. They do not believe in the Word, life after death, or anything related to heaven or the church. Because they have a light that is merely earthly, they believe that nature arises from itself, not from God. They see what is false as true and sense what is evil as good.

[9] (i) The inner and outer levels discussed here are the inner and outer levels of our spirit. Our body is only an element added on the outside as a container for all the above. Our body does nothing on its own—it acts on behalf of the spirit that is inside it.

It is important to know that after our spirit parts company with our body, it still thinks, wills, speaks, and acts. Thinking and willing remain our inner level and speaking and acting then become our outer level.

6. *People who are merely earthly and sense-oriented.*

402

Only a few know what "sense-oriented people" are and what they are like, even though it is an important thing to know. Therefore I will describe them.

(a) "Sense-oriented people" are people who judge everything on the basis of their physical senses—people who will not believe anything unless they can see it with their eyes and touch it with their hands. What they can see and touch they call "something." Everything else they reject. Sense-oriented people, then, are earthly in the lowest way.

[2] (b) The inner levels of their mind, levels that see in heaven's light, are closed inside people like this to the point where they see nothing true related to heaven or the church. This is because their thinking occurs on an outermost level and not inside, where the light is spiritual.

[3] (c) Since the light they have is dense and earthly, people like this are inwardly opposed to things related to heaven and the church, although they are outwardly able to speak in favor of them. If things related to heaven and the church give these people ruling power, they are even capable of speaking ardently in favor of them.

[4] (d) Sense-oriented people are able to reason sharply and skillfully, because their thinking is so close to their speech as to be practically in it—almost inside their lips; and because they attribute all intelligence solely to the ability to speak from memory.

[5] (e) Some of them can defend whatever they want. They have great skill at defending things that are false. After they have defended falsities convincingly, they themselves believe those falsities are true. They base their reasoning and defense on mistaken impressions from the senses that the public finds captivating and convincing.

[6] (f) Sense-oriented people are more deceptive and ill-intentioned than others.

[7] (g) The inner areas of their mind are foul and filthy because they use them to communicate with the hells.

[8] (h) The inhabitants of hell are sense-oriented. The deeper in hell they are, the more sense-oriented they are. The sphere of hellish spirits is connected to our sense impressions through a kind of back door.[622]

[9] (i) Sense-oriented people do not see anything that is genuinely true in the light. Instead, on every topic they debate and argue whether it is so. From a distance their arguments sound like the grinding of teeth.[623] The sounds of teeth grinding are actually the result of falsities colliding with

each other, and falsity and truth in collision as well. This makes it clear what "the grinding" or "gnashing of teeth" means in the Word.[624] Teeth correspond to reasoning based on mistaken impressions from our senses.

[10] (j) The educated and the scholarly who are deeply convinced of falsities—especially people who oppose the truths in the Word—are more sense-oriented than others, although that is not how they seem to the world. People who are sense-oriented are the foremost developers of heresies.

[11] (k) For the most part, hypocrites, deceitful people, hedonists, adulterers, and misers are sense-oriented.

[12] (l) The ancients[625] had a term for people who debate on the basis of sense impressions alone and speak against genuine truths in the Word and the church: they called them serpents of the tree of the knowledge of good and evil.

Sense impressions mean things that impinge on our physical senses and are experienced by those senses. This point leads to a number of others:

[13] (m) We are in touch with the world by means of sense impressions and with heaven by means of impressions on our rationality, which transcend sense impressions.

[14] (n) Sense impressions supply things from the physical world that serve the inner realms of the mind in the spiritual world.

[15] (o) There are sense impressions that feed the intellect: they are various earthly objects that are labeled "material." There are sense impressions that feed the will: they are called the pleasures of the senses and the body.

[16] (p) Unless our thought is lifted above the level of our sense impressions, we have very little wisdom. Wise people think above the level of sense impressions. When our thinking rises above sense impressions, it enters a clearer light and eventually comes into the light of heaven. From this light we get the awareness of truth that constitutes real intelligence.

[17] (q) The ancients knew how to lift their minds above sense impressions and take their minds away from them.

[18] (r) If sense impressions have the lowest priority, they help open a pathway for the intellect. We then extrapolate truths by a method of extraction. On the other hand, if sense impressions have the highest priority, that pathway is closed and truths are not visible to us except as if they were in a fog or in the dark of night.

[19] (s) For wise people, sense impressions have the lowest priority and are subservient to things that are deep inside. For unwise people,

sense impressions have the highest priority and are in control. This type of person can truly be called sense-oriented.

[20] (t) There are sense impressions that we have in common with animals and sense impressions that we do not have in common with animals. The more we lift our thinking above sense impressions, the more human we are. Without acknowledging God and living by his commandments, however, none of us can lift our thinking above sense impressions and see the truths that relate to the church. It is God who lifts and enlightens us.[626]

When the Three Universal Categories of Love Are Prioritized in the Right Way They Improve Us; When They Are Not Prioritized in the Right Way They Damage Us and Turn Us Upside Down

First I will say something about the prioritization of the three universal categories of love: love for heaven, love for the world, and love for ourselves. Then I will talk about the inflow and integration of one into the other. Finally I will discuss the effect of their prioritization on our state.

403

These three loves relate to each other as do the three areas of the body: the highest is the head; the middle is the chest and abdomen; and our thighs, lower legs, and feet make up the third.[627] When our love for heaven constitutes the head, our love for the world constitutes the chest and abdomen, and our love for ourselves constitutes the lower legs and feet, then we are in the perfect state we were created to be in. In this state the two lower categories of love serve the higher category the way the body and everything in it serves the head.

Therefore when a love for heaven constitutes the head, this love flows into our love for the world, which is chiefly a love for wealth, and takes advantage of that wealth to do useful things; our love for heaven also flows through our love for the world into our love for ourselves, which is chiefly a love for having a high position, and takes advantage of that high position to do useful things. Therefore an inflow from one love into the next allows the three categories of love to join forces in order to do useful things.

[2] Surely everyone realizes that when people intend to do useful things because they are moved by spiritual love coming from the Lord (which is what "love for heaven" means), their earthly self uses its wealth

and other goods to achieve those useful things, and their sense-oriented self carries them out as part of its position and derives honor from so doing.

Surely everyone also realizes that all the things we do with our body we do from the state of mind in our head. If our mind has a love for acts of service, our body uses its limbs to perform acts of service. Our body will do this because our will and intellect have their primary structures in our head and the derivations of those primary structures in our body, so that our will is present in what we do and our thinking is present in what we say.

Likewise the reproductive impetus in a seed affects each and every part of a tree and uses those parts to produce pieces of fruit as its acts of service. Or for another example, fire and light inside a clear container make the container hot and bright. In people whose three categories of love have been prioritized in the right and proper way, their mind's spiritual sight and their body's physical sight are translucent to the light that flows in through heaven from the Lord, just as a pomegranate is translucent all the way through to the center where the seeds are stored.

Something comparable is meant by the following words of the Lord: "Your eye is the lamp of your body. If your eye is whole, that is, good, your entire body is full of light" (Matthew 6:22; Luke 11:34).

[3] No one whose reason is sound could condemn wealth. Wealth in the general body politic is like blood in us. No one whose reason is sound could condemn the levels of status that go with different jobs—they are the monarch's hands and the pillars of society, provided a spiritual love for status takes priority over an earthly and sense-oriented love for it. In fact, there are government positions in heaven and there is status that goes with them; but because the people who fill these positions are spiritual, the thing they love the most is to be useful.

404 We take on a completely different condition if love for the world or for wealth constitutes the head, meaning that this is our dominant love. Then love for heaven leaves the head and goes into exile in the body. People who are in this state prefer the world to heaven. They do indeed worship God, but they do so from a love that is merely earthly, a love that leads them to take credit for all their acts of worship. They also do good things for their neighbor, but they do them to get something back in return.

In the case of people like this, heavenly things are like the clothes in which they strut about, garments that we see as shining but angels see as drab. When love for the world inhabits our inner self and love for heaven inhabits our outer self, then love for the world dims all things related to the church and hides them as if they were behind a piece of cloth.

Love for the world or for wealth comes in many forms, however. It gets worse the closer it approaches to miserliness. At the point of miserliness the love for heaven becomes dark. This love also gets worse the closer it approaches to arrogance and a sense of superiority over others based on love for oneself. It is not as detrimental when it tends toward wasteful indulgence. It is even less damaging if its goal is to have the finest things the world has to offer, like a mansion, fine furniture, fashionable clothing, servants, horses and carriages in grand style, and things like that. With any love, its quality depends on the goal that it focuses on and intends to reach.

Love for the world and for wealth is like a dark crystal that suffocates light and breaks it only into colors that are dull and faded. It is like fog or cloudiness that blocks the rays of the sun. It is also like wine in its first stages—the liquid tastes sweet, but it upsets your stomach.

From heaven's point of view, people like this look hunchbacked, walking with their head bent down looking at the ground. When they lift their head toward the sky, they strain their muscles and quickly go back to looking downward. The ancient people who were part of the church called people of this kind "Mammons." The Greeks called them "Plutos."[628]

If, however, love for ourselves or love of power constitutes the head, then love for heaven goes down the body to the lower legs. The more this love grows, the more love for heaven moves through the ankles into the feet. If love for ourselves grows even more, love for heaven passes through the shoes and is trampled.

405

There is a love for power that comes from loving our neighbor and a love for power that comes from loving ourselves. People who have a love for power that comes from loving their neighbor are ambitious for power for the purpose of benefiting both the general public and individual citizens. In the heavens, in fact, power is entrusted to people like this. [2] If emperors, monarchs, and generals who were born and raised to be leaders humble themselves before God, they sometimes have less self-love than people who come from a lowly family and whose pride makes them long for superior status over others.

On the other hand, people who have a love for power that comes from loving themselves use love for heaven as their footstool. They put their feet on it in view of the crowd. If there is no crowd in sight, they either toss it in the corner or throw it out the door. Why? Because they love only themselves. As a result, they plunge the willing and thinking of their minds into self-absorption. Self-absorption is in fact a hereditary evil; it is the polar opposite of love for heaven.

[3] If we have a love for power that comes from loving ourselves, we also have evils that accompany that love. They are generally the following: despising others, jealousy, viewing people as our enemies if they do not show us special favor, hostility, hatred, vengefulness, mercilessness, savagery, and cruelty. Despising God is another such evil, as is despising the divine things that are the true insights and good actions taught by the church. If we give these things any honor, we only pay them lip service to prevent the church hierarchy from attacking our reputation and to stave off verbal abuse from everyone else.

[4] Love for power is different for the clergy than it is for the laity. In the clergy this love surges upward, as long as it is given the reins, until they want to be gods. Lay people, on the other hand, want to be monarchs. That is how far the imagination of that love takes their minds.

[5] In spiritually well-developed people, love for heaven occupies the highest place and constitutes the head of what follows it; love for the world is beneath it and is like the torso below the head; love for themselves is below this love in the role of the lower legs. It follows then that if love for ourselves constitutes the head, we are completely upside-down. In that case we look to the angels like people sleeping with their heads on the ground and their rear ends up in the air. When people like this are worshiping, they look as if they are frolicking on all fours like panther cubs. Furthermore, they look like various kinds of two-headed creatures—the head on top has the face of a wild animal, while the other below it has a human face that is continually pushed down from above and forced to kiss the ground.

All people of this type are sense-oriented. They are like the people described above in §402.

All Individual Members of Humankind Are the Neighbor We Are to Love, but [in Different Ways] Depending on the Type of Goodness They Have

406 We are not born for our own sake; we are born for the sake of others. That is, we are not born to live for ourselves alone; we are born to live for others. Otherwise society would not be cohesive and there would be no good in it.

There is a common saying that we are all neighbor to ourselves.[629] The body of teaching on goodwill, however, shows how we should understand this. We are all supposed to provide ourselves with the necessities of life, such as food, clothing, a place to live, and many other things that are required by the civic life in which we participate. And we provide these things not only for ourselves but also for our loved ones, not only for the present but also for the future. If we do not provide ourselves with the necessities of life, we are in no state to practice goodwill, because we lack everything.

How we are to be neighbors to ourselves, however, can be shown through the following analogy: We should all provide our bodies with food. This has to come first, but the goal is to have a sound mind in a sound body. We also ought to provide our mind with its food, that is, things that build intelligence and judgment; but the goal is to be in a state in which we can serve our fellow citizens, our community, our country, the church, and therefore the Lord. People who pursue this goal are providing well for themselves to eternity.

These points make clear what is primary from the standpoint of time and what is primary from the standpoint of purpose. What is primary from the standpoint of purpose is the true overall goal.

This situation is like people building a house. They have to lay the foundation first, but the foundation is for the house, and the house is for living in. People who hold being neighbors to themselves as their first and foremost objective are like people whose main purpose is building the foundation rather than living in the house. Yet living in the house is the primary and ultimate purpose overall; the house and its foundation are only a means to an end.

Now I need to say what it is to love our neighbor. Loving our neighbor is intending and doing good not only to neighbors, friends, and good people but also to strangers, enemies, and evil people. But we exercise goodwill in our dealings with the latter in different ways than we do in our dealings with the former. We exercise goodwill in our dealings with our neighbors and friends by benefiting them directly. We exercise goodwill in our dealings with our enemies and evil people by benefiting them indirectly through our warnings, corrective action, punishments, and therefore efforts to improve them.

This could be illustrated as follows. Judges who punish wrongdoers because it is the just and legal thing to do have love for their neighbor. By

407

so doing the judges are straightening out the wrongdoers and are caring for people in the area by preventing the wrongdoers from doing them harm.

Everyone knows that parents who punish their children for doing what is wrong are showing them love; and on the other hand, parents who do not punish their children for doing what is wrong are showing love for evil traits in their children, which has nothing to do with goodwill.

For another example, suppose someone under the attack of an enemy repels the attacker and either strikes in self-defense or turns the attacker over to a judge to avoid being harmed. Say the victor maintains an intention nonetheless of becoming the attacker's friend. Then the victor is acting on the strength of goodwill. Even wars for the purpose of keeping the country and the church safe are not against goodwill. The ultimate purpose shows whether a given act is an expression of goodwill or not.

408 Fundamentally speaking, goodwill is wanting what is best for others. This desire resides in the inner self. When people of goodwill resist an enemy, punish a guilty person, or discipline evil people, clearly they do so through the medium of their outer selves. Therefore after the situation comes to an end, they go back to the goodwill that is in their inner selves. As much and as usefully as they can, they then wish the others well and benefit those others in a spirit of goodwill.

People who have genuine goodwill have a passion for what is good. In their outer selves that passion can look like rage and blazing anger, but it dies away and becomes calm as soon as their opponents come back to their senses. It is very different for people who have no goodwill. Their passion is a rage and a hatred that heat and ignite their *inner* selves.

409 Before the Lord came into the world, almost no one knew what the inner self was or what goodwill was. That is why in so many passages the Lord teaches love and goodwill. This is a distinguishing feature between the Old Testament or Covenant and the New.

In Matthew the Lord teaches that we are to do good to our adversaries and enemies and have goodwill toward them:

> You have heard the statement made to the ancients, "You are to love your neighbor and hate your enemy." But I am saying to you, love your enemies, bless the people who are cursing you, do good to the people who are hating you, and pray for the people who are hurting you and

persecuting you, so that you may be children of your Father who is in the heavens. (Matthew 5:43, 44, 45)

To Peter, who was asking how many times he should forgive someone who was sinning against him—whether he should give forgiveness as many as seven times—the Lord answered,

> I do not say as many as seven times, but as many as seventy times seven. (Matthew 18:21, 22)

I have also heard from heaven that the Lord forgives everyone's sins and never takes revenge or even assigns spiritual credit or blame, because he is love and goodness itself. Yet for all that, our sins are not washed away. Nothing washes our sins away except repentance. Since the Lord told Peter to forgive up to seventy times seven instances of sin, at what point would the Lord stop forgiving us?

Since goodwill resides in the inner self, where benevolence is felt, and then extends into the outer self, where good actions occur, it follows that people's inner selves are what we should love; and we should love their outer selves on the basis of their inner selves. Therefore we are to love people according to the type of goodness they have inside. It is the goodness itself, then, that is actually our neighbor.

410

The following situations may serve as illustration: When we choose ourselves a household manager out of three or four candidates, or we hire a servant, we investigate that person's inner self. We choose someone who is honest and faithful and prefer that candidate because of those qualities.

The same is true for monarchs or government officials. Out of three or four candidates, they select someone suitable for the job and reject the unsuitable, no matter whose looks they prefer or what the candidates say or do to win them over.

[2] Everyone is our neighbor, and people come in an infinite variety. Since we need to love them all as our neighbor for the type of goodness they possess, clearly there are genera and species of loving our neighbor, as well as higher and lower degrees of that love.

Since the Lord is to be loved above all else, it follows that the degrees of our love for our neighbors depend on their love for the Lord, that is, on the amount of the Lord or the amount from the Lord that our neighbors possess in themselves. That is also the amount of goodness they possess, since all goodness comes from the Lord.

[3] Nevertheless, since these degrees are within people's inner selves and these are rarely obvious to the world, it is enough to love our neighbor by the degree of goodness that we are aware of.

Now, these degrees are clearly perceived after death, since there the feelings in our will and the thoughts in our intellect form a spiritual sphere around us that others can sense in various ways. In this world, however, this spiritual sphere is absorbed by our physical body and is contained in the physical sphere[630] that pours out around us.

The Lord's parable about the Samaritan shows that there are degrees of love for our neighbor. The Samaritan had mercy on the person who had been wounded by robbers—a person whom both the priest and the Levite had seen and yet passed by. When the Lord asked which of the three seemed to have been a neighbor, the reply was "the one who had mercy" (Luke 10:30–37).

411 We read that we are to love the Lord God above all things, and our neighbor as ourselves (Luke 10:27). To love our neighbor as ourselves means not despising our neighbors in comparison with ourselves. It means treating them justly and not judging them wrongfully. The law of goodwill pronounced and given by the Lord himself is this:

> Whatever you want people to do for you, do likewise for them. This is the Law and the Prophets. (Matthew 7:12; Luke 6:31, 32)

This is how people who love heaven love their neighbor. People who love the world, however, love their neighbor on a worldly basis for a worldly benefit. People who love themselves love their neighbor in a selfish way for a selfish benefit.

The Neighbor We Are to Love Is Humankind on a Wider Scale in the Form of Smaller and Larger Communities and Humankind in the Aggregate as a Country of Such Communities

412 People who do not know what "our neighbor" really means think that it simply means an individual human being; benefiting that human being is loving our neighbor. Yet our neighbor, and love for our neighbor, also extends more widely than that—in fact it rises as the number of people increases.

Surely everyone understands that loving many people in a group involves more love for our neighbor than loving an individual member of that group. Therefore smaller and larger communities are also our neighbor, because they are a plurality of people. It follows that someone who loves a community loves the individuals who are part of that community; someone who wishes a community well and gives benefit to it cares for its individuals.

A community is like a person. In fact, the people who make up the community form a single body, in a sense. They are differentiated from each other like the parts of a single body. When the Lord looks at the earth, he sees an entire community as an individual person; the form of that individual person is based on the qualities of the people in the community. The Lord gives this sight to angels as well. In fact, I have been allowed to see a community in heaven completely in the form of an individual person; the person had the same proportions as people in the world.

[2] Love for a community is a fuller form of love for our neighbor than love for a single individual. This is clear from the fact that high positions are given to people according to their previous leadership of large groups. They have a level of status according to the job they do. In the world, in fact, positions in a hierarchy are considered to be higher or lower based on how wide a governmental responsibility these positions have over other people. The monarch is the person who has the widest government of all. Each person gets pay, glory, and general admiration according to the scope of the position and also the useful functions performed.

[3] But in this day and age, leaders may be useful and care for a community and still not love their neighbor. They perform functions and show concern for the sake of the world or themselves in order to deserve, or look as if they deserve, promotion to higher positions. Although these people may not be identified as such in the world, they are identified as such in heaven. People who have performed useful services out of love for their neighbor are put in leadership positions over a heavenly community as well; there they have splendor and honor. Yet still they do not take that splendor or honor to heart, just the usefulness. The rest, however, who were useful because they loved the world or themselves, are rejected.

Feeling love for our neighbor and acting on that love on an individual basis is one thing. Doing so on a plural or community basis is another. The difference between them is like the difference between the role of a citizen, the role of an official, and the role of a leader. It is also

413

like the difference between the person who traded with two talents and the person who traded with ten (Matthew 25:14–30).[631] It is like the difference between the value of a shekel and the value of a talent.[632] It is like the difference between the product of a grapevine and that of a whole vineyard, the product of an olive tree and that of an olive plantation, the product of a single tree and that of a whole fruit garden. Love for our neighbor also rises higher and higher within us, and as it rises, we love our community more than we love an individual and we love our country more than we love our community.

Now, because goodwill consists of wanting what is best for others and being of benefit to them, it follows that it is to be practiced in very similar ways toward a community as toward an individual person. We are to treat a community of good people differently than we treat a community of evil people. With the latter group, goodwill is to be practiced according to earthly impartiality; toward the former group, according to spiritual impartiality. But I will say more on these two kinds of impartiality elsewhere.[633]

414 Our country is our neighbor more than our community is, because our country consists of many communities. Love for our country is therefore broader and higher. Loving our country is also loving the well-being of the general public.

Our country is our neighbor because it is like a parent. We were born in it. It has nourished us and continues to nourish us. It has kept us safe from harm and continues to do so.

We are to do good to our country with love according to what it needs. Some of its needs are earthly and some are spiritual. Its earthly needs center on its civic life and order. Its spiritual needs center on its spiritual life and order.

We are to love our country not merely as much as we love ourselves; we are to love it more. There is a law written on the human heart that gives rise to the statement all just people say when they are in imminent danger of dying because of an enemy or some other cause. They say that it is a noble thing to die for their country.[634] They say that it is a glorious thing for soldiers to shed their blood for their country. They say this because that is how much one ought to love one's country.

It is important to know that if people love their country and benefit it because they wish it well, they love the Lord's kingdom after death. The Lord's kingdom is their country at that point. And those who love the Lord's kingdom love the Lord, since the Lord is everything to all his kingdom.

On an Even Higher Level, the Neighbor We Are to Love Is the Church, and on the Highest Level, Our Neighbor Is the Lord's Kingdom

We are born for eternal life and are introduced into it by the church. **415** Therefore we are to love the church as our neighbor on an even higher level [than we love our country]. The church teaches us the means that lead to eternal life and introduces us into that life. It leads us to eternal life by means of the true things in its body of teaching. It introduces us to that life through good ways to live.

This does not mean that we are to love the priesthood to a special degree or love the church on the priesthood's account. We are to love the church's goodness and truth, and love the priesthood on account of this goodness and truth. The priesthood only serves; it is to be honored according to its service.

We are to love the church as our neighbor on a higher level, even beyond our country, because our country initiates us into civic life but the church initiates us into spiritual life. Spiritual life is what sets us apart from a merely animal life.

What is more, our civic life is temporary. It comes to an end. Once it is over, it is the same as if it had not existed. Our spiritual life, on the other hand, is eternal, because it has no end. Spiritual life has a quality of reality therefore that civic life does not have. The difference between them is like the difference between what is finite and what is infinite— there is no ratio between them. Eternity is an infinity of time.

The Lord's kingdom is the neighbor to which we are to give the high- **416** est level of our love, because the Lord's kingdom means the church across the entire world, also known as "the communion of saints."[635] It includes heaven as well.

People who love the Lord's kingdom love all in the whole world who acknowledge the Lord, have faith in him, and have goodwill toward their neighbor; they also love all who are in heaven. People who love the Lord's kingdom love the Lord above all else. They have more love for God than others do. This is because the church in the heavens and on earth is the Lord's body. They are in the Lord and the Lord is in them. Loving the Lord's kingdom, then, is fully loving their neighbor. People who love the Lord's kingdom not only love the Lord above all else; they also love their neighbor as themselves. Love for the Lord is a universal love. It affects every aspect of spiritual life and also every aspect of earthly life. This is because love for the Lord dwells in the highest reaches of us, and things at the top flow into things lower down and bring them to life in the same way that our will flows into all our intentions and actions, and our intellect flows into all our thoughts and conversations. Therefore the Lord says,

> Seek first the kingdom of the heavens[636] and its justice. Then all these things will be added to you. (Matthew 6:33)

The kingdom of the heavens is the Lord's kingdom, as the following passage in Daniel shows:

> Behold, there was someone coming with the clouds of heaven—someone like *the Son of Humankind.* He was given dominion, glory, and a kingdom. All people, nations, and tongues will worship him. His dominion is a dominion of an age that will not pass and his kingdom is one that will not perish. (Daniel 7:13, 14)

Loving Our Neighbor Is Not in Fact Loving the Person but Loving the Goodness That Is inside the Person

417 Surely everyone knows that people are not people because they have a human face and body—they are people because they have wisdom in their intellect and goodness in their will. The higher the quality of this wisdom and goodness, the more human the people are.

When people are born they are more brutish than any animal. They become human through being instructed. If they are responsive to the instruction, a mind forms within them. People are human because of their mind, depending on its particular nature.

There are animals that have faces that are close to human, but they have no faculty for higher understanding or for taking any action on the basis of that understanding. They act on an instinct that is activated by their earthly love. One difference between animals and people is that animals express in sound the feelings belonging to their love, while people speak their feelings as transferred into thought. Animals turn their faces downward and look at the ground, while people look at the sky in all directions, their faces lifted up.

From these points we can draw the following conclusion: the more we base what we say on sound reasoning and the more we focus on the time we will spend in heaven, the more human we are. Conversely, the more we base what we say on twisted reasoning and focus only on the time we are to spend in the world, the less human we are. In the latter case, we are still human, but only potentially rather than actually, since all people have the power to understand things that are true and to intend actions that are good. Even if we have no intention of doing what is good or understanding what is true, we nonetheless retain the ability to ape and mimic human qualities on the outside.

The reason goodness is our neighbor is that goodness belongs to our will and the will is the underlying reality of our life. Truth is our neighbor, too, but only to the extent that it emanates from something good in our will. Goodness that belongs to the will takes shape in our intellect and visibly presents itself there in the light of reason. **418**

All our experience shows that goodness is our neighbor. We love people for the quality of their will and intellect, that is, the goodness and justness in them. For example, we love monarchs, princes, generals, officials, consuls, civic leaders, and judges for the judgment they show in their words and actions. We love church leaders, ministers, and their assistants for their knowledge, integrity of life, and passion for the well-being of souls. We love army generals and commanders under them for their fortitude and prudence. We love retailers for their honesty. We love workers and servants for their faithfulness. For that matter, we love a given species of tree for its fruit; the soil for its level of fertility; a stone for its preciousness; and so on.

Strange as it may seem, it is not just honest people who love goodness and justness in others. Dishonest people do too, because they do not fear losing reputation, respect, or wealth at the hands of honest people. The love that dishonest people have for goodness is not love for their neighbor, however—dishonest people do not inwardly love any others outside themselves unless those others serve them somehow.

Loving goodness in another person from goodness in ourselves is genuine love for our neighbor. In that situation the two goodnesses embrace and form a partnership.

People who love what is good because it is good and love what is true because it is true have supreme love for their neighbor, because they love the Lord who is goodness itself and truth itself. Love for goodness, love for **419** truth, and love for our neighbor come from nowhere else. Love for our neighbor, then, has a heavenly origin.

It is the same thing whether you say "goodness" or "usefulness." Therefore doing good things is doing useful things. The amount and quality of usefulness that a given good thing has determines the amount and quality of its goodness.

Goodwill and Good Actions Are Two Distinct Things: Wishing People Well and Treating Them Well

420 All people have an inner level and an outer level. Their inner level is called the inner self and their outer level is called the outer self. Nevertheless, someone who does not know what the inner and outer selves are could believe that our inner self is the source of our thinking and willing and our outer self is the source of our speaking and action. These are indeed inner and outer aspects of us, but they do not constitute the essence of our inner and outer selves. The human mind is indeed commonly held to be the inner self, but in actuality the mind is divided into two regions. One of the regions is spiritual; it is higher and farther within.[637] The other is earthly; it is lower and farther outside. Our spiritual mind focuses principally on the spiritual world. It deals with the things in that world, whether they are the kind that exist in heaven or the kind that exist in hell. (Both kinds are in the spiritual world.) The earthly mind, on the other hand, focuses principally on the earthly realm. It deals with the things in this world, whether good or evil.

All our action and speaking emanates from the lower region of our mind through a direct route. Ultimately, however, it comes from the higher region of our mind, although the route is indirect because the lower region is closer to the senses in our body, while the higher region is farther away from them. This division within our mind exists because we have been created to be spiritual and earthly at the same time, and therefore to be human, not animal.

These points make it clear that people who focus primarily on themselves and worldly things are external people. They are earthly not only in body but also in mind. People who focus primarily on things that relate to heaven and the church are internal people. They are spiritual in both mind and body. They are spiritual in body as well because their actions and words come from their higher mind, which is spiritual, through their lower mind, which is earthly. (As people generally know, effects come from our body, while the causes that produce those effects come from our mind; the cause shapes every aspect of the effect.)

It is obvious that the human mind has been divided in this way from the fact that people are able to pretend, to flatter, to be hypocritical, or to playact. They can agree with what someone else is saying and nevertheless view it as ridiculous. They do the former in their lower mind, the latter in their higher one.

These things enable us to see how we are to understand the statement that goodwill and good works are two distinct things: wishing people well and treating them well. That is, they are formally distinct, like the mind that does the thinking and willing and the body through which the mind speaks and acts. In fact, they are essentially[638] distinct as well, because the mind itself is divided into an inner region that is spiritual and an outer region that is earthly, as I said just above.

Therefore if the things we do come from our spiritual mind, they come from wishing others well, or goodwill. If, however, they come only from our earthly mind, they come from a form of wishing others well that is not genuine goodwill. It can appear to be goodwill in its outer form and yet not be genuine goodwill in its inner form. Goodwill that exists in an outer form alone does indeed present the look of goodwill, but lacks its essence.

This point could be illustrated by an analogy with seeds in the ground. Every type of seed gives rise to a shoot, but those shoots are either useful or useless, depending on their species. The same is true for spiritual seed, that is, for truth in the church that comes from the Word. A body of teaching grows out of this truth—a useful body of teaching if it is made out of genuine truths, a useless one if it is made out of truths that have been falsified. The same thing applies to goodwill that is exercised as the result of wishing our neighbors well, whether we wish them well for our own sake or for a worldly reason or for the sake of our neighbor in a narrower or a broader sense. If we wish our neighbors well for our own sake or for a worldly reason, our goodwill is not genuine. If we wish our neighbors well for their sake, our goodwill is genuine. See many statements that address these topics in the chapter on faith, especially in the discussion showing that "goodwill" is benevolence toward others; that "good works" are good actions that result from benevolence (§374); and that goodwill and faith are transient and exist only in our minds unless,

421

when an opportunity occurs, they culminate in actions and become embodied in them (§§375–376).

Goodwill Itself Is Acting Justly and Faithfully in Our Position and Our Work and with the People with Whom We Interact

422 Goodwill itself is acting justly and faithfully in our position and our work, because all the things we do in this way are useful to the community; and usefulness is goodness, and goodness in an impersonal sense is our neighbor. As I have shown above [§§412–414], our neighbor is not only individual people but also our community and the country as a whole.

For example, if monarchs lead the way for their subjects by setting an example of doing good, if they want their people to live by the laws of justice, if they reward people who live that way, if they give all people the consideration they deserve, if they keep their people safe from harm and invasion, if they act like parents to their countries, and take care for the general prosperity of their people—these monarchs have goodwill in their hearts. The things they do are good actions.

Priests who teach truths from the Word and use truths to lead to a goodness of life, and therefore to heaven, are practicing goodwill in very important ways, because they are caring for the souls of the people in their church.

Judges who make decisions on the basis of justice and the law, and not because of bribery or because someone is their friend or relative, are caring for the community and for the individual—for the community, because their decisions influence it to stay obedient to the law and fearful of breaking it, and for the individual, because their decisions allow justice to triumph over injustice.

Business people who act with honesty and without fraudulence are caring for the neighbor they do business with. So are workers and craftspeople when they do their work uprightly and honestly rather than falsely or deceptively. The same goes for everyone else—for ship captains and sailors, for farm workers and servants.

423 This is goodwill itself because it can be defined as follows: goodwill is doing good to our neighbor daily and constantly—not only to our neighbor as an individual but also to our neighbor collectively. The only way to do this is through practicing goodness and justice in our position and work and with the people with whom we have any interaction, because these are things we do every day. When we are not doing them, they still stay in our minds all the time; we think about them and intend to do them.

People who practice goodwill in this way become better and better forms of goodwill. Justice and faithfulness shape their minds and the practice of goodwill shapes their bodies. Over time, because of their form, they get to the point where everything they want and think about relates to goodwill. In the long run, they become like the people mentioned in the Word who have the law written on their hearts [Jeremiah 31:33]. Such people also take no credit for what they are doing since they are not thinking about receiving credit for it; they are thinking about their duty. In their view, acting this way is the right thing for citizens to do.

Nevertheless, we are completely incapable of acting on the basis of spiritual justice and faithfulness *on our own.* We all inherit from our parents the trait of doing what is good and just for our own sake or for worldly reasons. None of us hereditarily does these things for the sake of goodness and justice. Therefore only when people worship the Lord, and function from the Lord while they seem to be functioning on their own, do they attain spiritual goodwill and become saturated with it as the result of constant practice.

Many people behave justly and faithfully in their jobs, and yet although they are doing works of goodwill in this way, they still have no goodwill in themselves. Their love for themselves and for the world is in control rather than love for heaven. If love for heaven happens to be present at all, it is under their other loves like a slave under a master, like a foot soldier under a commander, like a doorkeeper standing by the door.

424

Acts of Kindness Related to Goodwill
Consist in Giving to the Poor and Helping the Needy,
Although with Prudence

It is important to distinguish between work-related acts of goodwill and incidental acts of kindness. "Work-related acts of goodwill" means those practices of goodwill that come straight from goodwill itself, since goodwill itself is a function of the work that we do, as I have shown just

425

above. "Acts of kindness," however, refers to helpful acts that are done outside of our work.

They are called acts of kindness because we are free to do them as we please, and when we do them, the recipients see them as kindnesses and nothing else. We do them according to the reasons and intentions we have in mind as benefactors.

It is a common belief that goodwill consists solely of giving to the poor, helping the needy, caring for widows and orphans, and making contributions to build, enhance, and endow hospices, hospitals, hostels, orphanages, and especially church buildings. Many of these actions, however, are not integral to the exercise of goodwill; they are extraneous to it.

People who consider goodwill to be good deeds of these kinds cannot help taking credit for them. Although people may claim aloud that they do not want any credit for their good deeds, nevertheless inside them lies the belief that they deserve credit. This is perfectly obvious after death when people like this list the things they have done and demand salvation as their reward. They are then investigated to find out what origin their actions had and what quality their actions possessed as a result. Whatever origin the actions had—whether they came from arrogance, or from a hunger for fame, or from a wish to be seen as generous, or from a desire to win friends, or from some merely earthly tendency, or from hypocrisy— they are judged on the basis of that origin, because the quality of the origin lies within the actions. Genuine goodwill, however, emanates from people who have become steeped in it through doing work based on justice and judgment without the goal of being repaid, in accordance with the Lord's words (Luke 14:12, 13, 14). People of genuine goodwill refer to the donations listed just above [not as goodwill itself but] as acts of kindness and also duties, although they are related to goodwill.

426   As is generally recognized, there are people who do acts of kindness that seem to the world like the very picture of goodwill, with the result that these people believe they have performed acts of genuine goodwill. They look at their own acts of kindness the way many Catholics look at indulgences[639] that have absolved them of their sins. They believe heaven ought to be granted to them since they are regenerated as a consequence; yet in fact they do not consider acts of adultery, hatred, revenge, fraud, or fleshly craving of whatever kind to be sinful. They indulge in such acts whenever they like.[640] But in that case, their good actions are like paintings of angels and devils at a party together, or like boxes made of lapis lazuli that have poisonous snakes inside them. It is completely different if people do the same acts of kindness but abstain from the evils just listed because these evils are the enemies of goodwill.

Nevertheless, doing kindnesses is enriching in many ways—especially giving to the poor and to people who are begging. By acts like these, young men and women, male and female servants, and simple people of all kinds are initiated into the exercise of goodwill. These actions are outward habits that help the givers absorb the benefits of goodwill. They are the beginnings of goodwill; they are like fruit not yet ripened. For people who afterward develop proper concepts of goodwill and faith, these habits become like fruit fully ripe. People like this come to regard the things they used to do from simplicity of heart as things they are now obliged to do.

Nowadays, kindnesses like these are seen as the central acts of goodwill that are referred to in the Word as "good works." The reason for this is that many times in the Word goodwill is characterized as giving to the poor, helping the needy, and taking care of widows and orphans. Up until now people have not known that the letter of the Word mentions only things that are external and are in fact the outermost aspects of worship; people have not realized that these external things have meanings that are spiritual and internal. On this last point, see the chapter above on Sacred Scripture (§§193–209). Those passages make it clear that mentions of the poor, needy, widows, and orphans in the Word do not [literally] refer to such people; they refer to people who are spiritually poor, needy, widowed, or orphaned. For "the poor" meaning people who have no concepts of goodness or truth, see *Revelation Unveiled* 209. For "widows" meaning people who have been separated from truths and yet long for them, see §764 there; and so on.

People who are born compassionate and yet do not make their earthly acts of compassion spiritual by doing them out of genuine goodwill tend to believe that goodwill is giving to any poor person and helping any needy person without first finding out whether the poor or needy person is good or evil. They say this is not necessary, because God notices only the helpful gesture and the act of mercy. After death, however, people like this are identified and completely separated from people who have done prudent kindnesses related to goodwill. The people who have done kindnesses based on a blind idea of goodwill do just as many kindnesses for the evil as for the good. The evil use the kindnesses to do evil things and harm good people. In that case the benefactors share the responsibility for harming good people.

Doing an act of kindness for an evildoer is like giving bread to a devil; the devil will turn it into poison. All bread that is in the hand of a devil is poison. If it is not, the devil will turn it into poison by diverting the act of kindness to an evil purpose.

It is as if you handed your enemy a sword, and the enemy killed someone with it. It is as if you gave a shepherd's staff to a human wolf to bring the sheep into the pasture; yet the human wolf, staff in hand, drove the sheep away from the pasture into the wilderness and slaughtered them there. It is as if you gave leadership and control to a thief whose sole focus was keeping an eye out for things to steal; the thief would create rules and make decisions based primarily on the abundance and value of the loot.

There Are Obligations That Are Related to Goodwill. Some of Them Are Public; Some Relate to the Household; and Some Are Personal

429 Acts of kindness related to goodwill and obligations related to goodwill are distinguished from each other thus: The former belong to those things that we may or may not do of our own free choice and the latter to those that we must of necessity do. Nevertheless the obligations related to goodwill mentioned here do not mean the obligations connected with our job in our country or republic, such as the obligation a minister has to minister and the obligation a judge has to judge, and so on. They mean the obligations we all have regardless of the jobs we do. These have a different origin and flow from a different intention. These obligations are done with goodwill by people who have goodwill; they are done without goodwill by people who have none.

430 *Public obligations that are related to goodwill* are primarily the paying of taxes. These taxes are not to be confused with obligations connected with our jobs. Spiritual people pay their taxes with a different feeling at heart than people who are merely earthly. Spiritual people pay taxes in a spirit of goodwill, because the taxes are collected to preserve the country and protect both it and the church. The taxes also pay for administration by government officials whose salaries and stipends have to be paid out of the public treasury. Therefore people who hold their country and their church as their neighbor pay taxes uncoerced, of their own free will, and consider it wrong to cheat or avoid them. People who do not hold their country or church as their neighbor, on the other hand, perform their tax-paying obligations unwillingly and with resistance. As often as the opportunity arises, they cheat and conceal their assets, because the neighbor they focus on is their own household and their own skin.

Household obligations that are related to goodwill are a husband's obligations to his wife and a wife's obligations to her husband; also a father and mother's obligations to their children and the children's obligations to their father and mother; and the obligations of the male and female heads of a household to their male and female servants, and the obligations of the latter to them. Because these obligations have to do with child rearing and management of the estate, there are so many of them that a mere list would fill a large book. For all of us, what moves us to fulfill these obligations is a different love from the one that is operative in our work. A husband's obligation to his wife and a wife's obligation to her husband come from and depend on marriage love. A father and mother's obligations to their children come from a parental love that is instinctive in everyone. Children's obligations to their parents come from and depend on another love that is closely linked with obedience under obligation. The obligations male and female heads of a household have to their male and female servants come from a love of overseeing, which depends on each person's individual state of mind.

431

[2] Marriage love, however, and love for our children, along with the obligations and the fulfillment of the obligations involved in these loves, do not produce a love for our neighbor the way the fulfillment of our work-related obligations does. This is because instinctive parental love is just as present in evil people as in good people; in fact, it is sometimes stronger in evil people. It also exists in animals and birds, which could never attain goodwill. It is a known fact that bears, tigers, and snakes love their offspring as much as sheep and goats do; and owls love theirs as much as doves love theirs.

[3] As for parents' obligations to their children in specific, these obligations are inwardly different for people who have goodwill and people who do not, although the obligations look the same on the outside. For people who have goodwill, their love for their children is connected to their love for their neighbor and for God. They love their children for the children's manners, abilities, interests, and potential for serving the public. People who have no goodwill, on the other hand, have an instinctive parental love that is disconnected from goodwill. Many of them love their children even more if the children are evil, poorly behaved, and

deceitful than if they are good, well behaved, and careful; such parents love children who are useless to the public more than children who are useful to it.

432   There are also many *personal obligations related to goodwill,* such as paying workers, paying interest on loans, honoring agreements, taking care of deposited valuables, and other things like that. Some of these obligations fall under criminal law, some fall under domestic law, and some fall under moral law. In the case of these obligations, too, people who have goodwill and people who do not, differ in their mindsets. People who have goodwill fulfill these obligations justly and faithfully because it is a principle of goodwill that people should act justly and faithfully toward everyone with whom they have any business or interaction (see §§422 and following above). The same obligations are fulfilled quite differently by people who have no goodwill.

The Recreations Related to Goodwill Are Lunches, Dinners, and Parties

433   As we all know, social lunches and dinners are customary everywhere. They are planned for various reasons. For many people they serve to build friendship or promote family togetherness; they serve for enjoyment, for fundraising, and for showing gratitude. They are also a corrupting influence used for persuading people to join some faction. Those in power use them to build their own reputations. Courts of monarchs use them to put on a magnificent display.

The only lunches and dinners that relate to goodwill, however, are those that involve people who love each other because they share a common faith. In early times, Christians used to have social lunches and dinners for exactly this purpose. Called feasts, they were instituted to lift and unite Christians' hearts and spirits.[641] The *dinners* they held stood for the associations and connections people formed when the church was first being established, because the evening when the dinners would occur has that meaning. The *lunches* they held, however, stood for people coming together in the second phase of the church's establishment, because that is what morning and daytime mean.

While they were at the table, they would have conversations on various subjects—both domestic and civic issues. In particular, they would discuss topics related to the church. Because the events were feasts of goodwill, the conversations would entail goodwill and its forms of joy and happiness. The spiritual atmosphere that prevailed during these feasts was an atmosphere of love for the Lord and for their neighbor. This atmosphere would lift their individual minds, soften their tones of voice, and allow a celebratory feeling from deep in their hearts to fill their senses.

We all have a spiritual atmosphere that emanates from the feelings derived from our love, and from the thinking prompted by those feelings. This atmosphere deeply affects other people, especially during feasts. It emanates from people's faces and their breathing.

The fact that lunches and dinners, or feasts, stood for such meetings of the mind is the reason they are named so many times in the Word. In the spiritual meaning this is exactly what these meals stood for. In the supreme sense this is what the Passover dinner among the children of Israel stood for; the same is true of the banquets during other Jewish festivals, as well as the meals from the sacrifices next to the tabernacle.[642] In those instances, the bond between people was represented by breaking bread and sharing it, and by drinking from the same cup, which people passed around among them.

As for *parties,* there were some that were held in the early church by people who referred to themselves as a "family in Christ." These were parties that related to goodwill, because the people felt a spiritual kinship. These parties were also a source of comfort during times of adversity in the church; they were celebrations of the church's growth; and they served as a rest for the soul from study and work, and a chance to have conversations on different topics. Because these parties flowed from spiritual love as their source, they were rational and moral with a spiritual origin.

434

Today friends have parties. The goal these events focus on is to have fun talking and to enjoy stimulating conversation. This leads to an expansion of mind, a liberation from limited thinking, a rejuvenation of the bodily senses, and a restoration to wholeness.

Parties related to goodwill do not yet exist, however, for the Lord says that at the close of the age, meaning the end of the church,

Injustice will increase and goodwill will grow cold. (Matthew 24:12)

The reason is that the church has not yet acknowledged the Lord God the Savior as the God of heaven and earth, and has not yet gone to him directly as the only source from which genuine goodwill emanates and flows.

Parties, however, where there is no friendship emulating goodwill to bring minds together are nothing but a pretense of friendship, a false witness to love for others, a seductive ploy to place others under obligation, and an indulgence in physical pleasures, especially sensory ones. People get carried away by these parties the way a ship gets carried away by its sails and a strong current; flatterers and hypocrites stand at the helm with the tiller in their hands.

The First Step toward Goodwill Is Removing Evils; the Second Step Is Doing Good Things That Are Useful to Our Neighbor

435 Among teachings on goodwill the following point is primary: the first step toward goodwill is not to do evil to our neighbor. A secondary point is to do good to our neighbor. This is like a doorway to the teachings on goodwill.

As people generally know, evil dwells in the will of every human being from birth. Because all evil targets someone nearby or far away, including the wider community and the country, it follows that hereditary evil is evil against our neighbor on every scale.

On the basis of reason itself we can all see that the less we remove the evil that dwells in our will, the more the good we do is pregnant with that evil, because then evil exists inside the goodness like a kernel in a shell or the marrow in a bone. Therefore although good things that someone does in that state appear to be good, they are nevertheless not good inside. They are like a shiny shell containing a nut that has been consumed by worms. They are like a white almond that has rottenness inside it, so that rotten streaks have crept up to the surface.

[2] Intending evil and doing good are two things that are intrinsically opposite to each other. Evil comes from hatred for our neighbor and good comes from love for our neighbor. Or to put it another way, evil is an enemy to our neighbor and goodness is our neighbor's friend. The two cannot exist in a single mind, that is, there cannot be evil in our inner self and goodness in our outer self. If there were, the goodness on the outside would be like a wound that has been superficially treated, beneath which there lies the pus of an infection.[643] We ourselves would then be like a tree whose roots are unsound; it produces pieces of fruit that outwardly look tasty and beneficial, although inwardly they are rotten and useless. Our good deeds would also be like pieces of rejected slag,

superficially polished and beautifully colored, which are offered for sale as precious stones. Briefly put, these good deeds would be like the eggs of an owl mistaken for the eggs of a dove.

[3] It is important to know that the good things people accomplish with the body come from the spirit or the inner self. The inner self is their spirit, which lives after death. Therefore when [evil] people cast away the body that formed their outer self, they are made up of nothing but their own evils. They enjoy these evils and steer away from goodness as a threat to the way they live.

[4] The Lord teaches in many passages that we cannot do good things that are intrinsically good before evil has been removed from us:

> Do people gather grapes from thornbushes or figs from thistles? A rotten tree cannot produce good fruit. (Matthew 7:16, 17, 18)

> Woe to you, scribes and Pharisees. You clean the outside of the cup and the plate, but the insides are full of plundering and self-indulgence. Blind Pharisee, first clean the inside of the cup and the plate, so that the outside may become clean as well. (Matthew 23:25, 26)

And in Isaiah,

> Wash yourselves. Remove the evil of your actions. Stop doing evil. Learn to do what is good; seek [good] judgment. Then if your sins had been like scarlet, they will become as white as snow. If they had been red as crimson, they will be like wool. (Isaiah 1:16, 17, 18)

This point can be illustrated further by analogies:[644] Suppose someone keeps a leopard and a panther in an apartment and, as the one who feeds them, is able to live safely with them. No one else can visit unless their owner first removes these wild animals. Guests invited to the table of the king and queen would not forget to wash their faces and hands before attending. Anyone must first purify ore with fire and remove slag before getting pure gold or silver. Everyone separates the tares or weeds from the harvested wheat before taking it into the barn. Everyone cooks some of the juice out of raw meat before it becomes edible and is set on the table. Everyone knocks the grubs and caterpillars off the leaves of a tree in the garden to prevent them from devouring the leaves and causing a loss of fruit. Does any man love a young woman and propose to marry her if she is riddled with malignancies or covered all over with pustules and varicose veins, no matter how much she puts makeup

436

on her face, wears gorgeous clothing, and makes an effort to be attractive by saying nice things and paying compliments?

The need for us to purify ourselves from evils, and not to wait for the Lord to do it without our participation, is like a servant coming in with his face and clothes covered in soot or dung, approaching his master and saying, "Lord, wash me." Surely his master would tell him, "You foolish servant! What are you saying? Look, there is the water, the soap, and a towel. Don't you have hands? Don't they work? Wash yourself!"

The Lord God is going to say, "The means of being purified come from me. Your willingness and power come from me. Therefore use these gifts and endowments of mine as your own and you will be purified."

437   There is a belief nowadays that goodwill is just our doing good, and if we do that, we are not doing evil. The idea therefore is that the first step toward goodwill is to do good and the second step is not to do evil. This is completely upside-down, however. The first step toward goodwill is to remove evils and the second step is to do good, because there is a law that is universal to the spiritual world and also therefore to the physical world: The less evil we intend, the more good we intend. Therefore the more we turn away from hell (from which all evil ascends), the more we turn toward heaven (from which all goodness descends). The more we reject the Devil, then, the more we are accepted by the Lord. People cannot stand between the Devil and the Lord with a flexible neck and pray at the same time to each of them. People like this are those whom the Lord meant when he said,

> I know your works, that you are neither cold nor hot. It would have been better if you were cold or hot; but since you are lukewarm and neither cold nor hot I am about to spew you out my mouth. (Revelation 3:15, 16)

Could anyone leading a troop of soldiers join a battle between two armies and fight on both sides at once? Can we focus on doing evil to our neighbors and also doing good to them? Would our evil not then lie hidden inside our good actions? Although evil that conceals itself does not appear in our actions, it is still obvious from many things when we reflect on it in the right way. The Lord says, "No servant can serve two masters. You cannot serve God and Mammon"[645] (Luke 16:13).

438   Still, none of us can purify ourselves from evils by our own power and our own force. On the other hand, neither can we purify ourselves without having power and force as if they were our own. If we did not

have apparent power, none of us could fight against the flesh and its cravings, although we have all been ordered to do so. In fact, we could not even think about battling them. We would let our mind go into evils of every kind. We would be held back from actually doing evils only by the laws of justice that have been passed in the world and the penalties they prescribe. Inside we would be like tigers, leopards, or snakes that utterly fail to reflect on the cruelty that their hearts enjoy.

Clearly then, because we are rational in a way that animals are not, we have to resist evils using the powers and abilities the Lord gives us, although as far as we can tell, those powers and abilities appear to be our own. The Lord gives us all this illusion in order to regenerate us, attribute goodness to us, forge a partnership with us, and save us.

As Long as We Believe That Everything Good Comes from the Lord, We Do Not Take Credit for the Things We Do As We Practice Goodwill

It is damaging for us to take credit for things we do for the sake of our salvation. Hidden within our credit-taking there are evil attitudes of which we are unaware at the time: denial that God flows in and works in us; confidence in our own power in regard to salvation; faith in ourselves and not in God; [the delusion that] we justify and save ourselves by our own strength; contempt for divine grace and mercy; rejection of reformation and regeneration by divine means; and especially disregard for the merit and justice of the Lord God our Savior, which we then claim as our own. In our taking credit there is also a continual focus on our own reward and perception of it as our first and last goal, a stifling and an extinction of love for the Lord and love for our neighbor, and total ignorance and unawareness of the pleasure involved in heavenly love (which takes no credit), while all we feel is our love for ourselves.

People who put their own reward as the first priority and salvation as the second, and therefore seek salvation as a reward, turn the proper arrangement upside down. They drown their inner desires in self-absorption and physically pollute them with evils belonging to their flesh. For this reason, goodness that we do to earn merit looks to the angels like a rust-colored plant disease, while goodness that we do not do to earn merit looks a rich purplish-red.

The Lord teaches in Luke that we are not supposed to do good for the purpose of getting a reward:

> If you benefit people who benefit you, what grace do you have? Rather, love and benefit your enemies, and lend [to people] expecting nothing back. Then your reward will be large, and you will be children of the Highest, since he is kind to the ungrateful and the evil. (Luke 6:33–36)

It is also taught in John that we cannot do anything truly good except from the Lord:

> Live in me and I [shall live] in you. As a branch cannot bear fruit on its own unless it lives in the vine, neither can you unless you live in me, because without me you cannot do anything. (John 15:4, 5)

> We cannot receive anything unless it is given to us from heaven. (John 3:27)

440   On the other hand, if people think about going to heaven and decide that they should therefore do what is good, this is not the same as making rewards their main goal or taking credit for their good deeds. People who love their neighbor as themselves and love God above all else have these thoughts because they have faith in the Lord's words that their reward will be great in heaven (Matthew 5:11, 12; 6:1; 10:41, 42; Luke 6:23, 35; 14:12, 13, 14; John 4:36); that people who do good things are going to possess as an inheritance a kingdom prepared since the founding of the world (Matthew 25:34); and that all are paid back for what they have done (Matthew 16:27; John 5:29; Revelation 14:13; 20:12, 13; Jeremiah 25:14; 32:19; Hosea 4:9; Zechariah 1:6; and elsewhere). What these people have is not confidence in a reward because they deserve it; they have faith in the promise of grace.

The pleasure of doing good to their neighbor *is* their reward. The angels in heaven feel this pleasure. It is a spiritual pleasure that is eternal. It immeasurably surpasses every earthly pleasure. People who have this pleasure do not want to hear about getting credit—they love doing good and feel joy in it. It depresses them if someone thinks they are doing it to get something in return. They are like people who benefit their friends for friendship's sake; who benefit their siblings for their siblings' sake; who benefit their spouse and children for their spouse's and children's sake; who benefit their country for their country's sake—people whose actions are based on friendship and love. People who do these good things state with conviction that they did not do it for themselves; they did it for the others.

It is completely different for people who focus on getting a reward as the primary goal of what they do. They are like those who strike up a friendship to get money; they give gifts, do favors, and profess their love as if it were heartfelt, but when they do not get what they were hoping for, they turn their backs, drop the friendship, and join up with the other's enemies and detractors.

They are like wet nurses who breastfeed babies only for the money. While the parents are looking, they kiss the babies and stroke them, but as soon as they are unsatisfied with the quality of the food they are given or do not get paid whatever they ask, they reject the babies, treat them roughly, beat them, and laugh at their crying.

[2] They are like people who focus on their country because they love themselves and the world. They say they intend the country's well-being and are devoting their lives to it, but if they do not receive promotions and wealth as rewards, they bad-mouth the country and become allies with its enemies.

They are like shepherds who take care of sheep only because of the money. If they do not get their money on time, they take their staffs and drive the sheep off the pasture into the wilderness. Priests who perform their duties only for the stipend involved are like these shepherds.[646] Clearly, they do not care at all about the salvation of the souls that are under their care and guidance.

[3] It is the same with government officials who focus only on the status and the income from their job. When they do something good, it is not for the public good but for the pleasure they take in loving themselves and the world, which they inhale as the only form of good.

The same sort of attitudes are possible in any line of work. The goal or purpose is the determining factor throughout. If the means employed in a given pursuit fail to achieve the goal, they are abandoned.

[4] People who are looking for the reward of salvation that they feel they deserve behave similarly. After death they demand heaven with tremendous confidence. Once it is discovered that they have no love for God or their neighbor, they are sent to teachers who instruct them about faith and goodwill. If they reject what they are taught, they are exiled to be with people like themselves, some of whom are enraged at God because they have not been given their rewards. They call faith a figment of the imagination.

These are the people who are meant in the Word by "hired workers," who were given extremely menial jobs in the entrances to the Temple.[647] From a distance [in the spiritual world] these people look as if they are splitting logs.

442 It is extremely important to realize that goodwill is closely linked to faith in the Lord. The quality of the faith determines the quality of the goodwill. For the point that the Lord, goodwill, and faith form a unity in the same way our life, our will, and our intellect form a unity, and that if we separate them, each one crumbles like a pearl that is crushed to powder, see §362 and following above. Also see the point that goodwill and faith come together in good actions, §§373–377. From those teachings it follows that the quality of our faith determines the quality of our goodwill; and the quality of our faith and goodwill combined determines the quality of our actions.

Now, if we believe that everything good that we do as if we are doing it on our own actually comes from the Lord, then we are the instrumental cause of that good and the Lord is its principal cause.[648] These two causes seem to us to be one thing, but in fact the principal cause affects every aspect of the instrumental cause. It follows then that if we believe that everything truly good comes from the Lord, we do not take credit for what we do. The more developed this faith becomes in us, the more the Lord takes away our fantasies about getting credit for what we have done. In this state we can practice goodwill abundantly without a fear of taking credit. Eventually we sense the spiritual pleasure in goodwill. Then we become averse to taking credit because doing so is damaging to our life.

It is easy for the Lord to erase people's idea that they deserve credit, provided those people attain goodwill primarily through working justly and faithfully in the position, business, or line of work they are in and with the people with whom they interact (see §§422, 423, 424 above). If, however, people believe that they attain goodwill through making charitable donations and helping the needy, it is difficult to rid them of the idea that they deserve credit, because as they make those contributions their desire for reward and credit, although obvious to them at first, becomes less noticeable [to them] as time goes by.

A Life of Goodwill Is a Moral Life That Is Also Spiritual

443 We all learn from our parents and teachers to live a moral life, that is, to behave like civil human beings. We learn to discharge the duties of an honorable life, which are related to the various virtues that constitute the essence of being honorable. We also learn to discharge these dutiful acts through the outward forms called manners. As we advance in age, we learn to add the exercise of rationality, and we use that rationality to enhance the morality of our life.

The moral life in youths up to early adulthood is earthly. After that it becomes increasingly rational. People who reflect on the question can see that a moral life is the same thing as a life of goodwill, which is behaving well to our neighbor and regulating our life to keep it from being contaminated with evils (as follows from the points made above in §§435–438). Nevertheless, in the first phase of our lives, our moral life is a life of goodwill on the outermost level, that is, only in the outward, most superficial part of our life, but not deeper within it.

[2] There are four phases to our lives. We pass through them as we go from infancy to old age. The first phase is when our behavior follows other people's instructions. The second is when our behavior is our own, and our intellect restrains us. The third is when our will pushes our intellect and our intellect restrains our will. The fourth is when our behavior is deliberate and purposeful.

These phases of our lives are phases of the life of our spirit, however; they do not necessarily relate to our body. Our body can behave morally and speak rationally, and yet our spirit can intend and think things that are the opposite of morality and rationality. It is clear from pretenders, flatterers, liars, and hypocrites that this is the nature of our earthly self. Clearly, people like this have a dual mind—their mind can be divided into two parts that do not agree.

It is different for people who have benevolent intentions and think rational thoughts, and as a result do good things and speak rationally. These are the type of people meant by "the simple in spirit" in the Word. They are called simple because they are not dual.[649]

[3] These statements clarify the proper meaning of the outer self and the inner self; they show that we cannot conclude from other people's morality in their outer self that they have morality in their inner self. Their inner self could be turned in the opposite direction. It could be hiding the way a turtle hides its head in its shell or the way a snake hides its head in its coils. In that case their supposedly moral self is like a robber who spends time both in the city and in the woods; in the city the robber behaves like a moral person, but in the woods, like a thief.

It is completely different for people who are inwardly moral, whose spirit is moral, and who attained that nature by being regenerated by the Lord. Such people constitute the type meant by the phrase "spiritually moral."

444 When our moral life is also spiritual, it is a life of goodwill, because the practices involved in a moral life and in a life of goodwill are the same. Goodwill is wishing our neighbors well and therefore treating them well. This is also a moral way of life. The following statement by the Lord is a spiritual law:

> All things whatever that you want people to do for you, do likewise for them. This is the Law and the Prophets. (Matthew 7:12)

This same law is universally applicable to a moral life as well. But listing all the practices related to goodwill and comparing them with the practices related to a moral life would require many pages. Just take six commandments from the second tablet of the Ten Commandments for an illustration—it is clear to everyone that they are principles for a moral life. (As for their containing all aspects of loving our neighbor, see §§329, 330, and 331 above.)

The following statement in Paul makes it clear that goodwill fulfills all the commandments:

> Love each other, for those who love others have fulfilled the law. The commandments that you are not to commit adultery, you are not to kill, you are not to steal, you are not to bear false witness, you are not to covet, and anything else that has been commanded, are included in the following saying: "You are to love your neighbor as yourself." Goodwill does not do evil to its neighbor. Goodwill is the fullness of the law. (Romans 13:8, 9, 10)

People who think only with their outer selves cannot help being astounded that the seven commandments on the second tablet[650] were proclaimed by Jehovah on Mount Sinai in such a miraculous way, given that these same rules were legal principles of civic justice in all the countries on earth, including Egypt, where the children of Israel had just come from. No country can survive without these rules.

The reason why Jehovah proclaimed them, however, and wrote them with his own finger on tablets of stone was that they are rules not only for all civic communities and therefore rules for a moral earthly life, they are also rules for all heavenly communities and therefore rules for a moral spiritual life. Acting against these rules then is acting not only against other people but also against God.

445 If we could see what a moral life is in its essence, we would see that it is a life in accordance with human laws and divine laws at the same time.

Therefore people who live by both sets of laws as one law are truly moral and live a life of goodwill.

Anyone who wants to grasp the nature of goodwill is capable of doing so by looking at the nature of outward moral life. Just copy the outward moral life you have in civil interaction into your inner self so that your inner willing and thinking parallel the actions of your outer self, and you will see a model of goodwill.

A Bond of Love That We Form with Others without Considering Their Spiritual Nature Is Damaging after Death

A "bond of love" is an inner friendship in which we love not only other people's outer selves but also their inner selves without investigating what their inner selves or spirits are like. We should investigate this to see whether the feelings in their minds relate to loving their neighbor and loving God and are therefore compatible with angels in heaven or whether they relate to forms of love that go against their neighbor and God and are therefore compatible with devils. **446**

Many people form deep bonds of love like this, for a variety of reasons and purposes. This is different from friendship with someone's outer persona alone, which we develop for the sake of various physical and sensual pleasures and different types of social interaction. This second type of friendship can be formed with anyone, even with a jester who jokes around at a duke's table. I am calling this latter type of friendship simply "friendship" while the former type I am calling a "bond of love," because friendship is an earthly connection but love is a spiritual connection.

A bond of love like this is damaging after death, as we can see from the state of heaven, the state of hell, and the state of our spirit in relation to both. **447**

The state of heaven is that it has been divided into countless communities according to all the different feelings of love for what is good. Hell on the other hand has been divided according to all the different feelings of love for what is evil.

After we die and become spirits, we are immediately attached to the community that shares our dominant love, based on the way we lived in the world. This community is in heaven if love for God or for our neighbor was primary among all the things we love. We are assigned to a community of hell if love for ourselves or for the world was primary among all the things we love.

After we have entered the spiritual world—which happens as a result of our dying and our physical body being laid to rest in the grave—we next spend a while being prepared for the community to which we have been assigned. This preparation is a matter of our rejecting things we love that do not agree with our primary love. During this same period of time, people are separated from each other—friends are separated, followers are separated from their leaders, parents are separated from their offspring, and siblings are separated from each other. Then we all become deeply attached to people similar to ourselves with whom we are going to live a life that is both shared and is truly our own to eternity.

During the first part of this preparation people meet and talk in a friendly way as they had in the world. Little by little, however, they are separated from each other. It happens without their realizing it.

448 People who have forged a bond of love with each other in the world, however, cannot be separated in an orderly way (as other people are) to become part of a community that relates to their life. People with bonds of love are spiritually bonded in a deep way. They cannot be pulled apart, because they are like branches that have been grafted onto other branches. If one of them is inwardly in heaven but the other is inwardly in hell, they are stuck together much like a sheep that is tied to a wolf, a goose that is tied to a fox, or a dove that is tied to a hawk. The one who is inwardly in hell arouses hellish impulses in the one who is inwardly in heaven.

One among the many things that are recognized in heaven is that good people can be influenced to have evil impulses, but evil people cannot be influenced to have good impulses. (The reason is that we all have evil qualities from birth.) Good people who are stuck to evil people have their deeper levels closed off as a result, and both are pushed down into hell in pairs. There the good person suffers hardships. Finally, after a period of time she or he is released and then starts to prepare for heaven.

I have been allowed to see bonds like this, especially between siblings and relatives, but also between leaders and followers. Many had bonds of love with their admirers. The members of these pairings had opposite feelings and different natures. I saw some of them that looked like goats with leopards, kissing each other and swearing allegiance to their former friendship. Then I sensed that the good people were absorbing pleasure in evils. I saw the pairs holding hands and going into caves together. In the caves I observed herds of evil people hideous in form. To each other, though, the people there looked attractive because of the illusion they projected. After a little while, I heard the good people screaming in terror as if they were trapped. From the evil people, I heard rejoicing like that of enemies glorying over the spoils of war. I witnessed other horrible scenes as well.

I have heard that later the good members of these pairs, when they are released, are prepared for heaven through the steps of reformation, but they have more difficulty than others.

Something completely different happens to people who love what is good in another person—people who love the justice, judgment, honesty, or benevolence that comes from goodwill in the other person, and especially people who love the other person's faith in and love for the Lord. They love these qualities inside the other person independently of that person's outer qualities. Therefore if they do not find these same qualities inside the other person after death, they immediately withdraw from the friendship, and the Lord connects them to people who have a similar kind of goodness.

It might be worth saying that it is impossible for any of us to investigate the inner qualities of mind in people with whom we socialize and interact. But this type of investigation is not necessary provided we take care not to form bonds of love with just anyone. Outward friendship formed for the sake of various benefits does no harm.

449

There Are Such Things as Illegitimate Goodwill, Hypocritical Goodwill, and Dead Goodwill

Genuine, living goodwill does not exist unless it accompanies faith and unless both goodwill and faith jointly focus on the Lord. These three— the Lord, goodwill, and faith—are the three essential elements for salvation. When they are united, goodwill is goodwill, faith is faith, and the Lord is in them both and they are in the Lord (see §§363–367, 368–372 above). When these three elements are not united, goodwill is illegitimate, hypocritical, or dead.

From the time Christianity was first established, various heresies have arisen; some are still in existence today. Even these heresies have all recognized these three essential elements: God, goodwill, and faith. Without these three elements there is no religion.

450

As for goodwill in specific, it can be attached to any heretical faith—Socinian faith,[651] faith in one's own divine inspiration, Jewish faith, even idolatrous faiths. People in these faiths believe that they have goodwill since it looks the same in outward form; nevertheless, goodwill changes its quality depending on the faith it is attached or united to. (This point is clarified in the chapter on faith [§367].)

451 All goodwill that is not united to faith in the one God, who has a divine trinity inside, is *illegitimate*. Take for example the goodwill practiced by the modern-day church, which has faith in three persons of the same divinity in succession: the Father, the Son, and the Holy Spirit. This constitutes a faith in three persons, each of whom is a self-sufficient god, and thus it is a faith in three gods. Goodwill can be appended to this faith—its proponents have in fact done this—but goodwill can never become an integral part of it. Goodwill that is only appended to faith is merely earthly; it is not spiritual. Therefore it is an illegitimate goodwill.

The same applies to the goodwill in many other heresies: for example, the heresy of people who deny the existence of the divine Trinity and therefore turn to God the Father alone or the Holy Spirit alone, or turn to them both rather than to God the Savior. Goodwill cannot become integral to these people's faith. Whether goodwill becomes integral to those faiths or is merely attached to them, in either case the goodwill is illegitimate.

It is called illegitimate because it is like offspring from an unlawful affair, like Hagar's son by Abraham, who was thrown out of the house (Genesis 21:9 [and following]).

This kind of goodwill is like fruit that did not grow on a tree but was nailed there instead. It is like a carriage with horses that are attached to it only by the reins in the driver's hands; when the horses start to run, they pull the driver from his seat, leaving the carriage behind.

452 *Hypocritical* goodwill is what people have who in church or at home bow themselves down until their heads almost touch the floor before God, devoutly pour forth long prayers, wear holy expressions, kiss images of the cross and bones of the dead,[652] genuflect at graves, and mumble words of sacred veneration of God with their lips, but all the while they desire at heart to be worshiped themselves and intend to be adored as divinities.

They are like the people the Lord describes in the following words:

When you make charitable donations, do not sound a trumpet before you the way the hypocrites do in the synagogues and the streets in order to be glorified by people. If you pray, you are not to be like the hypocrites who love to pray standing in the synagogues and on the street corners so people can see them. (Matthew 6:2, 5)

Woe to you, scribes and Pharisees, hypocrites, because you close the kingdom of the heavens to people. For you yourselves do not go in, and you do not let others in who are trying to enter. Woe to you hypocrites, because you travel across sea and land to make one convert, and when you have made one, you make that convert two times more a child of hell than you are. Woe to you hypocrites, because you clean the outside of the cup and plate but the insides are full of plundering and self-indulgence. (Matthew 23:13, 15, 25)

Isaiah prophesied about you hypocrites correctly when he said, "This people honors me with its lips, but its heart is far from me." (Mark 7:6)

Woe to you hypocrites, because you are like invisible tombs that people do not know about as they walk over them. (Luke 11:44)

And other passages as well.

These people are like pieces of flesh without blood. They are like crows or parrots that have been taught to say the words of some Psalm. They are like birds that have been taught to sing the melody of some sacred hymn. The sound of their talking is like a hunter's birdcall.

Dead goodwill is what people have when their faith is dead. The nature of the faith determines the nature of the goodwill. (In the chapter on faith I showed that the two become one [§§336, 362–367].) It is clear from the Epistle of James (2:17, 20) that faith is dead in people who do no works.

Faith is also dead in people who do not believe in God but who do believe in people who are alive or dead, or who worship idols as being intrinsically holy, as non-Christians used to do. When people have this kind of faith, the religious offerings they make to miraculous statues (as they call them) for the sake of salvation, counting these donations as acts of goodwill, are no different than pieces of gold and silver put in the urns and coffins of the dead; in fact, these donations are like the morsels offered to Cerberus and the coin paid to Charon for passage to the Elysian fields.[653]

The goodwill that people have when they believe there is no God other than nature is not illegitimate, hypocritical, or dead. It is *nonexistent* because it is not attached to any faith. The term *goodwill* does not apply, because goodwill derives its quality from faith. From heaven's point of view, these people's goodwill is like bread made out of ashes, a cake made out of fish scales, or a piece of fruit made out of wax.

The Bond of Love between Evil People Is Actually a Deep Mutual Hatred

454 I showed above [§§401, 420] that we each have an inner level and an outer level and that our inner level is called our inner self and our outer level is called our outer self.

To those points I will add the following: Our inner self is in the spiritual world and our outer self is in the physical world. We have been created with this nature so that we can be associated with spirits and angels in their world and be able to think analytically as a result, and also so that we can be transferred from our world to the other world after we die.

"The spiritual world" means both heaven and hell. Since our inner self is present with spirits and angels in their world and our outer self is present with people, clearly we can be associated with spirits from hell and with angels from heaven. This faculty and ability differentiates us from animals.

The way we are in our inner self is the way we truly are. We are not necessarily the way we appear on the outside. Our inner self is our spirit. It acts through our outer level. The physical body that our spirit wears in the physical world is something added on so that we can reproduce and so that our inner self can be formed. Our inner self is formed in our physical body like a tree in the ground or a seed in a piece of fruit. (For a number of points about the inner and outer self see §401 above.)

455a [654] What evil people are like in their inner self and what good people are like in theirs can be seen from the following brief description of hell and heaven: Evil people's inner selves are connected with devils in hell. Good people's inner selves are connected with angels in heaven.

Because of the loves it has, hell enjoys the pleasures of all kinds of evil; that is, the pleasure in hatred, in revenge, in killing; the pleasure in looting and stealing; the pleasure in verbal abuse and blasphemy; the pleasure in denying God and desecrating the Word. These pleasures lie hidden in cravings on which we do not reflect. Evil people burn with these pleasures like torches on fire. The pleasures just listed are what the Word means by hellfire.

The pleasures in heaven, on the other hand, are the pleasure in loving our neighbor and the pleasure in loving God.

[2] Since hell's pleasures are opposite to heaven's, there is a huge gap between them. The pleasures of heaven flow down into this gap from above and the pleasures of hell flow up into it from below. While we are alive in the world we are in the middle of this gap so that we can stay in balance and in a state of freedom to turn ourselves toward heaven or toward hell. This gap is what is meant by the great gulf fixed between the people in heaven and those in hell (Luke 16:26).[655]

[3] These points show us the nature of the bond of love between evil people. In their outer selves, evil people simulate morality in order to expand their social network and explore where a potential exists for enjoying the pleasures that they love and that set their inner selves on fire. The only thing holding them back and limiting their actions is fear of the law and fear for their reputation and their life. Their friendship then is like a spider in a sugar bowl, a viper in a loaf of bread, a baby crocodile in a honey-cake, or a worm in spices.

[4] This is the nature of the friendship that evil people extend to anyone. The friendship between blatantly evil people, such as thieves, robbers, and pirates, is like family, as long as their minds have come together to target something to steal. During that time they kiss each other like kin and enjoy each other's company with dining, singing, dancing, and plotting someone else's ruin.

But in fact, deep inside themselves they all regard their companions as their enemies. Clever thieves see this enmity in their companions and are afraid of it. Clearly, then, there is no friendship between them; there is instead a deep hatred.

There are people who have not openly associated with evildoers or practiced a life of thievery, and who have instead lived a moral and civic life to gain various benefits; yet they have not bridled the cravings that dwell in their inner self. Such people are capable of believing that their own friendships are not like those I have been describing.

455b

Nevertheless, I know for a certainty that evil people have this type of friendship, because of the many examples I have observed in the spiritual world. It can be found to one degree or another in all people who reject faith and who scorn the church's holy practices as having no value for themselves, however much value they believe those practices may have for the general public. In some of these cases the enjoyment of hellish love lay hidden like fire smoldering in a dry log still covered by bark. In some cases it lay hidden like coals burning under the ashes. In some cases it lay hidden like wax torches that would readily burst into flame in the presence of fire. In other cases it was hidden in other ways.

This is the nature of all people who have rejected matters of religion from their heart. Their inner selves are in hell. As long as they are still alive in this world—unaware of their situation because of the morality they imitate on the outside—they do not recognize as their neighbor anyone but themselves and their own children. They look on others with either contempt (in which case they are like cats ready to ambush birds on the nest) or hatred (in which case they are like wolves who see dogs and devour them).

The point of including this was to make it possible to recognize the nature of goodwill through its opposite.

The Connection between Loving God and Loving Our Neighbor

456 People generally know that the law proclaimed on Mount Sinai was written on two tablets, one of which was about God and the other about humankind. People also know that in Moses' hand the two were a single tablet: the right-hand side contained writing concerning God, and the left-hand side contained writing concerning humankind, because if it was set before people's eyes in this way, the writing on both sides would be seen at once. Therefore the sides faced one another like Jehovah talking with Moses and Moses with Jehovah, face to face, as we read [Exodus 33:11; Deuteronomy 34:10].

The tablets were made in this way so that together they would represent God's connection to people and people's reciprocal connection to God. For this reason the law written there was called "the Covenant" and "the Testimony." The term "covenant" refers to the partnership and "testimony" refers to the life that follows the points agreed upon.

The union of the two tablets shows the connection between loving God and loving our neighbor. The first tablet covers all aspects of loving God; they are primarily that we should acknowledge one God, the divinity of his human manifestation, and the holiness of the Word; and that in worshiping him we are to use the holy things that come from him. (The fact that the first tablet covers the above is clear from the comments made in chapter 5 on the Ten Commandments [§§291–308].)

The second tablet covers all aspects of loving our neighbor. The first five of its commandments relate to our behavior, or what are called our "works." Its other two commandments relate to our will and to the origins of goodwill: they tell us that we should not covet what our neighbors have, and that by not doing so, we have their well-being in mind.

On the point that the Ten Commandments contain everything about how to love God and how to love our neighbor, see §§329, 330, and 331 above. That discussion also shows that in people who have goodwill the two tablets are connected.

It is different for people who only worship God but do not also perform good actions related to goodwill. These people are like covenant breakers. It is different again for people who divide God into three and worship each one separately. It is different again for people who go to God, but not in his human manifestation. These are the people "who do not enter through the door but instead climb up some other way" (John 10:1). It is different again for people who deny with conviction that the Lord is divine. All these types of people lack a connection to God and therefore lack salvation. The goodwill they have is illegitimate. This type of goodwill forms a connection that is not face to face but side to side or back to back.

[2] I will briefly explain how loving God and loving our neighbor are connected. With all of us, God flows into our concepts of him and brings us true acknowledgment of him. He also flows into us and brings us his love for people. If we accept only the first inflow but not the second, we receive that inflow with our intellect but not our will. We keep the concepts of God that we have without arriving at an inward acknowledgment of God. Our state is then like a garden in winter.

If we accept both types of inflow, however, we receive the inflow with our will and then our intellect—that is, with our whole mind. We then develop an inner acknowledgment of God that brings our concepts of God to life. Our state is then like a garden in spring.

[3] Goodwill makes the connection, because God loves every one of us but cannot directly benefit us; he can benefit us only indirectly through each other. For this reason he inspires us with his love, just as he inspires parents with love for their children. If we receive this love, we become connected to God and we love our neighbor out of love for God. Then we have love for God inside our love for our neighbor. Our love for God makes us willing and able to love our neighbor.

[4] We cannot do anything good if it does not seem to us that our power, willingness, and actions come from ourselves. Therefore we are

granted the appearance that they do. When we freely do something good as if we were acting on our own, this goodness is attributed to us and is taken as our response, and this forges the connection.

The situation here is like something active and something passive and the cooperation of the two that occurs when the passive element accepts the active one.

The situation is also like the intention present in people's actions, the thinking present in their speech, and the soul working from the inside on both the intention and the thinking. It is like the originating force that is present in a motion. It is like the prolific power present in the seed of a tree. That power acts from the inside on the various forms of sap that develop the tree all the way to the point of bearing fruit. Through the fruit the tree produces new seeds. It is also like the light in precious stones that is reflected depending on the textures of the interior. Different colors appear as a result, as if they were the stone's colors, but they are really the colors of the light.

458 These points clarify where the connection between loving God and loving our neighbor comes from and what it is like: God's love for people flows into us; when we receive that love and cooperate with it, it becomes love for our neighbor.

Briefly put, the connection accords with the following saying of the Lord's:

> On that day you will recognize that I am in my Father and you are in me and I am in you. (John 14:20)

And this saying:

> The people who love me are those who have my commandments and do them. I will love these people, manifest myself to them, and make a home with them. (John 14:21, 22, 23)

All the Lord's commandments relate to loving our neighbor. In summary form, they involve not doing evil to our neighbors, and instead doing them good. According to the Lord's words just quoted, people like this love God and God loves them.

Because love for God and love for our neighbor are connected in this way, John says:

> Those who keep the commandments of Jesus Christ live in him, and he lives in them. If any say, "I love God in every way," but hate their

brothers and sisters, they are liars. If they do not love their brothers and sisters, whom they see, how can they love God whom they do not see? This commandment we have from him: that people who love God also love their brothers and sisters. (1 John 3:24; 4:20, 21)

To these points I will add these memorable occurrences.

The first memorable occurrence. From far away I saw five halls.[656] They were surrounded with different kinds of light. The first hall was surrounded with a fiery light, the second with a yellow light, the third with a bright white light, the fourth with a light halfway between daylight and twilight. The fifth hall was scarcely visible, because it was standing in the shadow of evening.

On the roads I saw some people on horseback, some in carriages, some walking, and some running and hurrying. The people in a hurry were headed for the first hall, the one surrounded in fiery light. Upon my seeing all this, a longing to go there and hear what they were discussing took hold of me and urged me in that direction. I quickly got ready and joined the people hurrying to the first hall. I went in with them.

Just picture the huge crowd inside. Some of them were heading to the right and some to the left to sit on seats arranged along the walls. Near the front I saw a low platform. The man who was the chairperson for the event was standing on it with a staff in his hand, a hat on his head, and a coat that was dyed the color of the hall's fiery light.

[2] After people had gathered, he lifted up his voice and said, "Friends, today we are discussing what *goodwill* is. As each of you may know, goodwill is spiritual in essence and earthly in practice."

Immediately someone in the first row on the left side (the row where people with a reputation for being wise were seated) stood up and began to speak.

He said, "My opinion is this. *Goodwill is morality inspired by faith.*"

He supported his opinion in the following way: "Surely everyone knows that goodwill follows faith the way a female attendant follows her lady. Everyone knows that people who have faith are so spontaneously living the law, and therefore a life of goodwill, that they don't realize that the law and a life of goodwill are what they are living. If they realized this and then did it and were thinking they would be saved as a result,

459

they would pollute the sacred faith with their selfishness and cripple its effectiveness."

He said, "Doesn't this follow our dogma?" and looked at the people sitting at the sides, some of whom were clergy. They nodded. [3] "But is spontaneous goodwill," he continued, "anything other than the morality into which everyone is initiated from early childhood? This morality is intrinsically earthly, but it becomes spiritual when faith is the inspiration for it. Who else but God can tell from people's moral life whether they have faith or not—given that everyone lives morally? God alone, who infuses faith into us and seals it there, is able to recognize and tell the difference. Therefore I submit that goodwill is morality inspired by faith. Morality that comes from our faith is intrinsically effective for our salvation. Every other type of morality does not bring us salvation, because we practice it in order to earn merit. Therefore people who mix goodwill and faith all find themselves without lamp oil[657]—that is, people who connect goodwill and faith inwardly rather than attaching them together outwardly. Mixing and connecting goodwill and faith would be like a servant standing by the back seat of a carriage in order to get in beside a church leader. It would be like bringing a doorkeeper into the dining room to sit at the table next to a powerful, influential person."[658]

[4] Then someone from the first row on the right stood up and said, "My opinion is that *goodwill is religious devotion combined with compassion.* I support this opinion as follows: Nothing can appease God more than religious devotion from a humble heart. Religious devotion constantly asks God to give us faith and goodwill. The Lord says, 'Ask and it will be given to you' (Matthew 7:7). Therefore what we are given has both faith and goodwill in it.

"I say that goodwill is religious devotion combined with compassion, because all true religious devotion feels compassion. Religious devotion moves our heart to the point of groaning; and what is that groaning but compassion? The feeling does indeed pass after we are done praying, but it nevertheless returns when we pray again. And when it returns there is a religious quality to it, showing that we have goodwill.

"Now, anything that advances our salvation our priests attribute solely to faith and not to goodwill. What is left for us then except to ask for both faith and goodwill with religious devotion and fervent prayer?

"When I read the Word, all I could see was that faith and goodwill are the two means of being saved; but when I consulted the ministers in the church, I heard that faith is the only means and goodwill is nothing.

Then I saw myself as being at sea on a ship that was being tossed between two rocky outcroppings. Since I was afraid that the ship would be smashed, I climbed off into a rowboat and set forth. My rowboat is religious devotion—which, by the way, avails in every difficulty."

[5] After that person, someone from the second row on the right stood up and said, "My opinion is that *goodwill is doing good to everyone, whether honest or dishonest.* I support this opinion as follows: Goodwill is goodness of heart. A good heart has good intentions toward all, both the honest and the dishonest. The Lord said that we are to do good even to our enemies. So if you withhold your goodwill from someone, doesn't that part of your goodwill become no goodwill? Aren't you then like a person hopping along on one leg because the other leg has been amputated? A dishonest person is just as much of a person as an honest one is. From the perspective of goodwill, people are people. If someone is dishonest, what difference does that make to me?

"Goodwill is like the warmth of the sun. It gives life to animals both wild and tame. It treats wolves and sheep alike. It makes trees grow whether they are harmful or beneficial. It treats thorn bushes the same as grapevines."

At that point the speaker picked up a grape and said, "Goodwill is like this grape. Split it and what's inside will fall out." He split the grape and its contents fell out.

[6] After that statement someone from the second row on the left stood up and said, "My opinion is that *goodwill is doing all you can for your relatives and friends.* I support this opinion as follows: Surely everyone knows that goodwill begins from ourselves. We are each neighbor to ourselves. Our goodwill then moves outward from ourselves to the people closest to us—first our brothers and sisters, and then our other family members and relatives. Goodwill's progression has built-in limits then. People who are more remote than this are foreign to us. Deep inside ourselves, we don't recognize foreigners. They are alien to our inner selves. Siblings and blood relatives, however, are connected to us by nature. Friends are connected to us by familiarity, which is a second nature; therefore these too become our neighbor. Goodwill connects us to people on the inside and then on the outside. People who are not connected to us on the inside should be called only acquaintances of ours.

"All birds recognize their family members. They use sound rather than plumage to tell. At close range they also tell by the living aura emanating from the bodies of their family members. In birds this innate love and sense of connection is called an instinct. But we have the same thing. In relation to our loved ones this is truly an instinct of human nature.

"Does anything make for compatibility except blood? The human mind or spirit senses a blood relationship as if it could smell it. In this compatibility, and the harmonious feeling it generates, lies the essence of goodwill. On the other hand, incompatibility that causes antipathy is like having no blood relationship and therefore no goodwill.

"And because familiarity is a second nature and it too produces compatibility, it follows that goodwill is also doing good to our friends.

"If we have been at sea and then we dock at some port and hear that we have arrived in a foreign land whose language and customs we do not know, we feel out of tune with ourselves and have no enjoyable feeling of love for the local people. But if we hear that it is our own country, with a language and customs we know, we feel in tune with ourselves and have an enjoyable feeling of love, which is also the enjoyable feeling of goodwill."

[7] Then someone from the third row on the right stood up and said in a loud voice, "My opinion is that *goodwill is giving donations to the poor and helping the needy.* This is definitely goodwill, because the divine Word teaches that it is. What the Word declares allows for no contradiction.

"It is a pointless display to make donations to the rich and wealthy. There is no goodwill in it; instead the purpose is to be paid back. In it no genuine feeling of love for our neighbor is possible; it is an illegitimate feeling that may work on earth but does not work in heaven. Therefore poverty and need are to be the focus of our donations, because then the idea of a personal payback does not arise.

"In the city where I live, I know who the honorable and the dishonorable people are. I have observed that all the honorable people, when they notice a poor person in the street, stop and make a donation. All the dishonorable people, on the other hand, when they see a poor person off to the side, keep walking as if they were blind to the poor person and deaf to his or her voice. Everyone knows that the honorable have goodwill but the dishonorable do not.

"Someone who gives to the poor and helps the needy is like a shepherd who leads starving, thirsty sheep to something they can eat and drink. Someone who gives only to the rich and well-off is like someone who entertains the elite and presses food and wine on those who have had far too much already."

[8] After that, someone from the third row on the left stood up and said, "In my opinion, *goodwill is building hospices, hospitals, orphanages,*

and hostels, and maintaining them with donations. I support my opinion as follows: These forms of benefit and aid are public. They are leagues beyond private giving. In this case, goodwill becomes richer and more packed with an abundance of good things, and the reward we hope for on the basis of promises in the Word becomes enlarged—as we prepare and sow the field, so we reap. Isn't this a way of giving to the poor and helping the needy on a large scale? Who would not want glory from the world as a result, and also praises in the humble voices of the grateful people we have helped? Doesn't this lift our heart to its peak, and with it our feeling called goodwill?

"Rich people who ride instead of walking through the streets have no opportunity to turn their eyes toward the people sitting against the walls at the curbs and to hand them coins. Instead they make donations to places like these, which help many at once. Lesser people, however, who walk the streets and don't have these kinds of resources, do something else."

[9] Upon hearing this, someone from the same row suddenly drowned out this person's voice with an even louder tone and said, "Nevertheless, rich people shouldn't value the generosity and excellence of their goodwill more than a pittance that one poor person gives another, because we know that all who perform any action do so according to their role in society. A monarch does something worthy of a monarch, a commander something worthy of a commander, an officer something worthy of an officer, and an attendant something worthy of an attendant. Goodwill is not essentially measured by the excellence of one's role or of the gift itself, but by the fullness of feeling that led to it. Therefore a manual laborer who gives a single coin can be making a donation with more abundant goodwill than a ranking official who gives or wills an extensive collection of valuables. This fits the following statement: 'Jesus saw rich people placing their donations in the treasury. He also saw a poor widow throwing in two mites. He said, "Truly I tell you, this poor widow threw in more than all the others"' (Luke 21:1, 2, 3)."

[10] Then someone from the fourth row to the left stood up and said, "My opinion is that *goodwill is providing church buildings with an endowment and benefiting its ministers.* I support this opinion as follows: People who do this have something holy in mind and act on that holiness. They make their donations holy as well. Goodwill demands this because it is intrinsically holy. All the worship that takes place in church buildings is holy, for the Lord says, 'Where two or three are gathered together in my name, I am there in the midst of them' [Matthew 18:20].

As his servants, the priests minister for him. Therefore I conclude that donations to priests and to church buildings count for more than donations to other people and other things. Furthermore, part of the work of the ministry is blessing, which means that the donations are sanctified.

"Afterward nothing makes the mind more elated and cheerful than seeing one's donations in the form of as many sanctuaries."

[11] Then someone from the fourth row to the right stood up and said this: "My opinion is that *goodwill is the ancient Christian family feeling.* I support my opinion as follows: Every church that worships the true God begins with goodwill. So did the early Christian church. Because goodwill unifies people's minds and makes one mind out of many, early Christians called each other family, but family in Jesus Christ their God. Since they were surrounded at that point by barbarous nations that they feared, they made a communal life with what they had, which brought them a great and like-minded happiness. They met together every day and talked about the Lord God their Savior Jesus Christ, and over lunch and dinner they talked about goodwill. This led to a family feeling among them.

"After those times, however, schisms began to occur, and then came the unspeakable Arian heresy, which robbed many of the idea that the Lord's human manifestation was divine. That caused goodwill to break down and the family feeling to fade away.

"The truth is that all who worship the Lord in truth and do what he commands are family (Matthew 23:8)—family in spirit. Since nowadays people don't recognize what others are like in spirit, there is no reason for them to refer to themselves as a family.

"A family feeling based on faith alone is not real; still less real is a family feeling based on faith in another god besides the Lord God the Savior. The goodwill that causes a family feeling is not part of that faith. Therefore I have concluded that the ancient Christian family feeling was goodwill. It *was,* but it is no more. Nevertheless, I predict that it is going to return."

When this last point was made, a fiery light appeared from outside the east window and tinged the speaker's cheeks—something the gathering was astounded to see.

[12] Lastly, someone from the fifth row on the left stood up and asked permission to add something to the last speaker's remarks. The group gave permission. The statement was this: "My opinion is that *goodwill is forgiving anyone's wrongs.* I base my opinion on the usual conversation

among people as they approach the Holy Supper. At that moment some people say to their friends, 'Forgive the wrongs I have done,' figuring that this will satisfy goodwill's requirements. But I have thought to myself that this is only the semblance of goodwill, not a real form of its essence. Some who say this are themselves unforgiving people, and some put no effort into the pursuit of goodwill. People like this are not the people mentioned in the prayer the Lord himself taught us: 'Father, forgive us our wrongs, just as we forgive people who wrong us.'

"Wrongs are like wounds. Unless they are opened up and cleansed, pus gathers in them and infects neighboring tissues, creeping outward like a serpent and corrupting the blood on all sides.[659] It is the same with wrongs against our neighbor. If they are not removed by repentance and by living as the Lord commands, they remain and become more deeply entrenched.

"People who merely pray to God to remove their sins but don't do any repentance are like people who live in some city and are infected with a contagious disease. They go to the mayor and say, 'Master, cure us.' Surely the mayor is going to tell them, 'Why do you ask me to cure you? Go to a doctor, find out what medicine to take, get some from the apothecary, and take it. Then you'll be cured.' If people beg for their sins to be forgiven without doing any actual repentance, the Lord will tell them, 'Open the Word and read what I said in Isaiah: "Woe to a sinful nation, heavy with injustice. As a result, when you stretch out your hands I hide my eyes from you. Even if you increase your praying, I do not hear it. Wash yourselves. Remove the evil of your doings from before my eyes. Stop doing evil. Learn to do good," and then your sins will be removed and forgiven (Isaiah 1:4, 15, 16, 17, 18).'"

[13] After these speeches I raised my hand and asked whether I could offer an opinion even though I was a stranger. The chairperson put it to the group. After they agreed I said, "My opinion is that *goodwill is to act in all our work, and in every role we have, with judgment based on a love for justice—but only if that love comes solely from the Lord God the Savior.* All the definitions I heard from the people in the seats to the right and the left are well-known examples of goodwill. Nevertheless, as the chair of this gathering said at the outset, goodwill is originally spiritual. It is earthly only by derivation. When earthly goodwill is inwardly spiritual, to the angels it looks as clear as a diamond. When earthly goodwill is not inwardly spiritual, however, and is therefore merely earthly, to the angels it looks opalescent, like the eye of a cooked fish.

[14] "It is not up to me to say whether the well-known examples of goodwill that you have just presented one after the other are actions motivated by spiritual goodwill or not. There is one thing I can do, however. These examples of goodwill should contain something spiritual. I can state what that spiritual something must be like if they are to be earthly forms of spiritual goodwill.

"Those actions are spiritual if they are done with judgment based on a love for justice. That is, as we practice goodwill we check to see whether we are acting on the basis of justice. We use our judgment to tell.

"It is possible for us to do harm through our good deeds. It is also possible for us to do good through apparently evil deeds. For example, we do harm through a good deed if we give a needy robber money to buy a sword, even if the robber while begging doesn't say that that is what the money is for; or if we bail the robber out of prison and point the way to the forest, saying to ourselves, 'It is not my fault if the robber steals. I have helped another human being.'

"For another example, if we feed some lazy person and protect him or her from being forced to labor for work, and we say, 'Stay in a room at my house. Lie in bed. Why wear yourself out?' we are encouraging laziness. Likewise if we give dishonest friends and relatives of ours jobs in high places from which they can practice all kinds of malice. Surely anyone can see that these acts of goodwill are not done with any love for justice or with any judgment.

[15] "On the other hand, we can also do good through actions that look bad. Take for example a judge who lets a criminal go because the criminal is crying and pouring out devout words, praying for the judge to grant a pardon because the criminal is the judge's neighbor. The judge would be performing an act of goodwill by imposing the penalty established in the law, because this would stop the criminal from doing any further harm and being a threat to the community; and the community takes precedence as a form of the neighbor. It would also prevent the scandal that might arise if the judge decided to let the criminal go.

"Surely everyone knows that servants benefit if their masters punish them for doing something evil, and children benefit as well when their parents punish them for the same reason.

"Something similar is also good for the people in hell, all of whom love doing evil. It is good for them to be kept locked in prisons and to be punished when they do something evil. The Lord allows this for the sake of their correction. This happens because the Lord is perfect justice and does what he does with perfect judgment.

[16] "From these points you can clearly see why I made the statement I did: we act with spiritual goodwill when we base our actions on a love for justice, and use our judgment.

"The love has to come solely from the Lord God the Savior, because all goodness related to goodwill comes from the Lord. He says, 'Those who live in me and I in them bear much fruit, because without me you cannot do anything' (John 15:5); and that he has all power in heaven and on earth (Matthew 28:18). All love for justice and use of judgment comes from the God of heaven alone, who is justice itself, and who is the source of all our ability to judge (Jeremiah 23:5; 33:15).

[17] "In conclusion, let's review all the definitions of goodwill from the chairs to the left and right—that it is morality combined with faith; religious devotion combined with compassion; doing good to everyone whether honest or dishonest; doing all you can for your relatives and friends; giving donations to the poor and helping the needy; building hospitals and maintaining them with donations; providing church buildings with an endowment and benefiting their ministers; the ancient Christian family feeling; and forgiving anyone's wrongs. These are all outstanding examples of goodwill as long as they are done with a love for justice and with judgment. Otherwise they are not goodwill: they are only streams that have been cut off from a river or branches that have been pulled off a tree, since real goodwill is believing in the Lord and behaving justly and uprightly in all our work and in every role we have. People who receive a love for justice from the Lord and who practice justice with judgment are goodwill in its image and likeness."

[18] After I said that there was silence, like the silence of people who see something in their inner self and acknowledge the truth of it to some extent, but do not see it yet in their outer self. I noticed this in their faces.

Suddenly, however, I was taken out of their sight because I went back out of the spirit into my physical body. Because our earthly self wears a physical body, it is not visible to any spiritual person, meaning a spirit or an angel, and neither are they visible to it.

The second memorable occurrence. Once when I was looking around the spiritual world I heard a sound like teeth grinding together and a sound like hammering and also a whistling mixed in with both other sounds. I asked what they were. The angels who were with me said, "They are

460

meetings (which we label as diversions) where people have verbal battles with each other. Their arguments sound this way from a distance. From closer by they merely sound like arguing."

I went to the place and saw huts made of rushes plastered together with mud. I tried to look in a window [of one of the huts] but there was none. (I was not allowed in the door, because light would have flowed in from heaven and confused them.) Suddenly a window was created on the right side of the hut. Then I heard the people complaining because they were in the dark. Soon a window was created on the left side, and the window on the right was closed over. It seemed to them that the darkness gradually went away and that they were in their own light again.[660] After that I was given permission to go in the door and hear what was going on.

There was a table in the middle with benches around it for sitting, but instead all the people seemed to me to be standing on the benches, having a harsh dispute with each other about *faith and goodwill*. One side was arguing that the essence of the church is faith; the other side was arguing that the essence of the church is goodwill.

The people who saw faith as the essential thing said, "In the case of faith, we are dealing with God. And in the case of goodwill we are dealing with human beings. Therefore faith is heavenly and goodwill is earthly. Surely we are saved by heavenly things, not by earthly things. God is able to give us faith from heaven, because faith is heavenly, but goodwill is something we have to give ourselves, because goodwill is earthly. And what we give ourselves is not part of the church and therefore does not save us. Or do you think people could be justified before God by doing things that are said to be part of goodwill? Believe us when we tell you—by faith alone we are not only justified, we are also sanctified, as long as our faith is not defiled by our desire to earn merit through our acts of goodwill." And many more points like these.

[2] On the other side, the people who saw goodwill as the essence of the church had sharp retorts. They said, "Goodwill saves us, not faith. Surely God holds all people as beloved and wants what is good for all. How could God put this goodness into effect if not through other human beings? Does God let us merely tell people points related to faith but not perform acts of goodwill toward them? Don't you see that what you are saying about goodwill is absurd—calling it earthly? Goodwill is heavenly. Since you don't perform acts of goodwill, your faith is earthly. You actually do receive this faith of yours in the way a log or a stone[661]

would. You say you receive it through hearing the Word, but how can the Word do any work on you if all you do is hear it? How can the Word do any work on a log or a stone? Perhaps you were brought to life but you were totally unaware that it happened! What is that liveliness except your ability to say, 'Faith alone justifies us and saves us'? But you don't even know what faith is or which type of faith saves us!"

[3] Then someone whom the angel with me called a syncretist stood up. He took off his head-covering and put it on the table, but then quickly put it back on his head because he was bald.[662] "Listen to me," he said. "You are all wrong. It is true that faith is spiritual and goodwill is moral, but still they are connected. The Word connects them; then they are connected by the Holy Spirit; and finally they are connected by their effect, which could indeed be called obedience, but it is an obedience in which we have no part, because when faith enters us we are as unaware of it as a statue would be. I have thought long and hard about this. What I have finally come to is that we can receive faith (which is spiritual) from God, but God cannot put us in a state of spiritual goodwill any more than he could put a log in a state of spiritual goodwill."

[4] The people who believed in faith alone applauded these statements, but the people who believed in goodwill booed them. The proponents of goodwill said indignantly, "Listen, friend, you don't seem to know that there is such a thing as a moral life that is spiritual, as opposed to a moral life that is merely earthly. People who do good things that have their origin in God and yet do them as if they were acting on their own live a spiritual moral life. People who do good things that have their origin in hell and yet do them as if they were acting on their own live a merely earthly moral life."

[5] I mentioned before that their fighting sounded like teeth grinding together and like hammering with whistling mixed in. The arguments from the people who made faith the sole and essential thing in the church sounded like teeth grinding together. The arguments from the people who made goodwill the sole and essential thing in the church sounded like hammering. The whistling that was mixed in came from the syncretist. These people sounded like this at a distance because they had all spent their time in the world arguing but had not abstained from any evil; therefore none of them had done any good thing that had a spiritual origin. They were also completely unaware that truth is the essence of faith and goodness is the essence of goodwill; that truth

without goodness is not spiritually true, and goodness without truth is not spiritually good; and that therefore the two shape each other.

461 *The third memorable occurrence.* Once I was carried in spirit to a paradise in the southern part of the spiritual world. I observed that this paradise was more magnificent than all the rest I had seen up to that point. The reason for its magnificence was that a garden means intelligence, and all the people who are exceptionally intelligent are moved to the south.

The Garden of Eden of Adam and his wife has exactly this meaning. Their expulsion from the garden means being taken away from intelligence and therefore from wholeness of life as well.

As I was walking around in this southern paradise I noticed some people sitting under a laurel tree eating figs. I went over to them and asked if I could have some figs. They gave me some. In my hand, however, the figs turned into grapes! Since I was astounded by this, an angelic spirit who was standing next to me told me, "The figs became grapes in your hand because figs correspondentially mean good actions related to goodwill, and therefore to faith, in our earthly or outer self. Grapes, however, mean good qualities related to goodwill, and therefore to faith, in our spiritual or inner self. This happened to you because you love spiritual things. In our world everything happens, takes shape, and also changes according to correspondences."

[2] At that point an avid desire suddenly came over me to know how people can do what is good from God and yet do it completely as if they were on their own, so I asked the people eating figs how they understood this. They said, "We have no other way to understand this except to think that God produces this effect inside us and through us when we are unaware of it; because if we knew about it and did it, the good we did would be only something seemingly good that was actually evil inwardly. Everything that comes from ourselves comes from our self-interest, which is evil from the day we are born. How could goodness from God and evil from ourselves become united and move together into action? When it comes to salvation, our self-interest is constantly seeking to earn merit. The more merit our self-interest seeks, the more merit it takes away from the Lord; this theft is the ultimate injustice and ungodliness. Briefly put, if the goodness that God produces in us were to flow into something we wanted and did, we would pollute and desecrate that goodness in every way, which God would never allow. We can of course think that the goodness we do comes from God and call it God's goodness acting through us, but we don't actually understand that."

[3] Then I opened my mind and said, "You don't understand it, because your thinking is based on the way things appear, and thinking that is based on an appearance is mistaken. You have this mistaken view because you believe that everything we intend and think, and everything we do and say, is inside us and therefore comes from us, when in fact none of it is inside us except a condition that enables us to receive what flows in. We are not life in itself; we are just organs that receive life. The Lord is life in itself, as in fact he says in John: 'As the Father has life in himself, so he has also given the Son to have life in himself' (John 5:26; see also 11:25; 14:6, 19).

[4] "There are two things that constitute life: love and wisdom, or what is the same thing, goodness related to love and truth related to wisdom. These two qualities flow in from God. We receive them as if they were ours. In fact, because we feel them that way, they emanate from us as if they really were our own. The Lord grants us this feeling so that what flows in will have an effect on us, and be accepted and stay with us. All that is evil also flows in, not from God but from hell. We feel pleasure as we take evil in, because we were born that way. Therefore we receive no greater amount of goodness from the Lord than the amount of evil we have removed as if we were removing it on our own. It is our repentance and our faith in the Lord that does this removing.

[5] "Love and wisdom, and goodwill and faith, or (to put it even more generally) the goodness of love and goodwill and the truth of wisdom and faith, flow in. Things that flow in seem to us to be totally our own, and therefore they go out from us as if they were our own. The truth of this can be clearly seen by analogy with sight, hearing, smell, taste, and touch. Everything that is perceived by the organs of these senses flows in from outside us but feels like it is inside us. The same is true for our organs of inner sensation, with just one difference: things that are spiritual and intangible flow into our organs of inner sensation, while things that are earthly and tangible flow into our organs of physical sensation.

"Briefly put, each of us is an organ that receives life from God. Therefore we become receptive to goodness depending on how thoroughly we stop doing evil. The power to stop doing evil is something the Lord grants to every one of us. He gives us the ability to intend and to understand. Whatever we do intentionally, based on our understanding (or to put it another way, using our free will and following the reasoning of our intellect) becomes a permanent part of us. The Lord uses these abilities to bring us to a state of partnership with him; in this state he then reforms us, regenerates us, and saves us.

[6] "The life that flows into us comes from the Lord. This life is also called the spirit of God. In the Word it is called the Holy Spirit. The Word says that the Holy Spirit enlightens us and brings us to life, and even that it works inside us.663 This life is varied and modified, however, by the structure that is created in us by what we love.

"Another way to tell that all the goodness of love and goodwill and all the truth of wisdom and faith flow in rather than coming from ourselves is this: People who think that goodness and truth have been in us since creation eventually cannot avoid thinking that God poured himself into us and therefore we are partly gods. Yet people who think this and believe it become devils. When they are among us, they reek like corpses.

[7] "Further, what else is human action except the mind acting? Whatever the mind intends and thinks, it does and says through its organ, the body. Therefore when our mind is led by the Lord, our words and actions are also led by the Lord; our words and actions are led by the Lord when we believe in him.

"If this is not true, tell me—if you can—why the Lord has commanded us in a thousand passages in his Word to love our neighbor, to perform acts of goodwill, to bear fruit like a tree, to obey what he commands, and to do all this so that we will be saved. For another thing, why did he say that we are judged by the actions and works we have done— people who do good things being judged to heaven and to life while people who do evil things are judged to hell and to death?664 The Lord would not say things like these if everything we accomplished was done to earn merit and was therefore evil.665 It is important for you to know, therefore, that if the mind is goodwill, then the action is goodwill; but if the mind is faith alone, which is also faith separated from spiritual goodwill, the action is also that same faith."

[8] The people sitting under the laurel tree then said, "We understand that you have spoken the truth—we just don't understand what you said."

"You understand that I spoke the truth," I replied, "because of the general awareness that people have from the light that flows in from heaven when they hear something true. You don't understand it because of your own awareness, which is something people have from the light that flows in from the world. These two kinds of awareness, an inner one and an outer one, or a spiritual one and an earthly one, become united in people who are wise. You too can unite them if you focus on the Lord and remove evils."

Since they understood this point, I pulled some branches from a grapevine and held them out to these people. "Do you believe these are coming to you from me or from the Lord?" I said.

They said, "They are coming from the Lord by means of you."

The branches in their hands suddenly grew grapes![666]

As I was leaving, I saw a cedar table that had a book on it. It was under a thriving olive tree that had vines wrapped around its trunk. I looked more closely, and the book turned out to be one written through me called *Secrets of Heaven!*[667] I told the people that the fact that we are organs that receive life rather than life itself was fully demonstrated in that book; the book also shows that life itself cannot be fabricated, and thus cannot reside as a fabricated thing within a person, any more than light can in an eye.

The fourth memorable occurrence. I looked over to a seacoast in the spiritual world. There I saw a magnificent harbor. I went to it and examined it more closely. There were large and small vessels there carrying merchandise of every different kind. Boys and girls were sitting on them distributing the wealth to anyone who wanted it. They said, "We are waiting to see our beautiful sea turtles.[668] They will soon be coming up out of the sea to us."

Then I saw the sea turtles, large and small. They had little baby sea turtles riding on their shells, looking around at the surrounding islands. The parent turtles had two heads. One head was large and was covered in a shell like the shell on their body, which made them look reddish. The other head was small like a normal turtle's head. They would retract this smaller head into the front part of their body. By an unseen method, they would also put this smaller head inside their larger head.

I kept my focus, however, on their large, reddish heads. I noticed that these heads had faces like those of human beings. They were talking with the boys and girls on the seats in the boats and licking the children's hands. Then the boys and girls began stroking the sea turtles and giving them things: rich, wonderful food, and also expensive gifts such as silk for clothing, cypress wood for building material, purple cloth for beautification, and scarlet dye for dying cloth.

[2] When I saw these things, I was eager to know what they meant, because I knew that everything visible in the spiritual world is a correspondence and represents something spiritual having to do with feelings and thoughts.

462

Then people began talking to me from heaven, saying, "You know what the harbor represents, and also the boats, and the boys and girls on them. You don't know what the sea turtles represent."

They continued, "The sea turtles represent members of the clergy in the spiritual world who keep their faith completely separate from goodwill and its good works. Inwardly in themselves they assert that there is obviously no connection between faith and goodwill; instead the Holy Spirit enters into us through our faith in God the Father on account of the Son's merit and purifies our inner levels, including our will. As they see it, the human will is like an oval plane. When the action of the Holy Spirit comes near that plane, it veers around it to the left without touching it at all. The inner or higher part of the human character, then, belongs to God, while the outer or lower part is all our own. Nothing that we do appears before God—either good or evil. The good things we do don't appear, because we do them to earn merit; and the evil things we do don't appear, because they are evil. If our doings did appear before God, we would perish on both counts. Therefore we are allowed to intend, think, speak, and do whatever we want as long as we are careful before the world."

[3] I asked, "Is it acceptable to them to think about God as not being omnipresent or omniscient?"

The people from heaven said, "This is also acceptable as far as they are concerned, because if people have developed faith and have been purified and justified as a result, God doesn't see through to anything they think or intend. Such people keep in the inner core or higher region of their mind or character the faith that they originally accepted when they experienced the purifying operation of faith. Those spirits believe that sometimes the purifying operation of faith can come to us again without our knowing it.

"These beliefs are represented by the *small head* they pull into the front of their body or else insert into the *large head* when they are talking to lay people. They don't use their small head to talk to lay people. They use the large one that looks like it has something of a human face on the front of it. They base their conversation with lay people on the Word, discussing love, goodwill, good works, the Ten Commandments, and repentance. From the Word they quote practically everything it has to say on these subjects. Then they insert the small head into the large one. In their small head, they privately believe that all the things just mentioned don't have to be done for God's sake or for the sake of salvation, but just for the sake of public and private benefit.

[4] "Because they say smooth and elegant things based on the Word about these subjects, especially about the good news of the gospel, the actions of the Holy Spirit, and salvation, they appear to the people who hear them to be people of beauty and of greater wisdom than anyone else in the world. That is also why you saw that they were given luxuries and expensive items by the boys and girls sitting on the seats in the boats.

"These then are the people you saw represented as sea turtles. In your world, they are hard to differentiate from others except for the fact that they think they are wiser than everyone else and laugh at others—even people who have a similar view of faith as their own but don't share in their mysteries. They wear a particular insignia on their clothing that they use to identify themselves as set apart from others."

[5] The person speaking with me said, "I am not going to tell you what they feel on the other topics related to faith: predestination, free choice, baptism, and the Holy Supper. They don't make their views on these topics public, but we in heaven know what they are.

"This is what they are like in the world. After death no one can speak anything except what he or she really thinks. Therefore because they then cannot help speaking the insane things they think, they are considered insane and are thrown out of the communities they are in. Eventually they are sent down into the pit of the abyss mentioned in Revelation 9:2. They become mindlessly earthly spirits. They look like Egyptian mummies. A callus develops over the interiors of their mind, because even in the world they put a boundary around them.

"There is a hellish community of these people right next to the hellish community of Machiavellians.[669] They often go from the one community to the other—they call each other colleagues—but they leave because there is a difference between the two communities: they themselves have some religious spirit based on the act of justification by faith, but there is no religious spirit among the Machiavellians."

[6] After seeing them being thrown out of the communities they had been in and being gathered together to be sent down, I saw a boat with seven sails flying through the air. In it there were captains and sailors wearing purple robes. They had magnificent laurel wreaths on their caps. They were shouting, "Look at us in heaven! We are doctors decorated with purple and more laureled than all the rest! We are the wisest of all the clergy in Europe!"

I wondered what this could possibly be. I was told that these were the arrogant pictures and mental images called fantasies on the part of the people I had seen before as sea turtles and more recently as insane people being thrown out of their former communities and gathered together in one place.

At that point I felt an urge to talk to those people. I went to the place where they were staying, greeted them, and said, "Are you the people who see our inner and our outer levels as being disconnected; who see the Holy Spirit's operation on us within the realm of faith as being disconnected from the Holy Spirit's cooperation with us outside the realm of faith; and who therefore see God as being disconnected from us? In that case you have not only taken goodwill and its works away from faith, as many other professors among the clergy have done, but you have also done away with faith itself in the sense that [without goodwill and good works] people have no way to demonstrate their faith to God.

[7] "Let me ask: would you like me to address this issue with you on the basis of reason or on the basis of Sacred Scripture?"

"Start with reason," they said.

So I said, "How can the inner and outer selves in people be disconnected? Surely everyone sees based on general awareness (or is at least able to see) that all the things inside us extend and are continued to the outer parts of us, even into the outermost parts, in order to have their effect and do their work. What is on the outside of us exists for the sake of what is on the inside of us, to give it a place of termination and something to rest on in order to have continued existence, much the way a base supports a column.

"If there were no continuity and connection, the outermost things would fall apart and burst like bubbles in the air. God carries out millions of processes in us that we know nothing about. How would it help us to know about them? All we need is to pay attention to the outermost areas where we and our thinking and willing are together with God.[670]

[8] "I will illustrate this with an example: Do we know the inner functions involved in our speaking? Do we know, for example, how the lungs pull in air and fill the air sacs, bronchial tubes, and lobes with air? Do we know how the lungs expel that air into the trachea and there turn it into sound? Do we know how that sound is modified in our glottis with the help of our larynx? Do we know how the tongue then articulates the sound and the lips complete the articulation so that speaking occurs? All those inner functions, about which we know nothing, exist for the sake of one outer function: enabling us to speak. Break the continuity

between any one of those inner functions and the outer functions—
could we speak any more than a piece of wood can?

[9] "Take another example: Our hands are two of our extremities.
There are inner parts that extend into our hands from our head through
our neck, and then through our chest, shoulder blades, upper arms, and
lower arms. There are countless muscle tissues, countless arrays of motor
fibers, countless troops[671] of nerves and blood vessels, and a number of
bone joints with ligaments and membranes involved. Do we know anything about them? And yet every one of them is involved in making our
hands work. Suppose that as those inner parts reached our wrist they
were sent off in another direction to the left or right and did not run all
the way into our hands. Our hands would just dangle from our forearms
like disconnected things, bereft of spirit, and rot. In fact, believe it or
not, our hands would then be just like a body with its head cut off.

"It would be exactly the same with our mind and its two lives, the
will and the intellect, if the divine functions related to faith and goodwill
were to stop midway and not extend all the way into us. Truly, if that
were the case we would be less than brutes; we would be mere pieces of
dead wood shot through with rottenness.

"The points just made follow the lines of reason.

[10] "Now—if you are still willing to listen to me—the same points
also accord with Sacred Scripture. The Lord says, 'Live in me and I [shall
live] in you. I am the vine and you are the branches. Those who live in
me and I in them bear much fruit' (John 15:4, 5). Surely those fruits are
the good works that the Lord does through us and that we do on our own
from the Lord. The Lord also says that he is standing at our door and
knocking, and that if we open it, he will come in and will dine with us
and we with him (Revelation 3:20). The Lord gives us money and talents[672] so that we will trade with them and make a profit, and if we make
a profit he gives us eternal life (Matthew 25:14–34; Luke 19:12–26). The
Lord gives us all a reward according to our labor in his vineyard
(Matthew 20:1–16). But these passages are just a few. Whole volumes
could be filled with quotations from the Word that say we are to produce
fruit like a tree, to work on following the commandments, to love God
and our neighbor, and more.

[11] "I am aware, however, that your own intelligence as it truly is
cannot have anything in common with these quotations from the Word.
Although you yourselves quote them, your ideas nonetheless pervert

them. You cannot help it, because you deny that anything having to do with God could be shared with or joined to humankind. What then is left but all the rituals of worship?"

Later on I saw them in the light of heaven, which uncovers and manifests what people are really like. Then they did not seem as they had before. They were not flying through the air in a ship, as though through heaven itself. They did not look like they had fine purple robes or laurel wreaths on their heads. They were instead in a sandy place in clothes made out of rags, with something like fishnets wrapped around their waists that still showed their nakedness. Then they were sent down to the community near the Machiavellians.

NOTES

Notes

Notes to the Opening Biblical Quotations

1. The Latin phrase here translated "the Son of Humankind" is *Filius Hominis,* traditionally rendered "the Son of Man." Elsewhere in this edition it has sometimes been rendered "the Human-born One." It is difficult to estimate the original range of meaning of the term; it is used in one way in the Old Testament, but in another in the New Testament. The force of the phrase is literally "someone descended from the human race," "someone who was born human," and therefore "someone human." In the Old Testament, the phrase is almost always used in reference to a human being (as opposed to the Divine). Elsewhere in Daniel, for example, the term applies to Daniel himself (Daniel 8:17). Here, however, Swedenborg clearly takes the term as applying to Jesus Christ, which is arguably its usual denotation in the New Testament. (Following Swedenborg's use of these terms, in this edition the Hebrew Scriptures are referred to as the Old Testament, and the Greek Scriptures are referred to as the New Testament.) [JSR]

2. In the first edition, these two quotations occur on the verso (that is, the back) of the title page. For similarly placed scriptural quotations in Swedenborg's theological works, see the versos of the original title pages of *Secrets of Heaven* (1749–1756) and *Survey* (1769). Swedenborg's quotations of Scripture often show more editing and rearrangement than modern standards might allow. His Latin rendering of Revelation 21 here is a reordered combination of various verses and parts of verses. For a sense of what these quotations and their prominent placement in the work may have communicated to eighteenth-century readers, see the introduction, pages 74–75. [JSR]

Notes to §§1–3

3 (in §1). The "new heaven" and the "new church" are allusions to the quotation from Revelation 21:1 given at the beginning of the work (the new church being symbolized by the city Jerusalem). There are similar mentions of new heavens in Isaiah 65:17, 66:22, and 2 Peter 3:13. Swedenborg describes the heavens as being multiple rather than single and containing people of a variety of faiths and perspectives (see, for example, his 1764 work *Divine Providence* 253). Elsewhere in the present work he states that at the time of its writing he was witnessing the establishment of a new heaven—a specifically Christian heaven made up of people who had died in the recent past, arranged into numerous communities (§§107, 108, 119:3, 138). He uses the word "church" (Latin *ecclesia*) in a variety of senses. Sometimes it refers to a religious approach in the abstract, whether that occurs in an individual or in a group large or small; sometimes it refers more concretely to local or national Christianity, to all Protestants, or even to Christianity as a whole; and sometimes it applies even more broadly to all believers on earth of whatever faith. In this instance, however, as often elsewhere, Swedenborg is using the term historically to mean the core religious approach of a given age or era through which heaven was connected with humankind, of which he asserts there have been five

major instances, in the following sequence: the earliest (or "most ancient") church, the early (or "ancient") church, the Jewish church, the Christian church, and the new church (see §§760, 762, 786; see also Swedenborg's 1758 work *Last Judgment* 46 and notes; and *Divine Providence* 328). [JSR]

4 (in §1). This work opens with the language of simile and continues to be laden with similes throughout. In many instances, these similes are compound, in the sense that they liken one theological assertion to many concrete things or situations. Often these reflect common human experiences, but at times they are bizarre and hypothetical. The similes apparently reflect correspondences (on correspondences, see note 35); for Swedenborg's statements about the purpose and correspondential nature of his similes, see §§131, 215, 496, and 669. Furthermore, §371:8 suggests that at least some similes could be explained in far more detail if there were room to do so. For more on the nature and structure of the similes in this work, see Rose 1994. [JSR]

5 (in §1). Although the notion of angels is common to many religious traditions, Swedenborg's view of them is unusual. Rather than describing them as a genderless or separately created race, Swedenborg asserted that they were all once people in the physical universe (*Last Judgment* 14–22), and that they remain human in every respect after death (see his 1758 work *Heaven and Hell* 75; and his 1768 work *Marriage Love* 44:2). [JSR]

6 (in §1). Central to Swedenborg's psychology is the view that a human being has multiple levels, especially levels of the mind, and that these levels can be described equally well as being "higher" and "lower" or as being "inner" and "outer" (see §214 and note 455; see also his 1763 work *Divine Love and Wisdom* 205–206). Although the inner and the outer levels of the mind "act together," each level is sufficiently complete and distinct that higher levels are capable of looking objectively at what is going on in lower levels (see *True Christianity* 603; *Secrets of Heaven* 1954:2), and different levels within the same individual are capable of having opposing and conflicting values and intentions (see *Divine Love and Wisdom* 260; *Divine Providence* 111:2, 284). [JSR]

7 (in §1). "What is good" (Latin *bonum*) and "what is true" (Latin *verum*) and their respective equivalents "goodness," "good," or "the good," and "truth" or "the true" are the most frequently occurring terms in Swedenborg's theological works. Echoing ancient philosophical and ethical traditions, in Swedenborg's theology these concepts stand in a complementary relationship to all things: that is, absolutely everything, whether physical, psychological, or spiritual, relates to either goodness or truth or to a "marriage" of both (or to their opposites, "evil" and "falsity"). Their complementarity is so all-encompassing that in a chapter on the two, Swedenborg defines them only in terms of each other (see his 1758 work *New Jerusalem* 11–19, with further references in *Secrets of Heaven* 20–27). In Swedenborg's system, goodness encompasses affective qualities such as love, affection, desire, and goodwill, and corresponds to physical heat, while truth encompasses cognitive qualities such as wisdom, thought, perception, and faith, and corresponds to physical light (on "goodwill," see note 19; on "correspondences," see note 35). Swedenborg uses these terms almost algebraically to stand in for things ranging from the sublimely abstract to the utterly concrete (see for example §419, where goodness is explicitly defined as usefulness). [JSR]

8 (in §1). In Swedenborg's works, "the Lord" refers to Jesus Christ as God. A core concept in Swedenborg's theology is that there are not three persons in the Trinity; there is one person, whose soul is the unknowable Divine, whose human manifestation is Jesus

Christ, and whose operative influence is the Holy Spirit. Of the many names and terms from philosophical and biblical backgrounds that Swedenborg uses to denote God (the Divine Being, the Divine, the Divine Human, the One, the Infinite, the First, the Creator, the Redeemer, the Savior, Jehovah [see note 9], God Shaddai [see note 80], and many more), the most frequently occurring term is "the Lord" (Latin *Dominus*), a title rather than a name, meaning "the one in charge," and referring to Jesus Christ as the manifestation of the one and only God. For Swedenborg's brief explanation of his reasons for using "the Lord," see *Secrets of Heaven* 14. See also chapter 2 of the present work. [JSR]

9 (in §2:1). The phrase "from eternity" means before creation, that is, before time came into existence. The name "Jehovah" was often used by Swedenborg, following a Christian practice of his times, as a rendering of the tetragrammaton, יהוה *(yhvh)*, "YHWH," the four-letter name of God in the Hebrew Scriptures. A complex set of circumstances gave rise to the name "Jehovah." The Hebrew alphabet originally consisted only of consonants. It was not until the eighth century of the Common Era that a complete system of diacritical marks for Hebrew vowel notation was developed. When for any reason the consonantal text was held not to be suitable for reading as it stood, the vowels of an approved reading would be added to the consonants that stood in the text, whether the number of syllables in the two words matched or not. Since the sanctity of the name of God, YHWH, was felt to preclude its being pronounced, under most circumstances the word אֲדֹנָי *(ʾăḏōnāi),* "Lord," was substituted, and to indicate this, vowels closely resembling those of the name Adonai were added to YHWH: YeHoWaH. This combination of consonants and vowels was transliterated into Latin as "Jehovah." (Some English Bibles since then have adopted the name "Jehovah" while others have rendered the term as "Lord," so capitalized.) When the Hebrew text used the expression "the Lord YHWH," however, this was read as "the Lord God," and the divine name was given the vowels of the word אֱלֹהִים *(ʾĕlōhîm),* "God." This gave rise to the relatively rare reading of the name as "Jehovih," which Swedenborg occasionally employs (see for example §§82:2, 308), although in English Bibles it is more commonly expressed as "the Lord God," so capitalized. The currently accepted scholarly reconstruction of the original pronunciation of the tetragrammaton is "Yahweh": see *Theological Dictionary of the Old Testament* under "YHWH." Swedenborg, like others, relates the meaning of the name to the concept of being or "is-ness" (see §19:1; see also §9:2–3). [GFD, JSR]

10 (in §2:1). Although Swedenborg often speaks of "hell" in the singular, he also frequently uses the plural, "hells," by which he apparently means the many communities of hell, each of which is in effect a hell in smaller form (*Heaven and Hell* 542; see also §§584–588 in that work). [JSR]

11 (in §2:1). The term "glorify" here may be misunderstood by today's readers. It has two essential meanings: to *deem* glorious or ascribe glory to, and to *render* glorious or actually transform. It is the latter meaning that Swedenborg generally intends by "glorify" and "glorification" in relation to Jesus' human nature. Swedenborg makes explicit that glorification is a rendering divine or a uniting with the Divine (see §2:2; see also §§97, 105, 110:4, 114, 126, 128, 130:2, 154:6). Swedenborg apparently derives this usage from the Gospel of John. Although generally in the Bible the word "glorify" means to praise or extol (the first meaning just given) and Swedenborg occasionally uses the word in this sense (see §§16:1, 117), the Gospel of John often uses "glorify" in the second sense just given. For example, to say that the Holy Spirit had not yet come into existence because

Jesus was not glorified yet (John 7:39) clearly does not mean that Jesus was not praised yet; it means that he was not yet completely transformed, or rendered fully divine. [JSR]

12 (in §2:2). Swedenborg is here contrasting his theology with that of contemporary Christianity. The concept of essence first became a topic of philosophical debate in the time of the ancient Greeks. It later became central to many Christian debates about the nature of God. Although the Greek and Latin terms associated with this concept, οὐσία *(ousía)* and *essentia,* respectively, had many subtly different meanings within various traditions, Swedenborg seems to use the term *essence* rather broadly to mean "the inherent principle by which a thing is what it is." God's essence, then, is divinity—it is that which makes God God. Further on in the text, Swedenborg identifies God's essence more specifically as divine love and wisdom (§37). The term *person* (Latin *persona*), on the other hand, originally meant a mask used by an actor, and then came to mean a character or role performed. Early Christian philosophers adopted the term to differentiate the three parts of the divine Trinity: the Father, the Son, and the Holy Spirit. Elsewhere Swedenborg quotes three Trinitarian scholars in the spiritual world as defining "person" as follows: "The term *person* means that which is not a role of, or a quality in, someone else, but an entity subsisting on its own" (§17:3). Christians of Swedenborg's time would generally have agreed with him that God is one in essence, but would have disagreed that God is one in person. See also note 82. [JSR]

13 (in §2:2). The phrase "the divine design" (the Latin here is *ordo,* literally, "order," which is expressed more fully elsewhere in the original as *divinus ordo,* literally, "divine order") refers to a divinely ordained arrangement of things in relation to each other both in physical space (or spiritual state) and in physical time (or spiritual sequence). For a definition of the term, see §52 in the general context of §§49–70, 74. For a brief description of the divine design of the universe, see §75. [JSR]

14 (in §2:3). The Latin word here translated "partnership" is *conjunctio.* As later passages show (see especially §§99, 371), Swedenborg uses the word to denote the relationship that develops when two people or things come together, without either element losing its identity. Swedenborg uses the term of our relationship with the Lord, but also of the relationship between inanimate objects or qualities of the mind; in the latter cases, when "partnership" seemed an inappropriate term, it is rendered "connection" or "union" in this translation. [JSR]

15 (in §2:3). From ancient times, Christian theologians have used citation or quotation of individual passages from Scripture as a way of authenticating and substantiating their arguments. Though this use of the Bible's text as a goldmine for "proof-texts" was criticized by sixteenth-century humanist scholars (and, in Swedenborg's time, by an emergent new generation of interpreters of Scripture) as ignoring the context of a biblical reference, "proof-texting" remained a common practice among Protestant theologians, and testifies to the centrality of biblical authority in theological debate. See also pages 78–79 of the introduction. [RGE]

16 (in §3:1). Swedenborg's phrase "Jehovah God" (Latin *Jehovah Deus*) is derived from the Latin translation of the Bible he preferred, the 1696 edition of Sebastian Schmidt (1617–1696). The original phrase in Hebrew is יהוה אֱלֹהִים *(yhvh ʾĕlōhîm).* In English translations of the Bible, the phrase is more commonly rendered as "the Lord God," so capitalized (see, for example, Genesis 2:4). For more on the term "Jehovah," see note 9 above. [JSR]

17 (in §3:1). The expressions "the Word" (Latin *Verbum*) here, and "God with God" later in the same sentence, are allusions to the opening sentence of the Gospel according to John (John 1:1). Swedenborg generally follows Protestant tradition in using the term *the Word* in at least three interrelated meanings: (1) the eternal Word of God, which existed before creation (John 1:1–3); (2) the incarnate Word, born into time and space as Jesus Christ (John 1:14); and (3) the inspired Word of Scripture as truth revealed by God (compare Muller 1985, 324). In the present passage, Swedenborg is using the term in the first and second meanings just given. Usually, however, he simply means the Bible, or more specifically those books within the Bible that he found to have a spiritual meaning throughout, namely, the Pentateuch (Genesis, Exodus, Leviticus, Numbers, Deuteronomy), some other historical books (Joshua, Judges, 1 and 2 Samuel, 1 and 2 Kings), the Book of Psalms, the major and minor prophets (Isaiah, Jeremiah, Lamentations, Ezekiel, Daniel, Hosea, Joel, Amos, Obadiah, Jonah, Micah, Nahum, Habakkuk, Zephaniah, Haggai, Zechariah, Malachi), the Gospels (Matthew, Mark, Luke, John), and the Book of Revelation. Swedenborg's biblical canon, then, subtracted a number of books from the Protestant canon, much as the Protestant canon had done to the Roman Catholic canon. For further discussion, see Swedenborg's *Secrets of Heaven* 10325, and his 1758 works *New Jerusalem* 266 and *White Horse* 16. For his explanation that he did not generally include the works of the apostles or Paul in "the Word" because their style is doctrinal rather than wholly correspondential, see his letter to Gabriel Beyer (April 15, 1766), cited in Acton 1948–1955, 612–613. [JSR]

18 (in §3:2). Although Swedenborg here follows the general Christian view of his times in referring to "the Devil" as if there were a single evil force opposite God, in fuller discussions elsewhere he asserts that there is no such thing: instead he uses "the Devil" as a collective term for hell (see *Secrets of Heaven* 251:2; *Heaven and Hell* 311, 544); nor is there one supreme "Satan," or a "Lucifer," that is, an angel who was cast down and became the Devil (a concept based on Isaiah 14:12; see *Divine Providence* 27:1; *Last Judgment* 14). Swedenborg does, however, speak of two classes of people in hell, one called "satans," and the other called "devils," or "demons." The distinction is outlined in *Divine Love and Wisdom* 273 and *Divine Providence* 310:3, and mentioned in §281:12 of the present work and in *Heaven and Hell* 311:2. In general, "satans" are associated with false thoughts, love for the world, and justification of obsessions with evil, whereas "devils" are associated with demonic loves, love for oneself, and acting out obsessions with evil. Swedenborg consistently describes "devils" or "demons" as more profoundly wicked than "satans." [JSR]

19 (in §3:2). Much like "goodness" and "truth" (see note 7 above), "goodwill" (Latin *charitas*) and "faith" (Latin *fides*) are treated by Swedenborg as a pair. In §365:1 goodwill and faith are in fact defined together in terms of goodness and truth: "'Faith' means all the truth from the Lord that we perceive, think, and speak. 'Goodwill' means all the goodness from the Lord which moves us and which we then intend and do." A whole chapter of the present work is devoted to faith (chapter 6) and another to goodwill (chapter 7). Although often in Swedenborg's other works the term *goodwill* (sometimes elsewhere in this edition rendered *thoughtfulness* or *charity*) denotes or at least implies good actions toward others, in the present work Swedenborg distinguishes between goodwill and good works; see §374. For Swedenborg's report of a debate in the spiritual world on how to define goodwill, see §459. See also note 554 below. [JSR]

20 (in §3:2). In the original Latin edition, this section and the one before it (§§2–3) are set in significantly larger type than the text that comes before and after, either because Swedenborg wished to mark these sections for special attention or because of some typographical reorganization forced by changes made to the text late in the printing. The only other passage in large type in the entire work is §§344–345. [JSR]

Notes to Chapter 1, §§4–80

21 (in §4:1). Swedenborg also mentions this sending out of the twelve apostles or disciples in §108, and in §791, the last section of the main text of the work. In §791 he dates the event to June 19, 1770. Therefore the present passage and §108, which both describe this as happening "several months ago," were presumably added after the main text was finished, during a revision later in 1770. Publication of the work was begun in December 1770 and completed just before June 18, 1771 (see Acton 1948–1955, 738–740; see also the preface to the present volume, pages 21, 28–29). The term "spiritual world" may require some explanation. In Swedenborg's theological cosmology there are two worlds or universes, one physical and one spiritual, which are related to each other through correspondences (see the overview in §75; on correspondences, see note 35 below). Swedenborg uses "spiritual world" as an umbrella term that includes heaven, hell, and the intermediate "world of spirits" to which people first go after they die, before going to either heaven or hell (*Divine Love and Wisdom* 140). All people who have lived and died in the physical world now live in the spiritual world (*Heaven and Hell* 311–317). [JSR]

22 (in §4:1). For a discussion of eighteenth-century Christian views of the Trinity and how they contrast with Swedenborg's views, see the introduction, pages 77, 80–81, 86–90. For more on Swedenborg's perspective on the Trinity, see §§163–188. [JSR]

23 (in §4:2). The Latin word here translated "materialist philosophy" is *naturalismus,* for which the English cognate would be "naturalism." The term was used in Swedenborg's day to denote the beliefs of theologians and philosophers who put particular value on knowledge derived from observation and rational analysis (as opposed to divine revelation). See note 491. [RGE]

24 (in §4:3). Swedenborg uses the term "soul" (Latin *anima*) in a variety of ways that can be grouped into two basic meanings, one of which occurs much more than the other. The less frequent usage denotes an area within human beings that is above and out of the reach of the conscious mind—an incorruptible area where the divine life first flows into human beings (see, for example, §498 of the present work; see also his 1769 work *Soul-Body Interaction* 8; *Marriage Love* 46, 101, 158, 179, 260; compare what is said about our "inner core" in *Secrets of Heaven* 1999:3–4). More commonly the soul includes or is even equivalent to the mind or "spirit," that is, the seat of human will and intellect, or emotions and thoughts (which in Swedenborg's theology are spiritual, not material; see note 409). In the present passage, as elsewhere when the mind is not specifically mentioned as a separate entity from the soul, the second meaning seems to be intended. (On the terms "plant soul," "animal soul," and "rational soul," see note 175 below.) [JSR]

25 (in §4:3). Though the attribution to St. Athanasius (around 295–373) had been effectively challenged by Protestant scholars by Swedenborg's time, this fourth- or fifth-century creed (often called the *Quicunque Vult* from its opening words, "Whoever wants [to be saved]") was one of the three ancient creeds considered authoritative by Lutherans. Taking

their lead from Protestant reformers Martin Luther (1483–1546) and Philipp Melanchthon (1497–1560), Lutheran theologians put greater emphasis on the Athanasian Creed than did either Calvinist or Anglican theologians, and continued the pre-Reformation practice of its use in worship. See also the introduction, pages 86–87. For the full text of the creed in English, see Kolb and Wengert 2000, 24–25. [RGE]

26 (in §4:3). On the term "rational soul," see note 175. [JSR]

27 (in §5). Over the course of writing and publishing his theological works, Swedenborg came more and more to use the geometrical style of argumentation (also called axiomatic presentation), in which pithy statements are first presented without support, and then taken up one by one and discussed, illustrated, and corroborated. This style of argumentation is named for geometry—even though its content may not be in the least mathematical—because the best known work of ancient Greek geometry, *Elements of Geometry* by Euclid (flourished around 300 B.C.E.), was written in this axiomatic style. [JSR]

28 (in §5). A reference to two contradictory principles can be seen in points 3 and 4 in this list of propositions. One is the principle of *ethical relativism,* the belief that there is no objective means of determining that a given moral or religious principle is valid for all peoples and societies. Though ethical relativism is discussed at least as early as Plato (427–347 B.C.E.; see *Laws* 10:889–890 [= Plato 1952, 760]; compare Aristotle *Metaphysics* 1061b–1063b [= Aristotle 1952d, 590–592]), as a challenge to the traditions of western Europe it was particularly strong in the century before *True Christianity* was originally published. Whereas Europeans had formerly believed that the Christian religion was supreme and was a unique source of morality, they were steadily tested in this assumption by a stream of information brought back by global explorers and traders, especially reports about China's ancient, literate, and orderly society (see Anderson 2000, 307–309; Lovejoy 1960a, 99–110; Mungello 2005). In point 3, Swedenborg rejects the principle of ethical relativism by maintaining the universal validity of monotheism. The second principle to which Swedenborg refers here is *uniformitarianism,* the Enlightenment principle that all human reason operates in identical fashion the world over and will produce the same choices of laws and customs unless misled. In his discussion of point 4 (§11), Swedenborg likewise maintains that a single early revelation would have produced an identical religion throughout the world if it had not been perverted as it was diffused. For more on uniformitarianism, see Lovejoy 1960a, 79–82. Perhaps the most mordant attack on Christian religion on this basis was *Essai sur les moeurs* (Essay on Customs; 1756), a survey of the variation of beliefs throughout world history by the *philosophe* Voltaire (François-Marie Arouet; 1694–1778). A rich, classic study of eighteenth-century intellectual and artistic contacts between China and Europe in particular is Reichwein 1925, especially 75–96; see also the more recent discussion of Europe's encounter with the wider world in Marshall and Williams 1982, especially 67–184, on Asia. [JSR, SS]

29 (in §6:1). The Latin word here translated "earthly" is *naturalis,* literally, "natural." Swedenborg uses this word very broadly both of material things (including all that is human-made) and of the "lower" or "outer" of three levels of the mind or spirit, and therefore also of heaven (see, for example, §420). He frequently speaks of this three-tiered hierarchy of heavenly (sometimes translated "celestial"), spiritual, and earthly levels; less frequently does he apply these terms to divine qualities, as he does here. [JSR]

30 (in §6:1). The Latin term here translated "underlying reality" is *Esse,* the infinitive of the verb "to be" used as a noun. It is a philosophical term for basic existence or "is-ness" as an attribute. See also notes 84 and 86 below. [JSR]

31 (in §6:2). The phrase "the fullness of God" here might be an allusion to Ephesians 3:19, the sole use of the phrase in Scripture. The connection between the two passages is obscure, however. [JSR]

32 (in §8:1). "Inflow" (Latin *influxus,* traditionally translated "influx") is a term derived from philosophy that denotes a one-way influence of one level or entity on another. In Swedenborg's time and before, a vigorous debate had been going on about how the soul or nonmaterial aspect of a human being and the body or material aspect affect each other. In this debate, Swedenborg took a firm stand in favor of "spiritual inflow," the position that what is spiritual acts upon and affects what is physical, but what is physical does not act upon or affect what is spiritual (see his 1769 work *Soul-Body Interaction;* see also *Divine Providence* 314:1; *Secrets of Heaven* 6322:2). The reverse position was known as physical inflow. In his theological works, Swedenborg uses the term *inflow* of several one-way influences: the influence of a "higher" or spiritual part of a human being on a "lower" or earthly part; the influence of the spiritual world on the physical world (see for example *Divine Love and Wisdom* 340); the influence of the will on the intellect (see §§50, 395:3 in the present work, and *Divine Providence* 233:7; on the "will" and the "intellect," see note 39 below); and here, divine influence on human beings. [JSR]

33 (in §8:1). See §214:1 and note 455 below, which show how and why the terms "inmost" and "highest" are interchangeable in Swedenborg's theology. [JSR]

34 (in §8:2). For more on the rhythmic speech of spirits and angels, see Swedenborg's unpublished diary of 1745–1765, *Spiritual Experiences* (= Swedenborg 1998–2002) §3423; see also *Secrets of Heaven* 1648, in which this type of speech is compared to the Psalms. [JSR]

35 (in §8:3). The brief phrase "as that inflow comes down it takes forms that do not correspond" contains several terms that carry special meanings in Swedenborg's theological works. The term "inflow" is addressed in note 32 just above. The concept of correspondence is briefly defined in *Divine Love and Wisdom* 71 as "the mutual relationship between spiritual and earthly things." In its full formulation, it holds that there are two separate universes, one spiritual and one material, that are related to each other through similarity but not through any shared matter or direct continuity. The material world is caused by God through the spiritual world and therefore reflects that world; physical phenomena and events *offer images of*—that is, are "responsive to" or "correspond to"—spiritual phenomena and events. By the term "form," Swedenborg seems to mean simply the shape or condition of something, here something earthly or physical, although he at times also uses the term for the shape or condition of something spiritual (see also note 85 below). Forms, whether in nature or in earthly minds, that do not correspond are said to be unresponsive and unreceptive to a particular inflow from the spiritual world. [JSR, SS]

36 (in §8:3). The phrase "the three kingdoms of nature" refers to the animal kingdom, the plant kingdom, and the mineral kingdom. [JSR]

37 (in §8:3). Swedenborg holds that while humans have much in common with animals, the defining characteristics of humans are the faculties of will (or volition) and intellect (or discernment), which animals lack. On will and intellect, see note 39. For more on the distinction between humans and animals, see note 67. [JSR]

38 (in §9:1). In Swedenborg's hierarchical view of a human being (see note 6 above), the lowest level is "bodily," or physical and self-centered; it is preoccupied with one's own person and standing in society. The level one step above that is "worldly," or preoccupied with wealth. Each of these levels has its own driving motivation and values, or "love," and its own perspective on life. Later in the work (§395), Swedenborg clarifies that when people choose to give heavenly values and perspectives precedence over bodily and worldly ones, the heavenly self, the worldly self, and the bodily self in each individual work in harmony for that person's betterment; only if people willfully disregard heavenly values and perspectives will the lower loves and perspectives become dominant and damaging. Swedenborg does not, then, share the view of some Christian theologies that the body and the world, or our enjoyment of them, are intrinsically evil; when he speaks pejoratively of worldly and bodily loves or perspectives, the wider context of his works shows that he means the state those loves and perspectives take on when they have left their post, so to speak, and have mutinied against what is higher. [JSR]

39 (in §9:1). The term here translated "intellect" (Latin *intellectus,* traditionally translated "understanding," and elsewhere in this edition, "discernment") refers to one of two faculties of the human mind; the other is the "will" (Latin *voluntas,* elsewhere in this edition rendered "volition"). These faculties are possessed by all people; they are what make humans human. Common parlance might refer to them as our "mind" and our "heart"; more technical language might identify them as "cognitive" and "affective" functions. Later in the text Swedenborg gives them the following briefest of definitions: "the will is a vessel and a dwelling place for love, and the intellect is a vessel and a dwelling place for wisdom" (§37:2). He presents a partnership between the will and the intellect in which the will is dominant, as it is the true self or core of a person, while the intellect is an important and at times independent but often unheeded advisor to the will (see for example *Divine Providence* 209). To put this in terms of inflow, mentioned in note 32 above, there is an inflow from the will to the intellect, but not from the intellect to the will. For an overview of the relationship between the will and the intellect, see §397; for a detailed and extensive account of their interaction as analogous to that of the heart and the lungs, see *Divine Love and Wisdom* 394–431. [JSR]

40 (in §9:1). The "Christian confessional creed" referred to here and quoted just below in the text is the Athanasian Creed (see Kolb and Wengert 2000, 24.3–6, 15–16, 18–19). On the Athanasian Creed, see note 25 above. [JSR]

41 (in §9:2). Swedenborg frequently refers to "the Golden Age," a concept of great importance in Western thought from Greco-Roman antiquity to his day. For references to the Golden Age in antiquity, see note 375 below; for references in Swedenborg's day, see Helander 2004, 430–433. The Golden Age was viewed as a time of peace and plenty in which agriculture was unnecessary because nature readily provided food and in which there was no need for governments or armies because people lived in harmony. Swedenborg identifies the Golden Age with what he calls the "earliest" or "most ancient church," the first of the "five churches" (on the five churches, see note 3 above). The second of the five churches was the "early" or "ancient church," alluded to in the next sentence in the text. [JSR]

42 (in §9:2). In §279:4 of the present work and in *Secrets of Heaven* 66, Swedenborg asserts that the first chapters of Genesis (the first eleven chapters according to *Secrets of Heaven* 2897; the first seven according to his 1763 work *Sacred Scripture* 103:3) were copied

from an earlier, no longer extant revelation, which he calls the early or ancient Word (for a brief history of Swedenborg's statements about the ancient Word, see note 503 below). In §19:1 in this volume, and also in *Secrets of Heaven* 411 and 1343:1, Swedenborg cites these early chapters of Genesis as evidence that the name Jehovah was in use before the time of Abraham. [JSR]

43 (in §9:2). On "worldly loves" and "bodily loves," see note 38 above. [JSR]

44 (in §9:3). By "preclassical," Swedenborg means before the fifth century B.C.E. Modern philologists no longer support the long-standing notion of a linguistic connection between the names "Jove" and "Jehovah"; the word "perhaps" in this sentence of the text suggests Swedenborg may have been aware of such doubts in his own times. [JSR]

45 (in §9:3). Plato and Aristotle (384–322 B.C.E.) did not explicitly espouse this belief. It is, however, highly compatible with ancient Greek religious thought. The Greeks saw God as a predicative concept. That is, rather than maintain that God is wisdom, they would have asserted that wisdom is God. Virtually any quality or attribute within human conception could thus be assigned to divinity. To cite a specific instance: Aristotle writes, "We say . . . that God is a living being, eternal, most good, so that life and duration continuous and eternal belong to God; for this *is* God" (*Metaphysics* 1072b [= Aristotle 1952d, 603]). In other words, the attribution of life, duration, and eternity to God is possible because life, duration, and eternity *are* God—or again, because God can be predicated of them. (See Wilamowitz-Moellendorf 1920, 1:348, and Grube 1935, 150.) This predicative view of divinity allowed the Greeks easily to assign an attribute to one God rather than several; a Greek could comfortably speak of Athena as the god of wisdom or speak generally of wisdom being "the gods." Plato's view of God in particular is complex and requires some nuanced conjecture to reconstruct; see Grube 1935, 150–178, who denies that Plato is "ever fully monotheistic" (178). It can be said, all the same, that in general Plato simply does not concern himself with distinguishing between a single deity and plural deities. Swedenborg's assertion that the multiple deities of Greek religion are attributes of the One God can probably be traced back to research he recorded in the manuscript *Quotations on Various Philosophical and Theological Topics* (= Swedenborg 1976d). There Swedenborg took the following notes: "Plato affirms that heaven itself is his God or the God of gods," and "All things are full of the gods," referring to the spurious Platonic dialogue *Epinomis* 977–978 and 991, respectively (see Swedenborg 1976d, 245–246). The *Epinomis* dialogue approaches the notion that all the gods are subsumed in one, but avoids stating as much. Following this passage in Swedenborg's manuscript are quotations from various philosophers, including Hugo Grotius (1583–1645), Gottfried Wilhelm Leibniz (1646–1716), Nicolas de Malebranche (1638–1715), René Descartes (1596–1650), and Benedict de Spinoza (1632–1677). Several of these other quotations focus on the idea that God subsumes the rest of creation; for example, "God has attributes wherein . . . are contained all created things" (Spinoza, as quoted in Swedenborg 1976d, 344). Some of these philosophers cite pre-Christian thinkers. [SS]

46 (in §11:1). Here Swedenborg rejects one of the primary tenets of Deism, a philosophical outlook that during his lifetime could be defined roughly as a belief in God based on inborn knowledge, reason, and experience, without acceptance of revelation or traditional religion. [JSR]

47 (in §11:1). On the term "the Word," see note 17 above. Just as a garland is a ring or circlet of different things woven together, so the Word (roughly speaking, the Bible) is a

garland (Latin *corona*) of many books. The Latin word *corona* also means a crown, so although context suggests that the union of diverse elements is the chief metaphor here, the word may also be intended to convey the superiority of the Word over other revelations. The phrase "all the fullness of divinity dwells physically in him" is an allusion to Colossians 2:9. [JSR]

48 (in §11:1). This mention of a Christian axiom about the opposition between the earthly and the spiritual self may be an allusion to Galatians 5:17 (compare §327). [JSR]

49 (in §11:2). Though this reference to contemporary non-Christian theology remains somewhat obscure, it is likely that in referring here to the acknowledgment of "nature as God," Swedenborg is attacking pantheism, the belief that God and the material world are identical, inherent in which is the denial that God transcends the material world and abides beyond space and time. By those who identify God with the "innermost aspects of nature," he may perhaps mean that subset of pantheists who believed in an immanent divine principle in nature; by those who identify God with the "outermost aspects of nature," he may perhaps mean materialists who saw no inner spiritual operation in nature and reduced God to mere physical reality. The precise identification of the particular philosophers to whom Swedenborg alludes is probably irrecoverable. As a prime candidate, however, the Dutch philosopher Benedict de Spinoza is worth mentioning (though he was not always seen as a pantheist, but as an atheist). Spinoza stated, for example, that "Besides God, no substance can be nor can be conceived. . . . Hence it follows with the greatest clearness that God is one, that is to say . . . , in nature there is but one substance, and it is absolutely infinite" (Spinoza [1677] 1952, 359–360 = part 1, proposition 14). The Irish theological and political writer John Toland (1670–1722), who coined the English term *pantheist* in 1705, also promoted some pantheistic beliefs. For a brief discussion of the subject with further bibliography, see Kors 2003, 3:236–241 (under "Pantheism"). [SS]

50 (in §11:2). By the term "Entity of All" (Latin *Ens universi*), Swedenborg seems to mean "the universe as an objectified entity," or "the universe *qua* universe as God." The thinkers he refers to would thus be a subset of those who identified God with the natural world (see note 49 above); these particular "naturalists" attempted to disguise their beliefs or render them less objectionable by creating an imaginary "Entity of All" to worship in place of God. They did not believe in a transcendent deity—one that transcends, or exists beyond, space and time; they believed that every physical thing around us is God and is all there is of God. Swedenborg has more to say about them in *Secrets of Heaven* 4950: "They were questioned as to whether they believed in an 'Entity of All,' a Supreme Divine Thing, that had created everything; but from the thoughts they shared with me I could tell that what they believed in was a kind of inanimate thing devoid of life. From this I could see that it was not a creator of the universe they acknowledged, but rather nature. They even said they could not conceive of a living deity." (Translated by SS.) Swedenborg's point is that these people are worshiping merely inanimate physical reality, not the living, creative divinity that flows into that dead physical reality and informs it with life. The term "entity of the mind alone," or, in the Latin, *ens rationis,* was commonly used in Scholastic philosophy to denote a thing existing in the mind alone, as opposed to a *res extra mentem* ("a thing [existing] outside the mind") or (alternatively) an *ens reale* ("real entity"). Swedenborg is punning on the Scholastic term to make fun of the similar-sounding "Entity of All." [SS]

51 (in §12:1). Although this statement could be taken out of context to mean that reason is capable of seeing God by itself without the help of revelation, a different interpretation is suggested if the text in §11, which asserts that without revelation there would be no knowledge of God, is read with the text in §§273–276, which argues that all knowledge of God originated in revelation. Together they imply that once revelation has informed reason of the existence of God, whether directly from the page to the eye or very indirectly by centuries of tradition, reason can see corroboration in the phenomena of nature; if revelation had never been given to anyone on earth, however, no amount of nature study would originate the concept of God. [JSR]

52 (in §12:1). In his last five published theological works (*Revelation Unveiled* [1766], *Marriage Love, Soul-Body Interaction, Survey,* and the present work), Swedenborg uses the term "memorable occurrence" (Latin *memorabile,* plural *memorabilia,* traditionally translated "memorable relation") as a technical term for an extended narrative account of one of his spiritual experiences. [JSR]

53 (in §12:1). Swedenborg's theology holds that when human beings die, they experience a seamless transition from consciousness of the physical world to consciousness of the spiritual world (*Heaven and Hell* 445, 493). Swedenborg claims that he himself was granted the experience of dying while his body remained nonetheless alive; he wrote fairly detailed descriptions of this experience (see *Secrets of Heaven* 168–189, 314–319; *Heaven and Hell* 445–452). [JSR]

54 (in §12:1). As often in Swedenborg's accounts of memorable occurrences, the views expressed by the participants here seem a synthesis of various trends prevailing in Swedenborg's time. Specifically, here a theory about the reproductive powers of nature seems to have been substituted for a theory in dynamics (the laws of force, gravitation, and so forth) as they appear in contemporary models of cosmogony. One view of God's role in creation was that God had created the universe as a kind of elaborate machine that could run from inception without further intervention. This view is (somewhat inaccurately) called the Cartesian view, after the French philosopher René Descartes. A variation on this view held that the universe, though a mere mechanism, required a periodic readjustment, much as a clock mechanism needs winding and resetting. This view is generally called the Newtonian view, after the English natural philosopher Sir Isaac Newton (1642–1727); see his *Optics* 3:1 (= Newton [1717] 1952, 542), where he mentions in passing the eventual necessity of a "reformation" of the motion of the solar system due to the increase of "inconsiderable irregularities." The view described in this passage seems to be a blend of the Cartesian and Newtonian views transposed on reproduction. A third school, of which Swedenborg is an outspoken adherent, held that the universe has required the continual infusion of some kind of divine force from the time of creation onwards. [SS]

55 (in §12:1). The material from here to the end of §12 is adapted from parallel passages in *Divine Love and Wisdom* 351–357 and *Marriage Love* 416–421, with slight but intriguing differences among the three. In *Divine Love and Wisdom* Swedenborg simply presents the material in question as an expository prose passage without any introduction or frame. In *Marriage Love,* however, he presents it as the text of *Divine Love and Wisdom* read aloud at the request of angels in an account of a memorable occurrence in the spiritual world. In the present instance, he inserts it as a direct quotation from a speech he made in the spiritual world, without any reference to its earlier written forms. [JSR]

56 (in §12:3). When Swedenborg mentions here that insects have lungs, he is speaking loosely. In the next subsection he makes clear that he means they have "windpipes that function like lungs." [JSR]

57 (in §12:5). Swedenborg often speaks as though there were only one sun in the physical world, even though he was well aware that stars are suns (see §160:1 of this work, as well as *Secrets of Heaven* 9441: "It is known in the learned world that every star is like a sun in its own place"). It was surmised at least as early as the Greek philosopher Aristotle (384–322 B.C.E.) that stars were enormous bodies that we see from an immense distance (*On the Heavens* 289b–290b [= Aristotle 1952c, 381–382]). The notion of stars as the centers of individual solar systems was popularized in the seventeenth and eighteenth century by the French writer Bernard le Bovier de Fontenelle (1657–1757) in his *Entretiens sur la pluralité des mondes* (Conversations on the Plurality of Solar Systems, 1686; = Fontenelle [1686] 1990). For more on extrasolar systems, see note 131. [JSR, SS]

58 (in §12:7). The many references to bees and their behavior in Swedenborg's theological works attest to his interest in them and his sense that they reflected something heavenly (for similar mentions, see *Secrets of Heaven* 4776:5, 6323:2; *Heaven and Hell* 108; see also Swedenborg's unpublished manuscript of 1758–1759, *Revelation Explained* [= Swedenborg 1994–1997] §1198:4]. His information about bees came at least in part from the *Biblia Naturae* (The Book of Nature) of Jan Swammerdam (1637–1680), which was published posthumously in 1737–1738. The note Swedenborg wrote on the flyleaf of a copy he gave to his friend Anders Johan von Höpken (1712–1789) describes how Swedenborg saw creatures such as bees as evidencing the inflow of divinity into the material world (see Tafel 1877, 750; Swedenborg 1996, 2:607). [JSR]

59 (in §12:8). Swedenborg here dates his spiritual awakening (that is, his transition to consciousness of both the physical and the spiritual world) to some time around 1743. Neither the date of writing nor the date of his awakening can be established with certainty because this passage and §157 give the length of time as twenty-six years, whereas §§281 and 851 give twenty-seven years. In general, Swedenborg's spiritual awakening appears to have been a gradual process between 1743 and 1745. Swedenborg himself always assigns a single date to it, either directly or by giving a span of intervening time as he does here, but that date generally recedes the older he gets; that is, in the late 1740s, he places it in 1745; in the 1750s through 1766, he places it in 1744; and after 1766 he places it in 1743; see Tafel's recapitulation (Tafel 1877, 1118–1127). This receding date may have been the effect of simple forgetfulness, or it may have been the result of an evolving understanding of his past. [JSR]

60 (in §13:1). Alpha and omega are the first and the last letters of the Greek alphabet. For an explanation of their meaning and significance, see §19:2. [JSR]

61 (in §13:3). These two sentences are repeated almost word for word from §12:9. It is not clear whether this repetition was intended by Swedenborg as a kind of refrain or was a slip either in his manuscript copying or on the typesetter's part, as the result perhaps of picking up the previous page of the handwritten original. [JSR]

62 (in §13:3). The Latin terms translated here, and generally throughout this volume, as "purposes," "means," and "results" are *fines, causae,* and *effectus.* These terms have traditionally been translated as "ends," "causes," and "effects," respectively. [JSR]

63 (in §14:1). There are important resonances in Swedenborg's use of the expression "citizens of both worlds," one classically Augustinian and the other specifically Lutheran:

Augustine (354–430), in his *City of God,* describes the elect and reprobate as forming two eternal cities, which, though they mix and may be indistinguishable from each other on earth during the temporal life of humans, have different origins and destinations in the realm of the eternal; Luther developed the idea further in what has come to be called his "two kingdoms" doctrine. In Luther's understanding, every human is subject to God's authority in two ways: primarily, by the direct claim of God as sovereign; and secondarily, as an inhabitant of a world governed by God through temporal rulers. [RGE]

64 (in §14:2). On the will, see note 39 above. [JSR]

65 (in §14:2). For this use of the plural "satans," which is common in Swedenborg, see note 18 above. [JSR]

66 (in §14:3). By the "spirit" into which people come when they are at home alone, Swedenborg means their inner self or true nature, as opposed to their outer self or the outward persona they present to the world (see §156). It is this mind or spirit that survives death. For how the "spirit" relates to the "soul" in Swedenborg's theology, see note 24 above. For a more otherworldly application of the phrase "coming into one's spirit," see note 203. [JSR]

67 (in §14:3). Descartes had argued in the 1600s that animals were essentially machines (Descartes [1637] 1952a, 59), and Enlightenment philosophers later extended this assertion to humans as well, most noticeably Thomas Hobbes (1588–1679) in his work *Leviathan* (1651): "For seeing that life is but a motion of Limbs, the beginning whereof is in some principal part within, why may we not say that all automata (engines that move themselves by springs and wheels as doth a watch) have an artificial life? For what is the heart, but a spring; and the nerves, but so many strings; and the joints, but so many wheels, giving motion to the whole body, such as was intended by the Artificer?" (Hobbes [1651] 1952, 47). This hint was taken up in full by Julien Offray de La Mettrie (1709–1751) in his book *L'Homme machine* (Humanity as Machine [= La Mettrie [1748] 1994]) and Paul-Henri Dietrich, Baron d'Holbach (1723–1789) in his *Système de la nature* (System of Nature, 1770). Swedenborg, like other Christian thinkers, asserted that though humans have an outer nature that is like that of an animal, they possess eternal souls that live on after death, whereas animals do not (*Heaven and Hell* 39). For extensive discussion, with bibliography, of the machine—both actual automata and as symbol of humankind during the Enlightenment—see Schaffer 1999, 126–165. For a fuller discussion and refutation of the argument that humans cannot be immortal if animals are not, see *Secrets of Heaven* 4760:2, 5114:5. [JSR, SS]

68 (in §14:4). The expression "gathered to their people" is an allusion to an idiom of the Old Testament meaning to die (see Genesis 25:8, 17; 35:29; 49:29, 33; Numbers 20:24; 27:13; 31:2; Deuteronomy 32:50). In the Old Testament, however, the "people" to whom one is gathered are one's earthly relatives, whereas here they are one's spiritual associates. [JSR]

69 (in §15:1). The expression "communion of saints" is derived from the creeds; it is defined later in the text as the Lord's "church that is scattered throughout the entire world" (§307:1; see also §416). It has most frequently been understood to mean the community of the saved, whether on earth, in heaven, or in the ages to come. It is based in the communion between all believers in Christ, seen as bringing Christians into communion with each other as well. In an extension of this idea, the expression has

occasionally been extrapolated to mean the unity in holiness shared by the elect, the angels, and the whole company of heaven. This could explain Swedenborg's parallel use of the expression "communion of angels" in this passage. The individuals within each group are clearly seen as being in special relationship with other group members through God. [RGE]

70 (in §15:1). The term "the Regenerator" has a specific meaning in Swedenborg's theology. It refers to God as the cause of "regeneration," or the process of spiritual rebirth, in people. On regeneration, see chapter 10 (§§571–625) in the second volume of this work. [JSR]

71 (in §15:2). By the "appendix at the end of this work," Swedenborg meant a separate smaller title, which he planned to produce immediately after the present title, and in which he intended to discuss the spiritually bankrupt state of contemporary Christianity and its imminent replacement by a "new church" (see other mentions of the planned appendix in §§177:2, 4; 343; 627; 758; and a mention of a seemingly related possible future work in §123:2; see also the preface, page 29). At the time of Swedenborg's death, he left behind some manuscript fragments on such topics: *Sketch for "Coda to True Christianity," Draft for "Coda to True Christianity," Sketch for "End of the Age," Outlines for "End of the Age,"* and *Draft Invitation to the New Church* (items U178–U182 in Rose 2005, 503–505; see Swedenborg 1996). He did not, however, publish or even complete the promised appendix. [JSR]

72 (in §15:2). This characterization of the Trinity seems intentionally incongruous. The three figures come from two widely divergent traditions. The "ancient of days" is a term for God that occurs in one prominent story in the Old Testament (Daniel 7:9, 13, 22); the "high priest" was a leading cleric in the Jewish ecclesiastical hierarchy of Old and New Testament times (see, for example, Leviticus 21:10; Matthew 26:3); and Aeolus was a figure in Greco-Roman mythology—he was the god of the winds. [JSR]

73 (in §15:2). The Trinity actually was at times depicted in European art as a single human body with three heads, a representation that proved so repugnant that it was outlawed by the Roman Catholic Church in 1628, during the Counter-Reformation. See also note 521. [SS]

74 (in §16:1). The word "justification" here is shorthand for the Protestant concept of "justification by faith alone." For an explanation of this concept, see the introduction, pages 90–92. See also note 252. [JSR]

75 (in §16:1). The bishop of this passage cannot be identified; certainly the image he describes, that of the persons of the Trinity as fully distinct realities occupying separate thrones, is not one that would have been considered orthodox even by the contemporary targets of Swedenborg's criticism. (Such images had appeared in early Christian art, however; see note 521.) Swedenborg uses the story to challenge overly literal understandings of the local presence of God and Christ in heaven; perhaps he has literalists of the Zwinglian persuasion in mind in his critique, for whom the local presence of Christ in heaven precluded any simultaneous sacramental presence on earth. For more on the view of the sacrament of the Eucharist taken by followers of Ulrich Zwingli (1484–1531), see notes 135, 275, and 315. [RGE]

76 (in §16:3). The material in single quotation marks is an allusion to the Athanasian Creed (see Kolb and Wengert 2000, 24.15–16). See also note 25 above. [JSR]

77 (in §16:4). A theme that recurs throughout Swedenborg's theology is that the option of lying is taken away after death; one can then only keep silence or speak honestly (see §111:1). [JSR]

78 (in §17:1). The Latin words here translated "to give spiritual credit or blame" are *quod imputet,* literally, "to impute," or "that he imputes." The related Latin noun *imputatio,* traditionally rendered "imputation," appears in this translation as "the assignment of spiritual credit or blame." See chapter 11 (§§626–666) in the second volume of this work; see also the preface, page 41, and introduction, pages 93–95. [JSR]

79 (in §17:2). In Lutheran Scholastic theology of the age before Swedenborg, the attributes of God's divinity were conventionally described as being either immanent (relating to God's essence) or as outwardly manifested. In a typical listing of the outwardly manifested attributes of God, Abraham Calov (1612–1686) identified them in his comprehensive study *System of Theology* (1655–1677) as omnipotence, omniscience, grace, justice, truth, and omnipresence (cited in Schmid 1889, 125). These "scholars with the sharpest wits" have confused outward with immanent attributes (or perhaps are not Lutheran theologians). [RGE]

80 (in §17:2). Swedenborg gives a detailed explanation of the term "God Shaddai" in *Secrets of Heaven* 1992, where he discusses the use of the term in Genesis 17:1 and elsewhere. In English translations the biblical term has generally been rendered "God Almighty," but Swedenborg argues that the name actually refers to God as the one who brings us into and out of crisis or challenge, and then consoles and comforts us. As was the custom in his day, Swedenborg referred to the Pentateuch (Genesis, Exodus, Leviticus, Numbers, and Deuteronomy) as the books of Moses. [JSR]

81 (in §17:2). Swedenborg here lists gods and goddesses of Greco-Roman mythology by their Roman names. Saturn was the god of agriculture; Jupiter, the supreme god; Neptune, the god of the sea; Pluto, the god of the dead, ruler of the underworld, and giver of wealth; Apollo, the god of prophecy, music, medicine, poetry, and the sun; Juno, the chief goddess, wife and sister of Jupiter, and the goddess of marriage; Diana, the goddess of hunting and childbirth; Minerva, the goddess of wisdom, invention, the arts, and martial ability; Mercury, the god of commerce, travel, and thievery, and messenger to the other gods; and Venus, the goddess of sexual love and physical beauty. [JSR]

82 (in §17:3). In his *Theological Commonplaces* (1591), Martin Chemnitz (1522–1586) defined *person* as formulated by classical Lutheran dogmatics as "an individual, intelligent, incommunicable substance, which is not sustained, either upon another or from another" (Chemnitz 1591, 1:39; cited in Schmid 1889, 144). The purpose of such a definition is to assert the individuality and uniqueness of personhood, and exclude the idea that persons could simply be different manifestations of the same entity. Swedenborg's interlocutors were more accurate here than previously in the question of God's immanent attributes (see note 79). See also note 12. [RGE]

83 (in §17:4). The connotation of the term *metaphysics* has shifted in a positive direction since Swedenborg's time. Then it often referred, as it does in the present passage, to a kind of philosophizing that was overly abstract and subtle. [JSR]

84 (in §18). The terms here translated "underlying reality" (Latin *esse,* literally, "to be," "is-ness," or "actual existence") and "essence" (Latin *essentia*) have long histories in western philosophy and theology. Swedenborg's usage of these terms differs somewhat

from the traditions he inherited. In those traditions, the term *essentia* often refers in a general way to that which makes something what it is (see note 12 above), while *esse* denotes something's actual existence; in this sense *essentia* is philosophically prior to or more fundamental than *esse*. In Swedenborg's theology, however, the roles are reversed. Particularly here in this chapter, *esse* is the most fundamental attribute—so much so that little can be said about it—while *essentia*, even the divine *essentia*, is more easily describable; see also §21 at the end. [JSR]

85 (in §18). *Substance* and *form* are technical terms stemming from ancient Greek philosophy. They were adopted by medieval Scholastic philosophers and were widely used in various senses by Enlightenment philosophers as well. Often equated with one another, even by the Scholastics, in most uses their definitions overlap. Furthermore, each of these terms could be more precisely specified; therefore the exact sense in which Swedenborg is using them may not be documentable. Rather than relying on the reader to understand arcane Scholastic distinctions, however, he generally uses terms in their immediate and commonsense meanings. "Substance," in Swedenborg's use, seems equivalent to what we would call a material. In using the word "form," Swedenborg is likely to be dispensing once again with Scholastic subtleties and referring approximately to the shape of a physical thing, as determined by the essence that informs the substance of which the thing is made. Thus (§20) he notes that "substance without form" is a "figment of the imagination"; that is, a material thing must have a physical shape. Finally, it is important to bear in mind that Swedenborg speaks of substance and form as belonging not only to the material world but to the spiritual world and even to the Divine as well (as he does here), where their analogs have similar effects (see §20; see also *Divine Love and Wisdom* 91, 257). For Swedenborg's discussion of these terms, see his unpublished work *Draft on Ontology* (= Swedenborg 1901). For further information, see Brown 1919, 398–413. [SS]

86 (in §18). In Swedenborg's theology, *esse*, here translated "underlying reality," is philosophically prior to or more fundamental than *essentia*, "essence" (see note 84). Likewise, *existere*, literally, "to stand out," here translated "capacity to become manifest," is philosophically prior to or more fundamental than *existentia*. The latter term means, if you will, "standing-out-ness," and is rendered "actual manifestation" in this translation. The basic philosophical sense of the term *existentia* is "that aspect of a being that stands out as distinct or particular, as against that which is undifferentiated or held in common." *Existere*, then, is the capacity of a being to take on this distinguishing or differentiating aspect. Here and elsewhere in this work, "underlying reality" and "capacity to become manifest" are paired together, as are the qualities to which they give rise: "essence" and "actual manifestation" (see especially §21). [GMC, JSR]

87 (in §19:1). On the term "Jehovah God," see note 16 above. [JSR]

88 (in §19:1). Here and throughout the rest of this volume, italicized material in biblical quotations represents Swedenborg's use of small capitals in the first edition to indicate emphasis. For more on Swedenborg's approach to biblical quotations, see pages 103–104. [JSR]

89 (in §19:1). The word "regeneration" here (Latin *regeneratio*) is not in the Bible Swedenborg generally used, Schmidt 1696; instead that text has the more familiar "generation" (Latin *generatio*). It is difficult to tell if the mention of "regeneration" here

is deliberate or not. On regeneration, see chapter 10 (§§571–625) in the second volume of this work. [JSR]

90 (in §19:2). Swedenborg was familiar with many languages. He was fluent in Swedish and Latin (which was still a spoken language during his lifetime) and had studied Greek and Hebrew. In addition, he had spent months in Germany and Denmark, over a year in France, over a year in Italy, and several years each in England and Holland, and had become familiar with each of the languages of those countries. His personal library contained works in many contemporary and ancient languages. (For a list of the works in Swedenborg's possession at the time of his death, less volumes that may have been kept by his heirs, see Alfelt 1969. A reconstructed collection of works that were in his library is held at the Swedenborg Library in Bryn Athyn, Pennsylvania.) [JSR]

91 (in §19:2). The work mentioned here, *Marriage Love,* was published by Swedenborg in 1768. [JSR]

92 (in §20). Biblical references to "children of God" or "sons of God" occur at Hosea 1:10; Matthew 5:9; Luke 20:36; John 11:52; Romans 8:16, 21; 9:8, 26; Galatians 3:26; 1 John 3:10; 5:2. References to those "born of God" occur at John 1:13; 1 John 3:9; 5:4, 18. [JSR]

93 (in §20). Swedenborg is probably referring here to natural religion, a religious perspective based on reason rather than revelation (for discussion and further bibliography, see Kors 2003, 3:142–150), or to pantheism (see note 49 above). He himself, despite his expressed respect for reason elsewhere, rejected natural religion as early as 1734, when he wrote: "Whatever is confirmed by Holy Scripture is in no need of confirmation from reason, from rational philosophy, or from geometry; this [confirmation] being already sufficiently implied in the fact of confirmation by the Infinite Himself" (*Basic Principles of Nature,* part 1, chapter 2 [= Swedenborg [1734] 1988a, 1:49]). [JSR, SS]

94 (in §20). For this belief in the accidental creation of the universe (including humankind), see, for example, the *philosophe* Denis Diderot (1713–1784): "The possibility of fortuitously engendering the universe is exceedingly small, but . . . the number of streams of [primordial] particles is infinite, that is to say, . . . the unlikelihood of such an event is more than set off by the multitude of streams" (Diderot [1746] 1953, 10, as translated in Pullman 1998, 150). A still earlier example could be cited—the real-life Savinien Cyrano de Bergerac (1619–1655), who attempted to compute the probabilities of such a random generation of the universe using a crude form of the mathematics of probability (Cyrano de Bergerac [1656–1662] 1968, 77, as cited in Pullman 1998, 373 note 85; for discussion, see Alcover 1970, 63). [SS]

95 (in §20). Thirty-seven years before the publication of *True Christianity,* Swedenborg had published an extensive theory of very much this kind, in which nondimensional points combine to form dimensional objects; see his scientific magnum opus of 1734, *Principia Rerum Naturalium* (Basic Principles of Nature, part 1, chapter 2 [= Swedenborg [1734] 1988a, 1:46–71]), and the brief overview in Jonsson 1999, 29–32. Compare the similar implicit criticism in *Divine Providence* 6; for commentary, see Swedenborg [1764] 2003b, 357 note 17. Swedenborg's resort to a nondimensional point in his scientific theories may have arisen out of a desire to dodge Descartes's rejection of atoms (as indivisible bodies) on the grounds that anything that has extension (dimension) in space must necessarily be further divisible (Descartes [1644] 1983, part 2, §20). However, Swedenborg was not comfortable with his theory from the moment he proposed it, as his own ambivalent language shows: Though he first insists that "this natural point is the same as the mathematical

point" because "the world is geometrical," he later hedges this statement by adding that this fundamental, simple point, "must be considered as non-geometrical, although it resembles what is geometrical" (*Basic Principles of Nature,* part 1, chapter 2 [= Swedenborg [1734] 1988a, 1:5]). He then laments his inability to articulate the complexity of the concept by adding: "I could wish that some other person, capable of the task, would favor us with a better or more just view of the subject. For my own part, I could willingly give up the further consideration of this first [point]. . . ." (*Basic Principles of Nature,* part 1, chapter 2 [= Swedenborg [1734] 1988a, 1:61]). For discussion, see Odhner 1951, 237–251, especially 242–243. [JSR, SS]

96 (in §20). In classical Greek mythology, the river Styx was the river of the underworld across which people were ferried into Hades; both the gods and people swore their most solemn oaths by it. The root of "Styx" in Greek denotes "hateful" and "gloomy." Tartarus, below Hades, was the lowest part of the infernal regions; it was widely used as a literary motif in the Neo-Latin literature of Swedenborg's time (see Helander 2004, 280). [JSR]

97 (in §21). By writing of God as "love in itself" in this passage, Swedenborg would not have been challenged by the dogmatic theologians of the Lutheran tradition, which also taught that all of the attributes of God were only "inadequate conceptions of the divine essence" and thus reflections of a deeper immanent reality in God (Quenstedt 1685, 1:284, cited in Schmid 1889, 121). [RGE]

98 (in §21). John 5:26 reads, "As the Father has life in himself, so he has granted the Son to have life in himself." [JSR]

99 (in §21). The Latin term here translated "actual manifestation" is *existentia.* See note 86 above. [JSR]

100 (in §22:3). Here Swedenborg may be referring to the long-held belief that the dark patches of the Moon's surface are bodies of water, similar to the oceans of Earth. The Greek biographer and moralist Plutarch (around 46–after 119 C.E.) expressed the notion that there were bodies of water on the surface of the moon (*Moralia* 935c). This idea went against the Aristotelian tradition, however, since Aristotle taught that the heavenly bodies are perfect spheres composed purely of unchanging substance (*On the Heavens* 270a–270b [= Aristotle 1952c, 351]). In later centuries as scientific instruments improved, Aristotle's view was again called into question. The astronomer Galileo Galilei (1564–1642), looking through his telescope, could see mountains, valleys, and even these apparent "seas"; see Galileo 1989, 43. German mathematician and astronomer Johannes Kepler (1571–1630) at first disagreed with Galileo, believing instead that the *light* patches on the moon were bodies of water and the *dark* patches continents; he later reversed his position and agreed with Galileo (Rosen 1965, 25–27). The modern nomenclature for such lunar features derives from the work of the Jesuit astronomer Giovanni Battista Riccioli (1598–1671), who in his 1651 *Almagestum Novum* called these patches *maria* ("seas") and gave them the names by which they are still known. See Whitaker 1999, 6, 7, 10–14, 19, 20; Winkler and Van Helden 1992, 195–217. [GMC]

101 (in §22:3). The reference to people's carrying religion in packs on their backs may be a reference to a motif of Greek and Roman literature—the proverbial pack on our back into which we put our faults. We can see the faults of others on their backs, but we cannot see our own, which may be even more numerous and grievous. See Aesop *Fables* 359 (= Aesop 1889; compare Jean de La Fontaine *Fables* [= La Fontaine

1909] 1:7:34–35); Babrius *Fables* 66; Phaedrus *Fables* 4:10; Catullus *Carmina* 22:21; Horace *Satires* 2:3:298–299; Persius *Satires* 4:23–24. The proverb is also quoted in a letter of 406 C.E. from Jerome (around 347–around 420) to Augustine (Letter 68, §2). The application here seems to be that though these people do carry religious concepts around with them, they keep them in the pack on their back where they are out of sight and thus never heeded. Compare §146. [SS]

102 (in §23:2). Vespasian (9–79 C.E.), as emperor of Rome (69–79), ordered the sacking of Jerusalem and the destruction of its temple in 70 C.E. [JSR]

103 (in §23:2). In this passage, Swedenborg is certainly referring to the long tradition of constructing automata (see note 546), but he may also be referring to an ancient tradition of deception in religion, whereby a statue or mask of a god or philosopher was secretly fitted with movable parts, or especially with a speaking tube through which a person in another room would speak the "divine oracle." Some scholars suspect that the most famous prophetic institution of classical antiquity, the Delphic Oracle, in fact employed this sort of deceptive device. In recent times several of these devices have come to light. The best-known example was discovered in the 1940s; it consists of a marble statue of the philosopher Epicurus (341–270 B.C.E.) that had been modified to hold a speaking tube so that the mouth emitted a voice. Though those testing it spoke from another room via a tube thirty-six feet (thirty-three meters) in length, modern-day listeners reported that the effect it produced was quite strange and convincing. The reconstruction is graphically described in Poulsen 1945, 178–195; it is also described in Lane Fox 1987, 135 note 44, in the context of other such ancient deceptions. The Greeks knew how to "animate" statues, a tradition that is referred to in Aristotle (*Politics* 1253b [= Aristotle 1952f, 447]) and actually demonstrated in Hero of Alexandria *Pneumatics* 28–30, 40, 54, 60, 70, 78. The sources of power for such devices were water and steam pressure. In Europe in the centuries just prior to Swedenborg's time, many scientists, such as Leonardo da Vinci (1452–1519), experimented with automata for the pleasure of their noble and royal patrons. Swedenborg would have been familiar with such devices. See also Douglas 1912–1913, 511–526. The reference to Satan, of course, alludes to the deception of Eve and Adam by the serpent in Genesis 3 (on Satan, see note 18 above). [GMC]

104 (in §24:1). For an extensive exposition of the spiritual sun in Swedenborg's theology, see *Divine Love and Wisdom* 83–172. The idea is traceable in his thought to at least the 1741 work *Dynamics of the Soul's Domain* (= Swedenborg [1740–1741] 1955) 2:§§255–267, and is mentioned in the 1745 work *Worship and Love of God* 56. [SS]

105 (in §24:1). Swedenborg quite often uses the term "substantial" to characterize spiritual "matter," while using "material" to characterize physical matter (see for example §798; *Marriage Love* 31, 328). [JSR]

106 (in §25:1). In this passage Swedenborg refers to an "oval of intensely shining light" that opens up the heavens for him. In detailing their religious experiences, writers from many times and places have described a point or window of light that opens into a heavenly vision of one sort or another. The shape commonly appears in the Christian iconographic tradition as the *mandorla,* the almond-shaped *aureole* or border surrounding either the Christ at his ascension, or the Virgin or Mary Magdalene at their respective assumptions, that is, as the heavens open up to receive them (see Hall 1994, 103). It symbolizes the glory of a sacred person and is also called *vesica piscis,* "fish bladder," on account of its

shape (Apostolos-Cappadona 1994, 226). In Christian art, the mandorla seems never to have been used to surround a living person, but only the souls of the glorified (Murray 1996, 300). It is unclear how widely these ideas were known during Swedenborg's time, although Christian art depicting these themes could be seen in churches all over Europe. For an example, see *The Transfiguration of Christ* (about 1441) by Fra Angelico (around 1400–1455) in the monastery of San Marco, Florence. [GMC]

107 (in §25:2). The expressions "a god from God" and "an eternally begotten god from God" denote the Christian concept of the Son, the expression "a god emanating from an eternally begotten god from God," the Holy Spirit. [JSR]

108 (in §26). Swedenborg is referring here to the Athanasian Creed. See note 25 above. [JSR]

109 (in §26). Winnowing is an ancient technique of separating the useful kernel of a grain from the inedible chaff; it is still employed in many parts of the world. After the grain has been threshed, a process in which the kernels are broken loose from the chaff, the product is then gathered into winnowing baskets. The contents are thrown into the air and caught again, the chaff being blown away by the wind. Sometimes a breeze is created with a fan or a piece of cloth. Winnowing is a very common religious symbol, appearing in the Bible as well as in the Qur'an, where chapter 51 is called the "winnowing wind." The wind is a traditional sign of the "Spirit," which here cleanses Swedenborg of mistaken thoughts or understandings. There are multiple threshing contexts in the Bible: Deuteronomy 25:4; Judges 8:7; 2 Kings 13:7; 1 Chronicles 21:20; Job 39:15; Isaiah 25:10; 28:27–28; 41:15; Jeremiah 14:5; Hosea 10:11; Amos 1:3; Micah 4:13; Habakkuk 3:12. Chaff is also mentioned: Job 21:18; Psalms 1:4; 35:5; Isaiah 5:24; 17:13; 29:5; 33:11; 41:15; Jeremiah 23:28; Daniel 2:35; Hosea 13:3; Zephaniah 2:2; Matthew 3:12; Luke 3:17. [GMC]

110 (in §28). Swedenborg's assertion of the limitations even of the most analytically capable human mind is both timeless and very much a part of Enlightenment thought. The historian of ideas Arthur O. Lovejoy notes: "The authors who were perhaps the most influential and the most representative in the early and mid-eighteenth century made a great point of reducing man's claims to 'reason' to a minimum, and of belittling the importance of that faculty in human existence; and the vice of 'pride' which they so delight to castigate was exemplified for them in any high estimate of the capacity of the human species for intellectual achievement, or in any of the more ambitious enterprises of science and philosophy" (Lovejoy 1960a, 68). This anti-intellectualism often existed side by side with a dependence on reason as humankind's only protection against the excesses of "passion," or the emotions. For a discussion of pride, humility, and anti-intellectualism as themes in Enlightenment thought, see Lovejoy 1960a, 62–68. See also note 604. [SS]

111 (in §28). Swedenborg is here describing an experiment well known and much repeated in his time, performed to demonstrate the effect of a vacuum on living creatures. It is the subject of a famous painting by Joseph Wright of Derby (1737–1797) titled *An Experiment on a Bird in the Air Pump* (1768), now in the National Gallery, London. [JSR]

112 (in §28). Swedenborg is probably thinking here of Cleombrotus of Ambracia, whose dates are not known, but who was alive at the time of Socrates' death (399 B.C.E.; see Plato *Phaedo* 59c [= Plato 1952, 221]) and was a pupil of the Greek philosopher Plato. The Roman philosopher Marcus Tullius Cicero (106–43 B.C.E.) mentions that Cleombrotus threw himself into the sea after reading Plato's *Phaedo* on the immortality of the soul (Cicero *Tusculan Disputations* 1:34:84; see also Callimachus *Epigrams* 25). [SS]

113 (in §29:1). For a brief summary of Swedenborg's concept of space and time, with extensive references to other relevant passages, see Gregory R. Johnson's comment in Kant [1766] 2002, 162 note 35. The view of space and time taken by Immanuel Kant (1724–1804) is similar in some respects: "Space does not represent any property of things in themselves . . . It is therefore from the human point of view only that we can speak of space, extended objects, etc. . . . . Time is not something which subsists of itself, or which inheres in things as an objective determination" (Kant [1781] 1952, 24–27 = §§2–7). On Kant's views, see also Jammer 1993, 131–139. A full comparison between Kant and Swedenborg on this topic, however, would be a complex undertaking, as would any determination of Swedenborg's possible influence on Kant. On space in Swedenborg, see also Pendleton 1957, 161–177, 204–221, 225–243; Odhner 1958, 301–314. [SS]

114 (in §29:1). From the point of view of an observer on the earth, over the course of each year the sun appears to move from one constellation of the zodiac to the next. With the gradual adoption of the heliocentric model of the solar system in the 1600s, however, this motion of the sun had come to be recognized as only an appearance caused by the earth's annual orbit around the sun. From the point of view of a putative observer at the sun, the earth itself would seem to move through the constellations of the zodiac as it progresses through the year, passing through the constellation opposite the one where the sun appears from the point of view of an observer on the earth. It is the point of view of an observer at the sun that Swedenborg uses here in citing the zodiac as the background and context for the earth's orbit. [JSR]

115 (in §29:1). By the statement that these elements are "extended," Swedenborg means "extended in three dimensions in space," that is, that they "take up" space. Although adumbrated in earlier philosophy (see Aristotle *Physics* 209b–210a, 211a–212a [= Aristotle 1952e, 288, 290–291]; Hobbes [1651] 1952, 270–271 = chapter 46), the concept of extension first became of critical importance to philosophical debate in the writings of René Descartes, who drew a contrast between matter, which possessed extension, and mind, which did not (Descartes [1641] 1952b, 130–133). Any educated reader of the eighteenth century would have instantly recognized this commonplace philosophical term. [SS]

116 (in §29:2). Swedenborg shared the belief of his times that there is an atmosphere rarer or finer than air, called "ether," which interpenetrates everything (see, for example, §339 below). It is (1) a term for "upper air" or "upper atmosphere" (*Revelation Unveiled* 907; *Marriage Love* 188:3); (2) a medium of light analogous to air as the medium of sound (see *Secrets of Heaven* 4523:1, 6013:2, 6057:1; and §§32:8, 79:2–6 in the present work); and (3), following the hypothesis of both Isaac Newton and Christiaan Huygens (1629–1695), a supporting structure for the universe of mechanical action and a hypothetical cause of gravity (Swenson 1972, 9–10), a use that Swedenborg echoes in §30. As a substance supposedly more refined than other matter, ether was also considered by some to be the stuff of which souls, angels, and spirits are made, for which reason some people called them "ethers" (see *Marriage Love* 315:11). Thus the Greek physician Galen (129–around 200 C.E) taught that the human soul was ultimately derived from the ethereal (upper atmospheric) regions, whence eternal spirit is inhaled and refined, and the *psychic spirits* are produced for use in the brain and the nerves, primarily for perception. This "pneumatic physiology" is described in Galen's treatise *On the Usefulness of the Parts of the Body* (= Galen 1968). In his *Life of Apollonius of Tyana,* the Greek philosopher

Philostratus (around 170–around 245 C.E.) taught that the ether was the divine element of the human soul (see Philostratus *Life of Apollonius* 3:34; compare 42). This is the sense in which the word is used in this passage (though Swedenborg does not subscribe to this view). [GMC, JSR]

117 (in §29:2). On the use of "substantial" to describe spiritual matter, see note 105 above. [JSR]

118 (in §29:3). In classical Lutheran dogmatics, God's infinity was understood as an expression of God's uniqueness; unlike every other being, God transcends all bounds and cannot be limited in space or time (see Schmid 1889, 116). [RGE]

119 (in §30:2). The word "taste" here and just below refers to the components in the tasted object that key into the receptors in the physical organs supplying the sensation of taste. This is why "taste" is seen here as an active force impinging on the passive receptors, in a parallel to the way light and sound impinge on the passive eye and ear, respectively. Swedenborg discusses his theory of taste extensively in *Draft on the Five Senses* (= Swedenborg 1976b) §§649–678; there §§654–656 relate in particular to what we would today call the molecules that we taste and the oral receptors into which they fit. See *Worship and Love of God* 50 note i for a similar reference to substances (as opposed to modulations of the atmosphere, which Swedenborg believed both light as well as sound to be) that produce smell and taste through their impact on the respective sensory organs. The mention of taste in this context is striking because elsewhere Swedenborg distinguishes it sharply from other senses. Spirits, for instance, do not have taste, but rather a sense analogous to it (see *Secrets of Heaven* 1516); or, in an alternative view, though they do have taste, it has a spiritual rather than a physical basis (see *Revelation Explained* [= Swedenborg 1994–1997] §618). One of the earliest theories describing the mechanism of taste as consisting of keys fitting into receptors was ascribed to the Greek philosopher Empedocles (around 492–434 B.C.E.) in Theophrastus *On the Senses* 7–12. [SS]

120 (in §30:2). For theories about ether in Swedenborg's day, see note 116 above. [JSR]

121 (in §30:2). By "both brains" Swedenborg means both the cerebrum (the expanded anterior portion of the brain) and the cerebellum (the small dorsally projecting portion of the brain between the brain stem and the back of the cerebrum). [JSR]

122 (in §31:1). This definition of God's infinity as immensity in regard to space and eternity in regard to time is a conventional one in Lutheran dogmatics; the Danish theologian and bishop of Sjælland, Jesper Rasmussen Brochmand (1585–1652), used extremely similar language in his *Comprehensive System of Theology* (see Brochmand 1633; Schmid 1889, 119). [RGE]

123 (in §31:3). Perhaps this is a nod to the apocryphal statement by St. Augustine that God spent the time before the creation of the world making hell for those who ask meaningless questions. For a similar statement by Luther, see note 171. [RGE]

124 (in §31:3). By "inner angels" here Swedenborg presumably means angels of the inner or higher heavens. For the correlation between "inner" and "higher," see note 6. [JSR]

125 (in §32:1). An entry in one of Swedenborg's notebooks (Swedenborg 1976d, 353) demonstrates that he was aware that the principle that no two substances can be exactly alike appears several times in the philosophy of Gottfried Wilhelm Leibniz. The first reference to this principle occurs in Leibniz's *Discourse on Metaphysics* (Leibniz 1956, §9; see also Leibniz 1881, §9). It is now called Leibniz's Law or "the identity of indiscernibles"

(that is, the sameness of things that cannot be distinguished from one another). It is sometimes said to depend upon another principle of Leibniz, the principle of sufficient reason, which (simply stated) holds that nothing exists without a reason. That is, Leibniz would aver that God would have no reason to create a thing if another thing identical to it already existed. However, other justifications can be found in Leibniz's philosophy. Some philosophers distinguish further between Leibniz's Law and the identity of indiscernibles, and argue that Leibniz did not advance either, but a related concept; see Feldman 1970, 510–522, for a rigorous analysis, and Curley 1971, 497–501, for a rebuttal. The question of whether two things can be exactly identical has a long pedigree; see, for example, the discussion by Cicero in his *Academica* 2:54–56. For further discussion of the identity of indiscernibles, see Black 1952, 153–164; Ayer 1954, 26–35; Hacking 1975, 249–256; O'Leary-Hawthorne 1995, 191–196; Zimmerman 1997, 305–309. [SS]

126 (in §32:1). By "substantial" here, Swedenborg may mean spiritual; see note 105 above. [JSR]

127 (in §32:1). The Greek astronomer Hipparchus (around 190–after 126 B.C.E.) noticed that at the time of the vernal equinox the sun rises at a slightly different position every year against the background of the fixed stars (see Ptolemy *Almagest* 3.1). He and subsequent Greek astronomers accounted for this motion from their earth-centered perspective by postulating a separate sphere of celestial motion as a cause. Nicolaus Copernicus (1473–1543) was the first to propose that this motion was due to a peculiarity of the Earth's rotation, namely, that the "pole" of the earth's motion is not fixed, but wobbles like the axis of a toy top (see his *On the Revolutions of the Heavenly Spheres* [Copernicus [1543] 1952]; see also Goldstein 1994, 189–197). The cycle of this movement, which is called precession, takes about twenty-six thousand years to complete. Although here Swedenborg expresses doubt about the exact repetition of the cycle, astronomers in his time were well aware of this phenomenon. [GMC]

128 (in §32:2). Swedenborg here echoes (without fully quoting) an ancient Latin saying; among its first occurrences in western literature is Terence *Phormio* 454, a work of the second century B.C.E. Since then the phrase has generally been rendered *quot capita, tot sententiae* (as many opinions as heads); *quot capita, tot sensus* (as many meanings as heads); or *quot homines, tot sententiae* (as many opinions as people). Swedenborg's version is *quot capita, tot animi* (as many minds as heads). The meaning is the same in every case: there are as many opinions as there are people to think them. [JSR]

129 (in §32:3). This statement reflects the common belief of the times that all animals were created at the beginning and have persisted since then. Nevertheless in a later passage and elsewhere we find a somewhat different idea, namely, that harmful animals such as crocodiles, leopards, wolves, rats, and poisonous snakes were not part of creation, but came into being after it (see §78:5; *Divine Love and Wisdom* 336; *Revelation Explained* [= Swedenborg 1994–1997] §1201:3). [JSR]

130 (in §32:3). Swedenborg's reference to "many" planets is an understatement. Over a twenty-year period of unchecked reproduction, a single plant that occupies one square inch and bears a hundred seeds each year would yield a number of plants sufficient to cover 10^{22} (ten thousand million million million) earth-sized planets. [JSR]

131 (in §32:5). There is a long tradition in the West prior to Swedenborg of a belief in many worlds and many solar systems, beginning from classical thinkers onward. Anaximander of Miletus (around 610–547 B.C.E.) is perhaps the best-known thinker to

have taught that the worlds are infinite in number. Aristotle, however, offered a cogent argument in *On the Heavens* 270b (= Aristotle 1952c, 362), based on the idea that there can be only one center of gravity, that ours is the only world system. Medieval Christian theologians could not accept this Aristotelian doctrine, since it places a limit on God, the Infinite and Eternal, which is one of the reasons Aristotle's philosophy initially was out of favor with the Church. A major question for these thinkers was: How can God's grace extend to this infinity of worlds? The Jewish thinker Hasdai Crescas (1340–1410), an opponent of Aristotelianism, was very influential among subsequent Christian thinkers, such as Nicholas of Cusa (1401–1464), Marsilio Ficino (1433–1499), Giovanni Pico della Mirandola (1463–1494), and Giordano Bruno (1548–1600; see Wolfson 1971, 117–118, 214–217, 472–476; Harvey 1998, 8–18). Crescas cited the Talmudic teaching that God governs eighteen thousand worlds, and he speculated that the worlds may actually be infinite in number, each with its own center of gravity. The most notorious of the "infinite worlds" thinkers was Giordano Bruno, who was not a scientist, and who understood the new Copernican astronomy only slightly. In his 1584 *De l'infinito universo e mondi* (On the Infinite Universe and Worlds), he set forth the argument that the universe is infinite, that it contains an infinite number of worlds, and that all of these worlds are inhabited by intelligent beings. This heresy would eventually bring him nine years of torture at the hands of the Inquisition and finally lead him to the stake in 1600 (Greenberg 1950, 56–65; Singer 1968; Armitage 1948). See also note 57. [GMC]

132 (in §32:5). Swedenborg is here referring to his 1758 work *Other Planets.* In that work (§§127–129) as well as later in the current work (§64) and in *Heaven and Hell* 192 he asserts that he was able through nonphysical travel to visit other planets and interact with their inhabitants. The idea of life on other planets grew widespread during the second half of the eighteenth century; for more on this and how Swedenborg's view of life on other planets relates to other ideas at the time, see Crowe 1986. [JSR]

133 (in §32:8). This seems to be a specifically Swedenborgian idea, derived from Swedenborg's cosmogonic theories (compare *Divine Love and Wisdom* 173–178, 183). He certainly borrows terminology from the earlier scientific tradition, such as the ideas that the air is the atmosphere closest to the planet and the ether is the rarified substance above the air; but the concept of an "aura" as the rarest of atmospheres is not prominent in that tradition. For more on the ether, see note 116 above. [GMC]

134 (in §33). This may be a reference to the Greek philosopher and mathematician Zeno of Elea (around 495–around 430 B.C.E.), who taught that every magnitude is divisible into an infinite number of magnitudes (see Simplicius *In Aristotelis de Physica Commentarii* 139–141), and whose famous paradox concerns the infinite subdivision of space. Then again, it may be a reference to the Aristotelian perspective in the ancient debate between those who supported the "atomic hypothesis," namely, the view that matter could not be divided below indivisible atoms, and those who supported the idea of infinite divisibility; see Kenyon 1994. [GMC, JSR]

135 (in §33). John Calvin (1509–1564) and Ulrich Zwingli held to the principle that the finite cannot contain the infinite *(finitum non capax infiniti),* specifically in relation to the notion of the infinite divinity of the Son being contained in the finite bread and wine of Christian Communion. The principle was rejected by Luther; see the discussion in note 275; see also note 245. It is striking that Swedenborg does not here connect the

phrase with the Lutheran understanding of the Communion. It appears in a similar discussion of the infinite and the eternal in *Secrets of Heaven* 3404:2. For a very ancient formulation of a similar notion, see Aristotle *Physics* 266a (= Aristotle 1952e, 353): "In no case is it possible for an infinite force to reside in a finite magnitude." [JSR, SS]

136 (in §33). In the first edition here the words "my works" are set in small capitals as if they were a title. Scholars have been puzzled by this reference, and have identified three candidates to be the works in question: (1) *Basic Principles of Nature* (1734), part of a multivolume set, and possibly to be taken in conjunction with *The Infinite* (1734), another small work published at the same time (Acton 1995, 43–44); (2) *Worship and Love of God* (1745), which might rank as "works" in the plural inasmuch as it was published in two separate parts (Gorman 1885, viii–ix); and (3) *Divine Love and Wisdom* (1763) and *Soul-Body Interaction* (1769). In fact, this description of God limiting his infinity into substances and ultimately forming inert elements closely matches part 4 of *Divine Love and Wisdom,* especially §§290–295, 300, 302–304, and *Soul-Body Interaction* throughout (see the convenient summary in §2 of that work); furthermore both works are cited in the previous paragraph of the main text here. Therefore his reference to "my works on creation" could be taken to mean those works. By contrast, *Basic Principles of Nature, The Infinite,* and *Worship and Love of God* do not discuss the instrumentality of the spiritual sun in creation in the specific terms used here. However, insofar as elements of this exposition can be seen in all of the works mentioned, Swedenborg may not be referring exclusively to any one of the enumerated candidates. For example, in *Basic Principles of Nature,* part 1, chapter 2, §1 (= Swedenborg [1734] 1988a, 1:46), he writes, "What is finite . . . takes its origin from what is infinite"; and in both that work and *The Infinite* he concludes that the "least natural entity" (which today we might call the first or most elementary physical particle or substance) "derived its origin from the Infinite" (*The Infinite* 4 = Swedenborg [1734] 1965, 30). *Worship and Love of God* is couched in a more complex symbolism, but in it Swedenborg is clearly holding to the same principle that the finite stems from the Infinite. Thus the reference to "my works on creation" can be read as meaning "all those works of mine in which I wrote on creation." Gorman 1885, vii–ix, sees a similar reference to Swedenborg's pretheological works in the phrase *ex scriptis de inhabitatione ejus [mundi],* "from the things that have been written concerning the inhabiting of the world," in *Soul-Body Interaction* 9. For an extensive discussion of Swedenborg's teachings on creation, see Odhner 1964; the topic has also been discussed in *The New Philosophy* in articles too numerous to list. See also Lamm 2000, 247–250. [JSR, SS]

137 (in §34:2). The original text of this paragraph seems somewhat unbalanced, but the reasons for that imbalance are not clear. There is a simile for the sorts of things loved by the second and third group and another simile for the nature of their intellect. In the case of the first group, however, there is only one simile, which applies to the sorts of things they love; there is no simile for the nature of their intellect. [JSR]

138 (in §34:3). Modern readers may be misled by the assumption that glass is generally so clear as to be virtually invisible; such was not the case in earlier times. Glass is understood to be a dark substance in several parallel passages in Swedenborg (see *Divine Providence* 318, where it is specifically called *vitrum nigrum,* "black glass"; and *Marriage Love* 233, *True Christianity* 334, where it is paired with black stone). In other cases its complete transparency must be specified by adjectives such as *purum* ("pure"), *pellucidum* ("clear"),

or *crystallinum* ("crystalline"); see especially *Marriage Love* 103 and *True Christianity* 839, in which windows are specifically described as being made of crystal glass. [SS]

139 (in §34:3). Although Swedenborg occasionally mentions Satan in casual references, as he does here and at the end of §23, his theology does not in fact accept the existence of a lone Devil or Satan in opposition to God; see note 18 above. [JSR]

140 (in §35:3). Acton 1938, 9–15, points out that this man proves to be an adherent of the theory of the nebular hypothesis of the origin of the solar system (see note 141 below). The German philosopher Immanuel Kant advanced this theory as early as 1755 in his book *Theorie des Himmels* (Theory of the Heavens), and the present passage would suggest that the theory was well known to Swedenborg. [SS]

141 (in §35:7). In his cosmological works, Swedenborg had argued that the planets ("the expanse") arose from an explosion of a crust built up on the surface of the sun ("the center")—that is, that the "expanse" came from "the center." The nebular hypothesis of the origin of the solar system advanced by Immanuel Kant (see note 140 just above) maintained the reverse: a nebula or cloud of cold gas ("the expanse") contracted to form the planets and finally the sun ("the center"). The scholar described in this memorable account does not dare to openly espouse his own cherished Kantlike theory, which is that "before the sun existed there was something," that is, the nebula; and that "of its own accord it flowed together into some order," that is, it coalesced to form the sun. It is worth noting that though Swedenborg is sometimes seen as the originator of the nebular hypothesis (for example, see Lachièze-Rey and Luminet 2001, 151), he here emphatically disavows it. That said, however, it should also be observed that in Swedenborg's treatment in this passage the dispute takes on a philosophical and theological import higher than that of mere competition between cosmological theories; in particular, it stands for a refutation of the belief that the origin of the universe can be found in nature, or (generally stated) that effect produces cause. The nesting and interweaving of symbols is very complex. For a fuller discussion of the cosmological aspects of the passage, see Acton 1938, 9–15; for Swedenborg's early cosmological theories, see *Basic Principles of Nature,* part 3, chapter 4 (= Swedenborg [1734] 1988a, 2:251–272), and *Worship and Love of God* 9–11. [SS]

142 (in §35:8). The Latin phrase here translated "continuing to exist is the same as perpetually coming into being" was a common theological maxim (see *Secrets of Heaven* 3483:2, 5084:3; see also *Marriage Love* 380:8; *Soul-Body Interaction* 4). Swedenborg frequently built on it (see §§46, 224:1 in the current work; *Secrets of Heaven* 775:2, 3648:2, 4322, 4523:3, 5116:3, 5377, 6040:1, 6482, 9502, 9847, 10076:5, 10152:3, 10252:3, 10266; *Heaven and Hell* 106, 303; *Divine Love and Wisdom* 152; *Soul-Body Interaction* 9:1). The notion is referred to as a commonplace in part 5 of *Discourse on Method* by Descartes: "It is an opinion commonly received by the theologians, that the action by which [God] now preserves [the universe] is just the same as that by which He at first created it" (Descartes [1637] 1952a, 55). Elsewhere Descartes offers this explanation: "The present time has no causal dependence on the time immediately preceding it. Hence, in order to secure the continued existence of a thing, no less a cause is required than that needed to produce it at the first" (Descartes [1641] 1952b, 131). Catholic philosopher Thomas Aquinas (1224 or 1225–1274) makes a similar statement about all "creatures," that is, created things: "The being of every creature depends on God, so that not for a moment could it subsist [have independent existence], but would fall into nothingness were it not kept in being by the operation of the Divine power" (*Summa Theologiae* 1:104:1; translation in Aquinas 1952,

535). In support of his position, Aquinas in turn cites another Church Father, Gregory the Great (540–604), specifically his *Moralia in Job* (Ethical Disquisitions on Job) 16:37; he is probably thinking of Gregory's statement there that "All things subsist in him [God]. . . . No created thing avails in itself either to subsist or to move." This Scholastic theory of perpetual creation is also discussed by the Anglo-Irish philosopher George Berkeley (1685–1753) in his work *The Principles of Human Knowledge* (Berkeley [1710] 1952, §46). It should perhaps be emphasized that the concept of the ongoing re-creation of the universe is by definition outside the pale of modern science, whereas in Swedenborg's view it can be taken as a scientific axiom. In other words, along with other aspects of the Swedenborgian principle of divine inflow, it is radically different from typical modern assumptions about the functioning of the universe. [JSR, SS]

143 (in §35:10). The mention here of two centers and two expanses refers to "life" and "nature" as two separate worlds, one spiritual, one physical. [JSR]

144 (in §37:3). Here and in §41:3 of the present work Swedenborg reverses a pattern that generally obtains in his previous theological works. In his work on marriage of three years earlier, women are generally said to be related to volition and love, while men are said to be related to intellect and wisdom (*Marriage Love* 33, 91, 160, 187, 218:2, 296:1). Here and in §41:3 the correspondence is the other way around (see also §377, where the love-related terms "goodwill" and "goodness" are said to play the role of father, and the wisdom-related terms "faith" and "truth" the role of mother). Passages in other works, however, bridge these two points of view and suggest how both may be simultaneously true: one declares that men are inwardly forms of love but outwardly forms of wisdom, and women are inwardly forms of wisdom but outwardly forms of love (*Marriage Love* 32); the other suggests that the relationship of love and wisdom to male and female is opposite in the so-called heavenly kingdom of heaven to that relationship in the so-called spiritual kingdom of heaven (*Secrets of Heaven* 8994:4). [JSR]

145 (in §37:3). Just as Swedenborg categorizes animals in ways that are unfamiliar to modern readers (see notes 129 and 159), he sees birds as being of two basic types: birds that come out by day, and birds that only come out in the evening or the night. In the latter group he includes creatures such as bats that are no longer thought of as birds (see also §332:2; *Divine Providence* 167). In Swedenborg's theology, birds that can see and therefore fly in the evening or the night have a very dark connotation. [JSR]

146 (in §38:2). Swedenborg refers here to the land of Canaan as the lush and verdant place of biblical times, "a land flowing with milk and honey" (Exodus 3:8). [JSR]

147 (in §38:2). In Swedenborg's day a "hydra" was any terrifying serpent or reptile; a "prester" was a serpent whose bite was believed to cause death by swelling. [JSR]

148 (in §38:3). For a more detailed discussion of these bundles, using the example of nerve fascicles, see §351. [JSR]

149 (in §40). The motif of a faint, deceptive light or glimmer recurs frequently in Swedenborg's theology. The Latin term for it here is *lumen fatuum* (literally, "foolish glimmer"); elsewhere it appears as *lux fatuus* or *ignis fatuus* (literally, "foolish light" and "foolish fire," respectively). In this volume alone, *lux fatuus* is mentioned at §§42; 61; 69:1; 94; 155; 162:2–3; 176; 334:4, 8; 335:1; 339:2; 346; and 385:3; and *ignis fatuus* at §110:1. The *lumen fatuum, lux fatuus,* and *ignis fatuus* were the "spectral lights" or "spook lights" believed by some to herald death. There are many folklore traditions

that associate the lights with the spirits of the dead, and such lights are often reportedly seen on or around battlefields where many people are known to have died at once. These mysterious lights often appear in marshes, but also occasionally over regular terrain. The traditional explanation is that, at least in the case of marshes, they are produced by spontaneous ignition of swamp gases. This is the explanation that seems most likely to have been known to Swedenborg; see §385:3. See Ross 1986, 10; Lang 1901, 343–344; Newell 1904, 39–60. [GMC, JSR]

150 (in §41:2). On "reformation" and "regeneration," two phases of the transformation of the individual from being earthly or hellish to being heavenly, see chapter 10 (§§571–625) in the second volume of this work. [JSR]

151 (in §41:2). Both "Lucifer" and "the dragon" are biblical allusions to the Devil. For Lucifer, see Isaiah 14:12; for the dragon as the Devil and Satan, see Revelation 20:2. The dragon plays a prominent role in Revelation 12 and 13 as well. On the stance of Swedenborg's theology in regard to the Devil, see note 18 above. [JSR]

152 (in §42). The Latin terms here translated "adolescence" and "early adulthood," *pueritia* and *adolescentia,* have frequently been mistranslated in earlier English versions of Swedenborg's works. They have been rendered as "childhood" and "adolescence" or "youth," respectively; but Swedenborg makes the dividing line between these ages explicit: *pueritia* lasts until the twentieth year of age, and is followed by *adolescentia* (*Secrets of Heaven* 10225), which would begin then in one's twenties. [JSR]

153 (in §43:2). "Michael" (Revelation 12:7) and "Gabriel" (Daniel 8:16; 9:21; Luke 1:19, 26) are angels mentioned by name in the Bible; see note 464. On "the Devil" and "Satan," see note 18. [JSR]

154 (in §43:2). The Latin word here translated "the people" is *subjectis,* literally, "the subjects." In philosophical terminology of the time, "subjects" referred to thinking beings, and "objects" to nonthinking beings. [JSR]

155 (in §44). Anthropomorphizing not only animals but also plants (Helander 2004, 443–444) was a common literary technique in the Swedish Neo-Latin literature of Swedenborg's time. [JSR]

156 (in §45). It is important to note that these descriptions are the way things appear *in the light of heaven,* which Swedenborg also refers to as "the light of truth" (§186). He explains elsewhere that in the faint, deceptive light of hell, things look more agreeable and normal to the spirits there (§281:12). [JSR]

157 (in §46). The "final cause" is one of four main categories of cause introduced by Aristotle *Physics* 194b–195b (= Aristotle 1952e, 271–272); it is equivalent to the purpose for which something exists or is created. "Intermediate causes," then, are methods or means of achieving the final cause or purpose. For a fuller discussion, see note 576. [JSR]

158 (in §48:1). Compare *Revelation Unveiled* 875:1, another memorable occurrence that begins with an exchange between an angel from the east of heaven and an angel from the south. [JSR]

159 (in §48:2). From an early period Western Europe was home to a belief—shared by Swedenborg—that all minerals, plants, and animals were arranged in a hierarchy within their respective kingdoms, and even within individual categories within those kingdoms. This hierarchical world system is known as the Great Chain of Being. The classic study on this topic is Lovejoy 1960b; it refers to the term "Great Chain of Being"

as "the sacred phrase of the eighteenth century," though some Enlightenment thinkers as early as the French philosopher René Descartes (Lovejoy 1960b, 188) and as late as Voltaire rejected the concept (Voltaire [1764] 1962, 163–166 [under "Great Chain of Being"]). The English writer Sir Thomas Elyot (1490?–1546) illustrates this belief:

> Beholde also the ordre that god hath put generally in al his creatures, begynnyng at the moste inferiour or base and assendynge upwarde: he made not only herbes to garnisshe the erthe, but also trees of a more eminent stature than herbes, and yet in the one and the other be degrees of qualitees; some pleasant to behold, some delicate or good in taste, other holsome and medicinable, some commodious and necessary. Semblably [similarly] in byrdes, bestis, and fisshes, some be good for the sustinance of man, some beare thynges profitable to sondry uses, other be apte to occupation and labour; in diuerse [some] is strength and fiersenes [fierceness] only; in many is both strength and commoditie; some other serue for pleasure; none of them hath all these qualities, fewe haue the more part of many, specially beautie, strength, and profite. But where any is founde that hath many of the said propreties, he [it] is more set by [esteemed] than all the other, and by that estimation the ordre of his [its] place and degree euidentlye apperethe [appears]; so that euery kynde of trees, herbes, birdes, beastis, and fisshes, besyde theyr diuersitie of fourmes, haue . . . a peculier disposition appropered [assigned as proper] unto them by god theyr creatour: so that in euery thyng is ordre, and without ordre may be nothing stable or permanent; and it may nat be called ordre except it do contayne in it degrees, high and base, accordynge to the merite or estimation of the thyng that is ordered. (Elyot [1531] 1907, 4)

For example, falcons with their long wings were considered noble, while short-winged goshawks and sparrow-hawks were considered ignoble (see *Oxford English Dictionary* under "ignoble"). See also subsection 13 of the current passage, where the distinction is applied to different kinds of seeds; and also §94 and note 249. For an extensive discussion of this belief in order and degrees as it appears in Elizabethan times, see Tillyard 1959. [JSR, SS]

160 (in §48:8). The Enlightenment period saw tremendous interest in the question of the extent to which knowledge was innate in humans; see the discussion at note 549. Thinkers of the time determined to settle the question empirically by either directly or indirectly studying the behavior of feral children—those who had been deprived of human contact from birth, or at least at some period during their childhood. Swedenborg's cousin-in-law, the taxonomist Carolus Linnaeus (1707–1778), created an entire subgenus *Homo Ferus* ("Wild Human") based on the evidence provided by such feral individuals as Peter of Hanover (1713?–1785) and Marie-Angélique Memmie Leblanc (1711?–1775). The traits reported here—for instance, inability to speak, lack of knowledge about proper human food, disinterest in the opposite sex—were reported of these feral individuals. The response of the scientific community in Europe to these people is described in Douthwaite 2002, 21–69; see especially page 32. The conclusions drawn and the apprehensions created by these studies reflected the values and concerns of the age. On feral children in general, see Candland 1993. [SS]

161 (in §48:8). For passages that help explain what Swedenborg means here by "mindlessly physical" (Latin *corporeus*), see §§381:1, 402. [JSR]

162 (in §48:9). In a memorable occurrence a little later in the present work, Swedenborg is told that the animals seen in the spiritual world are reflections of the feelings of people nearby (§78:1–2). [JSR]

163 (in §48:13). The word "human" shares the same root as the Latin *humus*, "earth." Likewise the Hebrew word אָדָם *('ādām)*, meaning "Adam" or "human," shares a root with the word אֲדָמָה *('ădāmā)*, which means "soil" or "ground." [GMC]

164 (in §48:20). This description parallels ancient Greco-Roman images of the messenger god, also known as Hermes and Mercury. See Kerényi 1986 for a general resource on Hermes. [JSR, SS]

165 (in §49). On the "divine design," see note 13 above. [JSR]

166 (in §53). The Latin words for "substance" and "subsist" in this sentence are a noun and a verb with the same root. They are used here in the philosophical sense of "(a thing) having a separate or independent existence." See also §17:3 and note 82. [JSR]

167 (in §53). On hellish plants and animals, as well as hell itself, coming into existence after creation, see §§78:5, 490; see also *Divine Love and Wisdom* 336; *Revelation Explained* (= Swedenborg 1994–1997) §1201:3. [JSR]

168 (in §55). As a member of the Swedish House of Nobles, Swedenborg was keenly interested in economic legislation, writing several memoranda on the subject during his long career; one example is translated in Acton 1948–1955, 537–544. He could not have been unaware that a new theme of economic theory, if not practice, in Western Europe during the Enlightenment was that laws governing trade should be flexible and nonrestrictive. During this period mercantilism, a rigid economic program that was the counterpart of political absolutism, was being challenged by the theory that would someday be known as laissez-faire or free trade. In France in particular, François Quesnay (1694–1774) offered an economic analysis known as Physiocracy (from Greek roots meaning "the rule of nature"). The Physiocrats held that natural laws of economics should be allowed to operate and that state interference should be ended; they actually succeeded in enacting some of their proposed reforms in the 1760s. The movement toward laissez-faire found its most acute and eloquent theoretician only after Swedenborg's death, when the Scot Adam Smith (1723–1790) published *An Inquiry into the Nature and Causes of the Wealth of Nations* in 1776. For brief overviews of the economic theory of the period, see Anderson 2000, 115; Kors 2003, 2:77–79. For more detail, see Dumont 1977, 40–108; Roll 1961, 54–198; and for the full treatment, Schumpeter 1954, 73–376. [SS]

169 (in §58). See Luther's complaint about this type of assertion in note 171 below. [SS]

170 (in §58). Earlier in this paragraph where goat people and sheep people are mentioned, Swedenborg implies that the belief of his times goes against a New Testament parable (Matthew 25:31–46). In that parable the Son of Humankind sits in judgment and separates people, as a shepherd separates sheep from goats; he places on his right the sheep, or the just, who have treated others well and will therefore go into eternal life, but places on his left the goats, or the unjust, who have not treated others well and will therefore go into everlasting punishment. Here and in several other passages in the present volume, goats have an evil connotation (§§72:1, 3; 74:5; 95; 113:4; 316; 328); but in still other passages they are associated with goodness (§§78:1; 200:2; 388:1, 3; 431:2; 448).

At the end of the paragraph Swedenborg similarly contrasts a dove person with an owl person. Doves have long been a symbol for mildness and meekness; in Swedenborg's works owls, and particularly horned owls and screech owls, are generally characterized as fierce and hellish (see for example §78:5). [JSR]

171 (in §58). This paragraph is full of biblical allusions. The mention of the eating of the fruit by Adam alludes to Genesis 3:6; the killing of Abel by Cain, Genesis 4:8; David's census of the people, 2 Samuel 24:1–10; the building of shrines for idols by Solomon, 1 Kings 11:7–8; and the desecration of the Temple by the kings of Judah and Israel, 2 Kings 16:8, 14, 17–18; 18:15–16; 2 Chronicles 26:16–19. Here Swedenborg uses for his own purposes a stock argument leveled against Christianity by Deists (see note 46), namely, "If God is omnipotent, why does he allow anyone to fall into damnation?" But it is important to distinguish between Swedenborg's use of this argument and that of the Deists. The latter, although they too generally believed in God, propounded this argument to challenge and even ridicule written revelation and the notion of God's interference in human affairs (Kors 2003, 1:338–339). For examples of such ridicule, see Voltaire's *Philosophical Dictionary* under "History of Jewish Kings and Chronicles" and "Moses" (= Voltaire [1764] 1962, 306–307, 400–405). Similar criticisms can also be seen in the best-selling *Dictionnaire historique et critique* of the fideist Pierre Bayle (1647–1706); for example, see the marginal notes for the article "David" (= Bayle 1740, 2:254–255). Swedenborg agrees that this argument points up an absurdity, but finds the source of that absurdity not in revelation but in the contemporary understanding of God's omnipotence. Finally, it should be noted that arguments of this kind will have been familiar to contemporary readers of both old and new theology and philosophy; see, for example, the trenchant comment in Luther's *Table Talk* (= Luther 1848) §§66–67:

> If a man ask, Why God permits that men be hardened, and fall into everlasting perdition? let him ask again: Why God did not spare his only Son, but gave him for us all, to die the ignominious death of the cross, a more certain sign of his love towards us poor people, than of his wrath against us. Such questions cannot be better solved and answered than by converse questions. . . . Let, therefore, his good will be acceptable unto thee, oh, man, and speculate not with thy devilish queries, thy whys and thy wherefores, touching God's words and works. For God, who is creator of all creatures, and orders all things according to his unsearchable will and wisdom, is not pleased with such questioning. . . . When one asked, where God was before heaven was created? . . . I said: He was building hell for such idle, presumptuous, fluttering, and inquisitive spirits as you.

See also Swedenborg's *Spiritual Experiences* (= Swedenborg 1998–2002) §4322. [JSR, SS]

172 (in §58). By the term "ancient gentiles" Swedenborg is referring here to the non-Jewish people of the Greco-Roman world. See also *Secrets of Heaven* 4280:2. [JSR]

173 (in §58). Swedenborg here mentions four myths found in the *Metamorphoses* of Ovid. Elsewhere Swedenborg presents the work as evidence that ancient peoples knew correspondences (see his unpublished manuscript *Draft of "Sacred Scripture"* [= Swedenborg 1997b] §7:3). Here, however, he emphasizes the unrealism and absurdity of these myths in order to question and challenge contemporary views of divine omnipotence. The myth of Deucalion and Pyrrha is found at Ovid *Metamorphoses* 1:313–415; the myth of Apollo and

Daphne, at 1:452–567; the myth of Diana and the hunter (Actaeon), at 3:138–252; and the myth of the maidens of Parnassus (the nine Muses), at 5:250–299. [JSR]

174 (in §60). By "glands" here, Swedenborg means what are now called brain cells or neurons, terms that did not exist at the time. Before turning to theology, Swedenborg had spent years studying and writing works on human anatomy. The brain was a particular focus of his research and an area in which he made several discoveries long before other researchers in the field, including the functions of the cerebral cortex, the corpus callosum, and the pituitary gland (see Gross 1999, 429–445, for overview and further bibliography). [GMC, JSR]

175 (in §63). The idea of a "plant soul" is as old as Aristotle and Galen, and a discussion of its role in biology (as then understood) would have been part of the general education of an intellectual such as Swedenborg. First discussed by Aristotle in *On the Soul* 413a (= Aristotle 1952g, 643), the notion is further developed by Galen for medical discussion in *On the Natural Faculties,* book 1. Creatures partake of various types and combinations of soul, according to their place in the order of creation. There were three souls: plant soul (or "nutritive" soul), animal soul, and rational soul. They corresponded (roughly) to the three types of "spirits," or very fine fluids (see note 467), that were thought to circulate within the bodies of animals, performing various life functions. The plant soul is the power we have in common with plants, namely, the capacity of our bodily tissues to derive nourishment from food and grow as if on their own. The animal soul is, among other things, the capacity that we share with other animal beings for self-locomotion and perception or sensibility. Finally, the rational soul is possessed by humankind alone among the created beings and is the basis of the human intellect. A being possessed of a rational soul also possesses the two lower souls and could not exercise the intellect if the lower souls were impaired. See also note 467. [GMC]

176 (in §63). On the meaning of "extended," see note 115 above. [JSR]

177 (in §63). Swedenborg made the first two points in §30, but does not discuss the third. The only thing comparable is §6:2, where Sacred Scripture is linked with "the fullness of God," a phrase that occurs in Ephesians 3:19. [JSR]

178 (in §64). Swedenborg collects his accounts of these experiences in his 1758 work *Other Planets.* [JSR]

179 (in §64). The three figures mentioned here, Martin Luther, John Calvin, and Philipp Melanchthon, were all major Protestant reformers. Luther and Calvin were the founders of the two principal branches of Protestant Christianity, which are commonly called Lutheran and Calvinist accordingly; Melanchthon was a friend of Luther's and author of the first systematic presentations of Reformation theology. See also §§796–799 in the second volume of this work. [JSR]

180 (in §64). Robert Smith (1689–1768), the writer of a book on optics that Swedenborg is known to have read (see Swedenborg 1976d, 473–477), states this principle as follows: "What is the apparent distance between two objects in any situation or between one object and the spectator himself, but the apparent extension of intermediate objects? And since they are seldom seen alone . . . it cannot be doubted, but we estimate their distances from one another and from our selves by our ideas of the magnitudes of those intermediate objects" (Smith 1738, 1:49). In *De Inquirenda Veritate* (On the Necessary Inquiry into Truth; second edition 1691), the French Cartesian philosopher Nicolas de Malebranche

makes the following statement: "When . . . I see a bell tower off in the distance, in the same field of vision I usually see a number of fields and houses intervening; but because I judge by the distance to those fields and houses, noticing that the bell tower is even farther away than they are, I take the bell tower to be more distant, larger, and taller than if I had seen it by itself. Nevertheless the image the tower forms in the inner part of my eye is the same size whether there are intervening fields and houses or not" (Malebranche 1691, 41). [JSR]

181 (in §67). The phrase "efficient cause" here is a reference to the theory of causation adopted by Aristotle and the medieval Scholastic philosophers. It is one of the four main categories of cause that Aristotle introduced (*Physics* 2:3 [= Aristotle 1952e, 271–272]). The "efficient cause" of something is the force or agent that creates it. On other types of cause, see note 576. [JSR]

182 (in §71:1). As mentioned above in note 21, Swedenborg divides the spiritual world into three main areas, which, listed in descending vertical order, are heaven, the world of spirits, and hell. The "lower earth" is the lowest area of the world of spirits; as such it contains people who have died but have not yet gone to their final home in either heaven or hell; see also *Heaven and Hell* 513; *Revelation Unveiled* 845:2; *Secrets of Heaven* 4728. For other memorable occurrences that Swedenborg experienced in the lower earth, see §§332–334 in the present volume. Swedenborg's descriptions give the impression that it is a kind of underground world or system of caves beneath the surface of the world of spirits. Here a chasm opens up giving access to it; in another memorable occurrence (§332:1) he climbs down a ladder to reach it. [JSR]

183 (in §71:1). The mention here of an evil spirit's ability to change his form into that of an angel of light is an allusion to 2 Corinthians 11:14: "Satan himself transforms himself into an angel of light." [JSR]

184 (in §71:2). The Latin phrase here translated "a heaven in miniature and a world in miniature" is *Micro-Uranos & Microcosmus,* literally, "micro-heaven and microcosm." The concept of a human being as a miniature world appears at least as early as the Neo-Platonic commentator Ambrosius Theodosius Macrobius (late fourth century C.E.), who wrote, "Natural philosophers say that the world is a vast human being and that a human being is a little world" (*In Somnium Scipionis* 2:12:11). For references to this popular concept in the fifteenth to eighteenth centuries, see Helander 2004, 434–444; Gatti 2002, 368–372, 375–380. *Micro-Uranos* is a related but much rarer term, which may even have been coined by Swedenborg himself. [JSR]

185 (in §71:3). Swedenborg alludes here to two biblical stories: that of Lot's wife, who looked back longingly in her flight from God's destruction of Sodom and in consequence was turned into a pillar of salt (Genesis 19:26); and that of the idol Dagon (1 Samuel 5:2–5). [JSR]

186 (in §71:3). For an explanation of the concept of "justification," see the introduction, pages 90–92. See also note 252. [JSR]

187 (in §71:3). The word "jot" here is probably an allusion to Matthew 5:18. See also note 480. [JSR]

188 (in §71:4). The name "Reed Sea" (*mare Suph* in the original Latin) is a biblical allusion to what is more generally known as the Red Sea (Exodus 10:19). [JSR]

189 (in §72:1). Swedenborg refers here to a longstanding debate among Calvinists about the nature of Christ's atonement and the extent of predestination. The followers of Jacob Arminius (1560–1609), called "Arminians," taught that God had predestined

only the saved, not the damned; that Christ had died for all, not simply the elect; and that human free will is capable of accepting or rejecting divine grace. Though condemned by a synod of the Dutch church at Dort in 1618–1619, Arminian ideas continued to have importance in both Dutch and English Protestantism. Based as it was on Calvinist principles not held by Lutherans, the Arminian controversy would have been mainly known to Swedenborg through his travels and wide circle of acquaintances in the Netherlands and England. [RGE]

190 (in §72:1). This sentence contains multiple biblical allusions. On "Lucifer" and "the dragon," see note 151 above. On "goats," see Matthew 25:31–33 and note 170; "archangels" are mentioned in Jude 9 and 1 Thessalonians 4:16. [JSR]

191 (in §72:2). This mention of our being like a stone or dead wood in spiritual matters is an allusion to Luther's words quoted in *The Book of Concord* (see Kolb and Wengert 2000, 548.20, 548–549.24), though ultimately the derogatory comparison to stone and dead wood goes back to Jeremiah 2:27. [JSR]

192 (in §72:2). The mention of goat's wool is an allusion to the Latin expression *de lana caprina rixari*, "to dispute about goat's wool," that is, about something of no value. It appears notably in the Roman poet Horace (65–8 B.C.E.), probably as a quotation of an existing proverb; see his *Epistles* 1:18:15. Its continued use as a common Latin proverb may be illustrated by two of its more significant instances: the Renaissance scholar Erasmus (1466?–1536) cites it in passing in the preface to his *Praise of Folly* (Erasmus [1511] 1971, 59); and it was the title of a satire by the notorious Giacomo Casanova (1725–1798) published in the year after *True Christianity*. Compare §335:2 of the present work. [SS]

193 (in §72:3). The "tip of one letter" is a reference to the tiny stroke at the top of each Hebrew letter. It has traditionally been translated "tittle." See also §278. [JSR]

194 (in §73:1). Octavian Augustus (63 B.C.E.–14 C.E.) and Nero Claudius Caesar (37 C.E.–68 C.E.) were Roman emperors. Presumably Swedenborg alludes here to generally held impressions of their differing approaches to holding supreme power: Augustus's establishment of peace, law, and order, as contrasted with Nero's infamous cruelty and irresponsibility, including the murders of his mother and his wife. [JSR]

195 (in §73:4). The Latin word here translated "angel guardians" is *cherubos*, traditionally translated "cherubs." Angel guardians in the Bible were unearthly, winged, awe-inspiring figures: the four "living creatures" described in Ezekiel 1 and 10; the guardians of the Garden of Eden (Genesis 3:24); the guardian figures carved in gold over the ark of the covenant (Exodus 25:18–21); and figures sewn into the curtains and veils of the tabernacle (Exodus 26:31) and carved on the walls and doors of the great temple in Jerusalem (1 Kings 6:29, 32, 35). Swedenborg mentions their ability to fly, and cites Scripture as saying that Jehovah sits or rides on them (Psalms 18:9, 10; 80:1; 99:1). He describes their function and meaning as having to do with protection; see §260. Here and in §134:5 they appear at the end of a memorable occurrence. [JSR]

196 (in §74:1). The references here to various classes of society and to hats of various kinds seem to be allusions to contemporary Swedish politics. The mention of an ecclesiastical class and other classes of society is reminiscent of the structure of the Swedish parliament (or "Diet") at the time. It was divided into four estates, or classes: the ecclesiastical, the noble, the merchant, and the peasant class. The mention of hats and caps echoes the nicknames for the two main factions within the Swedish government of that period, the "Hats" and the "Caps." The people who named themselves the Hats did so

because they saw themselves as dressed and ready for action, including war; they named their opponents the Caps, as if to say their opponents were dressed (with nightcaps) for bed. At the end of the memorable occurrence Swedenborg explains that the hats and caps correspond to the people's relative level of intelligence. [JSR]

197 (in §74:2). There is a shift from the plural "we" earlier in the paragraph to the singular "I" here. There are quite often such shifts in Swedenborg's representation of dialog in the spiritual world. They may be related to his assertion that in that world a group can speak through a single individual in such a way that both the group and the individual feel autonomous; see *Secrets of Heaven* 5983, 5985–5987. [JSR]

198 (in §74:2). The "leviathan" mentioned in this biblical allusion to Isaiah 27:1 is a huge and powerful sea monster, also mentioned in Job 41:1; Psalms 74:14; 104:26. [JSR]

199 (in §74:2). A "Gordian knot" means a complicated, unsolvable tangle or problem. Legend has it that the original Gordian knot was tied by a King Gordius of Phrygia in central Asia Minor. The knot (or knots), made of cornel-bark, was the central part of a display; it fastened a yoke to a wagon. An oracle stated that whoever could untangle the knot would rule Asia. Alexander the Great (356–323 B.C.E.) is said to have discovered a solution to the problem of the Gordian knot when he visited Phrygia in 333 B.C.E., although extant ancient sources give three different versions of what he did: he slashed it in half with his sword; or he cut through the outer fibers of the knot with his sword to reveal the ends, which had been tucked inside; or he simply pulled the knot off the wagon pole. See Arrian *Anabasis of Alexander* 2:3; Bosworth 1980, 186–187. The first, and most dramatic, of these explanations is the one Swedenborg gives here; it has generally been favored by tradition as the most representative of Alexander's character. For Alexander's throwing the knot to the ground and crushing its fibers with his heel, however, Bosworth's commentary cites no ancient support (see Bosworth 1980, 186–187). These details may instead be an oblique allusion on Swedenborg's part to the prediction in Genesis 3:15 that Adam's descendant (often taken to mean the Messiah) would bruise the serpent's head with his heel. [JSR]

200 (in §74:4). Swedenborg mentions at the end of the memorable occurrence (§74:5) that these people are seen as wearing caps because they are of lesser intelligence. By contrast, elsewhere in his theological works Swedenborg states that those of simple faith are actually often wiser than the erudite (*Secrets of Heaven* 4754; *Heaven and Hell* 86, 313, 602; *Divine Love and Wisdom* 361). [JSR]

201 (in §74:5). For more on the parable of the goats and the sheep alluded to here, see note 170. [JSR]

202 (in §75:7). It is curious that Swedenborg makes no mention here of a volume he had published eight years earlier that extensively addresses these very points, namely, *Divine Love and Wisdom,* especially the first four of its five parts, §§1–357. He mentions the work by name earlier in the text: see §§20, 33, 37:2. [JSR]

203 (in §76:1). The Latin phrase here translated "I came into my spirit" is *factus sum in spiritu,* literally, "I became in spirit." The same Latin phrase is used in *Revelation Unveiled* 36 and 228 as a literal rendering of the Greek expression of Revelation 1:10 and 4:2, ἐγενόμην ἐν πνεύματι *(egenómēn en pneúmati),* again literally, "I became in spirit," which John uses of his revelatory experiences. The phrase here means that Swedenborg shifted consciousness from his body in the physical world to his spirit in the spiritual

world. Swedenborg uses the same phrase elsewhere for shifting consciousness over to his spirit (see §112:1 of the present work; *Marriage Love* 326:1), and a similar phrase, *a spiritu factus sum in corpore,* literally, "I became from my spirit into my body," for shifting back to awareness of his body (§112:7). [JSR]

204 (in §76:1). Swedenborg himself describes the birth of the universe from a cosmic egg in poetic terms in *Worship and Love of God* 9–10; see also §9 note d there. The *Worship and Love of God* passage has its precursor in the scientific work *Basic Principles of Nature* part 3, chapter 4 (= Swedenborg [1734] 1988a, 2:251–272). There Swedenborg cites classical authors in illustration of the metaphor, including Aristophanes *The Birds* 693–703. For an extensive discussion on the origins of the symbol of the cosmic egg and its use in Swedenborg, see Jonsson 2004, 53–68. Of particular interest here is that Swedenborg reports a point of view that contradicts concepts utilized in his scientific works; see also notes 95, 206. [SS]

205 (in §76:1). The language of this and the previous sentence echoes the Scholastic commonplace *ex nihilo nihil fit,* "from nothing, nothing comes to be"; see the Scholastic philosophers Anselm of Canterbury (1033–1109) *Monologium* 8; and Aquinas *Summa Theologiae* 1:45:1, 2 (= Aquinas 1952, 1:242–243). They in turn derived it from Aristotle (see specifically *Physics* 191b [= Aristotle 1952e, 267]; *Metaphysics* 1062b [= Aristotle 1952d, 591]; and generally *On Generation and Corruption* 317b–319b [= Aristotle 1952a, 413–416]), and ultimately from Melissus of Samos (flourished around 444–441 B.C.E.), who used the principle to argue against the existence or possibility of change. The angels use the argument here, as Swedenborg does elsewhere (see for example *Divine Love and Wisdom* 55), to dispute the idea that God created the world *ex nihilo,* "out of nothing." [JSR, SS]

206 (in §76:2). Swedenborg seems to be referring negatively here to his own *Basic Principles of Nature,* commonly known as his *Principia,* a conjectural work on the process of creation published in Leipzig in 1734 (= Swedenborg [1734] 1988a). It is not clear to what extent he includes in this reference those passages in later works that were written after his spiritual awareness had begun. These include *Worship and Love of God* 9–15, *Notes on the Creation Story* (= Swedenborg 1927–1951a) §§1–10, and *Draft on Divine Wisdom* 168, traditionally known as *The Angelic Idea of Creation* (= Swedenborg 1997a, §168). For the chronological difficulties of the passage, however, see note 208. [JSR]

207 (in §76:2). On the dating of Swedenborg's spiritual awakening, see note 59 above. [JSR]

208 (in §76:2). The chronological sequence here cannot be taken strictly, as Swedenborg lists data about creation that he had accepted long before his spiritual awakening, namely, that people pass upon death into the spiritual world (see *Draft on the Soul and the Body* [= Swedenborg 1984] §76), and that there are two suns (see *Dynamics of the Soul's Domain* [= Swedenborg [1740–1741] 1955] 2:§§257, 260, 261; and Pendleton 1901, 121–122). [JSR]

209 (in §76:5). In his accounts of memorable occurrences, Swedenborg sometimes mentions leaving his house or home and then returning there again (see §159:7; *Marriage Love* 326:1, 329:1), without making explicit where that house or home was. A few indications suggest that although these journeys are spiritual, the home he mentions is his home in the physical world, or an analog of it in the world of spirits (see *Marriage*

Love 329:1, 3, in which students in the spiritual world are able to follow Swedenborg home and see him writing, talk with him, and then go back to their teacher; angels do likewise in §159:7 of the present work). On the existence of the same places in the spiritual world as in our physical world, see *Spiritual Experiences* (= Swedenborg 1978) §§5092–5094. [JSR]

210 (in §77:1). The introductory details here allude (in a contrary fashion) to the beliefs of followers of the school of Epicurus, who claimed that all earthly phenomena had natural rather than divine causes. In support of this belief the Epicureans pointed out that although thunder was supposed to be caused by the gods, in fact it never occurred except when clouds—a natural cause of thunder—were present. The setting Swedenborg describes, in which lightning is seen and thunder is heard from a clear sky, are an implicit refutation of the materialist view. For contrasts and parallels in classical literature, see Aristophanes *Clouds* 370–430; Lucretius *De Rerum Natura* book 6, especially 6:247–248 and 6:400–422; Vergil *Georgics* 1:487; Ovid *Fasti* 3:369; Seneca *Naturales Quaestiones* 2:18, 2:26:7; Lucan *Bellum Civile* 1:530; Martial *Epigrammata* 9:24:4; Suetonius *Titus* 10. A poem by the Roman Epicurean poet Horace is of special interest as a comparison to this passage; in it Horace abandons his Epicureanism in favor of religious belief after hearing thunder sound in a cloudless sky (see Horace *Odes* 1:34). Although different in force, the English expression "like a bolt out of the blue" and the Swedish *som en blixt från en klar himmel*, "like lightning from a clear sky," are probably dim echoes of this point of contention in the ancient skirmish between the Epicureans and those who believed in divine action. [SS]

211 (in §77:2). On the "world of spirits," see note 21 above. [JSR]

212 (in §77:6). For the structure of the world of spirits, see note 182 above. [JSR]

213 (in §78:1). Although the connection between cause and effect is only subtly expressed, apparently the forthcoming demonstration is a reward to Swedenborg for his services to a neighboring community (see §76). [JSR]

214 (in §78:3). On the term "extended" here, see note 115 above. [JSR]

215 (in §79:1). By "the Christian world" here Swedenborg means Europe and its colonies. The individual philosophers in this section mouth beliefs typical of natural philosophy during the Enlightenment. The first insists that nature must have always existed because its complete absence would be impossible. The second recounts a Kantian theory of cosmogenesis similar to the nebular hypothesis (see note 141), in which a cloud of gas condenses to form solid matter. (The vortices he mentions are a feature of a Cartesian system of celestial mechanics that unsuccessfully competed with the gravitational system formulated by Isaac Newton; they were whirls in the ether [see note 116] supposed to be the cause of the orbiting of the movement of celestial bodies. See Aiton 1972 for a complete history of the idea.) The third describes a theory in which an initial chaotic mass breaks open and spews forth the sun and other components of the solar system. However, the details of the dispute are not as important as the common assumption of its participants that a godless nature is sufficient to explain the existence and origin of the universe; all of the views are confuted by the one individual who insists that "Since nature is part of the universe, God then was also the Creator of all nature" (§79:4). Ultimately the philosophers are revealed as insane (§79:6). [JSR, SS]

216 (in §79:1). This mad philosopher happens randomly to utter an opinion with which Swedenborg agrees—that there is no such thing as a vacuum. See *Divine Love*

and Wisdom 82; and for commentary on that passage, see Swedenborg [1763] 2003a, 272–273 note 63. [SS]

217 (in §79:3). Etna (of eastern Sicily) and Vesuvius (of southern Italy) were the most famous active volcanoes known to classical antiquity. [JSR]

218 (in §79:6). It was not unusual in medieval art to depict the moment of death by showing the soul (usually in the form of a miniature human) departing through the deceased's mouth. For an example, see the church mural painted about 1240 in Ballerup, Denmark, of the Devil seizing the soul of a dying man as it exits his mouth (Mills-Kronborg 04-006). [RGE, SS]

219 (in §79:6). Plato may be one of "the wise" mentioned here. According to the Myth of Er, as related in book 10 of Plato *Republic* 614–620 (= Plato 1952, 437–441), souls are constantly reincarnated, even choosing the lives they will lead the next time they are born. See also the poetically told myths in Plato's *Phaedrus* and *Timaeus,* where the reincarnation of the soul is described in very different terms (Plato *Phaedrus* 248–249 [= Plato 1952, 125–126]; Plato *Timaeus* 42 [= Plato 1952, 452–453]). It is an open question to what extent these myths were accepted by Plato, or by Socrates, in whose mouth Plato puts them. On the subject of what Plato actually believed about immortality, see Patterson 1965. As the reader will see in §171 below, Swedenborg considers reincarnation "nonsense" and an "absurd notion." See also *Heaven and Hell* 256. [JSR, SS]

220 (in §79:7). By "loves" here, Swedenborg means values or motivations that determine one's priorities. Physical loves, then, assign the highest priority to worldly and fleshly desires and concerns. See also §§403–405 of the present work and note 38 above. [JSR]

221 (in §80:1). In classical mythology, sirens were minor divinities of the sea and of death. Part woman, part bird, they lured sailors to their doom by their sweet, irresistible singing, or by offering knowledge not otherwise accessible to mortals; see, for example, Homer *Odyssey* 12:39–54, 158–200. Christian writers adopted them as a symbol for the alluring power of sexual pleasure. Swedenborg uses the term to refer to a type of spirits, usually female (*Secrets of Heaven* 1983:3) but sometimes male (*Spiritual Experiences* [= Swedenborg 1978] §5486), who are expertly deceptive, manipulative, and seductive. They come largely from a European and Christian background (*Secrets of Heaven* 2744:2; *Spiritual Experiences* [= Swedenborg 1978] §4635) and were adulterous and devoid of conscience during their lives on earth (*Spiritual Experiences* [= Swedenborg 1998–2002] §3699). Endowed with magical powers (*Secrets of Heaven* 831), including the power to transform their own appearance, as indicated here, they are described by Swedenborg as being among the worst spirits in hell (*Spiritual Experiences* [= Swedenborg 1978] §5486). [JSR]

222 (in §80:1). In classical mythology, Venus fell so deeply in love with Adonis that she left heaven to be with him. She was devastated when he was savaged by a wild boar. For exhaustive treatment of the classical Adonis figure, see Fraser 1922, 376–403. [JSR]

223 (in §80:2). Here the siren crowns the satan with the laurel in an act reminiscent of the crowning of victors at athletic games. In addition to being a sign of victory of various kinds since ancient times (in which context it appears in §48:20), the laurel wreath also came to be associated with a university degree (although probably because of a false or punning etymological derivation of *bachelor* from *bacca lauri,* "berry of the laurel"). On the ancient origin of crowns and wreaths as symbols of victory, see Onians 2000, 376–377. [JSR]

Notes to Chapter 2, §§81–137

224 (in §81). The "letters" of the apostles mentioned here are the New Testament Epistles. The Apostles' Creed, a redaction of the Old Roman Creed, had been authoritative and widely used since the eighth century C.E. It was one of three pre-existing creeds adopted by Lutheranism. See Kolb and Wengert 2000, 21–22. [JSR]

225 (in §81). The Latin phrase here translated "the underlying divine reality" is *Divinum Esse,* literally, "the divine to be" or "the divine is-ness" or "the divine actual existence." See note 84. [JSR]

226 (in §81). Because the term "the Father" has only occurred to this point in the text in quotations of other sources—whether the Bible, a creed, or someone in a memorable occurrence—it may seem surprising or somewhat ironic, given Swedenborg's strong statements against any tripersonal understanding of the Trinity, that he here adopts the same language himself. Later in the text (§97) he explains that by "the Father" he means "the Divine," that is, God's divine nature, which was eventually united to Jesus' human nature. [JSR]

227 (in §81). The Latin phrase here translated "when he was being emptied out" is *status exinanitionis Ipsius,* literally, "his state of exinanition." Exinanition is a Lutheran theological term for Christ's self-emptying or self-renunciation (see Muller 1985 under "*exinanitio*"). On "being glorified," see note 11 above. [JSR]

228 (in §82:2). On the term "Jehovih," see note 9 above. [JSR]

229 (in §82:3). The Latin words here translated "have not had intercourse" are *virum non cognosco,* literally, "am not knowing a man." This use of a verb that ordinarily means "to know" to mean "to have intercourse with" is derived from a parallel expression in Greek. See, for example, the following statement in Matthew 1:25 about Joseph and Mary: οὐκ ἐγίνωσκεν αὐτὴν ἕως οὗ ἔτεκεν υἱόν *(ouk egínōsken autēn héōs hoû éteken huión),* literally, "he was not knowing her until she gave birth to a son." This Greek expression is derived in turn from an expression with the same dual meaning in Hebrew (יָדַע *[yāḏaʿ]*); see, for example, Genesis 4:1. [JSR]

230 (in §82:3). Swedenborg refers here to a long-held theory of reproduction that had found new support shortly before his time. Known as spermism, this theory held that in reproduction the sperm supplies the essential element that is to become the offspring, while the egg supplies only material nourishment for its growth. Aristotle had long ago expressed this theory (*On the Generation of Animals* 730a–731a [= Aristotle 1952b, 270–271]), but in the seventeenth century the Dutch microscopist Antoni van Leeuwenhoek (1632–1723), among others, had found experimental evidence that seemed to support it. Describing one such observation in a letter to the secretary of the Royal Society in London on March 18, 1678, Leeuwenhoek wrote: "If your Harvey [William Harvey, 1578–1657, discoverer of the circulation of the blood and investigator of the reproductive processes] and our de Graaf [Reinier de Graaf, 1641–1673, discoverer of the follicles of the ovary] had seen the hundredth part [of what I have observed] they would have stated as I did that it is exclusively the male semen that forms the foetus and that all that the woman may contribute only serves to receive the semen and feed it" (Leeuwenhoek 1941, 335). For more on eighteenth-century theories of reproduction, see Farley 1982; Pinto-Correia 1997. [GMC, JSR]

231 (in §82:3). Swedenborg may have two reasons for saying that Catholics and Protestants are *dreaming* that Jesus' soul came from his mother, that is, that he was merely human: one is that to Swedenborg this view was clearly wrong and was contradicted by

Scripture; but he may also be referring to the fact that this view was not generally openly espoused. [JSR]

232 (in §83). *Sabaoth* is a Hebrew term (צְבָאוֹת *[ṣəḇāʾôṯ]*) meaning "legions" or "armies." *Jehovah Sabaoth* means "Jehovah of the Legions," the legions being the "heavenly host"—either the angels or, when viewed on a more concrete level, the sun, moon, and stars; on the name "Jehovah," see note 9 above. The reason Swedenborg at times presents the term in a transcription of the Hebrew rather than translating it into Latin may be that this is approximately the form in which it appears in his Latin Bible. [JSR]

233 (in §84). In this passage Swedenborg refers to an important stream of Christian theological reflection, particularly as expressed by the medieval teacher Anselm of Canterbury, whose *Cur Deus Homo?* (Why Did God Become Human?—completed 1099) was a summary of the arguments for the assertion that the salvation of humankind required as a logical necessity that God be incarnated in human form. [RGE]

234 (in §84). The simile Swedenborg gives here reflects the perspective of the western European readership he naturally assumed for his theological works, written as they were in Neo-Latin. During the period at which he wrote, European states were vying to control India and its lucrative trade by armed means. By 1771 in particular, the British were gaining the upper hand: they had defeated the Dutch in 1759, consolidated their several victories over the French in the Treaty of Paris in 1763, and held Behar, Bengal, Circars, and Madras. [SS]

235 (in §85:1). For more on the expression "Jehovah God," see note 16. [JSR]

236 (in §87). As in §367:4, Swedenborg here repeats an illustration from a more detailed analysis of the action of the heart and lungs in *Divine Love and Wisdom;* see in particular §399 there. His main assertion is that the heart on its own supports basal, nonconscious bodily functions, but requires the simultaneous action of the lungs to initiate higher-order functions such as sensation and conscious movement. As proof he offers the examples of those who suffocate or are submerged (without suffering loss of heart function), as well as fetuses in the womb; he ascribes the absence of their power of conscious thought specifically to the absence of breathing. (Although Swedenborg was aware that fetuses move from time to time in the womb [see for example §§48:9, 335:7], he apparently classed such bodily movements with those that do not require higher-order intellect.) For the ancient Greek and Roman belief that the intellectual faculties were centered in the lungs, see Onians 2000, 35–42. [JSR, SS]

237 (in §87). "Anakim" and "Nephilim" are two plural words for giants taken from the Hebrew עֲנָקִים *(ʿănāqîm)* and נְפִילִים *(nəp̄îlîm)*. For the Anakim, see Deuteronomy 1:28; 2:10, 11, 21; 9:2; Joshua 11:21, 22; 14:12, 15; for the Nephilim, see Genesis 6:4; Numbers 13:33. For evil spirits that Swedenborg refers to as the Anakim and the Nephilim, see *Secrets of Heaven* 580–583; 1673:1–2; 7686. [JSR]

238 (in §88). For passages elsewhere explaining that "the Father" means the divine goodness, see *Secrets of Heaven* 2803, 3704. [JSR]

239 (in §90). The German philosopher Christian Wolff (1679–1754) posited the existence of a "simple substance," which forms the basis for all the matter in the universe (Wolff 1730, §794). For the report of an exchange in the spiritual world between Leibniz, Wolff, and Swedenborg on the topic of this simple substance, see *Draft of "Supplements"* (= Swedenborg 1997b, 160 = §§286–287 [Rogers's numbering] = §§262–264 [Potts's numbering]). See also Swedenborg 1976d, 319. [JSR]

240 (in §91). The Latin words here translated "divine miracles as opposed to magical miracles" are set in small capitals in the original Latin as follows: de MIRACULIS DIVINIS, & de MIRACULIS MAGICIS. Some have taken these words as the title of a forthcoming work by Swedenborg. If it was indeed Swedenborg's intent to produce such a work, it may perhaps be represented by a portion of the brief manuscript *Sketch for "Coda to True Christianity,"* which ends with five numbered points on miracles of both kinds (see Swedenborg 1996, 1:21–22). Whether Swedenborg was planning a whole separate title on this topic, however, or a mere chapter in the appendix to *True Christianity* (see note 71) is moot. [JSR]

241 (in §92). On this concept of reproduction, see note 230. [JSR]

242 (in §92). Although Swedenborg uses the singular, "language," here, his statement about the meaning of "angel" applies equally well to the Hebrew of the Old Testament (מַלְאָךְ *[mal'āk]*) and to the Greek of the New Testament (ἄγγελος *[ángelos]*). [JSR]

243 (in §92). The unusual plural "faces" here reflects a plural in the Latin of Swedenborg's first edition *(facierum),* a reading also found in the Latin translation of the Bible by Sebastian Schmidt, which Swedenborg favored (Schmidt 1696). It derives from a Hebrew idiom, פָּנִים *(pānîm),* meaning "presence." [JSR]

244 (in §94). Catholic Christians had for centuries seen Mary as having a particular importance among the saints, an importance demonstrated by Christian artists, who depicted Mary as a queen in heaven, often seated near or being crowned by her son Jesus. This was rooted theologically in the special role Mary played as the human mother of Jesus, and her uniqueness in Christian salvation history as the human chosen by God to bear the divine child. Martin Luther, though critical of positions that tended to give Mary a particular role in salvation itself as a "coredemptrix" with Christ, nonetheless honored her as the first of Jesus' followers and, as such, as a model of the church. [RGE]

245 (in §94). By "Arianism," Swedenborg is referring to a heresy of early Christianity, attributed to the Alexandrian priest Arius (around 250–around 336 C.E.), in which the human Son, Jesus, was seen as subordinate to the divine Father. It is the Athanasian Creed that most completely condemns this view. (See also note 25.) By "Socinianism" he means the sixteenth-century Unitarian teaching of the Italian theologians Lelio (1525–1562) and Fausto (1539–1604) Sozzini, or Socinus, who rejected the Trinitarian formulations both of the early church and of their Protestant reaffirmation. (See also the introduction, pages 87–88.) It is unclear what Swedenborg means by "Calvinism in its original form," since there was little difference between Calvin and any other Trinitarian theologian on the relationship of the divine and human natures in Christ. It is likely that Swedenborg is here expressing a generalized Lutheran prejudice against Calvinist rejection of the Lutheran teaching of the "communication of natures," which sought to protect the concept of Christ as an undivided unity by postulating that wherever he was present in his divine nature he was also present in his human one. This dispute between Lutherans and Calvinists focused on the narrower question of the nature of Christ's "presence" in the eucharistic elements. By lumping this particular catalog of "heresies" together with Judaism and materialist philosophy (both of which would also see Jesus as purely human) Swedenborg is trying to lift up and emphasize the divinity, not the humanity, of Christ. For more on Calvin, see note 179; for more on materialist philosophy, see note 23. [RGE]

246 (in §94). Arius was a heretical priest of Alexandria who taught that the human Jesus was subordinate to the divine Father (see also note 245). His views were repudiated

by the Council of Nicaea (325 C.E.) called by the Roman emperor Constantine the Great (around 285–337) to resolve a number of theological issues in early Christianity. [RGE]

247 (in §94). In Christian terminology, a "hypostasis" is a person of the Trinity. Therefore the term "hypostatic union" denotes the union of divine and human natures within the one person of Jesus Christ. [JSR]

248 (in §94). For collections of biblical passages on the relationship between the Son and the Father, along with further discussion, see §§107:2–3, 339:2, 370:1–2. [JSR]

249 (in §94). The Latin adjectives here translated "precious" and "of little value," *nobilis* and *ignobilis,* would be literally rendered "noble" and "ignoble." See note 159. [JSR]

250 (in §95). Swedenborg simplifies the theological issue here, but is basically correct in noting that the Christian theological consensus identified the atoning death of Christ on the cross as the locus of redemption. This was understood in the theological tradition as being a "satisfaction" of the guilt or debt justly owed by a fallen and sinful humanity to its righteous Creator and judge. Many metaphors have been employed by Christian thinkers to express this transaction, including those of Christ as willing victim, as sacrificial lamb, as payment of ransom, and as conquering victor over death. [RGE]

251 (in §95). For more on the parable of the goats and the sheep alluded to here, see note 170. [JSR]

252 (in §96). Though many of these ideas Swedenborg criticizes are common to Protestantism, this particular emphasis on recognition of one's inability to make oneself righteous before God, and thus on one's abject need for mercy and forgiveness, is a particular emphasis of Lutheranism. No doctrinal point was more commonly taught, reflected upon, or preached in Lutheran churches than this one: that salvation depends on God's prior action of gracious forgiveness; a person is not (and cannot become) righteous in oneself, but only as God has decided to impute righteousness to one for Christ's sake. This act, by which God declares to be righteous that which is by nature fallen and unrighteous (which Lutheran theology calls "imputed" or "forensic" righteousness), is at the heart of the Lutheran doctrine of "justification by faith," for it is by faith that one understands the remarkable thing God has done for one for Christ's sake. In taking this line of criticism, Swedenborg lays an axe to Lutheranism's theological roots. [RGE]

253 (in §96). The "scribes" in ancient Judaism were professional interpreters of the Law (see note 387). They were often linked with "Pharisees," who were an ancient Jewish sect known for their scrupulous observance of written and traditional law. Both groups are heavily criticized in the New Testament for hypocrisy. [JSR]

254 (in §98). On "justification by faith alone," see the introduction, pages 90–92. See also note 252 just above. [RGE]

255 (in §98). The parallel in the modern edition of Kolb and Wengert 2000 is found at 24.28, 25.32–35. [JSR]

256 (in §98). The centrality of this point to the whole work is suggested by similar material in the epilogue at the end of the second volume. [JSR]

257 (in §99). Where the translation reads "earth" here, the Latin original has "tree," which makes no sense in context. John Chadwick, in his translation of this work, suggested "ground"; see Swedenborg [1771] 1988b, 1:126 and note 1. [JSR]

258 (in §101). The Formula of Concord was a Lutheran statement of doctrine formulated by a committee of prominent German theologians in 1576 and 1577, comprising two parts: the Epitome (which briefly described the current controversies) and the Solid

Declaration (a longer discussion of the points needing reemphasis and reformulation). Its main purpose was to bring harmony among Lutherans on some disputed points, and to differentiate some Lutheran teachings more clearly from their Calvinist counterparts. The Formula strongly reaffirmed the authority of Scripture, of the three ancient creeds, and of the Lutheran confessional statements that preceded the Formula. See Kolb and Wengert 2000, 486–660; see also the introduction, pages 84–85. [RGE]

259 (in §101). The page numbers given here refer to the 1756 Leipzig edition of *The Book of Concord;* see *Concordia* 1756. The parallels in the modern edition of Kolb and Wengert 2000 are found at 511.13 and 619.19. [JSR]

260 (in §102:3). In the original Latin edition, this whole paragraph is set off in double quotation marks, both at the beginning and the end, and also at the beginning of every line in between. Swedenborg used double quotation marks like these to highlight text for one of two main reasons: to indicate the extent of lengthy quotations and excerpts (whether noted as such, see §§121, 464, 516, 526, 722; or not, see §§102, 397–402, 846–851), or to draw attention to particularly noteworthy sections (see §§137, 336, 508). Modern paragraphing conventions had not emerged as of his day, and paragraph breaks in his works are minimal; in the first edition of this work most paragraph breaks mark the commencement of a new numbered section. Within a block of text, then, these double quotation marks would clearly indicate where special material begins and ends. In this case they mark a quotation; that is, the entire paragraph is repeated from Swedenborg's 1763 work *Supplements* 66. Another parallel statement occurs in the second volume of the present work at §827. Parallels to this statement also occur in Swedenborg's manuscripts: *Spiritual Experiences* (= Swedenborg 1978) §5834; and *Draft of "Supplements"* (= Swedenborg 1997b, 84–85 = §69 [Rogers's numbering] = §68 [Potts's numbering]). [JSR]

261 (in §103:1). For more on this permanent physical "border" for our spirits after death, see *Divine Love and Wisdom* 257, 388. See also Sewall 1909, 87–89, and Odhner 1933, 245, where Odhner holds that this border is what remains after the "inmost or finest substances of nature" have receded after death, and that they "serve as the 'cutaneous envelopment' for the spiritual body itself." [JSR, SS]

262 (in §103:2). Here Swedenborg makes the assertion that Jews look different from Christians because of their differing religious beliefs, reflecting a general assumption of thinkers in his era that shared traits manifest themselves in certain common, classifiable features of the physiognomy. He makes a similar statement in the second volume of the present work (§521:1). In eighteenth-century Sweden, harsh and even virulent statements against other religions were extremely common (see Helander 2004, 319–344). In that context, Swedenborg's comments of this kind seem relatively mild, but he nonetheless includes in this volume some statements that modern readers may find offensive or distasteful. With the exception of the present passage, in this volume Swedenborg's comments about Jews concern those of Old and New Testament times, and are no doubt based largely on passages in the Bible. To summarize these critical comments: Swedenborg asserts that Jews of that period were disinterested in anything spiritual, and therefore they were idolatrous (§205) and their worship was external (§109:2); they looked down on people who were not of their religion (§215:3); they falsified and desecrated their Scriptures (§§116:1, 121:2, 122, 246, 270), and similarly desecrated Jesus during the crucifixion (§§129, 130:3, 311, 342:3). See also Rose 2005, 81–82. In §121 Swedenborg sets such statements in a

wider context: he clarifies that not just Judaism but "the whole planet" was spiritually depraved at the time; hence the statement in §3:1 that at the time of Christ's coming, "total damnation stood threatening at the door." Swedenborg saw the Christian world in his own times as being in much the same state (§§3:1, 206). [JSR]

263 (in §103:2). On spiritual and physical heredity from fathers and mothers, see note 230. [JSR]

264 (in §104). On the process of being emptied out, traditionally referred to as exinanition, see note 227; on the process of glorification, see note 11. [JSR]

265 (in §106). The key Latin terms used in this discussion of various ages (with translations in parentheses) are as follows: *infantia* ("infancy"), *pueritia* ("childhood"), *ephebatus* ("teenage years"), *adolescentia* ("twenties"), and *juventus* ("thirties"). On the ages meant by *pueritia* and *adolescentia,* see note 152 above. *Juventus* was the last age before full adulthood. In Swedenborg's time, an individual's apprenticeship and other training would often last well into the thirties. [JSR]

266 (in §107:3). On the growing awareness of non-Christian religions and societies at the time this work was written, see note 28. [JSR]

267 (in §108). On the "lower earth," see note 182 above. [JSR]

268 (in §109:1). On the various ways in which Swedenborg uses the word "church," see note 3. Here Swedenborg means the first three of the five churches: the earliest or most ancient, the early or ancient, and the Jewish church. [JSR]

269 (in §110:1). The Latin phrase here translated "strange light" is *ignis fatuus,* literally, "foolish fire." For more on this topic, see note 149 above. [JSR]

270 (in §110:1). For more on the biblical allusion to Michael, see note 464; on the dragon, see note 151. [JSR]

271 (in §110:2). For more on the Christian concept of "person," see note 82. [RGE]

272 (in §110:8). Mixtures of iron filings with powdered sulfur in approximately equal amounts, wetted with water, have been used for centuries to create artificial "volcanoes" for the purpose of display. In these cases the earth serves to temporarily retain the escaping heat and gases and thus to increase the eventual explosion, which can be extremely hazardous. The chemical reaction is obtained only when the iron and sulfur are used in large quantities, and the reaction—which emits toxic sulfur dioxide gas—may take ten or twelve hours to produce. The effect is mentioned again in §113:2. [SS]

273 (in §111:2). The setting and people mentioned in this narrative account are less clearly identified than in most other such accounts. In brief, it appears to describe an interaction between three main groups of people: (1) "the participants" (Latin *congregati*), who seem to be hosting the event, in that they do all the testing and challenging of the other two groups and, incidentally, are the only ones to read out loud. Context suggests that they are knowledgeable, seasoned, and spiritually advanced spirits. (2) Protestants, who are further subdivided. Anglican clergy are part of the main Protestant group, while Lutherans are a separate subgroup. (3) Roman Catholics, including monks. The latter two groups appear to be relatively new to the spiritual world. The setting seems to place group 2 in the center and group 3 beside group 2, perhaps all on a large and deep stage; while group 1 surrounds them, perhaps in tiered seating. [JSR]

274 (in §111:9). Despite the fact that the present work was written in Latin, this quotation from *The Book of Common Prayer* is given in English, creating an effect that is obviously difficult to reproduce in an English translation. The spelling has been normalized

here; in the first edition of *True Christianity* the passage reads, "For, when we spiritualy eat the flesh of Christ and drinck the blood, then we dwel in Christ, and Christ in us." Swedenborg owned the 1711 edition of *The Book of Common Prayer;* in it this quotation reads, "For then we spiritually eat the flesh of Christ, and drink his bloud; then we dwell in Christ, and Christ in us" (*Book of Common Prayer* 1711, 31). [JSR]

275 (in §111:10). This passage refers to the Lutheran doctrine of the "communication of natures," which taught that where either the divine or the human nature of Christ could be thought to be present, the other nature existed as well. Developed in part to refute the Zwinglian and later Calvinist arguments that Christ could not be "really" (that is, humanly) present in the eucharistic elements because his humanity since the ascension was locally present in heaven, this doctrine is a Lutheran distinctive. Ironically, it is more an extrapolation from Luther than an actual teaching, and is not in fact defined in the text referred to here, the Augsburg Confession. The Augsburg Confession (1530) was the earliest and most important of the Lutheran statements of faith; the controversy over the natures in Christ was a later issue and was dealt with elsewhere in *The Book of Concord* (1580), the authoritative compilation of Lutheran doctrinal statements. The summary here reflects points made in section 8 of both the Epitome and the Solid Declaration (see Kolb and Wengert 2000, 509.5, 510.10, 511.15–16, 617.6, 617.9, 618.12, 619.19, 620.23, 621.27, 628.66). See also notes 135, 245, 258, and the introduction, pages 86–90. [RGE]

276 (in §111:12). The mention here of "tongues like little flames" is reminiscent of the Pentecost, when the followers of Jesus spoke in tongues (Acts 2:3). A memorable occurrence in another volume has a similar ending; see *Revelation Unveiled* 224:13. [JSR]

277 (in §112:1). In Roman mythology, Aurora was dawn or the goddess thereof, often pictured as having wings. The reference to her as having gold in her mouth is apparently derived from a punning etymology of her name, according to which it was made up of the Latin roots *aur-* ("golden") and *or-* ("mouth"). The Swedish proverb *Morgonstund har guld i mun* ("Morningtime has gold in [its] mouth," that is, rising early leads to wealth) should also be noted in this connection. [JSR]

278 (in §112:1). The phrase an "apple of discord" refers to an ancient myth: the goddess Discord, also known by her Greek name, Eris, threw an apple among a group of goddesses, stipulating that only the most beautiful could pick it up. The resulting quarrel over the apple ultimately escalated into the legendary Trojan War. [JSR]

279 (in §112:1). The work mentioned here, referred to as *Survey* in the present edition, was published by Swedenborg in 1769. It was indeed a little volume—just sixtyseven pages in the Latin version. Presenting itself as a precursor to *True Christianity,* it offers even sharper criticisms of contemporary Christian beliefs. See also the preface, pages 10–13. [JSR]

280 (in §112:3). According to the Lutheran teaching of the "communication of natures" in Christ, what could be said of one of the natures could logically be said of the other. See also note 275. [RGE]

281 (in §112:6). The translation here follows the reading of the first edition, *est,* "is," although that reading may be a typographical error for the usual *es,* "are" in the second person singular, as in "[you who] are in the heavens." The usual form is used slightly farther on in the text, in §113:5. For more on the abundance of typographical errors in the first edition, see the preface, page 29 and footnote 48. [JSR]

282 (in §113:1). This description is reminiscent in a number of ways of events described in the Book of Revelation. The mentions of a battle, armies, riders, red and black horses, and white horses have parallels there (Revelation 6:4, 5; 9:7, 9, 16, 17; 16:14; 17:14; 19:11, 14, 15, 18, 19, 21; 20:8). The text following this mentions Armageddon specifically, and refers to the relevant verse in the Book of Revelation. Yet there are elements here that stand in stark contrast to that apocalyptic setting and render the present description comical: riders that look like monkeys sitting backwards on their steeds, backing away from the fight even as they seem to be calling for battle. [JSR]

283 (in §113:1). The question "What do you see?" is reminiscent of the accounts of the prophets Jeremiah (Jeremiah 1:11, 13; 24:3), Amos (Amos 7:8; 8:2), and Zechariah (Zechariah 4:2; 5:2), who are asked by either an angel or the Lord, "What do you see?" when they are having visions, and are then told the meaning of those visions. [JSR]

284 (in §113:2). On this chemical interaction, see note 272 above. [SS]

285 (in §113:4). By "falsified truths" Swedenborg means statements from Scripture whose meanings have been twisted to support a principle that is false; his usual example is the doctrine of justification by faith alone. See *Revelation Unveiled* 566:5. On justification by faith alone, see note 252 and the introduction, pages 90–92. [JSR]

286 (in §113:6). This volume asserts here and in several other passages that while we cannot see God the Father, we can see Jesus Christ (see §§159, 279:3, 339). Two of these other passages (§§159:3, 339) clarify that it is the eye of our mind or spirit that has this ability. [JSR]

287 (in §113:7). Matthew 3:2 does indeed concern John the Baptist, and John is mentioned in Mark 1:14, but in the quotation from Mark here the name John has been substituted where Mark reads "Jesus." A similar substitution can be seen in a quotation from Luke 3:8 in *Divine Providence* 114. [JSR]

288 (in §114). Swedenborg's distinction between the priestly and royal "offices" or roles of Christ is a theological commonplace. In Calvinist (and later Lutheran) dogmatic theology, the offices were redefined as being three: prophet, priest, and king. Lutheran dogmatics tended to stress the priestly (or "mediating") office. By not mentioning the prophetic office (except somewhat obliquely in point 6 toward the end of this section in the text), Swedenborg seems to be taking a somewhat old-fashioned Lutheran position. [RGE]

289 (in §115). Swedenborg is here referring to his work *Last Judgment.* [JSR]

290 (in §116:3). The Latin word here translated "Hero" is *Heros.* In most English translations of the Bible, the equivalent word in the original is rendered "Mighty." [JSR]

291 (in §119:3). On the river Styx, see note 96 above. [JSR]

292 (in §120:1). Swedenborg explains in §64 that in the spiritual world the action of thinking of someone else with love establishes contact with that person. Therefore it is inevitable that people who have recently arrived in the spiritual world will come into contact with their friends and loved ones, whatever their inward nature may be. [JSR]

293 (in §120:2). Although piracy had reached its high point earlier, sometime between 1680 and 1730, it remained a major international concern at the time of this publication. See also note 533. [JSR]

294 (in §121:1). The work mentioned here, *Secrets of Heaven,* was published by Swedenborg in eight volumes between 1749 and 1756. In this passage he refers to §§1283–1328 of that work. [JSR]

295 (in §121:3). Swedenborg's citation of this passage from §3 earlier in the work and the citation just above from §2 show an imprecision similar to that which can be seen sometimes even in his quotations from the Bible (on Swedenborg's approach to biblical quotations, see pages 103–104). The Latin of the passages quoted here from §§2 and 3 shows a number of subtle differences from the Latin of §§2 and 3 themselves, particularly some minor omissions. [JSR]

296 (in §123:1). This might prove a somewhat frustrating statement for the eighteenth-century reader, even one living in London, since it would be difficult to access the book without the name of the London printer. One possible source of this information for a contemporary reader would have been the last page of the first edition of *Marriage Love,* which lists Swedenborg's earlier theological publications and mentions (in English as represented here) that they are still being sold by "Mistr. Hart. Printer, in Poppings Court Fleetstreet" and by "Mistr. Lewis, in Pater noster row near Cheapside." The latter, John Lewis, is identified as the printer of *Last Judgment* in Hyde 1906, 256, item 1166. [JSR]

297 (in §123:2). Swedenborg again presents the possibility of a future publication (see notes 71 and 240 above). Although this publication did not come about, he did begin to address the topic in a work left in manuscript fragments at the time of his death: see *Draft for "Coda to True Christianity"* 14–17 (= Swedenborg 1996, 1:37–41). [JSR]

298 (in §124:1). On the mention of God as having "faces" here, see note 243. [JSR]

299 (in §124:1). Swedenborg is here referring to mythical creatures, probably aware that they were only such. On "hydras," see note 147. A "dragon" was a large snake or serpent, and a "basilisk" was a serpent whose breath and even whose gaze was said to be fatal. [JSR]

300 (in §125). The diving bell (Latin *campana urinatoria*), a large weighted structure that trapped air under water for the use of divers, was invented in the sixteenth century. The best versions in Swedenborg's time were designed by an acquaintance of his, the English astronomer Edmond Halley (1656–1742); his contemporary and countryman Mårten Triewald (1691–1747) also published on the subject. See Halley 1716; Halley 1721; Triewald 1734; and Triewald [1734] 2004. [JSR]

301 (in §126). By taking the view that the union of Christ's divine and human natures was a gradual process, beginning at the Nativity and culminating at the Crucifixion, Swedenborg presented his contemporaries with a radically new interpretation of an old theological issue. Materialist philosophers would have downplayed the divine nature entirely; orthodox Protestants (or Catholics) would have insisted that the divine and human natures were coexistent in Christ, who was in turn coexistent with God the Father. [RGE]

302 (in §128). For more on the meaning of the term "glorification," see note 11. [JSR]

303 (in §130:3). For a summary of Swedenborg's statements in this volume regarding ancient Jews, see note 262. [JSR]

304 (in §132:1). By Swedenborg's time, Lutheranism was theologically divided between those who emphasized right teaching (often referred to as "the orthodox") and those who emphasized deep religious feeling and amendment of life (often called "Pietists"). Swedenborg is not simply referring to the teachings-oriented party here, though, since the issue at hand here was not one that divided the groups. [RGE]

305 (in §132:1). Such a depiction of an angry God may be found in an early work of Swedenborg, written during his transition from scientific to theological writing (*Worship and Love of God* 78); it is of course common in Christian imagery in general.

Contemporary Deists (see notes 46 and 171) complained that such an image runs counter to the assertion that God is compassionate and merciful, a charge that parallels Swedenborg's own objections here. [SS]

306 (in §133). Swedenborg's statement here that "everything about the church hinges on its concept of God and its view of redemption" is reminiscent of the statement fondly repeated by Lutheran theologians to the effect that the church "stood or fell" on the doctrine of justification by faith; that is, all other doctrines and understandings of God were to be seen in light of that fundamental axiom. See the introduction, page 91 note 25. [RGE]

307 (in §133). On justification, see the introduction, pages 90–92; see also note 252. Along with justification, "sanctification" was another step in what Protestant Scholastic theologians knew in Latin as the *ordo salutis* or the steps toward salvation (see note 354). It is part of the process after justification; in it the individual becomes holy and willingly does good works; see Muller 1985 under "*sanctificatio.*" [JSR]

308 (in §133). Swedenborg is referring here to a form of ancient Roman dictatorship held by three people at once. In fact, it arose on two occasions. The First Triumvirate began in 60 B.C.E, and included Julius Caesar (101–44 B.C.E.), Gnaeus Pompeius Magnus (106–48 B.C.E.), and Marcus Licinius Crassus (around 115–53 B.C.E.). The Second Triumvirate, which began in 43 B.C.E., consisted of Marcus Aemilius Lepidus (around 90–13 or 12 B.C.E.), Marcus Antonius (around 83–30 B.C.E.), and Gaius Octavius (later known as Caesar Augustus, and the same as the Octavian Augustus mentioned in §73:1). Both experiments ended disastrously in civil war. [JSR, SS]

309 (in §133). On Arianism and Arius, see notes 245 and 246. [JSR]

310 (in §134:3). The angel's ridicule of the paradoxical nature of the doctrine of justification would have been a double rejection from the Lutheran perspective: of the doctrine in itself, of course, but also of Luther's teaching that God's saving work in Christ was "hidden" under or behind the judgment on human sin that God's law and righteousness represented and is therefore *intentionally* paradoxical. [RGE]

311 (in §135:3). For biblical passages on mediation, see 1 Timothy 2:5; Hebrews 8:6; 9:15; 12:24. [JSR]

312 (in §135:5). Swedenborg notes that the words here translated "appeasement" and "mercy seat" have "the same meaning" because in Latin they are closely related: *propitiatio* (literally, "propitiation") and *propitiatorium* ("place of propitiation"), respectively. [JSR]

313 (in §136:1). Swedenborg reports another spiritual experience of five halls in §459. As the next paragraph explains, these halls (Latin *gymnasia*) are public buildings where various educated groups meet for the sake of discussion and debate. They are perhaps somewhat like the academies, learned societies, and debating clubs that developed in Europe during the seventeenth and eighteenth centuries (see McClellan 1985; Roche 1978). [JSR]

314 (in §136:2). For those who are meant by the "people on the right," see note 170. [JSR]

315 (in §136:4). This teaching about God's sameness on the highest and lowest levels has close parallels in Lutheranism. As in the debate between Luther and Zwingli over the "presence" of Christ in the Eucharist, Lutheran theologians taught that, as a consequence of the "communication of natures," Christ's spiritual ubiquity was accompanied by a human one. Wherever one nature of Christ could be said to be, the other could be as well. See also notes 135, 245, 275. [RGE]

316 (in §136:4). The first edition here presents four quotations, attributing them all to "David," and citing psalm and verse numbers for each. (Writers of Swedenborg's time often referred to the Psalms by the name of their general putative author, David.) The first two attributions in the original are mistaken however—they cite the correct chapter and verse, but the quotations come from Isaiah, not the Psalms. [JSR]

317 (in §136:5). The Latin word here translated "hand," *manus,* often denotes not only the hand but also the forearm up to the elbow. In his first published theological work also, issued twenty-two years before *True Christianity,* Swedenborg reported having seen such a hand appearing from heaven; see *Secrets of Heaven* 878:8. [JSR]

318 (in §137:1). This rather lengthy memorable occurrence is entirely marked off in the first edition with double quotation marks. On such marks, see note 260 above. Although such marks sometimes serve to indicate a quotation, the present passage has no known parallel in Swedenborg's other works; the double quotation marks here apparently serve instead to draw particular attention to the passage. A concept in Swedenborg's theology that is important for understanding this memorable occurrence is that each individual person living in the physical world has a like-minded spirit (that is, the soul of a deceased person) who is closely associated with him or her (see §380:3). Although elsewhere Swedenborg states quite emphatically that such spirits do not and must not know the identity of the people with whom they are associated (*Heaven and Hell* 292), in this case two of them do. A summary of this fairly complicated memorable occurrence may help orient the reader: A debate takes place in the world of spirits in a group whose members include some who served as Christian clergy at periods ranging between the dawn of Christianity and Swedenborg's own time. The question is whether Swedenborg's teachings are correct or not. The participants are divided into two main groups: a favorable group on the right consisting of clergy who lived before the Nicene Council (325 C.E.), and an unfavorable group on the left consisting of clergy who lived after that time. Four individuals speak: (1) a chairperson, who apparently called the council, who has cronies in the group on the left, and who is closely associated with a famous critic of Swedenborg who lives in earthly Germany; (2) an angel from the group on the right, who speaks in support of Swedenborg's teachings; (3) Swedenborg himself, who opposes his absent earthly critics as well as the chairperson; and (4) a spirit from the group on the left who is closely associated with a prominent critic of Swedenborg from Göteborg in earthly Sweden. (For conjectures as to the identities of the earthly critics, see notes 341 and 347.) As a result of the debate, some spirits move from the unfavorable group on the left to the favorable group on the right. [JSR]

319 (in §137:1). When Swedenborg mentions the "justification of the elect by that faith," he is implicitly including both Lutherans and Calvinists. If he had meant Lutherans alone, he could well have said simply "justification by faith" (the Lutheran core doctrine of God's gratuitous mercy—see also note 252 and the introduction, pages 90–92); if he had meant Calvinists alone, he could have said "justification of the elect" or the salvation of those predestined to that happy end. The locution Swedenborg chooses is an interesting and unusual one. [RGE]

320 (in §137:1). Protestant clergymen of Swedenborg's time wore either broad white linen "bands" at the throat or full starched linen "ruffs" as a badge of office. Neither was

originally exclusively clerical wear, but both were retained by clergy long after the lay fashions had changed. Over time, bands became more common than ruffs, due to their far easier manufacture and maintenance. For some traditionalist Lutheran clergy this change was unwelcome, particularly because Calvinist clergy (always less concerned about externals in worship) had abandoned ruffs far earlier, and the move from ruffs to bands was seen as a rejection of tradition. The conservative Lutheran churches of north Germany and Scandinavia have retained the ruff to some degree to this day. The mention in this passage of women's hair as a material for wigs is probably intended to be understood as a contrast with the material more commonly used for this purpose, horsehair, which did not curl when exposed to damp air. [RGE, SS]

321 (in §137:2). The chairperson is referring here to Swedenborg himself and harping on Swedenborg's lack of credentials in theology. A gown, a cap, and laurel would be signs of a university degree in theology qualifying one to preach and teach. Swedenborg did have a university degree, but not in theology, and was not a cleric or a professor. At the end of *True Christianity* Swedenborg briefly addresses the issue of his credentials (see §850). [JSR]

322 (in §137:2). On the river Styx, see note 96. Orion is a large constellation on the celestial equator; and Lucifer, the "light bringer," in this context means the planet Venus in its role as "the morning star." [JSR]

323 (in §137:2). See, for example, Calvin *Institutes* (= Calvin 1960) 1:11:12–13. This dramatic debate is between those open to new insights about God in Christ and those who are not. Swedenborg, by here going on to describe those who oppose any revision to their ideas as bewigged, clean-shaven, and wearing ruffs, is identifying them as Lutherans as surely as he does by cataloging the doctrines they defend. (See note 320 above.) [RGE]

324 (in §137:3). The original Latin edition of the present work generally lacks quotation marks that are used as we now employ them to differentiate between speakers. Most quoted material is indicated as a quote in other ways. As this passage stands in the Latin, the statement beginning with "Very wisely said" is clearly uttered by some in the group on the left, while the statement ending "bringing it back with you" is clearly said by the chairperson; but the original contains no overt indication of when the change in speaker takes place. The point that seems the most logical for the transition has been chosen in this rendering. [JSR]

325 (in §137:4). For Swedenborg's assertion that people who die at whatever age become young adults in heaven, see *Heaven and Hell* 414; see also *Revelation Explained* (= Swedenborg 1994–1997) §1000:4. [JSR]

326 (in §137:4). A "relic" was a treasured and venerated object—some part of the body or clothing, or a possession, of a saint or martyr in the medieval Roman Catholic tradition. Luther and Protestants in general condemned relics as unholy and contributing nothing toward salvation (see Kolb and Wengert 2000, 305.22–23, 399.91). The speaker here, though a Christian on earth before 325 B.C.E. and therefore centuries before Protestantism, apparently would agree with Protestant criticism of the veneration of relics. [JSR]

327 (in §137:4). Swedenborg himself elsewhere echoes this idea that Roman Catholics have the same beliefs as Protestants, but those beliefs are a less prominent focus for Catholics than the observation of rituals (*Survey* 105–108). [JSR]

328 (in §137:4). Vesta was Roman goddess of the hearth. The fire on the hearth in the temple dedicated to her worship at Rome was never allowed to go out. Girls between the ages of six and ten years old were eligible to become her attendants, or "Vestal virgins." In early times such priestesses served for five years, but later for thirty. If one of them during her service broke her vow of chastity or let the fire go out, she was to be buried or entombed alive. This punishment was inflicted many times in Roman history; for example in 215 B.C.E., when several Vestals were so executed. The uninterrupted worship of Vesta was identified with the continued existence of Rome; see Horace *Odes* 3:30:8. [JSR, SS]

329 (in §137:5). "The sacred tome" here means the Bible. [JSR]

330 (in §137:7). "Evangelical" here and elsewhere in this translation refers to the Lutheran religion or its adherents. [JSR]

331 (in §137:7). In §101 of the present work Swedenborg identifies the Formula of Concord as a section of a larger work of Lutheran Orthodoxy, as indeed it was and still is (see the introduction, pages 84–85, and note 258). Here in the text, however, and in §§137:9–10, 356, he uses the same phrase as the title of that whole larger work, although it was then generally titled *Concordia Pia* (see *Concordia* 1756), and is now titled the *Book of Concord* (see Kolb and Wengert 2000). [JSR]

332 (in §137:7). The parallels in the modern edition of Kolb and Wengert 2000 are found at 509–510.5 and 617.6. [JSR]

333 (in §137:7). The parallels in the modern edition of Kolb and Wengert 2000 to the first and last references here are found at 512.18 and 617.6. The second reference is apparently erroneous; there is no such quotation on page 673 of *Concordia* 1756. [JSR]

334 (in §137:7). The parallels in the modern edition of Kolb and Wengert 2000 are found at 510.10 and 619.19. [JSR]

335 (in §137:7). Modern parallels for these passages are found not in Kolb and Wengert 2000, but in the *Catalog of Testimonies,* which no longer appears as part of *The Book of Concord:* see articles 1 and 2 (§§19–63) on "Majesty"; articles 3–5 (§§99 or 100–132); and articles 6–10, including the epilogue or conclusion at the end (§§143–181); they are included in *Triglot Concordia* 1921. [JSR]

336 (in §137:7). The parallels in the modern edition of Kolb and Wengert 2000 are found at 621.27–28 and 631.77–632.85. [JSR]

337 (in §137:7). The parallels in the modern edition of Kolb and Wengert 2000 are found at 626.55, 626.58, and 629.70. [JSR]

338 (in §137:7). The parallels in the modern edition of Kolb and Wengert 2000 are found at 511.15 and 618.12. [JSR]

339 (in §137:7). The parallel in the modern edition of Kolb and Wengert 2000 is found at 240.18. [JSR]

340 (in §137:7). The parallel in the modern edition of Kolb and Wengert 2000 is found at 58.2–4. For more on the Augsburg Confession, see note 275. [JSR]

341 (in §137:8). Evidence strongly suggests that the text is here referring to Johann August Ernesti (1701–1781). Ernesti was a well-known biblical scholar and editor of a journal that reviewed theological books; by 1771 Ernesti had reviewed Swedenborg's *Secrets of Heaven* (Ernesti 1760), his 1763 works *The Lord, Sacred Scripture, Life, Faith,* and *Supplements* (Ernesti 1763), and his 1766 work *Revelation Unveiled* (Ernesti 1766), and had reviewed another work that discussed Swedenborg's theology (Ernesti 1767). The evidence

that the famous man here is Ernesti comes from Swedenborg himself. In June 1771, after the publication of the present volume, Swedenborg learned that Ernesti had attacked him in the last-mentioned review (Ernesti 1767). There Ernesti conjectured that Swedenborg fabricated his clairvoyant experiences in order to deceive and laugh at his followers (Ernesti 1767, 874–875; see also note 342 below). In response Swedenborg printed a small broadside in late June 1771 and circulated it to acquaintances. (This printed sheet is referred to as *Reply to Ernesti*.) In its text Swedenborg declines to respond in kind but rather invites readers to see the end of *True Christianity* (§§846–851) and judge for themselves. He added a final paragraph that reads: "Furthermore a narrative account of a memorable occurrence written against this same Doctor Ernesti has been included in the aforementioned work, *True Christianity*, §137, pages 105 to 108. I recommend it to the reader" (translation by JSR from text in Swedenborg [1771] 1975d, 198). Two paragraphs later in the text here, the famous man is said to live near Luther's tomb. Ernesti lived in Leipzig, some forty miles from Luther's tomb in Wittenberg. In addition, Swedenborg's friend Johann Christian Cuno (1708–1796) mentions in a letter written on March 5, 1771, that Swedenborg had told him he had once "stoutly disputed" with a spirit closely associated with Ernesti (Cuno 1947, 165); although that letter does not mention this passage, it too lends some support to the identification of Ernesti as the famous man meant here. [JSR]

342 (in §137:8). This assertion that Luther "laughs when he looks upon his insane followers" is strikingly parallel to Ernesti's last critique of Swedenborg's theological works (Ernesti 1767, 874–875). In that review, Ernesti expresses the belief that Swedenborg's accounts of his spiritual experiences are "fictitious inventions" included in his works so that "in his heart he may laugh at the people (as also they deserve), who believe him and do not understand his artfulness" (this translation from Cuno 1947, 168). Yet Swedenborg was unaware of Ernesti's critique when he wrote and published this account (see note 341). Later in this work, Swedenborg reiterates that Luther changed his doctrinal position after death; see §796. [JSR]

343 (in §137:10). On the term "hypostatic union," see note 247 above. [JSR]

344 (in §137:10). The parallel in the modern edition of Kolb and Wengert 2000 is found at 619.17–621.30. [JSR]

345 (in §137:10). The parallel in the modern edition of Kolb and Wengert 2000 is found at 24.28, 24.32, 24.34–35. [JSR]

346 (in §137:11). For Arius, see notes 245 and 246. For the Council of Nicaea and Constantine the Great, see note 246. [JSR]

347 (in §137:12). The eminent man in Göteborg mentioned here is Erik Lamberg (1719–1780), who was bishop of Göteborg at the time. Swedenborg so identified the eminent man to his friend Johann Christian Cuno (although Swedenborg could not remember Lamberg's name at that moment), and Cuno wrote "bishop of Göteborg" in the margin of his copy of *True Christianity* next to this spot in the text ("History" 1890, 214). Although a later hand added to the same margin the name of Olof A. Ekebom (1716–1784), that identification is incorrect: Ekebom was the dean, not the bishop, of Göteborg. Bishop Lamberg had indeed accused Swedenborg of Muhammadanism: on November 16, 1769, Lamberg sent a letter to a friend, which was later incorporated into the minutes of the Göteborg Consistory. It spoke of Swedenborg's teachings as a "doctrinal system, which is . . . tinged with Mohammedanism" (Tafel 1877, 311). Tafel (1877, 1133) reports that Lamberg had been previously unwilling to tackle Swedenborgianism,

but was influenced to do so by Dean Ekebom, who strongly opposed Swedenborg. The charge of "Mohammedanism" probably arose out of a simplistic comparison of Swedenborg's antitrinitarianism with the radical monotheism of Islam; since Islam had been Christian Europe's main enemy for centuries, and yet accurate knowledge of Islamic belief was not common in Europe at the time (see also note 564), Christians made such accusations against a variety of suspected heretics (see Helander 2004, 343–344; Kors 2003, 2:269). This may explain the strong reaction expressed in the next paragraph of the text. John Wesley (1703–1791), founder of Methodism, later made similar accusations against Swedenborg (see the preface, page 37; Lang 2000, 61; Wesley [1782] 1856, 421) in response to Swedenborg's teaching later in the present volume that evil spirits are allowed to have sexual intercourse (§281:11). [RGE, JSR]

348 (in §137:12). Vulcan was the ancient Roman god of terrestrial fire; therefore the reference means simply that the bishop should have burned the letter. This mythological way of referring to a commonplace event shows the heated and highly rhetorical flavor of this exchange. [JSR]

349 (in §137:12). Swedenborg here vehemently defends himself against the charge of so-called Muhammadanism, which was a serious one at the time (see note 347). Generally elsewhere, however, Swedenborg writes more favorably about Islam. He sees divine providence in the spread of Islam to replace ancient idolatry with monotheism (see §833:4); he reports Muslim criticisms of Christianity with which he himself seems sympathetic (§831); and he states that the heavens include a multileveled realm for Muslims (*Divine Providence* 255:5). [JSR]

350 (in §137:12). In Revelation 3:18, the "Son of Humankind" gives this advice to the church of the Laodiceans: "I advise you to buy from me gold that has been refined in the fire so that you become rich; and white clothes for you to put on so that the shame of your nakedness will not appear; and also to anoint your eyes with eye salve, so that you will see." In Revelation 2:16 he gives this advice to the church in Pergamos regarding the Nicolaitans: "Repent; otherwise I will come to you quickly, and will fight against them with the sword that is in my mouth." The content and context of these passages amount to an implication that the bishop was complacent; ignorant of his own spiritual poverty, nakedness, and blindness; and in need of repentance. [JSR]

Notes to Chapter 3, §§138–188

351 (in §138). For a more detailed account of what happens to people when they die, see *Heaven and Hell* 445–452; *Secrets of Heaven* 168–189, 314–319. For quite a different account, see §160 of the present work. [JSR]

352 (in §138). "The Sacred Order" here means clergy in general. The name may derive from the division of the Swedish parliament into four estates known as "orders" (see Helander 2004, 209, under "*ordines*"; see also note 196 above). The Sacred Order was the ecclesiastical estate, which included bishops and clergy of various levels. Compare similar expressions in §§160:3, 181. [JSR]

353 (in §138). The Latin word here translated by the phrase "fanatics who have believed they were divinely inspired" is *enthusiastae,* literally, "enthusiasts." In Swedenborg's day, "enthusiasm" was a charge readily and frequently made against radicals of various kinds who claimed personal spiritual authority and knowledge of the will of God; see Kors 2003, 2:1–7. [JSR]

354 (in §138). This list of divine actions and powerful effects is much like Protestant Scholastic theology's *ordo salutis,* or steps toward salvation. Although the specific steps and their arrangement would vary from system to system, the following is a general model: calling, regeneration, adoption, conversion, faith, justification, renewal, sanctification, and perseverance (see Muller 1985 under "*ordo salutis*"; see also note 307 above). [JSR]

355 (in §141). In eighteenth-century Europe, many pulpits were eight to twelve feet above the congregation and included a staircase for clergy to climb into them. [JSR]

356 (in §141). Swedenborg refers here to the Roman republic of the decades before 27 B.C.E. (that is, before the beginning of the Roman Empire). The consul was one of two chief magistrates ruling the Roman Republic; the senate was the Republic's supreme council of state; and the advocate for the common people, or "tribune of the plebs," was an officer elected to protect the people from the arbitrary exercise of power by the patrician magistrates. Even after emperors (the Caesars to which Swedenborg here refers) began to hold power, these offices continued, but no longer retained the same authority. [JSR, SS]

357 (in §142). On this list of divine actions and powerful effects, see note 354. [JSR]

358 (in §146). On "inflow," see note 32. [JSR]

359 (in §146). On this metaphor of people carrying religious attitudes in packs on their backs, see note 101. [SS]

360 (in §146). The "Society of Jesus," also known as the Jesuits, was a Roman Catholic order founded by Ignatius of Loyola (1491–1556) in 1534. The Jesuits were a common object of disparagement in contemporary Protestant Sweden (see Helander 2004, 332–334). On the need for stairs to reach the high pulpits of the day, see note 355. [JSR]

361 (in §147). In Latin translations of the Bible, the passages cited here use the word *simplex* ("simple" or "single," in the sense of something that is not compounded of two or more elements) where modern English translations generally read "good." [JSR]

362 (in §151). On the unusual plural, "satans," here, see note 18. [JSR]

363 (in §153:3). John 15:26 reads, "When the Comforter comes, the Spirit of Truth whom I am going to send you from the Father, he will testify about me." [JSR]

364 (in §153:3). By the "Greek Church," Swedenborg probably means Eastern Orthodox Christianity in general. Although Swedenborg frequently mentions Protestant and Roman Catholic Christianity, his only other mentions of the "Greek Church" occur in §647:3 and *Survey* 18. [JSR]

365 (in §154:2). "Evangelical" here means Lutheran, while "Reformed" means Calvinist. On Luther, Calvin, and Melanchthon, see note 179. For the historical development of these factions over time, see MacCulloch 2003. [JSR]

366 (in §154:4). On free choice, see chapter 8 in the second volume of the present work (§§463–508). [JSR]

367 (in §154:5). By "the part of our mind that enables us to have volition and perception," Swedenborg probably means both the will and the intellect. See note 39. [JSR]

368 (in §154:6). By the "soul" here Swedenborg means the mind. See note 24. [JSR]

369 (in §156). Elsewhere Swedenborg differentiates evil spirits into satans and devils; see note 18. [JSR]

370 (in §156). Swedenborg is speaking here in general terms of the brain and the nerves. By "primary structures" he means cells within the brain, and by "extensions of these primary structures" he means the nerves that connect the brain to all parts of the

body, bringing in sensory information and sending out signals that occasion voluntary action. [GMC, JSR]

371 (in §157:1). On the dating of Swedenborg's spiritual awakening, see note 59. [JSR]

372 (in §157:3). Supplying exact references for these passages is unnecessary, as this paragraph constitutes a summary of the entire Book of Revelation. [JSR]

373 (in §159:5). For most of these Greco-Roman gods and goddesses, see note 81. Themis (the only one not listed in that earlier passage) was the goddess of custom. An early proponent of the idea that the gods were originally rulers who were deified after death was Euhemerus, a Greek writer of the fourth century B.C.E. The idea was imported into Christianity by Lactantius (around 240–around 320 C.E.). See Lactantius *Divine Institutes* 1:11:33–1:15:33 (= Lactantius 2003, 83; see also note 78 there); Block 1876, 60–69. [JSR]

374 (in §159:6). On Socinianism and Arianism, see notes 245 and 246. [JSR]

375 (in §159:7). By the "first and second ages," Swedenborg (and the angels) probably means the Golden and Silver Ages, mentioned in Hesiod *Works and Days* 109–126; Vergil *Eclogues* 4; and especially in Ovid *Metamorphoses* 1:89–112; see also note 41 above. Swedenborg discusses these ages in §762 of the present work and in several of his other works, including *Worship and Love of God* 1–2; *Secrets of Heaven* 1551:1, 5658:2, 10355:2–3; *Heaven and Hell* 115; and *Marriage Love* 75–76. He equates these ages with the earliest or most ancient church, and the early or ancient church (on the five churches, see note 3), both of which occurred before the times recorded in the Old Testament. [JSR]

376 (in §159:7). The letters alpha and omega were, respectively, the beginning and end of the Greek alphabet; and the Lord is called the Alpha and the Omega in Revelation 1:8, 11; 21:6; 22:13; see also §19. This identification of the Lord with all things from the beginning to the end bears on the meaning of the Latin phrase *Deus non sit vox trium syllabarum,* here translated "God is not a three-letter word." (Though the phrase could be literally rendered "God is not a word of three syllables," the term *syllaba,* "syllable," is generally used by Swedenborg in the sense of the English word "letter.") The statement is puzzling on its face, for in Latin it seems to be saying "The word *Deus* is not a three-letter word," which is self-evident. Swedenborg may be intimating that God is spelled with three letters in the spiritual world, or acknowledging that it is so spelled in some other language he does not specify—Swedish, for instance, in which it appears as *Gud.* Clearly, however, the sense intended is that God is not *merely* a three-letter word, just as the sentence before this asserted that God is not merely "a figment of our imagination." The implication is that no matter how many letters are used to spell the word God, he is in fact the entire alphabet of reality. [JSR, SS]

377 (in §160:2). The description in this passage, which looks objectively at what happens to people's spirits just after their bodies die, is strikingly different from the subjective accounts given elsewhere (see *Secrets of Heaven* 168–189, 314–319; *Heaven and Hell* 445–452). [JSR]

378 (in §160:2). The directions of the compass given here are somewhat confusing, but can be reconciled if Swedenborg is describing a whole area with an eastern, a western, and a southern region, all of which lie to his north. The western region is to his left and he is looking at a road to the north, while the southern region is nonetheless in front of him. Elsewhere Swedenborg explains that directions in the spiritual world are

difficult to describe because angels remain facing east no matter which way they turn (*Heaven and Hell* 141–144). [JSR]

379 (in §160:3). "Our Sacred Order" means the clergy; see note 352. [JSR]

380 (in §160:4). Swedenborg mentions this same basic question in *Secrets of Heaven* 6971:2; in fact, in *Heaven and Hell* 1 he states it as a motivation for his writing and publishing that book. The question is also an allusion to Luke 16:19–31. [JSR, SS]

381 (in §160:5). In Swedenborg's day, mummy powder, made from ground-up Egyptian mummies, was a popular and much-used medicine that came in many forms. Mummy powder was commonly mixed with other ingredients to make a tincture, elixir, or even a balsam, and was thought to be an effective remedy against vertigo, epilepsy, palsy, wasted limbs, and ulcers. Applied to wounds, it was thought to prevent necrosis. It was also used nonmedically in a number of ways, for example, as an ingredient in paint. Its use continued into the early twentieth century. See Aufderheide 2003, 515–536. [GMC, JSR]

382 (in §160:5). For the eighteenth-century view of the similarities and differences between humans and animals, see note 67. [JSR]

383 (in §160:6). This thought is also expressed in §14:3. It would be an understatement to say that political theory in the eighteenth century saw religion, whatever its verity, as necessary to preserving morality and hence social order. In particular, the threat of punishment in the afterlife for crime committed during life was seen as the only applicable deterrent in society in general. Even as dedicated a skeptic of organized religion as the French *philosophe* Voltaire said of the belief in God that "this sublime system is necessary to humankind; / it is the sacred bond of society. / . . . . If God did not exist, it would be necessary to invent him," that is, to maintain social order (Voltaire [1768] 1877–1885, 10:402–405, lines 16–17, 22). Swedenborg was in fact criticized by those who believed his description of hell would make it less effective as a deterrent; see the preface, pages 36–37. See also note 347. For a very ancient formulation of this thought, see Critias (around 460–403 B.C.E) fragment 1 (= Diggle 1998, 771–772). [SS]

384 (in §161:1). This is a reference to the Protestant doctrine of "justification by faith"; see the introduction, pages 90–92. See also note 252. [JSR]

385 (in §161:1). The greater or lesser value this researcher assigns to these books and their countries of origin suggests that he was a rigorous Calvinist; see also note 189. [JSR]

386 (in §161:3). John 14:6 reads, "I am the way, the truth, and the life. No one comes to the Father except through me." [JSR]

387 (in §162:2). The mention of the "works of the Law" here is a reference to Romans 3:28; the Law (so capitalized) means the books of Genesis, Exodus, Leviticus, Numbers, and Deuteronomy. For other meanings of "the law," see §262 at the end, and §288. [JSR]

388 (in §162:3). This passage reflects the ancient belief that the eyes emit perceptual rays, making vision possible. The visual ray was like an extension of the body's sensory apparatus. This was known as the extramission theory of vision. This idea first surfaces in western literature in fragments by Empedocles. Plato was another prominent early proponent of the theory; he taught that the eye had a fire of its own that, when combined with external light, would produce vision. Galen also supported extramission, and had a physiological model of the eye to support it. Also implicit here is the ancient belief that the soul's fire is visible in the eyes of a living creature. The soul was thought

to be composed of fire and ether, the latter of which was the highest and subtlest of the five traditional elements. Thus the soul combined the heat and active character of fire with the eternal character of the ether. Although by Swedenborg's time science had long refuted the extramission idea of vision, through the definitive work of Johannes Kepler in his *Optics* (1604), and although Swedenborg shows awareness that vision occurs when light from objects impinges on the eye (see §461:5), vestiges of the ancient theory remain in passages such as these. See Lindberg 1976; Park 1997, 34–50. [GMC]

389 (in §162:4). Whether the word "archangels" spoken here by these spirits represents an actual belief on their part in such creatures or not, it is not a belief shared by Swedenborg. With the possible exception of angel guardians, or cherubs (see note 195), Swedenborg does not share the medieval view that there were nine orders of spiritual beings. Although there are hierarchies or governmental structures among angels (*Heaven and Hell* 213, 218), there are no separate beings called archangels in his theology (see *Revelation Explained* [= Swedenborg 1994–1997] §735:2). [JSR]

390 (in §162:6). Without ever specifying exactly what the form is, Swedenborg mentions "the form of heaven" or "a form like heaven" in almost a hundred descriptions of spiritual objects in his published theological works. The phrase is occasionally plural, and apparently these forms are varied (*Marriage Love* 14:2). The chief characteristics of these forms are that they are "human," they incorporate a great variety of elements into one harmonious arrangement, and each element can be viewed as the central one; see *Secrets of Heaven* 4040, 4043, 6607, 9846, 9877. Even household utensils in the spiritual world may have this form (*Marriage Love* 137:7). [JSR]

391 (in §162:7). This description of someone's being knocked unconscious by touching the Word may be compared with a similar occurrence in §209:3. [JSR]

392 (in §162:7). The Latin of the first edition here makes no sense as it stands. A passage that is parallel with it, however, supplies a word that is apparently missing here. The bracketed emendation is imported from that parallel passage (*Revelation Unveiled* 566:7). On the "activation of faith," see note 612 below. [JSR]

393 (in §163). Touchstones have long been used to test or assay the purity of gold and silver, at least since the Greeks of the sixth century B.C.E. They are made of black siliceous stone. A sample of gold or silver of unknown purity is rubbed on the stone next to a sample of known purity. Nitric acid is then applied to dissolve the impurities from the test sample, leaving pure metal, and the two rubbings can be compared. Assaying by touchstone is a highly subjective method, though useful since it does not destroy the object. See Oddy 1983, 52–59; Eluère 1986, 58–61. [GMC]

394 (in §165:3). Lynceus and Argus are both figures from Greco-Roman mythology. Lynceus, one of the Argonauts, was known for having exceptional eyesight. Argus had a hundred eyes, only two of which slept at a time. [JSR]

395 (in §169). On Vestal virgins, see note 328. [JSR]

396 (in §171). Swedenborg believed that each individual has but one life in this world, and then passes on to spend eternity in the spiritual world. In that world, the individual retains his or her essential personality. As evidence he cites conversations he had with people who had died many centuries ago, who were still in the spiritual world and had the same character as before (*Heaven and Hell* 363). He also explains that rare instances of memory leakage from spirits to humans are the cause of experiences such as déjà vu that lead people to believe in reincarnation (*Heaven and Hell* 256). In the

allusion to the theory that humans souls were created at the beginning of the world, Swedenborg is probably referring to the Myth of Er, a theory of reincarnation described by Plato; see note 219. [JSR]

397 (in §172:1). A "posthumous child" was one born after the father had died. The implication seems to be that Christianity was already in some sense dead before the Athanasian Creed came into being. [JSR]

398 (in §173:1). The rumen is a component of the digestive system of animals classified as ruminants. Cows, for instance, have a three-chambered fore-stomach, consisting of a rumen, reticulum, and omasum; the rumen, the largest and most significant part, enables the cow to digest the fibrous cellulose that is the principal component of grasses and other plants, its main diet. The cow regularly regurgitates plant matter from the rumen for further chewing (rumination), which assists in the digestive process by breaking down the food into smaller particles. This analogy between the functions of the mental faculties and the compartments of a ruminant's stomach ultimately derives from the complicated Aristotelian model of mental function. In accordance with Aristotle's detailed account in *On the Soul* (especially books 2 and 3 = 412a–435b [= Aristotle 1952g, 643–688]), the processes of thought were called, collectively, "abstraction," since, according to the Aristotelian view, the principal function of the mind is to abstract general knowledge from particular sensory data. External stimuli impinge upon one of the sense organs, such as the eyes, which extracts a sensible "impression" and passes it on to the *sensus communis* ("common sense"), where it is combined with impressions from other senses to yield a single perceptible representation. Representations from all the senses are then passed to the *imaginative faculty*, which acts as a sensible memory. The *fantasia*, which serves as a kind of mental mirror, associates these ideas coherently. The *cogitative faculty* draws inferences from the associations made in the fantasia. And finally, the *memory faculty* retains the results of this process for future recall. The last two faculties are closely associated in the organism, so that ideas can be recalled from the memory and further cogitated upon to produce new insight, which is then stored in the memory. Such further thought usually occurs when the mind is not otherwise engaged in gathering new sensory experience, just as the cow ruminates when resting. See Smith 1992; Clarke and Dewhurst 1972; Harvey 1975; Wedin 1988. Birds are mentioned in this passage probably on account of their habit of regurgitating food for their young, not because their digestive system in any way resembles that of a ruminant's. [GMC]

399 (in §174:2). On Arius, Constantine the Great, and the Council of Nicaea, see note 246. [JSR]

400 (in §174:2). On the term "hypostatic union," see note 247 above. [JSR]

401 (in §175). On the Apostles' Creed, see note 224. The quotation from it that follows in the text is condensed but faithful. [JSR]

402 (in §176). In Swedenborg's 1734 work *Basic Principles of Nature,* part 3, chapter 4, §7 (= Swedenborg [1734] 1988a, 2:263–272), he quotes extensively from a list (Gregory 1702, 171) of more than twenty new stars (known generally as novas, but in the case of extremely bright stars, as supernovas) compiled by the astronomer David Gregory (1659–1708). The list begins in the time of Hipparchus; mentions new stars observed by Tycho Brahe (1546–1601), for which see further Brahe 1573, and by Johannes Kepler, for which see further Kepler 1606; and extends through 1670. Both the appearance and disappearance of these stars are described in the cited passage. The phenomenon is mentioned

again in *True Christianity* 348; see also *Worship and Love of God* 9 note d. Beekman 1902, 76–96, on Swedenborg's treatment of new stars, is of philosophical and historical interest, although its science is dated; it gives further references to passages on the topic in Swedenborg's scientific works. [JSR, SS]

403 (in §176). In the image of the bird flying in outer space or a deer running through the air, Swedenborg is drawing on the literary motif of impossibility established by classical Greek and Roman writers. Compare, for example, Archilochus [Diehl] 74:6–9; and Horace *Odes* 1:2:7–12; *Epodes* 16:34. This figure of speech—the exaggerated representation of the impossible—is called *adynaton*. [SS]

404 (in §177:2). The "Holy Supper" (Latin *Sancta Caena*) is Swedenborg's preferred way of referring to Holy Communion or the Eucharist—the ritual consumption of bread and wine initiated by Jesus Christ at his last supper and widely practiced in Christian denominations. Swedenborg devotes a chapter to it in the second volume of this work (§§698–752). [JSR]

405 (in §177:2). On this appendix, see note 71. [JSR]

406 (in §177:4). Swedenborg refers here to various policies decided by Roman Catholic councils. "Indulgences" are declarations of absolution from sin granted by the Catholic Church for various reasons. Their origin is somewhat shadowy; they are sometimes traced to a plenary forgiveness of sins granted to all who went on the First Crusade, issued by Pope Urban II (1035–1099) at the Council of Clermont in 1095. Over time they were subject to much abuse, and the granting of indulgences in exchange for money became a celebrated Protestant objection to the Catholic Church during the Reformation. The sale of indulgences was abolished by Pope Pius V (1504–1572) in 1567, though indulgences are still considered by the Catholic Church to be part of its infallible doctrine. "Splitting the Eucharist" refers to the Roman Catholic doctrine that the sacrament of the Eucharist can be completely effective even if the communicant receives only the bread and not the wine. Over a period of many centuries before the mid-1500s, this doctrine led to the denial of the wine to the laity. Protestant reformers strenuously objected to this doctrinal position and the resulting practice. [SS]

407 (in §177:4). This is a reference to the Synod of Dort (or Dordrecht) in the Netherlands, an international council of Calvinist churches, which embraced predestination as the first of five doctrinal points agreed upon (see §489:1). See also note 189. The reference to setting this doctrine up as an icon in front of all Calvinist church buildings is something of a taunt. Religious icons have played an important role in the Roman Catholic and Eastern Orthodox religious traditions. When Calvinists and Lutherans broke away from Catholicism, there was widespread iconoclasm, or smashing of icons (MacCulloch 2003, 150–151). [JSR]

408 (in §178). On Jupiter, Juno, Neptune, and Pluto, see note 81. [JSR]

409 (in §178). The notion that "birds fly in God, animals walk on God, fish swim in God" is a reference to pantheism; see note 49. On the ether, see note 116. The notion mentioned in passing here—that thoughts are modifications of the ether—is the same conclusion arrived at (somewhat randomly) in §79:5 by a group of giddy philosophers in the spiritual world. The English physician David Hartley (1704–1757) proposed a theory that shares features of the one described here. According to Hartley's *Observations on Man, His Frame, His Duty, and His Expectations* (1749), external sensory excitation is

transmitted via impulses through solid nerve matter to solid cerebral matter, where it sets up a vibration that in turn makes a superfine ethereal fluid within the brain tremble. These "tremblings"—modifications of the ethereal component of the brain—produce "traces," if repeated frequently; and these traces are what we know as our thoughts. Though Swedenborg's acquaintance with this particular theory is not documented, it stands as an example of the type of materialistic explanation of the thought process to which he refers in this passage. (On Hartley's theories and their influence, see Porter 2003, 348–361.) Swedenborg himself once held a similar theory, which he expounded in *Small Vibrations* (= Swedenborg [1717] 1976c, 1–7), published in 1717, and in two unpublished manuscripts, the only surviving of which is *Another Draft on Small Vibrations* (= Swedenborg [1717] 1976c, 9–76), written sometime during the period 1719–1720. Elsewhere in his scientific writings Swedenborg seconded this insistence that thought was purely material in nature (*Rational Psychology* [= Swedenborg 2001a] §152), but distinguished between thought as it takes place during earthly life and the superior intelligence of the soul, which survives death (*Rational Psychology* [= Swedenborg 2001a] §525). In his developed theology, he makes a similar distinction between material thought and spiritual thought (see for example *Secrets of Heaven* 10551:5). Thus his emphasis here: the materialist sees thought as *only* a variation in the ether—that is, as exclusively material—and does not allow for the existence of spiritual thought. For more on the contrast between spiritual and material thinking, see §§30:1, 280:5 in the present volume. [JSR, SS]

410 (in §178). The points of view presented here echo the bitter sarcasms that some Enlightenment philosophers leveled against revealed religion, in particular describing it as a human fabrication intended only to make and keep the people subservient to the priests and the powerful. See note 383 above. [JSR]

411 (in §178). For a memorable occurrence reinterpreting the relationship between reason and faith, see §508 in the second volume of this work. [JSR]

412 (in §179). A little further on in the text, Swedenborg cites the following chapters in the Book of Revelation: 6, 11, 12, 13, 16, 16, and 14, with that repetition and in that order. When Swedenborg mentions seven chapters here, he may have counted chapter 16 twice, since he cites it twice. [JSR]

413 (in §179). A stadium (plural: stadia) was an ancient Greek unit of distance equal to about 607 feet, or 185 meters. Sixteen hundred stadia, then, would be around 184 miles, or 296 kilometers. [JSR]

414 (in §181). On the "Sacred Order," see note 352. [JSR]

415 (in §181). The reference to divine truths being written in "silver letters" is strikingly reminiscent of the Codex Argenteus or Silver Bible, which was written in silver letters on purple vellum. It was donated to the University of Uppsala in 1669. See Kleberg 1984. Swedenborg attended the university from 1699 to 1709. [JSR]

416 (in §182:3). Apollo was the Greek god of prophecy and oracles; he was later identified strongly with the faculty of rationality. For a similarly negative identification of Apollo with the human mind cut off from divine influence, see *Worship and Love of God* 73–74. [SS]

417 (in §182:3). On leviathans, see note 198. [JSR]

418 (in §183:3). The Supralapsarians were Calvinists who believed that even before creation or the Fall God had already predestined people yet unborn to either heaven or

hell. The opposing point of view was held by Infralapsarian Calvinists, who believed that predestination occurred only after creation and the Fall. [JSR]

419 (in §184). Although it is impossible to know what examples Swedenborg had in mind, some of the phenomena used as analogies for the Trinity over the centuries are the triangle in plane geometry; the tetrahedron (a solid of which each face is three-sided) from solid geometry; fire (said to be composed of light, heat, and smoke) or water (which can take the form of steam, liquid water, and ice) from physics; and a single sheet of cloth or paper that remains one piece though folded three times. A paper cube unfolded to a configuration of 4 × 3 squares is also said to represent the cross, of which the crossbar of three squares represents the Trinity. Which example from arithmetic Swedenborg had in mind is particularly obscure, although the contrast between $1 \times 1 \times 1 = 1$ and $1 + 1 + 1 = 3$ is a possibility. [SS]

420 (in §185:2). This description is strikingly evocative of the beast from the sea in the Book of Revelation (13:2), which was like a leopard, and had feet like a bear's, and a mouth like a lion's. See also §187:2 of the present work. [JSR]

421 (in §185:4). The preacher alludes here to the story of Lot's wife in Genesis 19:26; see note 185. [JSR]

422 (in §186). The closure of the right-hand side of these people's higher levels probably indicates that the hearts or wills of such individuals are closed to what is good, though their intellects or minds remain open to it; see *Divine Love and Wisdom* 127, 270:2; *Revelation Unveiled* 386; *Marriage Love* 316:5. [JSR]

423 (in §187:2). Frogs have a universally negative meaning in Swedenborg's theology and are generally associated with hell. See §§45, 78:5, 120:1; see also *Secrets of Heaven* 7351; *Revelation Unveiled* 702; *Revelation Explained* (= Swedenborg 1994–1997) §1000; *The Old Testament Explained* (= Swedenborg 1927–1951b) §3557. [JSR]

424 (in §187:3). In Swedenborg's theological works mentions of the "east wind" seem to carry two functions: one is a biblical allusion to the potentially destructive, often hot and desiccating wind mentioned in the Old Testament as coming overland to the Holy Land from across the desert to the east, withering vegetation on land and disrupting ships on the Mediterranean (see for example Genesis 41:6; Exodus 10:13; 14:21; Jeremiah 18:7; Ezekiel 27:26; Hosea 13:15). The other is a related phenomenon in the spiritual world (see *Secrets of Heaven* 842, 7679; *Last Judgment* 61). [JSR]

425 (in §187:4). The Latin word for "tent" here and throughout this passage is *tabernaculum,* a word that would also remind the Latin reader of the "tabernacle," the sacred tent placed at the center of the tribes of Israel when they encamped during their wandering in the wilderness; see Exodus 25:8–9. [JSR]

426 (in §188:2). In the present work Swedenborg frequently criticizes the Christian councils of the past, beginning with, and reserving for special blame, the Council of Nicaea in 325 C.E. (§§94, 136:3, 176, 177, 489:1, 638). In what almost becomes a refrain, Swedenborg repeatedly urges the reader not to trust councils (§§176, 177, 489:1). Yet here we see a Christian (primarily Protestant; see §188:4–5, 8 and note 429) council in the spiritual world, at the conclusion of which its participants are led in glory to the new Christian heaven (§188:13). In §176 Swedenborg clarifies that councils can be useful provided they "go directly to the God of the church." [JSR]

427 (in §188:2). On the phrase "have not had intercourse," see note 229. [JSR]

428 (in §188:3). On the name "Jehovah Sabaoth," see note 232. [JSR]

429 (in §188:4). The mention of Roman Catholics hiding behind the altar suggests that this conference in the spiritual world was primarily for Protestant Christians. Further confirmation comes in subsection 5, in which a clergy person mentions a creed that has been accepted "by the entire Christian world including the Roman Catholics." [JSR]

430 (in §188:6). In another memorable occurrence, Swedenborg himself gives examples of this parallel of Father and Son with soul and body (§112:5). [JSR]

431 (in §188:9). The "Old Covenant" means the Old Testament. Likewise in the second sentence farther on in the text, the "New Covenant" means the New Testament. See also §285 at the end. [JSR]

432 (in §188:13). The mention of wedding garments here at the conclusion of this memorable occurrence alludes to two stories in the Bible: the parable of the wedding feast, at which a person without a wedding garment was thrown out (Matthew 22:11–12); and the end of the Book of Revelation with its suggestions of an impending wedding (Revelation 19:7–9; 21:2, 9; 22:17). See also §380:4; *Revelation Unveiled* 881, 960. [JSR]

Notes to Chapter 4, §§189–281

433 (in §189). With the exception of the memorable occurrences at the end, this entire chapter closely parallels Swedenborg's 1763 work *Sacred Scripture.* [JSR]

434 (in §193). Swedenborg does not specify which of the five memorable occurrences at the end of the chapter (§§277–281) he means. Chadwick (see Swedenborg [1771] 1988b, 1:256) supplies a reference to §280. Nevertheless, the language used in the author's index of memorable occurrences for §277 (see item 30 in that index, which is found at the end of the second volume of this work)—*Verbum, quale id in se est,* literally, "the Word, such as it is in itself"—suggests that §277 is the intended reference. This also accords with Swedenborg's promise here to "show" what the Word's spiritual core is. In §277, that core is not named or explained, but is presented in an image of large purses containing a significant quantity of silver. [JSR]

435 (in §195). It is possible that "divine wisdom" here should read "wisdom about what is true" instead, which is the reading found in the precursor to this chapter (see *Sacred Scripture* 6), and the reading implied by parallelism with the mention of "love for what is good" in the preceding sentence. [JSR]

436 (in §195). This passage (and a similar statement in §212) is a striking departure from all Swedenborg's previous statements on the structure of heaven. In other descriptions in his theological works, Swedenborg speaks consistently of two kingdoms and three heavens (see *Heaven and Hell* 20–28, 29–40). Occasionally he mentions a third kingdom but identifies it as composed of people on earth rather than in heaven (see for example *Divine Love and Wisdom* 232). Here, however, he speaks of a third kingdom of heaven—something not mentioned in *Sacred Scripture* 6, from which this section is otherwise borrowed. The identification of the three kingdoms with the three heavens is also somewhat surprising, given other statements that differentiate the two kingdoms from the three heavens (see Swedenborg [1763] 2003a, 279 note 120). [JSR]

437 (in §196:1). The Latin word here translated "gems" is *diademata,* plural of *diadema,* which is normally taken to mean a crown or headband, but which Swedenborg, in another treatment of this same passage from the Book of Revelation, explains as meaning a gem or precious stone; see *Revelation Unveiled* 540. [JSR]

438 (in §197). A cubit was a varying ancient measurement based on the distance from the elbow to the tips of the fingers—about 18 to 22 inches, or 43 to 56 centimeters; therefore 144 cubits was roughly 240 feet, or 73 meters. [JSR]

439 (in §197). A distance of twelve thousand stadia is approximately 1380 miles, or 2220 kilometers; see note 413. [JSR]

440 (in §197). See note 439. [JSR]

441 (in §199). The Latin word here translated "young women" is *virgines,* a word from which our English word "virgin" derives. The Latin word, however, connotes someone who is marriageable, young, and female, while the English word "virgin" has evolved to mean a sexually inexperienced person of either gender and any age. [JSR]

442 (in §200:2). Swedenborg here assigns five animals just three meanings. From other passages it becomes clear that innocence is represented by lambs (*Secrets of Heaven* 10132); goodwill is represented by sheep (*Secrets of Heaven* 9263:4); and earthly feelings are represented by goats (*Revelation Explained* [= Swedenborg 1994–1997] §730:43), calves (*True Christianity* 623:1), and oxen (*Secrets of Heaven* 9090). In other passages goats are said to represent evil people; see note 170. [JSR]

443 (in §201). The juxtaposition of these two seemingly contradictory sentences suggests that "no one has known until now" does not mean that no one on earth has ever known what correspondence is, but rather that no one in Swedenborg's times and in his world has known. [JSR]

444 (in §201). Swedenborg here echoes the prevailing view of his times that Egyptian hieroglyphics were a symbolic and pictorial language, a concept that dated back to the Greek historian Diodorus Siculus of the first century B.C.E. and the Greek philosopher Plotinus (205–270). [JSR]

445 (in §201). The Feast of Unleavened Bread, the Feast of Tabernacles (also known as the Feast of the Ingathering, Feast of the Booths, Sukkoth, Succoth, or Sukkot), and the Feast of First Fruits were three major sacred holidays in the ancient Jewish calendar. For the biblical description of these events, see Leviticus 23:4–14, 33–44; for Swedenborg's explanation of their inner meaning, see the references in note 446. [JSR]

446 (in §201). *Secrets of Heaven* discusses the inner meaning of burnt offerings and sacrifices in §§923, 2180, 2805, 2807, 2830, 3519, 6905, 8680, 8936, and 10042; of food offerings in §10079; of drink offerings in §§4581 and 10137; of the tabernacle and its contents in §§9455–9577, 9592–9692, and 9710–9789; of the three annual feasts in §§9285–9301; and of the priesthood and sacred clothing of Aaron and the Levites in §§9804–9966. [JSR]

447 (in §204). For a summary of Swedenborg's statements in this volume regarding ancient Jews, see note 262. [JSR]

448 (in §205). For a summary of Swedenborg's statements in this volume regarding ancient Jews, see note 262. [JSR]

449 (in §206). The content of this section may have been designed to undermine complacency in Swedenborg's Christian readers. It follows a criticism of Jews—a type of criticism with which Swedenborg's Christian readership was very familiar and apparently comfortable (see note 262; see also Helander 2004, 341–343)—with criticism of Christians. [JSR]

450 (in §208). The Latin word here translated "angel guardians" is often rendered "cherubs" in current English translations of the Bible. See note 195. [JSR]

451 (in §209:3). For a detailed account of someone's being knocked unconscious by touching the Word, see §162:5–7. [JSR]

452 (in §209:5). These words come from two plural Hebrew words, אוּרִים *('ûrîm)* and תֻּמִּים *(tummîm),* which are transliterated as *Urim* and *Thummim* in Swedenborg's Latin text (as they commonly are in English as well); they mean "the lights" and "the perfections." See Exodus 28:30; see also §218 in the present work. Aaron was the first high priest of ancient Judaism; he was commanded to have a breastplate, or ephod, with Urim and Thummim on it, through which he would receive answers to questions he had posed to God. [JSR]

453 (in §212). On the three heavens as three kingdoms, see note 436. [JSR]

454 (in §213). On the tabernacle, see note 425. The objects mentioned here—the ark of the covenant (described in Exodus 25:10–22), the golden lampstand (Exodus 25:31–40), the golden incense altar (Exodus 30:1–10), and the table of showbread (Exodus 25:23–30)—were the only furnishings in the two areas inside the tabernacle. For the curtains, see Exodus 26:1–14; for the veils and pillars, and the arrangement of furniture within the tabernacle, see Exodus 26:31–35. See also §§220, 283–284. [JSR]

455 (in §214:1). An example of such a "collapsed object" might be a hand telescope. If the large end of the telescope were placed lens down on a table top and the telescope were fully extended upward, it would illustrate elements in a sequential arrangement: starting at the upper end, the narrowest cylinder would be first, the middle-size cylinder would be next, and the widest of all would be last. If the small end were then pushed down, collapsing the telescope into its most compact form, it would illustrate the same elements, but now in a simultaneous arrangement. The cylinder that was first and at the top would now be in the center, and the "later" cylinders would now surround it. Swedenborg's frequent allusions to "inner" and "higher" as opposed to "outer" and "lower" elements suggest that this manner of visualizing the contrast between the simultaneous and the sequential captures an important facet of the way spiritual reality is both above and within physical reality, and that it helps to show how the stages that have led up to something are also present within it; see *Divine Providence* 12. [JSR]

456 (in §216). On the "Urim," the "Thummim," Aaron, and his ephod, see note 452. [JSR]

457 (in §220). On the tabernacle, see note 425; on the lampstand, the incense altar, and the table for showbread, see note 454. The most holy place in the tabernacle contained only the ark of the covenant, with the Ten Commandments ("the law written on two tablets") inside it (Exodus 26:33). On angel guardians, see note 195. [JSR]

458 (in §222). By "the historical Word," Swedenborg means Genesis, Exodus, Leviticus, Numbers, Deuteronomy, Joshua, Judges, 1 and 2 Samuel, and 1 and 2 Kings. By "the prophetic Word," he means Psalms, Isaiah, Jeremiah, Lamentations, Ezekiel, Daniel, Hosea, Joel, Amos, Obadiah, Jonah, Micah, Nahum, Habakkuk, Zephaniah, Haggai, Zechariah, and Malachi. For more on "the Word" and why certain books of the Bible are missing from this list, see note 17. [JSR]

459 (in §223). Technically, as Swedenborg probably knew, the Hebrew word for Nazirite, נָזִיר *(nāzîr),* primarily means "separated" or "consecrated." The denotation "hair" is not far to seek linguistically, however. Several of the rules for Nazirites involved growing or shaving their hair (see Numbers 6:1–21); and the related word נֵזֶר *(nēzer)* in Jeremiah 7:29 means "hair." [JSR]

460 (in §224:1). On continuing to exist as equivalent to perpetually coming into being, see note 142. [JSR]

461 (in §224:4). John 1:3, 10 reads, "All things were made by the Word, and nothing that was made was made without it." [JSR]

462 (in §225). The Latin word here translated "body of teaching" is *doctrina,* literally, "teaching." It has traditionally been translated "doctrine." Swedenborg elsewhere suggests that a given denomination has only a single *doctrina* (§227; *Life* 27). [JSR]

463 (in §228). Although in many other passages Swedenborg reiterates the idea that nakedness means deprivation or ignorance of truth (see for example *Revelation Unveiled* 706), he also indicates elsewhere that angels in the highest heaven and angels who have true marriage love are naked (see *Heaven and Hell* 178, 280, 341:3; *Spiritual Experiences* [= Swedenborg 1978] §§5179–5180). In the latter case, their nakedness means innocence and indicates that they have truth written on their hearts. For a discussion that clarifies the fact that nakedness may have either of two meanings, depending on the context, see *Revelation Explained* (= Swedenborg 1994–1997) §240:2. Swedenborg asserts that the same is true for the meaning of most words in Scripture; note, for example, the repeated use of the phrase "in an opposite sense" in §§250, 251 of the present work. [JSR]

464 (in §233). In the Christian theology of Swedenborg's day, Michael and Raphael were considered to be archangels, a higher order of being than angels. Michael is mentioned in the Protestant canon of the Bible (see Revelation 12:7). Raphael is not mentioned in the Protestant canon, but plays a prominent role in the apocryphal Book of Tobias. There Raphael says that he is one of seven angels who stand before the Lord (Tobias 12:15). Swedenborg's theology lacks archangels; see note 389. [JSR]

465 (in §236:1). Because the laws generally known as the "Ten Commandments" actually consist of a declarative statement and some fourteen imperative statements, religious scholars over time have differed over the numbering (MacCulloch 2003, 141–142). Swedenborg follows the Augustinian-Lutheran numbering, although he does seem aware that there are disputes about the numbering (§325). He is well aware that Scripture refers to them not as "Ten Commandments" but as "Ten Words" (§§286, 325). [JSR]

466 (in §237). Swedenborg is using the word "chyle" here not in its more usual sense of the emulsified or dissolved form of fatty substances that have been reduced for absorption via the lacteal lymph vessels in the small intestine, but in a rarer sense as the soupy substance in the stomach that results after digestive juices have acted on food before absorption by the stomach or intestines. The point here, then, is that the same food once broken down provides different systems in human and animal bodies with the specific nourishment they need. [GMC, JSR]

467 (in §237). Here Swedenborg plays on an analogy between human anatomy and that of plants: both are seen as circulating a "sap," the tree in its tissues, conveying it from the trunk to the branches, and the human in its nerve fibers. Long prior to Swedenborg, the nerves were thought to contain a fluid (considered by some to be the same as the cerebrospinal fluid in the cerebral ventricles), which the brain pumped through them in analogy with the blood circulatory system. The nerves were thought to convey three types of "spirits": the "psychic" spirits, which are the agency of the rational soul in the body; the "animal" spirits, which mediate bodily motions; and the "plant" spirits, thought to underlie the body's organism, and to account for the body's natural healing.

See Manzoni 1998, 103–152; Quin 1994, 393–395; Rocca 1997, 227–239; and note 175. Swedenborg describes several orders of sap for the plants, which seem to reflect a similar tripartite structure. Sap as it first is drawn out of the ground is thick, or crude, and most subject to gravity. As the sap is refined in the plant, it becomes finer, and eventually fine enough for use by the extremities of the plant. There the fruit and seeds of the plant are produced, and the seeds, as the kernels of the plants' offspring, require the purest nourishment. [GMC]

468 (in §237). This passage reflects a premodern belief about how minerals are formed within the earth—a process extremely mysterious to ancient people, since it required such a great length of time that no one could directly observe it. Many alchemical and mystical theories about this process had been developed; they still persisted in Swedenborg's day, and as a government supervisor of Sweden's mining industry, Swedenborg would have been very familiar with them. In sum, the earth was thought to be a vast womb in which minerals form from raw mineral substances in underground veins. (The term still used to describe the surrounding rocky substance from which the ore is extracted is *matrix* [Latin for "womb"].) One theory held that there was a great abyss of water under the solid crust of the earth and that currents within the abyss had transported minerals to their locations underground (Laudan 1987, 45–46, 66; Oldroyd 1996, 17, 32, 34, 50; Emerton 1984, 201–205); some such theory seems to be echoed here. The minerals listed here appear in rank according to their nobility in the alchemical scheme (on this concept of nobility, see note 159). In the case of the substances in the body and in the plant kingdom, elements are ranked according to the extent that they move upward into finer and more sublime regions, becoming finer in the process (see note 467); similarly, the ranking of minerals reflects the process of extraction. For example, just as animal spirits (see note 506) in the body are the refined substance of the soul that has been distilled from the coarser blood, so iron, a base metal, is what remains after the nobler elements have been harvested. See Collier 1934, 399–427; Laudan 1987, 42–69. [GMC, JSR]

469 (in §241:2). On "the historical Word" and "the prophetic Word," see note 458. [JSR]

470 (in §245). This statement about the formative role played by teaching that is whole and pure is probably an allusion to *The Book of Concord;* see Kolb and Wengert 2000, 42.2, 43.2, 308.9, 356.5, 445.39–41, 446.47, 526.1, 529.14. [SS]

471 (in §247:4). Admah and Zeboiim were cities destroyed along with Sodom and Gomorrah (see Deuteronomy 29:23). [JSR]

472 (in §250). The phrase inserted in brackets here is taken from the original version of this passage, *Sacred Scripture* 84. Its insertion seems warranted, in that the next sentence in the text here contains a mention of "water" that is otherwise without a referent. [JSR]

473 (in §252). In the ensuing quotations, the Latin words here translated "joy" and "rejoice," *gaudium* and *gaudeo* (a noun and the verb from which that noun is derived), are treated by Swedenborg as interchangeable. [JSR]

474 (in §253). Although there are two bodies of text to which this title may be referring, Swedenborg did not publish anything with the exact title *Teachings on the Lord the Redeemer.* One candidate is Swedenborg's 1763 work *Teachings for the New Jerusalem on the Lord* (generally referred to as *The Lord*). Another candidate is chapter 2 of the present work, which is titled "The Lord, the Redeemer." Yet another possibility, and in some ways the most likely, is that Swedenborg intended to refer to both of the texts just

mentioned, and the printer, who was remarkably careless in the production of this work, left out some overlapping words. Both treatments address the point cited here, that "Jehovah" and "God," or "Jehovah" and "the Holy One of Israel," appear in many biblical passages together and yet mean One Being; see §§82–83, 93 in this volume; *The Lord* 34, 38, 40. [JSR]

475 (in §257). In Swedenborg's day the conversion from the earth-centered to the sun-centered view of the universe was still sufficiently recent that the illusion of the sun's rotation around the earth was a common illustration in discussions of truth and certitude; see Voltaire [1764] 1962, 159 (under "*Certain, Certitude*"): "If you had asked the whole world before the time of Copernicus: 'Did the sun rise today? Did it set?' all men would have answered you: 'We are absolutely certain of it.' They were certain, and they were wrong." The most significant instance of this controversy, to which Swedenborg may be alluding here, was the infamous trial of the astronomer Galileo Galilei in 1633. Galileo was accused by the Roman Catholic church of "having held and believed a doctrine which is false and contrary to the divine and Holy Scripture; that the Sun is the center of the world and does not move from east to west, and the earth moves and is not the center of the world" ("Sentence" 1989, 291). For more on Galileo, see Santillana 1970; Shea and Artigas 2003. [JSR, SS]

476 (in §257). Swedenborg makes the same assertion that the stars do not shift positions relative to one another in *Worship and Love of God* 6 note b. Compare Aristotle's similar statement in *On the Heavens* 270b (= Aristotle 1952c, 361). Strictly speaking, this view is not correct—the stars do in fact move relative to one another, though to a viewer on Earth such motion is gradual and almost imperceptible. The first report of this type of stellar motion, called proper motion, was published in 1717 by the British astronomer Edmond Halley; see Halley 1717, 736–738. The discovery has been described as one of the greatest advances in astronometry during the Enlightenment (Cook 1998, 349). In terms of Swedenborg's argument in this passage, his apparent ignorance of Halley's somewhat obscure report is trivial; but it is surprising given his passion for astronomy, and it is of some biographical interest because he met several times with Halley while in London in 1712 (Sigstedt 1981, 23). This insistence on the immutability of the stellar positions is also somewhat at odds with his awareness that stars do sometimes appear and disappear; see note 402. [SS]

477 (in §258). It is possible that Swedenborg's three fanciful comparisons have risen to a crescendo and that he does actually expect the reader to picture a miniature snake; but given that snakes do not spawn in almonds and fly through the air when they hatch, another explanation is possible. The context suggests that the Latin words *coluber*, which is here translated "snake," and *colubellus*, "tiny snake," refer to the larvae of the meal moth, which infest almonds in the shell. When the nut is opened they thrash about violently, and the frass (chewed material) from the nut may blow free into the eyes. (Such larvae, referred to as worms, are mentioned in §435:1.) It is possible that Swedenborg chose the image of the snake, rather than that of a worm, because of the correspondential association of the snake or serpent with people who trust to sense information and to knowledge derived from it rather than to revelation. For this correspondence, see *Secrets of Heaven* 196, where Swedenborg also mentions the flying serpents found in the Bible (Isaiah 14:29; 30:6, discussed in *Divine Providence* 340). [SS]

478 (in §259). See *Heaven and Hell* 488:2, 586. [JSR]

479 (in §261). For the correlation of the last with the outermost level in Swedenborg's theology, see §214 and note 455. [JSR]

480 (in §262). The Latin word here translated a "little letter" is *jotha,* a reference to the smallest letter in Greek, the iota (ι), and the related smallest letter in Hebrew, the yod (׳). It has traditionally been translated "jot." For the meaning of "the tip of one letter," see note 193. See also §278. [JSR]

481 (in §262). On "the law" as meaning the whole of Scripture, see also §288. Contrast note 387. [JSR]

482 (in §265:1). For more on "the ancient Word," see §§266, 279, and note 503. [JSR]

483 (in §265:1). "The historical portions of our Word" is equivalent to "the historical Word"; see note 458. [JSR]

484 (in §265:2). The Latin word here translated "the *Makers of Pronouncements"* is set in small capitals, a convention Swedenborg uses for emphasis and also for book titles; here it may serve both purposes. [JSR]

485 (in §265:2). In the first edition here Swedenborg transcribes Hebrew words into Latin using a Germanic spelling: *moschalim* and *maschal.* Since Swedenborg clearly intends the first of these words to be the plural of the second, he likely meant *meschalim* instead of *moschalim,* as a transcription of the Hebrew word מְשָׁלִים *(məšālîm),* the singular of which is מָשָׁל *(māšāl),* "a proverb." The forms *meshalim* and *mashal* used in the translation thus represent a normalized English and corrected version of what is found in the original. [JSR, GFD]

486 (in §268). The contrast Swedenborg is making here is not between "Christians" and "Catholics" but between "Christians who read the Word" and "Catholics." Swedenborg elsewhere repeats the charge that Catholics do not read the Bible—a charge made by many Protestants of Swedenborg's time. This charge was probably based on the 1564 Tridentine Index of forbidden books, which banned the reading of vernacular Bibles without permission from the local bishop, and the 1596 Roman Index, which banned vernacular Bibles altogether (see MacCulloch 2003, 393–394, 565–566). [JSR]

487 (in §268). In *Divine Providence* 255, Swedenborg maintains that "most" Muslims (that is, in the mortal world) view Jesus as greater than Muhammad, an erroneous statement that seems to be based on misinformation concerning Islam that was current in Europe at the time. (See Swedenborg [1764] 2003b, 378 note 229.) The Latin text here, however, is somewhat ambiguous: Swedenborg may be implying that there are two classes of Muslims, those who acknowledge the Lord as the greatest prophet and those who do not; the former are the ones he explicitly locates in the area surrounding the chest. But in any case he is concerned here only with Muslims in the afterlife. [SS]

488 (in §270). On Catholics not reading Scripture, see note 486 just above. [JSR]

489 (in §270). For a summary of Swedenborg's statements in this volume regarding ancient Jews, see note 262. [JSR]

490 (in §273). The position that Swedenborg mentions here is typical of so-called natural religion, which arose during the seventeenth and eighteenth centuries as a reaction to "revealed religion," especially mainstream Christianity, with its emphasis on the need for Scripture. Natural religion argued that reason without the aid of revelation was

capable of arriving at certainty about the existence of God, and even about an afterlife in which virtue is rewarded and vice is punished. It also held that morality could be derived on the basis of reason rather than revealed divine law. Its exponents included Richard Bentley (1662–1742), Samuel Clarke (1675–1729), and William Derham (1657–1735), who all lent their voices to the cause in the Boyle lectures, a series (most celebrated in the years 1692–1731) established by the scientist Robert Boyle (1627–1691) to defend the Christian religion against atheism. For a brief sketch of the history of the idea, see Kors 2003, 3:142–150; for a general study, see Byrne 1989. [JSR, SS]

491 (in §273). Swedenborg is referring here to materialist philosophers in Christian Europe, who held that matter alone exists. Examples include the French thinkers Julien Offray de La Mettrie, Denis Diderot, and Paul Henri Dietrich d'Holbach. For summary and bibliography, see Kors 2003, 3:26–31. See also note 23. [JSR]

492 (in §273). Aristotle (384–322 B.C.E.) was a Greek philosopher; Marcus Tullius Cicero (106–43 B.C.E.) and Lucius Annaeus Seneca (4 B.C.E.–65 C.E.) were Roman philosophers. [SS]

493 (in §273). On natural theology, or natural religion, see note 490. [JSR]

494 (in §274). This mention of the spirit's rejoining its corpse and skeleton is a reference to a Christian belief, based on an interpretation of such passages as Revelation 20:12–13, that at the time of the Last Judgment, people's souls will be reunited with their bodies—an idea that Swedenborg criticizes as ludicrous (see for example *Marriage Love* 29). [JSR]

495 (in §275). On the attributes of God becoming understood as individual gods in ancient times, see note 45. On Jehovah, see note 9. On the possible relationship between the names Jove and Jehovah, see note 44. [JSR]

496 (in §275). Though Swedenborg seems to be referring specifically to Greco-Roman culture in this sentence, it is interesting that the features he mentions could indeed be illustrated from many cultures, as the wider context suggests. The myth of an ancient flood, for instance, can be found in the Akkadian, Aztec, and Indian legend, among many others. Given the restriction to examples strictly from Greco-Roman myth, however, the following could be cited: The Paradise of Greek mythology was called Elysium or the Elysian fields, and also the Islands of the Blessed; it was mentioned by Homer and other ancient poets (Homer *Odyssey* 4:561–569; Hesiod *Works and Days* 167–173). The Roman poet Ovid (43 B.C.E.–17 C.E.) tells of a worldwide flood in which "all is sea, but with no shore" (*Metamorphoses* 1.262–317 [= Ovid 1993, 14]). By the term "sacred fire" Swedenborg is presumably referring to the fire kept perpetually burning for Vesta, goddess of the hearth (see note 328). The four ages are most prominently treated in Ovid *Metamorphoses* 1:89–150. [JSR, SS]

497 (in §276). Pegasus was an immortal winged horse in Greco-Roman mythology. Mount Parnassus was the site of the oracle of Delphi in ancient times and was thus sacred to Apollo. Mount Helicon was known as the home of the Muses; Pegasus is said to have created the Hippocrene spring frequented by those goddesses by stamping his foot on the mountainside. [JSR]

498 (in §276). This is a reference to the infamous Tower of Babel. [JSR]

499 (in §276). The story of Goliath, the giant champion of the Philistines, who was killed by the young David, is told in 1 Samuel 17. [JSR]

500 (in §278). On the tips of Hebrew letters, see note 193. [JSR]

501 (in §278). In two Hebrew Bibles that Swedenborg owned (Arias Montanus 1657; Reineccius 1739), Psalms 32:2 reads: אַשְׁרֵי אָדָם לֹא יַחְשֹׁב יְהוָה לֹו עָוֹן וְאֵין בְּרוּחוֹ רְמִיָּה (ʾašrê ʾāḏām lō yaḥšōḇ yəhôvā lô ʿāvôn vəʾên bərûḥô rəmîyā). The meaning of the words in the verse is "Blessed are those to whom Jehovah will not charge sin, and in whose spirit there is no guile." [JSR]

502 (in §278). This passage has earlier parallels in the manuscript works *Spiritual Experiences* (= Swedenborg 1978) §5620 and *Draft of "Sacred Scripture"* (= Swedenborg 1997b) §4, and in the published work *Sacred Scripture* 90; the last of these was the source of the present passage. The information that the dot in Hebrew makes the consonant hard and the absence of a dot makes it soft was accurately reflected in the first of these references. The two later references, however, omitted some words and created the opposite impression, which is not accurate. [JSR]

503 (in §279:1). Swedenborg here alludes to the fact that his knowledge about the ancient Word developed in stages over time. (On "the ancient Word," see §266 of the present work.) Extant passages bear this out. In volumes published in 1750 and 1751, Swedenborg wrote briefly about the two ancient books discussed here (see *Secrets of Heaven* 2686:1, 2897), but made no mention of an ancient Word. Such a mention first occurred in the draft work *Revelation Explained* 1177:3, which was begun in 1759 (see Swedenborg 1994–1997). A few years later in a draft written in 1762 (see *Draft of "Sacred Scripture"* [= Swedenborg 1997b] §15), some six or seven years before Swedenborg began writing the present volume in late 1768, he mentioned information received from angels regarding the ancient Word. A small chapter on the ancient Word was included in the finished work *Sacred Scripture* 101–103. Then in 1766, in *Revelation Unveiled* 11, Swedenborg first mentioned the "news" that the ancient Word still existed on earth at that time, in the populous area north of the Great Wall of China then known as Great Tartary; he closes that passage by addressing the reader directly: "Ask about it in China, and perhaps you will find it there among the Tartars" (translated by JSR). See also note 504. [JSR]

504 (in §279:4). It is hard to tell here whether Swedenborg is referring to the history and geography of the physical or of the spiritual world, or both. If the context is the physical world, this passage may refer to the Mongolians who lived north of the Great Wall, and to the Ming Dynasty (1368–1644), during which the Great Wall was significantly enlarged and fortified. The Mongols at that time believed that the mother of Chinese emperor Yung-lo (1360–1424) had been a Mongol and that he was therefore a blood relative of theirs (Waldron 1990, 75; Shaw 1937). This passage might refer instead, however, to Manchuria and its relationship with the China of Swedenborg's own times, which was ruled by the Manchu or Ch'ing dynasty (1644–1912). This seems less likely, however, since Manchuria was off to the northeast and farther from the Great Wall; and compared with Mongolia, its regions were less populous, and its inhabitants less powerful and less threatening to China (Careri 1719, 4:400–401). [JSR]

505 (in §280:1). Swedenborg repeatedly claimed that he lived and functioned in both the material and the spiritual world at once (see §§157, 281, 695:2, 851; *Secrets of Heaven* Genesis 16 preface:3, 9439; *Heaven and Hell* 577:3; *Marriage Love* 1). Here he indicates that he was in control of this variable status. See note 508. [JSR]

506 (in §280:2). Swedenborg is perhaps referring to the notion held by some that the soul was a distillation of grosser elements circulating in the body. He here rejects the idea

that the soul itself can ever be refined out of a material substance; some intermediary substance is required between the purely spiritual and the physical or material. According to a theory he himself held—a complex variation on ideas about the operation of the soul that had been current for some time—this intermediary substance consisted of "animal spirits," also called "the spirituous fluid," a superfine fluid permeating all parts of the body. (See note 467.) In the lower parts and extremities the animal spirits were mixed with the grosser fluids, such as blood; as these grosser fluids circulated back to the brain, they ran through finer and finer vessels (becoming more and more "subtle") until only the animal spirits were left to come in contact with the soul; they would then cycle back through the body, instantly carrying the soul's spiritual impulses to the physical tissues. Swedenborg's theory of the animal spirits, which was derived almost purely through a priori reasoning, varied widely over his career, sometimes incorporating other life fluids that acted in conjunction with the animal spirits. Odhner 1933, 234–249, traces these variations from Swedenborg's fullest discussion in *Dynamics of the Soul's Domain* (= Swedenborg [1740–1741] 1955) to the brief summary in *Worship and Love of God* (especially §96) and on into the theological works (see for example *Secrets of Heaven* 4227:3; *Divine Providence* 296:14, 336). [SS]

507 (in §280:4). The Lord is called the Alpha and the Omega (the first and last letters of the Greek alphabet) in Revelation 1:8, 11; 21:6; 22:13. Compare note 376. [JSR]

508 (in §280:7). Swedenborg here emphasizes the uniqueness of his living in two worlds at once. Elsewhere, however, he indicates that all human beings are created to have similar experiences, and humankind used to have them long ago, but selfishness and worldliness now get in the way:

> The Lord created us to be capable of communicating with spirits and angels while still living in our bodies, as people actually did in the earliest times. After all, we are one with spirits and angels, being ourselves spirits clothed in flesh. Over time, though, people have immersed themselves so deeply in narcissistic and worldly concerns that almost nothing else interests them, and so the path has closed; but as soon as the concerns for our person that absorb us drop away, it opens and we find ourselves among spirits, living life together with them. (*Secrets of Heaven* 69; translation by Lisa Hyatt Cooper)

The apparent contradiction between the present statement and the one just quoted hinges on the frame of reference, much like the similar apparent contradiction about the knowledge of correspondences (see §201 and note 443). [JSR]

509 (in §280:8). When Swedenborg mentions "primary structures" and "derivatives of primary structures," he is usually speaking of the brain and nerves, respectively (see §§30:2, 156, and note 370). Here he clearly is using the same terminology metaphorically of spiritual substance and physical substance. See also §365; *Divine Providence* 6. [JSR]

510 (in §280:9). On "apparent time and space" in the spiritual world, see §29 and note 113. [JSR]

511 (in §281:1). On the dating of Swedenborg's spiritual awakening, see note 59. [JSR]

512 (in §281:1). For Swedenborg's account of what happens to people between the moment of death and their "coming back to their own life" on the third day afterward, see the passages listed in note 351. [JSR]

513 (in §281:10). The Latin phrase here translated "accursed dust" is *pulvis damnatus*, literally, "damned dust." Swedenborg also mentions this infernal dust in *Divine Love*

and Wisdom 341, where he indicates that it causes vomiting, headaches, and loss of consciousness. [JSR]

514 (in §281:11). John Wesley, the founder of Methodism, was strongly critical of the teachings in this specific passage; see the preface, pages 36–37, and note 347. [JSR]

515 (in §281:12). For more on the difference between satans and devils, see note 18. [JSR]

Notes to Chapter 5, §§282–335

516 (in §285). In *Revelation Explained* (= Swedenborg 1994–1997) §1026:3, Swedenborg clarifies that the first three commandments (by the Augustinian-Lutheran reckoning; see note 465) appear on the first stone tablet, the fifth through tenth commandments occur on the second tablet, and the fourth commandment bridges the two tablets. See also note 650. [JSR]

517 (in §286). Although English Bibles do not all read "the ten words" at the passages Swedenborg cites here, the Latin Bible he preferred (Schmidt 1696) in every case reads *decem verba,* "the ten words." [JSR]

518 (in §291). For a general idea of what Swedenborg means by "the historical and the prophetical parts of the Word," see note 458. [JSR]

519 (in §292). Baal, Ashtoreth, Chemosh, Milcom, and Beelzebub were gods and goddesses of the Canaanite nations mentioned in the Old Testament. The Israelites worshiped Baal at one point (Judges 2:13), and Solomon himself worshiped Asthoreth, Chemosh, and Milcom at various times (see 1 Kings 11:5–7). Baal was a male fertility god, often portrayed as a bull, who had power over thunder and lightning (for one of his many mentions in the Bible, see Judges 2:13). Asthoreth was a fertility or mother goddess, sometimes identified with Astarte. Chemosh was a sun god. Milcom, also known as Moloch (mentioned as a separate god at 1 Kings 11:7), was the Canaanite god of wealth. Beelzebub was a demon whose name means "Lord of Flies" (see 2 Kings 1:2); he is called the Prince of Devils in Matthew 12:24, and in later Christian tradition he was a lieutenant of Satan among the fallen angels (see Milton *Paradise Lost* 1:81). [JSR, SS]

520 (in §292). For Saturn, Jupiter, Neptune, Pluto, and Apollo, see note 81. Athena was the Greek goddess of wisdom and warfare, equivalent to the Roman Minerva; see Kerényi 1978. [JSR]

521 (in §296:4). Swedenborg had doubtless seen examples of just such a representation of the Trinity. In early Christian art, the Trinity was sometimes represented by three male figures. One of the earliest examples is the so-called Dogmatic Sarcophagus in the Vatican Museo Pio Cristiano in Rome; it dates from the fourth century. (This interpretation is, however, contested by Engemann 1976, 157–172.) The Bibliothèque Nationale in Paris has many illuminated manuscripts with the same iconography (see Mss. Latin 757, page 229 verso, from 1380). That iconography was superseded in some cases by the representation of the Trinity as one body having three faces (an example can be found in the Chateau de Chillon in Lausanne), but more commonly by the depiction of the Father and Son as separate human figures and the Holy Ghost as a dove (see Matthew 3:16). The latter iconography became standard; see, for example, *The Trinity,* about 1390–1396, by the Florentine Agnolo Gaddi (died 1396), in the Metropolitan Museum of Art. See also note 73. [SS]

522 (in §297). On the name "Jehovah," see note 9. [JSR]

523 (in §297). For a memorable occurrence involving efforts to pronounce the name Jesus, see §110. [JSR]

524 (in §299). Exodus 23:20–21 reads, "Do not provoke [the angel]. He will not tolerate your error, because my name is in him." Isaiah 63:16 reads, "You, Jehovah, are our Father; our Redeemer from everlasting is your name." [JSR]

525 (in §301). All these stories recount or relate to healings that Jesus performed on the Sabbath: Matthew 12:10–14, Mark 3:1–9, and Luke 6:6–12 concern the healing of a man with a withered hand; Luke 13:10–18, the healing of a woman who had been bent over; Luke 14:1–7, the healing of a man with edema; John 5:9–19, the healing of a man who had had a paralyzing infirmity for thirty-eight years (an action defended by Jesus in John 7:22, 23); and John 9:14, 16, the healing of a man born blind. [JSR]

526 (in §303). This reading of this verse, "the peace of the Lord" (Latin *pax Domini*), is not found in biblical sources and may or may not be intentional on Swedenborg's part. This verse in his preferred Latin Bible, Schmidt 1696, reads *pax domui huic,* "peace to this house." The printers may have misread *Domini* ("of the Lord") for *domui huic* ("to this house"). [JSR]

527 (in §307). The Latin phrase here rendered "the children of the wedding," *filii nuptiarum,* is found in Latin Bibles in Matthew 9:15, Mark 2:19, and Luke 5:34; in some English Bibles this phrase is rendered "the friends of the bridegroom." Examples of the Latin phrase "children of God," *filii Dei,* occur in John 1:12; Romans 8:14, 16; and Galatians 3:26; see also Galatians 4:5–7. The phrase "born of him" alludes to John 1:13, as well as 1 John 3:9, 4:7, and 5:18. [JSR]

528 (in §308). Compare the similar parental imagery in the cosmogony in Swedenborg's *Basic Principles of Nature,* part 3, chapter 5 (= Swedenborg [1734] 1988a, 2:275–276), and in the transitional work of 1745, *Worship and Love of God* 7, 11. [SS]

529 (in §311). For a summary of Swedenborg's statements in this volume regarding ancient Jews, see note 262. [JSR]

530 (in §314). "Babylon" here refers to the Roman Catholic church (compare *Revelation Unveiled* 631); this was an interpretation of the symbolism of the Book of Revelation common among Protestants in Swedenborg's day. [SS]

531 (in §316). By "misuse" here (Latin *abusus,* literally, "abuse") as a cause of impotence, Swedenborg presumably means masturbating as a misuse of seminal fluid; the term evolved into a later euphemism, "self-abuse." Two works published by others during Swedenborg's lifetime had caused widespread fear throughout Europe of the ill-effects of masturbation. *Onania* [1715], which went through twenty-two editions in its first twenty-two years, first made the assertion echoed here that masturbation causes impotence (along with a host of other health problems); and Tissot 1758, originally published in Latin but very soon translated into several European languages, supplied reinforcement to the idea. See Pinto-Correia 1997, 94–95; Laqueur 2003, 13–16, 29, 35. The precepts of classical medicine supplied a plausible basis for some of these beliefs about the deleterious effects of masturbation. Semen was thought to be produced from the same substance that circulated in the nerves, which made reason and conscious thought possible. Semen was, therefore, soul-material, and to spend it was to shed vitality and strength. If spent in excess, whether by too frequent intercourse or other means, the mental and perceptual faculties of the body would be harmed, and the body itself debilitated. See Hippocrates *On the Sacred Disease;* Galen *On Semen;* Phillips 1973, 24–25, 124. [GMC]

532 (in §316). Satyrs and priapuses were figures of Greco-Roman mythology. Satyrs were lustful, half-human, half-animal beings who lived in the forest. Priapus was the

god of procreation and was associated with the male genitalia; Swedenborg uses the plural here to mean lascivious male creatures. [JSR]

533 (in §317). True piracy was conducted by stateless brigands against anyone with the misfortune of running afoul of them (see note 293); by contrast, privateering was state-sanctioned piracy against merchant vessels of an enemy power, with the purpose of disrupting enemy trade. Captains who had been commissioned as privateers carried letters of marque from their sovereign authorizing their vessels to prey on enemy ships. See Starkey 1989, 279–286; Statham 1910; Swanson 1991. [GMC]

534 (in §320). The modern reader may be expecting the masks in this metaphor to be beautiful and thus conceal physical ugliness or corruption; but Swedenborg is thinking of garish masks, and his point is exactly the reverse: that false and heretical beliefs, like gaudy masks, are in fact ugly, whereas true beliefs, like the honest good looks of natural human facial features, are not. [SS]

535 (in §326). On scribes and Pharisees, see note 253. [JSR]

536 (in §329:3). The words in brackets are Swedenborg's interpolated explanation. In the first edition, they are set in parentheses in a different style of type from the surrounding quotation. [JSR]

537 (in §330). For more on effective and ineffective ways of getting rid of evil, see *Life* 108–113. [JSR]

538 (in §331:2). The beard of the barley is a long tassel of inedible fibers that project from the head, or grains. [SS]

539 (in §332:1). For more on the "lower earth," see note 182. [JSR]

540 (in §332:1). The Latin word here translated "providers of arguments" is *confirmatores,* literally, "confirmers" or "reinforcers." As the reader will see, it refers to people who are able to present convincing arguments of the truth of any proposition, however false. Such people were perhaps even more prevalent in Swedenborg's day than they are now, in part because the primary method of education was the Scholastic debate, in which students were called on to take up any position and argue it as convincingly as they could. See also note 542. [JSR]

541 (in §333:1). The scholars here targeted may be merely idle practitioners of Scholastic disputation (see note 542) or adherents of skepticism—the reliance on active disbelief as a basis for philosophy. Skeptics can be typified by such figures as Pierre Bayle, Denis Diderot, and David Hume (1711–1776), who in the seventeenth and eighteenth centuries were building on the classical tradition of the Greek skeptic, Pyrrhon of Elis (around 365–257 B.C.E.), and were questioning received knowledge; see Kors 2003, 4:78–86. Bayle did so in order to set religious belief on a foundation of faith alone; Diderot did so in order to dethrone religion from its basis of faith. In the text just below the scholars described are also associated with materialism. [JSR, SS]

542 (in §333:3). Formal debate traces its genealogy to the rhetorical exercises of the classical world, as best exemplified in the comprehensive training manual, *Institutio Oratoria* (Institutes of Oratory) of Marcus Fabius Quintilianus (around 35–96 C.E.). Students would practice arguing in favor of or against a thesis proposed by the teacher. These exercises were intended to prepare young men for careers in the law and politics. This tradition was taken up as a standard teaching device by the Scholastics of medieval times. Gradually, the structure of formal debate took the form it was to have from the Renaissance until the present: A thesis is proposed; each of two persons or teams argues

in favor of or against the thesis, in succession; each side is then given a chance to respond to the arguments of the other side. In formal rhetorical training, a speaker is taught the proper order of presenting his material—in the absence of an adversary, he must anticipate objections and counterarguments to his own statements. Contrived debates have been a literary device for teaching philosophy and other subjects since Plato wrote his dialogues. There was a great revival of interest in classical styles of debate in Europe during the lifetime of Swedenborg. During that period, and almost up until modern times, people attended public debates or read accounts of them as a form of entertainment; hence the mention of an audience here. See §334; see also Conley 1990, 188–234. [GMC]

543 (in §333:4). "Statues of salt" is an allusion to Lot's wife (Genesis 19:26); see note 185. [JSR]

544 (in §334:2). An educational goal in Swedenborg's day was to develop the individual's ability to argue opposing positions equally well; see note 542 above. [JSR]

545 (in §334:4). On "faint, deceptive light," see note 149; on the glow supposedly given off by cats' eyes at night, see §162:3 and note 388 there. [JSR]

546 (in §334:7). Some readers may be surprised to find a mention of robots (Latin *automata*) in an eighteenth-century text; but they were a familiar concept in Swedenborg's day and even long before. Self-operating humanoid mechanisms are mentioned in the Western tradition at least as early as Homer's *Iliad* 18:417–420. See also note 103. [SS]

547 (in §335:1). On "faint, deceptive light," see note 149. [JSR]

548 (in §335:1). Swedenborg here makes an intriguing distinction between merely having visions of phenomena in the spiritual world, as he does in the first part of this memorable occurrence, and actually entering into the experience in his spiritual body and seeing it directly with his spiritual eyes. [JSR]

549 (in §335:1). Swedenborg's life occurred at the latter end of a great debate about knowledge that took place between two groups of philosophers. On one hand are the Rationalists, represented by René Descartes (*Meditations on First Philosophy,* 1641), Benedict de Spinoza (*The Principles of Cartesian Philosophy,* 1663; *On the Improvement of the Understanding,* 1677), and to some extent Gottfried Wilhelm Leibniz, though much of his work was not published in his lifetime (*Discourse on Metaphysics,* written in 1685, but not published until 1846; *The New System,* 1695; *New Essays on Human Understanding,* written in 1704, but not published until 1765). Leibniz appears at the end of the memorable occurrence along with Christian Wolff (for more on Wolff, who has been considered, rightly or wrongly, a follower or at least an expositor of Leibniz, see notes 239, 552). On the other hand are the Empiricists, represented chiefly by John Locke (1632–1704; *Essay Concerning Human Understanding,* 1689) and David Hume (*A Treatise of Human Nature: Being an Attempt to Introduce the Experimental Method of Reasoning into Moral Subjects,* 1739–1740, Hume's principle philosophical work, the main arguments of which were rewritten in popular style in both *Philosophical Essays Concerning Human Understanding,* 1748, and *An Enquiry Concerning the Principles of Morals,* 1777). The Rationalists were impressed with the fact that some knowledge seems to be possessed universally and independent of sense experience, such as innate moral or religious sense, self-evident principles, and necessary truths that are more general than particular experiences. Therefore the Rationalists took it as axiomatic that humans are born with some necessary truths already in their souls. This argument was a

refinement of the ancient Platonic notion of innate knowledge of the eternal Forms (see especially the *Phaedrus,* the *Theatetus,* and the *Republic*). The Empiricists countered with the observation that all knowledge seems to derive from sense experience or intellectual manipulation of such ideas. They produced compelling arguments that the doctrine of innate ideas was superfluous: all our ideas rest ultimately on sense experience. Their approach has much in common with that of the ancient skeptical tradition. On this clash between views, see Kors 2003, 1:396. Swedenborg's position in the debate is basically that humankind does not possess inborn knowledge; that is, that all knowledge must be gained from analyzed sensory input. He does, however, hold to a theory that the soul has some kind of innate intuition and intelligence that allow it to analyze and order sensory data, or as the angel describes it here, "a faculty for knowing, understanding, and becoming wise, as well as a tendency to love not only knowledge, understanding, and wisdom but also [one's] neighbor and [one's] God" (§335:7). For Swedenborg's discussion, see, in addition to the current passage, his pretheological *Dynamics of the Soul's Domain* (= Swedenborg [1740–1741] 1955) 2:§294, where he quotes Locke in support of this theory; and, from his theological period, *Secrets of Heaven* 2577. In another pretheological work, *Worship and Love of God* 53 note q, he argues that the innate ability to sense moral and spiritual good was lost in the Fall, and that since then humans have possessed an innate understanding of good only in the external senses; it enables them to perceive only natural good (for instance, pleasing harmonies or tastes). This theory, however, is to some extent contradicted by the later passage *Secrets of Heaven* 3304:2. See also Woofenden 1971, 23; Lamm 2000, 266–269. [GMC, SS]

550 (in §335:2). For the meaning of "goat's wool," see note 192. The Latin phrase here translated "beards in a clean-shaven age" is *barba hujus saeculi,* literally, "the beard of this age." As Swedenborg notes elsewhere (§137:1), in his time and place beards were not considered fashionable. [JSR]

551 (in §335:3). The material in brackets is based on an interpolated parenthetical cross-reference in the first edition; that cross-reference points to the original page 11, where §12:7 occurs. Swedenborg usually inserted cross-references in his works before any pages were typeset, using section numbers (which do not change in typesetting) rather than page numbers (which do). It was highly unusual for him to provide an internal cross-reference to a specific page; his having done so here means, of course, that he inserted or changed the reference after page 11 of the book was typeset. [JSR]

552 (in §335:7). Gottfried Wilhelm Leibniz was a German philosopher who, as indicated in note 549, participated in the international scholarly debate about innate ideas. Christian Wolff was another German philosopher and a contemporary of Swedenborg's. Wolff has been considered a partner with Leibniz in a common philosophical program, but their views differed in significant respects (see Corr 1975, 241–262, with extensive bibliography in the notes). Historians of philosophy have tended to agree with the opinion expressed here by Swedenborg that Wolff was the lesser of the two. Though in his younger days Swedenborg often reacted to the influence of Wolff in determining his own views (see for example Swedenborg 1923), ultimately he came to reject much of Wolff's philosophy. Wolff is also mentioned by Swedenborg in *Spiritual Experiences* (= Swedenborg 1978) §§4727, 4728, 4744, 4757, 4851, 6018, 6049; *Other Planets* 38; *Draft of "Supplements"* (= Swedenborg 1997b) §§262–263. [JSR, SS]

Notes to Chapter 6, §§336–391

553 (in §336:1). By "the ancients" here Swedenborg presumably means the people of the "early" or "ancient church," whom he speaks of as inhabiting the Middle East in pre-Biblical times (see §§202–204). [JSR]

554 (in §336:1). The Latin word here translated "goodwill" is *charitas,* traditionally translated "charity," and as "thoughtfulness" elsewhere in this edition of Swedenborg's works. Although the term has appeared before in the work, in this chapter and the next it becomes a central focus. The term is presented in this work as something Swedenborg assumes will be vague to his original audience (see the helpful array of definitions for it in the debate in §459) and as something that has been mistaken for mere giving to the poor and other forms of philanthropy (§425). In statements in this work and elsewhere in Swedenborg's theological corpus, "goodwill" is defined as a spiritual feeling (*Secrets of Heaven* 7131) of love for our neighbor (*Secrets of Heaven* 362; *Revelation Unveiled* 128), with a specific mention of loving our neighbor as ourselves (*Secrets of Heaven* 1798:2). Swedenborg also reports that it is defined by a wise person in the spiritual world as loving to do what is good (*Revelation Unveiled* 655:5). Understandably, then, goodwill is often associated with loving *action* or *treatment* of others (*Faith* 13). More specifically it is defined as both *willing* and *doing* what is good, just, and right in every action (*Heaven and Hell* 364). It is most abstractly defined as intending and loving what is true (*Secrets of Heaven* 3876, 3877). Although goodwill is generally portrayed in Swedenborg's other theological works as involving activity, in the present work it is carefully distinguished from good works, although they are interdependent: goodwill is a feeling or attitude in the inner self while good works are actions of the outer self (§§374:1, 408, 421 in the present work). See also note 19. [JSR]

555 (in §336:2). In the first edition, the whole of what is designated subsection 2 is marked off with double quotation marks at the beginning and end of the passage, and at the beginning of every line. On the uses of these marks, see note 260. Here they presumably serve for emphasis, since the passage has no known parallel. [JSR]

556 (in §339:1). On "ether," see note 116. [JSR]

557 (in §339:1). On Arianism and Socinianism, see notes 245 and 246. [JSR]

558 (in §339:1). On birds dying in vacuum pumps, see note 111. [JSR]

559 (in §339:1). Aeolus, god of the winds in Greco-Roman mythology, is described in Vergil *Aeneid* 1:52–83 as confining the winds in the cave that forms his home, though they are raging to escape and destroy the world. Swedenborg's meaning, then, is that this type of faith can be trapped in the mind, but it is uncomfortable there and leaves as soon as it can. [JSR]

560 (in §339:2). On "materialist philosophy," see note 23. [JSR]

561 (in §339:3). This is the lone statement in the theological works originally published by Swedenborg to the effect that particular statements were written in the presence of others in the spiritual world; his unpublished diary of spiritual experiences, however, contains some two dozen similar statements, beginning with the first spiritual experience recorded in the work of that name (*Spiritual Experiences* §1a [= Swedenborg 1998–2002, 1]; compare §§169, 200, 273, 396, 418, 511, 696, 741, 760, 1076, 1877, 2255, 2262, 2283, 2393, 2505, 2919, 2946, 3128, 3476, 3772, 5292 in that work). [JSR]

562 (in §342:1). On the phrase "have not had intercourse," see note 229. [JSR]

563 (in §342:3). For a summary of Swedenborg's statements in this volume regarding ancient Jews, see note 262. [JSR]

564 (in §342:3). Although accurate information about Islam was hard to come by in the Europe of Swedenborg's times, he seems to have been aware that in general Muslims, though devoted to Muhammad as the author of the Qur'an, did not view him as a divine being. He characterizes worship of Muhammad as aberrant for Muslims; see §§830, 833. For other comments on Islam in this volume, see notes 349 and 487. [JSR]

565 (in §343). For more on this promised "appendix," see note 71. [JSR]

566 (in §345). In the original Latin edition, this section and the one before it (§§344–345) are set in significantly larger type than the text that comes before and after, either because Swedenborg wished to mark these sections for special attention or more likely because of some typographical reorganization forced by changes made to the text late in the printing. The only other passage in large type in the entire work is §§2–3. [JSR]

567 (in §346). Swedenborg here lists seven diseases of the eye. The Latin names for the second and fourth diseases could be misleading if taken too literally, since over the centuries from the time Swedenborg wrote this passage they have significantly changed in meaning; see King 1906, 10–11. The second disease, "cataract," is called in Latin *glaucoma,* a word identical to the English word "glaucoma," but meaning what is now called a cataract. Conversely, the fourth disease, which involves "a loss of transparency in the anterior chamber," is called in Latin *cataracta,* but is not what is now called a cataract. On "faint, deceptive light," see note 149. [JSR]

568 (in §348). On stars that appear and then grow dim, see note 402. [JSR]

569 (in §351:2). The reference here seems to be to philosophers who believed that ideas are created by the projection of external objects via light rays into the brain through the eyes, in the manner of the images projected on the screen of a modern-day cinema. The word *idea* itself comes from the Greek word for a thing that "has been seen," and the concept of ideas as the direct effect of a sense perception such as is caused by light entering the eye has a long history. Any specific identifications here would be conjectural, and in any case the philosophers in question would have taken exception to this simplistic characterization of their views. With that caveat, examples that might be listed are: Lucretius *On the Nature of Things* 4:722–817, and Epicurean and Stoic philosophy generally; Hobbes [1651] 1952, 49 = 1:1, 258 = 4:45; and Locke [1689] 1952, 2:1:3. For a rejection of ideas as images formed in the eye similar to that offered by Swedenborg, see Spinoza [1677] 1952, 2:49:scholium: "An idea . . . is not an image of anything." [SS]

570 (in §351:3). On Swedenborg's referring to brain cells as "glandular" tissue, see note 174 above. [JSR]

571 (in §354:1). The truths of faith just listed here in the text coincide with the topics of chapters 1–3 and 6–11 of this work itself. [JSR]

572 (in §356). The parallels in the modern edition of Kolb and Wengert 2000 are found at 544.7, 545.11–12, 547.20–549.25, and 554.53–556.62. [JSR]

573 (in §357). Although these quotations do not mention "goodwill" (Latin *charitas*) specifically, Swedenborg considers goodwill to be equivalent to loving one's neighbor (see the title of chapter 7), an attitude explicitly mentioned in both of these quotations. [JSR]

574 (in §358). The reading of the first edition here, Latin *exitus aquarum,* "springs of waters," was later corrected by the author himself in the margins of his own copy to read *exitus viarum,* "the ends of the streets." For more on typographical errors in the original and Swedenborg's corrections, see the preface, page 29 and footnote 48. [JSR]

575 (in §359). Although Swedenborg's language is usually gender inclusive, here he specifies a man (Latin *vir*) in authority. [JSR]

576 (in §360:1). Here as often Swedenborg assumes that his readers will be familiar with definitions of various kinds of cause developed by the Greek philosopher Aristotle and the medieval Scholastic philosophers. Aristotle introduced the four main categories of cause (*Physics* 194b–195b [= Aristotle 1952e, 271–272]); they can be described in simplistic terms with respect to an artifact such as a statue that is being carved from stone. The *material cause* is what the artifact is made of, the stone. The *efficient cause* is the agent that makes the artifact, the sculptor. The *formal cause* is the quality gained by the material that is being made into the sculpture, its "statueness." The *final cause* is the purpose for which the statue is made. Beyond Aristotle's basic causes the Scholastic philosophers defined many more, including the two mentioned here: the *instrumental cause,* a secondary cause that is an instrument or tool serving a primary cause (the hand with which the sculptor works, for example), and the *principal cause,* a cause that works by means of the power of its own form and (in this example) makes the resulting statue like itself. Here the point is that secondary causes (the heat and light of the material world) are activated by the primary causes (the love and truth of the spiritual world) that operate through them. See also notes 157 and 181. [JSR, SS]

577 (in §361:3). The temple of Diana (also known as Artemis) in Ephesus, one of the seven wonders of the ancient world, is thought to have been one of the largest and most magnificent temples of all time. It was destroyed in 262 C.E. [JSR]

578 (in §362:3). Swedenborg has already discussed faith in chapter 6, starting at §336 and proceeding to this point. He continues to discuss it through §391. He treats goodwill in chapter 7 (§§392–462); free choice in chapter 8 (§§463–508); reformation and regeneration in chapter 10 (§§571–625); assignment of spiritual credit or blame in chapter 11 (§§626–666); repentance in chapter 9 (§§509–570); baptism in chapter 12 (§§667–697); and the Holy Supper in chapter 13 (§§698–752). [JSR]

579 (in §366:2). See, for example, §77:3–6. Swedenborg makes similar assertions at *Divine Love and Wisdom* 425; *Divine Providence* 86, 167; *Revelation Unveiled* 765:2; *Marriage Love* 498. [JSR]

580 (in §367:5). Until the seventeenth century, and to some extent even through the eighteenth, it was believed that under certain circumstances living creatures, especially smaller ones such as bees and worms, are spawned in nonliving matter like the bloodless flesh mentioned here. This belief arose naturally from the observation of maggots hatching in dead animals. For a history of the concept, called spontaneous generation or abiogenesis, see Farley 1977. [JSR]

581 (in §367:6). The medical ideas of this passage are consistent with the teachings of Galen, who recommended a balanced consumption of foods and described the ill effects of an imbalanced diet. See Grant 2000. [GMC]

582 (in §367:7). St. Vitus's Dance (also known as St. Guy's Dance, St. Anthony's Dance, and St. John's Dance), which is now often taken to mean Huntingdon's chorea, referred to a different malady in Swedenborg's day: *choreomania* ("dancing frenzy"), which was a nervous or emotional phenomenon that affected people during the late Middle Ages (a time roughly corresponding to the end of the Black Death) up to the early Enlightenment (the seventeenth century). Those afflicted seemed to dance uncontrollably and, when in groups, to engage in all sorts of unrestrained and

licentious activities. It was called by the name of St. Vitus because processions of choreomaniacs would often end at the local shrine of St. Vitus, who was thought to have special powers to bless those thus afflicted. The specific variant of choreomania referred to in this passage was tarantism, which is actually named for the city of Taranto, Italy, near where tarantism was thought to be most common during the hot summer months. The name tarantism was often associated, however, with the belief that the symptoms of the disorder were caused by the bite of a tarantula or a wolf spider, due to a sudden acute pain felt at its onset. (Swedenborg gives this etiology in *Draft on the Fiber* [= Swedenborg 1976a] §§543–544, where he discusses the disease at length.) It was believed that it could be cured only by frenzied dancing to music: the afflicted person would "dance" until, exhausted, he or she collapsed in a sweat, at which time the "cure" was supposed to be effected. A related term is *tarantella,* denoting a musical piece whose intense and rousing rhythms are intended to stimulate a dancing cure in the sufferer. See Rosen 1968, 196–205; Sirois 1982, 218. [GMC, SS]

583 (in §367:7). The Latin word here translated "a suffocating nightmare" is *incubus* (from the Latin *incubare,* "to lie on"). In medieval folklore, an incubus was a nightmare personified as a demon thought to lie on sleeping people, sometimes with sexual, sometimes with murderous, intent. Swedenborg rarely uses the word, and never in an overtly sexual context. In one passage he uses it to mean simply a nightmare involving a great pressure or sense of weight on the chest, without any apparent demonic connotations (see §482:2). In another passage he identifies evil spirits as the cause of such a nightmare (see *Spiritual Experiences* [= 1998–2002] §3364). For Swedenborg's discussion of this as a disease, see *Draft on the Fiber* (= Swedenborg 1976a) §§534–536. On the phenomenon of the incubus in world culture, see *Sleep Paralysis* 2005, 5–145. [JSR, SS]

584 (in §370:1). Burning mirrors fascinated ancient military technologists from the time it was discovered that a parabolic mirror redirects the parallel rays of the sun in such a way as to focus them at a single point. Archimedes (around 287–212 B.C.E.), the ancient Greek scientist and mathematician, devised such mirrors. See Simms 1977, 1–24; Toomer 1976. [GMC]

585 (in §371:3). One of the long-standing theories about faith to which Swedenborg perhaps alludes here holds that there would be no purpose in Christ's commandment to have faith (Mark 11:22) if it were possible to know God by rational means; otherwise, he would have enjoined his followers to discover God through reason. By this way of thinking, the mere commandment to be faithful is *prima facie* evidence of the exclusivity of the role faith plays in salvation. All attempts at deliberately acquiring faith are thus seen as paradoxical. Swedenborg's practical emphasis on building faith by using the rational mind to accumulate and assimilate religious truths flies in the face of this theory. [SS]

586 (in §371:4). The phrase "column of air" used in this passage is still employed to describe air pressure in terms of the weight of a hypothetical column of air extending upwards into the atmosphere. That is, the pressure of air in pounds per square inch (or kilograms per square centimeter) at sea level is the weight of a hypothetical column of air one square inch (or one centimeter) in cross-sectional area extending to the limit of the atmosphere (about fifty miles [eighty meters] or so into space). See Torricelli 1897; Middleton 1964, 4, 25, 66. [GMC]

587 (in §375). There are numerous classical references to Fama (also known as Ossa or Pheme in Greek); see especially Vergil *Aeneid* 4:173–197; Ovid *Metamorphoses*

12:39–63. She is described as having wings and many eyes and being capable of rapid, massive growth, but is not given the specific attributes Swedenborg here ascribes to her; nor does she appear with them in art, though the possibility that Swedenborg saw some such representation cannot be ruled out. This seems to be a pastiche of literary tropes and symbols common in alchemical and other art. The laurel wreath is a symbol of victory; see note 223. The horn of plenty, or cornucopia, is symbolic of the material rewards that are a consequence of success; it is usually associated with the allegorical figure Abundantia (Abundance); for an example, see Ripa [1758–1760] 1971, 1:34; see also *The Soul's Domain* (= Swedenborg [1744–1745] 1960) §23. The ghostliness of the mythological figure is a trope perhaps adopted from such passages as Homer *Odyssey* 11:206–208 and Vergil *Aeneid* 2:792–794, 6:700–702, in which the shades of departed loved ones slip through the grasp of the hero. It should also be recalled that the emblematic distinctions among various mythological figures such as the Muses, Abundance, Prosperity, Happiness, and Fame were blurred by the simple fact that artistic representations of them were frequently not labeled. [JSR, SS]

588 (in §377). On goodwill as father and faith as mother, see §37:3 with note 144, and §41:3. [JSR]

589 (in §378:2). Swedenborg here begins a list of people and movements that have attacked the Christian church. The mention of Corinth at the end of this paragraph may refer to a disturbance caused in the Christian group there by someone's involvement in incest; see 1 Corinthians 5:1; 2 Corinthians 2:5–8. [JSR]

590 (in §378:2). The Marcionites rejected the Old Testament and held that Christ was not the son of the Old Testament God but of another God. The Noetians were a third-century sect that believed the Father was the only person in the godhead. The Valentinians were followers of the second-century Gnostic heretic Valentinus (around 100–around 152), who taught that there were three redeeming beings, and that Christ, the Son of Mary, did not have a real body and did not suffer. The Encratites were early Christians who abstained from flesh, wine, and marriage. The Cataphrygians were a second-century sect that followed Montanus (flourished around 156–172) in believing that Christ ascended to heaven with his spirit but not his body. The Quartodecimans were a group that celebrated Easter on the Jewish Passover whether it fell on a Sunday or not. The Alogians were an ancient sect that denied that Jesus Christ was the divine Logos (or Word; see John 1:14), and rejected the Gospel of John. The Catharans were a sect or sects that professed superior purity. The Origenists, or Adamantines, arose in the second century; they believed in three layers of allegorical meaning within Scripture, the pre-existence of souls, and eventual salvation for all. The Sabellians were followers of a third-century heretic who believed that there was no difference between the Father, the Son, and the Holy Spirit; they were instead simply three modes of manifestation. The Samosatenians were followers of Paul of Samosata (bishop of Antioch 260–272), who made a distinction between the Son or Logos on the one hand, which was a shapeless being incapable of manifestation, and Christ on the other, who was merely an inspired human being. The Manicheans were a sect from the third to fifth centuries with mixtures of Christian and non-Christian beliefs. The Meletians were followers of Meletius, Bishop of Lycopolis in Egypt during the early fourth century. Meletius was accused of sacrificing to idols and performing ordinations in areas beyond his own diocese. The Arians were followers of Arius; see notes 245 and 246. [JSR]

591 (in §378:2). The Donatists were a schismatic sect begun in 311, which believed that holiness must reside in the clergy and in the people of the church if they are to remain members of it. The Photinians were followers of Photinus (died 376), who believed that Christ was not essentially divine, but became so by a divine emanation. The Semi-Arians, or Acatians, were people who held that the Son was of a similar substance but not the same substance as the Father. The Eunomians taught that the Son is completely unlike the Father and that the Father is entirely comprehensible. The Macedonians were followers of Macedonius, bishop of Constantinople (342–346, 351–360 C.E.), who denied the divinity of the Holy Spirit. The Nestorians were a Christian group that divided Christ into two persons, one divine and one human. The Predestinarians believed in predestination to heaven or hell. The term "Papist" was generally applied derogatively by non-Catholics to any who advocated the supremacy of the pope, that is, to Roman Catholics. The Zwinglians were followers of Ulrich Zwingli who practiced an extreme asceticism and disputed Luther's assertion that God is present in the bread and wine of communion. The Anabaptists were a sect in Germany started in 1521; they believed in rebaptism. The Schwenkfeldians were followers of a Protestant mystic named Kaspar von Schwenkfeld (1490–1561) who broke away from Lutheranism and refused its sacraments; they held that the Scriptures are transitory and separate from the eternal Word. The Synergists were people who believed that human will cooperates with divine grace in salvation. On Socinianism, see note 245. The Antitrinitarians rejected the Trinity. Quakers believe in the presence and leading of the Holy Spirit and the equality of all religions; in practice they are pacifists with a spirit-led approach to worship. The Herrnhuters, also known as the Moravians, broke away to create a church based more on conduct than doctrine, with an emphasis on evangelization. In 1744 Swedenborg spent some time with this last group himself; see his posthumously published work *Journal of Dreams* (= Swedenborg 2001b) §§142, 192. [JSR]

592 (in §378:2). On Luther, Melanchthon, and Calvin, see note 179. [JSR]

593 (in §379:1). See §214:1 and note 455 above, which show how and why the terms "inner" and "higher" are interchangeable in Swedenborg's theology. [JSR]

594 (in §379:5). On touchstones, see note 393. [GMC]

595 (in §380:2). On Arians and Socinians, see notes 245 and 246. Many thinkers of the Enlightenment expressed views similar to those Swedenborg mentions here; for just one example, see the ironic article "Divinity of Jesus" in Voltaire's *Philosophical Dictionary* (Voltaire [1764] 1962, 240–241). [JSR, SS]

596 (in §380:3). Five of Swedenborg's first six theological titles advertise that their contents are based on things Swedenborg had seen or heard or both (see the full titles listed on pages 105–106). His emphasis on experience addressed the Enlightenment interest in moving away from received authority and tradition toward knowledge based on empirical evidence. Therefore throughout his theological works Swedenborg repeatedly emphasizes, as he does here, that he speaks from experiential knowledge. [JSR]

597 (in §380:4). On piracy, see notes 293 and 533. [JSR]

598 (in §380:4). On wedding garments, see note 432. [JSR]

599 (in §381:4). For a full discussion of the notion of the two ways leading into the mind, see *Revelation Explained* (= Swedenborg 1994–1997) §208:3. The imagery of the hinged door can also be found in *Worship and Love of God* 56: "Our minds are able to turn, as though they were hinged, in two directions—inward and outward (or upward and downward). . . . Into them flow two lights; one, which is called the spiritual, comes

from the Supreme and his Love; the other is the material, from the sun of our world and its heat. These lights meet together in our minds, and from their meeting they become like centers of the entire universe—of heaven and earth. From these centers we are allowed to walk forth with new vision into all the outlying regions of the universe." In *Worship and Love of God* 73, as in the present passage, the powers of the material world are described as overwhelming the mind and barring it so that it cannot open upward to heaven. Compare also *True Christianity* 366 and *Marriage Love* 146. [SS]

600 (in §382). Swedenborg here describes a notable trend in some eighteenth-century philosophic thought. Such atheistic materialism was to be found primarily among the French *philosophes;* the chief atheists among them included Julien Offray de La Mettrie; Denis Diderot; Claude-Adrien Helvétius (1715–1771); Paul-Henri Dietrich, Baron d'Holbach; and Nicolas-Antoine Boulanger (1722–1759). Slightly younger followers of the atheist movement were editor Jacques-André Naigeon (1738–1810); poet Pierre-Sylvain Maréchal (1750–1803); astronomer Joseph-Jérôme Le François de Lalande (1732–1807); and his student, the astronomer, mythologist, and ex-priest Charles François Dupuis (1742–1809). See Kors 2003, 1:94–97. [SS]

601 (in §385:2). "Arcanists" comes from the Latin root *arcanum,* meaning a mystery or secret. During the eighteenth century, it was applied to people who knew the industrial secret of making certain kinds of pottery, in particular porcelain. Its exact application here is obscure; it presumably simply means "people who believe they know secrets," or "people who believe in a mystery." [JSR, SS]

602 (in §386:1). Swedenborg often speaks of spirits as having one appearance at a distance and another when seen close at hand (see for example §441 at the end; *Marriage Love* 42:2, 75:4, 137:1, 512:2). In §388:3 in the present work, Swedenborg writes: "Everything in the spiritual world, when seen from a distance, has an external appearance that is based on correspondences." [JSR]

603 (in §386:1). The Latin is not entirely logical, as neither angel could "reach the other" without the other angel simultaneously reaching him or her; but the sense it gives of each angel trying to go farther in his or her attempt to reach the other is clear. This attempt serves not only to color the account with gentle humor, but also to prefigure the conversation about to take place concerning whether love or wisdom comes first. [JSR]

604 (in §387:1). The angel here expresses a thought similar to that which Socrates claimed to have been taught by divine oracle: "He . . . is the wisest who, like Socrates, knows that his wisdom is in truth worth nothing" (Plato *Apology* 23 [= Plato 1952, 203]). Although humility about the value of human knowledge is an age-old theme, Enlightenment thinkers were particularly prone to an anti-intellectualism that went hand-in-hand with their craving after knowledge; see the discussion at note 110. Swedenborg here goes on to remark on his own progress toward this humility: "I had often thought about this myself. At first through book-learning [that is, by reading about the limitations of human wisdom in authors such as Plato], later through my own perception of it, and finally because I saw it in an inner light, I had come to acknowledge that we have very little wisdom" (§387:2). At an earlier stage of his career, Swedenborg hoped that human scientific research could attain a knowledge of one of its great mysteries, the operation of the soul, by mastering a higher, generalized form of knowledge he called "the mathematical philosophy of universals." As of 1739 he still claimed that this kind of philosophical algebra was within human reach

(Notes about a Pathway to Knowledge of the Soul [= Swedenborg 1992] §4). Over the next decade, as he progressed through his spiritual enlightenment, he gave up this dream in the face of an increasing humility about the powers of the unaided human mind. [SS]

605 (in §387:2). The original Latin sentence here lapses out of normal sentence structure into a string of phrases without verbs, as if to convey a kind of breathless wonder. [JSR]

606 (in §388:1). On "the dragon," see note 151. In this memorable occurrence Swedenborg at times refers to "the dragon" in the abstract, at times to one spirit as "the dragon," and at times to multiple spirits as "dragon spirits." [JSR]

607 (in §388:1). On satyrs and priapuses, see note 532. [JSR]

608 (in §388:2). On the world of spirits, see note 21. [JSR]

609 (in §388:4). The Latin word here translated "double-talk" is *mussitatio,* which has been adopted into the English language as the word "mussitation." The term is used here of misleading verbal sophistry, but comes from a root meaning to murmur or mutter. [JSR]

610 (in §388:5). The words "essential" and "formal" are used here in their philosophical senses, which relate to essence and form. On Swedenborg's use of the term *essence,* see notes 12 and 84; on form, see notes 35 and 85. [JSR]

611 (in §388:6). Swedenborg states elsewhere that all evil spirits in the hells appear upside down to angels (*Secrets of Heaven* 9128:3; *Revelation Explained* [= Swedenborg 1994–1997] §1143:4; compare *Revelation Unveiled* 655:6). For a somewhat comical description of how this appears, see *Marriage Love* 79:3; for a rather gruesome description, see *Worship and Love of God* 75. [JSR]

612 (in §389:4). The phrases "activation of faith" (Latin *fides actu*) and "ongoing state of faith" *(fides statu)* relate to the Protestant doctrine of justification by faith. According to that doctrine, an individual's faith is not acquired through some process but instead goes from being potential to being activated or actualized by grace without any cooperation on the individual's part. This activation of faith then leads to an ongoing state of faith, which includes further stages of progress in faith. See Muller 1985 under *"actus fidei."* See also §390:1, 2 a little later on in the text. [JSR]

613 (in §389:7). A "miter" is a tall pointed hat with two peaks. In Swedenborg's day it usually served as part of a bishop's regalia. [JSR]

614 (in §390:2). The "three sole things that bring salvation" are stated or implied in the preceding paragraph: grace, the merit of Christ, and the work of the Holy Spirit. [JSR]

615 (in §391:2). The connection between the lack of vegetation around the clergyman's companions and their saying that inside themselves they have nothing related to the church is that, as Swedenborg asserts a number of times, in the spiritual world one's surroundings correspond to one's inner state (§78:1–3; *Heaven and Hell* 109, 111). All vegetation relates to wisdom and intelligence; grass specifically corresponds to the least and lowest form of true faith (*Revelation Unveiled* 401). See also §259 in the present work. [JSR]

616 (in §391:3). A "Reformed Christian" probably means a Calvinist here; see also note 365. [JSR]

Notes to Chapter 7, §§392–462

617 (in §393). The Latin phrase here translated "a costly education" is *talenta & minas eruditionis,* literally, "talents and minas of erudition." Both talents and minas were units

of weight and money used in ancient Greece, Rome, and the Middle East. At different times and places, a talent ranged from fifty-seven to eighty-eight pounds (twenty-six to forty kilograms) of gold, silver, or copper. A mina was a sixtieth of a talent. [JSR]

618 (in §396). For a discussion of the New Testament parable of the wise and foolish young women, see §199. [JSR]

619 (in §399:1). The identification of love as our life is a key teaching of Swedenborg's; see, for example, *Divine Love and Wisdom* 1. Compare also his pretheological work *Worship and Love of God* 67:4: "Without love there is no life; and . . . the quality of our life matches the quality of our love." [JSR, SS]

620 (in §400:7). Swedenborg may be referring back to ancient Roman emperors who were deified during their lifetimes; he is certainly also referring to the Roman Catholic clergy, as this was a standard Protestant charge against them, and one that he himself makes elsewhere (see for example *Revelation Unveiled* 263:2, 738:2). [JSR]

621 (in §401:4). On satans, see note 18. [JSR]

622 (in §402:8). The Latin phrase here translated "through a kind of back door" is *a tergo,* literally, "from the back" or "at the back." [JSR]

623 (in §402:9). For a spiritual experience in which Swedenborg heard the grinding of teeth from such people, see §460. [JSR]

624 (in §402:9). The gnashing or grinding of teeth is mentioned in Job 16:9; Psalms 35:16; 37:12; 112:10; Lamentations 2:16; Matthew 8:12; 13:42, 50; 22:13; 24:51; 25:30; Mark 9:18; Luke 13:28; and Acts 7:54. See also Swedenborg's explanations in *Secrets of Heaven* 4175; *Heaven and Hell* 575. [JSR]

625 (in §402:12). The phrase "serpents of the tree of the knowledge of good and evil" at the end of this paragraph is an allusion to Genesis 2 and 3. Therefore the "ancients" mentioned here are not the ancient Greeks or Romans but the people of the early or ancient church; see note 553. Compare the mention of "the ancient people who were part of the church" at the end of §404. [JSR]

626 (in §402:20). The entirety of §§397–402 is marked with double quotation marks at the beginning of every line; on such marks, see note 260. Here they indicate extensive quotations from Swedenborg's 1758 work *New Jerusalem.* For the references in detail, see the table of parallel passages at the end of the second volume of this work. [JSR]

627 (in §403:1). In this brief outline of the body, Swedenborg does not mention the arms and hands, and does not indicate to which area they would belong. Although arms and hands are extremities like legs and feet, it appears from another passage that Swedenborg considers them an extension of the torso (see *Secrets of Heaven* 10241; compare *Secrets of Heaven* 7442:3), and therefore part of the second category here. [JSR]

628 (in §404). Mammon, originally an Aramaic word for wealth or property, was taken over into Greek as a name for the god of wealth; it occurs in Matthew 6:24 and Luke 16:9, 11, 13. The Greek word πλοῦτος *(ploûtos)* also meant wealth or riches, and is related to the name of the god Pluto; see note 81. In both cases, the plural is unusual. [JSR]

629 (in §406). The Latin proverb here translated "We are all neighbor to ourselves," *Quisque sibi proximus,* is of unknown provenance and antiquity. It can also be found in a Latin epigram by Georg Carolides (1569–1612), the court poet of Prague (Carolides 1597, 229). It was likely based on a maxim of Roman law, *Proximus sum egomet mihi,* "I am always next as regards my own interest," which applied to cases in which, for instance, an executor could properly pay a debt owed to himself from an estate before

discharging others. In this latter version it is quoted by the Roman comic poet Terence (185 or 186–159? B.C.E.) in *Andria* 4:1:12, and so made its way into Western literature; for example, it appeared in 1633 in somewhat altered form, though still in Latin, in *The Jew of Malta* 1:1:194 (= Marlowe 1994, 10), by the English playwright Christopher Marlowe (1564–1593). An eighteenth-century lexicographer and collector of proverbs, Nathan Bailey (?–1742), connects the latter form (that is, *Proximus sum egomet mihi*) not only with Terence but with the Greek Φιλεῖ δ᾽ ἑαυτοῦ μᾶλλον οὐδεὶς οὐδένα *(Phileî d᾽ heautoû mâllon oudeìs oudéna),* "No one loves anything more than him- or herself" (Bailey [1721] 1917, 6). Swedenborg's version of the proverb appears again in §459:6. [SS]

630 (in §410:3). For more on the physical sphere exuded from the human body, see *Marriage Love* 171; *Divine Love and Wisdom* 293. [JSR]

631 (in §413). The Gospel story Swedenborg cites here mentions five talents rather than ten; Swedenborg may be conflating this account with Luke 19:11–27, a similar parable in which ten minas are given out for trade (see Luke 19:13). On minas and talents, see note 617. [JSR]

632 (in §413). In ancient Hebrew weights and measures, a talent was worth three thousand shekels. On talents, see note 617. [JSR]

633 (in §413). Swedenborg's promise here to say more later about earthly and spiritual impartiality (Latin *aequitas*) is not strictly speaking fulfilled. This is the last occurrence of that Latin word in his published works; in fact, this passage contains three out of only four uses of the word in Swedenborg's entire published theological corpus (the other is in *Secrets of Heaven* 5130:2). There are related thoughts, however, in §§407–408, 410, 428, and especially §459:14–15. [JSR]

634 (in §414). The Latin phrasing of the passage about dying for one's country leaves little doubt that Swedenborg is echoing Horace *Odes* 3:2:13: *Dulce et decorum est pro patria mori* (It is a sweet and glorious thing to die for one's country). In neither Horace's use nor Swedenborg's does the phrase have the irony it was later to acquire in *"Dulce et Decorum Est,"* a poem by Wilfred Owen (1893–1918) about the horrors of World War I (Owen 1963, 477–478). [JSR, SS]

635 (in §416). On "the communion of saints," see note 69. [JSR]

636 (in §416). Although modern English Bibles generally read "the kingdom of God" in this passage, "the kingdom of the heavens" is a translation of an alternate reading found in some Greek manuscripts of the New Testament and in Schmidt 1696, the Latin Bible Swedenborg preferred. [JSR]

637 (in §420). On the intrinsic relationship between "higher" and "farther within" in Swedenborg's theology, see §214:1 and note 455 above. [JSR]

638 (in §421). The words "formally" in the previous sentence and "essentially" here are used in their philosophical meanings; see note 610 and the cross-references there. [JSR]

639 (in §426). On "indulgences," see note 406. [JSR]

640 (in §426). Charges like this regarding indulgences were no doubt very familiar to Swedenborg's original readers. The Protestant Reformation first began as a campaign by Martin Luther against indulgences; see MacCulloch 2003, 118–122. [JSR]

641 (in §433). In Swedenborg's day the early Christian tradition of the love-feast was enjoying a revival among break-away Protestant groups, especially the United Brethren, or Herrnhuters, whom Swedenborg mentions in passing in §378:2 (see note 591). See also Ramirez 2004. [JSR]

642 (in §433). On the major festivals or feasts of the ancient Jewish calendar, see note 445. A portion of the sacrifices made outside the tabernacle was to be given to the priests as food (Leviticus 7:28–36). [JSR]

643 (in §435:2). The relationship between pus and infection was not yet entirely clear in Swedenborg's day. Some experiments with injection of pus that resulted in death suggested that pus itself caused infection. A theory in existence since the twelfth century was that there are two different types of pus: "laudable" pus, which is white or yellow and heralds healing; and thin, pink, or red pus associated with spreading inflammation, cellulitis, and gangrene (Duffin 1999, 217–219). The latter is the type of pus meant here and in §459:12. [JSR]

644 (in §436). The remainder of this passage is excerpted from §331. A few analogies are omitted, and a word or two here or there is changed, but it is largely identical. [JSR]

645 (in §437). On Mammon, see note 628. [JSR]

646 (in §441:2). This passage may be an allusion to Ezekiel 34:1–10, especially verse 5. [JSR]

647 (in §441:4). The term "hired workers" is evidently a reference to the Gibeonites who are made slaves to the house of God in Joshua 9:21–27. Hewing wood is specifically mentioned as one of their menial tasks. A possible reason Swedenborg refers to them here as "hired workers" instead of "slaves" (see Joshua 9:23) is that, as he mentions elsewhere (see *Secrets of Heaven* 1110), people who are the spiritual equivalent of the Gibeonites do good deeds not out of love or any desire to be useful but merely to earn themselves salvation. [JSR, SS]

648 (in §442). On the terms "instrumental cause" and "principal cause," see note 576. [JSR]

649 (in §443:2). Although there is no exact reference in Scripture to "the simple in spirit," Swedenborg may be referring to Matthew 5:3, "Blessed are the poor in spirit," or to Luke 8:15. He may also mean more generally passages in the Latin Bible that speak of simplicity: Psalms 19:7 (which is Psalms 19:8 in Latin Bibles); 116:6; 119:130; Matthew 6:22; 10:16; Luke 11:34; Philippians 2:15. Swedenborg mentions elsewhere that the simple at heart are often wiser than the learned and complex; see, for example, *Secrets of Heaven* 4754. [JSR]

650 (in §444). The mention of seven commandments here includes the fourth commandment (by the Augustinian-Lutheran reckoning; see note 465), which is elsewhere said to bridge the two tablets; see note 516. Below in the text (§456) Swedenborg indicates that the two tablets were joined as one, yet also faced each other, with the first tablet on the right and the second on the left, presumably because Hebrew is written from right to left. [JSR]

651 (in §450). On the Socinian faith, see note 245. [JSR]

652 (in §452). For more on "bones of the dead," or relics, see note 326. [JSR]

653 (in §453). Swedenborg here chides certain Christians for their idolatrous practices by comparing those practices to ancient pagan ideas. In Greek mythology, the dying soul would have to pay a coin to Charon, the ferryman, in order to be ferried across the river Styx (on the Styx, see note 96). The gate of Hades itself or the underworld was guarded by Cerberus, a monstrous dog with many heads (anywhere from one to fifty, but most accounts indicate three). The morsels offered to Cerberus are an allusion to

Greek and Roman myths concerning the "sop to Cerberus." The morsel pacified the beast so that it would allow a living visitor to hell to come and go; see, for example, Vergil *Aeneid* 6:417–421, where the morsels are medicated in order to put Cerberus to sleep. On the Elysian fields, see note 496. [JSR]

654 (in §455a:1). In the first edition, this section and the following one are both numbered 455. [JSR]

655 (in §455a:2). In Luke 16:26, Abraham in heaven, speaking for himself and Lazarus, a pauper, addresses a rich man in hell: "Between us and you a great gulf has been established so that those who want to cross from here to you cannot, and those who are there cannot cross over to us." [JSR]

656 (in §459:1). Swedenborg reports another spiritual experience involving five halls in §136. See also note 313. [JSR]

657 (in §459:3). The phrase "without lamp oil" is a reference to Matthew 25:1–12, especially verse 3; see §199. [JSR]

658 (in §459:3). The social divisions of Swedenborg's time were far more rigid than those of today; the mingling of different social classes indignantly suggested here would have been unthinkable. [GMC]

659 (in §459:12). On pus as an infective agent, see note 643. [JSR]

660 (in §460:1). This account is largely copied from *Revelation Unveiled* 386. For some reason, however, a final lengthy sentence of that earlier version is omitted here, even though it helps to clarify why the window on the right darkened the room, while the window on the left brightened it. It reads as follows: "It became dark when a window was created on the right side because light from heaven that flows in on that side affects our *will*. It became light when a window on the right side was closed over and a window was created on the left side because light from heaven that flows in on the left side affects our *intellect*. The intellect in every one of us can receive the light of heaven provided that the evil in our will is closed over" (translated by JSR). [JSR]

661 (in §460:2). This mention of "a log or a stone" is an allusion to a Lutheran doctrine of human spiritual powerlessness, based ultimately on the Bible; see note 191 and the quotation in §356. The spirit here portrays that doctrine as a kind of self-fulfilling prophecy. [JSR]

662 (in §460:3). In Swedenborg's day "syncretist" was a pejorative term for someone who attempted to reconcile opposing branches of the church to each other, but in ineffective or superficial ways. For the symbolism of baldness, see §§74:5, 223. [JSR]

663 (in §461:6). For biblical passages on the Holy Spirit's effect on and in people, see §143. [JSR]

664 (in §461:7). The "life" and "death" referred to here are spiritual, not physical. In §369:3, Swedenborg defines spiritual death as "earthly life without spiritual life." [JSR]

665 (in §461:7). Swedenborg apparently means that although everything that comes from us *alone* is credit-seeking and evil, good actions whose ultimate source is God do come into realization through us, and in that sense we can be said to produce something other than what is merely credit-seeking and evil. He is contrasting his theology with that of those who believe no works can be good; see further in §462. [JSR]

666 (in §461:8). In a largely parallel memorable occurrence published five years earlier (*Revelation Unveiled* 875:9–15), there are minor differences with this account. One is

that in the earlier account Swedenborg pulled branches from the laurel tree under which the people were sitting, and when they came to this insight, the laurel branch blossomed (*Revelation Unveiled* 875:15). [JSR]

667 (in §461:8). Another difference between this account and its predecessor (see note 666) is that in the earlier account, the book on the table is said to be *Divine Love and Wisdom* and *Divine Providence* (in a combined volume; see *Revelation Unveiled* 875:15). Both *Secrets of Heaven* and *Divine Love and Wisdom* contain material on human beings as organs that receive life rather than life-forms in their own right; see the lists of internal cross-references on this topic in *Secrets of Heaven* 3318:2, 7406; see also *Divine Love and Wisdom* 4–6, 55–60. [JSR]

668 (in §462:1). With the exception of a handful of words here and there from other languages, Swedenborg wrote his theological works in Latin. This passage contains one of those exceptions. After the Latin word here translated "sea turtles," *testudines* (singular *testudo*), Swedenborg inserted in parentheses the word *skillepadde,* which means "turtle" in Swedish, his native tongue. (The modern Swedish equivalent is *sköldpadda.*) While it is not clear why he did so, the likely explanation is that he intended the Swedish word as a gloss to prevent a misreading or misunderstanding at the first occurrence of the Latin word. The fact that he chose Swedish to indicate the gloss, rather than some other more common European language, suggests that *True Christianity* may have been aimed primarily at a Swedish audience. [JSR, SS]

669 (in §462:5). Niccolò Machiavelli (1469–1527) was a Florentine statesman and writer who by Swedenborg's day had become notorious for his views regarding political expediency and his efforts to attack and overthrow not only Christianity but also all forms of religion and theology (Kors 2003, 3:316–317). During Swedenborg's lifetime, Frederick II of Prussia (1712–1786) published an influential tome against Machiavelli: see Frederick II 1981; see also Meinecke 1957. [JSR]

670 (in §462:7). For more on this concept of deeper areas within us in which God is completely in control and outer areas in which we share control with God, see *Divine Providence* 198–200. [JSR]

671 (in §462:9). This passage contains a sustained military metaphor in the Latin, in Swedenborg's description of the hands and their muscles. *Phalanges* ("arrays [of soldiers]") and *manipuli* ("troops") are terms derived from Greek and Roman military usage. *Manipulus* ("maniple") literally meant one third of a cohort, and so one thirtieth of a legion; see Campbell 1994, 4–6; Goldsworthy 1996, 33–38. Implied here is the image of the brain as the general commanding the extremities as soldiers. [GMC]

672 (in §462:10). The Latin words here translated "money and talents" are *minas & talenta,* literally, "minas and talents" (see note 617). Minas are the units of trade in Luke 19:12–26; talents in Matthew 25:14–34. As early as classical times, however, the word "talent" also meant a special ability. [JSR]

Works Cited
in the Notes

Acton, Alfred. 1938. "Swedenborg and the Nebular Hypothesis." *The New Philosophy* 41:9–15.

———. 1948–1955. *The Letters and Memorials of Emanuel Swedenborg.* 2 vols. Bryn Athyn, Pa.: Swedenborg Scientific Association.

Acton, Alfred, II. 1995. "What Were They Fighting about? A Review of the Argument over the Nature of Spiritual Creation." *The New Philosophy* 98:43–62.

Aesop. 1889. *Fabulae Aesopicae Collectae.* Edited by Karl Halm. Leipzig: Teubner.

Aiton, E. J. 1972. *The Vortex Theory of Planetary Motions.* New York: American Elsevier.

Alcover, Madeleine. 1970. *La Pensée philosophique et scientifique de Cyrano de Bergerac.* Geneva: Librarie Droz.

Alfelt, Lennart O. 1969. "Swedenborg's Library: An Alphabetical List." *The New Philosophy* 72:115–126.

Anderson, M. S. 2000. *Europe in the Eighteenth Century, 1713–1789.* 4th ed. Harlow, U.K.: Pearson Education.

Apostolos-Cappadona, Diane. 1994. *Dictionary of Christian Art.* New York: Continuum.

Aquinas, Thomas. 1952. *Summa Theologiae.* Translated by the Fathers of the English Dominican Province and revised by Daniel J. Sullivan. Vols. 19–20 of *Great Books of the Western World.* Chicago: Encyclopedia Britannica.

Arias Montanus, Benedictus. 1657. *Biblia Universa et Hebraica.* Leipzig: C. Kirchner.

Aristotle. 1952a. *On Generation and Corruption.* Translated by H. H. Joachim. In vol. 8 of *Great Books of the Western World.* Chicago: Encyclopedia Britannica.

———. 1952b. *On the Generation of Animals.* Translated by A.S.L. Farquharson. In vol. 9 of *Great Books of the Western World.* Chicago: Encyclopedia Britannica.

———. 1952c. *On the Heavens.* Translated by J. L. Stocks. In vol. 8 of *Great Books of the Western World.* Chicago: Encyclopedia Britannica.

———. 1952d. *Metaphysics.* Translated by W. D. Ross. In vol. 8 of *Great Books of the Western World.* Chicago: Encyclopedia Britannica.

———. 1952e. *Physics.* Translated by R. P. Hardie and R. K. Gaye. In vol. 8 of *Great Books of the Western World.* Chicago: Encyclopedia Britannica.

———. 1952f. *Politics.* Translated by Benjamin Jowett. In vol. 9 of *Great Books of the Western World.* Chicago: Encyclopedia Britannica.

———. 1952g. *On the Soul.* Translated by J. A. Smith. In vol. 8 of *Great Books of the Western World.* Chicago: Encyclopedia Britannica.

Armitage, Angus. 1948. "The Cosmology of Giordano Bruno." *Annals of Science* 6:24–31.

Aufderheide, Arthur C. 2003. *The Scientific Study of Mummies.* Cambridge: Cambridge University Press.

Ayer, A. J. 1954. "The Identity of Indiscernibles." In *Philosophical Essays*. New York: St. Martin's Press.

Bailey, Nathan. [1721] 1917. *Divers Proverbs with Their Explication and Illustration Compiled and Methodically Digested As Well as for the Entertainment of the Ignorant and for the Benefit of Young Students, Artificers, Tradesmen & Foreigners Who Are Desirous Thorowly to Understand What They Speak, Read, or Write.* New Haven: Yale University Press.

Bayle, Pierre. 1740. *Dictionnaire historique et critique.* 5th ed. 4 vols. Amsterdam: Leide. First edition: 1697, Amsterdam: Reinier Leers.

Beekman, Lillian. 1902. "Swedenborg on the Appearance and Disappearance of New Stars." *The New Philosophy* 5:76–96.

Berkeley, George. [1710] 1952. *The Principles of Human Knowledge.* In vol. 35 of *Great Books of the Western World.* Chicago: Encyclopedia Britannica.

Black, Max. 1952. "The Identity of Indiscernibles." *Mind* 61:153–164.

Block, R. de. 1876. *Évhémère: Son Livre et sa doctrine.* Brussels: Hector Manceaux.

Book of Common Prayer. 1711. London: Charles Bill and Thomas Newcomb.

Bosworth, A. B. 1980. *A Historical Commentary on Arrian's History of Alexander.* Vol. 1. Oxford: Clarendon.

Brahe, Tycho. 1573. *De Nova et Nullius Aevi Memoria Prius Visa Stella.* Copenhagen: Laurentius Benedicti.

Brochmand, Jesper Rasmussen. 1633. *Universae Theologiae Systema.* Copenhagen: Martzanianus.

Brown, Reginald W. 1919. "The Fundamental Concept of Substance, and of Its Form and Activity." *The New Philosophy* 22:398–413.

Bruno, Giordano. 1584. *De l'infinito universo et mondi.* Venice [London: J. Charlewood].

Byrne, Peter. 1989. *Natural Religion and the Nature of Religion: The Legacy of Deism.* London: Routledge.

Calov, Abraham. 1655–1677. *Systema Locorum Theologicorum.* Wittenberg: Andreas Hartmann, Johann Röhner, Michael Wendt, Christian Schroedter, Johann Wilcke.

Calvin, John. 1960. *Institutes of the Christian Religion.* Edited by John T. McNeill and translated by Ford Lewis Battles. 2 vols. Philadelphia: Westminster.

Campbell, J. B. 1994. *The Roman Army, 31 B.C.–A.D. 337: A Sourcebook.* New York: Routledge.

Candland, Douglas Keith. 1993. *Feral Children and Clever Animals: Reflections on Human Nature.* New York: Oxford University Press.

Careri, Gemelli. 1719. *Voyage du tour du monde.* Translated by L.M.N. 6 vols. Paris: Etienne Ganeau.

Carolides von Carlsperg, Georg. 1597. *Farrago Symbolica Sententiosa Perpetuis Distichis Explicata.* Prague: Adam.

Casanova, Giacomo. 1772. *Lana caprina, epistola di un licantropo indiritta a S. A. la signora principessa J.L.n.P.C.* Bologna.

Chemnitz, Martin. 1591. *Loci Theologici.* 3 vols. Frankfurt: Joannes Spies. English translation: *Loci Theologici,* translated by J.A.O. Preus, St. Louis, Mo.: Concordia Publishing House, 1989.

Clarke, Edwin, and Kenneth Dewhurst. 1972. *An Illustrated History of Brain Function.* Berkeley, Ca.: University of California Press.

Collier, Katharine B. 1934. *Cosmogonies of Our Fathers: Some Theories of the Seventeenth and the Eighteenth Centuries.* New York: Columbia University Press.

Concordia Pia et Unanimi Consensu Repetita Confessio Fidei. 1756. Leipzig: Grossiana.

Conley, Thomas M. 1990. *Rhetoric in the European Tradition.* New York: Longman.

Cook, Alan. 1998. *Edmond Halley: Charting the Heavens and the Seas.* New York: Oxford University Press.

Copernicus, Nicolaus. [1543] 1952. *On the Revolutions of the Heavenly Spheres.* Translated by Charles Glenn Wallis. In vol. 16 of *Great Books of the Western World.* Chicago: Encyclopedia Britannica.

Corr, Charles A. 1975. "Christian Wolff and Leibniz." *Journal of the History of Ideas* 36:241–262.

Crowe, Michael J. 1986. *The Extraterrestrial Life Debate, 1750–1900: The Idea of a Plurality of Worlds from Kant to Lowell.* Cambridge: Cambridge University Press.

Cuno, J. C. 1947. *J. C. Cuno's Memoirs on Swedenborg.* Translated by Claire E. Berninger. Bryn Athyn, Pa.: Academy Book Room.

Curley, E. M. 1971. "Did Leibniz State 'Leibniz' Law'?" *The Philosophical Review* 80:497–501.

Cyrano de Bergerac, Savinien. [1656–1662] 1968. *L'Autre Monde: Histoires comique des états et empires de la lune; Histoire comique des états et empires du soleil.* In *Les Oeuvres libertines de Cyrano de Bergerac.* Geneva: Slatkine Reprints. Reprint of the Paris edition of 1921.

Descartes, René. [1637] 1952a. *Discourse on the Method of Rightly Conducting the Reason.* Translated by Elizabeth S. Haldane and G.R.T. Ross. In vol. 31 of *Great Books of the Western World.* Chicago: Encyclopedia Britannica.

———. [1641] 1952b. *Meditations on First Philosophy.* Translated by Elizabeth S. Haldane and G.R.T. Ross. In vol. 31 of *Great Books of the Western World.* Chicago: Encyclopedia Britannica.

———. [1644] 1983. *Principles of Philosophy.* Translated by Valentine Rodger Miller and Reese P. Miller. Dordrecht: Reidel.

Diderot, Denis. [1746] 1953. *Pensées philosophiques.* In *Selected Philosophical Writings,* edited by J. Lough. Cambridge: Cambridge University Press.

Diggle, J., ed. 1998. *Tragicorum Graecorum Fragmenta Selecta.* Oxford: Oxford University Press.

Douglas, J. Bruce. 1912–1913. "Human Automata in Classical Tradition and Mediaeval Romance." *Modern Philology* 10:511–526.

Douthwaite, Julia V. 2002. *The Wild Girl, Natural Man, and the Monster: Dangerous Experiments in the Age of the Enlightenment.* Chicago: University of Chicago Press.

Duffin, Jacalyn. 1999. *History of Medicine: A Scandalously Short Introduction.* Toronto: University of Toronto Press.

Dumont, Louis. 1977. *From Mandeville to Marx: The Genesis and Triumph of Economic Ideology.* Chicago: University of Chicago Press.

Eluère, C. 1986. "A Prehistoric Touchstone from France." *Gold Bulletin* 19(2):58–61.

Elyot, Thomas, Sir. [1531] 1907. *The Boke Named the Gouernour.* New York: E. P. Dutton.

Emerton, Norma E. 1984. *The Scientific Reinterpretation of Form.* Ithaca, N.Y.: Cornell University Press.

Engemann, Josef. 1976. "Zu den Dreifaltigkeitsdarstellungen der frühchristl. Kunst: Gab es im 4. Jh. anthropomorphe Trinitätsbilder?" *Jahrbuch für Antike und Christentum* 19:157–172.

Erasmus, Desiderius. [1511] 1971. *Praise of Folly.* Translated by Betty Radice. New York: Penguin.

Ernesti, Johann August. 1760. Review of *Secrets of Heaven,* by Emanuel Swedenborg. *Neue Theologische Bibliothek* 1:515–527.

———. 1763. Review of *The Lord, Sacred Scripture, Life, Faith,* and *Supplements,* by Emanuel Swedenborg. *Neue Theologische Bibliothek* 4:725–733.

———. 1766. Review of *Revelation Unveiled,* by Emanuel Swedenborg. *Neue Theologische Bibliothek* 7:685–692.

———. 1767. Review of *Vollständige Einleitung in die Religion und gesamte Theologie,* vol. 4, by Heinrich Wilhelm Clemm. *Neue Theologische Bibliothek* 8:860–892.

———, ed. 1760–1769. *Neue Theologische Bibliothek.* Vols. 1–10.

Farley, John. 1977. *The Spontaneous Generation Controversy from Descartes to Oparin.* Baltimore: Johns Hopkins University Press.

———. 1982. *Gametes and Spores: Ideas about Sexual Reproduction, 1750–1914.* Baltimore: Johns Hopkins University Press.

Feldman, Fred. 1970. "Leibniz and 'Leibniz' Law.'" *The Philosophical Review* 79:510–522.

Fontenelle, Bernard le Bovier de. [1686] 1990. *Conversations on the Plurality of Worlds.* Translated by H. A. Hargreaves. Berkeley, Ca.: University of California Press.

Fraser, James George. 1922. *The Golden Bough: A Study in Magic and Religion.* New York: Macmillan.

Frederick II. 1981. *The Refutation of Machiavelli's "Prince": Or, Anti-Machiavel.* Translated by Paul Sonnino. Athens, Ohio: Ohio University Press.

Galen. 1968. *Galen on the Usefulness of the Parts of the Body* (De Usu Partium). Translated with commentary by Margaret Tallmadge May. Ithaca, N.Y.: Cornell University Press.

Galileo Galilei. 1989. *Sidereus Nuncius, or the Sidereal Messenger.* Translated by Albert Van Helden. Chicago: University of Chicago Press.

Gatti, Hilary, ed. 2002. *Giordano Bruno: Philosopher of the Renaissance.* Burlington, Vt.: Ashgate.

Goldstein, B. R. 1994. "Historical Perspectives on Copernicus's Account of Precession." *Journal of the History of Astronomy* 25:189–197.

Goldsworthy, Adrian Keith. 1996. *The Roman Army at War: 100 B.C.–A.D. 200.* Oxford: Clarendon Press.

Gorman, Thomas Murray. 1885. "Address to the Reader." In *On the Worship and Love of God,* [translated by John Clowes]. London: Kegan Paul, Trench.

Grant, Mark. 2000. *Galen on Food and Diet.* New York: Routledge.

Greenberg, Sidney. 1950. *The Infinite in Giordano Bruno, with a Translation of His Dialogue Concerning the Cause, Principle, and One.* New York: King's Crown Press.

Gregory, David. 1702. *Astronomiae, Physicae, et Geometricae Elementa.* Oxford: Sheldonian Theater.

Gross, Charles G. 1999. "Emanuel Swedenborg: A Neuroscientist before His Time." *The New Philosophy* 102:429–445.

Grube, G.M.A. 1935. *Plato's Thought.* London: Methuen.

Hacking, Ian. 1975. "The Identity of Indiscernibles." *The Journal of Philosophy* 72:249–256.

Hall, James. 1994. *Illustrated Dictionary of Symbols in Eastern and Western Art.* Illustrated by Chris Puleston. London: John Murray.

Halley, Edmond. 1716. "The Art of Living under Water." *Philosophical Transactions* 29:258–267.

———. 1717. "Considerations on the Change of Latitude of Some of the Principal Fixt Stars." *Philosophical Transactions* 30:978–990.

———. 1721. "An Addition to the Description of the Art of Diving or Living under Water." *Philosophical Transactions* 31:521–523.

Hartley, David. 1749. *Observations on Man, His Frame, His Duty, and His Expectations.* 2 vols. London: Richardson.

Harvey, E. Ruth. 1975. *The Inward Wits: Psychological Theory in the Middle Ages and Renaissance.* Warburg Institute Surveys, 6. London: University of London Press.

Harvey, Warren Zev. 1998. *Physics and Metaphysics in Ḥasdai Crescas.* Amsterdam: J. C. Gieben.

Helander, Hans. 2004. *Neo-Latin Literature in Sweden in the Period 1620–1720.* Uppsala: Uppsala University.

"History of Swedenborg's Reply to Ernesti." 1890. *New Church Life* 10:213–215.

Hobbes, Thomas. [1651] 1952. *Leviathan.* In vol. 23 of *Great Books of the Western World.* Chicago: Encyclopedia Britannica.

Holbach, Paul-Henri Dietrich, Baron d'. 1770. *Système de la nature, ou des lois du monde physique et du monde moral.* London.

Hume, David. 1748. *Philosophical Essays Concerning Human Understanding.* London: A. Millar.

———. [1739–1740] 1999. *A Treatise of Human Nature: Being an Attempt to Introduce the Experimental Method of Reasoning into Moral Subjects.* Kitchener, Ont.: Batoche.

———. [1777] 2004. *An Enquiry Concerning the Principles of Morals.* Amherst, N.Y.: Prometheus Books.

Hyde, James. 1906. *A Bibliography of the Works of Emanuel Swedenborg, Original and Translated.* London: Swedenborg Society.

Jammer, Max. 1993. *Concepts of Space: The History of Theories of Space in Physics.* 3rd ed. New York: Dover Publications.

Jonsson, Inge. 1999. *Visionary Scientist: The Effects of Science and Philosophy on Swedenborg's Cosmology.* West Chester, Pa.: Swedenborg Foundation.

———. 2004. *A Drama of Creation: Sources and Influences in Swedenborg's "Worship and Love of God."* West Chester, Pa.: Swedenborg Foundation.

Kant, Immanuel. 1755. *Allgemeine Naturgeschichte und Theorie des Himmels oder Versuch, von der Verfassung und dem mechanischen Ursprunge des ganzen Weltgebäudes nach Newtonischen Grundsätzen abgehandelt.* Königsberg and Leipzig: Petersen.

———. [1781] 1952. *The Critique of Pure Reason.* Translated by J.M.D. Meiklejohn. In vol. 42 of *Great Books of the Western World.* Chicago: Encyclopedia Britannica.

———. [1766] 2002. *Kant on Swedenborg: Dreams of a Spirit Seer and Other Writings.* Edited by Gregory R. Johnson and translated by Gregory R. Johnson and Glenn Alexander Magee. West Chester, Pa.: Swedenborg Foundation.

Kenyon, Ralph E., Jr. 1994. *Atomism and Infinite Divisibility.* Dissertation, University of Massachusetts Amherst.

Kepler, Johannes. 1604. *Ad Vitellionem Paralipomena, Quibus Astronomiae Pars Optica Traditur; Potissimum de Artificiosa Observatione et Aestimatione Diametrorum Deliquiorumque; Solis et Lunae, cum Exemplis Insignium Eclipsium . . . Tractatum Luculentum et Modo Visionis, et Humorum Oculi Usu, contra Opticos et Anatomicos.* Frankfurt: Marnium & Heredes Aubrii.

———. 1606. *De Stella Nova in Pede Serpentarii, et Qui sub Ejus Exortum de Novo Iniit, Trigono Igneo.* Prague: Paul Sessius.

Kerényi, Karl. 1978. *Athene: Virgin and Mother in Greek Religion.* Translated by Murray Stein. Dallas, Tex.: Spring Publications.

———. 1986. *Hermes: Guide of Souls: The Mythologem of the Masculine Source of Life.* Translated by Murray Stein. Dallas, Tex.: Spring Publications.

King, J.B.S. 1906. "The Scientific Terminology of Swedenborg's Time." *The New Philosophy* 9:5–12.

Kleberg, Tönnes. 1984. *Codex Argenteus: The Silver Bible at Uppsala.* 6th ed. Uppsala: Uppsala University Library.

Kolb, Robert, and Timothy J. Wengert, eds. 2000. *The Book of Concord.* Minneapolis: Fortress Press.

Kors, Alan Charles, ed. 2003. *Encyclopedia of the Enlightenment.* 4 vols. New York: Oxford University Press.

La Fontaine, Jean de. 1909. *The Fables of La Fontaine.* Translated by Elizur Wright. London: George Bell and Sons.

La Mettrie, Julien Offray de. 1748. *L'Homme machine.* Lyde.

———. [1748] 1994. *Man a Machine; and, Man a Plant.* Translated by Richard A. Watson and Maya Rybalka, with an introduction and notes by Justin Leiber. Indianapolis: Hackett.

Lachièze-Rey, Marc, and Jean-Pierre Luminet. 2001. *Celestial Treasury: From the Music of the Spheres to the Conquest of Space.* Translated by Joe Loredo. Cambridge: Cambridge University Press.

Lactantius. 2003. *Divine Institutes.* Translated by Anthony Bowen and Peter Garnsey. Liverpool: Liverpool University Press.

Lamm, Martin. 2000. *Emanuel Swedenborg: The Development of His Thought.* Translated by Tomas Spiers and Anders Hallengren. West Chester, Pa.: Swedenborg Foundation.

Lane Fox, Robin. 1987. *Pagans and Christians.* New York: Knopf.

Lang, A. 1901. "Spectral Lights." *Folk-Lore* 12:343–344.

Lang, Bernhard. 2000. "On Heaven and Hell: A Historical Introduction to Swedenborg's Most Popular Work." In *Heaven and Its Wonders and Hell,* by Emanuel Swedenborg, translated by George F. Dole. West Chester, Pa.: Swedenborg Foundation.

Laqueur, Thomas W. 2003. *Solitary Sex: A Cultural History of Masturbation.* New York: Zone Books.

Latin Manuscripts. Bibliothèque Nationale de France, Paris.

Laudan, Rachel. 1987. *From Mineralogy to Geology.* Chicago: University of Chicago Press.

Leeuwenhoek, Antoni van. 1941. *The Collected Letters of Antoni van Leeuwenhoek.* Edited, illustrated, and annotated by a committee of Dutch scientists. Vol. 2. Amsterdam: Swets and Zeitlinger.

Leibniz, Gottfried Wilhelm. 1881. *La Monadologie.* Annotated by Émile Boutroux. Paris: C. Delgrave.

———. 1956. *Discourse on Metaphysics.* In *Philosophical Papers and Letters,* translated and edited by Leroy Loemker. 2 vols. Chicago: University of Chicago Press.

———. 1981. *New Essays on Human Understanding.* Translated and edited by Peter Remnant and Jonathan Bennett. New York: Cambridge University Press.

———. 1991. *Discourse on Metaphysics and Other Essays.* Edited and translated by Daniel Garber and Roger Ariew. Indianapolis: Hackett.

———. [1695] 1997. *The New System.* In *Leibniz's New System and Associated Contemporary Texts,* translated and edited by R. S. Woolhouse and Richard Francks. New York: Oxford University Press.

Lindberg, David C. 1976. *Theories of Vision from al-Kindi to Kepler.* Chicago: University of Chicago Press.

Locke, John. [1689] 1952. *Essay Concerning Human Understanding.* In vol. 35 of *Great Books of the Western World.* Chicago: Encyclopedia Britannica.

Lovejoy, Arthur O. 1960a. *Essays in the History of Ideas.* New York: G. P. Putnam's Sons.

———. 1960b. *The Great Chain of Being: A Study of the History of an Idea.* New York: Harper & Row.

Luther, Martin. 1848. *Table Talk.* Translated by William Hazlitt. London: D. Bogue.

MacCulloch, Diarmaid. 2003. *The Reformation.* New York: Penguin Group.

Malebranche, Nicholas. 1691. *De Inquirenda Veritate.* Geneva: Society.

Manzoni, T. 1998. "The Cerebral Ventricles, the Animal Spirits and the Dawn of Brain Localization of Function." *Archives Italiennes de Biologie* 136(2):103–152.

Marlowe, Christopher. [1633] 1994. *The Jew of Malta.* Edited by Peter J. Smith. London: Nick Hern.

Marshall, P. J., and Glyndwr Williams. 1982. *The Great Map of Mankind: Perceptions of New Worlds in the Age of Enlightenment.* Cambridge, Mass.: Harvard University Press.

McClellan, James E. 1985. *Science Reorganized: Scientific Societies in the Eighteenth Century.* New York: Columbia University Press.

Meinecke, Friedrich. 1957. *Machiavellism: The Doctrine of Raison d'État and Its Place in Modern History.* New Haven: Yale University Press.

Middleton, William Edgar Knowles. 1964. *The History of the Barometer.* Baltimore: Johns Hopkins Press.

Mills-Kronborg Collection of Danish Church Wall Paintings. Index of Christian Art, Princeton University.

Muller, Richard A. 1985. *Dictionary of Latin and Greek Theological Terms, Drawn Principally from Protestant Scholastic Theology.* Grand Rapids, Mich.: Baker Book House.

Mungello, D. E. 2005. *The Great Encounter of China and the West, 1500–1800.* 2nd ed. Lanham, Md.: Rowman and Littlefield.

Murray, Peter. 1996. *The Oxford Companion to Christian Art and Architecture.* New York: Oxford University Press.

The New Philosophy. 1899– (vols. 1–). Urbana, Ill./Philadelphia: Swedenborg Scientific Association.

Newell, William W. 1904. "The Ignis Fatuus, Its Character and Legendary Origin." *Journal of American Folklore* 17:39–60.

Newton, Isaac. [1717] 1952. *Optics.* 2nd ed. In vol. 34 of *Great Books of the Western World.* Chicago: Encyclopedia Britannica.

Oddy, A. 1983. "Assaying in Antiquity." *Gold Bulletin* 16(2):52–59.

Odhner, Hugo Lj. 1933. "The History of the 'Animal Spirits,' and of Swedenborg's Development of the Concept." *The New Philosophy* 36:218–223, 234–249.

———. 1951. "Christian Wolf and Swedenborg." *The New Philosophy* 54:237–251.

———. 1958. "Space and Spiritual Extense." *The New Philosophy* 61:301–314.

———. 1964. *Creation: Doctrinal Essays.* Bryn Athyn, Pa.: Academy Publication Committee.

Oldroyd, David R. 1996. *Thinking about the Earth: A History of Ideas in Geology.* London: Athlone.

O'Leary-Hawthorne, John. 1995. "The Bundle Theory of Substance and the Identity of Indiscernibles." *Analysis* 55(3):191–196.

Onania; or The Heinous Sin of Self-Pollution, and All Its Frightful Consequences, in Both Sexes, Considered . . . [1715]. [London: n.p.].

Onians, Richard Broxton. 2000. *The Origins of European Thought about the Body, the Mind, the Soul, the World, Time, and Fate: New Interpretations of Greek, Roman, and Kindred Evidence, Also of Some Basic Jewish and Christian Beliefs.* 2nd ed. Cambridge: Cambridge University Press.

Ovid. 1993. *The Metamorphoses of Ovid.* Translated by Allen Mandelbaum. New York: Harcourt Brace.

Owen, Wilfred. 1963. *"Dulce et Decorum Est."* In *The Mentor Book of Major British Poets,* edited by Oscar Williams. New York: New American Library.

Park, David. 1997. *The Fire within the Eye: A Historical Essay on the Nature and Meaning of Light.* Princeton: Princeton University Press.

Patterson, Robert Leet. 1965. *Plato on Immortality.* University Park, Pa.: Pennsylvania State University Press.

Pendleton, Charles R. 1957. "The Concept of Space." *The New Philosophy* 60:161–177, 204–221, 225–243.

Pendleton, W. F. 1901. "The Credibility of Swedenborg's Science." *New Church Life* 21:113–135.

Phillips, Eustace Dockray. 1973. *Greek Medicine.* London: Thames and Hudson.

Pinto-Correia, Clara. 1997. *The Ovary of Eve: Egg and Sperm and Preformation.* Chicago: University of Chicago Press.

Plato. 1952. *The Dialogues of Plato.* Translated by Benjamin Jowett. In vol. 7 of *Great Books of the Western World.* Chicago: Encyclopedia Britannica.

Porter, Roy. 2003. *Flesh in the Age of Reason: The Modern Foundations of Body and Soul.* New York: W. W. Norton.

Poulsen, Frederik. 1945. "Talking, Weeping, and Bleeding Sculptures: A Chapter of the History of Religious Fraud." *Acta Archaeologica* 16:178–195.

Pullman, Bernhard. 1998. *The Atom in the History of Human Thought.* Translated by Alex Riesinger. Oxford: Oxford University Press.

Quenstedt, Johann Andreas. 1685. *Theologia Didactico-Polemica.* Wittenberg: J. L. Quenstedt and E. Schumacher.

Quin, C. E. 1994. "The Soul and the Pneuma in the Function of the Nervous System after Galen." *Journal of the Royal Society of Medicine* 87(7):393–395.

Ramirez, Frank. 2004. "Holy Ground." *Christian History and Biography* 84:29–30.

Reichwein, Adolf. 1925. *China and Europe: Intellectual and Artistic Contacts in the Eighteenth Century.* New York: Alfred A. Knopf.

Reineccius, Christian. 1739. *Biblia Hebraica ad Optimas Quasque Editiones Expressa cum Notis Masorethicis et Numeris Distinctionum in Paraschas et Capita et Versus . . .* Leipzig: Lanckisi.

Riccioli, Giovanni Battista. 1651. *Almagestum Novum Astronomiam Veterem Novamque Complectens.* 3 vols. Bologna: Benatius.

Ripa, Cesare. [1758–1760] 1971. *Baroque and Rococo Pictorial Imagery: The 1758–60 Hertel Edition of Ripa's "Iconologia."* Edited by Edward A. Maser. New York: Dover Publications.

Rocca, Julius. 1997. "Galen and the Ventricular System." *Journal of the History of the Neurosciences* 6(3):227–239.

Roche, Daniel. 1978. *Le Siècle des lumières en province: Académies et académiciens provinciaux 1680–1789.* 2 vols. Paris: Mouton.

Roll of Ipsden, Eric Roll, Baron. 1961. *A History of Economic Thought.* 3rd ed. Englewood Cliffs, N.J.: Prentice-Hall.

Rose, Jonathan S. 1994. "Similes in Emanuel Swedenborg's *Vera Christiana Religio* (1771)." In *Acta Conventus Neo-Latini Hafniensis.* Binghamton, N.Y.: Medieval & Renaissance Texts & Studies.

———. 2005. "Annotated Bibliography of Swedenborg's Writings." In *Emanuel Swedenborg: Essays for the New Century Edition on His Life, Work, and Impact,* edited by Jonathan S. Rose and others. West Chester, Pa.: Swedenborg Foundation.

Rosen, Edward. 1965. *Kepler's Conversation with Galileo's Sidereal Messenger.* New York: Johnson Reprint Corporation.

Rosen, George. 1968. *Madness in Society: Chapters in the Historical Sociology of Mental Illness.* Chicago: Chicago University Press.

Ross, Sylvia. 1986. "Spectral Armies from Yorkshire's Past." *Earth* 1:10.

Santillana, Giorgio de. 1970. *The Crime of Galileo.* Chicago: University of Chicago.

Schaffer, Simon. 1999. "Enlightened Automata." In *The Sciences in Enlightened Europe,* edited by William Clark, Jan Golinski, and Simon Schaffer. Chicago: University of Chicago Press.

Schmid, Heinrich. 1889. *The Doctrinal Theology of the Evangelical Lutheran Church, Exhibited and Verified from the Original Sources.* Translated by Charles A. Hay and Henry E. Jacobs. Philadelphia: Lutheran Bookstore.

Schmidt, Sebastian. 1696. *Biblia Sacra sive Testamentum Vetus et Novum ex Linguis Originalibus in Linguam Latinam Translatum.* Strasbourg: J. F. Spoor.

Schumpeter, Joseph A. 1954. *History of Economic Analysis.* Edited by Elizabeth Boody Schumpeter. New York: Oxford University Press.

"Sentence of Galileo Galilei, 22 June, 1633." 1989. In *The Galileo Affair: A Documentary History,* translated by Maurice A. Finocchiaro. Berkeley, Ca.: University of California Press.

Sewall, Frank. 1909. "Swedenborg's Doctrine of 'The Purer Parts of Nature.'" *The New Philosophy* 12:75–91.

Shaw, S. J. 1937. "Historical Significance of the Curious Theory of the Mongol Blood in the Veins of the Ming Emperors." *The Chinese Social and Political Science Review* 20:492–498.

Shea, William R., and Mariano Artigas. 2003. *Galileo in Rome: The Rise and Fall of a Troublesome Genius.* New York: Oxford University Press.

Sigstedt, Cyriel Odhner. 1981. *The Swedenborg Epic: The Life and Works of Emanuel Swedenborg.* London: Swedenborg Society. First edition: 1952, New York: Bookman Associates.

Simms, Dennis L. 1977. "Archimedes and the Burning Mirrors of Syracuse." *Technology and Culture* 18:1–24.

Singer, Dorothea Waley. 1968. *Giordano Bruno, His Life and Thought, with Annotated Translation of His Work, "On the Infinite Universe and Worlds."* New York: Greenwood Press.

Sirois, François. 1982. "Perspectives on Epidemic Hysteria." In *Mass Psychogenic Illness: A Social Psychological Analysis,* edited by M. Colligan, J. Pennebaker, and L. Murphy. Hillsdale, N.J.: L. Erlbaum Associates.

Sleep Paralysis. 2005. In *Transpersonal Psychiatry* 42(1):5–145. Thousand Oaks, Ca.: Sage Publications.

Smith, A. Mark. 1992. "Picturing the Mind: The Representation of Thought in the Middle Ages and Renaissance." *Philosophical Topics* 20:149–170.

Smith, Adam. [1776] 1982. *The Wealth of Nations.* 2 vols. Edited by R. H. Campbell and A. S. Skinner. Indianapolis: Liberty Fund.

Smith, Robert. 1738. *A Compleat System of Opticks.* 2 vols. Cambridge.

Spinoza, Benedict de. [1677] 1952. *Ethics.* Translated by W. H. White; revised by A. H. Stirling. In vol. 31 of *Great Books of the Western World.* Chicago: Encyclopedia Britannica.

———. [1677] 1958. *On the Improvement of the Understanding.* Translated by Joseph Katz. Indianapolis: Bobbs-Merrill.

———. [1663] 1998. *The Principles of Cartesian Philosophy.* Translated by Samuel Shirley. Indianapolis: Hackett.

Starkey, David J. 1989. "Eighteenth-Century Privateering Enterprise." *International Journal of Maritime History* 1:279–286.

Statham, E. P. 1910. *Privateers and Privateering.* London: Hutchinson & Co.

Swammerdam, Jan. 1737–1738. *Biblia Naturae, sive Historia Insectorum, in Classes Certas Reducta.* Translated into Latin from the Dutch by H. D. Gaubius. Leyden: I. Severinus.

Swanson, Carl E. 1991. *Predators and Prizes: American Privateering and Imperial Warfare, 1739–1748.* Columbia: University of South Carolina Press.

Swedenborg, Emanuel. 1889. *The Spiritual Diary of Emanuel Swedenborg.* Vol. 4. Translated by George Bush and revised and edited by James F. Buss. London: James Speirs.

———. 1901. *Ontology, or the Significance of Philosophical Terms.* Translated by Alfred Acton. Boston: Massachusetts New-Church Union. Reprint: Bryn Athyn, Pa.: Swedenborg Scientific Association, no date.

———. 1923. *Psychologica, Being Notes and Observations on Christian Wolf's Psychologia Empirica.* Latin-English edition by Alfred Acton. Bryn Athyn, Pa.: Swedenborg Scientific Association.

———. 1927–1951a. *The History of Creation as Given by Moses.* In vol. 1 of *The Word of the Old Testament Explained,* translated by Alfred Acton. Bryn Athyn, Pa.: Academy of the New Church. First edition: 1911, Bryn Athyn, Pa.: Academy of the New Church.

———. 1927–1951b. *The Word of the Old Testament Explained.* 10 vols. Translated and edited by Alfred Acton. Bryn Athyn, Pa.: Academy of the New Church.

———. [1740–1741] 1955. *The Economy of the Animal Kingdom, Considered Anatomically, Physically, and Philosophically.* 2 vols. Translated by Augustus Clissold. Bryn Athyn, Pa.: Swedenborg Scientific Association. First edition of this translation: 1845–1846, London: W. Newbery, H. Bailliere, and Boston: Otis Clapp. A more accurate translation of the title of this work is *Dynamics of the Soul's Domain.*

———. [1744–1745] 1960. *The Animal Kingdom, Considered Anatomically, Physically, and Philosophically.* 2 vols. Translated by James John Garth Wilkinson. [Bryn Athyn, Pa.]: Swedenborg Scientific Association. First edition of this translation: 1843–1844, London: W. Newbery. A more accurate translation of the title of this work is *The Soul's Domain.*

———. [1734] 1965. *Forerunner of a Reasoned Philosophy Concerning the Infinite, the Final Cause of Creation; Also the Mechanism of the Operation of the Soul and Body.* 3rd ed. Translated by James John Garth Wilkinson, with an introduction by Lewis F. Hite. London: Swedenborg Society. Revision of the 1847 edition, London: William Newbery.

———. [1771] 1975. *Reply to Dr. Ernesti.* In *Small Theological Works and Letters of Emanuel Swedenborg,* translated and edited by John E. Elliott. London: Swedenborg Society.

———. 1976a. *The Economy of the Animal Kingdom, Considered Anatomically, Physically, and Philosophically, Transaction III.* Translated by Alfred Acton. Bryn Athyn, Pa.: Swedenborg Scientific Association. First edition: 1918, Philadelphia: Swedenborg Scientific Association. A more accurate translation of the title of this work is *Dynamics of the Soul's Domain.*

———. 1976b. *The Five Senses.* Translated by Enoch S. Price. Bryn Athyn, Pa.: Swedenborg Scientific Association. First edition of this translation: 1914, Philadelphia: Swedenborg Scientific Association.

———. [1717] 1976c. *On Tremulation.* Translated by Carl Th. Odhner. Bryn Athyn, Pa.: Swedenborg Scientific Association. First edition of this translation: 1899, Boston: Massachusetts New-Church Union.

———. 1976d. *A Philosopher's Note Book.* Translated by Alfred Acton. Bryn Athyn, Pa.: Swedenborg Scientific Association. First edition: 1931, Philadelphia: Swedenborg Scientific Association.

———. 1978. *The Spiritual Diary of Emanuel Swedenborg.* Vol. 4, pages 91–494, and vol. 5. Translated by James F. Buss. New York: Swedenborg Foundation. First edition: 1889, London: J. Spiers.

———. 1984. *The Soul and the Harmony between Soul and Body.* In *Psychological Transactions and Other Posthumous Tracts 1734–1744,* translated by Alfred Acton. 2nd ed. Bryn Athyn, Pa.: Swedenborg Scientific Association.

————. [1734] 1988a. *The Principia; or, The First Principles of Natural Things.* 2 vols. Translated by Augustus Clissold. Bryn Athyn, Pa.: Swedenborg Scientific Association. First edition of this translation: 1846, London: W. Newbery.

————. [1771] 1988b. *The True Christian Religion.* Translated by John Chadwick. 2 vols. London: Swedenborg Society.

————. 1992. *The Way to a Knowledge of the Soul.* Translated by John James Garth Wilkinson. In *Scientific and Philosophical Treatises (1716–1740),* edited by Alfred H. Stroh. 2nd edition edited and rearranged by William Ross Woofenden. Bryn Athyn, Pa.: Swedenborg Scientific Association.

————. 1994–1997. *Apocalypse Explained.* 6 vols. Translated by John C. Ager, revised by John Whitehead, and edited by William Ross Woofenden. West Chester, Pa.: Swedenborg Foundation.

————. 1996. *Posthumous Theological Works.* 2 vols. Translated by John Whitehead and edited by William Ross Woofenden. West Chester, Pa.: Swedenborg Foundation.

————. 1997a. *On Divine Love and Divine Wisdom.* Translated by John C. Ager, revised by John Whitehead, and edited by William Ross Woofenden. In vol. 6 of *Apocalypse Explained.* West Chester, Pa.: Swedenborg Foundation.

————. 1997b. *Three Short Works.* Translated by N. Bruce Rogers. Bryn Athyn, Pa.: General Church of the New Jerusalem.

————. 1998–2002. *Emanuel Swedenborg's Diary, Recounting Spiritual Experiences during the Years 1745 to 1765.* 3 vols. Translated by J. Durban Odhner. Bryn Athyn, Pa.: General Church of the New Jerusalem. The first three volumes, in English, of the six volumes of Swedenborg's Latin work *Experientiae Spirituales,* edited by J. Durban Odhner (Bryn Athyn, Pa.: Academy of the New Church, 1983–1997). Further volumes forthcoming.

————. 2001a. *Rational Psychology.* Translated by Norbert H. Rogers and Alfred Acton. Bryn Athyn, Pa.: Swedenborg Scientific Association. Revision of 1950 edition, Philadelphia: Swedenborg Scientific Association.

————. 2001b. *Swedenborg's Dream Diary.* Edited by Lars Bergquist and translated by Anders Hallengren. West Chester, Pa.: Swedenborg Foundation.

————. [1763] 2003a. *Angelic Wisdom about Divine Love and about Divine Wisdom.* Translated by George F. Dole. West Chester, Pa.: Swedenborg Foundation.

————. [1764] 2003b. *Angelic Wisdom about Divine Providence.* Translated by George F. Dole. West Chester, Pa.: Swedenborg Foundation.

Swenson, Loyd R., Jr. 1972. *The Ethereal Aether.* Austin, Tex.: University of Texas Press.

Tafel, R. L. 1877. *Documents Concerning the Life and Character of Emanuel Swedenborg.* Vol. 2, parts 1 and 2. London: Swedenborg Society.

Theological Dictionary of the Old Testament. 1986. Edited by G. Johannes Botterweck and Helmer Ringgren, and translated by John T. Willis. Vol. 5. Grand Rapids, Mich.: William B. Eerdmans.

Tillyard, E.M.W. 1959. *The Elizabethan World Picture.* New York: Vintage Books.

Tissot, Samuel Auguste André David. 1758. *Tentamen de Morbis ex Manustupratione.* Lausanne: Bousquet. English version: *Onanism,* New York: Garland, 1985.

Toomer, G. J. 1976. *Diocles on Burning Mirrors.* New York: Springer Verlag.

Torricelli, Evangelista. 1897. *Esperienza dell'argento vivo.* Neudrucke von Schriften und Karten über Meteorologie und Erdmagnetismus, no. 7. Berlin: G. Hellmann. The

"Neudrucke von Schriften und Karten" series of individual reprints was collected into volumes and reprinted again by Kraus Reprint, of Nendeln, Liechtenstein, in 1969; the Torricelli material appears in volume 2 of this second reprint.

Triewald, Mårten. 1734. *Konsten at lefva under vatn.* Stockholm: Benjamin Gottlieb Schneider.

———. [1734] 2004. *The Art of Living under Water.* London: Historical Diving Society.

Triglot Concordia: The Symbolical Books of the Evangelical Lutheran Church: German-Latin-English. 1921. St. Louis, Mo.: Concordia.

Voltaire. [1768] 1877–1885. "Epître à l'auteur du livre des trois imposteurs." In vol. 10 of *Oeuvres complètes de Voltaire,* edited by Louis Moland. Paris: Garnier.

———. [1764] 1962. *Philosophical Dictionary.* Translated by Peter Gay. New York: Harcourt, Brace, & World.

———. [1756] 1963. *Essai sur les moeurs et l'esprit des nations.* 2 vols. Paris: Garnier Frères.

Waldron, Arthur. 1990. *The Great Wall of China: From History to Myth.* Cambridge: Cambridge University Press.

Wedin, Michael V. 1988. *Mind and Imagination in Aristotle.* New Haven: Yale University Press.

Wesley, John. [1782] 1856. "Thoughts on the Writings of Baron Swedenborg." In vol. 13 of *The Works of the Rev. John Wesley,* edited by Thomas Jackson. London: John Mason.

Whitaker, Ewen A. 1999. *Mapping and Naming the Moon: A History of Lunar Cartography and Nomenclature.* Cambridge: Cambridge University Press.

Wilamowitz-Moellendorf, Ulrich von. 1920. *Platon.* 2 vols. Berlin: Weidemann.

Winkler, Mary G., and Albert Van Helden. 1992. "Representing the Heavens: Galileo and Visual Astronomy." *Isis* 83:195–217.

Wolff, Christian. 1730. *Philosophia Prima, sive Ontologia.* Frankfurt: Libraria Rengeriana.

Wolfson, Harry Austryn. 1971. *Crescas's Critique of Aristotle: Problems of Aristotle's "Physics" in Jewish and Arabic Philosophy.* Cambridge, Mass.: Harvard University Press. First edition: 1929, Cambridge, Mass.: Harvard University Press.

Woofenden, William Ross. 1971. *Swedenborg's Concept of Love in Action: A Study of the Ethics of Emanuel Swedenborg (1688–1772).* Boston: Massachusetts New-Church Union.

Zimmerman, Dean W. 1997. "Distinct Indiscernibles and the Bundle Theory." *Mind* 106:305–309.

Biographical Note

EMANUEL SWEDENBORG (1688–1772) was born Emanuel Swedberg (or Svedberg) in Stockholm, Sweden, on January 29, 1688 (Julian calendar). He was the third of the nine children of Jesper Swedberg (1653–1735) and Sara Behm (1666–1696). At the age of eight he lost his mother. After the death of his only older brother ten days later, he became the oldest living son. In 1697 his father married Sara Bergia (1666–1720), who developed great affection for Emanuel and left him a significant inheritance. His father, a Lutheran clergyman, later became a celebrated and controversial bishop, whose diocese included the Swedish churches in Pennsylvania and in London, England.

After studying at the University of Uppsala (1699–1709), Emanuel journeyed to England, Holland, France, and Germany (1710–1715) to study and work with leading scientists in western Europe. Upon his return he apprenticed as an engineer under the brilliant Swedish inventor Christopher Polhem (1661–1751). He gained favor with Sweden's King Charles XII (1682–1718), who gave him a salaried position as an overseer of Sweden's mining industry (1716–1747). Although he was engaged, he never married.

After the death of Charles XII, Emanuel was ennobled by Queen Ulrika Eleonora (1688–1741), and his last name was changed to Swedenborg (or Svedenborg). This change in status gave him a seat in the Swedish House of Nobles, where he remained an active participant in the Swedish government throughout his life.

A member of the Swedish Royal Academy of Sciences, he devoted himself to scientific studies and philosophical reflections that culminated in a number of publications, most notably a comprehensive three-volume work on mineralogy (1734) that brought him recognition across Europe as a scientist and philosopher. After 1734 he redirected his research and publishing to a study of anatomy in search of the interface between the soul and body, making several significant discoveries in physiology.

From 1743 to 1745 he entered a transitional phase that resulted in a shift of his main focus from science and philosophy to theology. Throughout the rest of his life he maintained that this shift was brought about by Jesus Christ, who appeared to him, called him to a new mission, and opened his perception to a permanent dual consciousness of this life and the life after death.

He devoted the last decades of his life to studying Scripture and publishing eighteen theological titles that draw on the Bible, reasoning, and his own spiritual experiences. These works present a Christian theology with unique perspectives on the nature of God, the spiritual world, the Bible, the human mind, and the path to salvation.

Swedenborg died in London on March 29, 1772, at the age of eighty-four.